Impacts of
Science & Technology on Currency Internationalization

Impacts of Science & Technology on Currency Internationalization

Peter Guangping Zhang

Shanghai Bureau of China Banking and Insurance Regulatory Commission, China

World Scientific

NEW JERSEY • LONDON • SINGAPORE • BEIJING • SHANGHAI • HONG KONG • TAIPEI • CHENNAI • TOKYO

Published by

World Scientific Publishing Co. Pte. Ltd.
5 Toh Tuck Link, Singapore 596224
USA office: 27 Warren Street, Suite 401-402, Hackensack, NJ 07601
UK office: 57 Shelton Street, Covent Garden, London WC2H 9HE

Library of Congress Cataloging-in-Publication Data
Names: Zhang, Peter G., author.
Title: Impacts of Science & Technology on currency Internationalization / Peter Guangping Zhang, Shanghai Bureau of China Banking and Insurance Regulatory Commission, China.
Description: New Jersey : World Scientific, [2023] | Includes bibliographical references and index.
Identifiers: LCCN 2022018562 | ISBN 9789811254086 (hardcover) | ISBN 9789811254093 (ebook) | ISBN 9789811254109 (ebook other)
Subjects: LCSH: Foreign exchange. | International finance. | International trade. | Technological innovation--Economic aspects.
Classification: LCC HG3851 .Z478 2023 | DDC 332.4/5--dc23/eng/20220610
LC record available at https://lccn.loc.gov/2022018562

British Library Cataloguing-in-Publication Data
A catalogue record for this book is available from the British Library.

For any available supplementary material, please visit
https://www.worldscientific.com/worldscibooks/10.1142/12772#t=suppl

Desk Editors: Soundararajan Raghuraman/Lixi Dong

Typeset by Stallion Press
Email: enquiries@stallionpress.com

Foreword

Dr. Zhang has accomplished scrupulous analysis of the relationship between science and technology innovation and currency internationalization from a wide range of perspectives and utilized the epoch-making data analysis to successfully prove the strong correlation between the two. Zhang evaluates the status of Renminbi (Chinese yuan) internationalization from various perspectives to point out that there is extensive room to promote it further. He demonstrates clearly and powerfully that an improvement in China's science and technology innovation would be an integral factor in strengthening export competitiveness, thus promoting Renminbi internationalization. This is indeed a pioneering theory.

The author analyzes the science and technology status of the United States, Japan, and selected countries from Europe and Asia. From the perspective of Japanese researchers, the analysis of Japan in this book constitutes a new line of discovery, and the findings related to Japan's position in science and technology innovation are of great significance.

Based on the detailed analysis of the empirical data mentioned above, the author opines that it is necessary to realize the internationalization of the Renminbi in a manner consistent with the current extent of China's economic strength. Zhang delves into the current status of Renminbi internationalization through the close examination of empirical data and candidly details future challenges facing the internationalization of the Renminbi, such as insufficient data and the limitations of the internationalization of Chinese banks. In addition to the Renminbi internationalization, Zhang paints a picture of the current status of the internationalization of other major currencies using detailed analysis and evaluations, specifically from the perspective of science and technology innovations.

Zhang hypothesizes that with the continued growth in the Chinese economy, the Renminbi would hold a more prominent stage in the international marketplace; however, he also points out that the United States dollar will maintain its dominant position as the key global currency in the foreseeable future.

In such circumstances, the author argues that there is room for stronger financial cooperation between Japan and China. Enhancing such financial cooperation provides mutual benefits and win-win outcomes for both nations involved, promotes the internationalization of their respective currencies, and boosts the development of science and technology. It is therefore necessary and indispensable that both countries put in the effort to do so.

For international readers, this book is a valuable and rare work that imparts a wealth of information and knowledge concerning the international development of science and technology and its relationship to currency internationalization; it is a must-read for those who are contemplating the future of the internationalization of the world's major currencies, including the United States dollar, the Euro, the yen, the pound sterling, and the Renminbi.

This book is one that I recommend all to read attentively.

Yosuke Tsuyuguchi
Professor, Faculty of Economics
Teikyo University, Japan
May 24, 2022

Preface

Science and technology (sci-tech) have influenced world trade, world economy, and international finance for decades and even centuries. However, their specific impacts are seldom known, and related empirical studies are rare. With sci-tech continuously innovating, they will play more and more important roles in world geopolitics, world trade and world finance, etc. Thus, we must quantify and empirically explore how sci-tech influence such areas as mentioned above.

The purpose of this book is to explore how sci-tech influence world trade, foreign exchange, and currency internationalization in various ways. This book explores empirically how major world currencies might change their relative international positions with the continuing innovation and diffusion of sci-tech.

Currency internationalization is traditionally measured by the percentage share of average daily turnover of a particular currency in global foreign exchange market over the corresponding overall daily turnover of global foreign exchange market. Currency internationalization has been studied extensively worldwide in professional and academic arenas simply because global usage of currencies is realized and reflected in global foreign exchange market. Sci-tech internationalization needs to be quantified first in order to study its influence on world trade and currency internationalization accordingly. Sci-tech themselves are borderless in nature as they can be widely used anywhere in the world without any interference. Sci-tech, as a commodity, are borderless, yet their inventors and related businesses are bound by intellectual property laws of their own countries.

Sci-tech are challenging to measure because of its complexity, various types of patents are not easily comparable due to different criteria of patent authorities, and a great majority of patents are protected in various forms. Various forms of patent data updated by the World Intellectual Property Organization (WIPO) and other international organizations are the necessary background for patent internationalization, yet patent data cannot actually reflect technology levels of various economies because patent quality varies significantly across patent regulators. Following the measurement of currency internationalization, we can measure sci-tech internationalization of the major world currency issuers using international patent data and exports and imports data of charges for the use of IP. With measurements of both currency internationalization and sci-tech internationalization, we can find the relationship between currency internationalization and the sci-tech internationalization of major currency issuers.

Part I of this book introduces major factors affecting currency evaluation and currency internationalization. Chapter 1 introduces GDP, foreign trade, capital market, foreign exchange market, and other important factors influencing currency valuation and currency internationalization. Chapter 2 introduces investments in Research and Development (R&D), R&D investment distribution in critical fields, patent applications, and approvals of major countries to provide necessary background information for sci-tech internationalization measurement in following chapters.

Part II consists of six chapters, which define currency and sci-tech internationalization. Chapter 3 discusses trade settlement, foreign reserves, and other issues that affect currency valuation. Chapter 4 introduces traditional currency internationalization results of major world currencies in the past two decades. Chapter 5 first introduces international and regional patent data released by five regional IP offices of the European Patent Organization, the United States, Japan, South Korea, and China (IP5 offices), and discusses the distribution of patent families of IP5 patent offices, and concludes with defining and measuring patent internationalization.

Chapter 6 first introduces major components of world services trade, particularly export and imports of charges for the use of intellectual property (IP) of major economies. Chapter 6 continues by defining and then quantifying sci-tech originality sufficiency. Chapter 7 first defines and quantifies sci-tech originality capability (OC) using exports and imports of charges for the use of IP, and then defines and quantifies sci-tech internationalization of patent blocs through annual share of weighted patent families of one bloc over the total weighted patent families of the world.

The quality of international patents of different countries is not globally consistent and is difficult to calculate. Based on the analytical sci-tech results of Chapter 5, along with the ratios of sci-tech OC over patent OC of each patent bloc as weights of patent family of each patent bloc, Chapter 7 quantifies sci-tech internationalization of patent blocs through annual share of weighted patent families of one bloc over the total weighted patent families of the world.

Chapter 8 first studies the impacts of sci-tech OC and sci-tech internationalization on exports, net exports, and current accounts of top world economies and then explores the implications of sci-tech OC on gross national products (GDP) and its major components. Empirical results show that imports of charges for the use of IP provide necessary sci-tech from international market for economic development. They can contribute to GDP nearly as much as exports of charges for the use of IP for most major economies. The synergy generated by exports and imports of charges for the use of IP for economic development shows that the efficient coordination or combination of exports and imports of charges for the use of IP can generate more influence of sci-tech on GDP and its major components for most major advanced economies. It is noticeable that total factor productivity (TFP) is primarily the contribution of sci-tech in the United States and to a lesser degree in Japan and other developed economies.

Part III of this book introduces various aspects of Chinese Renminbi (RMB, Chinese yuan or CNY) internationalization. Chapter 9 introduces the developments of major offshore CNY/RMB centers worldwide and their contribution to potential CNY internationalization in the future. Chapter 10 presents major offshore CNY markets and their contribution to CNY internationalization. Chapter 11 introduces offshore asset distributions of major currency issuers and bank internationalization of global banks. Chapter 12 introduces CNY internationalization in the past few years.

Part IV is the last and critical part of this book. Chapter 13 first analyzes correlation coefficients between sci-tech internationalization and currency internationalization. The average positive correlation coefficients between sci-tech internationalization and currency internationalization are generally more than 90%, indicating significantly mutual supporting relationship between these two internationalizations. Careful reasoning and analysis show that the unusual or non-intuitive average correlation coefficient between the above two factors was 90.27% of 2010, higher than the corresponding average correlation coefficient 89.69% of 2007 which is due to the nominal value rather than the real-change-hand-turnover of foreign exchange derivatives trading. By reducing the nominal turnover of foreign exchange derivatives, better results of currency internationalization are obtained with the target that the overall average correlation coefficients between the two factors are the greatest. Corresponding to the better correlation coefficients between currency internationalization and sci-tech internationalization, we calculate the better currency internationalization measures.

Chapter 14 uses results of sci-tech internationalization of Chapter 7 and currency internationalization of Chapter 4, analyzes the mutual impacts of sci-tech internationalization and currency internationalization, and finds empirical evidence that the former has more impacts on the latter, indicating the overall importance of sci-tech internationalization on currency internationalization.

Chapter 15 defines currency OC following the concept of sci-tech OC of Chapter 6 and then finds empirical evidence of mutual impacts among sci-tech OC, currency OC, sci-tech internationalization, and currency internationalization. The results show that sci-tech OC has a more significant impact on currency OC, sci-tech internationalization has a greater impact on sci-tech OC, and sci-tech internationalization has a more substantial effect on currency OC, providing evidence that sci-tech internationalization is the most critical factor of the above four factors.

Chapter 16 finds an alternative way to better forecast relative long-term currency internationalization to overcome subjective issues such as choosing historical data periods. The new method uses the product of sci-tech OC and nominal GDP world share of a currency issuer as a substitute for foreign exchange turnover of the currency. As sci-tech OC largely determines export capability and nominal GDP world share represents import ability of any currency issuer, their product can represent the trade capability of any currency issuer. Empirical results show that the product of sci-tech OC and nominal GDP world share are highly correlated with foreign exchange turnovers of major currencies. Since economic and sci-tech OC growth rates are relatively stable for most major currency issuers, sci-tech OC and nominal GDP world share can be more accurately predicted. Therefore, forecasting results using this new method is more reliable than results using historical foreign exchange turnovers.

Finally, net exports of charges for the use of IP of any economy are natural results of its sci-tech OC or sci-tech internationalization. Yet, currency internationalization also plays an essential role in determining net exports of charges for the use of IP because net exports of charges for the use of IP denominated in terms of currencies. The last chapter also analyzes contributions of sci-tech and currency to net exports of charge for the use of IP of major world currency issuers. Results show that the higher the internationalization level of a currency, the higher its contribution to its issuer's net export of charges for the use of IP, which gives us a deeper understanding of sci-tech and currency internationalization.

After the manuscript of this book was handed over to the publisher over a month ago, I thought of applying exotic options from my earlier book, *Exotic Options — A Guide to Second Generation Options*, first published in 1997, to the analysis of technology progress. Most exotic options or correlation options are mostly over-the-counter options that came into existence over three decades ago in major world financial centers. If we regard exports and imports of charges for the use of IP as assets, prices of some correlation options give us relative advantages of science and technology of one economy over another. I have published a number of related academic papers in this area recently. Sensitivity parameters of related options provide us with many sophisticated parameters to measure science and technology, and the application of these options into the analysis of technology deepens most regression or statistical results of this book into the domain of mathematic analysis. As most of these results are highly mathematical, I decided not to include them in this book for the time being.

Attempts to introduce sci-tech into economics and finance are relatively new, the effectiveness of the empirical results in this book may be limited because of the number of data observations. Yet, these results provide us a deeper understanding of the interactions between sci-tech and currency internationalization, and the critical roles of sci-tech on economies, trade, net exports, current accounts, currency valuation, etc. Future studies can extend to impacts of sci-tech OC and internationalization on stock market capitalization, GDP growth, etc. As these attempts are new, discoveries may lay grounds for new lines of research within the discipline of international economics and finance. Finally, the list of acknowledgment is rather long as I owe many professionals worldwide a great deal in the past two decades and more, and I will acknowledge many of them in detail at the end of this book.

Guangping (Peter G.) Zhang
Shanghai
January 16, 2022

About the Author

Dr. Peter Guangping (Peter G.) Zhang obtained his BS and MS in Computer Science in the Chinese Mainland, before being sent to study in the United States in 1987. He has served as Manager, Senior Associate, or Vice-President in various financial institutions, including MMS International (Standard & Poor's Group), the Union Bank of Switzerland (New York Branch), and the Chemical Bank (Head Office) in New York City. After working for the Chase Manhattan Bank (Tokyo Branch) as a Vice-President for about 3 years, he broadened his expertise to financial law at Harvard Law School. He joined Shanghai Futures Exchange in 2003 as Chief Financial Engineering Advisor and Senior Director of Research & Development Center of the Exchange. He joined the newly established Supervisory Cooperation Department for Banking Innovation of China Banking Regulatory Commission (CBRC) in November 2005 as Deputy Director General and re-allocated to CBRC Shanghai Bureau as Deputy Director General in October 2007. He began to serve as a counselor to Shanghai Municipal Government since 2021. As an experienced financial expert he published many articles and books in English and Chinese. His representative books include *Exotic Options — A Guide to 2nd Generation Options* (2nd Edition 1998); *Chinese Yuan (RMB) Derivative Products* (English Edition, 2004), *Chinese Yuan Internationalization and Product Innovation* (First Edition in 2010 and 10th Edition in 2021). He has completed a series of research papers on the impacts of science and technology on international trade, foreign exchange trading, and currency internationalization based on quantitative measures of science and technology originality capability and science and technology internationalization in the past 2 years.

Acknowledgments

I have benefited greatly from many friends and professionals both domestically and internationally in the past quarter of a century. It is impossible to list them all in a short list. This book is largely based on my earlier publications both in English and Chinese in the past two decades and I have owned a lot to many of my friends who have helped to make such books possible.

First of all, I want to thank Jade Lu of SPD Silicon Valley Bank for her comments and suggestions for earlier versions of this book; I want to thank Kevin Yang from Standard Chartered Bank, Dora Liu Ming Hua, Henry Cao and Stephanie D Zhang from Deloitte, Yinru Wang and Stella Fu from PWC, Thomas Chen and James Chen from KPMG and Dr. Jian Huang, VP of S&P Group for their help in discussing and refining various versions of this book.

Help from Prof. Yosuke Tsuyuguchi is especially acknowledged. I want to thank my friends Dr. Feridun Hamdullahpur, Raymond Qu, Darren Buckley, Megan Hu, Andrew Paul Swain, Mr. Huang Feng, Mr. Nie Ming and Michelle Zou from China for their special help in publication of this book. I also want to thank Wei Wang, Tim Huang, Wenjie Zhang, John Zhang, Jie Huang, Guiyu Zhang, Cang YongTao, Arthur Zou, and Ting Zou for their help and encouragement in the publication of this book.

I need to thank Peter Foo, Mark Yang, and Zhong Wei from UOB and Kyle Tan and Mark Yang from DBS, especially for their help in discussing a number of issues and collecting various types of data for this book.

Finally, I want to thank Madhanaumar, Soundararajan Raghuraman, Nandhakumar Krishnan, Britney Jiang, Rebecca Fu, and Angela Lixi Dong from World Scientific Publishing Co Pte Ltd for their high professionalism which has been well maintained and improved steadily since my earlier books *Barings Bankruptcy & Financial Derivatives* and *Exotic Options — A Guide to Second Generation Options* were published by World Scientific over 20 years ago.

Guangping (Peter G.) Zhang
April 26, 2022

Contents

Foreword v

Preface vii

About the Author xiii

Acknowledgments xv

Part I **1**

Chapter 1 Major Factors Affecting Currency Internationalization 3

Chapter 2 Science and Technology: The Cornerstones for Currency Internationalization 23

Part II **65**

Chapter 3 Global Trade and Cross-Border Payment and Settlement 67

Chapter 4 Currency Internationalization 109

Chapter 5 PCT Patents: The Backbone of International Technology 179

Chapter 6 Development of Global Trade in Services and Charges for Use of Intellectual Property 239

Chapter 7 Science and Technology Originality Capability and Internationalization Measures 295

Chapter 8 Impacts of Science and Technology on Trade, Current Accounts, and Others 333

Part III **361**

Chapter 9 Development and Current Status of Offshore CNY Centers 363

Chapter 10 Offshore CNY Markets 413

Chapter 11 Overseas Assets and Bank Internationalization of Major Currency Issuers 459

Chapter 12 Current Status of Major International Currencies 491

Part IV **549**

Chapter 13 Mutually Supportive Relationship between Science & Technology Internationalization and Currency Internationalization and Better Currency Internationalization Measure 551

Chapter 14 Mutual Impacts of Sci-tech Internationalization and Currency Internationalization 577

Chapter 15 Currency Originating Capability and Relationships among Currency Originality Capability, Currency Internationalization, and Sci-tech Originality Capability 623

Chapter 16 Future Changes of Major Currency Internationalization and Market Development 649

Concluding Remarks 691

Index 695

Part I

Chapter 1

Major Factors Affecting Currency Internationalization

There are many factors affecting currency valuation and currency internationalization. Academic and professional books and articles have thoroughly studied most of these factors; we do not intend to repeat them here. Yet, many of these factors are so crucial to currency internationalization that we cannot judge international positions of major currencies in the future without knowing their recent magnitudes and future fluctuations. The purpose of this chapter is to introduce significant factors that affect currency internationalization and provide essential background information for future analysis in this book.

1.1 Gross Domestic Product

The Gross Domestic Product (GDP) of any economy is the most critical factor affecting its currency valuation and international position. Two popular methods are widely used to measure GDP worldwide: one converts GDP into domestic currency using a foreign exchange rate and the other uses the purchasing power parity (PPP) theory to measure GDP. We will briefly introduce GDP data using these two methods released semi-annually by the International Monetary Fund (IMF).

1.1.1 *Gross National Product by foreign exchange rate conversion*

The most popular GDP data used worldwide is the Gross Domestic Product calculated by foreign exchange rate conversion. Table 1.1 gives GDP world share of five major currency issuers in 2020, calculated using data released by the IMF in April 2021. Table 1.1 shows that the US world share of GDP was 24.76%, making it the largest economy globally. If we look back at historical data, we can find that the US world GDP share was 34.70% in 1985, the highest in the past four decades, yet the share decreased gradually to the lowest point at 21.14% in 2011 because of the 2008 financial crisis and other reasons; it increased slightly to 24.61% in 2016 and remained at about the same level in the past few years. Chapter 16 will forecast the US GDP world share in the next two decades using historical data to predict the currency internationalization positions of significant currencies.

Table 1.1 shows that the Chinese GDP world share was 17.42%, 2.14% higher than the Eurozone share of 15.28%. The IMF data show that the Chinese economy surpassed the Eurozone for the first time in 2018, becoming the second largest economy globally since then; Eurozone, Japan, and the UK were the third, fourth, and fifth most significant economies in the world, respectively. India surpassed the UK to become the fifth largest economy in the world in 2019; yet, India's GDP fell behind the UK again in 2020 because of COVID-19.

1.1.2 *GDP by PPP*

The second popular GDP estimation method is the PPP theory. Table 1.1 gives PPP GDP world share using data released by the IMF in April 2021. Table 1.1 shows that the Chinese PPP GDP share was 18.34%, 2.44% higher than that of the second largest US GDP share of 15.90%, followed by Eurozone, Japan, and the UK with share of 12.05%, 4.04%, and 2.25%, respectively, with world rankings as the third, fifth, and eighth. The largest economies in the world such as Indian, Russian, and Brazilian's PPP GDP share were 6.77%, 3.11%, and 2.40% with rankings as the fourth, sixth, and seventh in the world in 2020. If Eurozone is not ranked as a whole economy, then the UK would be classified as the ninth economy as the UK PPP GDP share was lower than German and French share of 3.42% and 2.28%.

Table 1.1: World Share of GDP, Trade, and Other Factors of Major Currency Issuers in 2020 (Unit: %)

Currency Issuer	US (%)	Eurozone (%)	Japan (%)	UK (%)	China (%)	Others (%)
GDP (Foreign Exchange Conversion)	24.76	15.28	5.97	3.21	17.42	33.37
GDP (PPP)	15.90	12.05	4.04	2.25	18.34	47.42
Commodity Trade Volume	13.44	16.28	4.37	3.26	16.50	46.15
Commodity Export Volume	10.61	17.95	4.66	2.80	19.16	44.82
Commodity Import Volume	16.66	15.29	4.26	3.82	14.57	45.41
International Payment	38.73	36.70	3.59	6.50	1.88	12.60
Total Debt	25.86	18.12	9.36	4.56	16.42	25.68
Government Debt	30.21	17.45	12.88	4.05	10.74	24.67
International Bond Value*	9.13	35.69	1.96	12.34	0.86	40.02
Stock Market Capitalization	41.04	7.78	6.09	3.67	11.07	30.35
Securitization Ratio	216.37	66.51	133.07	149.23	82.96	118.73
Stock Market Capitalization	36.74	5.11	4.43	1.51	21.54	30.67
Annual Turnover of Stock Market	38.87	4.16	4.87	2.33	25.08	24.69
World Bank Voting Rights	16.53	19.07	7.15	3.92	4.61	48.72
IMF Voting Rights	17.45	22.13	6.48	4.24	6.41	43.29
IMF Special Drawing Rights (SDRs)	41.73	30.93	8.33	8.09	10.92	0.00
Foreign Exchange Daily Trading Value Worldwide**	44.15	16.14	8.40	6.40	2.16	22.75
Foreign Exchange Daily Trading Value Locally**	16.51	8.43	4.52	43.09	1.64	25.82

Source: GDP data based on world GDP data released by the IMF in April 2021; trade volume data based on the trade data of major countries published by the OECD. Stats in April 2021; the stock market capitalization and turnover data from the World Federation of Exchanges; debt data are calculated using related estimated debt ratios of the International Institute of Finance (IIF, 2021) of 2020; International debt ratios were calculated using the data released by Bank for International Settlements (BIS) for 2020 Q3; Foreign exchange volume share was calculated using daily average trading data for April 2019 from BIS Triennial data updated in December 2019; World Bank voting rights, IMF voting rights and SDRs data from World Bank and IMF official websites; **cross-border currency trade share data from the Society for Worldwide Interbank Financial Telecommunication (SWIFT) in January 2021.**

***calculated using data released by IMF website; **calculated using "Triennial Central Bank Survey of Foreign Exchange and over-the-counter (OTC) Derivatives Markets in 2019 by Bank for International Settlements (BIS).**

1.1.3 *Some useful related comparisons*

According to the IMF data released from 2014 to 2019, Chinese PPP GDP surpassed the US for the first time in 2014, the former as 4.36% higher than the latter, and the former was 33.39% and 56.04% higher than the latter in 2020 and 2024 (forecast by IMF), respectively; however, the newly released IMF data in October 2020 and April 2021 show that the Chinese/US PPP GDP ratio was reduced to 4.28%, 32.03%, and 54.38% in 2014, 2020, and 2024. Yet, the aforementioned ratios were significantly reduced to −1.86%, 1.39%, 15.34%, 9.32% in 2014, 2017, 2020, and 2024, respectively, with IMF data updated in April 2021. These findings change the well-known assertion that China surpassed US as the largest economy in 2014. The margin between the top two economies was dramatically reduced. The more significant signal was that the ratio between the two economies will reach the highest level of 5.76% in 2023, declining gradually to 4.28% in 2026 using the IMF forecast data for the two economies. These dramatically modified results give us the impression that the IMF PPP GDP data are questionable as the changes cannot be explained satisfactorily.

1.2 Foreign Trade

Foreign trade is the most crucial part of the world economy and international finance. Traditionally, foreign trade mainly stands for commodity trade, yet services trade has played a more critical role in world trade in the past few decades. We will introduce the two kinds of trade briefly in this section.

1.2.1 *Commodity trade*

Commodity trade has been the most important factor affecting foreign exchange trading, and thus the most important factor affecting currency valuation and currency internationalization. According to the World Trade Organization (WTO) data, the world commodity trade grew at an average annual rate of 10.3% from 1948 to 1983, more than twice as high as world GDP for the same period; world commodity trade grew at an average annual growth rate of 6.6%, higher than nominal world GDP yearly growth rate of 5.8% from 1983 to 2019. The world commodity trade/GDP ratio grew from 32.15% in 1983 to 46.86% in 2008 and declined to around 40% in 2020. Table 1.1 gives the world commodity trade share of five major economies in 2020.

Table 1.1 shows that China's commodity export share was 19.16% (excluding intra-EU export), 8.55% higher than the US share of 10.61% in 2020. China's commodity import share was 14.04% (excluding intra-EU import), 2.02% lower than the US share of 16.06%; China's total commodity trade share was 16.50%, 3.06% higher than the US share of 13.44%. China's commodity trade surpassed the US for the first time in 2014 and remains the world's largest commodity trade country since then, with the only exception being 2015. Eurozone was the world's second largest commodity trade region in 2020 (we use Eurozone's trade with countries outside Eurozone); Japan remains the fourth largest trade country since 2004, and the UK remains the fifth largest commodity trade country if we take Eurozone as a whole region. We will discuss more about the commodity trade of significant economies in Chapter 3.

1.2.2 *Trade in services*

Compared to world commodity trade, world services trade is relatively small in magnitude, yet its share in world trade has been increasing over the past few decades. Table 1.2 gives the services exports and imports of major economies from 2001 to 2020. Table 1.2 shows that the ratio of world services trade over world commodity trade declined slightly from 26.3% in 2001 to 24.1% in 2012 and increased to 32% in 2019 steadily with average annual growth of 1.1%, indicating that services trade has been growing faster than commodity trade since 2012.

Table 1.2 also shows that the US is by far the most significant services trade exporter, services trader, and net services exporter in the world for most years with world share of services trade over 11%; and the UK has been ranked second following the US services export and net export. Although Eurozone is ranked largest in services trade, its net services export is not equal to that of the UK; Japan's services export and import are mostly ranked fifth and sixth, and Japan's net services trade changed from negative to positive in 2017 and its net export was less than India's net services export in 2019; China's services export was ranked fourth following Eurozone, US, and the UK in 2019; China's services import was ranked third following Eurozone and US, and China's services trade was ranked fourth following Eurozone, US, and UK. Yet, China's services trade deficit was ranked the highest of all the major economies with a percentage share as high as 80% of the world in 2019.

Table 1.2: Services Exports and Imports of Major Economies in Selected Years from 2001 to 2020 (Unit: billion USD, %)

Country/Region	2001	2007	2012	2014	2016	2019	2020	2001–2007 Annual Growth Rate	2007–2014 Annual Growth Rate	2014–2019 Annual Growth Rate
Export										
US	274.3	488.4	655.7	741.1	758.9	845.2	692.1	10.1	7.2	2.2
UK	128.1	322.1	324.4	374.0	348.1	616.2		16.6	2.5	8.7
Germany	85.4	211.8	252.5	299.4	285.7	346.6		16.3	5.9	2.5
China	**90.1**	**125.4**	**201.6**	**219.1**	**208.4**	**244.4**	**208.0**	**5.7**	**9.7**	**1.8**
Japan	**64.7**	**121.6**	**137.0**	**163.8**	**175.7**	**207.3**	**157.5**	**11.1**	**5.1**	**4.0**
India	17.3	86.6	145.5	157.2	161.8	214.4		30.8	10.4	5.3
Eurozone	520.0	1,160.2	1,336.3	1,564.6	1,492.9	1,852.7		14.3	5.1	2.9
OECD	1,261.5	2,661.2	3,173.6	3,635.0	3,513.7	4,212.7		13.2	5.3	2.5
World	1,686.4	3,033.1	4,602.2	5,211.1	5,045.5	6,093.7		10.3	9.4	2.6
World services export/World commodity export	27.0	25.7	24.7	27.3	30.1	32.5		−0.8	1.0	2.9
Import										
US	213.5	372.6	452.0	480.8	509.8	595.4	458.3	9.7	4.3	3.6
UK	104.5	214.8	196.3	222.1	210.8	283.4		12.8	0.6	4.1
Germany	141.7	259.4	294.3	332.1	307.9	369.4		10.6	4.2	1.8
China	39.5	129.1	281.3	432.9	441.5	505.5	453.6	21.8	22.3	2.6
Japan	111.1	158.7	184.7	192.6	176.7	196.2	190.6	6.1	3.3	0.3
India	20.1	70.2	79.9	81.1	95.9	130.6		23.2	2.4	8.3
Eurozone	528.9	1,103.5	1,224.5	1,437.8	1,393.3	1,738.4		13.0	4.5	3.2

OECD	1,208.7	2,393.6	2,763.1	3,093.5	3,008.8	3,657.3		12.1	4.4	2.8
World	1,640.5	2,916.0	4,378.7	5,014.7	4,774.6	5,767.5		10.1	9.5	2.4
World services import/World commodity import	25.6	24.0	23.4	26.3	29.3	31.4		−1.1	1.5	3.0
World services trade/World commodity trade	26.3	24.8	24.1	26.8	30.3	32.0		−1.0	1.3	3.0
Net Export										
US	60.8	115.8	203.7	260.3	249.1	249.8	233.9	11.3	14.5	−0.7
UK	23.6	107.3	128.1	151.9	137.3	332.8		28.7	6.0	14.0
Germany	−56.3	−47.6	−41.8	−32.7	−22.2	−22.8		−2.8	−6.1	−5.8
China	50.6	−3.7	−79.7	−213.8	−233.1	−261.1	−245.6	−35.3	96.6	3.4
Japan	−46.4	−37.1	−47.7	−28.8	−1.0	11.2	−33.1	−3.7	−4.1	14.6
India	−2.8	16.4	65.6	76.1	65.9	83.8		34.3	29.1	1.6
Eurozone	−8.9	56.7	111.8	126.8	99.6	114.3		36.2	14.4	−1.7
OECD	52.8	267.6	410.5	541.5	504.9	555.4		31.1	12.5	0.4
World	45.9	117.1	223.5	196.4	270.9	326.2		16.9	9.0	8.8
Net Export Share of the World										
US	132.5	98.9	91.1	132.5	92.0	76.6		−5.60	5.61	−11.19
UK	51.4	91.6	57.3	77.3	50.7	102.0		6.70	−2.38	4.94
Germany	−122.7	−40.6	−18.7	−16.6	−8.2	−7.0		13.67	4.00	1.93
China	110.2	−3.2	−35.7	−108.9	−86.0	−80.0		−18.90	−17.62	5.76
Japan	−101.1	−31.7	−21.3	−14.7	−0.4	3.4		11.57	2.84	3.62
India	−6.1	14.0	29.4	38.7	24.3	25.7		3.35	4.12	−2.61
Eurozone	−19.4	48.4	50.0	64.6	36.8	35.0		11.30	2.69	−5.90
OECD	115.0	228.5	183.7	275.7	186.4	170.3		18.91	7.87	−21.09

(*Continued*)

Table 1.2: (*Continued*)

Country/Region	2001	2007	2012	2014	2016	2019	2020	2001–2007 Annual Growth Rate	2007–2014 Annual Growth Rate	2014–2019 Annual Growth Rate
Services Trade Share of the World										
US	14.7	14.5	12.3	11.9	12.9	12.1	11.4	−0.03	−0.42	0.04
UK	7.0	9.0	5.8	5.8	5.7	7.6		0.34	−0.53	0.35
Germany	6.8	7.9	6.1	6.2	6.0	6.0		0.18	−0.29	−0.03
China	3.9	4.3	5.4	6.4	6.6	6.3	6.6	0.06	0.35	−0.01
Japan	5.3	4.7	3.6	3.5	3.6	3.4	3.5	−0.10	−0.20	−0.02
India	1.1	2.6	2.5	2.3	2.6	2.9		0.25	−0.05	0.12
Eurozone	31.5	38.1	28.5	29.4	29.4	30.3		1.09	−1.45	0.18
OECD	74.2	85.0	66.1	65.8	66.4	66.4		1.79	−3.19	0.11

Source: World Development Indicator, World Bank, 2019; data of US, China, and Japan are from official websites of the three countries.

1.2.3 *Commodity trade and trade in services*

We earlier introduced commodity trade and services trade separately, here we still need to put them together in terms of world trade. China surpassed the US in commodity trade volume in 2014. However, the US remained the world's largest trade country until 2019 as the US services trade of $1.441 trillion was $690.7 billion more than the Chinese services trade of $0.750 trillion the same year. At that time, Chinese commodity trade volume of $4.567 trillion was $406.9 billion more than the US commodity trade of $4.169 trillion. Also, the US trade $5.612 trillion in 2019 was $283.6 billion more than the total Chinese volume of $5.336 trillion in the same year.

As the US commodity trade and services trade decreased significantly by 9.2% and 21.4%, respectively, from 2019 to 2020, total US trade fell 12.4% to $4.936 trillion. The Chinese commodity trade increased by 1.5% to $4.646 trillion, and the services trade declined by 16.8% to 0.618 trillion, the total Chinese trade was $5.263 trillion the same year, $326.4 billion more than the corresponding total US trade in 2020. Thus, China's total trade surpassed the US for the first time in 2020.

1.3 Share of Global Payment of Major Currencies

GDP and trade are two primary factors affecting currency valuation. Yet, their effects on currency valuation are reflected in global payments, and global price of significant currencies somehow reflects the international positions of currencies. Table 1.1 shows that the US dollar and Euro are the top two currencies for global payment with a combined world share of 75.43% in December 2020, indicating that these two currencies are the world's dominant currencies for international payment. The British pound, Japanese yen, and Chinese yuan are three currencies with world payment share of 6.50%, 3.59%, and 1.88% in December 2020. The total percentage of the top five currencies was as high as 87.4% simultaneously, and the share of all other currencies was merely 12.6%, implying that significant world currencies primarily dominate global payment.

If we compare the international payment share and commodity trade share of five major currencies in Table 1.1, we find the ratio of global payment share of USD over the percentage of US commodity trade share in Table 1.1 was 360.1%, and the proportions for Euro and pound were 281.8% and 249.5%, respectively, indicating that these three currencies were used not only for their trade settlement but also for trade settlement of other currency issuers; the corresponding ratio for Japanese yen was 102.6%, indicating that Japanese yen was used mainly for its trade settlement; and the corresponding percentage for Chinese yuan was as low as 14.2%, meaning that yuan was used to settle only a small fraction of Chinese commodity trade, the majority of Chinese commodity trade was paid with USD, Euro, and other major currencies.

1.4 Debt Market

The debt market includes the government sector, non-financial corporate sector, financial sector, and household sector. According to a recent report from the Institute of International Finance (IIF, 2021), total global debt reached the highest level of $281 trillion by 2020, 3.32 times the world GDP and 2.55 times the world stock capitalization by the end of 2020. We will introduce significant sectors of the world debt market briefly in this section.

1.4.1 *Government debt*

Government debt is the largest sector of all four sectors of debt. Table 1.1 shows that the US government debt share of the world reached 30.21%, or $26.92 trillion in 2020, followed by Eurozone and Japan with share of 17.75% and 12.88%; the share of China and UK was 10.74% and 4.05%, respectively, in the same period; the total share of these top three currency issuers was 60.54%, indicating that the top three world currencies are highly indebted. The government debt/GDP ratio of the US, Eurozone, and Japan reached 128.6%, 120.4%, and 227.3% in 2020. The high indebtedness of major world currency issuers has somewhat worried the world of the worthiness of these currencies.

1.4.2 *International debt*

International debt represents only a relatively small share of world debt. Table 1.1 shows that total global debt of $26.24 trillion was only 9.65% of the entire world debt of $272 trillion estimated by IIF. Table 1.1 gives the world share of international debt of major currency issuers by the end of Q3 2020. Table 1.1 shows that the Eurozone had the most significant global debt of $9.365 trillion or 35.69% of the total world international debt of $26.242. The UK had the second largest amount of international debt of $3.237 trillion or 12.34% of the total world international debt, followed by the US with 9.13%; Japan's share of global debt was merely 1.96%, lower than the share of Canada and Australia (3.81% and 2.16%); and China's share was 0.86%, lower than the share of Norway and Sweden (0.97% and 1.76%). It is noticeable that the offshore centers, particularly the Cayman Islands and Hong Kong SAR, had world share of international bonds of 8.36% and 1.35%, reflecting their unique roles in the international financial markets.

1.5 Stock Market

The stock market is a critical sector of world financial markets. Stock market capitalization reflects financial wealth accumulation, and the stock market has an essential role in supporting research and development. We will briefly introduce stock market capitalizations and turnovers of major stock markets of the world.

1.5.1 *Stock market capitalization*

Although COVID-19 had severe impacts on the world trade and GDP, world stock market capitalization increased by 18.5% to $110.35 trillion, or 130.5% of world GDP in 2020 (world securitization ratio), 23.9% higher than the 2019 ratio of 106.6%. Table 1.1 shows that the US share of stock market capitalization was 41.04%, which is not only the highest of all countries but also 12.44% higher than the total share of Eurozone, Japan, UK, and China's 28.61%; the US securitization ratio (market capitalization/GDP) of 216.37% was also the highest of all currency issuers; the market capitalization share of China, Eurozone, and Japan was 11.07%, 7.79%, and 6.09%, respectively, ranking second, third, and fourth. It is noticeable that market capitalization share of the UK of 3.67% was not only the lowest of the five currency issuers but also significantly lower than the corresponding share of Hong Kong SAR 5.56%.

1.5.2 *Stock market turnovers*

Market turnover stands for the total trading value of a market over a certain period, generally within a year. Table 1.1 gives the stock market turnover share of the five currency issuers in 2020. Table 1.1 shows that the US share of stock market turnover was 38.21%, which was not only the highest of all countries but also 3.20% higher than the total share of Eurozone, Japan, UK, and China's 35.01%.

1.6 Voting Rights in Major International Organizations

Voting rights of major currency issuers are important factors reflecting a currency's relative weight in prominent international organizations. Table 1.1 shows the major currency issuers' rights and special drawing rights (SDR) of major international organizations.

1.6.1 *The World Bank*

Table 1.1 shows that the US has the highest voting rights of 16.53% in the World Bank as a country, yet its voting rights were 2.54% lower than the total voting rights of the 19 member countries of Eurozone (19.07%); Japan, China, and the UK have voting rights of 7.15%, 4.61%, and 3.92% in the World Bank.

1.6.2 *International Monetary Fund*

Table 1.1 shows that the US has the highest voting rights of 17.45% in the IMF as a country, yet its voting right was 4.68% lower than the total voting rights of the 19 member countries of the Eurozone (22.13%); Japan, China, and UK have voting rights of 6.48%, 6.41%, and 4.24%, respectively, in the IMF.

1.6.2.1 *SDR of IMF*

SDR of currencies reflect the relative "importance" of major currencies in the IMF. Table 1.1 also gives the SDR of five major international currencies in the IMF. Table 1.1 shows that the USD SDR of 41.75% was the highest in the IMF, a little lower than the corresponding weight of USD foreign exchange average daily turnover in world foreign exchange markets in 2019. Euro SDR weight of 30.93% was almost twice as the corresponding weight of 16.14% of Euro foreign exchange average daily turnover in world foreign exchange market in 2019. Although Chinese yuan's corresponding weight at 2% was ranked third, the weight was 2.16% of the corresponding weight of USD foreign exchange average daily turnover in world foreign exchange markets in 2019. Corresponding yen's SDR of 8.33% was almost the same as related weight of 8.40% of yen foreign exchange average daily turnover in world foreign exchange markets in 2019. British pound SDR of 8.09% was ranked fifth, noticeably higher than the corresponding weight of 6.40% of pound foreign exchange average daily turnover in world foreign exchange markets in 2019.

1.7 Foreign Exchange Market

There are many kinds of international uses of currencies such as in trade settlement, foreign direct investments, and international aid. Yet, any national use of a currency is reflected in the currency's foreign exchange transactions. Thus, the foreign exchange trading volume of any currency in the world foreign exchange marketplace is the best way to measure its internationalization. We will briefly introduce the main components of foreign exchanges and their magnitudes in this section.

1.7.1 *Significant components of foreign exchange market*

There are two primary components of the foreign exchange market, namely the spot or cash market and derivatives market. We will briefly introduce the foreign exchange market in this section.

The spot or cash market of the foreign exchange market is simply the exchanges or transactions of one currency for another currency at the current exchange rate. The traditional foreign exchange transactions from the Bank for International Settlement (BIS) show that spot transactions were the only transactions in the international foreign market before 1989. With the introduction of foreign exchange derivatives trading, the share of spot foreign exchange average daily trading volume in the world foreign exchange market declined to 28.8% in 2007. However, its share increased slightly to 34.7% in 2013. It declined steadily to 27.5% in 2019.

With the increasing popularity of forwards and options, particularly foreign exchange swaps, foreign exchange derivatives trading has become even more critical in the world foreign exchange market. The same data from the BIS show that the share of foreign exchange derivatives average daily trading volume over the average daily trading volume of the world foreign exchange market grew from 52.7% in 1992 to 71.2% in 2007; it declined slightly to 65.3% in 2013 after the 2008 world financial crisis, yet it rose to 72.5% in 2019.

1.7.2 *Domestic foreign exchange trading*

Local foreign exchange trading simply stands for the total foreign exchange trading, or domestic currency trading with foreign currencies and foreign exchange trading among foreign currencies within a country or a region. Table 1.1 shows that the UK's share of local average daily foreign exchange trading volume was 43.09% in 2019, the highest in the world, reflecting the unique position of London's largest foreign exchange trading center; the share of the US was 16.51%, second only to that of the UK. Although there are 19 member countries in the Eurozone, the total share of Eurozone average daily foreign exchange trading volume was only 8.43% in 2019, lower than not only the share of the UK and the US but also just more than the share of Singapore (7.71%) and Hong Kong SAR (7.62%). The share of Japan was 4.52%, lower than the share of Singapore and Hong Kong SAR; the share of China was 1.64%, which was not only lower than all the currencies mentioned above but also lower than the share of Switzerland (3.32%).

1.7.3 *Foreign exchange trading worldwide*

As all international uses of any currency are reflected in its foreign exchange trading, the share of the currency in world foreign exchange average daily trading volume is one of the best measures of the currency's internationalization. Table 1.1 gives the percentages of five major international currencies in world foreign exchange trading volume. Table 1.1 shows that the USD is by far the world's top international currency as its trading share in the world foreign exchange market was 44.15%, not only higher than any other currency but also 11.05% higher than the total trading share of all other four currencies at 33.10%, indicating USD's relative monopoly in world foreign exchange market. The Euro's trading share of 16.14% in the world foreign exchange market was second only to USD, and higher than the sum of share of Japanese yen and

British pound at 14.80%; Japanese yen and British pound were ranked third and fourth with share at 8.40% and 6.40%, respectively. The percentage of Chinese yuan at 2.16% was not only lower than all the above four major world currencies but also lower than the share of Australian dollar (3.38%), Canadian dollar (2.52%), and Swiss franc (2.48%), indicating that yuan's internationalization position is still far away from matching Chinese economic and trade positions.

1.8 An Aggregating Factor and Its Intuitive Explanation

The share of daily average trading value of any currency of world's daily average trading value is the best way to measure the currency's internationalization; thus, the average daily foreign exchange trading volume share is the final result of the internationalization of any currency. Yet, all factors from Section 1.1 to Section 1.7 are contributors or potential factors for currency internationalization. The arithmetic averages of the rankings of these factors for each currency can also give us accurate information for the potentiality of internationalization for each currency. Table 1.3 gives us the orders of each element from Section 1.1 to Section 1.7 in Table 1.1, the arithmetic average ranking, and the comparisons with the daily average trading volume share in Table 1.1.

Table 1.3 shows that the arithmetic ranking of USD, Euro, yen, and pound was 1.44, 2.56, 3.63, and 3.94, respectively, or 0.44, 0.56, 0.63, and 0.94 higher than their rankings according to daily average trading value share of first, second, third, and fourth positions, or all the top four world currencies were over-ranked to various degrees, especially the British pound was over-ranked by almost one ladder position. Yet the arithmetic ranking of the Chinese yuan of 3.31 was lower than the third-ranked world currency, yen's 3.63, meaning the yuan has the potential to be classified as the third currency instead of yen if the above factors from GDP, trade, international payment, debt market, stock market, and others played their traditional roles in foreign exchange trading.

The sum of the above four over-ranking-ness parameters 0.44, 0.56, 0.63, and 0.94 of the four major currencies at 2.57 may be explained as the total over-ranking-ness of the four top world currencies together, or the four top world currencies together were over-ranked by over two ladder positions in 2019 at the cost of under-rankingness of yuan.

Table 1.3: Rankings and Arithmetic Average Rankings of Factors from Section 1.1 to Section 1.7 in Table 1.1 of Major Five World Currency Issuers

Currency Issuer	**US**	**Eurozone**	**Japan**	**UK**	**China**
GDP (Foreign Exchange Conversion)	1	3	4	5	2
GDP (PPP)	2	3	4	8	1
Commodity Trade Volume	3	2	4	5	1
Commodity Export Volume	3	2	4	6	1
Commodity Import Volume	1	2	4	5	3
International Payment	1	2	4	3	5
Total Debt	1	2	4	5	3
Government Debt	1	2	3	5	4
International Bond Value	3	1	4	2	12
Stock Market Capitalization	1	3	4	6	2
Securitization Ratio	1	5	3	2	4
Stock Market Capitalization	1	4	3	6	2
Annual Turnover of Stock Market	1	4	3	6	2
World Bank Voting Rights	1	2	3	5	4
IMF Voting Rights	1	2	3	5	4
IMF Special Drawing Rights (SDRs)	1	2	4	5	3
Arithmetic Average Ranking	1.44	2.56	3.63	4.94	3.31
Foreign Exchange Daily Average Trading Value Worldwide	1	2	3	4	8
Arithmetic Average Ranking — Foreign Exchange Daily Average Trading Value Ranking	0.44	0.56	0.63	0.94	–4.69

Source: GDP data based on world GDP data released by the IMF in April 2021; trade volume data based on the trade data of major countries published by the OECD. Stats in April 2021; the stock market capitalization and turnover data from the World Federation of Exchanges; debt data are calculated using related estimated debt ratios of the International Institute of Finance (IIF, 2021) of 2020; International debt ratios were calculated using the data released by Bank for International Settlements (BIS) for 2020 Q3; Foreign exchange volume share was calculated using daily average trading data for April 2019 from BIS Triennial data updated in December 2019; World Bank voting rights, IMF voting rights and SDRs data from World Bank and IMF official websites; cross-border currency trade share data from the Society for Worldwide Interbank Financial Telecommunication (SWIFT) in January 2021.

Australian dollar, Canadian dollar, and Swiss franc were each over-ranked by one ladder position as the fifth, sixth, and seventh ranked world currencies in 2019. Thus, yuan was five ladder positions under-ranked in 2019. The primary reason for the under-rankingness of the yuan was the result of the majority of Chinese trade being settled in USD and other major world currencies rather than the yuan, as explained earlier in the international payment section. The deeper reason was that most Chinese commodity exports were from foreign enterprises in China. These foreign exporters prefer to settle their exports in their currencies rather than the Chinese yuan to avoid foreign exchange risk. We will discuss and analyze related issues later in this book.

1.9 Science and Technology

Besides the above well-known factors affecting currency valuation and currency internationalization, there is another factor — science and technology (sci-tech) — that is extremely important and affects almost all of the aforementioned factors, and in turn acts as currency valuation and currency internationalization as we introduced briefly in the preface of this book. Sci-tech affect and even lead exports as no products can be exported without being recognized. Exports then determine international settlements as exporters prefer to settle their products with their currencies to avoid foreign exchange rates. In turn, exports affect current accounts and currency valuation and finally affect currency internationalization. All the above effects are intuitive, yet empirical evidence is missing in the existing literature. This book's primary purpose is to find empirical evidence as to how sci-tech affect currency valuation and currency internationalization through quantifying originality capability and sci-tech internationalization.

1.10 Conclusion

Currency internationalization is a complicated issue to study and to forecast as many factors are affected by it. We introduced significant traditional factors that affect currency internationalization such as GDP, international commodity trade, and services trade that largely involve global settlement and payment, debt market, stock market, and foreign exchange trading, and these factors affect currency internationalization in different “weights”, or its importance in determining currency internationalization should be significantly different. Although there are many types of international uses of currencies, all international uses of currencies are reflected in the foreign exchange trading of all currencies. Thus, sharing of these daily foreign exchange trading values of a currency in the world foreign exchange market is a good measure of currency internationalization as it avoids the complex problem of giving weights to various factors as shown in Table 1.1.

Although the weights of various factors in Table 1.1 are different and challenging to obtain, the simplest way to weigh all the factors the same, or the simplest arithmetic average ranking of significant factors other than foreign exchange trading may give us some intuitive results. Results in Table 1.3 show that all top four world currencies are somewhat over-ranked. The yuan is significantly under-ranked mainly because majority of the Chinese trade is settled with the USD and other major currencies rather than yuan. With the progress in science and technology, more share of Chinese business will be settled with Chinese yuan, its under-rankingness will be reduced gradually, and its international position will be closer to its rational level as shown in Table 1.3.

Bibliography

Arslanalp, S., Wei Liao, Shi Piao, and D. Seneviratne, China's Growing Influence on Asian Financial Markets, *IMF Working Paper, Asia and Pacific Department, WP/16/173*, August 2016.

Chang Shu, Dong He and Xiaoqiang Cheng, One Currency, Two Markets: The Renminbi's Growing Influence in Asia-Pacific, *BIS Working Papers No. 446*, Monetary and Economic Department, Bank for International Settlements, April 2014, http://www.bis.org.

Fratzscher, M. and A. Mehl, China's Dominance Hypothesis and the Emergence of a Tri-polar Global Currency System. *CEPR Discussion Paper No. 8671*, November 2011.

Henning, C., Choice and Coercion in East Asian Exchange Rate Regimes, Peterson Institute for International Economics, *Working Paper*, 2012, pp. 12–15.

International Institute of Finance (IIF), COVID Drives Debt Surge — Stabilization Ahead?, *Global Debt Monitor*, February 17, 2012.

Li, Zengxin, Long Way to CNY Internationalization — An Interview with Zhu Min, Deputy Managing Director of International Monetary Fund, *Century Weekly*, February 2011, pp. 52–55.

Rafiq, S., When China Sneezes Does ASEAN Catch a Cold, *IMF Working Paper No.16/214*, November 10, 2016.

Shu, C., N. Chow and J.-Y. Chan, Impact of the Renminbi Exchange Rate on Asian Currencies, *China Economic Issues*, No. 3/07, Hong Kong Monetary Authority, January 2007.

Subramanian, A. and M. Kessler, The Renminbi Bloc is Here: Asia Down, Rest of the World To Go?, Peterson Institute for International Economics, *Working Paper No. 12–19*.

Winning, N. and W. Horobin, IMF's Strauss Kahn Wants the Yuan in SDR, *Dow Jones News Wires*, February 19, 2011.

Zhang, Guangping (Peter G.), *CNY Derivative Products* (Fourth Edition), China Financial Publishing House, 2016.

Zhang, Guangping (Peter G.) and Tan Ziyang, *CNY Derivative Products* (Tenth Edition), China Financial Publishing House, 2021.

Chapter 2

Science and Technology: The Cornerstones for Currency Internationalization

Economy and trade are the foundations for currency valuation and internationalization, whereas science and technology (sci-tech) are economical and trade development foundations. Over the past decades, scientific and technological advancement has played an unquestionable leading role in driving global economic and trade development, and this role will grow increasingly important in decades to come. Developed countries invest in developing countries to expand their export markets and promote economic and trade growth. In recent years, developed countries have increased their investments in research and development (R&D) to maintain their globally leading position in sci-tech to guarantee their driving seats in export trade. Scientific and technological innovations require investments, yet investments alone cannot achieve efficiency if the necessary management system is not implemented correctly. In recent years, trade disputes between the US and China, especially since the second half of 2019 when the conflicts escalated, have made China realize the necessity and essentiality of science and technology.

Innovation is always the main driving force for human progress, and scientific and technological innovations are the most crucial part. Scientific and technological innovations have influenced societies for centuries. Nowadays, scientific and technological innovations have permeated every aspect of our lives. This impact will become stronger as time goes on since scientific and technological innovations directly impact the real economy. The essence of finance is to serve the economy, and scientific and technological innovations constitute the foundation for financial services. This chapter briefly introduces the size of global investments in R&D for over a decade. Sectors in which investments impacted R&D on patents, R&D and technology content in export products, the relationship between technology content in export products and export settlement in the local currency, and the remarkable R&D progress China has made and relevant issues *need to slim down*. Lastly, this chapter discusses the vital role scientific and technological innovation plays in promoting currency internationalization.

2.1 R&D Investment by Major Countries and Regions

R&D investment is an important marker of the ability of a country or an institution in scientific and technological innovations and an important indicator of competitiveness. Table 2.1 shows R&D investments made by the top 20 countries from 2004 to 2018 and R&D investment as a percent of a country's GDP in a given year.

2.1.1 *R&D Investment as a percentage of GDP*

As shown in Table 2.1, the world's top four economies, namely the US, China, Japan, and Germany, are also the top four R&D spenders; R&D investment rankings of other major economies also mirror their rankings in GDP. Notably, South Korea moved up to fifth place in R&D investment rankings in 2018, surpassing the UK and France, whereas its GDP ranking for the same year is No. 10. From 2004 to 2018, South Korea recorded a 10.6% compound annual growth rate (CAGR) in R&D spending, nearly twice the country's nominal GDP CAGR (5.7%) over the same period, making it No. 1 in R&D investment increase among the 16 developed economies covered by the table. South Korea has certainly put great emphasis on R&D over the years. However, South Korea's share of world GDP only increased to 1.99% in 2018 from 1.81% in 2004, remaining at No. 10. The findings demonstrate that R&D investments need adequate management to grow.

Table 2.1: R&D Investment in the Top 20 Economies and R&D Investment as % of a Country's GDP in Given Year from 2004 to 2018 (Unit: billion USD, %)

Country/ Amount	**2004**	**2008**	**2012**	**2014**	**2016**	**2018**	**2004–2018 CAGR***
US	3,056.4	4,072.4	4,343.5	4,764.6	5,165.9	5,840.0	4.7
China	237.6	664.3	1,631.5	2,126.2	2,379.6	3,037.0	20.0
Japan	1,458.8	1,681.2	1,990.7	1,649.2	1,553.2	1,617.5	0.7
Germany	681.6	969.6	1,011.7	1,113.5	1,011.3	1,222.0	4.3
South Korea	200.9	327.1	514.6	636.6	634.2	827.6	10.6
France	443.2	601.5	597.7	649.1	549.2	613.3	2.3
UK	372.8	474.4	431.1	508.3	453.2	493.2	2.0
Australia	113.6	253.3	341.4	300.7	229.3	260.0	6.1
Canada	205.1	288.2	324.9	309.9	264.4	268.8	2.0
Italy	189.9	279.1	265.2	290.0	257.2	291.8	3.1
Switzerland	105.3	150.5	212.9	234.7	226.4	240.6	6.1
Brazil	64.5	191.5	277.8	312.2	227.0	243.7	10.0
Sweden	130.5	180.7	181.1	182.9	168.6	185.5	2.5
Netherlands	117.6	153.8	160.8	176.0	156.5	197.8	3.8
India	53.7	103.0	136.0	143.1	154.0	176.4	8.9
Spain	110.8	214.1	170.6	169.2	146.0	175.6	3.3
Russia	68.0	173.5	226.7	220.8	140.1	165.3	6.5
Israel	52.5	93.9	106.9	129.0	143.7	183.5	9.3
Austria	65.2	110.6	119.3	136.3	123.5	144.5	5.9
Belgium	66.7	99.1	112.8	127.6	121.6	153.1	6.1
Eurozone	1,806.9	2,661.6	2,647.9	2,879.5	2,545.9	3,019.1	3.7
EU	2,043.3	3,037.5	3,039.5	3,293.2	2,923.0	3,479.8	3.9
Total	7,794.5	11,081.9	13,157.2	14,180.0	14,104.9	16,337.2	5.4
Global	8,709.4	12,714.0	15,308.8	16,478.9	16,234.6	19,649.7	6.0
% of the global total	89.5	87.2	85.9	86.0	86.9	83.1	

Country/ of GDP	**% 2004**	**2008**	**2012**	**2014**	**2016**	**2018**	**2004–2018 Annual Change**
US	2.50	2.77	2.68	2.72	2.76	2.84	0.024
China	1.21	1.45	1.91	2.03	2.12	2.19	0.069
Japan	3.03	3.34	3.21	3.40	3.16	3.26	0.017

(Continued)

Table 2.1: (*Continued*)

Country/ of GDP	% 2004	2008	2012	2014	2016	2018	2004–2018 Annual Change
Germany	2.43	2.60	2.87	2.87	2.92	3.09	0.048
South Korea	2.53	3.12	4.03	4.29	4.23	4.81	0.163
France	2.09	2.06	2.23	2.28	2.22	2.20	0.008
UK	1.54	1.62	1.59	1.66	1.68	1.72	0.013
Australia	1.85	2.40	2.21	2.05	1.90	1.81	−0.003
Canada	2.00	1.86	1.78	1.72	1.73	1.57	−0.031
Italy	1.05	1.16	1.27	1.34	1.37	1.40	0.025
Switzerland	2.67	2.71	3.19	3.31	3.37	3.41	0.053
Brazil	0.96	1.13	1.13	1.27	1.26	1.29	0.024
Sweden	3.39	3.49	3.28	3.14	3.27	3.34	−0.003
Netherlands	1.79	1.62	1.92	1.98	2.00	2.16	0.027
India	0.76	0.86	0.74	0.70	0.67	0.65	−0.008
Spain	1.04	1.32	1.29	1.24	1.19	1.24	0.014
Russia	1.15	1.04	1.03	1.07	1.10	0.99	−0.012
Israel	3.88	4.35	4.16	4.17	4.51	4.95	0.077
Austria	2.17	2.57	2.91	3.08	3.13	3.17	0.072
Belgium	1.81	1.92	2.27	2.39	2.56	2.82	0.072
Eurozone	1.78	1.89	2.10	2.13	2.13	2.21	0.031
EU	1.79	1.87	2.08	2.11	2.11	2.18	0.028
Global	1.99	2.00	2.04	2.07	2.13	2.27	0.021

Source: Data for 2014–2019 is calculated based on World Development Indicators (WDI) of the World Bank.

*CAGR stands for compound annual growth rate.

2.1.2 *Distribution of R&D investment in developed and developing countries*

It is noteworthy that out of the top 10 economies in 2019, there are three developing countries. In contrast, only one developing country — China — is among the top 10 R&D spenders, as shown in Table 2.1. Besides, the other developing countries (Mexico, Indonesia, Turkey, and Saudi Arabia) among the world's top 20 economies in 2018 do not find a place in Table 2.1.

However, four small and medium-sized economies, Sweden, Israel, Austria, and Belgium, are listed among the top 20 R&D spenders, which shows their emphasis on R&D. In general, developing countries are ranked lower in R&D investment compared with their rankings in GDP, which is a proof that most developing countries have potential to increase their R&D investment.

2.1.3 *R&D investment as a percentage of GDP*

R&D investment as a percentage of GDP demonstrates the priority level of R&D in that country. Table 2.1 also provides R&D investment as a percentage of GDP in significant R&D spenders from 2004 to 2018. Israel and South Korea are the top two countries in terms of R&D investment as a percentage of their respective GDPs, which exceed 4.5%. Next are Sweden, Switzerland, Japan, Austria, and Germany with 3–4%; the US comes in at No. 8, standing at roughly 3%; the last two countries are India and Russia with less than 1% R&D investment.

2.2 Landscape of R&D Investors

2.2.1 *Companies of major countries and regions entering top 2,500 companies of the world*

The latest editions of the *EU Industrial R&D Investment Scoreboard* show that the total number of companies entering the world's top 2,500 companies are from the US and the EU. However, the 2020 *EU Industrial R&D Investment Scoreboard* listed the UK outside of the EU; as Brexit was not finalized, we will consider the UK inside of the EU in 2019. China and Japan changed 6, −3, 29, and −9 from 769, 551, 507, and 318 to 775, 421, 536, and 209 to 775, 548, 536, and 309, respectively, indicating significant changes in companies with more R&D investment in the four major groups.

2.2.2 *Distribution of R&D investment by major countries and regions*

According to the latest two editions of the *EU Industrial R&D Investment Scoreboard*, total R&D investment of major US companies grew 11.26%

from 2018 to 2019, higher than the annual growth rate of total R&D investment of 9.81% for 2,500 companies in the same period. The US share of 2,500 companies grew from 37.95% to 38.45%, indicating the dominant position of the US companies in the R&D of the world. The share of total EU companies (including UK companies in 2019) declined from 28.86% to 24.43% in the same period. The percentage of Chinese companies grew from 11.71% to 13.14% in the same period as a result of a high growth rate of 23.26% of total R&D investment of major Chinese companies (more than twice the corresponding total R&D investment of 2,500 companies of 9.81% from 2018 to 2018), surpassing Japanese share of 12.70% for the first time in 2019. The percentage of Japanese companies declined from 13.29% to 12.70%.

It is noticeable that besides China, the largest developing country in the world, the number of companies entering the top 2,500 companies from other developing countries declined from 39 to 31 from 2018 to 2019. Their total share of R&D investment as a percentage of total world R&D investment dropped from 0.91% to 0.80%, even adding share of China, total R&D investment of companies entering the top 2,500 companies increased from 12.62% to 13.94% in the same period, showing that R&D investment has mainly been the business of developed economies.

2.3 Global R&D Investment by Sector

2.3.1 *Global R&D investment growth by sector*

According to the latest two editions of the *EU Industrial R&D Investment Scoreboard* from 2019 to 2020, the total R&D investment of the top 2,500 firms grew 9.87% to 904.7 billion EER from 2018 to 2019, as shown in Table 2.2. Total R&D investment in ICT services, industrials, health industries, and ICT producers grew 20.50%, 9.08%, 8.89%, and 8.67%, respectively, in the same period. EU investment in ICT industries reflects that ICT services are a significant contributor to worldwide R&D growth, which will continue.

2.3.2 *Global R&D investment by sector*

The previous section shows R&D investment growth in major sectors. Table 2.2 shows global R&D investment by sector in 2019. As we can see from Table 2.2, the top two sectors in terms of R&D spending were ICT producers and health industries, accounting for 23.0% and 20.5%, respectively, of the year's total. ICT services followed, making up 16.9% of the total; automobiles and other transport came in fourth, accounting for 16.3%; industry, chemicals, and aerospace and defense accounted only for 5.5%, 2.6%, and 2.3%, respectively. ICT producers and services together accounted for 39.9% of the total, demonstrating the dominant position of information technology in attracting investment.

We can also calculate R&D-related projects as a share of the total announced projects by sector during 2010–2018, according to the World Investment Report 2019 published by the United Nations Conference on Trade and Development (UNCTAD). Investments in pharmaceutical, software and IT services, chemicals, electrical and electronics, and automotive and aerospace accounted for 17%, 15%, 14%, 11%, and 9% of the total. R&D investments in machinery and equipment, food, beverages and tobacco, rubber and plastic, other manufacturing, extractives, and non-tech services only accounted for 6%, 5%, 5%, 4%, 3%, and 2%, respectively, all below the average of 6%. These data are representative of the distribution of global R&D investment over the last decade.

2.3.3 *Distribution of types of R&D investment by company size*

The previous section describes the distribution of global R&D investment by sector. Similarly, it is also meaningful to analyze the distribution of global R&D by investment type. Table 2.3 presents the types of R&D investment by EU companies of various sizes. Though it only covers EU companies, it can still shed light on the situation in other countries and regions. As shown in Table 2.3, R&D investment varies with the size of a company. Smaller companies focus on basic research and software development to prepare for converting new concepts into new products. In comparison, larger companies heavily invest in applied research and market adaptability as they are often more internationalized and thus must adapt to local markets.

Echoing Table 2.3, Table 2.4 shows that different sectors have different R&D priorities. Types of R&D investment in eight technology-related sectors are presented in Table 2.4. As we can see, the majority of R&D investments in health industries, chemicals, industrials, and ICT producers

Table 2.2: Industrial Classifications Applied in Eight Industrial Groups (2019)

Sector/Region	Sector Classification	No. of Firms	R&D (Billion Euro)	% of Total R&D	R&D per Firm
Aerospace & Defense	Aerospace; Defense	45	20.6	2.3	457.0
ICT Producers	Computer Hardware; Electrical Components & Equipment; Electric Equipment; Electric Office Equipment; Semiconductors; Telecommunications Equipment	461	208.5	23.0	452.3
ICT Services	Computer Services; Internet; Software; Mobile Telecommunications	322	152.8	16.9	474.7
ICT	ICT Providers & ICT Services	783	361.3	39.9	461.5
Health Industries	Biotechnology; Health Providers; Medical Equipment; Medical Supplies; Pharmaceuticals	530	185.6	20.5	350.2
Industrials	Aluminum; Containers & Packaging; Diversified Industrials; Deliveries; Industrial Machinery; Iron & Steel; Non-ferrous Metals; Transportation Services	291	49.4	5.5	169.9
Automobiles & Other Transport	Auto Parts; Automobiles; Commercial Vehicles & Trucks; Tires	187	147.3	16.3	787.7
Chemicals	Commodity Chemicals; Specialty Chemicals	130	23.1	2.6	178.0
Others	Alternative Energy; Banks and Others	534	117.2	13.0	219.5
Total		2,500	904.7	100.0	361.9

Source: Table 1.2 of *The 2020 EU Industrial R&D Investment Scoreboard*, https://iri.jrc.ec.europa.eu.

were dedicated to applied research/technology development, accounting for 59%, 51%, 32%, and 27%, respectively. In particular, health industries and chemicals put over half of their R&D investments into applied research/technology development; aerospace and defense and ICT services allocated 40% and 37%, respectively, of their R&D investments to

Table 2.3: Distribution of EU Types of R&D Investment by Company Size (2018)

Type of R&D Investment/ Company Size by No. of Employees	%	Nearly 2,500	2,501–10,000	10,001–50,001	In % Over 50,000
Applied research/technology development	36	34	26	31	41
Development for market launch	16	23	21	13	17
Development for adapting products to local markets	15	10	7	14	17
Basic research	9	15	9	9	10
Development of software/data	8	15	7	14	4
Acquisition of machinery, equipment, software & buildings	6	2	25	7	2
Others	10	2	5	13	9

Source: Figure 24 in the *2019 EU Survey on Industrial R&D Investment Trends*, https://iri.jrc.ec.europa.eu.

development for market launch. ICT services, ICT producers, and industrials distributed 31%, 10%, and 9%, respectively, to the development of software/data. Chemicals, industrials, and ICT producers spent 17%, 10%, and 9%, respectively, on fundamental research. The above data show different sectors have different concentrations of R&D investment.

2.4 Global Ranking of Companies by R&D Investment

R&D investments in developed countries are mainly company-funded, so ranking companies by R&D investment ranking can also reflect the extent to which companies from different countries and regions value technology. Table 2.5 presents the top 20 R&D investing companies in 2019 and introduces them from country perspectives, R&D investment amount, R&D intensity, ranking change in 2019 and ranking change from 2013 to 2019.

2.4.1 *Distribution of the top 20 R&D investors by country and sector*

As reported in Table 2.5, among the top 20 R&D investors, there are 10 companies based in the US, showing the leading position of the US

Table 2.4: Distribution of EU Types of R&D Investment by Sector (2018)

Sector	Aerospace & Defense	Automobiles & Other Transport	Chemicals	Health Industries	ICT Producers	ICT Services	Industrials	In % Others
Applied research/technology development	15	9	51	59	27	15	32	31
Development for market launch	**40**	12	7	9	17	37	17	11
Development for adapting products to local markets	39	2	20	6	25	9	24	19
Fundamental research	6	2	17	7	9	5	10	14
Development of software/data	0	2	2	1	10	31	9	5
Acquisition of machinery, equipment, software & buildings	0	2	4	2	11	2	6	15
Others	0	71	0	15	2	0	1	4

Source: Figure 24 in the *2019 EU Survey on Industrial R&D Investment Trends*, https://iri.jrc.ec.europa.eu.

Table 2.5: Top 20 R&D Investing Companies in 2019 and Ranking Change from 2013 to 2019 In billion EUR

Ranking	Name	Country	Industry	R&D Investment	R&D Intensity	Ranking Change 2013 to 2019
1	Alphabet	US	Software & computer	23.16	24.37	8
2	Microsoft	US	Software & computer	17.15	14.18	1
3	Huawei	China	Technology & hardware	16.71	31.23	23
4	Samsung	South Korea	Electronic and electrical equipment	15.52	8.27	−2
5	Apple	US	Technology & hardware	14.44	13.92	30
6	Volkswagen	Germany	Automobiles & parts	14.31	4.88	−5
7	Facebook	US	Software & computer	12.11	32.39	94
8	Intel	US	Technology & hardware	11.89	−1.34	−4
9	Roche	Switzerland	Pharmaceutical & biotechnology	10.75	5.87	−3
10	Johnson & Johnson	US	Pharmaceutical & biotechnology	10.11	5.38	−2
11	Daimler	Germany	Automobiles & parts	9.63	6.51	−1
12	Toyota Motor	Japan	Automobiles & parts	9.06	5.87	−5

(*Continued*)

Table 2.5: *(Continued)*

Ranking	Name	Country	Industry	R&D Investment	R&D Intensity	Ranking Change 2013 to 2019
13	Merck US	US	Pharmaceutical & biotechnology	8.23	–4.45	–1
14	Novartis	Switzerland	Pharmaceutical & biotechnology	7.71	–5.38	–9
15	Gilead Sciences	US	Pharmaceutical & biotechnology	7.39	97.86	53
16	Pfizer	US	Pharmaceutical & biotechnology	7.37	6.12	–1
17	Honda Motor	Japan	Automobiles & parts	6.83	0.34	3
18	Ford Motor	US	Automobiles & parts	6.59	–9.76	–1
19	BMW	Germany	Automobiles & parts	6.42	–6.84	–6
20	Robert Bosch	Germany	Automobiles & parts	6.23	0.65	–4

Source: The *2020 EU Industrial R&D Investment Scoreboard*, https://iri.jrc.ec.europa.eu.

in R&D: four in Germany, two in Switzerland, two in Japan, one in China, and one in South Korea. Regarding sector distribution of the top 20 R&D investors, seven companies come from automobiles and parts, displaying the unchanged leading position of this traditional sector in R&D innovation. However, the declining general budgets of these companies (six of the seven automobiles and parts distributors in Table 2.5) fell in ranking; only Honda Motor is an exception as its ranking increased from 20th to 17th. The total R&D investment of these seven companies of €59.1 billion was significantly lower than the total R&D investment of the top four companies of €72.6 billion in Table 2.5. This indicates the declining role of the automobile sector mentioned above in R&D investment; six companies from pharmaceuticals and biotechnology with a total R&D investment of €51.6 billion; three from technology and hardware with a total R&D investment of €43.0 billion, three from software and computer companies with total R&D investment of €58.4 billion, and one from electronic and electrical equipment. Software, computer, and electrical equipment companies are generally classified as high-tech companies, with a total R&D investment of €117.0 billion, 6.4 billion more than the total R&D investment of 13 automobiles and parts and pharmaceuticals, indicating the extreme importance of high-tech companies in making R&D investment.

2.4.2 *R&D intensity of the top 20 R&D companies*

Table 2.5 also provides the R&D intensity (R&D/sales ratio) of the top 20 R&D companies. As we can see from Table 2.5, the R&D intensity of high-tech and pharmaceutical companies is generally higher than automobiles and parts companies, all of which have around 5%. It is noticeable that Facebook and Gilead Sciences, two US companies, had the two most significant ranking increases of 94 and 53 and two high R&D investment intensities of 19.24% and 37.0%.

2.4.3 *Rank change of the top 20 R&D companies*

In Table 2.5, 13 out of the top 20 R&D investors dropped in the ranking from 2013 to 2019, including six from automobiles and parts, five from pharmaceuticals and biotechnology, one from technology and hardware, and one from electrical equipment. Facebook, Gilead Sciences, Apple, and Huawei gained 94, 53, 30, and 23 places, respectively, from 2013 to 2019, showing their fast growth in R&D spending.

2.5 Global Distribution of Patents and Changes

Patents represent a company's R&D investment performance and constitute a company's competitiveness, and total patents represent the general development status of the science and technology of a country. Following an introduction to the landscape of R&D investments of significant companies by country/region, this section presents the number of patents filed and authorized worldwide in the last decade. Table 2.6 provides the number of patents filed by major countries and regions, total patent filings by a country/region as a percentage of the world's total, and GDP created per item of patent and changes over 2001–2019.

2.5.1 *Distribution of patents*

In Table 2.6, the number of patents filed by China increased to 289,383 in 2008 from 63,450 in 2001, representing its contribution to the world's total increasing from 4.4% to 15.0%. The country's CAGR in patents reached 24.2%, over five times higher than the world's average (4.1%) over the same period, ranking No. 1 worldwide.

- The contribution of the EU and Japan dropped over the same period.
- The CAGR of the US recorded 4.9%, slightly higher than the world's average (4.1%), and its contribution to the world's total rose by 1.2% cumulatively.
- Other countries and regions outside China, the US, Japan, and the EU realized a CAGR of 5.3%, and their contribution increased by 2.1% cumulatively.

From 2008 to 2019, China realized a CAGR of 19.1%, lower than the previous period (2000–2008). However, China's CAGR doubles the worldwide average of 5.9%; its contribution to the world's total increased to 43.4% from 15.0%, making it the top patent applicant globally. China's contribution was double that of the US, which came in second, manifesting China's significant patent achievements over the last decade.

Table 2.6: Number of Patents Filed by Major Countries and Regions, No. of Patents by a Country/Region as % of the World's Total, and GDP Per Patent and Changes (2001–2019)

No. of Patents (Thousand)	2001	2005	2008	2011	2014	2017	2018	2019	2001–2008 CAGR (%)	2008–2019 CAGR (%)
China	63.5	173.3	289.8	526.4	928.2	1,381.6	1,542.0	1,400.7	24.2	19.1
US	326.5	390.7	456.3	503.6	578.8	607.0	597.1	621.5	4.9	3.5
Japan	440.2	427.1	391.0	342.6	326.0	318.5	313.6	308.0	−1.7	−2.6
EU	271.8	272.8	283.1	277.1	291.8	305.9	311.6	315.9	0.6	1.2
Other countries and regions	354.8	439.2	509.7	508.5	547.5	549.4	562.0	578.2	5.3	1.4
Global	1456.8	1703.2	1930.0	2158.2	2672.2	3162.3	3326.3	3224.2	4.1	5.9
No. of Patents as % of World's Total	**2001**	**2005**	**2008**	**2011**	**2014**	**2017**	**2018**	**2019**	**2001–2008 CAGR (%)**	**2008–2019 CAGR (%)**
China	4.4	10.2	15.0	24.4	34.7	43.7	46.4	43.4	19.1	12.5
US	22.4	22.9	23.6	23.3	21.7	19.2	18.0	19.3	0.7	−2.2
Japan	30.2	25.1	20.3	15.9	12.2	10.1	9.4	9.6	−5.5	−8.0
EU	18.7	16.0	14.7	12.8	10.9	9.7	9.4	9.8	−3.4	−4.4
Other countries and regions	24.4	25.8	26.4	23.6	20.5	17.4	16.9	17.9	1.1	−4.2
Global	100	100	100	100	100	100	100	100		

(*Continued*)

Table 2.6: (*Continued*)

GDP Created per Piece of Patent (In mm USD)	2001	2005	2008	2011	2014	2017	2018	2019	2001–2008 CAGR (%)	2008–2019 CAGR (%)
China	21.0	13.2	15.8	14.2	11.3	8.9	9.0	10.2	−4.0	−5.9
US	32.4	33.4	32.2	30.9	30.3	32.2	34.5	34.5	−0.1	0.7
Japan	9.9	11.3	13.1	18.2	15.0	15.5	16.1	16.7	4.0	2.1
EU	33.2	52.9	68.0	66.4	64.2	56.9	60.4	58.5	10.8	−1.2
Other countries and regions	23.7	29.8	39.8	50.8	50.2	48.6	49.1	48.3	7.7	2.0
Global	23.1	28.0	33.1	34.1	29.6	25.6	25.8	27.1	5.3	−2.5

Source: Calculated according to the country-based patent statistics updated in Jan 2021 on the website (www.wipo.int) of World Intellectual Property Organization (WIPO) and country-based GDP statistics updated in Apr 2020 by the International Monetary Fund (IMF).

2.5.2 *Distribution of patents by sector*

Table 2.6 provides the distribution of patents by country/region, while Table 2.7 presents significant patents as a share of total patents in major countries and regions during 2009–2019. We can calculate the distribution of patents by major sectors in those countries and regions from the two tables.

According to Table 2.7, in terms of patent contribution to ICT industries, which represent the most potential and fastest growing sector, China, although ranking world No. 1 in the total number of patents, is not only far behind the US but also lagging behind Japan and the world's average. During 2009–2019, China's patent contribution to this sector even declined by 2.45%. Similarly, the decrease in patent contribution also happened in pharmaceuticals and biotechnology, and automobile industries. Apart from the three major sectors, China's patent contribution to other sectors increased remarkably by 6.97% from 2009 to 2019. The above analysis reflects that China's patent performance in the three main sectors is far from satisfactory even if its total number of patents is vast.

As for the US, the world's leading country in science and technology, its patent contribution to ICT industries increased by 0.13% from 2009–2019 and remained high at 37.90%. Countries that prioritize their R&D do so as it has substantial growth opportunities. Its contribution to the automobile industry is even higher than last year. The country's total contribution to the three main sectors remained nearly unchanged, only increasing by 0.35% over the decade. This manifests the leading position of the US in the three technology-intensive sectors.

2.6 The Meaning of a Narrowing Smiling Curve of Industrial Chain and What It Tells Us

Decades ago, the international derivatives market put forward volatility smiles, implying volatility patterns against strike prices for a given expiration (see options terminology in Chapters 10 and 16). Generally, options (at-the-money options) whose strike price is identical to the underlying asset's price have low implied volatility; those whose strike price differs substantially from the underlying security price have high implied volatility. The result is a skewed "smile" when graphing implied volatilities against strike prices for a given expiry.

Table 2.7: Major Patents as a Share of Total Patents in Major Countries and Regions over 2009–2019

China	**2009**	**2011**	**2013**	**2015**	**2017**	**2018**	**2019**	**2009–2019 % Change**
ICT and relevant industries	24.90	23.24	19.61	17.49	19.12	17.88	22.44	−2.45
Chips	3.23	3.35	2.58	1.93	1.60	1.62	1.93	−1.30
Pharmaceutical & biotechnology	7.41	6.82	5.91	6.41	4.87	3.97	3.66	−3.75
Automobiles and relevant industries	8.13	8.07	8.26	8.00	7.59	7.43	7.37	−0.76
Other industries	59.56	61.87	66.22	68.10	68.42	70.71	66.53	6.97
Japan	**2009**	**2011**	**2013**	**2015**	**2017**	**2018**	**2019**	**2009–2019 % Change**
ICT and relevant industries	26.70	26.42	24.74	22.91	21.52	20.64	20.27	−6.43
Chips	5.64	5.98	5.79	4.72	4.03	3.81	3.66	−1.98
Pharmaceutical & biotechnology	3.29	3.10	3.40	3.41	3.77	4.07	4.03	0.74
Automobiles and relevant industries	6.66	6.64	7.04	6.90	7.14	7.13	6.99	0.33
Other industries	63.36	63.84	64.82	66.78	67.57	68.17	68.71	5.36
US	**2009**	**2011**	**2013**	**2015**	**2017**	**2018**	**2019**	**2009–2019 % Change**
ICT and relevant industries	37.78	37.06	39.75	39.73	38.65	37.47	37.90	0.13
Chips	4.97	5.35	5.28	5.48	5.34	5.16	5.15	0.18
Pharmaceutical & biotechnology	6.05	5.94	5.19	5.04	5.21	5.33	5.53	−0.52
Automobiles and relevant industries	4.89	4.89	5.19	5.32	5.54	5.82	5.63	0.74
Other industries	51.29	52.12	49.87	49.91	50.61	51.38	50.94	−0.35

(Continued)

Table 2.7: (*Continued*)

EU	**2009**	**2011**	**2013**	**2015**	**2017**	**2018**	**2019**	**2009–2019 % Change**
ICT and relevant industries	16.55	16.47	17.90	18.44	19.97	19.52	19.29	2.74
Chips	1.96	2.20	2.20	1.96	2.09	1.98	1.95	0.00
Pharmaceutical & biotechnology	5.05	5.90	4.59	4.38	5.23	5.32	5.70	0.65
Automobiles and relevant industries	7.31	7.32	8.23	8.41	8.96	8.43	7.93	0.61
Other industries	71.09	70.31	70.34	69.49	68.90	69.78	67.08	−4.01
Global	**2009**	**2011**	**2013**	**2015**	**2017**	**2018**	**2019**	**2009–2019 % Change**
ICT and relevant industries	26.43	25.53	24.56	23.15	22.68	21.62	24.30	−2.12
Chips	4.40	4.43	4.00	3.29	2.85	2.69	2.94	−1.46
Pharmaceutical & biotechnology	6.37	6.39	5.79	6.21	5.77	5.11	5.21	−1.16
Automobiles and relevant industries	6.40	6.51	7.00	7.04	6.95	6.96	6.87	0.46
Other industries	60.80	61.58	62.65	63.60	64.60	66.31	63.62	2.82

Source: *The 2020 EU Industrial R&D Investment Scoreboard*, https://iri.jrc.ec.europa.eu. In Table 2.6, ICT (Information, Computer and Telecommunication) and relevant industries include the following seven types of technologies published by the WIPO: audiovisual technology, telecommunications, digital communication technology, basic communication processing technology, computer technology, information technology management methodology, and semiconductor technology. Pharmaceuticals and biotechnology include pharmaceuticals and biotechnology; automobiles and relevant industries include the following three types of technologies: control technology, material, and metallurgical technology, and engine, transmission, and turbine technology, given the specificity of semiconductor technology, we will list out patents of this technology separately.

2.6.1 *The meaning of a smiling curve of the industrial chain*

The industrial chain can be presented in a graph with an X-axis for different stages of production and a Y-axis for value-added. Specifically, the X-axis covers a value chain comprising a full range of activities, such as developing new products, producing parts and components, producing module parts and components, assembling, sales, brand marketing, and relevant sales services. In general, profits are generated by assembling. The middle part of a value chain is the lowest. In contrast, the two ends of a value chain, the development of new products and brand marketing, can yield higher profits, resulting in the "smiling" appearance of the value chain (Jian Zhaoquan and Wu Zhuoshen, 2011).

The narrowing of a smiling curve of the industrial chain, meaning that the two ends of the curve become steeper and higher, shows that product development and brand marketing activities have become more profitable, and assembling and other production-related activities have become less profitable. This proves the increasingly important position of R&D and branding in an industrial chain.

2.6.2 *Hidden champion is the cornerstone of manufacturing*

While the profits from the two ends of a value chain are growing, the stage only next to product development is hailed as the "hidden champion" of manufacturing, covering essential parts and components, materials, industrial software, etc. These products are "hidden" inside the end products, making them hard to be noticed or attract consumers' attention (Zhu Wenhao, 2019). But without these hidden products, the end products cannot be manufactured. The so-called hidden champion, or essential parts and components and basic materials, is an integral part of some industries and the cornerstone of the manufacturing sector, making it an indicator of manufacturing prowess. China has a complete industrial system and is ahead of the world in most sectors, but its basic industries' contribution to GDP is unsatisfactory. From 2013 to 2017, the contribution from the value-added of China's primary industries (mainly including essential parts and components, computer numerical control, and instrumentation) to the world's total declined to 6.92% from 11.54%, further widening the gap with the US and Japan. The increasing constraints from core essential parts and components, fundamental materials, and critical processes have become the main bottlenecks for China to become a manufacturing powerhouse (Zhu Wenhao, 2019). Therefore, while improving R&D investment efficiency to make it more market- and enterprise-oriented, China should also promote R&D in essential industries.

2.7 GDP Per Item of Patent Worldwide and Changes

As a significant R&D outcome, patents represent a company's competitiveness and contribute to economic growth. Table 2.6 reports contribution per item of patent to GDP.

According to the table, from 2001 to 2008, GDP per patent worldwide remained around $28 million, making patents a great GDP contributor; during 2001–2008, EU GDP per patent rose by 105.0% to $68 million, and the number dropped by 11.4% to $58.5 million in 2019. Though the total number of patents is not that high, the EU ranked No. 1 in terms of GDP per patent, proving the high quality of its patents over 2001–2019. US GDP per patent remained around $32 million, lower than that of EU but higher than the world's average, showing the country's regular patent contribution to economic growth. Other countries and regions apart from China, the US, Japan, and the EU saw their GDP per patent decreasing continuously, maintaining at $49 million.

As shown in Table 2.6, Japan ranked the lowest in terms of GDP per patent. The number showed an upward trend during 2001–2019, up by 68.7% cumulatively. China's GDP per patent continued to decline, down by 51.4% cumulatively during 2001–2019 to $10.2 million. This reflects that although China has shown remarkable growth in the total number of patents, it needs to improve its quality.

2.8 China's R&D Achievements in the Past 10 Years

As reported in Table 2.1, China surpassed Japan in 2013 in terms of total R&D investment, ranking No. 2 globally, and has remained in this position since 2013. Three years earlier, China overtook Japan to become the world's second largest economy in 2010. The table shows from 2004 to 2018, China achieved a CAGR of 20.0% in R&D investment, the highest in the world, 6.8% higher than the CAGR (13.2%) of nominal GDP and 11.4% higher than its trade CAGR (8.6%). This manifests how much the country and its leaders have valued scientific and technological innovations. In 2018, China's R&D investment as a percent of GDP increased to 2.19%, showing the country's continuous emphasis on and promotion of scientific and technological innovations.

Still, according to Table 2.7, China has harvested great results from its R&D investments. In 2011, China overtook the US in terms of the total number of patents, making it the world's No. 1 patent applicant; besides, its CAGR in the number of patents vastly exceeded the world's patent CAGR, showing a promising trend in enhancing its R&D capacity. Continuous R&D investments have driven significant growth in the number of patents, laying a solid foundation for economic transformation and high-quality development.

In 2017, China recorded RMB 1.76 trillion in R&D expenditure, nearly 80% of which came from its companies. In particular, 136,000 high-tech companies in China spent RMB 900 billion on R&D in 2017, accounting for 68% of the country's total company-funded R&D (*Economic Daily*, 2019). The significant increase in company-funded R&D has invigorated China's R&D efforts, and R&D investments to high-quality economic growth will make more contributions.

2.9 Main Issues in China's R&D Investments

While seeing that China has made significant achievements in R&D, we should also be aware of the gap between China and leading countries and keep trying to achieve better results.

2.9.1 *Low concentration of R&D investment*

According to the *2019 EU Industrial R&D Investment Scoreboard*, there were only two Chinese companies among the top 50 R&D investing companies in 2019, namely Huawei and Alibaba. In 2018–2019, the number of Chinese companies among the top 2,500 R&D investors climbed from 438 to 504, the highest increase in the world. However, the average R&D spending of these Chinese companies only rose to RMB 214 million from RMB 186 million, only 57% of the 2,500 companies' average, ranking the lowest among major countries and regions. A low concentration of R&D investment can hardly generate scale effects or play a leading role in major technology fields.

According to the statistics, "136,000 high-tech companies in China spent RMB 900 billion on R&D in 2017, accounting for 68% of the country's total company-funded R&D" (*Economic Daily*, 2019). From the data reported in Table 3.4, we can calculate that the average R&D expenditure of 135,600 medium-sized companies was nearly RMB 2.4 million in 2017 (minus 438 large companies in Table 2.4 from the total 136,000 and minus $88.52 billion spent by the 438 large companies from the total RMB 900 billion). The remaining RMB 423.53 billion is thus attributed to small companies with a size of about RMB 300,000 (assuming the average R&D spending of small companies is RMB 1.4 million). Therefore, R&D investments by large, medium, and small-sized Chinese companies accounted for 43.5%, 24.5%, and 32.0%, respectively, of the total RMB 900 billion. It is necessary to support small and medium-sized companies in scientific and technological innovation as it will immediately impact increasing employment. Still, they can hardly play a direct and influential role in making scientific and technological breakthroughs or improving China's international competitiveness.

2.9.2 *Unsatisfactory R&D and patent performance in key technologies*

As shown in Table 2.6, though China ranks high in the number of patents, its contribution to the highest potential sectors, including ICT and pharmaceuticals and biotechnology, is far from satisfactory.

Over 2009–2019, the number of patents in these two sectors as a share of China's total patents cumulatively decreased by 7.01% and 3.44%, respectively. In contrast, China's patents outside the three major R&D sectors exceeded the global level and Japan's contribution to the country's total and quickly overtook the US in this regard; this means China has to make more efforts to enhance R&D performance in crucial technologies.

2.9.3 *Weak spots in core technologies to be strengthened*

According to the results presented above, the fastest growing industries for R&D investment in recent years are ICT producers and services. The ICT sector is closely related to the highest potential technologies such as robotics and artificial intelligence, which will profoundly influence the global economy and trade, society, and people's lives. The core technology related to ICT is the chip, namely the integrated circuit (IC) and semiconductor-related technologies. As shown in Table 2.6, except for the EU, the other three major economies like China, the US, and Japan saw a decrease in the total number of semiconductor patents as a percentage of the country's total. Besides, China ranked the world's lowest in chip R&D in 2018. This is further evidence that China needs to increase R&D investment in core technologies like chips even if its total number of patents filed has skyrocketed since 2010.

According to the statistics published by the General Administration of Customs of China, China's IC imports rose by 3.8 times to $312.06 billion in 2018 from $81.55 billion in 2005, with a CAGR recording 10.9%. This points toward the country's high dependence on foreign chips and strong market demand over the same period, as the trade deficit of IC in China continued to increase to $227.42 billion from $67.16 billion, with a CAGR up to 9.8% in 2018. The ratio of China's IC trade deficit to its trade surplus of goods was 53.9% on average, reflecting that the IC trade deficit has seriously impacted the country's total trade surplus. The 17.2% growth in IC imports during 2016–2018 revealed that "China learned a bitter lesson from its attempts to build its own leading IC companies" (*The Straits Times*, July 15, 2019). In 2019, China's IC imports decreased to $305.55 billion, down by 2.1% year on year; accordingly, the trade deficit of IC fell by 10.3%, showing that trade disputes have taken a substantial toll on this sector. Hopefully, China can take this opportunity to shore up its weak spots in IC and other core technologies.

2.9.4 *Patent contribution to China's GDP to be increased*

According to Table 2.6, China ranks the world's No. 1 in the number of patent filings, but its GDP per patent ranks the lowest, showing a downturn trend over 2001–2019, down by 51.4% cumulatively. In contrast, GDP per patent recorded an increase of 76.2%, 68.7%, and 6.5%, respectively, in Europe, Japan, and the US, and 10.7% worldwide. Countries outside of the EU, Japan, the US, and China also increased by 103.8% over the same period. These data reflect China's patents are low in technology content and less market-oriented, so there is still much room for improvement.

2.9.5 *Contribution of R&D investments and patents to intellectual property to be improved*

According to statistics provided in the World Investment Report 2019 issued by the UNCTAD, the global patents index and patent royalties index increased by over 60% cumulatively from 2010 to 2018, higher than the increase in the services trade index (by about 50%) and goods trade index (by about 20%), respectively. This reflects the fact that intellectual property (IP) has been growing faster than trade. According to the US Bureau of Economic Analysis (BEA), the net income of IP in the US was about $72.6 billion in 2018, accounting for nearly one-third of the country's trade surplus in services and becoming the second largest surplus sub-item of the country. Such a high IP income represents returns on high R&D investments made by the US. It also shows a positive cycle of the US in maintaining its leading role in technology fields. During 2015–2019, China ranked as the world's No. 2 in terms of total R&D investments, but its trade deficit of IP continued to climb to $27.7 billion from $20.9 billion, recording a CAGR of 7.3%. This shows that China's R&D investments have generated many research papers and patent filings, but those research papers and patents have not done much to change its trade deficit of IP. R&D investments need to be market-oriented. Only by serving products and the market can R&D investments develop positively and sustainably.

2.9.6 *University R&D needs to be more practical and market-oriented*

Researchers, graduates specializing in various academic fields, and universities constitute a vital driver of R&D innovations. According to a report from the United Nations Educational, Scientific and Cultural Organization (UNESCO, 2019), higher education-funded R&D investments in the US, Japan, Canada, France, and South Korea in 2017 accounted for 4%, 5%, 10%, 2%, and 1% of its total investments. In contrast, universities in China barely provided any source of R&D funds. The number of R&D investments used by universities in the US, Japan, Canada, France, and South Korea took up approximately 13%, 12%, 40%, 20%, and 8%, respectively. In contrast, Germany and China recorded separately at 17% and around 7% in this regard. This shows that universities in the top R&D spenders are not the primary source of R&D funds, but they are essential participants in R&D activities and users of R&D funds. In addition, universities in different countries show different levels of participation in R&D activities.

According to the *China Statistics Yearbook* published on the National Bureau of Statistics website, government R&D grants used by universities in China accounted for 39.7% of the country's total in 2017, increasing from 34.6% in 2010. Chinese universities' proportion of R&D expenditure to total government R&D grants rose from 47.0% to 52.0%. Chinese universities participate in more state-led R&D activities than their counterparts in most developed countries. With many R&D funds, Chinese universities have achieved positive results in research papers and patents. The global ranking of China's knowledge creation capacity rose from No. 37 in 2000 to No. 7 in 2016, boasting the most innovation achievements (National Innovation Index Report 2018). Nonetheless, during 2007–2016, China's ranking in the development of industrial clusters and the coordination between enterprises and universities remained unchanged at No. 18 and No. 22, respectively. This reflects that Chinese universities have neither built a close connection with the market nor established deep cooperation with enterprises *in addition to* publishing papers and filing patents.

2.9.7 *Innovation performance remains stable with a slight decline*

The above-cited National Innovation Index Report 2018, compiled by the Chinese Academy of Science and Technology for Development, provides eye-catching results in innovation performance assessment. According to this report, during 2000–2016, China's R&D innovation barely played any role in improving labor productivity and GDP per unit energy (with the rankings declined from No. 39 to No. 37 and from No. 39 to No. 36, respectively). The proportion of high-tech exports to total manufacturing exports climbed to No. 6 from No. 16. However, as stated above, during 2005–2018, the ratio of China's IC trade deficit alone to its trade surplus of goods was nearly 60% on average, indicating that contribution from other high technologies apart from IC to exports is somewhat limited. From 2001 to 2016, China's knowledge-intensive service industry's added value as a share of GDP moved up from No. 35 to No. 12 worldwide, and the ranking of the added value from its knowledge-intensive sectors as a share of the world's total also improved significantly, moving up from No. 8 to No. 2. As mentioned above, China's GDP per patent is decreasing, the contribution to GDP per item of research paper is also going downward. The remarkable growth in the number of reports and patents is gratifying indeed, but we may need to re-evaluate their quality.

2.10 R&D Spending of Major Listed Companies

The stock market is the embodiment of a modern country's financial wealth. The wealth accumulation in the stock market has become an important supporter and driver of consumption in Western developed countries. The distribution and transfer of stock market wealth in different sectors can reflect a country's value orientation. The market capitalization of listed companies in a country/region and the distribution of listed companies by sector can largely reflect how investors in the country/region evaluate the future potential of different sectors. This section will provide a brief analysis of R&D investments by the top 30 companies from the US, the EU, Japan, and China listed in the Fortune 500 in 2020 to determine how much these countries and regions value science and technology. Since most companies appearing in the Fortune 500 are listed companies except for the rare case of Huawei, the largest company in a country/region listed in the Fortune 500 is also the largest listed company of the country/region in most cases.

2.10.1 *R&D investments by major US companies*

The 30th largest US company ranks No. 69 on the Fortune 500 list in 2020, showing that the revenue size of US companies remains very significant. Among these top 30 US companies, three are in the energy sector, five in financial, three in telecommunications, three in motor vehicles and parts, six in commerce and retailing, seven in health care, and three in IT. Amazon, Apple, Alphabet, and Microsoft rank No. 9, 12, 29, and 47 globally, and No. 2, 4, 11, and 21, respectively, in the US. Of them, Alphabet, Microsoft, and Apple are among the world's top 10 R&D investors. Ford Motor and General Motors also rank among the top 20 R&D investors worldwide. This demonstrates that both high-tech and traditional companies in the US have made substantial investments in R&D. Notably, there are only five financial companies among the top 30 US companies. Berkshire Hathaway ranks No. 6, followed by JPMorgan Chase (No. 17), Fannie Mae (No. 24), Bank of America (No. 25), and Wells Fargo (No. 30). This shows that financial companies are not as advantageous in revenue size compared with other major US companies.

2.10.2 *R&D investments by major EU companies*

The 30th largest EU company ranks No. 175 on the Fortune 500 list in 2020, showing that large EU companies are generally slightly smaller in revenue than their US counterparts. Among the top 30 EU companies, nine are in the financial sector, five in energy, six in motor vehicles and parts, one in high technology, and nine in others. Of the nine financial companies, there are five insurers (Allianz, AXA, Generali, Aegon, and Munich Re), three banks (Banco de España, Crédit Agricole, and BNP Paribas), and one diversified financials provider (Exor). The six automobile companies are Volkswagen, Daimler, BMW, Robert Bosch, Peugeot, and Renault. Siemens from Germany is deemed as the only high-tech company in the EU. Among the above companies, Volkswagen, Daimler, BMW, Robert Bosch, Renault, and Peugeot all ranked among the top 50 R&D investors worldwide in 2018–2019, and Bosch was the world's 20th R&D investor. In conclusion, most R&D investments are devoted to the traditional automobile sector in the EU, while high-tech companies are fewer whose ranking in terms of R&D investment even dropped during 2004–2019.

2.10.3 *R&D investments by major Japanese companies*

The 30th largest Japanese company ranks No. 300 on the Fortune 500 list in 2020, showing that large Japanese companies are much smaller in overall revenue than their EU peers. Among the top 30 Japanese companies, seven are in financials, four in motor vehicles and parts, four in electronics and electrical equipment, two in energy, eight in retailing and trade, one in high technology, and four in others. Of the seven financial companies, there are five insurance companies (including Nippon Life) and two banks (MUFG Bank and SMBC). The four automobile companies are Toyota, Honda Motor, Nissan Motor, and Denso. The solo high-tech company is SoftBank Group. The four companies in electronics and electrical equipment are Hitachi, Panasonic, Sony, and Mitsubishi Electric. All four automobile companies were listed among the top 50 R&D investors in 2018/2019; two traditional electrical giants, Panasonic and Sony, also rank among the top 50 R&D investors worldwide. Hitachi and NTT rank No. 58 and No. 87 worldwide in terms of R&D spending. SoftBank is, in fact, an investment company rather than a high-tech one, which was the No. 111 R&D investor worldwide in 2018–2019, with an R&D investment of only 1.7%, much lower than that of automobile companies. Like the EU, Japan puts most of its R&D investment into traditional sectors like automobiles and electronics instead of high-tech companies.

2.10.4 *R&D investments by major Chinese companies*

The total number of Chinese companies in Fortune 500 of 2020 increased to 129 and surpassed the corresponding total number 129 of US companies for the first time in history. Of these Chinese companies, six were in the financial sector, seven in energy and electricity, three in motor vehicles and parts, three in high technology, and 12 in others; of the six in financials, and two insurance companies (Ping An Insurance and China Life Insurance) and four banks (Industrial and Commercial Bank of China, China Construction Bank, Bank of China, and Agricultural Bank of China). Of the seven energy and electricity companies, Sinopec and CNPC are the world's second and fourth largest companies, respectively. The three high-tech companies are Huawei, JD.com, and Hon Hai. The three automobile companies are SAIC Motor, Dongfeng Motor, and FAW Group. The other 10 companies are mainly sizable state-owned construction and chemical enterprises. Of the three Chinese automotive companies, SAIC Motor and Dongfeng Motor are the No. 71 and No. 241 R&D investors worldwide, respectively, with an R&D intensity of 1.9% and 4.5% separately, much lower than that of their EU and Japanese counterparts. Huawei is the only high-tech company among the top 30 Chinese companies and the only Chinese company among the world's top 50 R&D investors. CNPC, Sinopec, China Railway, China Railway Construction, China Communications Construction, Power Construction Corporation of China, and China State Construction Engineering, all large state-owned enterprises, rank No. 81, 156, 100, 84, 113, 131, and 72 worldwide, respectively, by R&D investment.

The total R&D investments of the above seven companies, €10.49 billion, are only 75% that of Huawei over the same period; only by adding the amount by the above two large automotive companies, the nine companies' total, namely €13.13 billion, is almost equivalent to Huawei's over the same year. Their R&D intensity is merely 1.1%, not even 10% of Huawei's. In summary, large Chinese companies have a long way to catch up with their EU and Japanese counterparts in terms of R&D investment, not to mention their US peers. It is insufficient to emphasize core technologies and competitiveness rhetorically, but it is vital to significantly increase R&D investments to deliver better results.

2.10.5 *Profitability gap needs to be narrowed*

Chinese companies occupy 133 places on the Fortune 500 list for 2020, overtaking the US of 121 companies, demonstrating the rapid growth of Chinese companies in recent years. These 133 Chinese companies are 10.9% and 45.3% smaller than the 121 US companies in total revenues and profits. It demonstrates there is a clear gap between companies of the two countries in terms of profitability.

2.11 Inspirations by Huawei

I once visited Huawei Technologies Shanghai R&D Center 3 years ago for research purposes. This trip allowed me to have a direct observation of this company. I was surprised to know that most of its revenue came from overseas markets from years ago. In 2018, the US began to sanction ZTE and other Chinese technology companies. Huawei was one of the 70 affiliates to the "Entity List" in May 2019, restricting it from buying components from American companies. Under the current situation, we did a deeper analysis of Huawei.

2.11.1 *Steady R&D investments*

According to the 2020 R&D investment statistics of the world's top 2,500 R&D investors published by the EU in 2020, Huawei spent €16.71 billion on R&D in 2019, ranking third of all 2,500 companies, first among the top five Chinese companies included in the top 2,500 list (the other four Chinese companies rank from No. 26 to No. 66 on the list). Huawei's R&D investment was 13.2% larger than the four other Chinese companies combined (€14.77 billion). The average R&D intensity of these four companies was merely 5.6% in 2019, not even 40% of Huawei's R&D intensity.

Inputs will not necessarily bring outputs, but zero investment indeed ends up in zero output. Huawei has made significant R&D investments and developed strict management rules and execution capacity to effectively generate R&D inputs. Since being incorporated in Shenzhen in 1987 with just RMB 20,000 initial capital, Huawei has grown into a global tech giant with a revenue of over $100 billion, ranking No. 49 worldwide by revenue in 2019 (Fortune 500 ranking). It is also the 16th largest company and biggest private company in China. Besides, Huawei has become a global leader in the 5G mobile communication technology. Huawei could not become what it is today if it failed to take the right strategy to make short-term profits or make intensive R&D investments unswervingly.

According to Huawei's (Huawei Annual Report, 2020) data, it spent RMB 141.9 billion R&D in investment in 2020, equivalent to $20.56 billion with an R&D intensity of 15.9% higher than its intensity of 15.3% in 2019.

2.11.2 *Serving China and serving humanity*

On May 16, 2019, the Bureau of Industry and Security under the United States Department of Commerce added Huawei to the "Entity List." To respond to the ban imposed by the US, Ren Zhengfei, Founder and CEO of Huawei, received interviews from many media in Shenzhen on May 21. This is a man who has kept a low profile for decades. In one of the interviews, Mr. Ren said, "but in the end, we will embrace with each other and contribute to humanity together," which tells us the development philosophy that Huawei has upheld over the last decades: serving China and serving humanity.

2.11.3 *Implication of Huawei internationalization to CNY internationalization*

While valuing R&D investment and scientific and technological innovation, Huawei has also improved *management* to become a global leader in science and technology advancement. Its experiences and lessons are worth learning for other Chinese companies. In particular, shortly after gaining a firm foothold in the domestic market, Huawei began to expand its international markets. Its success in increasing its presence in major countries and regions is also worth learning for other Chinese companies. Huawei's internationalization, primarily how it promotes its 5G technology globally, can provide some insights into promoting RMB internationalization.

2.12 Fintech

As science and technology develop rapidly, the traditional financial sector will be challenged. With the increasing application of science and technology in finance, the number of bank outlets and employees will reduce irreversibly, and the business models of the financial sector will be materially changed. This section will briefly introduce how Fintech has developed and what issues it faces.

2.12.1 *Definition of Fintech*

As the name suggests, Fintech is a portmanteau of "finance" and "technology," but different institutions have different definitions for it. Fintech refers to integrating new technologies and the financial sector to drive financial products, services, channels, and management in a more convenient, customized, and intelligent way (Li Lin, 2017). Fintech creates products and services at the juncture of technology and financial services, seeking to challenge the existing processes and products that dominate the marketplace (H2 Ventures and KPMG, 2018). The former definition is more general while the latter is more narrowly defined, but the latter emphasizes the power of Fintech. In essence, Fintech refers to financial innovations driven by technology. Such financial innovations include those made by neo-banks and those made by the traditional financial sector in embracing new technologies to improve its operating efficiency. The former is revolutionary and the latter reformative.

2.12.2 *The catalog of Fintech*

According to H2 Ventures and KPMG (2019), the Catalog of Fintech is as follows: payment, lending, wealth management, insurance, neo-bank, and cross-sector multiple offerings. In 2019, among companies included in the "Top 50" and "Emerging 50", two sub-lists of Fintech 100, those from the above six sectors accounted for 27%, 15%, 19%, 17%, 9%, and 13% separately, showing that the application of science and technology varies with sectors. According to Citi GPS (2016) statistics, global capital invested in Fintech companies by segment includes 73% in retailing and SMEs, 10% in asset management and wealth, 10% in insurance, and 3% in large corporates. The banking sector far overtakes other sectors in terms of R&D investment (median IT expense as a share of business entity revenue recorded 8.7% in the banking sector, far higher than that of other industries according to the 2018 report of Citi GPS).

2.12.3 *Distribution of world's leading Fintech companies*

In the *2019 Fintech 100: Leading Global Fintech Innovations* (H2 Ventures and KPMG), 100 Fintech companies were selected based on the amount and growth rate of capital raising. The distribution of the 100 Fintech companies by country is as follows: US has 15, UK 11, and China 10; India 8, Australia 7, and Germany 5; Japan 4, Singapore 4, France 4, and Brazil 4; Spain 3 and Israel 3; Canada 2, Belgium 2, Indonesia 2, Vietnam 2, and South Korea 2; Argentina 1, Luxembourg 1, Sweden 1, Lithuania 1, Turkey 1, Malta 1, Finland 1, Nigeria 1, UAE 1, Cambodia 1, Thailand 1, and New Zealand 1. These figures show that developed countries still play a leading role in Fintech and China ranks among the first tier of the list. Besides, more and more Fintech companies in cutting-edge fields are born in emerging countries.

2.12.4 *Issues of Fintech*

While enabling and creating benefits for financial institutions, the rapid growth of Fintech has gradually blurred the boundary of financial businesses. The financial risks can be transmitted across sectors and time, causing new challenges for monetary policies, the stability of the financial market, and financial regulations (*The Development Program of Fintech* (2019–2021) issued by People's Bank of China on August 22, 2019, on its website). Since the boundary of financial innovations has become ambiguous, some fintech companies on the Fintech 100 list have violated regulatory rules, and some even do not have a banking license. Whether these companies can continue to develop is in doubt. Only by strictly obeying relevant laws and regulations can fintech companies genuinely embark on a healthy and sustainable development road.

2.13 Technology-Powered Transformation of Traditional Financial Industries and Prospects of Fintech

KPMG has issued the *Fintech 100* report for five consecutive years, a good reference for us to learn about the development of Fintech worldwide. However, this report only focuses on innovation activities by neobanks in the financial sector without discussing how traditional financial industries have used technology to improve operating efficiency. Fintech companies indeed have played a role in driving global Fintech development (Citi GPS, 2019), posing challenges to traditional financial industries. Nonetheless, the weak capital strength of these neo-banks makes it hard for them to compete with conventional financial institutions sitting on trillions of US dollars of capital. The latter can achieve better results by leveraging technology. Therefore, we should also pay attention to the technology-powered transformation of traditional banks, insurance companies, and securities institutions.

2.13.1 *Transformation of traditional financial industries in major developed countries and regions*

It is difficult to get access to data about the transformation of traditional financial industries. US banks' technology and communication operating expenditure (Opex) as a percentage of total Opex rose to over 2% during 2009–2013 and dropped under 2% in 2014 before rallying again to 2.5% from 2014–2016, reflecting that the US banking sector started to transform itself after the financial crisis. In contrast, Australian and EU banks fall far behind the US in this regard (EU banks' number was negative during 2011–2015 and rose to only 0.25% in 2016).

Relying on self-R&D can be a way for banks to realize technology-powered transformation. They can also invest in new technology companies with venture capital (VC) backgrounds. Table 2.8 presents the number of Fintech companies with a venture capital background funded by significant banks worldwide from 2015 Q3 to 2016 Q3. It shows that the cooperation between Citi (US) and two Spanish Banks (BBVA and Banco Santander) with VCs has played a leading role in global Fintech innovations. Of the banks included in Table 2.8, nine European banks invested in 28 Fintech companies in total, five US banks invested in 19 Fintech companies, three large Japanese banks invested in 10 Fintech companies, and one Chinese Bank (Bank of China) invested in only one Fintech company. These figures reflect that central EU, US, and Japanese banks try to transform themselves by investing in Fintech companies together with VCs. They use the products and services developed by these Fintech companies to improve their operating efficiency and help these Fintech companies expand their global presence to gain more returns.

Table 2.8: Number of Fintech Companies with a VC Background Invested by Significant Banks Worldwide over 2015 Q3–2016 Q3

Citi	8	PNC	2
Banco Santander	8	Capital One	2
BBVA + Propel	8	Mizuho Capital	2
Goldman Sachs	7	Wells Fargo	1
MUFG Bank	5	JPMorgan Chase	1
UBS	3	Bank of China	1
SMBC	3	Société Générale	1
ING	2	BBVA	1
HSBC	2	BNP Paribas	1
US	19	Europe	28
Japan	10	Others	1

Source: 2017 Investment Themes: A Wind of Change by Citi GPS. BBVA, short for Banco Bilbao Vizcaya Argentaria, is a Spanish bank, the world's 32nd largest bank in 2018 and 33rd most prominent in 2019; BBVA + Propel is a joint venture of BBVA and Propel, a VC firm.

Just as the US leads global innovations in science and technology, its banking sector also shows the cooperation between banks and VCs to invest in Fintech companies. Table 2.9 provides the number of Fintech companies supported by central US banks from 2009 to 2016. As we can see, Citi invested in 14 Fintech companies from 2009 to 2016: 10 of them were solely invested by Citi or jointly invested with VCs; the other four were invested together with Goldman Sachs and Morgan Stanley. The number of Fintech companies supported by Citi has overtaken that of Bank of America (which acquired Merrill Lynch after the financial crisis), JPMorgan Chase, and Wells Fargo combined (11), proving Citi's dominant position in Fintech around the US and even around the whole world.

According to Table 2.9, Goldman Sachs and Morgan Stanley invested in 18 Fintech companies in total, accounting for over 70% of the other four investment banks combined (25), demonstrating the strength of the two investment banks in driving Fintech development. Over half of the 18 Fintech companies invested in by the two investment banks were together

Table 2.9: Number of Fintech Companies Invested by Major US Banks over 2009–2016 Q3

Bank	No. of Fintech Companies Invested	No. of Joint Ventures	Bank	No. of Fintech Companies Invested	No. of Joint Ventures
Citi	14	4	Bank of America/ Merrill	4	3
Goldman Sachs	10	5	JPMorgan Chase	4	3
Morgan Stanley	8	4	Wells Fargo	3	1

Source: Citi GPS (2917).

with other commercial banks, which helps diversify risks while promoting products and services of these Fintech companies through the commercial banks. By comparing Table 2.8 with Table 2.9, we can find that the number of Fintech companies invested in by Citi and Goldman Sachs during the five quarters from 2015 Q3 to 2016 Q3 far exceeded half the number they invested, respectively, during 2009–2016 Q3, showing an accelerating pace of US banks in Fintech investments.

2.13.2 *Fintech development in China*

Under the joint promotion by the People's Bank of China (PBOC) and relevant institutions, the banking sector in China has actively made exploratory efforts in architecture transformation and the fundamental studies and application of new technologies. One result was an innovation in architecture transformation upgrading from conceptualization to rolling out, breakthroughs in independent innovations, big data analytics, and cloud computing, among other new technologies being widely used to reshape business models and service procedures ("Leading Group Meeting of 2018 Banking Technology Award Appraisal Held in Beijing", the website of PBOC, September 19, 2019). These show a promising trend of Fintech development in China. During 2017–2018, the top five Chinese banks successively signed strategic cooperation agreements with Baidu, Alibaba, Tencent, JD.com, and Suning.com, embarking on explorations into Fintech. Other central banks also started to explore Fintech in varying degrees (Liu Bin, 2019).

New Fintech companies have expanded at full steam in new financial service fields or encroached upon traditional economic segments, while traditional financial companies have also been actively studying and embracing technology. Nonetheless, the Chinese banking sector has not yet gathered momentum in cooperating with VCs to invest in Fintech companies. More needs to be done to propel Fintech with market forces.

2.13.3 *Prospect of Fintech*

Smart Bank (Li Lin, 2017), *Future Banking* (KPMG and Alibaba Cloud Research Center, 2019), *Bank of the Future: The ABCs of Digital Disruption in Finance* (Citi GPS, 2018), and *Bank X: The New New Banks* (Citi GPS, 2019) all think that the development of Fintech in traditional banking industries is promising and that non-traditional enterprises are leading the way and pushing forward the frontier of Fintech in a profound manner. On August 22, 2019, the PBOC issued the *Development Program of Fintech*, which specifies critical tasks for supporting the healthy and orderly development of Fintech over 2019–2021 as follows: promote the appropriate application of Fintech and regulate the selection of key generic technologies, application scenarios and security control to fully improve Fintech application; enable financial services to improve both quality and efficiency, rationally utilize Fintech approaches to enrich service channels, improve product supply, reduce service cost, optimize financing service, improve the quality and efficiency of financial services, and allow more people and enterprises to enjoy the well-being of Fintech innovations better, and then promote the healthy and sustainable development of the real economy; enhance technical defense capability of financial risk; apply Fintech in improving the capabilities to identify, warn and handle cross-market, cross-industry and cross-region financial risks, to strengthen network risk management and control, and financial information protection, to prevent new-technology-application risk; enhance prudential supervision on Fintech, establish and improve fundamental rule system of regulation with following efforts in monitoring, analysis and evaluation, and strengthen the professionalism, consistency and penetration of financial supervision. Following these guidelines, Fintech will embark on a healthy development road in China.

2.14 R&D Investment of Banks

2.14.1 *R&D investment of major banks*

R&D investment of banks around the world may enhance our understanding of Fintech introduced above. The number of banks in the top 2,500 companies for R&D investment declined from 36 in 2015 to 24 in 2019. The share of total R&D investment of these banks over total assets of the 2,500 companies declined from 1.67% to 1.21%, indicating that banks are minor players in direct R&D investments and their role in world R&D investment has been on the downward trend.

Most banks with high R&D investment among the 2,500 companies are from Europe. Of the 24 banks in the 2019 list, 21 banks were European banks, two banks were Australian banks, and one was Canadian bank, indicating that European banks pay much greater attention to R&D investment than banks in any other continent.

Science and technology are the foundations of the economy and trade. Science and technology-backed economies and businesses can firmly prop up exports, thus supporting the local currency. We have already discussed how vital the economy and trade foundations are for currency internationalization in this chapter, so we will not elaborate on this point.

According to global trade statistics for recent decades, the growth rate of trade in services has significantly surpassed that of trade in goods, showing the focus of the global economy and trade turning from goods to services. According to relevant statistics provided in Chapter 6, during the three decades since 1988, trade-in ICT services as a percent of global trade in services continued to grow faster than other services fields. IP has become an increasingly important part of the trade-in services, reflecting the significant contribution from R&D to trade-in services. The trade-in services outside ICT and IP, including financial, transportation, construction, and other commercial services, are closely correlated with the development of science and technology of different degrees. In short, R&D has made a significant contribution to trade in services, thus providing essential support for RMB internationalization.

As shown in Chapter 3, which introduces international empirical research results regarding the relationship between technology content of exports and settlement in the local currency, the higher technology content the exports have, the higher the proportion of export settlement in local currency. This means if a country has not reached a certain international level in terms of science and technology strength, the balance of its export settlement in local currency will not increase, regardless of how significant its export volume is. Therefore, the advancement in scientific and technological innovations plays a central role in improving the technology content of exports and elevating a country's place in the global industrial chain, thus becoming the core of local currency internationalization. We can build a solid foundation for independent economic and trade development and RMB internationalization by effectively promoting scientific and technological innovations.

2.15 Conclusion

Economy and trade are the foundations of a currency, whereas science and technology are the foundations of economy and trade. Without the independent advancement in science and technology, a country cannot gain independence in developing its economy and trade, leaving itself under the heel of others, and its local currency can hardly become an independent and significant international currency. This chapter has introduced the distribution of global R&D investments by country/region and sector over the last few decades. We have seen that China has become the world's second largest R&D investor, corresponding to its global status in the economy and trade. China has also progressed rapidly in delivering scientific and technological papers and patents over the years, greatly improving its capability in scientific and technological innovations. However, such significant R&D investments have not brought out a high R&D intensity, and China's R&D investments in the highest potential sectors grow relatively slow, demonstrating that its R&D investments have not been well market-oriented. China's total R&D investments as a percentage of GDP have reached the highest level among developing countries and close to the level of developed countries. That said, the performance of such investments is far from satisfactory, so more improvements are needed. In particular, China's substantial R&D investments and rapid increase in the number of essays and patents have not proven their value in exports for the use of intellectual property (we will study and compare such issues in Chapter 5). It is an urgent task for Chinese companies to align their R&D investments and management with domestic and overseas markets.

Revenues and profits of high-tech companies have been increasing faster than energy, automobile, and other traditional sectors, particularly R&D investments of US high-tech companies that have outperformed the conventional sectors of the US economy. In contrast, the financial industry has a more significant share among top EU and Japanese companies; R&D investments in the EU and Japan are more concentrated on the traditional automobile sector, whereas high-tech companies have become a more prominent force. Energy companies in China and the US enjoy similar status among large companies, but financial companies are placed higher in China than their peers in the US, EU, and Japan. In terms of R&D investments, traditional automobile companies in China still have a large gap with their peers in the US, EU, and Japan. Large state-owned enterprises have allocated a particular share of R&D investment, but R&D intensity is barely satisfactory, making it hard to obtain technological breakthroughs. Most Chinese companies are fully aware of the importance of competitiveness in science and technology. Still, they are yet to put their plans into action to catch up with their counterparts in developed countries and regions.

Bibliography

Chinese Academy of Science and Technology for Development, National Innovation Index Report 2018, 2018, www.most.gov.cn,most.gov.cn.

Citi GPS, Digital Disruption: How Fintech is Forcing Banking to a Tipping Point, March 2016.

Citi GPS, 2017 Investment Themes: A Wind of Change, January 2017.

Citi GPS, Bank of the Future: The ABCs of Digital Disruption in Finance, March 2018.

Citi GPS, Bank X: The New New Banks, March 2019.

Economic Daily, Chinese Companies' R&D Investments Recorded Nearly 2 Trillion RMB in 2018 — Largely Improving their Innovation Capabilities, May 25, 2019.

European Union, The 2016 EU Industrial R&D Investment Scoreboard, 2017, www.ijr.jrc.europa.eu.

European Union, The 2017 EU Industrial R&D Investment Scoreboard, 2018, www.ijr.jrc.europa.eu.

European Union, 2018 EU Industrial R&D Investment Scoreboard, 2019, www.ijr.jrc.europa.eu.

H2 Ventures and KPMG, 2018 Fintech100: Leading Global Fintech Innovators, 2018.

Jian Zhaoquan and Wu Zhuoshen, A Study on the Paths for the Manufacturing Sector to Provide Services — Based on the Theory of Smiling Curve, Science of Science and Management, December 2011.

KPMG and Alibaba Cloud Research Center, Future Banking — A New Start for Chinese Banking Sector under the DT Era, July 2019.

Li Lin *et al.*, Smart Bank — New Service Model for Future Banking, China Financial Publishing House, 2017.

Liu Bin, 2018 Progress in Banking Digitalization and Prospects into 2019, Strategic Planning Department of Shanghai Pudong Development Bank, 2019.

United Nations Educational, Scientific and Cultural Organization, Global Investments in R&D, Fact Sheet No. 54, June 2019.

UNCTAD, World Investment Report 2019, 2019, www.un.org/publications.

UNESCO Institute for Statistics, Global Investment in R&D, UIS Fact Sheet No. 54, June 2019, www.un.org/publications.

Zhu Wenhao, Hidden Champion is the Cornerstone of a Manufacturing Power, *Economic Herald*, July 2019 (244). www.un.org/publications.

Part II

Chapter 3

Global Trade and Cross-Border Payment and Settlement

Economy and trade are the fundamentals for currency valuation, and international trade settlement is the simplest and most basic essence of currency internationalization. This chapter first introduces the development of international trade in the past decade, and then focuses on the development of China's foreign trade and Chinese Yuan's (Renminbi, RMB or CNY) cross-border settlement to make a general assessment of the basis of RMB internationalization.

3.1 Development of Global Trade

Trade changes the world. British economist William Stanley Jevons (1865) said there is no doubt that trade develops with its invisible strength, converging different parts of the world into a network of transactions with each other. The unique potential of each region will be helpful to the others. "In fact, without trade, it would be impossible for Europeans to have the motivation in the constant expansion around the world. Without trade, it would be impossible for Europeans to accumulate enough wealth to maintain their world hegemony for three or four centuries" (*The World That Trade Created, Society, Culture and the World Economy, 1400 to the Present*, by Kenneth Pomeranz and Steven Topik, 2012). More than 200 years ago, classical economists had recognized the importance of international trade to economic development and put forward many new theories about international trade. These theories have become the essential content of economics, and this chapter will not repeat them.

3.1.1 *Development of global trade after World War II*

There are two stages of sustained growth in modern international business: one is from the mid-19th century to the outbreak of World War I and the other is from World War II to the present. We will mainly introduce the development of international trade after World War II. According to WTO data, from 1948 to 1983, the average annual growth rate of global trade in goods was as high as 10.3%, more than double the growth rate of the world economy in the same period. From 1983 to 2012, international trade increased from $3.72 trillion to $38.0 trillion, with an average annual growth rate of 8.1%, 1.6% higher than the average nominal growth rate of 6.5% of the world economy in the same period. However, the total volume of world trade fell continuously to $32.32 trillion in 2012–2016, with an average annual decline of 5.3% over the 3 years before rebounding by 10.7% in 2015–2017. Despite the trade frictions between the US and China and the US with other trading partners, global trade increased by 10% to $39.34 trillion in 2018, compared to 2017, and international trade in goods shrank 2.9% in 2019 due to the intensification of global trade frictions.

3.1.2 *Development of global trade in recent years*

In a speech in Shanghai in 2012, Robert Mundell mentioned that the third economic prosperity in human history should be from 2002 to 2008. He thinks this is the greatest boom in history. People can see that almost all countries globally, especially China and other developed and developing countries, enter a period of rapid development. According to the IMF data, except Afghanistan, Iraq, South Sudan, and Zimbabwe lack corresponding data due to war and other reasons, all countries have achieved varying degrees of growth. The GDP growth rate of 142 countries and regions in the world (accounting for more than three-fourth of the total number) exceeds the global growth rate, showing the scene of global prosperity at this stage. Amid such economic prosperity, the development of international trade has also reached an unprecedented level. According to data released by the WTO, from 2002 to 2008, global trade volume increased from $13.23 trillion to $32.68 trillion, with an average annual compound growth rate of 16.3%; this is the fastest growth period since World War II. Over the same period, the world's nominal GDP grew at an average annual rate of 10.7%, 5.6% slower than trade growth. Impacted by the global financial crisis, the development of world trade has slowed down significantly since 2008. From 2008 to 2013, the average annual growth rate of world trade was only 3.2%. Lower than one-fifth of the previous 6 years' average annual growth rate, the average annual compound growth rate was 0.7% from 2013 to 2018. Global exports and imports fell by 3% and 2.9%, respectively, in 2019, reflecting the impact of trade frictions on international trade.

3.1.3 *Changes in the global trade dependence degree*

According to the latest data released by the WTO and the updated world economic data by the IMF, from 1983 to 2008, the world trade dependence degree, the aggregate world trade volume to GDP, gradually increased from 33.5% to 51.4%. After the global financial crisis outbreak, the growth rate of world trade began to slow down in 2009, and the international trade dependence degree fell back to 39.8% in 2009. After that, it rebounded to 50.3% in 2011 but continuously fell back to 42.7% during 2011–2016. Then it rallied to 43.4% in 2016–2019, which is significantly lower than its high of 47% in 2008.

3.1.4 *Distribution of global trade*

Table 3.1 shows the global trade distribution among major countries and regions from 1963 to 2019. Table 3.1 shows that during the two decades from 1963 to 1983, China's trade share increased by only 0.1%. During the decade from 1983 to 1993, China's trade share increased by 1.45%, slightly lower than that of the US of 1.53% in the same period, indicating that China's trade growth was relatively slow at the initial stage of the reform and opening-up. From 1993 to 2003, China's trade increased by 3%, ranking the highest among the major trading bodies, showing the accelerated growth of China's trade in the middle of the reform and opening-up. The cumulative share increased by 5.3% in the decade of 2003–2013. It shows that China's entry into the WTO became an important driving force for the development of China's foreign trade. In 2014, China's total trade volume surpassed the US for the first time, becoming the world's largest trading body. China held the ranking during 2014–2018 except for 2016 when China ranked second to the US. However, from 2013 to 2018, China's share of global trade increased by

Table 3.1: Global Trade Distribution (1963–2019) (Unit: USD trillion, %)

Import/Region or Country	**1963**	**1973**	**1983**	**1993**	**2003**	**2011**	**2012**	**2013**	**2014**	**2015**	**2016**	**2017**	**2018**	**2019**
Global total	0.16	0.59	1.88	3.79	7.69	18.53	18.74	19.05	19.13	16.79	16.29	18.04	19.87	19.24
Share of the United States	11.4	12.3	14.3	15.9	16.9	12.2	12.5	12.2	12.6	13.8	13.8	13.3	13.2	13.4
Share of China	0.9	0.9	1.1	2.7	5.4	9.4	9.7	10.3	10.2	10	9.8	10.2	10.8	10.8
Share of Germany	8	9.2	8.1	9	7.9	6.8	6.2	6.2	6.3	6.3	6.5	6.4	6.5	6.4
Share of Japan	4.1	6.5	6.7	6.4	5	4.6	4.7	4.4	4.2	3.9	3.7	3.7	3.8	3.7
Share of Britain	8.5	6.5	5.3	5.5	5.2	3.7	3.7	3.5	3.6	3.7	3.9	3.6	3.4	3.6
Share of Eurozone				31.3	30.9	25.3	23.2	23.2	23.4	22.9	23.6	23.6	23.8	23.6
Share of the BRICS countries	8.7	7	7.9	5.4	8.5	15.7	16	16.5	14.6	15.2	14.6	15.5	16.1	16.1
Share of BRICS countries except China	7.8	6.1	6.7	2.7	3.1	6.2	6.3	6.2	4.3	5.2	4.8	5.2	5.3	5.4
Export/Region or Country	**1963**	**1973**	**1983**	**1993**	**2003**	**2011**	**2012**	**2013**	**2014**	**2015**	**2016**	**2017**	**2018**	**2019**
Global total	0.16	0.58	1.84	3.68	7.38	18.34	18.51	18.95	18.99	16.53	16.03	17.73	19.48	18.89
Share of the United States	14.9	12.3	11.2	12.6	9.8	8.1	8.4	8.3	8.5	9.1	9.1	8.7	8.5	8.7

(*Continued*)

Table 3.1: (*Continued*)

Export/Region or Country	1963	1973	1983	1993	2003	2011	2012	2013	2014	2015	2016	2017	2018	2019
Share of China	1.3	1	1.2	2.5	5.9	10.4	11.1	11.7	12.3	13.8	13.1	12.8	12.8	13.2
Share of Germany	9.3	11.7	9.2	10.3	10.2	8	7.6	7.6	7.9	8	8.3	8.2	8	7.9
Share of Japan	3.5	6.4	8	9.9	6.4	4.5	4.3	3.8	3.6	3.8	4	3.9	3.8	3.7
Share of Britain	3.2	3.8	4	4.6	4.1	2.8	2.5	2.9	2.7	2.8	2.6	2.5	2.5	2.5
Share of Eurozone					34	25.7	24.4	24.7	25.1	25	26	25.7	25.6	25.6
Share of the BRICS countries	9.4	7.3	8.9	6.3	10	16.9	17.3	17.9	15.7	19.1	18.1	18.2	18.4	18.8
Share of BRICS countries except China	8.1	6.3	7.7	3.8	4.1	6.5	6.3	6.2	3.4	5.3	5	5.4	5.7	5.6
Import/Region or Country	**1963**	**1973**	**1983**	**1993**	**2003**	**2011**	**2012**	**2013**	**2014**	**2015**	**2016**	**2017**	**2018**	**2019**
Global total	0.32	1.17	3.72	7.46	15.07	36.87	37.25	38	38.12	33.32	32.32	35.78	39.34	38.13
Share of the United States	13.1	12.3	12.8	14.3	13.5	10.2	10.4	10.3	10.6	11.5	11.5	11.1	10.9	11.1
Share of China	1.1	0.9	1.2	2.6	5.6	9.9	10.4	11	11.3	11.9	11.4	11.5	11.8	12

(*Continued*)

Table 3.1: (*Continued*)

Import/Region or Country	1963	1973	1983	1993	2003	2011	2012	2013	2014	2015	2016	2017	2018	2019
Share of Germany	8.6	10.4	8.7	9.7	9	7.4	6.9	6.9	7.1	7.1	7.4	7.3	7.2	7.1
Share of Japan	3.8	6.4	7.4	8.1	5.7	4.6	4.5	4.1	3.9	3.8	3.9	3.8	3.8	3.7
Share of Britain	5.9	5.2	4.7	5.1	4.7	3.2	3.1	3.2	3.1	3.3	3.2	3	3	3
Share of Eurozone					32.4	25.5	23.8	23.9	24.2	24	24.8	24.7	24.7	24.6
Share of the BRICS countries	9	7.2	8.4	5.8	9.2	16.3	16.7	17.2	15.1	17.1	16.3	16.8	17.3	17.5
Share of BRICS countries except China	7.9	6.2	7.2	3.2	3.6	6.4	6.3	6.2	3.8	5.3	4.9	5.3	5.5	5.5

Source: The data for 1963–2013 are calculated based on quarterly trade data released by the WTO for significant trading partners and major intercontinental imports and exports. The data for 2014–2019 are calculated based on trade data from different countries and regions published on the organization's website (www.wto.org).

only 0.8%, 0.2% higher than the 0.6% growth rate of the US in the same period. It shows the impact of the slowdown in global trade growth and the renewed growth of US trade on China after the US started to exit from quantitative easing (the average annual compound growth rates internationally and of the US and China in goods trade are 0.1%, 1.3%, and 1.6%, respectively, from 2013 to 2019; the share of the US in global trade fell by 4% from 1993 to 2003, while it increased by 0.75% in 2019).

3.2 The Main Settlement and Financing Currencies in Global Trade and Their Distribution

3.2.1 *Share and ranking of global settlement currencies*

Global trade needs to be settled in a currency acceptable to both parties. The payment function is the primary embodiment of a currency's international function. Although currency settlement data under global trade are difficult to obtain, trade items dominate the international settlement of currencies. Therefore, the role of currency in global payment is similar to that in trade settlement. The Global Interbank Financial Telecommunications Association (Society for Worldwide Interbank Financial Telecommunication, SWIFT) is the world's largest financial payment institution, which publishes monthly data on the amount and share of payments made in various currencies in global financial markets. Table 3.2 shows the percentage of international payments in the world's top 20 currencies from January 2012 to June 2020.

Table 3.2 shows that the USD and the Euro are the world's main payment currencies, with a combined share of 70–80%, indicating the importance of the two currencies in the global payment system. From January 2012 to August 2015, the Euro settlement fell by 16.84% to 27.2%, while the share of USD settlement increased by 15.09% to a historical high of 44.82%. It shows the substitutability of the two currencies in terms of the payment function. From August 2015 to June 2020, Euro payments increased by 6.90–34.10%, while the percentage of the USD dropped by 4.49–40.33%. The two currencies' share in global payment gets closer. The share of Sterling and JPY fell by 1.37% and increased by 0.98%, respectively, but the two currencies remained the third and fourth largest payment currencies in the world. From January 2001 to August 2015, the share of CNY settlement sustainably increased to 2.79%, rising from the

Table 3.2: Share and Ranking of the Top 20 International Currencies (2012–2020 June) (Unit: %, ranking)

Currency/ Time	January 2012	December 2012	December 2013	December 2014	August 2015	December 2015	December 2016	December 2017	December 2018	December 2019	June 2020
USD	29.73	39.76	39.52	44.64	44.82	43.89	42.09	39.85	41.57	42.22	40.33
Euro	44.04	33.34	33.22	28.3	27.2	29.39	31.3	35.66	32.98	31.69	34.1
GBP	9	8.68	9.13	7.92	8.45	8.43	7.2	7.07	6.76	6.96	7.08
JPY	2.48	2.45	2.56	2.69	2.76	2.78	3.4	2.96	3.36	3.46	3.74
RMB	0.25	0.57	1.12	2.17	2.79	2.31	1.68	1.61	2.07	1.94	1.76
CAD	1.81	1.97	1.9	1.92	1.79	1.7	1.93	1.57	1.84	1.98	1.75
HKD	0.95	1.09	1.11	1.27	1.41	1.17	1.31	1.22	1.44	1.46	1.47
AUD	2.08	2.11	1.89	1.79	1.6	1.5	1.55	1.39	1.57	1.55	1.44
THB	0.82	0.83	0.8	0.88	1.04	0.81	0.93	0.94	0.91	1.09	1.04
SGD	1.03	1.03	0.96	0.9	0.89	0.85	0.85	0.84	1.03	1.05	1.01
NOK	0.93	0.84	0.76	0.72	0.65	0.66	0.64	0.64	0.66	0.66	0.84
SEK	1.05	0.96	0.96	0.78	0.84	0.93	1.06	0.8	0.76	0.76	0.77
CHF	1.36	1.91	1.29	1.39	1.55	1.56	1.53	1.26	0.81	0.78	0.76
PLN	0.27	0.54	0.56	0.49	0.51	0.51	0.5	0.54	0.53	0.47	
MYR							0.43	0.41	0.49	0.46	0.37
DKK	0.54	0.45	0.48	0.4	0.4	0.37	0.4	0.35	0.35	0.38	0.37
NZD	0.33	0.35	0.37	0.39	0.4	0.32	0.33	0.34	0.31	0.32	0.34
SAR	0.48	0.4	0.39	0.45	0.46	0.39	0.38	0.4	0.39	0.36	0.29
MXN	0.31	0.39	0.42	0.39	0.37	0.37	0.35	0.32	0.29	0.32	0.27
TRY	0.27	0.27	0.32	0.32	0.26	0.24		0.25			
Ranking of RMB	20	14	8	5	4	5	6	5	5	6	5

Source: The website (http://www.swift.com) of the Society of Worldwide Interbank Financial Telecommunication (SWIFT). The MYR did not enter the top 20 before 2016. The blank indicates that the corresponding currency did not enter the top 20 at that time.

20th to the fourth place. However, from August 2015 to December 2016, the percentage of CNY settlements dropped from 2.79% to 1.68%. The ranking fell back to sixth place. Since 2017, the share of RMB settlement has hovered around 2%, maintaining fifth or sixth place.

3.2.2 *The relationship between currency payment and trade settlement*

During 2012–2019, the average share of USD settlement was 2.82 times higher than that of the United States trade, while the average share of the Euro is only 31.4% higher than that of the Eurozone trade. The average percentage of Sterling is 1.49 times higher than that of the UK trade, while the average share of JPY is only 75% of that of Japanese trade. The data show that among the top four international currencies, the position of the USD and Sterling in the global settlement system is significantly higher than that of their goods trade. In comparison, the position of the Euro is only slightly higher than that of Eurozone goods trade. The position of JPY in the global settlement is marginally lower than that of its goods trade. It is worth noting that the share of RMB settlement to China's goods trade internationally increased from 5% to 19.4% in 2012–2015, but dropped to 16.2% in 2016–2019, back to the level of the summer of 2014. It shows that the RMB still has great potential in trade settlement and will be further discussed in the following introduction of RMB cross-border transactions.

3.2.3 *Changes in the share and ranking of RMB global payments in recent years*

Table 3.2 and related data show that in January 2012, the share of RMB in the global settlement was only 0.25%, ranking 20th. In December 2012, the share of RMB in global payments more than doubled to 0.57%, rising to 14th place. In June 2013, the share of RMB further rose to 0.87%, reaching 11th place. In December 2013, the share of RMB rose further to 1.12%, ranking eighth. In June 2014, the share of RMB in global settlement rose to 1.55%, rising to seventh place for the first time. In December 2014, the share of RMB payment increased to 2.17%, maintaining seventh place. In August 2015, the percentage of RMB payments rose to 2.79%, surpassing the JPY's share of 2.76% for the first time, becoming the world's fourth largest payment currency, yet the share of RMB cross-border payments globally has continuously dropped since August 2015. The global ranking fell from fourth to sixth in December 2016 and remained in the fifth or sixth position since December 2017 (see Figure 3.1).

3.2.4 *Forecast on the changes in the share and ranking of international currencies settlement*

Using the data in Table 3.2, we can calculate the monthly changes in the share of global payments for different currencies from January 2012 to June 2020, and we can use these monthly changes to estimate the share of other currencies in global payments and their corresponding rankings from 2020 to December 2028. The related results are given in Table 3.3. Table 3.3 shows that the Euro and the USD will remain the top two payment currencies in the world for many years to come, and the RMB will replace the Sterling and JPY by June 2028 and December 2028 to become the fourth and third largest payment currencies in the world, respectively.

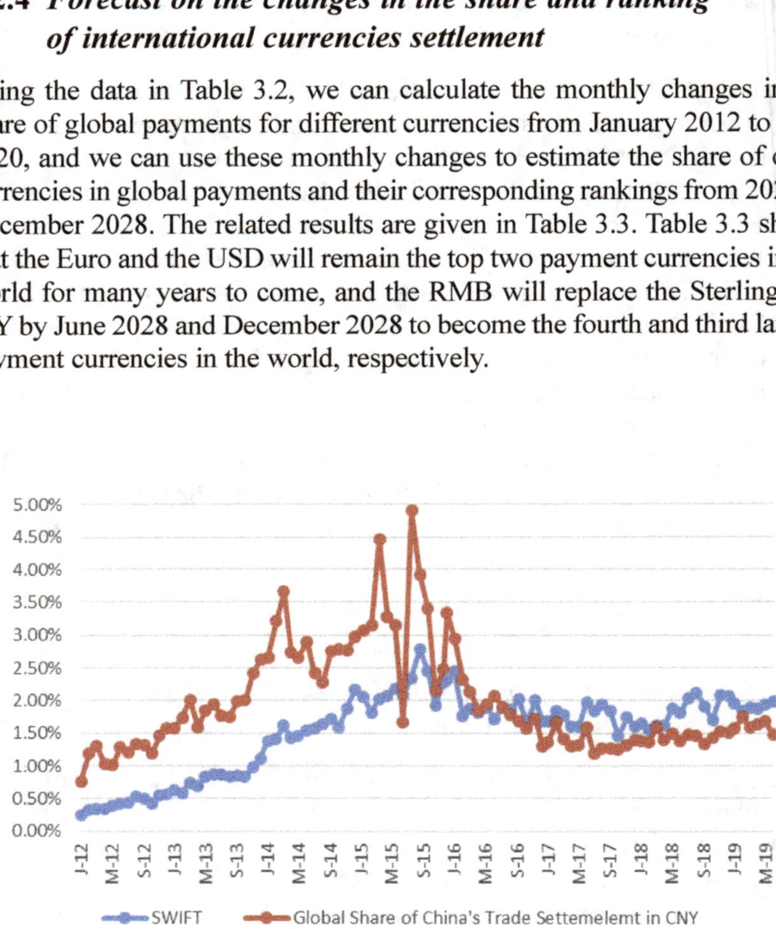

Figure 3.1: Comparison of the Share of RMB in Global Payments and Trade by Month

Source: Payment share data are from Table 3.2. RMB cross-border trade data are calculated based on its cross-border trade settlement data published monthly by the People's Bank of China, monthly trade data published by General Administration of Customs, and the share of China's trade since 2012 given in Table 3.1.

Table 3.3: Average Monthly Share in Global Payments of Major Currencies in Different Periods (Unit: %)

Currency/ Month	Share of Settlement in June 2020	Share of Settlement in December 2020	Share of Settlement in December 2021	Share of Settlement in December 2022	Share of Settlement in December 2025	Share of Settlement in December 2027	Share of Settlement in June 2028	Share of Settlement in December 2028
USD	40.33	40.37	40.44	40.52	40.75	40.91	40.95	40.99
Euro	34.1	34.15	34.25	34.36	34.67	34.88	34.93	34.98
GBP	7.08	6.98	6.8	6.62	6.1	5.77	5.7	5.62
JPY	3.74	3.85	4.07	4.31	5.1	5.71	5.87	6.04
RMB	1.76	1.9	2.21	2.56	4.02	5.43	5.86	6.32
CAD	1.75	1.74	1.71	1.68	1.6	1.55	1.54	1.53
AUD	1.47	1.5	1.56	1.62	1.83	1.98	2.02	2.06
HKD	1.44	1.4	1.33	1.27	1.09	0.98	0.96	0.93
SEK	1.04	1.06	1.09	1.12	1.23	1.3	1.32	1.34
SGD	1.01	1.01	1.01	1	1	0.99	0.99	0.99
THB	0.84	0.84	0.84	0.84	0.84	0.84	0.84	0.84
CHF	0.77	0.76	0.74	0.72	0.66	0.62	0.61	0.6
NOK	0.76	0.71	0.63	0.56	0.39	0.3	0.28	0.27
PLN	0.47	0.49	0.53	0.57	0.71	0.82	0.85	0.88
MYR	0.37	0.36	0.35	0.33	0.29	0.27	0.26	0.26
SAR	0.37	0.37	0.36	0.35	0.32	0.3	0.3	0.3
NZD	0.34	0.34	0.34	0.34	0.33	0.33	0.33	0.33

(Continued)

Table 3.3: (*Continued*)

Currency/ Month	Share of Settlement in June 2020	Share of Settlement in December 2020	Share of Settlement in December 2021	Share of Settlement in December 2022	Share of Settlement in December 2025	Share of Settlement in December 2027	Share of Settlement in June 2028	Share of Settlement in December 2028
DKK	0.29	0.28	0.27	0.26	0.23	0.21	0.21	0.2
MXN	0.27	0.26	0.25	0.24	0.21	0.19	0.18	0.18
TRY	0.25	0.24	0.24	0.23	0.22	0.21	0.21	0.21

Source: The monthly cross-border payment share of different currencies from December 2012 to December 2020 is calculated according to the data in Table 3.2. It is assumed that the future cross-border payment ratio of different currencies will be calculated according to the monthly share change from December 2012 to June 2020. The difference in the average monthly share of the MYR is calculated from the average monthly change from December 2016 to June 2020 in Table 3.2. The change in the average monthly allocation of the TRY is calculated from the average monthly change from December 2012 to December 2017 in Table 3.2.

3.2.5 *The development of offshore CNY centers and the distribution of CNY settlement in recent years*

In recent years, offshore CNY centers developed rapidly. In addition to Hong Kong, the largest offshore center, Singapore, London, South Korea, the United States, Taiwan China, Australia, France, Luxembourg, Germany, Macao, Japan, Malaysia, Netherlands, and more than a dozen of offshore CNY centers are developing one after another. The establishment and development of these offshore CNY centers show overseas confidence in CNY. They also lay a solid base to promote CNY cross-border settlement and internationalization.

Trade finance is also an essential embodiment of the international function of a currency. Most of the five countries and regions that use RMB for trade finance are Mainland China and Hong Kong, Singapore, Germany, and Australia. According to the data released by SWIFT in July 2020, the share of RMB trade finance in global rose rapidly from 1.89% in January 2012 to a peak of 8.66% in October 2013, declining year by year since 2014. As of June 2020, RMB trade finance global share is 1.95%, ranking third after the USD (86.52%) and the Euro (6.62%). The dramatic changes in RMB trade finance around 2014 may be related to the launch of quantitative easing in the United States and the end of the years of CNY appreciation.

3.3 The Prominent Opinions and Empirical Research Results of the Monetary Theory of Global Trade Settlement

Many complex factors affect the choice of settlement currency in global trade. A large amount of research has been done in the international academic community. There are three choices of currencies for international trade settlement: the exporting country's currency, the importing country's currency, and the third country's currency. Since the 1970s, the choice of international trade settlement currency has received more and more attention from scholars. Factors of international trade settlement over the past 30 years can be summarized: (1) the currency of the exporting country is likely to be chosen as the settlement currency than the currency of the importing country; (2) the trade between developed and developing countries is settled in the currencies of developed or third countries; (3) commodities with high heterogeneity (high technical goods relative to homogeneous goods and primary goods) are usually settled in the exporting country's currency. Homogeneous and primary goods tend to be denominated and settled in a major international currency with low transactional costs; (4) the currencies of countries with a larger share in the global trade are more likely to be used as settlement currencies; (5) the currencies of countries with relatively low inflation rates and inflation volatility are likely to become trade settlement currencies; (6) robust currencies are more likely to become trade settlement currencies; (7) currencies of countries with relatively sound foreign exchange markets and banking systems are more likely to be used for trade settlement.

Factors (1) and (4)–(6) above support the RMB to become a cross, border settlement currency as China's share in global trade is very high. China has become the largest exporter and second largest importer in 2010 and has become the world's largest trading body since 2014, and the inflation rate is relatively low. RMB has been relatively strong for more than 8 years from 2002 to 2010, and RMB depreciated against the USD for only half a year after the outbreak of the global financial crisis. It was devalued against the USD after 2014 within a specific limit. Factors (2), (3), and (7) are the weaknesses of the RMB being a cross-border settlement currency.

On the whole, China is still a developing country. Although the technological content of exported products has improved in recent years, most of them are still homogeneous goods and primary goods. Therefore, only by improving China's sci-tech level to improve the position of China's exported products in the global supply chain, we can effectively improve the share of RMB in cross-border settlement. Compared with the developed countries and many developing countries, China's foreign exchange market needs further improvement. In addition to the factors above, the dimensions affecting the choice of settlement currency are foreign exchange market risk and hedging, trade volume, industrial structure of the country where the exporter is located. Market share, demand price sensitivity, margin cost hedging, importers' domestic economic stability, and other factors also influence settlement. Readers may refer to Bacchetta and Van Wincoop (2005), Witte (2006), Novy (2006), Ligthart and Silva (2007), Goldberg and Tille (2010) and other related literature and research. We will not go into further details. With the continuous development of RMB cross-border settlement and the accumulation of relevant data, the research in such fields will increase rapidly in the next few years.

3.4 Development and Global Distribution of China's Foreign Trade

Table 3.1 shows that since the reform and opening-up, China's foreign trade has increased. Notably, after China joined the WTO in 2001, the development of foreign trade further accelerated. This section will briefly introduce China's foreign exchange development and global distribution over the past 30 years.

3.4.1 *China's foreign trade slows down from the rapid development*

Table 3.4 shows China's foreign trade volume, export, import, trade balance, and its annual changes, as well as the ratio of foreign trade volume to GDP from 1981 to 2020. In the early years of reform and opening-up in 1981, China's trade grew at an average annual compound rate of 13%, and the degree of trade dependence (the ratio of trade volume to GDP) increased from 15.1% to 37.9%. However, since China's entry into the WTO in 2001, the average annual compound growth rate has more than doubled to 27.4% in 2007 compared with the previous 20 years. The degree of trade dependence also increased to 60.9%, indicating the strong momentum in the development of foreign trade. However, from 2007 to 2019, China's foreign trade's average annual compound growth rate decreased to 6.4%. The degree of trade dependence also dropped to 31.9%, indicating the slowing down of China's trade after the global financial crisis.

3.4.2 *The distribution of China's foreign trade across Asia, Europe, Americas, and other continents*

In the following, we will analyze the distribution of China's trade in and across the continents to see the potential of implementing the "Belt and Road Initiative" to promote trade growth in different regions. Table 3.5 shows the distribution of China's trade across Asia, Europe, the Americas, and other continents from 2002 to 2019.

Table 3.5 shows that from 2002 to 2011, the share of trade between Asia and China declined from 58.4% to 52.2%. In 2011–2013, it rebounded slightly to 53.5%, and in 2013 to the first half of 2019, it

Table 3.4: China's Foreign Trade Volume, Export, Import, Trade balance, and Its Annual Changes, and the Ratio of Foreign Trade Volume to GDP (1981 to 2020) (Unit: USD billion, %)

						Compared with the Same Period Last Year±%		
Year	**Import and Export**	**Export**	**Import**	**Trade Balance**	**Trade Volume/ GDP**	**Import and Export**	**Export**	**Import**
1981	44.02	22.01	22.02	−0.01	15.10			
1985	69.60	27.35	42.25	−14.90	22.30	12.10	5.60	17.70
1990	115.44	62.09	53.35	8.75	29.00	10.60	17.80	4.80
1995	280.86	148.78	132.08	16.70	38.10	19.50	19.10	19.90
2000	474.30	249.20	225.09	24.11	39.00	11.00	10.90	11.30
2001	509.65	266.10	243.55	22.55	37.90	7.50	6.80	8.20
2002	620.77	325.60	295.17	30.43	42.00	21.80	22.40	21.20
2003	850.99	438.23	412.76	25.47	50.90	37.10	34.60	39.80
2004	1,154.55	593.33	561.23	32.10	58.70	35.70	35.40	36.00
2005	1,421.91	761.95	659.95	102.00	61.60	23.20	28.40	17.60
2006	1,760.44	968.98	791.46	177.52	63.50	23.80	27.20	19.90
2007	2,176.18	1,220.06	956.12	263.95	60.90	23.60	25.90	20.80
2008	2,563.26	1,430.69	1,132.56	298.13	55.70	17.80	17.30	18.50
2009	2,207.54	1,201.61	1,005.92	195.69	43.10	−13.90	−16.00	−11.20
2010	2,974.00	1,577.75	1,396.25	181.51	49.00	34.70	31.30	38.80
2011	3,641.86	1,898.38	1,743.48	154.90	48.40	22.50	20.30	24.90
2012	3,867.12	2,048.71	1,818.41	230.31	45.10	6.20	7.90	4.30
2013	4,158.99	2,209.00	1,949.99	259.02	43.20	7.50	7.80	7.20
2014	4,301.53	2,342.29	1,959.24	383.06	40.80	3.40	6.00	0.40
2015	3,953.03	2,273.47	1,679.56	593.90	35.20	−8.00	−2.90	−14.10
2016	3,685.56	2,097.63	1,587.93	509.71	32.80	−6.80	−7.70	−5.50
2017	4,107.14	2,263.35	1,843.79	419.55	34.00	11.40	7.90	16.10
2018	4,622.42	2,486.68	2,135.73	350.95	34.50	12.50	9.90	15.80
2019	4,577.70	2,499.46	2,078.25	421.21	31.90	−1.00	0.50	−2.70
2020	2,029.69	1,098.75	930.95	167.80	31.20	1.50	0.50	2.70

Source: Calculated according to the data on the website of the General Administration of Customs (www.customs.gov.cn). The data for 2020 are for the first half of the year.

continued to decline to 51.7%, still accounting for more than half of the total share, indicating the importance of Asia to China's trade. Europe is China's second largest trading partner. Trade between Europe and China rose to 20% from 2002 to 2008, fell to 17.6% from 2008 to 2015, and rebounded to 19.2% from 2016 to 2019. North America is China's third largest trading partner. From 2002 to 2011, the share of trade between North America and China declined to 13.6%, marking a cumulative decrease of 3.3%, second only to Asia's 6.2% in the same period. However, the share of trade between China and North America rebounded from 2011 to 2017, rising by 1.9–15.5%. Latin America, Africa, Oceania, and the Pacific Islands are China's fourth, fifth, and sixth most prominent trading partners. The share of trade between these regions and China rose from 2002 to 2019. The share of trade between the three areas and China increased by 4.0%, 2.6%, and 2.4%, respectively, indicating the importance of the three regions to China's trade. From 2007 to 2019, the total share of China's trade with Asia, Africa, and Latin America accounted for an average of 63.4%, indicating the importance of the four continents to China's foreign trade.

It is worth noting that, affected by the trade friction between the United States and China, the share of trade between China and North America decreased by 2.2% from 2017 to 2019, while the share of trade between China and other continents outside Asia increased by varying degrees. Among them, the most significant percentage increase is the trade with Europe, which increased by 0.8%, followed by a rise of 0.6% with Latin America.

3.4.3 *The comparison between China and Japan's distribution of foreign trade across continents*

The previous section gives the distribution of China's trade among significant continents, which is of great significance for forecasting China's foreign trade development in the future. However, we will get other implications compared with Japan's trade distribution before and after the global financial crisis. Using the data published on the website of the Japanese External Trade Organization (www.jetro.go.jp), we find that from 2004 to 2008, before the global financial crisis, Japan's share of trade with Asia fell from 47% to 45%, and the share with North America and Europe fell from 21.1% and 15.6% to 16.5% and 12.9%, respectively.

Table 3.5: The Distribution of China's Foreign Trade across Asia, Europe, Americas, and Other Continents (Unit: USD billion, %)

Year/ Trading Partner	Total	Asia	Europe	North America	Latin America	Africa	Oceania and the Pacific Islands
2002	620.77	58.4	17.8	16.9	2.9	2	2
2003	850.99	58.2	18.6	16	3.2	2.2	1.9
2004	1,154.55	57.6	18.3	16.1	3.5	2.6	2
2005	1,421.91	56.8	18.5	16.2	3.6	2.8	2.2
2006	1,760.40	55.7	18.8	16.3	4	3.2	2.1
2007	2,173.73	54.6	19.7	15.3	4.7	3.4	2.3
2008	2,563.26	53.3	20	14.4	5.6	4.2	2.6
2009	2,207.53	53	19.4	14.9	5.5	4.1	3.1
2010	2,974.00	52.6	19.3	14.2	6.2	4.3	3.3
2011	3,641.86	52.2	19.3	13.6	6.6	4.6	3.6
2012	3,867.12	52.9	17.7	13.9	6.8	5.1	3.5
2013	4,158.99	53.5	17.6	13.8	6.3	5.1	3.7
2014	4,301.53	52.9	17.7	13.9	6.8	5.1	3.5
2015	3,953.03	53	17.6	15.5	6	4.5	3.4
2016	3,685.56	52.9	18.4	15.3	5.9	4.1	3.5
2017	4,107.14	51.8	18.4	15.5	6.3	4.1	3.9
2018	4,622.42	51.5	18.5	15.1	6.6	4.4	3.9
2019	4,577.70	51.7	19.2	13.3	6.9	4.6	4.4
2020	2,029.69	52.1	19.5	12.8	6.8	4.1	4.5

Source: Calculated according to the data on the website of the General Administration of Customs (www.customs.gov.cn). The data for 2020 are for the first half of the year.

The share of trade between Japan and the Middle East continued to rise from 7.6% to 13%. The trend is similar to that of China in the same period. However, after the global financial crisis, Japan's share of trade with Asia rebounded significantly from 45% to 50.2% in 2008–2011, and its share with North America and Europe fell further from 16.5% and 12.9% to 14.3%, and 12.0%, respectively. At the same time, the share of trade with the Middle East also fell from 13.0% to 11.1%. The trend indicates that the focus of Japan's business has gradually returned to Asia after nancial crisis. The recovery of trade between Japan and Asia also has cations for China's foreign trade.

Implication of the difference in China and Japan's distribution of foreign trade across continents

ıanges in the distribution of global trade of China and Japan before :er the global financial crisis show that the focus of Japan's interna- :rade has returned to Asia after the crisis. In contrast, China's global 'ith regions outside Asia gradually increased as foreign trade recov- 2011. Table 3.5 shows that although the share of trade between and Asia remains more than 52%, if we subtract the false trade ı China onshore and other regions of China given in Table 3.6, then 'e of trade between China and Asia declined from 56% to 50.7% –2007, below 50% to 49.7% for the first time in 2008, and further l to 48.9% in 2011. It shows that while Japan has returned to Asia ; global financial crisis, China has moved toward the world at a ɔace, similar to a state in which Japan's share of Asian trade was ıntly lower than 50% before the financial crisis. The difference in l indicates the increased resilience of China against the financial is also the result of the sustained growth of China's economy and l the further promotion of omni-directional, multilevel, and wide- opening-up to the world. In recent years, dealing with East Asia ; for about 48% of Japan's foreign trade, while China's share with a has dropped to less than one-third to that of Japan. This will be liscussed in the following section when introducing and analyzing ibution of China's trade across Asia.

China's major trading partners

.6 shows the share of trade between China's main trading partners ına from 2002 to 2019. Table 3.6 indicates that the European Union intained China's largest trading partner position since 2003, and ted States has maintained the status of China's second largest trad- :tner until 2018. However, due to the impact of trade frictions n the United States and China, the share of trade between the States and China is lower than that of ASEAN for the first time in making it the third largest trading partner of China. As the main component of the European Union, the total economic output of the Eurozone accounted for more than 70% of the European Union in recent years. In 2019, the share of trade between China and the Eurozone reached 11.4%, close to the 11.8% of the United States. The share of trade between ASEAN and China has maintained a rising trend over the past decade. ASEAN has become the fastest growing trading partner among China's top nine trading partners, which shows the importance of ASEAN to China's foreign trade.

Table 3.6 shows that Japan maintained its position as China's third largest trading partner from 2002 to 2011, but its share of trade with Chin has declined the most since 2002. ASEAN replaced Japan's position a China's third largest trading partner in 2011, and Hong Kong further over took it from 2012 to 2016. By 2017, Japan surpassed Hong Kong agai and retook its position as China's fourth largest trading partner. Over th past decade, the decline in the share of trade between Mainland China an Hong Kong is second only to Japan, with a cumulative decline of nearl 5%, and has maintained the mainland's fifth largest trading partner statu over the past few years. South Korea's trade volume with China exceede $100 billion for the first time in 2005, maintaining its position as the sixt largest trading partner for many years. The trade between Taiwan Chin and Mainland China exceeded $100 billion for the first time in 2006 an has maintained its position as the mainland's seventh largest trading part ner for many years. The trade volume between Australia and Chin exceeded $100 billion for the first time in 2011, and trade with China ha increased significantly in recent years. Since 2017, it has become th eighth most significant trading partner of our country. The region "China in Table 3.6 represents the trade volume of China's export to domesti sales, which is next to Taiwan China and has maintained its position a China's "eighth largest trading partner" as of 2016.

In 2017, the trade volume between China and Vietnam exceede $100 billion for the first time, making it the ninth largest trading partne of China after Australia. In addition to the main trading partners listed in Table 3.6, the trade volume between Malaysia, Brazil, Russia, and China has slightly exceeded $100 billion in 2019, making them the 10th to 12th largest trading partners of our country. Table 3.6 also shows that in the first half of 2020, while ASEAN overtook the European Union to become China's largest trading partner for the first time, Vietnam surpassed Australia for the first time to become China's eighth largest trading partner. With the implementation of trade agreements between the 10 ASEAN

Table 3.6: China's Major Trade Partners and Their share in China's Foreign Trade (2002–2020) (Unit: %)

Year/ Trading partner	EU	America	Eurozone	ASEAN	Japan	Hong Kong	South Korea	Taiwan China	Australia	Vietnam	Mainland China
2002	14.7	15.7	11.8	8.8	16.4	11.2	7.1	7.2	1.7	0.5	2.4
2003	15.5	14.9	12.5	9.2	15.7	10.2	7.4	6.9	1.6	0.6	3
2004	15.3	14.7	12.4	9.2	14.5	9.8	7.8	6.8	1.8	0.6	3.4
2005	15.2	14.9	12.4	9.2	13	9.6	7.9	6.4	1.9	0.6	3.9
2006	15.7	14.9	12.5	9.1	11.8	9.4	7.6	6.1	1.8	0.6	4.2
2007	16	13.9	13	9.3	10.9	9.1	7.4	5.7	2	0.7	4
2008	16.2	13	13.1	9	10.4	7.9	7.3	5	2.3	0.8	3.6
2009	16	13.5	13	9.7	10.4	7.9	7.1	4.8	2.7	1	3.9
2010	15.6	13	12.8	9.9	10	7.8	7	4.9	3	1	3.6
2011	15.1	12.3	12.4	10	9.4	7.8	6.7	4.4	3.2	1.1	3.4
2012	14.1	12.5	10.8	10.4	8.5	8.8	6.6	4.4	3.2	1.3	3.7
2013	14.1	13.2	10.7	11.2	7.9	10.1	6.9	5	3.5	1.6	4
2014	14.1	12.5	10.8	10.4	8.5	8.8	6.6	4.4	3.2	2	3.7
2015	14.1	13.2	10.6	11.2	7.9	10.1	6.9	5	3.5	2.4	4
2016	14.8	14.1	11	12.3	7.5	8.3	6.9	4.9	2.9	2.7	3.5
2017	15	14.2	11.2	12.5	7.4	7	6.8	4.9	3.3	3	3.2
2018	14.8	13.7	11.2	12.7	7.1	6.7	6.8	4.9	3.9	3.2	3.2
2019	15.4	11.8	11.4	14	6.9	6.3	6.2	5	3.7	3.5	2.8
2020	14.3	13.2	12	14.6	6.9	5.6	6.2	5.5	3.6	4	2.8

Source: Calculated according to the data on the website of the General Administration of Customs (www.customs.gov.cn). The data for 2020 are for the first half of the year.

partners and the five countries (China, Japan, South Korea, New Zealand, and Australia), trade between China and ASEAN will continue to grow. China's trade with Japan, South Korea, and Australia will also have better conditions for development.

3.4.6 *The distribution of China's trade among the five major regions of Asia*

As Asia is an essential region for China's foreign trades, this will be the region where CNY internationalization will proceed fast. This section introduces major Chinese trading partners in Asia. Table 3.7 shows the trade distribution between China and five regions of Asia from 2002 to 2019. Table 3.7 shows East Asia is China's largest trading partner in Asia. However, the share of East Asia in China's foreign trade declined, from 75.2% to 53.2% during 2002–2019, with a drop of around 22%. Southeast Asia is China's second largest trading partner in Asia; its trade with China has not only sustained but also shown considerable growth trend over the past decade, accounting for 27.1% of China's trade with Asia, with a cumulative increase of 11.3%, which shows the importance of this region to China's foreign trade. West Asia is China's third largest trading partner in Asia. From 2002 to 2014, the share of West Asia in China's total foreign exchange increased against Asia as a whole. However, due to the significant drop in international crude oil prices since 2014, the share of trade between this region and China declined and did not recover until recent years. South Asia is China's fourth largest trade in Asia. Its trade with China is in an upward trend. From 2002 to 2019, the share of trade between South Asia and China in China's total trade with Asia has more than doubled from 2.4% to 5.7%. Central Asia is China's fifth largest trade area in Asia, and the share of trade between the region and China continued to rise from 2002 to 2013. However, similar to West Asia, trade between the region and China declined to 1.5% in 2016 due to a drop in raw material and crude oil prices since 2013 but rose slightly to 2.0% since 2016.

Due to issues such as trade frictions between the United States and China, China's trade share with East Asia decreased by 3.0% in 2019. Its trade share with Southeast Asia, West Asia, and Central Asia increased by 2.4%, 0.4%, and 0.2%. In comparison, trade with South Asia decreased by 0.2%, showing the changes in China's trade in all major regions of Asia.

Table 3.7: Distribution of China's Trade among the Five Major Regions of Asia (Unit: USD billion, %)

Year/ Region	Total	East Asia	Southeast Asia	West Asia	South Asia	Central Asia
2002	19.17	75.20	15.80	5.90	2.40	0.70
2003	27.29	73.40	16.70	6.50	2.60	0.90
2004	36.94	72.20	17.00	6.70	3.10	0.90
2005	44.15	70.20	17.40	7.70	3.60	1.20
2006	52.54	68.40	17.80	8.70	3.80	1.30
2007	61.99	65.70	18.40	9.50	4.60	1.80
2008	70.26	62.30	18.20	11.90	5.20	2.40
2009	60.35	62.00	19.70	10.90	5.30	2.20
2010	83.50	61.00	20.10	11.30	5.50	2.10
2011	100.41	58.80	20.40	13.10	5.50	2.20
2012	204.49	61.40	19.60	12.30	4.50	2.30
2013	222.49	61.10	19.90	12.40	4.40	2.30
2014	204.49	65.50	23.50	14.30	5.20	2.20
2015	209.56	59.00	22.50	11.20	5.30	1.60
2016	194.81	59.20	23.20	10.40	5.70	1.50
2017	212.57	57.30	24.20	10.90	5.90	1.70
2018	238.11	56.20	24.70	11.50	5.90	1.80
2019	236.66	53.20	27.10	11.90	5.70	2.00
2020	238.66	53.60	28.20	11.70	4.90	1.60

Source: Calculated according to the data on the website of the General Administration of Customs of China (www.customs.gov.cn).

3.4.7 *China's main trading partners in Asia and its potential*

The previous section introduced the distribution of China's trade in the five major regions of Asia, and now we will introduce China's main trading partners in Asia by country/region. Table 3.8 shows China's 25 major trading partners in Asia from 2008 to 2020 as well as their share of total trade in China and trade dependence on China. The total trade volume between these trading partners with China exceeded $2.17 trillion in 2020, or 91.1% of total trade of Asia with China the same year. Table 3.8 shows that since 2008, the trade between these 25 countries and regions with China has accounted for more than 90% of the total trade between

China and Asia, indicating that these countries and regions play an essential role in the trade between China and Asia.

Table 3.8 shows that of China's top three trading partners in Asia, the trade share with Japan, Hong Kong, and South Korea decreased by varying degrees from 2008 to 2020, while trade share with Taiwan China slightly increased. Of all 25 major Asian trading partners of China, Vietnam trade share with China increased the most, 6.56% from 2008 to 2020, as a result its trade dependence with China increased from 50.8% in 2008 to 56.42% in 2020, second only to Hong Kong's dependence of 80.02% at the same time. The largest decreases in trade dependence with China were noted with Hong Kong, Turkmenistan, Iran, Myanmar, South Korea, and Bangladesh with decreases over 2%. The aggregate share of the 25 major Asian trading partners in the total trade volume between China and Asia dropped to 91.07% in 2020, slightly higher than the ratio 91% in 2014. The aggregate trade dependence of the 25 trading partners with China has dropped slightly to 12.58% in 2020 from 12.80% in 2008.

Table 3.8 shows that Turkey, India, Iran, Israel, and Bangladesh show still less than 5% dependence on trade with China, indicating that these countries have great potential for trade growth with China. In addition, Japan, Indonesia, Qatar, and Saudi Arabia's trade dependence with China is only between 5% and 10%, indicating potential for developing trade between China and these countries.

3.5 Brief Introduction to CNY Trade Settlement before and after the Official Launch of CNY Cross-Border Trade Settlement Pilot Project

3.5.1 *RMB trade settlement before the launch of RMB cross-border trade settlement pilot program*

China officially launched the RMB settlement pilot project for import and export in July 2009. But in fact, RMB has been used to settle trade and other transactions with neighboring countries since many years ago. The RMB has nearly achieved free circulation in economies such as Pakistan, Vietnam, Myanmar, and Laos, enjoying a status close to the USD. Since October 1, 1997, small-amount boundary goods trade began to apply for an export tax refund following the measures for Administration of Export Tax Refund (Exemption) (from now on referred to as the "measures") issued by State

Table 3.8: China's Main Trading Partners in Asia and Their Share and Trade Dependence on China (2008–2020) (Unit: USD billion, %)

Year/ Trading Partner	2008	2014	2019	2020	Trade in 2008/ GDP	Trade in 2019/ GDP	Trade in 2020/ GDP
Japan	21.00	13.70	13.30	13.31	6.30	6.10	6.29
Hong Kong	16.00	16.50	12.20	11.72	111.10	77.20	80.02
South Korea	14.70	12.80	12.00	11.95	19.90	17.50	17.49
Taiwan China	10.20	8.70	9.60	10.93	35.80	38.90	39.01
Vietnam	1.50	3.70	6.80	8.06	50.80	61.90	56.42
Malaysia	4.20	4.50	5.20	5.50	32.40	33.90	38.77
Thailand	3.30	3.20	3.90	4.13	18.80	17.30	19.65
Singapore	4.10	3.50	3.80	3.73	26.20	24.80	26.21
India	4.10	3.10	3.90	3.67	3.40	3.20	3.23
Indonesia	2.50	2.80	3.40	3.28	6.30	7.20	7.40
Saudi Arabia	3.30	3.00	3.30	2.81	7.90	10.00	9.57
Philippines	2.30	2.00	2.60	2.56	15.60	17.10	16.88
United Arab Emirates	2.20	2.40	2.10	2.06	13.60	12.00	13.88
Iraq	0.20	1.30	1.40	1.26	11.40	14.90	17.53
Kazakhstan	1.40	1.00	0.90	0.90	7.80	12.90	13.01
Myanmar	0.20	1.10	0.80	0.79	25.70	28.30	23.25
Oman	0.90	1.10	1.00	0.78	24.90	29.50	29.50
Israel	0.40	0.50	0.60	0.74	3.80	3.80	4.36
Bangladesh	0.30	0.60	0.80	0.66	7.10	5.80	4.82
Iran	2.20	2.30	1.00	0.62	9.00	5.00	2.35
Kuwait	0.50	0.60	0.70	0.60	9.80	12.60	13.24
Qatar	0.20	0.50	0.50	0.46	4.20	5.80	7.46
Turkey	0.20	1.00	0.90	0.27	2.50	2.80	0.91
Turkmenistan	0.10	0.50	0.40	0.27	24.10	19.50	13.76
Total amount	96.40	91.00	91.80	91.07	12.80	12.10	12.58

Source: Trade data from the website of the National Bureau of Statistics (www.stats.gov.cn) and the website of General Administration of Customs (www.customs.gov.cn). The degree of trade dependence is calculated from GDP data of various countries and regions published on the International Monetary Fund website in October 2019.

Administration of Taxation. However, one of the documents to be provided for a tax refund following the measures is the Certificate for Foreign-Exchange Verification (special copy of export tax rebate) for receiving foreign exchange (USD). More than 85% of Yunnan's small-amount boundary goods trade with Myanmar, Laos, and Vietnam are settled in RMB ("Yunnan small-amount boundary goods trade development urgently needs the state's policy support for RMB settlement of export tax rebates," according to the Yunnan provincial government website, www.yn.gov.cn/yunnan, China).

In 2004, RMB accounted for about 90% of the boundary goods trade between China and Mongolia, 81% in the boundary goods trade between China and Vietnam, 45% in the boundary goods trade between China and North Korea, and 15% in the boundary goods trade between China and Russia (Liu, 2008). In 2004, RMB settled through the cash account bank in the boundary goods trade between China and Mongolia was RMB 1.166 billion, reaching RMB 2.732 billion in 2005, RMB 3.446 billion in 2006, and RMB 6.869 billion in 2007. The RMB cannot be used directly in Russia but primarily for boundary goods trade settlement (Li Dongrong, 2009).

On the whole, before the pilot project of RMB cross-border trade settlement was implemented in July 2009, the share of RMB usage brought by international trade to China's domestic money supply and China's total import and export volume was still meager. Non-neighboring Asian economies, Europe, the United States, and other regions rarely use RMB for settlement (except for tourism RMB exchange and payment). Boundary goods trade only accounts for a small part of the total trade between China and neighboring countries; as the government has not published relevant data of RMB settlement in border trade, it is difficult to estimate the share of RMB in China's trade settlement. Wang Chengji (2012) studied the RMB trade settlement before the RMB cross-border trade settlement pilot project in 2009 and provided some relevant data and analysis, which will not be discussed here. The major indices of RMB cross-border trade settlement have been released regularly since 2010, which we will analyze and study in detail in the following section.

3.5.2 *Policy preparation for RMB cross-border trade settlement*

As early as the 1990s, China and its neighboring countries began to use RMB for settlement in boundary goods trade, but the scope of use was relatively small. In 2009, the Chinese government began to accelerate the promotion of RMB trade settlement. After years of exploration and review, the executive meeting of the State Council formally decided on April 8, 2009, to carry out a pilot project of RMB cross-border trade settlement in Shanghai, Guangzhou, Shenzhen, Zhuhai, Dongguan, and other cities. It is a crucial step toward RMB internationalization, which is constructive to gradually improve its international position. On July 1, 2009, the pilot measures for the Administrative Rules on Pilot Program of RMB Settlement of Cross-border Trade Transactions were released to provide a foundation for implementing the RMB cross-border trade settlement. On July 3, 2009, the PBOC issued the Detailed Rules for implementing the Administrative Measures for the Cross-border RMB Trade Settlement Pilot Project. On July 6, 2009, the launching ceremony of the RMB cross-border trade settlement project was held in Shanghai. At the same time, the first foreign trade settled in RMB was also executed on the same day. If you are interested, please refer to Shi Liya (2018) for the introduction and analysis of the RMB trade settlement pilot project.

On June 22, 2010, the PBOC and six other regulatory bodies jointly issued Notice on Issues Related to Expansion of RMB Cross-Border Trade Settlement Pilot Project. The pilot project has been expanded from four cities to 20 provinces (autonomous regions and municipal cities). Overseas regions have been expanded from Hong Kong, Macao, and ASEAN to all countries and regions. The notice also clarified that the pilot project covers cross-border trade settlements in goods, services, and other current account items. On August 24, 2011, the PBOC announced that the pilot project of RMB cross-border trade settlement would be extended nationwide, marking the full implementation of the initiative from the pilot project.

3.5.3 *Result of pilot project of RMB cross-border trade settlement in the initial stage*

The RMB cross-border trade settlement was not very active at the initial stage of the pilot project, i.e., the second half of 2009. From implementing the RMB cross-border trade settlement pilot project in early July to the end of 2009, the total RMB cross-border trade settlement is only 3.59 billion yuan. However, with various supporting measures gradually put in place, the cross-border RMB trade settlement entered a track of sustained and significant growth from the first quarter of 2010, which we will introduce in detail in the following section.

3.6 The Achievement of CNY Cross-Border Trade Settlement

After less than half a year of exploration and running, RMB cross-border trade settlement gradually moved onto the right track. RMB cross-border trade settlement has made gratifying achievements in 2010, especially in 2011 and 2012. Table 3.9 shows RMB cross-border trade settlement and its share of the corresponding total trade from the first quarter of 2010 to the second quarter of 2021. The calculations behind this table which will be introduced in the following sections, are complex.

3.6.1 *Overall progress of RMB cross-border trade settlement*

Table 3.9 shows that from 2010 to 2015, the share of RMB cross-border settlement in China's total trade sustainably rose from 2.5% to 29.5%. However, the share of RMB cross-border trade settlement fell to 21.5% and 15.7%, respectively, in 2016–2017 and slightly rebounded to 16.8% and 19.1% in 2018 and 2019. The data show that the cross-border CNY trade settlement pilot project has achieved gratifying results in the past 9 years. Still, the significant decline in the total settlement volume and share since 2016 is worth greater attention.

Table 3.9 shows that from the first quarter of 2010 to the second quarter of 2011, the share of RMB cross-border settlement in total trade kept growing from 0.4% to 7%. RMB import settlement maintained a higher growth trend in the same period from 0.8% to 11%. Due to the expectation of depreciation of RMB abroad at the end of the third quarter of 2011, the share of RMB trade settlement decreased for the first time. Although the share of RMB settlement in imports slowed down due to the re-emergence of the expectation of RMB depreciation, the export settlement maintained a sound momentum of growth. The share of RMB trade settlement of total trade continued to grow from 6.7% in the third quarter of 2011 to 28% in the first quarter of 2014, surpassing one-fourth for the first time. In the same period, the share of import settlement continued to grow from 9% to 38.3%, and the share of export settlement continued to rise from 4.7% to 18%. Affected by RMB depreciation expectation, in the second and third quarters of 2014, the share of RMB settlement of total trade fell to 24.9% and 22%, respectively. Then from the third quarter of 2014 to the third quarter of

Table 3.9: CNY Cross-Border Trade in Goods, Services and Other Current Account Settlement Volume and Share (2010Q1–2021Q2) (Unit: CNY billion, %)

Time	Settlement Trade	Settlement Export	Settlement Import	Settlement Import/ Settlement Export	Share of Trade Settlement	Share of Export Settlement	Share of Import Settlement
2010Q1	18.35	2.14	16.22	7.58	0.40	0.10	0.80
2010Q2	48.66	6.72	41.94	6.24	1.00	0.30	1.80
2010Q3	126.48	16.42	110.06	6.70	2.40	0.60	4.50
2010Q4	312.85	36.67	264.31	7.21	5.50	1.20	10.40
2011Q1	360.32	39.82	320.50	8.05	4.90	1.50	8.30
2011Q2	597.25	103.78	305.25	2.94	7.00	3.40	11.00
2011Q3	583.41	156.90	262.67	1.67	6.70	4.70	9.00
2011Q4	540.29	269.46	180.82	0.67	7.40	8.40	6.20
2012Q1	580.40	229.17	320.84	1.40	10.10	8.40	11.80
2012Q2	671.55	275.90	386.27	1.40	10.70	8.30	13.40
2012Q3	798.96	405.29	393.67	0.97	12.60	11.80	13.50
2012Q4	885.54	370.92	451.04	1.22	12.70	10.60	15.20
2013Q1	1,003.90	416.71	587.21	1.41	16.40	13.00	20.00
2013Q2	1,039.90	471.78	568.12	1.20	16.30	13.90	19.10
2013Q3	1,116.20	440.07	656.21	1.49	17.00	12.70	21.20
2013Q4	1,470.00	458.09	1,011.91	2.21	21.80	12.50	32.70

(Continued)

Table 3.9: *(Continued)*

Time	Settlement Trade	Settlement Export	Settlement Import	Settlement Import/ Settlement Export	Share of Trade Settlement	Share of Export Settlement	Share of Import Settlement
2014Q1	1,651.30	541.59	1,109.71	2.05	28.00	18.00	38.30
2014Q2	1,618.70	687.75	930.95	1.35	24.90	19.60	31.30
2014Q3	1,545.60	656.18	889.42	1.36	22.00	16.80	28.50
2014Q4	1,740.90	845.84	895.06	1.06	24.80	21.30	29.40
2015Q1	1,654.60	905.54	749.05	0.83	29.90	28.80	31.20
2015Q2	1,716.50	889.01	827.49	0.93	28.80	26.20	32.20
2015Q3	2,089.20	1,187.72	901.48	0.76	32.80	32.30	33.60
2015Q4	1,774.00	715.90	1,058.10	1.48	26.60	18.40	38.00
2016Q1	1,344.40	527.22	817.18	1.55	26.40	18.20	37.30
2016Q2	1,324.80	536.23	788.57	1.47	22.50	15.90	31.20
2016Q3	1,360.40	492.72	867.68	1.76	21.20	13.40	31.60
2016Q4	1,197.90	454.75	743.15	1.63	17.30	11.60	24.50
2017Q1	994.20	458.16	536.04	1.17	16.10	13.90	18.60
2017Q2	1,161.60	521.72	639.88	1.23	16.80	13.50	21.00
2017Q3	1,077.20	566.80	510.40	0.90	15.00	14.30	15.90
2017Q4	1,127.00	559.44	567.56	1.01	14.90	13.30	17.00
2018Q1	1,058.98	554.70	504.28	0.91	15.70	15.70	15.60

(Continued)

Table 3.9: (*Continued*)

Time	Settlement Trade	Settlement Export	Settlement Import	Settlement Import/ Settlement Export	Share of Trade Settlement	Share of Export Settlement	Share of Import Settlement
2018Q2	1,258.42	628.27	630.15	1.00	17.10	15.80	18.60
2018Q3	1,392.60	698.97	693.63	0.99	17.00	16.00	18.20
2018Q4	1,400.00	706.62	693.38	0.98	17.10	15.50	19.00
2019Q1	1,291.71	712.67	579.04	0.81	18.40	18.90	17.80
2019Q2	1,505.95	743.83	762.12	1.02	19.60	17.80	21.80
2019Q3	1,602.34	802.74	799.60	1.00	19.40	17.70	21.50
2019Q4	1,640.00	804.53	835.47	1.04	19.10	16.90	21.70
2020Q1	1,460.00	718.03	741.97	1.03	22.20	21.50	22.90
2020Q2	1,620.00	810.00	810.00	1.00	21.10	18.50	24.60
2020Q3	1,820.00	892.83	927.17	1.04	13.27	11.96	14.83
2020Q4	1,870.00	919.67	950.33	1.03	12.71	11.24	14.56
2021Q1	1,700.00	851.67	848.33	1.00	11.85	11.13	12.67
2021Q2	1,900.00	951.86	948.14	1.00	11.95	11.28	12.70
2010	506.34	61.96	432.53	6.98	2.50	0.60	4.60
2011	2,081.27	569.96	1,069.24	1.88	8.80	4.60	9.40
2012	2,936.45	1,281.28	1,551.82	1.21	12.00	9.90	13.50
2013	4,630.00	1,786.65	2,823.45	1.58	17.90	13.00	23.30

(*Continued*)

Table 3.9: (*Continued*)

Time	Settlement Trade	Settlement Export	Settlement Import	Settlement Import/ Settlement Export	Share of Trade Settlement	Share of Export Settlement	Share of Import Settlement
2014	6,556.50	2,731.36	3,825.14	1.40	24.80	19.00	31.80
2015	7,234.30	3,698.17	3,536.12	0.96	29.50	26.20	33.90
2016	5,227.50	2,010.91	3,216.59	1.60	21.50	14.50	30.60
2017	4,360.00	2,106.12	2,253.88	1.07	15.70	13.70	18.10
2018	5,110.00	2,588.56	2,521.44	0.97	16.80	15.80	17.90
2019	6,040.00	3,063.77	2,976.23	0.97	19.10	17.80	20.80
2020	6,770.00	3,340.53	3,429.47	1.03	13.29	12.16	14.60
2021H1	3,600.00	1,803.53	1,796.47	1.00	11.90	11.21	12.68

Source: The basic data come from the implementation report of the People's Bank of China's monetary policy from the first quarter of 2010 to the second quarter of 2021 published on the website of the People's Bank of China (www.pbc.gov.cn) and the financial statistics report published by the People's Bank of China. Due to several changes in the data publication format, the import and export balance and the corresponding share calculation method in the fourth quarter of 2010 and the second quarter of 2011 to the second quarter of 2020 are explained in the text.

2015, the share of RMB trade settlement rebounded and reached a new high of 32.8%, and the corresponding share of export and import settlement reached 32.3% and 33.6%, respectively. However, from the third quarter of 2015 to the fourth quarter of 2017, the share returned to a downward trend and fell to an all-time low of 14.9%. Since the first quarter of 2020, the share gradually rose to 22.2%, equal to the second quarter of 2016.

3.6.2 *Volume of RMB cross-border trade settlement in imports and exports in the first three quarters of 2010*

The total volume of RMB cross-border trade settlement is essential, as is the export and import settlement distribution in total volume. Especially with the significant increase in cross-border RMB settlement, trade settlement will have a bigger impact on China's foreign exchange reserves and monetary policy. Without the export and import RMB cross-border trade settlement volume, it is difficult to see the impact of RMB cross-border trade settlement on China's trade surplus and foreign exchange reserves, making it difficult to judge the effect on China's monetary policy.

In fact, in the quarterly monetary policy execution report published by the People's Bank of China since the first quarter of 2010, the distribution of RMB settlement volume in exports and imports under goods and services trade was only directly given in the report published in the first quarter of 2011. It is difficult to directly obtain the RMB settlement volume in import and export for other quarters. After the second quarter of 2011, the People's Bank of China only published the RMB cross-border trade settlement's actual receipt and payment data. No RMB cross-border settlement data of imports and exports was published since then, making it difficult to forecast the change in the volume.

3.7 Comparison between the Share of Overseas RMB Cross-Border Payment and RMB Cross-Border Trade Settlement

Section 3.2 introduced the concept that a currency's global settlement data is a better substitute for its cross-border trade settlement data. RMB overseas payment data should also be a better substitute for RMB cross-border trade settlement data. Using the monthly RMB cross-border trade settlement data and the corresponding calculation methods in Table 3.9, we can calculate the RMB cross-border trade settlement share in China's monthly total trade from January 2012 to December 2019. Using the share of China's foreign exchange globally from 2012 to 2021 given in Table 3.1, we can calculate the percentage of RMB cross-border trade settlement of the global trade during January 2012–December 2019. Figure 3.1 shows the comparison between the share of RMB cross-border trade settlement in world trade and the share of overseas RMB payments globally from January 2012 to June 2021.

Figure 3.1 shows that the global share of RMB cross-border trade settlement was constantly higher than the global share of RMB cross-border payment before 2016. From 2012 to 2016, the monthly average gap of the former to the latter was 185.6%, 135.9%, 74.2%, 48.2%, and 2.5%, respectively, indicating a positive trend of the convergence between the two. However, in 2017, the former was lower than the latter by 21.6% for the first time, indicating the decline in the status of global trade settlement in cross-border RMB payments in 2017. The former exceeded the latter by an average of 23.3% in the first three months of 2018. Although the concepts of RMB cross-border trade settlement in world trade and global share of RMB cross-border trade settlement are different, trade settlement is still the primary purpose of cross-border RMB settlement. The vast difference between the two shows that a large portion of RMB cross-border trade settlement has no corresponding cross-border payment. In other words, a considerable share of RMB cross-border trade settlement before 2015 was caused by false cross-border settlement, which has decreased significantly since 2016. The gap between the two still needs further discussion as the data accumulate in the future.

3.8 The Analysis of RMB Cross-Border Trade Settlement for Export and Import

The results in Table 3.9 show that the ratio of RMB import settlement and export settlement reached 7.91 times, 2.05 times, and 1.37 times, respectively, from 2010 to 2012, mainly due to the decline in the appreciation pressure of RMB against the USD at the time, indicating that the RMB cross-border settlement for imports and exports in 2010–2012 was reasonable. Although the ratio of import settlement to export settlement rebounded slightly to 1.79 in 2013–2015, it returned to a downward trend in 2013–2015 and fell to 1.30 for the first time in 2015, in line with the peak of the expectation on RMB depreciation against the USD in 2010–2015. It shows that the reasonable level of RMB import to export settlement returned with the reappearance of the depreciation pressure of RMB. Since 2017, the ratio returned above 1, consistent with the declining expectation of the RMB depreciation. These results show once again that RMB trade settlement is closely related to the appreciation and depreciation of RMB against the USD.

Data of Japanese trade settlement show that Japan's export settled in Japanese yen accounted for more than 10 times of Japan's import settled in Japanese yen from 1970 to 1980 (Sato, 1998). Among the seven factors in the choice of international trade settlement currency, except for factor (7), the other six factors support the Japanese yen to become the settlement currency of Japanese export trade. The higher share of Japanese yen settled exports to imports is because the major goods imported were energy and other raw materials (products with high homogeneity). These products were mainly denominated and settled in USD. Therefore, it was difficult to effectively promote the settlement of Japanese yen in imports. In addition to these theoretical explanations, a currency with clear appreciation expectations is likely to become the settlement currency for imports by its home country, as the exporters are more willing to hold it. When Japan began to implement the Plaza Agreement in 1985, the share of Japanese yen in import settlement increased significantly. The ratio of Japanese yen settled exports/imports dropped sharply from 12.3 times in 1980 to 5.4 times in 1985. In 1987, it further dropped to 3.2 times, which became the fastest increase in Japanese yen import settlement share. The share of Japanese yen import settlement continued to increase after 1987. Still, the pace was much more moderate than the period from 1985 to 1987, indicating that there was indeed an advantage in promoting local currency import settlement during a period of local currency appreciation.

As we calculated, in China's RMB cross-border trade settlement, the import settlement in 2010 is nearly seven times that of the export settlement, inconsistent with the first empirical result of international trade settlement currency choice in Section 3.3. It was precisely the opposite of the initial effect of the Japanese yen trade settlement 30 years ago. However, in recent years, China's energy imports and other raw materials are very similar to those of Japan 40 years ago. What is the reason for this opposite result? The answer has been given above: RMB cross-border import settlement is easier to develop because China's overseas "importers" are more willing to accept RMB under the pressure of overseas RMB appreciation. While we fully affirm the remarkable achievements of RMB cross-border trade settlement, the motivation of overseas "importers" to arbitrage between the two markets through trade settlement is worth attention.

3.9 Issues in the RMB Cross-Border Trade Settlement

RMB cross-border trade settlement has made remarkable achievements from 2010 to 2015, and the share of RMB cross-border trade settlement of the total trade volume in the same period increased from 2.5% to 29.5%. However, the RMB settlement ratio has followed a decreasing path after 2015 largely because of the depreciation trend of RMB since 2015 after the US withdrew from the quantitative easing programs.

3.9.1 *The significant difference between the data released by the People's Bank of China and the Hong Kong Monetary Authority*

Based on the RMB cross-border trade settlement data released by the People's Bank of China for the first three quarters of 2011, Table 3.9 estimates that the settlement amount of RMB cross-border trade settlement in the fourth quarter of 2011 was 540.29 billion yuan. RMB cross-border trade settlement volume through Hong Kong announced by the Hong Kong Monetary Authority for the same period was as high as 585.49 billion yuan, which was 45.2 billion yuan higher than the People's Bank of China's data or 8.4% higher. According to the financial statistics report of January 2012 released by the People's Bank of China, the total amount of RMB cross-border trade settlement in January 2012 was 128.4 billion yuan. The RMB cross-border trade settlement in Hong Kong in January 2012 was announced by the Hong Kong Monetary Authority at the end of February 2012 was 156.4 billion yuan, which was 28 billion yuan higher than the data released by the People's Bank of China or 21.8% higher. The corresponding data released by the Hong Kong Monetary Authority for May 2012 was also 7.4 billion yuan higher than that by the People's Bank of China or 3.4% higher. From June 2012 to July 2014, the RMB settlement data released in Hong Kong was constantly lower than that published by the People's Bank of China for more than 2 years. Still, in July and August 2014, the former was 1.8% and 8.5% higher than the latter, respectively, indicating that cross-border trade coordination between the two regions was still insufficient after 8 years of practice. The significant difference between the settlement data released by the local regulators persisted. It may be due to the different statistical methods between the two regions. The RMB cross-border trade volume settled in Hong Kong should not exceed the total amount announced by the People's Bank of China, not to mention higher by 20%.

3.9.2 *The difference between the data of RMB cross-border payment and RMB cross-border trade settlement*

Using the international trade share and global settlement data of major currencies and the trade data of the major currencies' home countries listed in Tables 3.1 and 3.2, we can compare the share of major currencies payment with the global share of countries' foreign trade. The comparison of the two tables shows that except for the USD, Sterling, Euro, Australian dollar, Swiss franc, Norwegian kroner, and New Zealand dollar, the share of payment of other currencies is lower than that of their home countries' foreign trade. This shows that the trade settlements of other currencies all depend on the major currencies to certain degrees. The difference between the share of RMB payment and China's share in global trade is the largest, exceeding 10%, showing that RMB has excellent potential for trade settlement.

3.9.3 *The pricing function of RMB has not improved with the growth of cross-border trade settlement*

Unlike other international currencies, which usually act as both pricing and settlement currency in cross-border trade, the pricing function of RMB has not yet improved with the growth of cross-border trade settlement. Many companies do not use RMB to price in cross-border trade but only as a payment currency. Since there are fewer RMB investment channels, the rationale for many foreign enterprises willing to choose RMB as the payment currency is mainly due to the expectation of RMB appreciation. In the future, as the expectation of two-way fluctuation of the RMB increases, the settlement brought by this expectation will decline. As a whole, it is not clear whether the volume of RMB cross-border trade settlement can maintain such strong growth momentum (Lu Ting, 2014).

3.10 The Future Development of RMB Cross-Border Trade Settlement

In the above context, we introduce and calculate the global share of China's foreign trade and the share of RMB cross-border trade settlement in China's foreign trade. Although the share of RMB trade settlement globally is still relatively low, it has made significant progress in recent years. In particular, in 2011, RMB trade settlement accounted for 0.88% of the global total, significantly exceeding the RMB foreign exchange trading volume share in the global total trading volume. It shows that RMB trade settlement has surpassed the global ranking of the RMB foreign exchange market since 2011. In 2012, the global share of RMB trade settlement exceeded 1% for the first time and reached 1.24%, higher than the RMB foreign exchange market ranking in the world. In 2013, the global share of RMB trade settlement was close to 2%, much higher than the worldwide share of 0.66% of RMB trading volume for the same year, indicating a large gap between the RMB foreign exchange market and RMB trade settlement 2013. The global share of RMB trade settlement was still near the level of 2% in 2016, significantly higher than the share of 1.1% of RMB trading volume in the global foreign exchange market, indicating that the progress of the RMB foreign exchange market and RMB cross-border trade settlement has been slow in recent years, which diverges from the potential of RMB internationalization.

RMB cross-border trade settlement is a necessary measure of RMB internationalization. However, the gradual implementation of RMB cross-border trade settlement has indirectly opened up new channels for the in-and-out flow of international hot money. The fact that the average annual growth rate of China's trade surplus exceeded 100% from 2004 to 2007 made more and more scholars and experts realize that without vigorous promotion of RMB cross-border trade settlement, the massive fund inflow through China's opening current items would push up the level of fixed asset investment in China (Li Dongping, 2008). On the contrary, when the fund turned to outflow in the fourth quarter of 2008 and the first quarter of 2009, China's economy was significantly affected, especially since the second half of 2014, when the United States withdrew from quantitative easing, most of the world's currencies depreciated against the USD. The capital withdrawals from the emerging markets caused great shock and impact on the economies.

The launch of the RMB cross-border trade settlement and foreign direct investment project created new channels for cross-border capital flows. Without the strengthened monitoring of cross-border capital flows, it will significantly impact China's economy and financial market. Therefore, in promoting RMB cross-border settlement, it is necessary to constantly improve the RMB regulatory framework, gradually initiate and strengthen the relevant supporting measures, and establish a monitoring and preventive mechanism for cross-border capital flows to enhance the ability to control the cross-border fund flow. In the opening of capital accounts in the future, the channels of cross-border capital flows will gradually increase, and the establishment of a monitoring and preventive mechanism for cross-border capital flows will be the task for many years to come. Even if the RMB capital account is fully opened in the coming years, the monitoring system of cross-border capital flows will be a necessary and permanent mechanism to ensure the smooth operation of China's economy.

3.11 Summary

This chapter introduced many measures and achievements of RMB internationalization, the development of the RMB offshore market, the opening of the RMB capital account, etc. All the data in the chapter show that gratifying achievements and progress have been made in RMB internationalization in recent years. In August 2015, RMB overtook the Japanese yen for the first time to become the world's fourth largest payment currency. However, we should be aware that RMB internationalization is still at the initial level compared with the process and outcome of Japanese yen internationalization. Moreover, since 2015, the level of RMB internationalization has been significantly affected by the monetary policy of the United States. While fully understanding the favorable economic and trade conditions in promoting RMB internationalization, we should also recognize that many issues exist: the depth and breadth of the domestic capital market needs to be improved, the interest rate markets need to be further implemented, the volume of the foreign exchange market needs to be significantly improved, and the monitoring and supervision system of cross-border funds needs to be further enhanced. It will take time to address these issues, step by step and in a well-planned path.

After entering the WTO, China's economy has been closely tied to the world economy, and those ties will be even closer in the future. The strong momentum in China's economy and trade after we became a member of the WTO has proved the strategic vision of decision makers. The internationalization of RMB closely links China's finance, economy, and other fields with the world. RMB internationalization is a relatively long-term process. Though we can use the experience of other countries as our reference, we still need to explore and improve in many fields to consistently promote RMB internationalization based on China's situation. Exploration is necessary, it must be carried out step by step and in a planned and orderly manner. In other words, there should be a medium- and long-term roadmap and timetable for RMB internationalization to serve China's medium- and long-term strategic development and the consistent improvement of the livelihood of Chinese people. The process should be coordinated with the development and stability of Asia's economy, trade, and financial markets.

Furthermore, it should pay attention to the connection between the reform of the international monetary and financial system and its global development. From these aspects, RMB internationalization is an unprecedented historic feat, which requires joint efforts from both China and abroad. Although "there is no readymade roadmap," we should formulate medium- and long-term strategic objectives, plans, and implementation details to promote RMB internationalization based on a reasonable outlook of the development of China's economy and the global economy, and make appropriate adjustments to adapt to changes in the domestic and international economies, trade and markets. The process of RMB internationalization should be the best reflection and measure in promoting a community with a shared future for mankind and the great rejuvenation of China. With joint efforts from various fields, we can achieve RMB internationalization in the next few years. The RMB's global position will gradually lift to the level equivalent to China's economic position in the world.

As the chapter shows, although the share of the trade between Asia and China in China's total trade has declined over the years, it is still the central part of China's foreign trade. The promotion of RMB cross-border trade settlement should first start in Asia. Other measures of RMB internationalization should also focus on Asia and then on Europe, Africa, Latin America, and North America. After years of promotion, the RMB will become the main settlement currency in Asia and then become the trading currency. In this way, the USD, Euro, and RMB will become the major currencies in the Americas, Europe, and Asia, respectively, achieving the ideal state of "currency tripolar."

To more accurately reflect the current state of global trade, on January 16, 2013, the OECD and WTO released a new statistics methodology of international trade for the first time in Paris, based on the added value of goods in different economies in the global supply chain. This method measures the contribution of other economies based on the added weight on a single global supply chain, which is more scientific than traditional statistical methods. Due to the short track record and the lack of comparable historical data of this methodology, it is challenging to compare trade between different economies, so this is not covered in this chapter. With the accumulation of data, we will follow this method in the future to give more scientific comparisons among different economies in the global economy and trade system.

Chapter 4

Currency Internationalization

The function of a currency in foreign exchange markets and capital markets is a crucial performance indicator and key measurement of its internationalization. It is necessary for us to have a basic understanding of how market liquidity and globalization of major currencies are currently measured so that we can be in an excellent position to analyze the status of RMB globalization and make predictions.

4.1 Major International Currencies in International Foreign Exchange Market

We introduce the liquidity of the global foreign exchange market, trading of major currency pairs, foreign exchange transactions between major countries, and other factors to discuss the status of worldwide currencies in the international foreign exchange market in this section.

4.1.1 *Distribution in turnover of currencies in the international foreign exchange market*

Foreign exchange markets are mostly over the counter (OTC), traded in the interbank market, their clients and among banks, therefore it is difficult to obtain as accurate annual data as securities turnover in organized worldwide exchanges. The most authoritative data about the global foreign exchange transactions come from the Bank for International Settlements (BIS), which releases data every 3 years on the average daily turnover of currencies in April of that year.

Table 4.1 gives the percentages of average daily turnover of key currencies in global foreign exchange trading markets from 1998 to 2019. As each exchange involves a pair of two currencies, the proportion of all currency transactions adds up to 200%. Based on these data, we can calculate the percentages of the key global currencies — USD, EUR, GBP, JPY, and others — in the international foreign exchange market. The results show that turnovers of the top four currencies accounted for 59.8% of global foreign exchange transactions (the sum of the four currencies' percentages, as shown in Table 4.1, divided by two) in 1998, and the percentages reached as high as 81.2% and 81.4% in 2001 and 2004, respectively, fell to around 77.6% from 2007 to 2013, and further dropped to 75.1% in 2019. The data reflect the monopolistic position of these four currencies in the global foreign exchange market.

As shown in Table 4.1, CNY turnover in the global foreign exchange market only accounted for 0.5% of the total in 2007, which was disproportionate to the fact that China contributed to 6.2% of the world's total GDP in the same year. The percentage of CNY was 0.9%, ranking 16th in the world in 2010, while China's GDP made up 9.2% of the global total and ranked second in the world. The ratio of CNY trade in the worldwide foreign exchange market increased to 2.2% in 2013, ranking ninth in the world the same year, while at the same time China's GDP contributed 12.7% of the global total. The ratio of CNY exchange increased further to 4% in 2016, which was more than 10% lower than the ratio of China's GDP of the global total, 15.2%. The proportion of CNY trade was further increased to 4.3% in 2019 while it still far behind the number of GDP contribution. By analyzing BIS's data, we found that the CNY turnovers in a few regions may have significant differences with the statistics compiled in London and other financial centers. After some reasonable adjustments, as shown in detail in Chapter 11, the actual ratio of CNY turnover in the global foreign exchange market should be 5.1% in 2019. Even so, this number is still more than 10% lower than the proportion of China's GDP of the global total. Having taken BIS's data into sole consideration, the international ranking of CNY trade rose from 16th to 8th from 2010 to 2019. However, according to the revised data in Chapter 11, the ratio of CNY exchange of the global total has already surpassed that of CHF and CAD, which puts CNY into sixth position in the same year.

Table 4.1: Proportions of Average Daily Turnovers of Major Currencies in the International Foreign Exchange Market (1998–2019) (Unit: %)

Year **Currency**	**1998**	**2001**	**2004**	**2007**	**2010**	**2013**	**2016**	**2019**
USD	86.8	89.9	88.0	85.6	84.9	87.0	87.6	88.3
EUR	—	37.9	37.4	37.0	39.0	33.4	31.4	32.3
JPY	21.7	23.5	20.8	17.2	19.0	23.0	21.6	16.8
GBP	11.0	13.0	16.5	14.9	12.9	11.8	12.8	12.8
AUD	3.0	4.3	6.0	6.6	7.6	8.6	6.9	6.8
CAD	3.5	4.5	4.2	4.3	5.3	4.6	5.1	5.0
CHF	7.1	6.0	6.0	6.8	6.3	5.2	4.8	5.0
CNY	0.0	0.0	0.1	0.5	0.9	2.2	4.0	4.3
HKD	1.0	2.2	1.8	2.7	2.4	1.4	1.7	3.5
NZD	0.2	0.6	1.1	1.9	1.6	2.0	2.1	2.1
SEK	0.3	2.5	2.2	2.7	2.2	1.8	2.2	2.0
KRW	0.2	0.8	1.1	1.2	1.5	1.2	1.7	2.0
SGD	1.1	1.1	0.9	1.2	1.4	1.4	1.8	1.8
NOK	0.2	1.5	1.4	2.1	1.3	1.4	1.7	1.8
MXN	0.5	0.8	1.1	1.3	1.3	2.5	1.9	1.7
INR	0.1	0.2	0.3	0.7	0.9	1.0	1.1	1.7
RUB	0.3	0.3	0.6	0.7	0.9	1.6	1.1	1.1
ZAR	0.4	0.9	0.7	0.9	0.7	1.1	1.0	1.1
TRY	NA	0.0	0.1	0.2	0.7	1.3	1.4	1.1
BRL	0.2	0.5	0.3	0.4	0.7	1.1	1.0	1.1
TWD	0.1	0.3	0.4	0.4	0.5	0.5	0.6	0.9
DKK	0.3	1.2	0.9	0.8	0.6	0.8	0.8	0.6
PLN	0.1	0.5	0.4	0.8	0.8	0.7	0.7	0.6
THB	0.1	0.2	0.2	0.2	0.2	0.3	0.4	0.5
IDR	0.3	0.2	0.2	0.2	0.2	0.4	0.3	0.4
Others	—	7.1	7.3	8.7	6.3	3.6	4.2	2.2
CNY*	0.2	0.6	0.0	0.0	0.7	1.3	4.0	5.2

Source: Updated data about average daily turnovers in April 2019 released by the BIS in December 2019 and data from previous years.

4.1.2 *Major currency pairs in international foreign exchange markets*

The daily turnovers of significant currency pairs in the global foreign exchange market, to certain degree, reflect the internationalism of involved currencies. Table 4.2 provides the turnovers and ratios of foreign exchange of significant currency pairs from 2001 to 2019. It shows that the foreign exchange between USD and the other three major currencies — EUR, JPY, and GBP — dominates the global foreign exchange markets. Total turnover of these three currency pairs accounted for 60.6% and 58.4% of the global foreign exchange trading in 2001 and 2004, respectively, and this number fell from 51.6% to 46.8% from 2007 to 2016, which shows that the proportion of the three major currencies fell to 50% of the global total in the foreign exchange market for the first time. Encouragingly, Table 4.2 shows that the USD/CNY currency pair became the sixth biggest currency pair of the world both in 2016 and 2019, and the CNY/EUR currency pair became the 13th currency pair against EUR, and its daily turnover reached $2.4 billion on average in 2019.

4.1.2.1 *Dominance of USD*

Although the ratio of USD-involved currency pairs dropped from 89.8% in 2001 to 85.6% in 2007 and fell further to 84.9% in 2010 as shown in Table 4.1, it rebounded, surpassing 85.6% in 2013 and even climbing up to 87.6% in 2016; the proportion hit a record high of 88.3% in 2019, even higher than the level seen in 2007 and before the financial crisis. This trend shows that the USD has regained its dominance witnessed before the financial crisis. Transactions of USD-involved currency pairs, as shown in Table 4.2, also reflect different currencies' global positions to a large extent. For example, the ratio of CNY/USD currency pair's transactions increased from 2.1% in 2013 to 4.1% in 2019 with its ranking moving up from eighth to sixth. Those results are close to the rankings of CNY's daily turnovers, as shown in Table 4.1.

4.1.2.2 *EUR/JPY currency pair*

Table 4.2 shows that the ratio of the average daily turnover between EUR and other currencies hovered around 37.5% from 2001 to 2007; although this proportion increased to 39.1% during the 2007–2010 period, it

Table 4.2: Average Daily Turnovers and Proportions of Major Currency Pairs (2001–2019) (Unit: USD billion, %)

Year	2001		2004		2007		2010		2013		2016		2019	
Currency Pair	**Amount**	**Share**	**Amount**	**Share**	**Amount**	**Share**	**Amount**	**Share**	**Amount**	**Share**	**Amount**	**Share**	**Amount**	**Share**
USD/EUR	372	30	541	28	892	26.8	1,099	27.7	1,292	24.1	1,172	23.1	1,583.6	24.0
USD/JPY	250	20.2	328	17	438	13.2	567	14.3	980	18.3	901	17.8	870.7	13.2
USD/GBP	129	10.4	259	13.4	384	11.6	360	9.1	473	8.8	470	9.3	630.4	9.6
USD/AUD	51	4.1	107	5.5	185	5.6	248	6.3	364	6.8	262	5.2	357.9	5.4
USD/CAD	54	4.3	77	4	126	3.8	182	4.6	200	3.7	218	4.3	287.3	4.4
USD/CNY	—	—	—	—	—	—	31	0.8	113	2.1	192	3.8	269.4	4.1
USD/CHF	59	4.8	83	4.3	151	4.5	166	4.2	184	3.4	180	3.6	228.1	3.5
USD/MXN	—	—	—	—	—	—	—	—	128	2.4	90	1.8	219.4	3.3
USD/SGD	—	—	—	—	—	—	—	—	65	1.2	81	1.6	125.3	1.9
USD/NZD	—	—	—	—	—	—	—	—	82	1.5	78	1.5	110.1	1.7
USD/KRW	—	—	—	—	—	—	58	1.5	60	1.1	78	1.5	109.7	1.7
USD/HKD	—	—	—	—	—	—	85	2.1	69	1.3	77	1.5	106.6	1.6
USD/SEK	—	—	—	—	570	1.7	45	1.1	55	1	66	1.3	104.6	1.6
USD/TRY	—	—	—	—	—	—	—	—	63	1.2	64	1.3	86.2	1.3
USD/INR	—	—	—	—	—	—	36	0.9	50	0.9	56	1.1	73.3	1.1
USD/RUB	—	—	—	—	—	—	—	—	79	1.5	53	1.1	66	1.0
USD/NOK	—	—	—	—	—	—	—	—	49	0.9	48	0.9	62.8	1.0
USD/BRL	—	—	—	—	—	—	25	0.6	48	0.9	45	0.9	62.3	0.9

(Continued)

Table 4.2: (*Continued*)

Year	2001		2004		2007		2010		2013		2016		2019	
Currency Pair	**Amount**	**Share**	**Amount**	**Share**	**Amount**	**Share**	**Amount**	**Share**	**Amount**	**Share**	**Amount**	**Share**	**Amount**	**Share**
USD/ZAR	—	—	—	—	—	—	24	0.6	51	1	40	0.8	62.3	0.9
USD/TWD	—	—	—	—	—	—	—	—	22	0.4	31	0.6	58.9	0.9
USD/PLN	—	—	—	—	—	—	—	—	22	0.4	19	0.4	24.7	0.4
USD/other currencies	199	16	307	15.9	612	18.4	446	11.2	214	4	215	4.2	319.7	4.9
EUR/GBP	27	2.1	47	2.4	69	2.1	109	2.7	102	1.9	100	2	130.7	2.0
EUR/JPY	36	2.9	61	3.2	86	2.6	111	2.8	148	2.8	79	1.6	113.5	1.7
EUR/CHF	13	1.1	30	1.6	62	1.9	71	1.8	71	1.3	44	0.9	72.7	1.1
EUR/SEK	—	—	—	—	24	0.7	35	0.9	28	0.5	36	0.7	36.2	0.5
EUR/NOK	—	—	—	—	—	—	—	—	20	0.4	28	0.6	33.5	0.5
EUR/AUD	1	0.1	4	0.2	9	0.3	12	0.3	21	0.4	16	0.3	18.4	0.3
EUR/CAD	1	0.1	2	0.1	7	0.2	14	0.3	15	0.3	14	0.3	15.1	0.2
EUR/PLN	^(	—	—	—	—	—	—	—	14	0.3	13	0.3	13.2	0.2
EUR/DKK	^(	—	—	—	—	—	—	—	13	0.2	13	0.2	10.7	0.2
EUR/HUF	^(	—	—	—	—	—	—	—	10	0.2	5	0.1	10.2	0.2
EUR/TRY	^(	—	—	—	—	—	—	—	6	0.1	4	0.1	3.9	0.1
EUR/CNY	^(	—	—	—	—	—	—	—	1	0	2	0	2.4	0.0

(*Continued*)

Table 4.2: *(Continued)*

Year	2001		2004		2007		2010		2013		2016		2019	
Currency Pair	**Amount**	**Share**	**Amount**	**Share**	**Amount**	**Share**	**Amount**	**Share**	**Amount**	**Share**	**Amount**	**Share**	**Amount**	**Share**
EUR/other currencies	20	1.6	38	1.9	83	2.5	102	2.6	51	0.9	65	1.3	84.6	1.3
JPY/AUD	—	—	—	—	—	—	24	0.6	46	0.9	31	0.6	35	0.5
JPY/CAD	—	—	—	—	—	—	—	—	6	0.1	7	0.1	7.2	0.1
JPY/NZD	—	—	—	—	—	—	4	0.1	5	0.1	5	0.1	6.3	0.1
JPY/TRY	—	—	—	—	—	—	—	—	1	0	3	0.1	5.7	0.1
JPY/ZAR	—	—	—	—	—	—	—	—	4	0.1	3	0.1	4.8	0.1
JPY/BRL	—	—	—	—	—	—	—	—	3	0.1	1	0	1.6	0.0
JPY/Other currencies	15	1.2	28	1.4	66	2	50	1.3	88	1.6	45	0.9	62.9	1.0
Other currency pairs	13	1.1	22	1.1	74	2.2	70	1.8	44	0.8	116	2.3	102.3	1.6
All currency pairs	1,239	100	1,934	100	3,324	100	3,971	100	5,357	100	5,067	100	6,590.4	100.0

Source: Compiled based on the revised data about the average daily turnover in April 2019 released by the BIS in December 2019 and the data from previous years.

dropped to 32.3% from 2010 to 2019, significantly lower than 37.5% recorded in the 2001–2007 period, reflecting the significantly negative impacts of the European debt crisis on the EUR. From 2016 to 2019, the ratio of turnover between EUR and GBP was higher than that of EUR and JPY, and there was a significant decline in the proportion of turnover between EUR and CHF. However, the ratio of turnover between EUR and other currencies increased slightly.

As shown in Table 4.2, the proportion of the average daily turnover between JPY and other currencies registered a drop of nearly 10% from 27.1% to 17.3% during the 2001–2007 period. Although this ratio recovered to 23.1% during the 2007–2010 period, it dropped to 19.8% in 2013. The ratio did not change much from 2016 to 2019, showing a medium-to-long-term drop compared with that in 2013. This mirrors Japan's sluggish trade and economy over the past two decades and indicates that Japan's aggressive economic stimulus efforts have had little effects on JPY foreign exchange markets.

4.1.2.3 *Influences of daily average turnover of major currencies on currency internalization*

As shown in Table 4.2, the standings of daily turnovers of USD/EUR, USD/JPY, USD/GBP, USD/AUD, and USD/CAD were the same as the rankings of six currencies, as indicated in Table 4.1. In 2016, the daily average turnover of USD/CNY reached $192 billion, for the first time higher by 5.6% than $180 billion of average turnover of USD/CHF, as seen in the same year. This percentage increased to 18.1% in 2019. Meanwhile, the difference between the average turnover of USD/CNY and that of USD/CAD dropped from 12.8% to 6.2%. These data show that the international ranking of CNY, as compared to USD, improved noticeably from 2016 to 2019, surpassing CHF and taking the seventh position. Additionally, it was catching up with CAD which ranked sixth. These data offer support for justifying the status of CNY internationalization in 2019, as shown in Chapter 11.

4.2 Geographical Distribution of International Foreign Exchange Trade

Geographical distribution of foreign exchange trade among countries and regions can provide vital information about the global foreign exchange

Table 4.3: Countries and Regions in Global Foreign Exchange Trade (1998–2019) (Unit: %)

	1998	2001	2004	2007	2010	2013	2016	2019	Change 2016–2019
UK	32.64	31.78	32.03	34.65	36.74	40.77	36.94	43.12	6.18
US	18.26	15.99	19.12	17.41	17.92	18.89	19.53	16.52	−3.01
Singapore	6.90	6.08	5.12	5.65	5.27	5.73	7.94	7.64	−0.30
Hong Kong	3.81	4.01	4.06	4.23	4.71	4.11	6.70	7.62	0.92
Eurozone	16.13	14.25	12.94	11.33	9.97	9.00	8.53	6.51	−2.02
Japan	6.97	8.96	7.95	5.84	6.19	5.60	6.13	4.53	−1.60
Switzerland	4.36	4.48	3.27	5.92	4.94	3.24	2.40	3.32	0.92
France	3.68	2.91	2.55	2.96	3.01	2.84	2.77	2.01	−0.76
China	0.01	0.00	0.02	0.22	0.39	0.66	1.12	1.64	0.52
Germany	4.74	5.36	4.62	2.37	2.15	1.66	1.79	1.50	−0.29
Australia	2.30	3.17	4.11	4.12	3.81	2.72	1.86	1.44	−0.42
Canada	1.81	2.60	2.27	1.50	1.23	0.97	1.31	1.32	0.01
Netherlands	2.04	1.79	2.00	0.58	0.36	1.68	1.31	0.77	−0.54
Denmark	1.34	1.40	1.61	2.06	2.39	1.76	1.55	0.76	−0.79
Luxembourg	1.08	0.77	0.56	1.02	0.66	0.77	0.57	0.69	0.12
South Korea	0.17	0.58	0.79	0.82	0.87	0.71	0.73	0.67	−0.06
Russia	0.33	0.56	1.14	1.17	0.83	0.91	0.69	0.56	−0.13
Saudi Arabia	0.11	0.12	0.08	0.10	0.15	0.10	0.12	0.55	0.43
Spain	0.95	0.48	0.53	0.40	0.58	0.64	0.50	0.49	−0.01
India	0.12	0.20	0.26	0.90	0.54	0.47	0.53	0.48	−0.05
Sweden	0.77	1.46	1.22	1.03	0.89	0.65	0.64	0.45	−0.19
Belgium	1.30	0.61	0.80	1.17	0.64	0.32	0.35	0.43	0.08
Norway	0.42	0.76	0.55	0.75	0.44	0.32	0.62	0.36	−0.26
Taiwan China	0.23	0.28	0.36	0.36	0.36	0.39	0.41	0.36	−0.05
South Africa	0.43	0.58	0.38	0.33	0.28	0.31	0.32	0.25	−0.07
Mexico	0.41	0.50	0.59	0.36	0.34	0.48	0.31	0.24	−0.07
Turkey	0.00	0.06	0.13	0.10	0.33	0.41	0.34	0.23	−0.11
Brazil	0.24	0.32	0.15	0.13	0.28	0.26	0.30	0.23	−0.07
Italy	1.36	1.03	0.90	0.88	0.57	0.35	0.27	0.21	−0.06

(*Continued*)

Table 4.3: (*Continued*)

	1998	**2001**	**2004**	**2007**	**2010**	**2013**	**2016**	**2019**	**Change 2016–2019**
Austria	0.56	0.49	0.56	0.44	0.39	0.23	0.29	0.19	−0.10
Thailand	0.15	0.11	0.12	0.15	0.15	0.19	0.16	0.17	0.01
Malaysia	0.05	0.08	0.06	0.08	0.14	0.17	0.13	0.12	−0.01
New Zealand	0.33	0.24	0.27	0.30	0.17	0.18	0.15	0.11	−0.04
Poland	0.13	0.30	0.25	0.22	0.16	0.11	0.14	0.11	−0.03
Chile	0.06	0.14	0.09	0.09	0.11	0.18	0.11	0.10	−0.01
Israel	0.05	0.09	0.19	0.20	0.20	0.12	0.12	0.09	−0.03
Indonesia	0.08	0.23	0.09	0.07	0.07	0.07	0.07	0.08	0.01
Finland	0.21	0.10	0.07	0.19	0.62	0.22	0.21	0.08	−0.13
Colombia	0.00	0.02	0.03	0.04	0.06	0.05	0.06	0.05	−0.01
Other countries/ regions	1.59	1.35	1.07	1.21	1.07	0.77	0.50	0.50	0.00
Europe	56.11	54.99	53.03	57.12	56.35	56.76	51.51	54.41	2.90
Europe outside UK	23.47	23.21	21.00	22.48	19.61	15.98	14.57	11.29	−3.28
Asia	18.60	20.65	18.91	18.42	18.84	18.20	24.04	23.86	−0.18
North America	20.50	19.10	22.00	19.30	19.50	20.30	21.20	18.08	−3.12
Other regions	4.80	5.40	5.80	5.00	4.90	4.30	2.90	3.65	0.75
Total	100.00	100.00	100.00	100.00	100.00	100.00	100.00	100.00	0.00

Source: Updated data released by the BIS in December 2019 regarding average daily turnover in April 2019 and data from previous years; data of Eurozone is the sum of foreign exchange transactions of 18 Eurozone countries which entered the rankings of foreign exchange transactions as published by the BIS in December 2019, except for the Republic of Malta.

market. Table 4.3 identifies 36 countries and regions most actively engaged in foreign exchange and their share of global foreign exchange for the 1998–2019 period.

4.2.1 *The front-runner status of the UK*

Although the UK has only been the world's fifth biggest economy for years and accounted for less than 4% of the world economy in recent years, it has maintained an unmatched position as an international financial center, especially for global foreign exchange trade. According to Table 4.3, around 32% of global foreign exchange trade took place in the UK during the 1998–2004 period; this ratio then increased to 34.65% during the 2004–2007 period, 36.74% during the 2007–2011 period and 40.77% during the 2011–2013 period, doubling that of the US, which was the world's prominent economy. Although this proportion dropped a bit in 2016, it rose to 43.12% in 2019, which was a relatively high level over the past two decades. This indicates that the UK's leading role in international foreign exchange trade has been noticeably reinforced.

A comparison of Tables 4.1 and 4.3 reveals that while an increasing amount of foreign exchange has taken place in the UK in recent years, GBP saw continuous drops in its share in worldwide foreign exchange trading, which indicates that a considerable ratio of foreign exchange trade conducted in the UK did not involve GBP, but was between other major currencies. The UK, the leading trading center for the global foreign exchange market, has shown interest in CNY internationalization and even made efforts to this end.

4.2.2 *Rising status of the US in foreign exchange trade*

It is not surprising to see the UK come out on top, but you may question the ratio of the UK's foreign exchange turnover in 2019 reaching the highest level since 1998, as shown in Table 4.3. It is well known that the foreign exchange trade in a certain region is closely correlated with changes in the assets of foreign-invested companies based in this region. Data from the BIS show that the cross-border asset volume in four international finance centers (the US, Singapore, Hong Kong, and Tokyo) increased by more than 10% from the end of the first quarter in 2016 to the end of the first quarter in 2019. During the same period, that number was only 9.1% for the UK, which made it the smallest among the top five international finance centers, showing the influences of Brexit on the assets outside the British territories in recent years. However, the total increase rate of the UK's daily average foreign exchange trade was as high as 48.6% from April 2016 to April 2019, as shown in Table 4.3, the highest among the top five international finance centers, which makes it 7.7% higher than the US's increase rate of 40.9% for the same period.

Besides, data about the global foreign exchange market given by the BIS every 3 years should be close to the results published by the central bank of each country or region in the same period. However, the UK's daily average foreign exchange transaction trade in 2019 published by the BIS was larger by 25.1% than the number of the same period published by the Bank of England and was almost three times greater when compared with 8.8%, which was the average difference among 2010, 2013 and 2016. This means that the UK's daily foreign exchange transaction volume in 2019, as published by the BIS, was too large, which led to an overlarge ratio on an international level, because that proportion should be within 40% for the UK in 2019. Due to the abnormal data about the UK's foreign exchange transaction market which is also the most prominent in the world, data regarding the foreign exchange transactions of key currencies in the UK also have some problems, leading to problematic global standings of major currencies. We will introduce and analyze the relevant problems in Chapter 12 while analyzing the global ranking of CNY in 2019.

The proportion of foreign exchange transactions in the US — the biggest economy — did not change a lot from 1998 to 2013 and hovered around 18%. However, the ratio increased by 0.54% to 19.43% in 2016 and exceeded 19% for the first time in the past 20 years. But it dropped to 16.52% in 2019. The mild fluctuations of the ratio of the US's foreign exchange transactions existed because most American financial institutions had set foreign exchange trading platforms in the UK and some of America's foreign exchange transactions were done in the UK. Although the percentage of foreign exchange transactions done in America has not changed significantly since 2017, the proportion of USD transactions of the foreign exchange transactions done in the US has increased significantly. Brexit will encourage more USD transactions to be done back in America.

4.2.3 *Eurozone's significantly decreased share of foreign exchange trade*

According to Table 4.3, the percentage of foreign exchange commerce taking place in 15 Eurozone countries saw a significant drop over the past 10 years. From 1998 to 2019, it experienced a significant decline from 16.99% to 6.51%. Furthermore, from 2016 to 2019, the percentage of foreign exchange commerce taking place in the Eurozone dropped by 2.02%, only second to the US which is 3.01%. Although as an integrated economy adopting the same currency, the Eurozone was only behind the US in terms of its ability to host foreign exchange trade, indicating that even though the EUR is the world's second largest currency, the Eurozone is likely to have greater potential to host foreign exchange trade.

4.2.4 *Singapore: The third largest foreign exchange center in the world and the largest in the Asia-Pacific region*

One of the most vital changes in the global financial market, especially in the international foreign exchange market, over the past decade occurred in 2013 when Singapore overtook Japan to become the world's third most prominent foreign exchange center and the biggest in the Asia-Pacific region. For over a decade, Singapore accounted for 0.3–0.4% of the world's economy, but it was a leader in the financial market in the Asia-Pacific region, especially in the foreign exchange market. Table 4.3 indicates that Singapore maintained the world's fourth and Asia's second biggest foreign exchange market for most of the time for more than a decade until 2010. In 2013, it surpassed Japan for the first time to become the world's third largest foreign exchange center and the biggest in Asia, and these standings remained the same from 2016 to 2019, which demonstrates Singapore's importance in foreign exchange markets in the Asia-Pacific region and in the world. Singapore has been preparing for offshore CNY trading for years and was authorized by the People's Bank of China as the second biggest offshore CNY trading center after Hong Kong at the beginning of 2013. The importance of Singapore in the global foreign exchange market and its measures to promote CNY globalization will help it play a significant role in pushing for CNY internationalization in the Asia-Pacific region, especially in ASEAN countries.

4.2.5 *Hong Kong: The fourth largest foreign exchange center in the world and the second largest in the Asia-Pacific region*

Hong Kong has been a crucial gateway to the global foreign exchange market for the Chinese mainland over the past three decades, and it has played a significant role in the process of China's reform and opening. As the biggest offshore CNY trading center, Hong Kong will continue to play a significant role in the process of CNY internationalization. For years, Hong Kong's GDP was higher than that of Singapore due to its population and territorial area. However, from 2010 to 2014, Singapore's economy grew at a significantly higher rate than that of Hong Kong, which ultimately paved the way for Singapore's GDP to overtake that of Hong Kong in 2010, although Hong Kong turned the table in 2015. As shown in Table 4.3, Hong Kong's ability to facilitate foreign exchange remained weaker than that of Singapore, though the gap is gradually narrowing. During the period from 2007 to 2010, Hong Kong saw its proportion of foreign exchange trade increase by 0.5% to 4.7%, while Singapore's percentage dropped from 0.3% to 5.3%, contributing to the narrowest gap between the two in over a decade. However, during the 2010–2013 period, instead of increasing, the share of Hong Kong decreased by 0.6% to 4.11%, reverting to the 2004 level. Singapore, on the other hand, saw its share grow by 0.46% to 5.73%. From 2016 to 2019, Hong Kong's foreign exchange trade once again entered an uptrend, and the percentage climbed up to 7.62%, for which its gap with Singapore narrowed to as small as 0.02%.

With the stimulations and promotions by China on offshore CNY settlements as well as other CNY businesses to Hong Kong foreign exchange businesses, according to the trend in the share of foreign exchange traded in Hong Kong and Singapore from 2007 to 2010, Hong Kong would overtake Singapore or even Japan to become the biggest foreign exchange center in Asia-Pacific region for the first time in 2013. However, Table 4.3 shows that at that time we were too optimistic about Hong Kong's foreign exchange market. However, Table 4.3 also shows that despite such a decrease, Hong Kong's rank in the global foreign exchange market moved up from seventh in 2010 to sixth in 2013, partially due to a significant drop of Switzerland in the ranking as it was hit hard by the global financial crisis, and its share of foreign exchange trade dropped drastically from 5.92% in 2007 to 3.24% in 2013. However, data in Table 4.3 are encouraging. The percentage of Hong Kong's foreign exchange improved by 3.51% from 2013 to 2019, the biggest growth in the world over the same period of time, which made it surpass Japan and become the second biggest foreign exchange commerce center in the region and the fifth biggest in the world.

4.2.6 *Significantly decreased share of Japan's foreign exchange trade*

As shown in Table 4.3, foreign exchange trade taking place in Japan displayed a general irreversible downward trend after 1998. Thus, Japan was replaced by Singapore as the world's third largest foreign exchange center and the biggest in the Asia-Pacific region. Later, in 2013, Japan was replaced by Hong Kong as the world's fourth largest foreign exchange center and the second biggest in the Asia-Pacific region. The unremitting gloom in Japan's economy during the past two decades was also represented in the global foreign exchange markets. Table 4.3 also shows that the proportion of Japan's foreign exchange trade dropped by 1.6% from 2016 to 2019, with its drop only smaller than that of US and Eurozone.

4.2.7 *China's share of foreign exchange trade and related issues*

As shown in Table 4.3, foreign exchange trade taking place in China was 0.22% in 2007, but it was increased to 0.39% in 2010, 0.66% in 2013, 1.12% in 2016, and 1.64% in 2019. Correspondingly, the ranking of CNY internationalism also moved up to 22nd, 16th, 13th, and 8th, reflecting the rapid growth of China in foreign exchange trade during the past 10 years. Table 1.1 gives the percentages and standings of China's economy, trade, and CNY foreign exchange market. As shown by the data in Table 4.3, compared to the proportions and standings of China's economy, trade and CNY's foreign exchange trade, the ranking of China's foreign exchange trade is not only significantly lower than the global ranking of China's economy and trade but also much lower than the ranking of CNY in the foreign exchange trade. It shows that the development of China's domestic foreign exchange market significantly lags CNY internationalization.

In Table 4.3, we can see that the ranking of China's foreign exchange trade is low, and China's increase of 4.5% is lower than that of UK, Hong Kong, and Switzerland. Additionally, the percentage of foreign exchange taking place in China is 1.64% in 2016, less than 25% of that in Singapore and Hong Kong in the same period. Such an inactive foreign exchange market mismatches China's economic and commerce status as well as China's CNY globalization, which has made it one of the bottlenecks for China's CNY internationalization efforts. Accelerating the development and activation of the domestic foreign exchange has also become an urgent task in promoting CNY globalization.

4.2.8 *Intercontinental distribution of global foreign exchange trade*

Table 4.3 shows the intercontinental distribution of global foreign exchange trade. The proportion of exchange commerce in Europe outside of the UK has witnessed a significant decline by 3.82% from 2016 to 2019, and its magnitude was even larger than the US's 3.01%. However, the percentage of exchange commerce in Europe (including UK) was still more than 50%. From 2013 to 2016, Asian foreign exchange trade increased by 5.75%. In 2016, for the first time, Asia replaced North America becoming the world's second biggest continent in foreign exchange trade, just behind the European continent. However, the percentage of Asian foreign exchange trade dropped to 23.86%. Even so, it was still the second biggest continent in terms of foreign exchange trade. It indicates that the Asian economy and trade scale also has a preliminary reaction in the global foreign exchange market. The percentages of South America, Africa, and Oceania in the global foreign exchange trading are very low and on a downward trend.

4.3 Activity of Major International Currencies in International Market of Foreign Exchange Derivatives

Despite a bad reputation following the global financial crisis, derivatives still play an important role in the global financial market. Zhang, Guangping (Peter G.) (2016) thought that for over a decade, the turnover of financial derivatives was significantly larger than that of bonds, foreign exchange, shares, and other traditional financial products in the global market. As observed above, the average daily turnover of the international foreign exchange market not only included traditional foreign exchange spot goods or spot trade but also foreign exchange forward trade, foreign exchange swaps, currency swaps, foreign exchange options, and other foreign exchange derivatives. In addition, foreign exchange derivatives have taken up a bigger market share than spot trade since 1992 (the BIS data show that foreign exchange derivatives trading surpassed spot

Table 4.4: Proportions of Total Average Daily Turnovers of Spot Transaction, Forward Transaction, and Foreign Exchange Swaps of Major Currencies (2007–2019) (Unit: %)

Year	2007			2013			2016			2019		
Currency	**Spot**	**Forward**	**Swap**	**Spot**	**Forward**	**Swap**	**Spot**	**Forward**	**Swap**	**Spot**	**Forward**	**Swap**
USD	29.7	10.9	59.4	36.4	12.6	43.6	31.2	13.5	48.7	29.0	15.2	49.9
EUR	36.9	12.1	51.1	42.2	10.0	42.9	32.7	11.2	50.7	28.9	12.0	53.6
JPY	40.4	12.1	47.5	49.7	10.0	27.0	36.0	13.8	41.8	32.5	13.1	46.5
GBP	32.5	10.0	57.4	35.9	11.0	47.8	32.5	14.2	47.1	28.4	12.9	52.6
AUD	25.7	10.0	64.3	42.4	10.8	39.6	41.0	11.7	39.6	38.2	11.9	41.8
CAD	29.7	11.8	58.6	38.3	14.8	41.3	40.1	13.2	39.6	36.7	12.9	43.9
CHF	42.2	10.1	47.7	30.6	9.8	54.1	23.5	12.3	61.5	26.2	11.1	59.4
CNY	61.4	31.3	7.4	28.4	23.5	33.4	33.4	13.8	42.6	34.1	12.5	48.1
SEK	20.7	10.0	69.3	28.7	12.5	55.9	30.0	11.9	52.6	30.7	12.5	52.8
NZD	29.4	11.3	59.3	37.0	10.9	47.6	38.8	10.7	41.7	38.6	11.7	39.4
MXN	37.4	11.7	50.9	42.0	10.2	42.8	44.3	12.4	37.1	42.4	11.2	38.2
SGD	22.5	7.9	69.6	27.4	14.3	53.6	30.4	8.7	55.4	31.2	10.1	54.3
HKD	18.4	7.0	74.6	26.9	9.6	61.3	25.3	6.9	65.5	24.4	11.3	59.7
NOK	18.4	9.7	71.9	27.9	13.2	55.9	34.1	9.4	51.8	35.1	12.5	47.4
KRW	44.7	29.4	25.9	30.3	37.2	24.9	34.5	41.7	16.7	23.1	54.6	14.2
TRY	61.4	11.4	27.2	22.4	13.8	55.5	27.0	8.1	54.1	33.9	7.5	49.8
RUB	70.7	5.0	24.3	42.8	10.3	43.2	40.7	10.2	45.8	46.8	13.7	36.1
INR	**42.6**	**27.5**	**29.8**	**28.9**	**46.2**	**19.1**	**32.8**	**39.7**	**22.4**	**41.6**	**86.9**	**20.6**

(Continued)

Table 4.4: (*Continued*)

Year	2007			2013			2016			2019		
Currency	**Spot**	**Forward**	**Swap**	**Spot**	**Forward**	**Swap**	**Spot**	**Forward**	**Swap**	**Spot**	**Forward**	**Swap**
BRL	50.2	47.3	2.5	28.9	46.2	19.1	25.5	52.9	2.0	19.8	60.1	0.8
ZAR	19.9	12.1	68.0	32.6	11.9	52.3	32.0	8.0	48.0	38.0	9.4	43.0
DKK	21.8	10.3	67.9	17.4	12.4	69.5	16.7	11.9	71.4	16.7	11.3	70.9
PLN	20.0	10.9	69.1	28.8	14.8	52.7	34.3	11.4	51.4	29.8	12.6	53.4
TWD	47.1	40.6	12.3	23.2	45.0	25.9	29.0	41.9	25.8	21.2	57.9	17.0
HUF	34.1	15.7	50.2	33.0	15.6	45.9	26.7	13.3	53.3	32.5	11.8	46.8
Others	43.7	39.3	17.0	31.8	30.6	31.1	31.0	26.3	33.6	35.7	27.4	31.4
All currencies	30.2	10.9	51.6	38.3	12.7	41.7	32.6	13.8	46.9	30.2	15.2	48.6

Source: Calculated according to data on average daily turnover in April 2019 released by the BIS in December 2019 and data from previous years.

trading for the first time in 1992). In fact, as early as more than a decade ago, traditional foreign exchange spot trade was no longer a crucial part of the foreign exchange market. In other words, foreign exchange trade is mostly composed of trade of foreign exchange derivatives. This section introduces the product composition for major international currencies in the global foreign exchange market. Table 4.4 shows percentages of foreign exchange spot trade, foreign exchange forward trade and foreign exchange swaps of 24 major currencies from April 2007 to April 2019.

4.3.1 *Comparison of foreign exchange spot goods/spot trade and foreign exchange derivatives*

Data from the BIS show that in 1992, spot trade in foreign exchange markets was lower than 50% for the first time, and the average daily turnover of foreign exchange swaps surpassed that of spot trade for the first time in 1995, which made foreign exchange swaps a major product in the foreign exchange market. During the period from 2001 to 2007, the share of spot trade continued to drop to a record low, only slightly above 30%. However, as shown in Table 4.4, under the impact of the global financial crisis, the share of foreign exchange swaps witnessed a significant slide in the global foreign exchange market from 2007 to 2013, while spot trade saw its share increasing noticeably, indicating a strong return to traditional products in the global foreign exchange market in a post-crisis era. From 2013 to 2016, foreign exchange swaps accounted for 46.9% again while spot transactions fell to 32.6%, close to the proportion seen in 2004. In 2019, the percentage of exchange rate swaps rose further to 48.6%, while that of foreign exchange spot trade fell to 30.2%. Table 4.4 also shows that foreign exchange derivatives in global foreign exchange markets fell from 69.8% in 2007 to 61.7% in 2013 and rebounded to 69.8% in 2019, reaching a peak value before the financial crisis. This demonstrates the importance of derivative products in the international foreign exchange market.

4.3.2 *Comparison of proportions of foreign exchange forward trade of different currencies*

Foreign exchange forward trade is the oldest and simplest form of derivatives trade in the global foreign exchange market. As shown in Table 4.4, although turnover of foreign exchange swaps continued to decline from

2007 to 2013, the share of turnover of foreign exchange forward trade continuously increased to 12.7%, and it further reached 15.2% in 2019, showing the upward trend of the global foreign exchange forward trade over the past 21 years (from 8.4% in 1998 to 10.9% in 2007). In Table 4.4, from 2007 to 2019, the average percentage of foreign exchange forward trade of 15 developed economies' currencies among 24 major currencies are close to that of the global average. While the proportions of foreign exchange forwards in nine emerging markets are higher than that of the globe, their percentages of foreign exchange swaps are significantly lower than the global level.

4.3.3 *Proportions of foreign exchange swaps of different currencies*

Foreign exchange swaps are the most vital product in a country's foreign exchange market. As shown in Table 4.4, the percentage of the average daily turnover of global foreign exchange swaps in the total average daily turnover decreased from 51.6% to 44.3% and further to 41.7% during the 2007–2013 period, indicating a return to traditional trade in the international foreign exchange market after the global financial crisis. However, the percentage returned to 46.8% and 48.6% in the 2016–2019 period, which covered almost half of whole foreign exchange market, showing that the adjustment after the financial crisis is over. Table 4.4 also shows that in 2019, the proportions of USD, EUR, GBP, and CHF and other major currencies' foreign exchange swaps are higher than the global average. Nevertheless, JPY, AUD, and CAD foreign exchange swaps are significantly lower than the global average to different extents, indicating that the activity levels of different major global currencies' foreign exchange swaps are different. In emerging markets, only the percentage of TRY, PLN, ZAR, and RUB foreign exchange swaps are close to or higher than the global level of 48.6%. But the proportions of other emerging countries' currency foreign exchange swaps are significantly lower than the global level. This demonstrates that there is still plenty of room for growth in those emerging countries' foreign exchange swap markets.

4.3.4 *Comparison of the proportions of different currencies' foreign exchange option markets*

In addition to foreign exchange forward trade and swap trade as shown in Table 4.4, two foreign exchange derivatives, namely, foreign exchange options and currency swaps, are traded in the global foreign exchange market. Foreign exchange options play a significant role in the foreign exchange market. According to data released by the BIS every 3 years, from April 1998 to April 2007, the average daily turnover of global foreign exchange options trade was only $87 billion, $60 billion, $119 billion, and $212 billion, accounting for 5.7%, 4.8%, 6.2%, and 6.4% of the total, respectively. From April 2007 to April 2010 and then to April 2013, average daily turnover of global foreign exchange options commerce was $207 billion and $337 billion, respectively, accounting for 5.2% and 6.3% of the total, indicating that the percentage of foreign exchange options commerce was equal to only half of the proportion of foreign exchange forward trade, as shown in Table 4.4.

Table 4.5 provides the proportions of chief global currency swaps and foreign exchange options commerce from April 2010 to April 2019. The percentage of average daily turnover of global foreign exchange options trade to daily turnover of global foreign exchange market increased from 5.2% to 6.3% from 2010 to 2013, then fell back to 4.5% from 2013 to 2019, slightly exceeding a quarter of percentage of global foreign exchange forward commerce — 15.2%. It indicates that when compared with foreign exchange swaps and foreign exchange forward trade, the scale of foreign exchange options trade is rather limited. As shown in Table 4.5, only the proportion of JPY foreign exchange options trade was significantly higher than that of the global average. However, the percentages of foreign exchange options trade of other major global currencies, such as USD, GBP, AUD, and CAD, are comparable to that of global foreign exchange options trade. Among the major emerging countries' currencies, the percentage of BRL foreign exchange options trade was as high as 15.7%. CNY foreign exchange option trade accounted for 4.7%, close to the 4.5% for global foreign exchange option trade. The percentages of TRL and INR foreign exchange options trade were slightly higher than the global level. The proportion of RUB foreign exchange options trade was only 2.4%, a bit higher than a half of the global level.

4.3.5 *Proportions and comparison of different currencies' swaps*

In addition to the three foreign exchange derivatives discussed above, which are foreign exchange forwards, swaps, and options, there is another foreign exchange derivative product in the global foreign exchange market — currency swaps. Currency swaps are one of the least traded foreign exchange derivative products in the international foreign exchange market, with average daily turnovers amounting to only $10 billion, $7 billion, $21 billion, and $31 billion from April 1998 to April 2007, accounting for 0.7%, 0.6%, 1.1%, and 0.9% of the total average daily turnovers, respectively. From April 2010 to April 2019, average daily turnover of currency swaps increased to $43 billion, $54 billion, $82 billion, and $108 billion, respectively, accounting for 1.1%, 1.0%, 1.6, and 1.6% of the total average daily turnovers, respectively. Although the currency swap market is small, it has grown faster than other foreign exchange derivatives in recent years. Table 4.5 also shows the share of currency swaps of major currencies in their total average daily turnovers from April 2010 to April 2019.

4.3.6 *A comparative study of the proportion of CNY foreign exchange derivatives and related issues*

Table 4.2 also shows that in 2007, CNY is one of the most traditional currencies among 24 currencies. CNY spot trade took up 61.4% of the total in 2007, only second to RUB's percentage of 70.7%. In the same year, CNY forward trade made up 31.3% of the total, which was next only to the corresponding proportions of BRL and TWD in the same year. CNY foreign exchange swaps accounted for 7.4% of the total, being the second lowest among 24 currencies just after BZL (2.5%), indicating the inactivity of CNY foreign exchange derivatives. However, in 2010, the share of CNY spot trade of total CNY trade dropped significantly to 23.7%, less than half the share seen in 2007 (61.4%). It was not only much lower than the share of spot trade (37.4%) in the global market in the same year but also lower than share of 18 currencies other than SEK, HKD, PLN, DKK, and NOK. This demonstrates that although there was some development in the market of CNY derivatives during the 2007–2010 period, the leap from the most "traditional" currency to a significantly "non-traditional" currency was unexpectedly impressive. Despite a recovery to 28.4% in the share of spot trade in total CNY trade in 2013, the share was still 10% lower than the global average of 38.3% in the same year. The share of forward trade as a percentage of total CNY trade fell to 23.5% in 2013, much closer to the global average of 12.7%,

Table 4.5: The Proportion of Daily Turnover of Major International Currency Swaps and Foreign Exchange Options in Total Foreign Exchange Transactions (April 2010–April 2019) (Unit: %)

Year	**2010**		**2013**		**2013**		**2019**	
Currency	**Swap**	**Option & Others**	**Swap**	**Option & Others**	**Swap**	**Option & Others**	**Swap**	**Option & Others**
USD	1.1	4.7	1.1	6.3	1.7	4.9	1.7	4.2
EUR	1.1	5.6	1.0	3.9	1.4	4.0	1.2	4.2
JPY	0.9	7.2	0.9	12.5	1.7	6.7	2.1	5.7
GBP	0.5	3.9	0.7	4.6	1.6	4.6	2.3	3.8
AUD	1.9	5.1	1.3	5.9	2.0	5.6	2.7	5.5
CAD	1.4	2.9	0.9	4.8	1.6	5.4	2.2	4.3
CHF	0.7	5.3	0.5	4.9	0.7	2.0	0.6	2.8
CNY	0.2	14.6	0.4	14.3	1.3	8.8	0.6	4.7
SEK	0.8	3.4	0.9	2.0	0.8	4.7	2.0	2.1
NZD	1.0	4.8	1.4	3.0	1.0	7.8	3.2	7.0
MXN	0.7	4.6	0.6	4.5	0.0	6.2	1.1	6.9
SGD	0.1	4.8	0.8	3.9	2.2	3.3	1.4	3.2
HKD	0.4	1.8	0.6	1.6	1.1	1.1	1.1	3.3
NOK	1.2	3.6	0.5	2.6	1.2	3.5	0.9	4.1
KRW	1.6	5.9	1.1	6.6	1.2	6.0	0.7	7.5
TRY	6.5	12.8	3.6	4.7	5.4	5.4	2.8	6.2
RUB	0.5	2.9	0.6	3.2	1.7	1.7	1.0	2.4
INR	0.1	9.9	0.6	5.2	0.0	5.2	0.3	4.9
BRL	1.4	17.1	4.3	18.1	3.9	15.7	2.6	16.2
ZAR	0.5	3.6	0.3	2.9	8.0	4.0	1.4	10.0
DKK	0.5	0.9	0.5	0.2	0.0	0.0	0.3	0.0
PLN	0.6	6.5	0.9	2.8	0.0	2.9	0.3	3.1
TWD	0.5	6.7	1.0	4.9	0.0	3.2	0.1	8.8
HUF	0.3	7.2	1.2	4.3	0.0	6.7	0.3	4.1
Others	0.2	0.5	0.8	5.7	2.6	6.5	0.7	4.7
All currencies	1.1	5.2	1.0	6.3	1.6	5.0	1.6	4.5

Source: Calculated by average daily turnover in April 2019 released by the BIS in December 2019 and data from previous years.

but it was still 10.8% higher than the latter. The share of foreign exchange swaps of total CNY trade increased to 33.4%, closer to the global average of 41.7%. From 2016 to 2019, the percentages of CNY foreign exchange spot trade, forward trade and swap trade became more reasonable in comparison with the global levels.

The above is data issued by the BIS. When comparing China foreign exchange market's spot, forward and swap trade data in recent years with above data, we can easily find the errors in CNY foreign exchange market's data in 2007–2019 published by IMF.

4.3.7 *Foreign exchange derivatives from global exchanges*

The main components of the global foreign exchange market are introduced above, namely, the major foreign exchange products and liquidity in the interbank OTC market. In fact, in addition to the interbank market, the exchange products trade in the global exchange markets, and foreign exchange futures and foreign exchange options also have certain market share.

4.3.7.1 *Brief introduction of the size of foreign exchange futures and options traded on global exchanges*

According to data published by the BIS, every 3 years from 1998 to 2013, the global foreign exchange futures and options transactions amounted to \$3.1 trillion, \$3.5 trillion, \$8 trillion, \$24.6 trillion, \$38.7 trillion, and \$35.6 trillion. The average daily turnover amounted to \$12.4 billion, \$14 billion, \$32 billion, \$98.4 billion, \$154.8 billion, and \$142.6 billion, accounting for 0.8%, 1.1%, 1.7%, 3%, 3.9%, and 2.7% of the daily turnover of the OTC Foreign Exchange Market, respectively, as shown in Table 4.2. According to data published on the BIS's website, the daily average turnover of foreign exchange futures and options trade on global exchanges were \$115 billion and \$294 billion in the 2016–2019 period, accounting for 2.3% and 4.5% of \$5.088 trillion and \$6.590 trillion of turnover of global interbank foreign exchange trade, respectively. These data demonstrate that from 1998 to 2019, the percentages of turnover of foreign exchange products traded on global exchanges and via inter banks were rising.

4.3.7.2 *Currency distribution of developed countries' foreign exchange futures and options traded on global exchanges*

The BIS has released its currency distribution of the transaction value of the foreign exchange futures and options traded on global exchanges since 2014. The BIS announced that the average daily turnovers, of global foreign exchange futures and options in 2014 and 2015 were $125 billion and $122 billion, respectively. The corresponding average daily turnovers of USD foreign exchange futures and options were up to $118 billion and $114 billion, accounting for as high as 94.4% and 93.4%. In April 2019, the percentage of USD dropped to 82.7% (bilateral calculations as per Table 4.1, the same as the following). In April 2019, the average daily turnovers of foreign exchange futures and options of EUR, JPY, GBP, AUD, CAD, CHF, and KRW accounted for only 30.6%, 21.5%, 10.1%, 8.3%, 4.8%, 3.1%, and 3.3%. The rankings are like those shown in Table 4.1 for interbank foreign exchange market turnover, while USD was in a higher monopoly position.

4.3.7.3 *Currency distribution of emerging market countries' foreign exchange futures and options traded on global exchanges*

In addition to currency distribution of developed countries' foreign exchange futures and options in recent years on global exchanges, the liquidity of foreign exchange futures and options of BRL, INR, RUB, and MXN in four chief emerging countries is lower but still impressive. In April 2019, the average daily turnovers of futures and options traded of the four currencies on global exchanges were as high as $11 billion, $6 billion, $8 billion, and $2 billion, respectively, accounting for 3.9%, 1.9%, 2.7%, and 0.6% of the global market, respectively. The proportions of BRL, INR, and MXN were significantly larger than the percentages of their interbank foreign exchange trade (as shown in Table 4.1). This demonstrates that the development of foreign exchange derivatives traded on those three countries' exchanges was impressive, and their liquidity was better than that of CNY foreign exchange futures and options trade on China's and overseas exchanges.

4.4 Support of Continuous Linked Settlement System for International Position of USD

As shown above, the global foreign exchange market is open 24 hours a day, with an average turnover of trillions of dollars per workday, and USD is in an absolute leading position in the market. USD has the world's highest liquidity for many reasons, and its continuous linked settlement (CLS) system plays the most vital role, which is an excellent reference for the internationalization of CNY. This section will simply introduce the global CLS system and its function.

4.4.1 *Foreign exchange settlement risk — Herstatt risk and establishment of continuous linked settlement institution*

As early as in 1974, when Bank of Herstatt in Federal Germany received a payment by Deutsche mark from Bank of America, due to the time difference between Germany and the US, Bank of Herstatt issued a receipt before they received the appropriate dollar amount, which eventually led to the bankruptcy of the bank. With the volume of foreign exchange markets increasing substantially, the risk of settlement in the global foreign exchange markets increased. To reduce the risk of settlement in the foreign exchange market, the CLS was incorporated in New York in 2002. CLS, supervised by the Federal Reserve, was designated by the US Financial Stability Oversight Council as a systemically important financial market function in 2012. CLS has played an vital role in the settlement of the global foreign exchange market for more than 10 years (CLS Group, www.en.wikipedia.org).

4.4.2 *Member and settlement currency of continuous linked settlement institution*

In 2002, CLS was an establishment with only 39 members and seven major global currencies for settlement. By November 2015, CLS had become the world's prominent foreign exchange settlement institution with 64 settlement members, 18 settlement currencies and 74 shareholders. There are more than 9,000 active participants from third markets. At present, 18 types of currency settlement of CLS include the following:

AUD, CAD, DKK, EUR, HKD, HUF, ILS, JPY, MXN, NZD, NOK, NZD, ZAR, KRW, SEK, CHF, GBP, USD. As shown in Table 4.1, except HUF and ILS, 16 currencies are among the world's 20 most active currencies in 2019. Total turnover of CLS's 18 currencies accounted for 93.2% of the total in global foreign exchange markets.

4.4.3 *Estimation of time of CNY being one of CLS currencies and influence*

When observing the above CLS 18 currencies, we found that CNY, INR, RUB, and BRL, four major currencies of the BRIC countries, are not CLS currencies. Any kind of currency needs to get written approval by the Federal Reserve to gain the qualifications to join the CLS system. The monetary policy direction of the monetary authorities in the US may also have a potential impact on this process. The accession of CNY to the CLS system also has a process. However, with the specified signed Sino-US memorandum of cooperation arrangements in CNY clearing banks, it is believed that Sino-US financial cooperation will take a new step. The process of CNY becoming a CLS currency will be accelerated. CNY becoming one of the CLS currencies is beneficial to the exchange trade of CNY against USD and other major currencies. Nevertheless, the Central Counterparties (CCP), used in CNY foreign exchange trading since 3 November 2014, needs to be constantly improved to better guard against Herstatt risk (Xu Qiyuan, 2016) and properly prepare for the gradual improvement of the international status of CNY.

4.5 Status of Major International Currencies in International Interest Rate Derivatives Market

Interest rate is the most vital market factor affecting the whole financial market or even the entire economy. Interest rate risk, therefore, is the most vital market risk in the financial market, which makes interest rate derivatives the most active risk management instruments in the financial market. On the other hand, interest rates are the foundation of foreign exchange rates, whose trends are determined by changes in interest rates. Therefore, the trading activity in interest rate derivatives of a currency in the market reflects, to a great extent, the international status of that currency. As the bonds market, especially the market for government bonds issued by developed countries, will continue to be an important component of the international financial market in the future, internationally traded interest rate derivatives are also set to play an increasingly significant role.

4.5.1 *Monetary distribution of the average daily turnover of global interbank interest rate derivatives*

Interest rate derivatives make up the world's prominent derivatives market and mainly include forward rate agreements, interest rate swaps, interest rate options, and other interest rate derivatives. Interested readers may refer to Zhang Guangping (2015) for details. Table 4.6 shows the monetary distribution of the average daily turnover of global interbank interest rate derivatives from April 1998 to April 2019. As shown in Table 4.6, between 2001 and 2013, the average daily turnover of EUR interest rate derivatives is more than that of USD, indicating that EUR is the most crucial currency of global interbank interest rate derivatives. However, from 2013 to 2019, EUR interbank interest rate derivatives' average daily turnover increased by 40%, but its percentage to the global total decreased from 49.03% to 24.42%. Meanwhile, USD interbank interest rate derivatives have long average daily turnover of 112.2%, accounting for an increase from 27.65% to 50.86%, USD replaced the EUR as the main currency of the global interbank interest rate derivatives. Furthermore, USD in global interbank interest rate derivatives' daily turnover increased sharply by 511.7%, and its percentage to the global total rose from 27.65% to 50.30%. As a result, USD replaced EUR and became the major currency for global interbank interest rate derivatives. More than that, the percentage of USD's interbank interest rate derivatives' daily average turnover to the global total was more than 50%, significantly exceeding the percentage of USD turnover in global foreign exchange market (44.2%). This shows that the international status of USD has further improved in recent years.

As shown in Table 4.6, in addition to the daily average turnover of USD interbank interest rate derivatives increasing substantially from April 2013 and April 2019, AUD and CAD interbank interest rate derivatives' daily turnover also increased by more than 30%. GBP and JPY interbank interest rate derivatives' daily average turnover increased by

Table 4.6: Proportion of Average Daily Turnover of On- and Off-Exchange Trade of Interest Rate Derivatives of Different Currencies in April (1998–2019) (Unit: %, USD trillion)

Year	1998	2001	2004	2007	2010	2013	2016	2019	Ranking in 2019
USD	26.68	31.02	33.88	31.59	31.83	27.65	50.88	50.30	1
EUR	—	47.38	44.96	38.91	40.60	49.03	24.03	24.42	2
GBP	6.26	7.52	8.77	10.20	10.39	8.08	8.89	8.27	3
AUD	1.14	1.71	1.16	1.11	1.78	3.29	4.05	6.17	4
JPY	10.29	5.58	4.50	8.11	6.04	2.99	3.11	3.28	5
CAD	2.71	1.17	0.74	0.92	2.35	1.29	1.46	1.39	6
SEK	0.66	1.06	1.28	1.95	0.98	1.56	0.71	0.94	7
NZD	0.11	0.09	0.19	0.39	0.18	0.21	0.97	0.86	8
CNY	0.00	0.00	0.00	0.01	0.09	0.61	0.37	0.51	9
NOK	0.66	0.62	0.81	0.47	0.73	0.40	0.56	0.47	10
KRW	0.00	0.01	0.03	0.28	0.80	0.52	0.49	0.41	11
CHF	3.51	1.32	0.96	1.10	0.99	0.62	0.52	0.40	12
ZAR	0.19	0.08	0.15	0.19	0.26	0.68	0.60	0.39	13
MXN	0.06	0.05	0.17	0.32	0.22	0.42	0.97	0.36	14
HKD	0.20	0.30	0.42	0.55	0.15	0.09	0.19	0.27	15
INR	0.00	0.01	0.04	0.21	0.11	0.28	0.22	0.25	16
SGD	0.00	0.07	0.26	0.22	0.21	0.16	0.45	0.23	17
PLN	0.00	0.05	0.06	0.11	0.07	0.32	0.22	0.13	18
BRL	0.00	0.04	0.08	0.10	0.14	0.71	0.26	0.12	19
HUF	0.00	0.00	0.01	0.07	0.01	0.11	0.30	0.12	20
MYR	0.00	0.00	0.00	0.02	0.01	0.08	0.11	0.03	21
CLP	0.00	0.00	0.00	0.00	0.01	0.05	0.15	0.02	22
CNY*	0	0	0	0.01	0.03	0.1	0.07	0.20	18
Global takeover	0.265	0.489	1.025	1.686	2.054	2.311	2.667	6.501	

Source: Calculated based on the average daily turnover of interbank interest rate derivatives released by the BIS in September 2019; CNY* ratio is calculated on the basis of domestic and overseas interbank data.

more than 20%. BRL interbank interest rate derivatives' average daily turnover fell by 11.2%, which reflected the significant influence of Brazil's economy dropping in the financial market. SEK interbank interest rate derivatives' average daily turnover fell by 6.2%, and the magnitude of its drop was smaller than that of BRL during the same period.

4.5.2 *The monetary distribution of futures and options for daily transactions on global exchanges*

Table 4.6 only shows the currency distributions of global interbank interest rate derivatives. In fact, unlike the global foreign exchange market, which is dominated by the interbank market, the global interbank interest rate derivatives market is much less liquid than that of interest rate derivative products traded on exchanges. Therefore, if we do not consider the currency distribution of interest rate derivatives traded at exchanges, we cannot fully understand the currency distribution of global interest rate derivatives. Table 4.7 shows the monetary distribution of average daily turnover of interest rate derivatives traded at global exchanges during 2014–2019.

Table 4.7 shows that the percentage of interest rate derivatives of USD traded on global exchanges was 73.86%, 23.56% higher than that of interbank interest rate derivatives (50.30%), indicating that USD is more popular in the global exchange rate trading derivatives market. However, the percentage of interest rate derivatives of the EUR traded in the global exchanges was 11.17% lower than that of interbank interest rate derivatives, suggesting that EUR interest rate derivatives traded in exchanges are less active in comparison with interbank interest rate derivatives. The difference between GBP, AUD, and CAD is rather small. On the other hand, the percentage of JPY exchange rate derivatives traded in exchanges was only 0.48%, 2.80% lower than that of interbank interest rate derivatives (3.28%). Its ranking was even behind BRL, showing that JPY interest rate derivatives traded in exchanges were less active in comparison with other interbank products. We can see significant findings regarding currency in Table 4.7. It shows that the ratio of average daily turnover of interest rate derivatives of BRL traded in exchange to the global total was 0.57%. It ranked sixth in April 2019, behind CAD of 1.04% but 0.09% higher than JPY of 0.48%. The development of interest rate derivatives of BRL traded on exchanges is not only higher than all other developing countries but also higher than many developed countries. This is worth learning and drawing lessons from.

Table 4.7: Money Distribution and Ranking of Interest Rate Derivatives, Average Daily Turnover of Global Exchange Transactions (2014–2019) (Unit: %, USD trillion)

	2014	**2015**	**2016**	**2017**	**2018**	**2019**	**Ranking in 2019**
USD	59.87	69.28	71.83	72.60	72.16	73.86	1
EUR	22.99	12.91	13.19	16.68	14.35	13.25	2
GBP	10.92	9.52	7.78	6.03	8.79	7.52	3
AUD	2.17	3.65	3.16	1.70	1.69	2.61	4
CAD	1.41	1.66	1.72	1.02	1.07	1.04	5
BRL	0.90	1.22	0.79	0.84	0.61	0.57	6
JPY	0.65	0.71	0.67	0.38	0.54	0.48	7
CHF	0.65	0.53	0.30	0.39	0.41	0.26	8
KRW	0.16	0.31	0.26	0.14	0.15	0.17	9
CNY	0.00	0.04	0.10	0.11	0.11	0.09	10
NZD	0.05	0.11	0.08	0.04	0.07	0.08	11
SEK	0.18	0.07	0.08	0.05	0.05	0.06	12
ZAR	0.00	0.00	0.02	0.01	0.01	0.01	13
NOK	0.02	0.00	0.02	0.00	0.00	0.00	14
CNY*	0.0035	0.0513	0.0972	0.1094	0.1001	0.0917	10

Source: www.bis.org — website of the BIS.To better compare the data of trade taking place in the interbank market and on exchanges, the average daily turnover in April of every year is chosen, and the proportion-related data are calculated based on the average daily data. CNY* refers to the turnover of China's domestic Government Bond futures. Due to rounding, it is possible that the proportion of China's CNY interest rate derivatives is larger than the percentage of CNY interest rate derivatives in the world.

4.5.3 *Monetary distribution of average daily turnover of interest rate derivatives traded on exchanges and interbank markets*

The above sections introduced the monetary distribution of the average daily turnover of interest rate derivatives on global exchanges and the interbank market. Based on the results of Tables 4.6 and 4.7, we can calculate the monetary distribution of the average daily turnover of interest rate derivatives on global exchanges and in the interbank market in April 2016, as shown in Table 4.8.

Table 4.8 shows USD interest rate derivatives' daily turnover accounted for as much as 63.13% of the world's total, 18.99% higher than the ratio of USD in the global foreign exchange market (half of 88.30% as total share was 200% because of double counting) in April 2019, as shown in Table 4.1. The result demonstrates that USD has a much higher role in the global interest rate derivatives market than in the global foreign exchange market. The percentages of EUR and GBP interest rate derivatives' average daily turnovers on exchanges and in the interbank market as a percentage of the global total accounted for 18.33% and 7.86%, respectively, 13.97% and 4.94% lower than the percentages of those two currencies in the global foreign exchange market (32.3% and 12.8%). The percentage of JPY interest rate derivatives' daily average turnover to the global total was only 1.75%, lower by 15.05% than the ratio of JPY in the global foreign exchange market in April 2019, as shown in Table 4.1. These show that major global currencies are in lower monopoly positions in the exchange rate market than in the foreign exchange market.

4.5.4 *Comparison of turnover ratio of CNY interest rate derivatives and related problems*

Table 4.6 shows that from April 2010 to April 2013, the percentage of interbank CNY interest rate derivatives' daily turnover as a percentage of the global total increased from 0.09% to 0.61%, and the ranking rose from 18th to 10th. Whereas in 2016, the percentage dropped to 0.38%, and its ranking fell to 15th, in 2019, these two numbers were 0.51% and ninth. These data show that the exchange of interbank CNY interest rate derivatives made fast and great progress over the past 10 years.

Since 2007, the quarterly monetary policy report released by the PBOC has provided the domestic CNY interest rate swap transactions in each quarter. Using these data and the CNY exchange rate against the dollar from April 2007 to April 2019, we can calculate that the domestic interbank CNY interest rate derivatives' daily turnovers were $117 million, $595 million, $2.25 billion, $5.5 billion, and $13.4 billion, respectively. In the first half of 2015, the City of London announced that the average daily turnover of CNY interest rate swaps in London was only a few million dollars, so the whole overseas interbank CNY interest rate swap as compared to the average daily turnover of the domestic market can be ignored. Therefore, using the domestic interbank CNY interest rate swaps average daily turnover as mentioned above, we calculated the percentage of CNY

Table 4.8: Distribution and Rankings of Currencies with $6.501 Trillion of Interest Rate Derivatives Products' Average Daily Turnover in Exchanges and Interbank Market (April 2016 and April 2019) (Unit: %)

Currency	Share in 2016	Ranking in 2016	Share in 2019	Ranking in 2019	Currency	Share in 2016	Ranking in 2016	Share in 2019	Ranking in 2019
USD	64.52	1	63.13	1	MXN	0.34	11	0.16	15
EUR	16.91	2	18.33	2	HKD	0.06	19	0.13	16
GBP	8.15	3	7.86	3	INR	0.08	18	0.12	17
AUD	3.46	4	4.23	4	SGD	0.15	16	0.11	18
JPY	1.51	6	1.75	5	CZK	0.01	26	0.08	19
CAD	1.63	5	1.20	6	PLN	0.06	20	0.06	20
SEK	0.30	12	0.46	7	HUF	0.10	17	0.06	21
NZD	0.39	8	0.43	8	THB	0.03	23	0.04	22
BRL	0.61	7	0.36	9	TWD	0.03	24	0.03	23
CHF	0.37	9	0.32	10	DKK	0.03	25	0.02	24
KRW	0.34	10	0.28	11	MYR	0.04	22	0.01	25
CNY	0.19	15	0.28	12	ILS	0.01	27	0.01	26
NOK	0.21	14	0.22	13	CLP	0.05	21	0.01	27
ZAR	0.22	13	0.18	14	CNY*	0.06	21	0.13	16

Source: Calculated using data from Tables 4.6 and 4.7.

interest rate swap transactions' daily turnover in the world from 2010 to 2019. The related results are shown in Table 4.6. Table 4.6 shows that CNY interbank interest rate derivatives' daily turnover are 0.09% in 2010, 0.61% in 2013, 0.38% in 2016, and 0.51% in 2019, which are significantly lower than CNY's percentages of foreign exchange share in Table 4.1, showing that CNY interest rate derivatives world share and rankings are considerably lower than CNY status in global foreign exchange market.

As shown in Table 4.8, average daily turnover of CNY in the global exchange and OTC interest rate derivatives market ranked 12th in 2019. The ranking was 16th if China's domestic data were considered. The standings moved up by three and five spots, respectively, in comparison with the position 3 years ago.

4.5.5 *Comparison of average daily turnover between global interchange and OTC interest rate derivatives and foreign exchange derivatives*

Table 4.7 shows that in April 2019, the average daily turnover of global interbank foreign exchange derivatives was 28.8% higher than the average daily turnover of global interbank interest rate derivatives. Since the average daily turnover of interest rate derivatives traded on global exchanges is much more active than that of interbank interest rate derivatives, the average daily turnover of interest rate derivatives exchanged on global exchanges is 56% higher than that of interbank interest rate derivatives in April 2019. Average daily turnover of global interest rate derivatives is 1.47 times higher than the average daily turnover of global foreign exchange derivatives. It shows that the global interest rate derivatives market is much larger than the corresponding foreign exchange derivatives markets, as shown in Table 4.8. If we use the average daily turnovers of global interest rate derivatives and foreign exchange derivatives for the purpose of calculation, USD's global ranking will be much higher than the ranking of USD in the global foreign exchange market, as shown in Table 4.1.

4.6 Investigating the Factors for Measuring Currency Internationalization

Factors used to determine the extent of internationalization of a currency discussed above include the share of special drawing rights in the

International Monetary Fund, weight of an international reserve currency, turnover ratios in the global foreign exchange market, status in the international foreign exchange and interest rate derivatives market, the size of the international bond market and bond circulation. In fact, there are also other indicators to this end, such as the status of a currency in offshore markets, the worldwide trade system, the international credit market, the direct investment system, and international aid, which will not be explained here. This demonstrates the complicated process of determining currency internationalization.

In *Non-International Currencies, Currency Internationalization and Capital Account Convertibility* (Yao Li, 2003), Li Yao proposes a model for measuring currency internationalization and concludes the CNY was 1.85% as internationalized as USD in 2000. Many domestic and overseas financial institutions and research institutions compiled and issued some related indices about CNY internationalization in recent years. These indices measure the internationalization of the CNY from different perspectives, but the vast majority are difficult to tell on the overall degree of internationalization of CNY. The Appendix gives a brief introduction and comparison of the release time, the publishing organization, the parameter range, and the research significance of these major indices, so we will not repeat them here.

In *The Reality, Approaches and Strategies of CNY Internationalization*, Li Yao uses a similar model and concludes the CNY was 2.0% as internationalized as USD in 2002. Although the use of a currency in different markets or fields does reflect how internationalized the currency is, measurement for different fields may vary, and it is difficult to determine the weight that should be given to a specific field. Therefore, using this model to determine currency internationalization is quite complicated, as a lot of data needed is hard to obtain. If currency internationalization can be measured by a simple parameter, with the use of simple data periodically released by international institutions, we will be able to easily determine how internationalized a currency is and have a rough idea of its changes. One of these simple methods is introduced in the following.

Although international demand for a currency is composed of demand for settlements, transactions, and risk management, all those kinds of demand have to be realized through foreign exchange trade eventually. For this reason, how active a currency is in the international foreign exchange market to a great extent reflects how internationalized the currency is. However, as countries may have varying sizes of economy, the size of its economy should be considered when currency's trading volume in the global foreign exchange market is to be used to determine currency internationalization.

Specifically, the share of foreign exchange turnover of a currency as a percentage of the world's total foreign exchange turnover divided by the share of its country's GDP share in the world's GDP can serve as a simple and easy parameter to measure currency internationalization. For instance, according to Table 4.1, the share of USD in the global foreign exchange market in 2007 was 42.8% (USD has a weight of 85.6% which should be divided by two to avoid duplicated calculation as a foreign exchange involves two currencies and percentages of all currencies add up to 200%), and the US contributed to 25.02% of the global GDP in 2007. Therefore, USD internationalization is measured at 42.8% divided by 25.02%, i.e., 171.1%. Using the same method, we find that CNY internationalization in 2007 is 3.7% (0.23% divided by 6.17% which is China's GDP contribution to the world), equivalent to 2.2% of USD's figure, and slightly higher than what was estimated by Li Yao for CNY internationalization in 2000 and 2002. In 2007, CNY internationalization level is only 2.2% of that of USD.

4.7 Influence of Difference between Foreign Exchange's Actual Daily Turnover and Its Nominal Turnover on the Measurement of Currency Internalization

4.7.1 *Foreign exchange derivatives' actual turnover*

Since the global application of all currencies is reflected by the global foreign exchange trade, the percentage of a currency's foreign exchange trade in the global market is the best measurement of this currency's internationalization. A variety of methods can be used to measure foreign exchange trade. As shown in Table 4.1, the average daily turnover of global foreign exchange trade includes traditional spot trade, foreign exchange forward trade, foreign exchange swap trade, currency swap trade, foreign exchange currency options trade and trade of other foreign exchange derivatives. Additionally, the turnover of these foreign exchange derivatives has made up more than 2/3 of daily average turnover of foreign exchange in the world, making them the major products in global foreign exchange trade. In fact, the daily average turnover of foreign exchange derivatives trade, as shown in Tables 4.1 and 4.6, is not the actual turnover which has already changed hands between buyers and sellers, it is the nominal turnover of all foreign exchange derivatives traded.

As a matter of fact, trading of foreign exchange forwards, foreign exchange swaps, currency swaps and foreign exchange options are not transacted with nominal amounts directly. Foreign exchange forwards, foreign exchange swaps and currency swaps are traded based on nominal amount by buyers paying deposits in ways approved by sellers, and the settlement is completed with the difference between agreed spot exchange rate and due exchange rate at the agreed payment time. In most cases, the amount to be paid is smaller than the deposit which is usually about 5%. As for the foreign exchange options trade, buyers of options pay an option premium to sellers, and the premium is usually lower than 5% of the nominal amount. In other words, among the daily average foreign exchange trade, the actual turnover of most foreign exchange derivatives is much lower than their nominal amount. As shown in Table 4.1, the daily average turnover in the global foreign exchange trade market is much larger than the actual trade amount, and it is inaccurate to measure the currency internationalization based on this. Some reasonable adjustments must be made.

4.7.2 *Reasonable estimation of foreign exchange's daily average turnover*

With the fast technological development, it is feasible to complete the statistics of global daily average turnover of foreign exchange trade from the technological perspective. However, most foreign exchange derivatives can be used for risk management or for speculation. Some financial institutions and enterprises, due to their trading strategies and risk management strategies, decide not to publish their trading positions, which makes it hard to do the statistics of global foreign exchange trade. Particularly, for foreign exchange forwards, swaps and options, the prices locked by different contracts are different, and the ratios of trade amount to the nominal amount can be different, which make the statistics of foreign exchange derivatives trade globally more complicated. In Table 4.1, the statistics of foreign exchange trade based on the nominal amount of foreign exchange derivatives are expedient, and the actual trade amount is exaggerated. In fact, the actual daily average turnover of foreign exchange trade in the world, as shown in Table 4.1, cannot be easily found out. But we can use some simple methods. By setting 5% of each foreign exchange forward and swap as the upper limit of deposit and 5% of each foreign exchange option premium as the upper limit, the nominal amount of foreign exchange derivatives in Tables 4.4 and 4.9 is used to estimate the upper limit of actual turnover of foreign exchange derivatives in the world. Plus, the daily average turnover of foreign exchange spot trade in Table 4.4 and the actual daily turnover of different currencies foreign exchange trade can be calculated. Results from 2007 to 2019 are displayed in Table 4.9.

4.7.3 *Comparison of foreign exchange's actual average daily turnover and nominal turnover, and the latter's limitations*

As shown in Table 4.9, the actual daily average turnover of foreign exchange market globally was $1.12 trillion, $1.61 trillion, $2.21 trillion, $1.83 trillion, and $2.22 trillion from 2007 to 2010, 2013, 2016, and 2019, respectively. These daily average turnovers amount to 33.73%, 40.55%, 41.28%, 36.03%, and 33.63% of the nominal daily average turnover of foreign exchange trade of $3.32 trillion, $3.97 trillion, $5.36 trillion, $5.07 trillion, and $6.60 trillion, as shown in Table 4.1. This demonstrates that the actual daily average turnover in the global foreign exchange market is much smaller than the nominal turnover. Thus, it is more reasonable to compare the actual daily average turnover of foreign exchange trade with the turnover in the stock market and the bond market. Besides, the percentages of actual daily average turnovers of global top eight currencies in the foreign exchange market as shown in Table 4.9, are close to the ratios of average daily nominal turnovers in the foreign exchange market, as shown in Table 4.1. However, the percentages of nominal turnover in Table 4.1 overestimate the ratio of USD in the world, underestimate the percentage of EUR from 2007 to 2013, overestimate the ratio of EUR in 2019, underestimate the ratio of JPY from 2007 to 2016, overestimate the proportion of JPY in 2019, underestimate the percentages of GBP in 2010 and 2016, and overestimate the percentages of GBP in 2013 and 2019. Although the ratios of different currencies do not differ significantly,

Table 4.9: Actual Average Daily Turnover of the Top Eight Currencies in the Global Foreign Exchange Market and Ratios (2007–2019, Assuming that the Actual Turnover of Foreign Exchange Derivatives is Only 5% of Nominal Turnover) (Unit: USD billion, %)

Turnover	2007	2010	2013	2016	2019	Annual Avg. Change
USD	892.99	1,296.09	1,839.29	1,540.10	1,894.02	6.47
EUR	460.60	733.17	805.85	573.68	691.19	3.44
JPY	224.33	322.70	643.29	430.53	397.64	4.89
GBP	167.13	227.71	246.96	233.73	269.96	4.08
AUD	61.13	120.53	209.26	154.22	183.84	9.61
CAD	43.70	84.37	93.92	112.44	132.30	9.67
CHF	94.97	99.65	101.02	66.66	97.75	0.24
CNY	9.28	9.43	38.23	74.29	106.30	22.53
Others	287.57	332.88	444.34	465.50	662.67	7.20
Global	1,120.85	1,613.26	2,211.08	1,825.58	2,217.84	5.85
Proportions	**2007**	**2010**	**2013**	**2016**	**2019**	**Annual Avg. Change**
USD	7.97	8.03	8.32	8.44	8.54	0.48
EUR	4.11	4.55	3.65	3.14	3.12	−0.83
JPY	2.00	2.00	2.91	2.36	1.79	−0.17
GBP	1.49	1.41	1.12	1.28	1.22	−0.23
AUD	0.55	0.75	0.95	0.85	0.83	0.24
CAD	0.39	0.52	0.43	0.62	0.60	0.17
CHF	0.85	0.62	0.46	0.37	0.44	−0.34
CNY	0.08	0.06	0.17	0.41	0.48	0.33
Others	2.57	2.06	2.01	2.55	2.99	0.35
Global	100.00	100.00	100.00	100.00	100.00	0.00

Source: Calculated using data from Tables 4.4 and 4.5.

it means a lot for the global standings of different currencies. The percentages of actual turnover of CNY foreign exchange in 2016 and 2019, which are 4.07% and 4.79% as shown in Table 4.9, are higher than the percentages of CHF (i.e., 4.07% and 4.79%), which means CNY should rank seventh in the world. However, according to the nominal turnovers of foreign exchange trade in the world as shown in Table 4.1, the standings of CNY (i.e., eighth) are lower than that of CHF.

Since the average daily nominal turnovers as shown in Table 4.1 significantly exaggerate the actual foreign exchange trade, it is safe to say that the actual daily average turnover in the global foreign exchange market is more reasonable than the nominal turnovers in Table 4.1. The exaggerated nominal turnover cannot reflect the actual internationalization level of a currency. In Chapter 14, those problems caused by those exaggerated nominal turnovers will be located and resolved. Even so, nominal turnover of foreign exchange trade has been widely used as a basis to measure a currency's internationalization for many years. In the following chapters of this book, the nominal turnover in Table 4.1 will also be used as the basis for the measurement of a currency's internationalization level. Meanwhile, the actual average daily turnover as shown in Table 4.9 will be regarded as the reasonable basis to measure a currency's internationalization level to find out the more reasonable relationship between currency internationalization and technological internationalization.

4.8 Measurement and Comparison of Internationalization of Major Currencies in 2007

As observed above, the importance of an international currency in the global foreign exchange market greatly reflects how internationalized a currency is, however the economy of its issuer is not considered. Currency internationalization can be better measured if the share of a country's economy in the world's economy is considered together with the percentage of a currency in the international foreign exchange market. Table 4.10 shows the share of the world's major currencies in the global foreign exchange trade and the contributions of their corresponding issuing countries or regions to the world's GDP in 2007. We chose 2007 to measure currency internationalization because 2007 is only 1 year away from the global financial crisis that took place in 2008, it was also the year when the BIS was set to release its triennial data on the international foreign exchange market.

In Table 4.10, the excess of foreign exchange share of a currency over GDP share of its issuer can reflect how internationalized the currency is, but the excess may be a positive or a negative number, which makes it

Table 4.10: Measurement and Comparison of Internationalization of Currencies of Major Countries and Regions in 2007 (Unit: %)

Currency	Foreign Exchange Share in 2007	GDP Share in 2007	Excess of Foreign Exchange Share over GDP Share	Foreign Exchange Share/GDP Share
USD	42.80	25.66	17.14	166.82
EUR	18.52	21.93	−3.41	84.44
JPY	8.62	7.72	0.91	111.74
GBP	7.43	5.06	2.37	146.79
AUD	3.31	1.68	1.63	196.79
CHF	3.41	0.80	2.61	427.39
CAD	2.14	2.58	−0.44	83.04
Total of seven currencies	86.24	65.43	20.81	131.80
NZD	0.95	0.24	0.71	402.53
SEK	1.35	0.82	0.53	164.76
HKD	1.35	0.37	0.98	360.74
NOK	1.05	0.70	0.35	150.89
SGD	0.58	0.32	0.27	184.79
Total of five currencies	5.29	2.44	2.84	216.39
MXN	0.66	1.85	−1.19	35.47
TRY	0.09	1.15	−1.06	7.80
KRW	0.58	1.86	−1.28	31.09
DKK	0.42	0.55	−0.13	76.29
PLN	0.38	0.75	−0.37	50.61
TWD	0.18	0.70	−0.51	26.09
HUF	0.03	0.24	−0.21	11.77
MYR	0.11	0.34	−0.24	31.21
CZK	0.08	0.32	−0.24	24.14
THB	0.10	0.44	−0.34	22.34
CLP	0.06	0.37	−0.31	15.01
ILS	0.03	0.31	−0.28	8.40
IDR	0.05	0.77	−0.71	6.89

(*Continued*)

Table 4.10: (*Continued*)

Currency	Foreign Exchange Share in 2007	GDP Share in 2007	Excess of Foreign Exchange Share over GDP Share	Foreign Exchange Share/GDP Share
Total of 13 currencies	2.75	9.64	−6.89	28.54
Total of nine currencies	1.54	6.22	−4.68	24.82
ZAR	0.46	0.51	−0.05	89.98
RUB	0.37	2.30	−1.93	16.27
INR	0.36	2.19	−1.84	16.19
BRL	0.20	2.42	−2.22	8.14
CNY	0.23	6.19	−5.97	3.65
Total of BRICS	1.61	13.62	−12.01	11.81
Total of BRICS excluding CNY	1.38	7.43	−6.04	18.62

Source: Data about share of foreign exchange trade are from Table 4.1; data about GDP share are calculated based on the data about each country and region's GDP released by the International Monetary Fund in April 2018.

hard to compare. The ratio of foreign exchange share to GDP share will always be positive, thus it better reflects the extent of currency internationalization.

4.8.1 *Measurement and comparison of internationalization of major international currencies in 2007*

As shown in Table 4.10, the foreign exchange share of the five major international reserve currencies all exceeded their countries' GDP share, with two other international reserve currencies — EUR and CAD — failing to show this positive excess. The total foreign exchange share of the seven international reserve currencies was as high as 86.2%, 21.1% higher than their countries' combined GDP share of 65.1%, with the ratio of the former to the latter amounting to as high as 132.4%, indicating the importance of these seven currencies in the global foreign exchange market.

The share of CHF foreign exchange trade in the world was 3.4%, significantly higher than Switzerland's GDP share of 0.8%, with the ratio of the former to the latter amounting to as high as 413%. This shows that despite a small economy, CHF is highly internationalized. Table 4.10 shows that with a high ratio of 203.1%, AUD came second after CHF in terms of currency internationalization. In addition, USD and GBP also witnessed high ratios of 171.8% and 140.5%, respectively, with JPY's ratio standing at 111.0%. The EUR and CAD were the least internationalized currencies among the seven reserve currencies, with their ratios at 83.5% and 85.1%, respectively.

4.8.2 *Measurement and comparison of internationalization of currencies of other major developed countries and regions in 2007*

Table 4.10 shows that currencies of the five major developed countries and regions, including NZD, all saw their foreign exchange share exceed their economies' GDP share, with their ratios of the former to the latter all exceeding 100%. Among them, NZD had the highest ratio amounting to 408.2%, followed by HKD's ratio of 371.5%, indicating the crucial role of Hong Kong as a regional financial center. The ratio of those five currencies' combined share to their economies' combined GDP's share reached as high as 217%, higher than the same ratio of the seven reserve currencies of 132.4%, indicating that despite smaller influence of those five currencies in the global foreign exchange market compared to the seven currencies, they were highly internationalized relative to the size of their economies. The ratios of foreign exchange share of SGD and SEK to GDP share of Singapore and Sweden were 188.5% and 160.9%, respectively, slightly lower than the combined ratio of the five currencies of 217%.

4.8.3 *Measurement and comparison of internationalization of currencies of other developed countries and regions in 2007*

A third group of currencies in Table 4.10 contains KAW, DKK, TWD, CZK, and ILS, currencies of five developed economies. Since Czech Republic was admitted to the developed economies in 2016, CZK has been listed as a currency of a developed economy. The percentages of those five currencies trade in the global foreign exchange market are low, and their percentages in the foreign exchange market are also lower than the ratios of their GDPs to the global total. The combined percentage of those five currencies in the global foreign exchange market is only 1.4%, while GDP of the economies of those five currencies account for 3.8% of the global total. The former percentage is smaller by 2.5% than the latter proportion, and the percentage of the former to the latter is only 35.8%. This shows that the internationalization of the currencies of those five developed economies is generally low.

4.8.4 *Measurement and comparison of internationalization of currencies of developing countries in 2007*

In Table 4.10, the 13 currencies starting from the MXN are the currencies of developing countries. The reason why we put these currencies into one group is that the share of these currencies' foreign exchange trade is lower than their economies' GDP contribution to the world. As shown in Table 4.10, of these 13 currencies, ZAR is the most internationalized, foreign exchange share of which is 88.6% of its economy's GDP share. Followed by HUF and PLN, the ratios of their foreign exchange share to their countries GDP share are 55.9% and 51.6%, respectively. The ratio of MXN foreign exchange trade's share to Mexico's GDP share is 36.2%. In the group of 13 currencies, the degrees of internationalization of BRL, TRY, INR, and CNY were the last four, and ratios of their foreign exchange share to their countries GDP share are only 8.2%, 7.7%, 6.8%, and 3.7%, respectively.

4.9 Changes in Internationalization of Major International Currencies since the Global Financial Crisis

As shown above, we used the ratio of a currency's foreign exchange trade share to its country's GDP share to measure how internationalized a currency is in April 2007. In this section, we will leverage global foreign exchange data released by the BIS in 2010 and 2016 to analyze and determine changes in internationalization of major currencies. Tables 4.11–4.14 give out results which are comparable to the results from 2010 to 2016, as shown in Table 4.10.

4.9.1 *Changes in internationalization of currencies of developed countries from 2010 to 2019*

Comparing the results of Tables 4.10 and 4.11, we found that from 2007 to 2010, the internationalization of CAD and EUR increased significantly. The difference between the two currencies' foreign exchange trade share and their GDP share in the world changes from negative to positive, and the ratio of their foreign exchange share to their GDP share increased to 101.6% and 108%, so that seven international reserve currencies' foreign exchange share is larger than the corresponding GDP share in 2010. At the same time, the degree of internationalization of the dollar has not declined but has rather increased to 187.0%; the percentage of GBP foreign exchange share to its GDP rose by 33.4% to 173.8%, demonstrating the biggest increase among the seven currencies. However, the degree of internationalization of CHF, AUD, and JPY have declined to varying degrees. The decline of CHF was 56.4%, the largest drop among seven currencies, showing the more severe impact of the financial crisis on CHF. The percentage of foreign exchange trade of seven international reserve currencies rose from 86.2% in 2007 to 87.6% in 2010, while the ratio of their countries' GDP to the global total fell by 5.6%. The ratio of those seven currencies' foreign exchange trade share to their countries' GDP share rose from 132.4% to 147.2%, showing that the overall degree of internationalization of the main international currency increased slightly during the 3 years after the financial crisis.

Comparing the results of Tables 4.11 and 4.12, we found that USD international status strengthened slightly from 2010 to 2013, while the international positions of EUR and CAD weakened slightly (i.e., the ratio of a currency's foreign exchange trade share to its country's GDP share falls below 100%); CHF's international position declined further because the percentage of CHF foreign exchange trade share to its country's GDP share dropped by 69.5% in comparison with that in 2010. Meanwhile, the ratio of JPY increased by 61.4% to 171.2% (mainly because of the devaluation of the JPY, resulting in a significant decline of Japanese GDP contribution to the world which was USD-denominated and a significant rise in the percentage of JPY foreign exchange trade). In 2013, the ratio of total foreign exchange trade share of the seven major currencies to their countries' GDP share further increased to 159%.

As shown in Tables 4.12 and 4.14, from 2013 to 2019, the internationalization of CAD increased significantly and USD's internationalization

Table 4.11: Comparison of Internationalization of Major Currencies in 2010 (Unit: %)

Currency	Foreign Exchange Share in 2010	GDP Share in 2010	Excess of Foreign Exchange Share over GDP Share	Foreign Exchange Share/GDP Share
USD	42.4	22.7	19.7	187.0
EUR	19.5	19.2	0.3	101.6
JPY	9.5	8.6	0.9	109.9
GBP	6.4	3.7	2.7	173.8
AUD	3.8	1.9	1.9	200.2
CAD	2.6	2.4	0.2	108.0
CHF	3.2	0.9	2.3	356.5
Total of seven currencies	87.5	59.5	28.0	147.1
NZD	0.8	0.2	0.6	361.3
SEK	1.1	0.7	0.4	147.9
HKD	1.2	0.3	0.8	341.3
NOK	0.7	0.7	0.0	101.5
SGD	0.7	0.4	0.4	197.7
Total of five currencies	4.4	2.3	2.1	191.8
KRW	0.8	1.7	−0.9	45.7
DKK	0.3	0.5	−0.2	58.1
TWD	0.2	0.7	−0.4	35.4
CZK	0.1	0.3	−0.2	30.4
ILS	0.1	0.4	−0.3	21.2
Total of five currencies	1.5	3.5	−2.0	41.6
MXN	0.6	1.6	−1.0	39.2
ZAR	0.4	0.6	−0.2	63.4
RUB	0.5	2.5	−2.0	18.2
INR	0.5	2.6	−2.1	18.3
PLN	0.4	0.7	−0.3	55.4
BRL	0.3	3.3	−3.0	10.2
TRY	0.4	1.2	−0.8	31.5

(*Continued*)

Table 4.11: (*Continued*)

Currency	Foreign Exchange Share in 2010	GDP Share in 2010	Excess of Foreign Exchange Share over GDP Share	Foreign Exchange Share/GDP Share
HUF	0.2	0.2	0.0	108.8
MYR	0.1	0.4	−0.2	35.6
THB	0.1	0.5	−0.4	18.6
CLP	0.1	0.3	−0.2	24.8
IDR	0.1	1.1	−1.1	6.6
CNY	0.4	9.2	−8.8	4.7
Total of 13 currencies	4.1	24.3	−20.2	16.8
Total of BRIC	1.7	17.6	−15.9	9.6
Total of BRICS	2.1	18.2	−16.1	11.3

Source: Data about share of foreign exchange trade are from Table 4.1; data about GDP share are calculated based on the data about each country and region's GDP released by the International Monetary Fund in April 2018.

weakened a bit (ratio of CAD foreign exchange trade share to Canada's GDP share increased by 29.7%, the biggest among the seven major currencies; meanwhile, the ratio for USD dropped by 19.2% to 180.5%, a bit higher than 171.8%, as shown in 2007), while the internationalization of the other six major currencies did not change significantly from 2013. The ratio of these seven major currencies' total foreign exchange trade share to their countries' GDP share dropped a bit from 15.9% as seen in 2013, but it was still as high as 155.6%.

4.9.2 *Changes in internationalization of currencies of other developed economies from 2010 to 2019*

By comparing Tables 4.10–4.12, we find that NZD, SEK, HKD, NOK, and SGD, five developed economies' currencies, have maintained their currency trade share higher than their GDP share from 2010 to 2013. The

Table 4.12: Comparison of Internationalization of Major Currencies in 2013 (Unit: %)

Currency	Foreign Exchange Share in 2013	GDP Share in 2013	Excess of Foreign Exchange Share over GDP Share	Foreign Exchange Share/GDP Share
USD	43.5	21.8	21.7	199.7
EUR	16.7	17.2	−0.5	97.0
JPY	11.5	6.7	4.8	171.2
GBP	5.9	3.6	2.3	165.1
AUD	4.3	2.0	2.3	218.2
CAD	2.3	2.4	−0.1	94.8
CHF	2.6	0.9	1.7	287.0
Total of seven currencies	86.8	54.6	32.2	159.0
NZD	1.0	0.2	0.7	402.2
SEK	0.9	0.8	0.1	116.7
HKD	0.7	0.4	0.4	200.9
NOK	0.7	0.7	0.0	105.4
SGD	0.7	0.4	0.3	175.5
Total of five currencies	4.0	2.4	1.6	164.1
KRW	0.6	1.7	−1.1	35.2
DKK	0.4	0.4	−0.1	87.5
TWD	0.2	0.7	−0.4	34.1
CZK	0.2	0.3	−0.1	65.1
ILS	0.1	0.4	−0.3	24.0
Total of five currencies	1.5	3.5	−2.0	42.8
MXN	1.3	1.7	−0.4	75.9
ZAR	0.6	0.5	0.1	116.4
RUB	0.8	3.0	−2.2	26.6
INR	0.5	2.4	−1.9	20.3
PLN	0.4	0.7	−0.3	51.2
BRL	0.6	3.2	−2.7	17.1
TRY	0.7	1.2	−0.6	53.2

(*Continued*)

Table 4.12: (*Continued*)

Currency	Foreign Exchange Share in 2013	GDP Share in 2013	Excess of Foreign Exchange Share over GDP Share	Foreign Exchange Share/GDP Share
HUF	0.2	0.2	0.0	120.0
MYR	0.2	0.4	−0.2	47.1
THB	0.2	0.5	−0.4	29.1
CLP	0.1	0.4	−0.2	40.8
IDR	0.1	1.2	−1.1	7.1
CNY	1.1	12.6	−11.5	8.9
Total of 13 currencies	6.6	28.0	−21.4	23.5
Total of BRIC	3.0	21.2	−18.3	13.9
Total of BRICS	3.5	21.7	−18.2	16.2

Source: Data about share of foreign exchange trade are from Table 4.1; data about GDP share are calculated based on the data about each country and region's GDP released by the International Monetary Fund in April 2018.

ratio of these five currencies' foreign exchange trade share to their economies' GDP share dropped slightly by 25.2% to 191.8% from 2007 to 2010 and further dropped by 27.7% to 164.1% from 2010 to 2013. However, this ratio rose by 46.1% to 210.2% from 2013 to 2016, close to 217.0% in 2007. It is noteworthy that the ratio of SGD foreign exchange trade share to Singapore's GDP share increased by 44.5% to 220.0% from 2013 to 2016, exceeding HKD's ratio of 203.6%. This demonstrates that the internationalization of SGD is higher than that of HKD.

By comparing Tables 4.10–4.12, we find that KRW, DKK, TWD CZK, and ILS, five developed economies' currencies, have maintained their currency trade share lower than their economies' GDP share between 2010 and 2013. Ratios of these five currencies' foreign exchange trade share to their economies' GDP share increased slightly to 41.6% and 42.8%, respectively, in the 2007–2010 period and in 2013. However, from 2013 to 2016, only DKK's foreign exchange trade share was slightly higher than Denmark's GDP share by 2.9%, and the ratio of these five

Table 4.13: Comparison of Internationalization of Major Currencies in 2016 (Unit: %)

Currency	Foreign Exchange Share in 2016	GDP Share in 2016	Excess of Foreign Exchange Share over GDP Share	Foreign Exchange Share/GDP Share
USD	43.8	24.7	19.1	177.5
EUR	15.7	15.8	−0.1	99.2
JPY	10.8	6.6	4.3	164.9
GBP	6.4	3.5	2.9	181.6
AUD	3.4	1.7	1.8	205.1
CAD	2.6	2.0	0.5	126.3
CHF	2.4	0.9	1.5	271.1
Total of seven currencies	85.1	55.2	29.9	154.3
NZD	1.0	0.2	0.8	417.9
SEK	1.1	0.7	0.4	162.6
HKD	0.9	0.4	0.4	203.6
NOK	0.8	0.5	0.3	170.1
SGD	0.9	0.4	0.5	220.0
Total of five currencies	4.7	2.3	2.5	210.2
KRW	0.8	1.9	−1.0	44.3
DKK	0.4	0.4	0.0	102.9
TWD	0.3	0.7	−0.4	45.1
CZK	0.1	0.3	−0.1	54.3
ILS	0.1	0.4	−0.3	32.8
Total of five currencies	1.8	3.7	−1.8	50.3
MXN	1.0	1.4	−0.5	67.1
ZAR	0.5	0.4	0.1	124.2
RUB	0.6	1.7	−1.1	33.8
INR	0.6	3.0	−2.4	19.0
PLN	0.3	0.6	−0.3	55.8
BRL	0.5	2.4	−1.9	21.1
TRY	0.7	1.1	−0.4	62.8

(Continued)

Table 4.13: (*Continued*)

Currency	Foreign Exchange Share in 2016	GDP Share in 2016	Excess of Foreign Exchange Share over GDP Share	Foreign Exchange Share/GDP Share
HUF	0.2	0.2	0.0	88.2
MYR	0.2	0.4	−0.2	45.4
THB	0.2	0.5	−0.4	33.0
CLP	0.1	0.3	−0.2	37.1
IDR	0.1	1.2	−1.1	8.1
CNY	2.0	14.9	−12.9	13.4
Total of 13 currencies	6.9	28.2	−21.3	24.4
Total of BRIC	3.6	22.0	−18.3	16.6
Total of BRICS	4.1	22.3	−18.2	18.5

Source: Data about share of foreign exchange trade are from Table 4.1; data about GDP share are calculated based on the data about each country and region's GDP released by the International Monetary Fund in April 2018.

currencies' total foreign exchange trade share to their economies' GDP share increased slightly to 50.3%, indicating that the internationalization of these five currencies increased slightly with little change after the financial crisis. As shown in Table 4.14, KRW took NOK's position in 2019, and difference between these five currencies' foreign exchange trade share and their economies' GDP share was within 1%.

4.9.3 *Changes in internationalization of currencies of developing countries since the global financial crisis*

We can conclude from Table 4.11 that, during 2010–2013, HUF's foreign exchange trade share was higher by 8.8% and 20.0% than Hungary's GDP share for two times. In 2013, ZAR's foreign exchange trade share was higher than South Africa's GDP share by 16.4%. Except for those two currencies, the other 13 currencies' foreign exchange trade share was

Table 4.14: Comparison of Internationalization of Major Currencies in 2019 (Unit: %)

Currency	Foreign Exchange Share in 2019	GDP Share in 2019	Excess of Foreign Exchange Share over GDP Share	Foreign Exchange Share/GDP Share
USD	44.2	24.5	19.7	180.5
EUR	16.2	15.6	0.6	103.7
JPY	8.4	5.9	2.5	141.7
GBP	6.4	3.2	3.2	197.4
AUD	3.4	1.6	1.8	208.1
CHF	2.5	0.8	1.7	310.7
CAD	2.5	2.0	0.5	124.5
Total of seven currencies	83.5	53.6	29.8	155.6
HKD	1.8	0.4	1.3	403.7
NZD	1.0	0.2	0.8	428.1
SEK	1.0	0.6	0.4	162.3
KRW	1.0	1.9	−0.9	52.4
SGD	0.9	0.4	0.5	211.6
Total of five currencies	4.8	3.2	1.6	150.2
NOK	0.9	0.5	0.4	184.0
MXN	0.9	1.4	−0.6	60.6
INR	0.9	3.4	−2.5	25.3
RUB	0.5	1.8	−1.3	29.7
ZAR	0.5	0.4	0.1	128.6
Total of five currencies	3.7	7.6	−3.9	49.0
TRY	0.5	0.8	−0.3	66.8
BRL	0.5	2.2	−1.7	23.9
TWD	0.5	0.7	−0.2	66.4
DKK	0.3	0.4	−0.1	79.0
PLN	0.3	0.7	−0.4	45.4
THB	0.2	0.6	−0.4	40.5
MYR	0.2	0.4	−0.2	47.8

(*Continued*)

Table 4.14: (*Continued*)

Currency	Foreign Exchange Share in 2019	GDP Share in 2019	Excess of Foreign Exchange Share over GDP Share	Foreign Exchange Share/GDP Share
HUF	0.2	0.2	0.0	104.3
CZK	0.2	0.3	−0.1	68.9
ILS	0.2	0.4	−0.3	35.1
CLP	0.1	0.3	−0.2	43.5
IDR	0.1	1.3	−1.1	11.2
CNY	2.2	16.3	−14.1	13.2
CNY*	2.6	16.3	−13.7	16.0
Total of 13 currencies	5.6	24.6	−19.1	22.7
Total of BRIC	4.1	23.8	−19.7	17.2
Total of BRICS	4.6	24.2	−19.6	19.2

Source: Data about share of foreign exchange trade are from Table 4.1; data about GDP share are calculated based on the data about each country and region's GDP released by the International Monetary Fund in April 2018. CNY* is calculated using data from Table 4.1.

lower than their economies' GDP share. Although the foreign exchange trade share of these 13 currencies increased from 3.1% to 6.9% from 2007 to 2013, the total share of their economies increased from 19.5% to 28.0%, and the ratio between them increased slightly from 16.1% in 2007 to 23.5%, demonstrating the slightly changed internalization level of major developing countries' currencies. From 2013 to 2016, among these 13 currencies, only ZAR's foreign exchange trade share was larger than South Africa's GDP share. The other 12 foreign exchange trade share was much smaller than their economies' GDP share. The total share of these 13 currencies' foreign exchange trade rose from 6.6% to 6.9%, while the total share of their economies increased slightly to 28.2%, which allowed their ratio to rise from 23.5% to 24.4%. From 2016 to 2019, in addition to CNY, only the difference between BRL's foreign exchange trade share and its economy's GDP share was larger than 1%, while others were within 0.5%, showing small overall changes.

4.9.4 *Comparison of changes of major developed economies' currency internationalization since the global financial crisis*

By comparing Table 4.10 with Table 4.14, we find that the foreign exchange trade share of seven major international currencies dropped by 2.7% to 83.5% from 86.2% during the 11 years after the global financial crisis, while their economies' GDP share dropped by 11.5% to 53.6% from 65.1%, and the latter's drop was 8.8% higher than the former. The ratio between the two shares increased by 23.2% to 155.6% from 132.4%. This means that the internalization level of these major international currencies improved because their economies' GDP dropped.

The total share of the foreign exchange trade of five developed economies' currencies (including NZD) dropped by 0.5% to 4.8%, while the total share of those five developed economies' GDP dropped by 0.2% to 3.2%, for which their ratio between those two shares increased by 19.8% to 211.6%. This means that the growth of the former was slower than the latter.

4.9.5 *Comparison of changes of major developing economies' currency internalization since the global financial crisis*

The total share of the foreign exchange trade of 13 emerging economies' currencies (including MXN) increased by 3.9% to 6.9% from 3.1%, while the total share of those 13 emerging economies' GDP increased by 8.5% to 24.4% from 16.1%. Both these shares did not increase a lot because the growth of those 13 emerging economies' GDP share was larger than that of 13 currencies' foreign exchange trade share. In 2019, the samples had some changes, but the share almost showed no change.

4.10 Changes in and Comparison of Internationalization of Currencies of BRICS Countries before and after the Global Financial Crisis

"Currencies of BRICS countries" in Tables 4.10–4.13 refers to currencies of five BRICS countries frequently identified by international media, namely,

Brazil, Russia, India, China, and South Africa, whose global influence was growing following the global financial crisis. In the sixth BRICS summit in Brazil in July 2014, leaders of BRICS countries announced to jointly build a BRICS bank. On July 21, 2015, the BRICS bank was officially launched in Shanghai. The bank was set up and run in 2015. In this section, we will address the measurement and comparison of the internationalization of five BRICS currencies before and after the global financial crisis.

4.10.1 *Overall GDP share of BRICS countries before and after the global financial crisis*

According to statistics released by the International Monetary Fund in April 2018, in 2007 which was 1 year before the global financial crisis, the GDP of BRICS countries made up only 13.6% of the world's GDP, 8.6% and 13.1% lower than the GDP share of the Eurozone and the US, respectively. However, the GDP share of BRICS countries increased to 18.2% in 2010, only slightly lower than that of the Eurozone (19.2 %), with a narrowed gap of 4.5% with that of the US (22.7%). In 2013, BRICS' GDP share continued to rise and reached 21.7%, surpassing the Eurozone's share of 17.2% for the first time and only 0.1% behind the 21.8% share of the US. In 2016, the share of BRICS's GDP in the world improved further to 22.3%, 6.5% higher than that of Eurozone but 2.3% lower than that of US. According to the predicted data released by the IMF in April 2018, the total GDP share of BRICS will reach 24.4% in 2018, larger than that of US (23.5%). The global economic influence of BRICS will strengthen further.

4.10.2 *Internationalization of currencies of BRICS countries in 2007 with a comparative study*

As shown in Table 4.10, the combined foreign exchange turnover of five BRICS currencies only accounted for 1.6% of the world's total in 2007, 12.0% lower than five BRICS countries' GDP share of 13.6% of the world. The ratio of these five currencies' foreign exchange trade share to these five countries' GDP share was only 11.8%, much lower than 13 emerging economies' currencies' ratio of 16.1% and even lower than one-third of five developed economies' currencies' ratio of 35.8%, as shown in Table 4.10. This indicates the low internationalization of BRICS currencies even when compared with developing countries.

4.10.3 *Internationalization progress of currencies of the five BRICS countries after the global financial crisis*

Table 4.11 shows that the foreign exchange trade share of the five BRICS currencies increased to 2.1% in 2010, and the GDP share of BRICS countries increased to 18.2%, for which the difference between those two shares enlarged to 16.1%. The ratio of these five currencies' foreign exchange trade share to these five countries' GDP share further dropped to 11.3%, lower than 30% of the corresponding ratio for the five developed economies' currency (including KRW), as shown in Table 4.11. In 2013, the foreign exchange trade share of the five BRICS currencies increased to 3.5%, and the GDP share of BRICS countries increased to 21.7%, further widening the gap between the two shares to 18.2%. The foreign exchange share/GDP share of the currencies saw a slight increase to 16.2%, but it was only slightly higher than two-thirds of 13 emerging economies' currencies' ratio of 23.5%, and lower than 40% of five developed economies' currencies' (including KRW) ratio of 42.8%, as shown in Table 4.11. In 2016, the share of foreign exchange trade of the five BRICS currencies increased to 4.1%, while their GDP share increased to 22.3%, and the difference between them expanded to 18.2% with the ratio between them increasing slightly to 18.5%, slightly higher than one-third of the five developed economies' currencies' corresponding ratio of 50.3%. Table 4.14 shows that the share of BRICS currencies' foreign exchange trade share further increased to 4.6% in 2019, while the share of BRICS countries' GDP increased to 22.3%, with the difference between those two shares widening to 19.6%.

The result indicates that the total foreign exchange turnovers of BRICS' currencies has delightfully increased during the 12 years from 2007 to 2019, but the growth of foreign exchange market is still much slower than their economic growth, which shows the level of their currency internationalization is still much lower than that of 13 emerging economies' currencies.

4.10.4 *Comparison of currency globalization for BRICS*

Table 4.10 shows that among the five currencies of BRICS, the ZAR has the highest globalization level. The ratio of ZAR foreign exchange trade share to South Africa's GDP share is 88.6%, more than six times higher than the total globalization level of BRICS (11.8%) in the same year.

Tables 4.11 and 4.13 show that although the globalization level of ZAR decreased a little in 2010, it still stood first among the BRICS countries. In 2013, the ratio of ZAR reached up to 116.4%, which exceeded 100% for the first time, not only exceeding the other four BRIC countries but also exceeding the ratios of EUR, CAD, NOK, and many other currencies of developed countries. In 2016, the ratio of ZAR foreign exchange trade share to South Africa's GDP share rose to 124.2%, exceeding the ratios of five developed economies' currencies including EUR, and KRW, and it ranked 12th in the world. In 2016, the globalization of RUB, BRL, and INR ranked from second to fourth among BRICS's currencies, and globalization of CNY remained the last one. In 2019, the ratio of ZAR foreign exchange trade share to South Africa's GDP share further improved to 128.6%, while the ratios of the other four currencies did not change a lot.

4.11 Internationalization of CNY before and after the Global Financial Crisis with a Comparative Study

According to GDP statistics released by the International Monetary Fund in October 2016, China's GDP share of five BRICS countries exceeded 50% for the first time to 52.4% in 2009 and exceeded 60% for the first time in 2014 to 60.7%. Following the measurement and comparison of internationalization levels of major international currencies, this section focuses on changes in CNY internationalization over a span from 2007 to 2016 and provides a comparative study of CNY and currencies of other developing countries.

According to Tables 4.10–4.13, in 2007, there was a huge gap between CNY's foreign exchange trade share of 0.23% and China's GDP share of 6.2%. In 2010, while CNY's foreign exchange trade share was 0.43%, China's GDP share was 9.2%, with the excess of the former over the latter reaching −8.8% from 5.9%. In 2013, CNY foreign exchange trade share rose significantly to 1.12%, and China's GDP share of the world was 12.7%, which increased their difference to −11.5%. In 2016, CNY foreign exchange trade share rose significantly to 1.99%, and China's GDP share was 15.3%, which increased their difference to −13.3%. Although the share of CNY foreign exchange trade was rising significantly from 2007 to 2013, the magnitude of this rise was smaller than that of China's GDP share. The ratio of CNY's foreign exchange trade share to China's GDP share increased from 3.7% in 2007 to 4.7% in 2010, the lowest ranking not only among five BRICS currencies but also among 30 currencies shown in Table 4.11. Table 4.12 shows that although this ratio increased to 8.8% in 2013, it still came last among five BRICS currencies and the second lowest in the standings in Table 4.12. Some progress was made. This ratio for CNY increased to 13.0% in 2016 and 13.2% in 2019. However, CNY was still the second lowest in the rankings of BRICS, and its gap with other currencies was still large.

4.12 Measurement of Currency Internationalization in a Relative Sense

Using the data in Tables 4.10–4.14 about internationalization of 30 currencies, we can easily produce the internationalization level of any currency relative to all other currencies. This section addresses the relativity of currency internationalization.

4.12.1 *Currency internationalization relative to USD*

Internationalization of any currency relative to USD can be easily shown by a fraction of USD as the denominator and the currency in question as the numerator. This section introduces currency internationalization in a relative way. Internationalization of different currencies relative to USD can be rendered with USD as the denominator. Table 4.15 shows such relativity for different currencies from 2007 to 2019.

Table 4.15 shows that the overall internationalization of seven international reserve currencies relative to USD slightly improved from 77.1% in 2007 to 78.7% in 2010 before increasing to 79.6% in 2013, 86.9% in 2016 and 86.2% in 2019. Relative internationalization of currencies of five developed countries and regions, including New Zealand, dropped significantly from 126.3% in 2007 to 82.2% in 2013 and rebounded to 83.2% in 2019, 3% lower than the relative internationalization level of seven reserve currencies (86.2%) in the same year. Internationalization level of five BRICS currencies relative to USD dropped slightly from 6.9% in 2007 to 6.1% in 2010 before rising steadily to 10.6% in the 2010–2019 period. The internationalization level of CNY to USD rose from 2.1% in 2007 to 7.3% in 2019. If the adjusted CNY (CNY*) were taken into consideration, its internationalization level had risen to 9.0% in

Table 4.15: Internationalization of Currencies of Major Countries and Regions Relative to USD (2007–2019) (Unit: %)

	2007	2010	2013	2016	2019
USD	100	100	100	100	100
EUR	48.6	54.3	48.6	55.9	57.4
JPY	64.6	58.7	85.7	92.9	78.5
GBP	81.8	92.9	82.6	102.3	109.4
AUD	118.2	107.0	109.3	115.6	115.3
CHF	240.3	190.6	143.7	152.8	172.1
CAD	49.5	57.7	47.5	71.2	69.0
Total of seven currencies	77.1	78.7	79.6	86.9	86.2
HKD	216.2	182.5	100.6	114.7	223.6
NZD	237.6	193.2	201.4	235.5	237.1
SEK	93.6	79.1	58.4	91.6	89.9
KRW	17.4	24.4	17.6	24.9	29.1
SGD	109.7	105.7	87.9	124.0	117.2
Total of five currencies	126.3	102.6	82.2	118.5	83.2
NOK	88.7	54.3	52.8	95.8	101.9
MXN	21.1	21.0	38.0	37.8	33.6
INR	9.7	9.8	10.2	10.7	14.0
RUB	9.1	9.7	13.3	19.0	16.4
ZAR	51.5	33.9	58.3	70.0	71.3
Total of five currencies	20.8	22.2	21.5	28.4	27.1
TRY	4.5	16.8	26.6	35.4	37.0
BRL	4.8	5.5	8.6	11.9	13.2
TWD	15.1	18.9	17.1	25.4	36.8
DKK	44.6	31.1	43.8	58.0	43.8
PLN	30.0	29.6	25.6	31.5	25.1
THB	12.6	10.0	14.6	18.6	22.4
MYR	11.3	19.0	23.6	25.6	26.5
HUF	32.5	58.2	60.1	49.7	57.8

(*Continued*)

Table 4.15: (*Continued*)

	2007	2010	2013	2016	2019
CZK	19.2	16.3	32.6	30.6	38.2
ILS	14.6	11.3	12.0	18.5	19.5
CLP	10.4	13.2	20.5	20.9	24.1
IDR	4.0	3.5	3.5	4.5	6.2
CNY	2.1	2.5	4.4	7.6	7.3
CNY*	2.1	2.5	4.4	7.6	9.0
Total of 13 currencies	9.4	9.0	11.8	13.7	12.6
Total of BRIC	5.1	5.2	7.0	9.3	9.6
Total of BRICS	6.9	6.1	8.1	10.4	10.6

Source: Calculation is based on data from Tables 4.10 to 4.14. CNY* data are calculated based on data from Tables 4.1 and 4.14.

2019. Internationalization of CNY relative to USD in 2007 and 2010 shown here is close to the results of internationalization of CNY relative to USD in 2000 and 2002 produced by Li Yao (2003) and the research team on CNY internationalization.

4.12.2 *Internationalization of CNY relative to other currencies*

Using the same methodology, we can put CNY internationalization data in Tables 4.10–4.13 as the numerator to easily get the changes in internationalization of CNY relative to other currencies from 2007 to 2019. The details are shown in Table 4.16.

Table 4.16 shows that internationalization level of adjusted CNY (CNY*) relative to seven international reserve currencies increased from 2.7% in 2007 to 10.4% in 2019. Meanwhile, internationalization level of CNY relative to NZD and other four developed economies' currencies increased from 1.7% in 2007 to 10.8% in 2019, and CNY's internationalization level relative to five developed economies' currencies, including NOK, increased from 10.1% to 33.0% in 2019. CNY's internationalization level relative to 12 emerging economies' currencies increased from 22.3% to 71.3%, and CNY's internationalization level relative to five

Table 4.16: Internationalization of CNY Relative to Other Currencies (2007–2019) (Unit: %)

	2007	2010	2013	2016	2019
USD	2.1	2.5	4.4	7.6	9.0
EUR	4.3	4.6	9.1	13.6	15.7
JPY	3.3	4.3	5.1	8.2	11.5
GBP	2.6	2.7	5.3	7.4	8.2
AUD	1.8	2.3	4.0	6.6	7.8
CHF	0.9	1.3	3.1	5.0	5.2
CAD	4.2	4.3	9.3	10.7	13.0
Total of seven currencies	2.7	3.2	5.5	8.7	10.4
HKD	1.0	1.4	4.4	6.6	4.0
NZD	0.9	1.3	2.2	3.2	3.8
SEK	2.2	3.2	7.5	8.3	10.0
KRW	12.1	10.2	25.0	30.5	30.9
SGD	1.9	2.4	5.0	6.1	7.7
Total of five currencies	1.7	2.4	5.4	6.4	10.8
NOK	2.4	4.6	8.3	7.9	8.8
MXN	10.0	11.9	11.6	20.1	26.8
INR	21.6	25.5	43.1	71.0	64.3
RUB	23.1	25.8	33.1	40.0	54.9
ZAR	4.1	7.4	7.5	10.9	12.6
Total of five currencies	10.1	11.3	20.5	26.8	33.2
TRY	46.7	14.9	16.5	21.5	24.3
BRL	43.8	45.5	51.2	63.9	68.2
TWD	13.9	13.2	25.7	29.9	24.5
DKK	4.7	8.0	10.0	13.1	20.5
PLN	7.0	8.4	17.2	24.1	35.9
THB	16.7	25.0	30.1	40.9	40.2
MYR	18.6	13.2	18.6	29.7	34.0
HUF	6.5	4.3	7.3	15.3	15.6
CZK	10.9	15.3	13.5	24.8	23.6

(*Continued*)

Table 4.16: (*Continued*)

	2007	2010	2013	2016	2019
ILS	14.4	22.1	36.7	41.1	46.2
CLP	20.2	18.9	21.5	36.4	37.3
IDR	52.5	71.4	125.7	168.9	145.2
CNY	100.0	100.0	100.0	100.0	123.3
CNY*	100.0	100.0	100.0	100.0	100.0
Total of 13 currencies	22.3	27.8	37.3	55.5	71.4
Total of BRIC	41.2	48.1	62.9	81.7	93.8
Total of BRICS	30.4	41.0	54.3	73.1	84.9

Source: Calculated based on data from Tables 4.10–4.14.

currencies of BRICS increased from 30.4% to 84.9% in 2019. All these are remarkable achievements.

4.13 Alternative Method for Measuring Currency Internalization

Tables 4.1 and 4.3 show the percentages of foreign exchange trade by currency and by country/region in the global foreign exchange market from 1992 to 2019. For any country and region, foreign exchange trade between its currency and other currencies usually takes up a prominent share, supplemented by trade between other currencies. This section starts by introducing the ratio of foreign exchange trade between a currency and other currencies in offshore markets to the currency's total onshore foreign exchange trade and then also introducing the share of a currency's offshore and onshore foreign exchange trade in the international foreign exchange market, followed by the calculation of the ratio of a currency's offshore foreign exchange turnover to its onshore foreign exchange turnover. In general, the higher the ratio, the higher the level of internationalization. As such, this can be an alternative way to measure currency internationalization.

4.13.1 *Proportions of foreign exchange trade between major currencies and other currencies taking place in their countries and regions' domestic foreign exchange markets in total foreign exchange ratio hosted by those markets*

Table 4.17 shows the global distribution of foreign exchange trade in major countries and regions. However, without any information on the amount of foreign exchange trade transacted between those countries and regions' own currencies and other currencies, it is difficult to determine the level of activity of those countries and regions' own currencies in their domestic foreign exchange markets and offshore foreign exchange markets. Table 4.17 shows the ratios of major international currencies' offshore foreign exchange trade's average daily turnover to the domestic foreign exchange trade's average daily turnover from 2007 to 2019.

4.13.2 *Changes in ratios of CNY domestic/offshore foreign exchange trade and related problems*

As shown in Table 4.16, based on data from the BIS, the ratio of CNY offshore foreign exchange trade to CNY domestic foreign exchange trade was as high as 14.01 in April 2007. Chapter 9 indicates that the offshore CNY market just started in August 2010, so the offshore CNY foreign exchange trade should have been zero in April 2007, which made the ratio of 14.1 an impossible number. The ratios of offshore CNY foreign exchange trade to the domestic CNY foreign exchange trade from April 2010 to April 2019, as shown in Table 4.16, demonstrate that it is reasonable to think that the fast development of the offshore CNY market from 2010 to 2019 contributed to the increased ratios. Analysis will be made in Chapter 12 regarding the progress of domestic and offshore CNY foreign exchange market over the past 2 years.

4.14 Conclusion

This chapter provides an overall introduction to the composition of major international currencies, foreign exchange products in those currencies and liquidity, and their internationalization. In addition, we have also

Table 4.17: Comparison of Ratios of Major Currencies' Offshore/ Domestic Foreign Exchange Trade's Daily Average Turnover (2007–2019)

	2007	2010	2013	2016	2019
USD	4.23	3.30	3.15	3.03	3.78
EUR	5.10	4.16	3.96	3.93	4.92
JPY	2.23	2.03	3.36	2.47	2.79
GBP	0.68	0.55	0.49	0.62	0.42
AUD	1.63	2.52	4.05	5.21	6.57
CAD	2.45	3.92	5.19	4.10	4.44
CHF	2.26	2.23	3.40	3.19	2.55
CNY	14.01	1.83	2.57	2.65	1.81
SGD	0.60	0.78	1.27	1.27	1.09
HKD	0.22	0.30	0.55	0.57	0.60
CNY	15.4	0.25	1.45	1.68	1.11
CNY*	15.4	0.25	1.45	1.68	1.56

Source: Calculation is based on the global foreign exchange data in April of every 3 years released by the BIS from 2007 to 2019. The Eurozone's data are calculated based on data from Austria, Belgium, Estonia, Finland, France, Germany, Greece, Ireland, Italy, Latvia, Lithuania, Luxembourg, the Netherlands, Portugal, Slovakia, and Spain, while data from Cyprus and Malta were missing. CNY* was calculated based on results shown in Table 4.1.

touched on currencies of other developed and developing countries and regions, foreign exchange products in those currencies and liquidity, and their internationalization. Our analysis shows that the international status of international reserve currencies is best reflected by their functions as trading and reserve currencies, with their spot trading, forward trading and swap trading all playing a significant role in the global foreign exchange market. International currencies with USD at the center have increasing rather than decreasing influence in the international market after the global financial crisis. Other than major international currencies, currencies of developed countries and regions also play an important role in the international market, despite a drop in internationalization of those currencies. The status of almost all currencies of developing countries and regions in the international market is disproportionately related to the economic status of those countries and regions, or in other words, the percentages of foreign exchange trade in almost all those currencies in the international market are lower than their countries and regions' GDP share in the world. This shows the need for those countries and regions to improve the international status of their currencies.

The measurement of currency internationalization is a complicated concept. An objective understanding of the changes in the level of internationalization of different currencies over time is not possible without an unbiased and scientific measuring methodology. In the course of on-going CNY internationalization in the years to come, measurement of CNY internationalization, especially one that enables comparison with other currencies, is of great significance to our work. If the level of internationalization of CNY relative to that of other currencies achieves our target set for a certain period, we will feel motivated to carry on the work. If it fails to do so, we can easily find the causes to adjust and improve our strategies and methods for an orderly and sound progress of CNY internationalization.

As the international functions of a currency are often manifested in various areas and involve numerous data and parameters in those areas, an accurate and comprehensive measurement of currency internationalization is difficult. However, no matter how many areas the international functions of a currency involve, improved performance in each area will certainly translate into higher activity of the currency in foreign exchange trading. Therefore, we measure the internationalization level of a currency indirectly by assessing how active the currency is in the global foreign exchange market. This chapter, with this methodology in mind, builds a simple and practical approach to measure currency internationalization which allows for the calculation of the internationalization of a currency or currency pair relative to other currency or currency pair.

With over a decade of development, especially after 2005 when a CNY exchange rate formation mechanism was implemented, tremendous progress has been made in areas such as domestic foreign exchange trading mechanisms and product innovation and launch, with increased liquidity for foreign exchange forwards, swaps, forward rate agreements, interest rate swaps, forward options, and other products. However, further growth of China's financial market necessitates a need for comparison not only with the past but also with the financial markets of other countries and regions so that the gap can be exposed. From the above discussions, we can see that significant gaps still exist between China and developed countries, and even between China and most of the developing countries in foreign exchange and interest rate markets. China still faces issues such as low product liquidity, ineffective market roles, and insufficient supply of on-exchange financial derivatives which urgently need to be resolved.

Using a simple measuring method, we calculated the extent of CNY internationalization as well as relative to other currencies from 2007 to 2019. Our results show that despite an increase in the internationalization level of CNY from 2007 to 2010, this level of internationalization runs counter to China's economic achievements in recent years, recording a significant gap from the internationalization level of currencies to developed countries and regions, and a smaller yet noticeable gap to that of currencies of developing countries and regions. Although CNY internationalization enhanced significantly from 2013 to 2019, it has a long way to go before it matches China's economic and trade status in the world and even reaches the level of BRICS' currencies.

Ever since 2009, China has been promoting CNY cross-border settlements, offshore issuance of CNY bonds, direct offshore investment using CNY and other businesses, with enormous progress made in those aspects. Despite such efforts, however, foreign exchange trading in China failed to register any growth during the same period, which makes it clear that while promoting CNY businesses globally, we need to place importance to the sound development of CNY foreign exchange markets as well, as new CNY businesses in the international market will lose strong market support and miss the steady and continuous growth target if a sound development of CNY foreign exchange markets is lacking. In other words, any measure for the purpose of promoting CNY internationalization should be accompanied in a coordinated fashion by the effort to achieve sound growth of CNY foreign exchange markets. We are confident that CNY will become far more internationalized in the years to come. Rome was not built in one day. While basking in the progress we have made, we should carry out earnest studies on the success of and lessons from developed and developing countries so that we can produce proper roadmaps and timetables for short-term (3–5 years), mid-term (5–8 years) and long-term (10–20 years) development of China's financial markets, financial products, and regulatory mechanisms, with the goal of the development of such products in China's financial markets, improving various mechanisms, increasing market activity, and giving full play to market roles. It is only in this way that we can let the financial sector better serve the real economy and lay a solid foundation for CNY internationalization. We will continue to discuss trends of CNY internationalization in other chapters.

Currencies' internationalization levels are reflected in areas where the currencies are applied on an international level. Wider application of currencies globally means a higher level of currencies' internationalization. However, it is hard to acquire accurate data of global application of currencies in all areas. Even if such data are available, ratios will be inconsistent in different areas. So, it will be difficult to accurately measure the internationalization levels of currencies. Although currencies are applied in a variety of areas on a global level, the international application of currencies can be reflected by data about the foreign exchange trade between a currency and other currencies. So, the share of a currency's average daily turnover in the global foreign exchange market is the best method to measure a currency's internationalization level. In the past two decades, 60% of the average daily turnover in the global foreign exchange market are the average daily nominal turnover of foreign exchange derivatives rather than the foreign exchange spot trade. Thus, as shown in Table 4.1, most of the daily average turnovers in the global foreign exchange market, including the average daily nominal turnovers of foreign exchange derivatives, are the trade of foreign exchange derivatives. The nominal turnover is not the turnover of actual trade which changes hand, but an exaggerated turnover. Thus, currency internationalization, as measured by the average daily nominal turnover in the global foreign exchange market, has many limitations. Related problems will be analyzed and discussed in Chapter 13 to find out the problems caused by these limitations. The best methods to measure the currency's internationalization level, which are like the actual turnover of foreign exchange trade as shown in Table 4.9, will be found out and proved.

Appendix: Introduction to Domestic and Offshore CNY Internationalization Indices

Since 2007, many domestic and offshore financial and academic institutions subsequently introduced various types of CNY internationalization indices. Table A4.1 lists names of institutions, names of indices, time of launch, scope of parameters, and purpose of research about CNY internationalization indices. This table indicates various indices have its own emphases. Some emphasize on offshore CNY market, e.g., HSBC offshore CNY foreign exchange index. Others emphasize offshore CNY bond and equity market, e.g., BOC offshore CNY index and future usage of CNY, e.g., DBS CNY drive index. These indices reflect and promote different aspects of CNY internationalization by introducing relevant products launched by institutions.

Table A4.1: Domestic and Offshore CNY Internationalization Indices

Names of Indices	Institutions	Frequency	Scope of Parameter	Purpose of Research
CNY index	SEM	Monthly since July 2007	Effects of SRD basket to trade and FDI Weighted average: USD, JPY, EUR, HKD, SKW, TWD, SGD, and GBP	Provide composite benchmark and underlying asset for foreign exchange futures and options Play information, investment, and evaluation functions
CNY effective foreign exchange index	SSI	Quarterly since interim 2010	Weighted average based on trade calculated by bilateral exchange rate: USD, EUR, JPY, HKD, AUD, GBP, RUB, CAD, and MYR	With the deep connection with international economy, bilateral rates are limited to affect the valuation of CNY. However, the change reflects the composite value of CNY and trend
CNY global index	SCB	Monthly since December 2010	Three offshore CNY centers (Hong Kong, London, and Singapore) Apply deposit, dim sum bond, CD, trade settlement and foreign exchange to evaluate wealth reserve, financing tools, international trade, and transaction channel	To quantify trend and scale of CNY activities, recognize acceptance of offshore CNY as reserve currency, more reference to use CNY as operation capital
Offshore CNY foreign exchange index	HSBC	March 2011	Single currency index, trade weighted referring to exchange rate and precious metal	To manage CNY position of investors and accelerate CNY internationalization with relevant CNY index products

(*Continued*)

Offshore CNY index	BOC	Quarterly since 2011	Composite weighted: offshore CNY deposits, offshore CNY loans, bond and equity denominated in CNY, foreign exchange reserve, and foreign exchange trading volume	Composite evaluation to stock scale of CNY, usage of CNY and financial instruments in offshore financial market
Cross-border CNY index	BOC	Quarterly since 2011, Monthly since April 2014	Indicators of current account, representative capital account and offshore circulation account	Usage level of CNY in cross-border transaction from the view of inflow and outflow
DBS CNY Drive index	DBS	Quarterly since 2012	Actual performance in last 12 months and future performance in future 12 months, demands for using CNY in the operation, trade, financing, and current accounts	More representative in corporations and evaluate CNY acceptance and penetration from perspective of corporations registered in Hong Kong
CNY internationalization index	Renmin University of China	Since 2012	Composite weighted: CNY credit, CNY bonds and notes, direct investment, and foreign reserve	With the subsequent opening capital account, CNY internationalization index is established to measure the level from perspective of payment and reserve to improve ability of management. The change of figure and structure in CNY internationalization index is main factors to evaluate CNY internationalization

Source: Websites of various indices from composite institutions.

Bibliography

International Monetary Fund, 2010, Review of the Method of Valuation of the SDR. Prepared by the Finance Department. In Consultation with the Legal and Other Departments, Approved by Andrew Tweedie, October 26, 2010.

Li, Yao, Non-International Currencies, Currency Internationalization and Capital Account Convertibility, *Financial Studies*, 2003.

Mihaljek, D. and Packer, F., Derivatives in Emerging Markets, *BIS Quarterly Review*, December 2010.

Triennial Central Bank Survey, Foreign Exchange and Derivatives Market Activity in April 2010, Preliminary Results, Monetary and Economic Department, September 2010.

Triennial Central Bank Survey, Report on Global Foreign Exchange Market Activity in 2010, Monetary and Economic Department, December 2010.

Xu, Qiyuan, How Does China Face Herstatt Risk, Research Center for International Finance Institute of World Economics and Politics, Chinese Academy of Social Sciences, 2016.049, August 1, 2016.

Zhang, Guangping (Peter G.) *CNY Derivatives* (Fourth Edition), China Finance Press, 2016.

Zhang, Guangping (Peter G.) and Thomas Chan, *Chinese Yuan Internationalization and Financial Products in China*, John Wiley & Sons, 2011.

Zhang, Guangping (Peter G.) and Yang, Jian, *Indian Financial Reforms and Experiences for China to Learn*, Research sponsored by Asian Development Bank, 2008.

Zhou, Xiaochuan, *Thoughts on Reform of the International Monetary System*, website of the People's Bank of China.

Chapter 5

PCT Patents: The Backbone of International Technology

Patents are the key accumulations of scientific and technological achievements, and the main component of intellectual property. Chapter 2 introduced the distribution of Patent Cooperation Treaty (PCT) applications in critical countries and regions, and in key technology areas of the past 10 years, which helps us understand patents. However, the number of patent applications cannot well represent the levels of technology in different countries or regions, in particular their global competitiveness, since patent grant management and approval procedures vary significantly across different countries or regions.

Based on patent family data published by the patent offices of China, Europe, Japan, Republic of Korea, and the US (hereinafter referred to as "the five offices") and World Intellectual Property Organization (WIPO), this chapter defines patent globalization or the science and technology competitiveness and provides a method for measurement. Relevant results can help us to understand the world situation of science and technology competition among chief countries and regions in the past decade, as well as the improvements and challenges of China's science and technology innovation ability. Further, they can help us to think about how to improve the level of scientific innovation and how to support the development of China's trade in the future.

5.1 Top Five Offices in the World and Their Cooperation

5.1.1 *Introduction of the top five offices*

The European Patent Office (EPO) was established in 1973 under the European Patent Convention (EPC), which was signed by the patent offices of the chief European countries. The EPC was updated on December 17, 1991, and November 29, 2000, respectively (EPO website: www.epo.org). At the end of 2018, the EPO had 38 EU member states, including 19 Eurozone member states, UK, Sweden, Switzerland, Turkey, etc. In 2018, the EPO spent €1.65 billion ($1.89 billion), of which research and examination accounted for 50.2% and 32.4%, respectively, for a combined share of 82.6%. As of 2018, the EPO has 6,696 employees from 35 European countries and manages patent applications, grants and matters related to European and worldwide cooperation of 38 member states (IP5, 2018).

The predecessor of the Japan Patent Office (JPO) was established to enforce the Trademark Law of Japan in 1884 and the Patent Monopoly Law of Japan in 1885. JPO has a certain degree of autonomy, is the authority to formulate, amend, and interpret ⟨Franchising Law⟩, ⟨Utility Model Law⟩, ⟨Design Patent Law⟩, and ⟨Commodity Law⟩, responsible for accepting, examining, and granting applications for the above-mentioned four types of patents. In terms of JPO functions, refer to its official website: www.jpo.go.jp. By the end of 2018, JPO had 2,780 employees and a yearly expenditure of JPY 310.4 billion ($2.83 billion), of which 32.2%, 26.5%, and 22.4%, respectively, accounted for general administration, complaint review and patent processing computerization, which together accounted for 81.1% (IP5, 2018).

The predecessor of the Korean Intellectual Property Office (KIPO) was established in 1948 as an office under the Ministry of Industry and Commerce of Republic of Korea. In 1979, KIPO joined WIPO. In 2000, it changed the name of the former Korea Industrial Property Office to the present Korean Intellectual Property Office. KIPO oversees the administration of Korean patents and trademarks and worldwide cooperation. In terms of KIPO, refer to www.kipo.go.kr. In 2018, KIPO's total expenditure was 702.28 billion won ($630 million), of which operating expenses and internal affairs accounted for 39.8% and 38.6%, respectively, and the combined two items accounted for 78.4%. As of 2018, KIPO has

1,667 employees and manages matters, such as Korean patents and trademarks and international cooperation (IP5, 2018).

China's Patent Law was adopted by the National People's Congress on March 12, 1984, and came into force on April 1, 1985, which was updated in January 1993 and July 2001, respectively (refer to the official website of China National Intellectual Property Administration (CNIPA), for details: www.cnipa.gov.cn). As of the end of 2018, CNIPA had 12,000 patent examiners. In 2018, CNIPA's total expenditure was RMB 6.30 billion ($920 million), of which the expenditure on patent examination and administrative, operation accounted for 77.5% and 13.2% of the total expenditure, respectively, accounting for 93.7% of the total expenditure (IP5, 2018).

The United States Patent and Trademark Office (USPTO), established in 1802, is an agency under the US Department of Commerce responsible for advising inventors and their inventions for patent protection, trade mark registration and intellectual property certificate (in terms of regulations and data of US patent and trademark, refer to the official website of USPTO: www.uspto.gov). By the end of 2018, the USPTO had 12,579 employees and spent $3.33 billion in 2018, of which 66.8% and 6.9%, respectively, were paid for wages and benefits and equipment, accounting for 73.7%.

5.1.2 *Cooperation among the top five offices*

From 1985 to 2008, EPO, JPO, and USPTO jointly published an annual report on "trilateral" patent-related data. In 2009, KIPO joined the cooperation of the three offices, thus forming the cooperation of the world's chief four patent offices and jointly publishing relevant patent data. Since 2012, CNIPA also joined the previous four collaborating offices, forming the framework for cooperation among the world's chief five patent offices, which work with WIPO to issue patent-related data from the top five offices and from other countries outside of the chief five offices, providing reliable information for us to understand and analyze global patents and related topics. In 2017, 2.8 million invention patent applications were received globally, including direct national applications, direct regional applications, and international patent applications filed through PCT, with 94% of the applications coming from countries and regions where the chief five offices are located. In addition, 91.1% of the 13.636 million valid patents in 2017 were under the management of the top five offices, while patents from other countries and regions accounted for only 8.9% (IP5, 2018), indicating the important influence of the chief five offices in the global patent area and the importance of the chief five offices' yearly patent reports.

5.1.3 *The top five offices: Comparison and implications*

As noted in the previous section, expenditure used for employee wages and welfare was the highest among the principal five offices. At the same time, JPO used for digital management of patent spending was accounted for the highest, which indicated that JPO's goal of "being the world's most rapid patent examination office with best service" was implemented in management action. In addition, according to 2018 yearly spending data of the principal five offices mentioned above, we can calculate that support cost of USPTO, EPO, JPO, CNIPA, and KIPO out of that of the leading five offices were 40.5%, 23.2%, 17.3%, 11.2%, and 7.7%, which was aligned with the sequence sorted by patent number of these five patent offices. This indicates that management cost of patent offices in main countries and regions and the amount of their patents also has a direct relationship.

5.2 PCT Patent Introduction

Most of the valid patents granted and maintained by the leading five offices are resident files. For example, valid patents filed in Europe, Japan, Republic of Korea, China, and the US accounted for 60%, 83%, 75%, 68%, and 50%, respectively, and 35% in other countries and regions; global resident patents accounted for 66.4% in 2017. However, international patent accounted for only 33.6%, but these foreign patents or international patents in global trade and other business activities play a more crucial role. The globalization of markets and production remains a major business trend. A PCT patent is a patent coordinated by global general standards, and cross-border patent application is an important connotation of the trend of economic and trade globalization.

The universal global patent standard is "Patent Cooperation Treaty" (PCT) signed in Washington in 1970, which was amended in 1979 and 2001, respectively. As of October 2, 2019, 153 countries and regions in the world have signed the treaty, which is the most significant sign of progress in the field of global patents (the official website of WIPO: www.wipo.int). The treaty provides detailed regulations and constraints on global cooperation among signatory countries and plays a crucial role in promoting global patent cooperation. China entered the treaty in January 1994, which laid a foundation for the worldwide cooperation of China's patents.

PCT patent is to meet the provisions of the Patent Cooperation Treaty, first by the patent applicant to its in-charge receiving office, by WIPO's International Bureau for global disclosure and by the global search unit for retrieval. This chapter introduces, compares, and analyzes the PCT patents of the chief five offices and other countries and regions by using the relevant global patent data from the top five offices and WIPO.

5.3 PCT Patent Distribution in Main Countries and Regions

5.3.1 *Distribution of PCT patent applications in main countries and regions*

Table 5.1 shows the number of PCT patent applications in the chief five offices from 2007 to 2019 and the yearly compound growth rate in relevant periods. Table 5.1 indicates that from 2007 to 2019, the number of global PCT patent applications maintained a relatively stable growth rate of slightly more than 4%; China has the biggest increase, with applications rising nearly 10-fold to 58,990, which surpassed the Republic of Korea, Europe, Japan, and the US for the first time in 2010, 2016, 2017 and 2019, respectively, to become the world's largest PCT patent applicant country, demonstrating China's impressive achievements in PCT patents over the past decade. From 2007 to 2019, the number of PCT patent applications in the Republic of Korea doubled the global average annual growth rate as 8.6%, while the average yearly growth rate in Japan also slightly exceeded the global growth rate. Europe's annual growth rate was relatively stable, but it was 1% lower than the global growth rate. The average yearly growth rate of the United States was only 0.5%, slightly more than 10% of the global growth rate, while the number of patent applications from other countries and regions outside of the chief five offices did not increase but declined slightly.

Table 5.1: PCT International Filings by Receiving Offices and Compound Annual Growth Rates (CAGRs) of Filings by Receiving Offices (2007–2019) (Unit: %)

Year \ Region	EPC	Japan	Korea	China	US	Others	Global
2007	26,061	26,935	7,060	5,400	54,595	39,876	159,927
2008	29,494	28,027	7,911	6,081	52,054	39,674	163,241
2009	27,360	29,291	8,025	8,000	46,055	36,671	155,402
2010	28,900	31,523	9,639	12,917	45,228	36,133	164,340
2011	30,893	37,972	10,413	17,471	49,366	36,322	182,437
2012	32,430	42,787	11,787	19,924	52,009	36,315	195,252
2013	32,036	43,075	12,439	22,927	57,678	37,125	205,280
2014	32,902	41,292	13,138	27,088	61,963	37,897	214,280
2015	34,151	43,097	14,593	31,044	57,419	36,551	216,855
2016	35,288	44,495	15,595	44,463	56,665	36,347	232,853
2017	36,619	47,425	15,789	50,657	56,256	36,599	243,345
2018	37,937	48,630	16,990	55,204	55,230	38,539	252,530
2019	37,999	51,652	18,885	60,997	56,230	39,594	265,357
2007–2011 CAGR	4.34	8.96	10.20	34.12	−2.49	−2.31	3.35
2011–2015 CAGR	2.54	3.22	8.80	15.46	3.85	0.16	4.42
2015–2019 CAGR	2.71	4.63	6.66	18.39	−0.52	2.02	5.18
2007–2019	3.19	5.58	8.54	22.39	0.25	−0.06	4.31

Source: Data from 2007 to 2019 are from IP5 statistical report 2019.

According to the data in Table 5.1, it can be calculated that from 2007 to 2019, the proportion of PCT international filings accepted by the leading five offices increased from 75.1% to 85.1% in the world, indicating the importance of the top five offices in global patent management.

5.3.2 *The proportion of PCT patent applications as a percentage of the total patent applications*

Data from the 2011–2018 Patent Report of leading five offices show that PCT patent applications accounted for about 3% of the total patent applications in China from 2006 to 2016, increased from 0.84% to 3.84% in 2017, yet decreased slightly to 3.74% in 2018, while the corresponding percentages in EPC States, US, Japan, Republic of Korea, and other countries and regions averaged 20%, 15%, 12%, 6%, and 8% in the same period (Report of Top Five Offices IP5, 2019, Figure 5.1). This implies that the proportion of PCT patent applications in China is the lowest. Most of the Chinese patents are applied domestically, while the patents applied and granted in China are only valid domestically, and it is difficult to play a role in the global market or even to replace foreign patents in China.

5.3.3 *Comparison of proportions of PCT patent granted by five offices*

Figure 5.4 of the 2019 reports of the principal five offices gives the proportions of PCT patents granted by the five patent offices from 2009 to 2019. Figure 5.4 shows that EPC-granted ratio grew steadily by 12% from 53% in 2009 to 65% in 2019; Japan-granted ratio grew steadily by 13% from 12% in 2009 to 25% in 2019; the US-granted ratio grew steadily by 10% from 11% in 2009 to 21% in 2019; Korea-granted ratio grew steadily by 3% from 17% in 2009 to 20% in 2019; and China-granted ratio declined steadily by 13% from 25% in 2009 to 12% in 2019.

5.3.4 *PCT patents granted by five offices*

Table 5.2 gives the total PCT patents granted by each patent office from 2009 to 2019. This table shows that despite the low yearly growth rates of PCT patents granted, the EPO has by far been the patent office that grants the largest number of PCT patents in the past decade, followed by JPO and USPTO. Although the number of PCT patents granted by CNIPA has been smaller than the above three offices, the CAGR of 22.05% was the highest from 2009 to 2014, and despite the lower CAGR of 6.20% between 2014 and 2019, the number of PCT patents granted by CNIPA is expected to surpass USPTO in the next decade or so.

The number of PCT patents granted by each office in Table 5.2 includes the PCT patents granted to overseas patent applicants within its jurisdiction as well as to domestic applicants. As such, from the number of PCT patents in Table 5.2, it is still difficult to see the number of PCT patents originating from the office, or the global competitiveness of

Table 5.2: PCT Patents Granted by and CAGRs of PCT Patents Granted in Five Offices (2009–2019)

Year \ Office	EPO	JPO	KIPO	CNIPA	USPTO
2009	14,501	3,515	1,364	2,000	5,066
2010	16,184	4,413	1,639	2,842	5,880
2011	17,609	6,076	1,770	3,494	6,911
2012	18,161	7,702	2,255	3,985	8,321
2013	18,581	8,615	2,363	4,585	9,805
2014	19,741	9,084	2,496	5,418	11,153
2015	21,174	10,343	2,919	5,277	10,910
2016	22,584	10,234	2,963	7,559	10,766
2017	23,541	11,198	3,118	7,105	11,253
2018	24,659	11,671	3,398	6,624	11,046
2019	24,699	12,945	3,777	7,320	11,584
CAGR from 2009 to 2014	6.36	20.91	12.84	22.05	17.10
CAGR from 2014 to 2019	4.58	7.34	8.64	6.20	0.76

Source: Calculated using the proportions data of Figure 5.4 PCT Activity-Receiving Office data of the 2019 reports of the principal five offices, www.fiveipoffices.org.

science and technology cannot be represented by PCT patents of each office.

5.4 Patent Family Introduction

The number of PCT patents granted by offices shown in Table 5.2 cannot give us comparative competitiveness of each office in science and technology, as shown earlier. All related PCT data in the 2019 and earlier yearly reports cannot give us necessary number of PCT patents originated from and granted by each office to compare the competitiveness of each office in science and technology. However, the annual reports of five offices give us much more detailed data of patent families than PCT patents, such data provide us with good sources to compare relative competitiveness of each office in science and technology.

5.4.1 *A brief introduction of patent family*

A patent family is a set of interrelated subsequent patent applications for priority claim in other regions, based on priority claim of an earlier application. It means when filing for a patent for the first time or soon after, the claim of priority is accepted and registered. After that, the patent is applied for and granted by different patent offices abroad. Patent family is not only recognized domestically but also abroad, which is important to protect the exportation products of the exclusive claimant. Patent family data of the principal five offices and other countries and regions, published by the top five offices and WIPO since 2000, are not only much more detailed than PCT patent data of the same period but also with specific data flows of subsequent filings of bloc of origin from which priority is claimed, such data provide us with valuable data to support the change in global competitiveness in science and technology of main patent offices.

5.4.2 *First filing distribution of patent families*

Crucial data of all the yearly reports of the five offices provide the first filings in "bloc of origin from which priority is claimed" from EPC, Japan, Korea, US, China, others, and global total. Table 5.3 gives the first filings of each bloc from 2000 to 2015. Table 5.3 shows that Japan and US had remained in the principal two highest positions in first filings from 2000 to 2008; China replaced US as the second bloc in first filings in 2009, and China surpassed Japan with the highest number of first filings of patent families in 2010, and China's first filing number reached the highest level of 965.137 thousand, or 52.3% of global total first filings in 2015, indicating the steady growth of patent families in China.

5.4.3 *Flows to subsequent filings in any other blocs*

Flows to subsequent filings of each bloc in any other blocs and in any other in the five blocs include critical data for patent families. Table 5.3 gives such data for each bloc from 2000 to 2015 and the corresponding average yearly growth rates in three consecutive 4-year periods from 2003 to 2015. Table 5.3 shows that the US and Japan had remained in the leading two positions in subsequent filings from 2000 to 2015 with the only exception of 2004 when the Japanese number of 75,416 slightly

Table 5.3: Distribution of First Filings and Flows to Subsequent Filings of Each Bloc from Which Priority is Claimed of Patent Families (2000–2015) (Unit: %)

Year/ Origin of Priority	First Filings in Origin	Flows to Subsequent Filings in Any Other Region	Flows to Subsequent Filings in Any Other Top Five Offices	Patent Families of Five Blocs	Percentages of Patent Families in Five Offices	Patent Families of Five Offices/ First Filings
2000						
EPC	130,928	58,399	47,383	3,803	22.93	2.90
Japan	384,201	65,455	63,406	6,263	37.77	1.63
Korea	72,753	7,872	6,961	1,229	7.41	1.69
US	161,786	79,190	53,823	4,971	29.97	3.07
China	25,261	2,093	852	36	0.22	0.14
Others	53,930	9,034	9,034	282	1.70	0.52
Global	828,859	222,043	181,459	16,584	100.00	2.00
2001						
EPC	120,050	52,525	47,801	5,470	23.20	4.56
Japan	382,815	63,664	62,596	8,711	36.95	2.28
Korea	73,546	8,504	8,216	1,491	6.32	2.03
US	174,979	73,575	54,794	7,417	31.46	4.24
China	29,959	1,173	1,057	78	0.33	0.26
Others	66,078	10,040	10,040	410	1.74	0.62
Global	847,427	209,481	184,504	23,577	100.00	2.78
2002						
EPC	118,120	59,140	47,406	6,392	23.36	5.41
Japan	365,204	67,674	64,815	9,666	35.33	2.65
Korea	76,440	11,518	10,329	2,060	7.53	2.69
US	179,642	81,695	57,576	8,723	31.88	4.86
China	39,671	2,111	1,418	125	0.46	0.32
Others	60,141	11,656	11,656	397	1.45	0.66
Global	839,218	233,794	193,200	27,363	100.00	3.26
2003						
EPC	125,129	50,308	47,340	6,928	22.94	5.54
Japan	358,184	70,118	68,532	10,013	33.16	2.80

Table 5.3: (*Continued*)

Year/ Origin of Priority	First Filings in Origin	Flows to Subsequent Filings in Any Other Region	Flows to Subsequent Filings in Any Other Top Five Offices	Patent Families of Five Blocs	Percentages of Patent Families in Five Offices	Patent Families of Five Offices/ First Filings
Korea	90,165	14,965	14,425	2,863	9.48	3.18
US	184,758	71,973	59,690	9,839	32.58	5.33
China	56,637	2,337	2,028	148	0.49	0.26
Others	58,298	13,157	13,157	409	1.35	0.70
Global	873,171	222,858	205,172	30,200	100.00	3.46
2004						
EPC	127,112	50,475	48,823	6,841	21.94	5.38
Japan	362,342	75,416	74,297	9,747	31.26	2.69
Korea	105,027	18,839	18,722	3,130	10.04	2.98
US	185,008	74,343	64,214	10,880	34.90	5.88
China	65,586	3,063	2,990	153	0.49	0.23
Others	53,106	13,325	13,325	426	1.37	0.80
Global	898,181	235,465	222,375	31,177	100.00	3.47
2005						
EPC	126,652	50,381	48,634	7,021	21.35	5.54
Japan	359,382	76,031	74,631	9,724	29.57	2.71
Korea	121,942	22,091	21,920	3,136	9.54	2.57
US	202,776	79,686	68,854	12,307	37.43	6.07
China	93,172	5,347	5,258	233	0.71	0.25
Others	50,285	14,885	14,885	460	1.40	0.91
Global	954,209	248,421	234,182	32,881	100.00	3.45
2006						
EPC	129,229	50,308	48,206	6,438	20.75	4.98
Japan	336,013	75,179	73,735	9,533	30.72	2.84
Korea	125,249	21,674	21,481	2,881	9.28	2.30
US	215,904	80,393	68,023	11,513	37.10	5.33
China	121,968	5,987	5,815	270	0.87	0.22
Others	67,018	15,346	15,346	395	1.27	0.59
Global	995,381	248,887	232,606	31,030	100.00	3.12

(*Continued*)

Table 5.3: (*Continued*)

Year/ Origin of Priority	First Filings in Origin	Flows to Subsequent Filings in Any Other Region	Flows to Subsequent Filings in Any Other Top Five Offices	Patent Families of Five Blocs	Percentages of Patent Families in Five Offices	Patent Families of Five Offices/ First Filings
2007						
EPC	131,364	49,715	47,406	6,085	21.44	4.63
Japan	321,375	74,495	72,885	8,278	29.17	2.58
Korea	128,438	21,101	20,904	2,366	8.34	1.84
US	234,043	79,992	67,427	10,916	38.47	4.66
China	152,299	7,794	7,585	367	1.29	0.24
Others	54,347	15,231	15,231	363	1.28	0.67
Global	1,021,866	248,328	231,438	28,375	100.00	2.78
2008						
EPC	132,401	48,635	46,771	6,704	22.30	5.06
Japan	317,528	70,509	69,208	7,794	25.92	2.45
Korea	126,691	18,824	18,652	2,057	6.84	1.62
US	223,045	77,292	66,396	12,700	42.24	5.69
China	194,005	9,129	8,967	393	1.31	0.20
Others	108,544	15,949	15,949	419	1.39	0.39
Global	1,102,214	240,338	225,943	30,067	100.00	2.73
2009						
EPC	132,568	49,097	46,894	7,113	21.75	5.37
Japan	282,359	67,726	66,431	8,477	25.92	3.00
Korea	126,988	19,318	19,078	2,343	7.16	1.85
US	213,093	77,308	66,751	13,560	41.46	6.36
China	228,456	11,448	11,191	706	2.16	0.31
Others	90,607	15,911	15,911	505	1.54	0.56
Global	1,074,071	240,808	226,256	32,704	100.00	3.04
2010						
EPC	117,916	50,534	48,308	6,600	19.93	5.60
Japan	276,156	76,326	74,517	9,117	27.54	3.30
Korea	131,461	22,172	21,948	2,813	8.50	2.14

Table 5.3: (*Continued*)

Year/ Origin of Priority	First Filings in Origin	Flows to Subsequent Filings in Any Other Region	Flows to Subsequent Filings in Any Other Top Five Offices	Patent Families of Five Blocs	Percentages of Patent Families in Five Offices	Patent Families of Five Offices/ First Filings
US	227,907	82,419	71,275	13,281	40.11	5.83
China	291,960	12,888	12,513	806	2.43	0.28
Others	75,585	17,434	17,434	491	1.48	0.65
Global	1,120,985	261,773	245,995	33,108	100.00	2.95
2011						
EPC	124,435	51,752	49,092	6,642	19.39	5.34
Japan	271,683	78,342	76,273	8,755	25.57	3.22
Korea	137,671	22,108	21,842	3,187	9.31	2.31
US	231,630	89,050	77,162	14,048	41.02	6.06
China	413,540	15,596	14,621	971	2.84	0.23
Others	71,808	19,068	19,068	643	1.88	0.90
Global	1,250,767	275,916	258,058	34,246	100.00	2.74
2012						
EPC	126,222	51,911	49,901	6,659	19.64	5.28
Japan	269,132	77,264	75,116	8,322	24.54	3.09
Korea	147,694	25,093	24,858	3,183	9.39	2.16
US	250,617	94,176	81,802	13,985	41.24	5.58
China	533,245	19,304	18,111	1,181	3.48	0.22
Others	80,343	20,022	20,022	581	1.71	0.72
Global	1,407,253	287,770	269,810	33,911	100.00	2.41
2013						
EPC	127,188	53,772	51,849	6,791	19.80	5.34
Japan	252,391	74,632	72,394	7,498	21.86	2.97
Korea	159,248	29,484	29,171	2,891	8.43	1.82
US	264,923	100,769	87,721	15,104	44.03	5.70
China	702,013	21,089	19,706	1,548	4.51	0.22
Others	88,645	19,531	19,531	471	1.37	0.53
Global	1,594,408	299,277	280,372	34,303	100.00	2.15

(*Continued*)

Table 5.3: (*Continued*)

Year/ Origin of Priority	First Filings in Origin	Flows to Subsequent Filings in Any Other Region	Flows to Subsequent Filings in Any Other Top Five Offices	Patent Families of Five Blocs	Percentages of Patent Families in Five Offices	Patent Families of Five Offices/ First Filings
2014						
EPC	128,438	54,952	53,253	7,051	20.91	5.49
Japan	245,343	74,823	72,651	7,547	22.39	3.08
Korea	163,185	29,828	29,522	2,743	8.14	1.68
US	260,984	93,209	81,678	13,830	41.02	5.30
China	798,074	23,054	22,003	1,977	5.86	0.25
Others	84,315	19,369	19,369	566	1.68	0.67
Global	1,680,339	295,235	278,476	33,714	100.00	2.01
2015						
EPC	127,357	54,285	51,632	6,964	21.46	5.47
Japan	237,574	70,957	68,662	7,027	21.66	2.96
Korea	166,376	29,634	29,362	2,703	8.33	1.62
US	260,274	94,229	82,686	13,175	40.61	5.06
China	965,137	25,107	22,916	2,050	6.32	0.21
Others	88,691	19,442	19,442	527	1.62	0.59
Global	1,845,409	293,654	274,700	32,446	100.00	1.76
2003–2007 CAGR	**First Filings**	**Any Other Region**	**Any Other Five Offices**	**Patent Family of Five Offices**	**Average Annual Percentage Change**	**Average Annual Change of Patent Family of Five Offices/ First Filings**
EPC	1.22	−0.30	0.03	−3.19	−1.00	−0.05
Japan	−2.67	1.53	1.55	−4.65	−0.29	−0.33
Korea	9.25	8.97	9.72	−4.65	1.47	−0.17
US	6.09	2.68	3.09	2.63	0.20	−0.01
China	28.06	35.14	39.07	25.49	−0.02	−0.01

Table 5.3: (*Continued*)

2003–2007 CAGR	First Filings	Any Other Region	Any Other Five Offices	Patent Family of Five Offices	Average Annual Percentage Change	Average Annual Change of Patent Family of Five Offices/ First Filings
Others	−1.74	3.73	3.73	−2.94	0.00	−0.17
Global	4.01	2.74	3.06	−1.55	0.00	0.00
2007–2011 CAGR						
EPC	−1.35	1.01	0.88	2.21	−0.51	0.18
Japan	−4.11	1.27	1.14	1.41	−0.90	0.16
Korea	1.75	1.17	1.10	7.73	0.24	0.12
US	−0.26	2.72	3.43	6.51	0.64	0.35
China	28.37	18.94	17.83	27.54	0.39	0.00
Others	7.21	5.78	5.78	15.37	0.15	0.06
Global	5.18	2.67	2.76	4.81	0.00	−0.01
2011–2015 CAGR						
EPC	0.58	1.20	1.27	1.19	0.52	0.03
Japan	−3.30	−2.44	−2.59	−5.35	−0.98	−0.07
Korea	4.85	7.60	7.68	−4.03	−0.24	−0.17
US	2.96	1.42	1.74	−1.59	−0.10	−0.25
China	23.60	12.64	11.89	20.54	0.87	−0.01
Others	5.42	0.49	0.49	−4.85	−0.06	−0.08
Global	10.21	1.57	1.57	−1.34	0.00	−0.24

Source: The 2019 reports of the top five offices, www.fiveipoffices.org.

surpassed the US number of 74,343; EPC states, Korea, and China remained in third, fourth, and fifth positions in subsequent filings from 2000 to 2015.

It is noticeable that China replaced the USA and Japan as the second and largest bloc of first filings in 2009 and 2010, respectively, and China's first filings reached the highest level of 956,137 in 2015, or 52.3% of world's total first filings in the same year, indicating a steady growth of patent families in China.

5.5 Patent Families and Patent Internationalization

The number of PCT patents granted by offices in Table 5.2 cannot give us comparative competitiveness of each office in science and technology as shown earlier, as all relevant PCT data in the 2019 and earlier yearly reports cannot give us the necessary number of PCT patents originated from and granted by each office to compare the competitiveness of each office in science and technology. However, the annual reports of five offices give us a much more detailed data of patent families than PCT patents, such data provide us good sources to compare relative competitiveness of each office in science and technology.

5.5.1 *Brief introduction of the number of patent families in main patent blocs*

Table 5.3 gives us the number of patent families originating in EPC states, Japan, Korea, the US, China, and other countries and regions from which priority is claimed and the patent families/first filing ratios of each bloc from 2000 to 2015. As Table 5.3 contains much information, Table 5.4 concentrates on the numbers of patent families of each bloc from 2000 to 2015 and estimates similar data for years from 2016 to 2020 based on historical data.

Table 5.4 shows that Japan had the highest number of patent families from 2000 to 2003, and its leading position was replaced by the US from 2004; EPC remained in third position in the number of patent families from 2000 to 2015. EPC states may replace Japan as the second bloc in patent families because Japanese parent families have been changing at lower average yearly growth rates. Korea remained in fourth position in patent families. The number of Chinese patent families was not only the lowest of all other four blocs from 2000 to 2015 but was also lower than the rest of the world from 2000 to 2006, indicating how much work needs to be done to catch up in this area.

Table 5.4: Distribution of Global Patent Families and the Average Annual Growth Rates of Patent Families in Each Office (2000–2019) (Unit: %)

Year/Bloc of origin from which priority is claimed	**EPC**	**Japan**	**Korea**	**US**	**China**	**Others**	**World**
2000	3,803	6,263	1,229	4,971	36	282	16,584
2001	5,470	8,711	1,491	7,417	78	410	23,577
2002	6,392	9,666	2,060	8,723	125	397	27,363
2003	6,928	10,013	2,863	9,839	148	409	30,200
2004	6,841	9,747	3,130	10,880	153	426	31,177
2005	7,021	9,724	3,136	12,307	233	460	32,881
2006	6,438	9,533	2,881	11,513	270	395	31,030
2007	6,085	8,278	2,366	10,916	367	363	28,375
2008	6,704	7,794	2,057	12,700	393	419	30,067
2009	7,113	8,477	2,343	13,560	706	505	32,704
2010	6,600	9,117	2,813	13,281	806	491	33,108
2011	6,642	8,755	3,187	14,048	971	643	34,246
2012	6,659	8,322	3,183	13,985	1,181	581	33,911
2013	6,791	7,498	2,891	15,104	1,548	471	34,303
2014	7,051	7,547	2,743	13,830	1,977	566	33,714
2015	6,964	7,027	2,703	13,175	2,050	527	32,446
2016*	7,047	6,651	2,594	12,965	2,414	501	32,172
2017*	7,131	6,295	2,489	12,759	2,842	477	31,993
2018*	7,216	5,959	2,389	12,556	3,346	454	31,919
2019*	7,302	5,640	2,293	12,356	3,939	432	31,962
2020*	7,389	5,338	2,200	12,160	4,638	411	32,135
2003–2007 CAGR	−3.19	−4.65	−4.65	2.63	25.49	−2.94	−1.55
2007–2011 CAGR	2.21	1.41	7.73	6.51	27.54	15.37	4.81
2011–2015 CAGR	1.19	−5.35	−4.03	−1.59	20.54	−4.85	−1.34
2015–2019* CAGR	1.19	−5.35	−4.03	−1.59	15.32	−4.85	−0.38

Source: The 2019 reports of the top five offices, www.fiveipoffices.org; the data for EPC States, Japan, US, and Korea from 2016 to 2020 are estimated using the compound annual growth rates from 2011 to 2015; data for China are estimated using the CAGR of 20.54% from 2011 to 2015 multiplied by the ratio, i.e., 20.54%/27.54% = 74.59% of the CAGR from 2011 to 2015 to the compound annual growth rate from 2007 to 2011 in order to maintain the declining growth pattern in the past 8 years prior to 2015. *Data from 2016 to 2020 are estimated using related CAGRs from 2003 to 2015.

5.5.2 *Ratios of patent family over first filings*

Table 5.3 gives the ratio of patent families over number of first filings in each bloc from 2000 to 2015. Table 5.3 shows that from 2000 to 2015, the proportion of the number of top five office family patents as a proportion of the number of first filings from Europe and US continued to increase from more than 3% to more than 5% and then kept at a high level of more than 5% without much change most of time. Japan grew from 1.63% to 3.30% during 2000–2010, yet it decreased to below 3% during 2010–2015. Republic of Korea grew from 1.69% in 2000 to 3.18% in 2003, and it decreased to 1.62% in 2015, almost the same as in 2000. The corresponding ratios in China has been the lowest around 0.2% and is still on a declining path, implying that the quality of first filings needs to be improved significantly in China.

5.5.3 *Evolution of patent internationalization in each bloc of patent origin*

Patent families are accepted worldwide and internationally, thus, like currency globalization, patent globalization of different blocs may be defined as the proportion of patent families in a bloc as a proportion of global patent families. Using the data from Table 5.4, we can find patent globalization of each bloc, and Table 5.5 gives us the results.

Table 5.5 shows that the US has maintained the leading position in patent globalization from 2004 and Japan and EPC have maintained the second and third positions from 2005 to 2015. These top three patent family originators had monopolized over 90% of world patent families from 2000 to 2002 and between 83% and 90% from 2003 to 2015, indicating the monopolistic positions of these regions in world patent families and in global technology.

5.5.4 *Relatively stable state of major patent originators*

Table 5.3 shows that average yearly growth rates of first filings, flows to subsequent filings in any bloc and in any other five blocs in EPC states, Japan, and the US were all at the lower single-digit levels, and even the average annual growth rates in Korea were in high single-digit levels, indicating that patent families in the leading three global patent originators basically reached a relatively stable growth trend.

Table 5.5: Patent Internationalization in Each Bloc (2000–2020)

Year \ Bloc of Origin from Which Priority is Claimed	EPC States (%)	Japan (%)	Korea (%)	US (%)	China (%)	Others (%)	Global Total (%)
2000	22.93	37.77	7.41	29.97	0.22	1.70	100.00
2001	23.20	36.95	6.32	31.46	0.33	1.74	100.00
2002	23.36	35.33	7.53	31.88	0.46	1.45	100.00
2003	22.94	33.16	9.48	32.58	0.49	1.35	100.00
2004	21.94	31.26	10.04	34.90	0.49	1.37	100.00
2005	21.35	29.57	9.54	37.43	0.71	1.40	100.00
2006	20.75	30.72	9.28	37.10	0.87	1.27	100.00
2007	21.44	29.17	8.34	38.47	1.29	1.28	100.00
2008	22.30	25.92	6.84	42.24	1.31	1.39	100.00
2009	21.75	25.92	7.16	41.46	2.16	1.54	100.00
2010	19.93	27.54	8.50	40.11	2.43	1.48	100.00
2011	19.39	25.57	9.31	41.02	2.84	1.88	100.00
2012	19.64	24.54	9.39	41.24	3.48	1.71	100.00
2013	19.80	21.86	8.43	44.03	4.51	1.37	100.00
2014	20.91	22.39	8.14	41.02	5.86	1.68	100.00
2015	21.46	21.66	8.33	40.61	6.32	1.62	100.00
2016*	21.90	20.67	8.06	40.30	7.50	1.56	100.00
2017*	22.29	19.68	7.78	39.88	8.88	1.49	100.00
2018*	22.61	18.67	7.48	39.34	10.48	1.42	100.00
2019*	22.84	17.65	7.17	38.66	12.32	1.35	100.00
2020*	22.99	16.61	6.85	37.84	14.43	1.28	100.00

Source: Calculated using data from Table 5.4. *Data from 2016 to 2020 are estimated using related previous CAGRs from 2003 to 2015.

5.5.5 *Comparison with China's patent internalization*

Table 5.4 shows that although the number of patent families originating in China was the lowest of all given offices from 2000 to 2015, the number increased by 3.11 times (the compound average yearly growth rate was 60.20%) from 36 in 2000 to 148 in 2003, and the number increased

1.48 times (the CAGR declined to 25.49%) from 148 in 2003 to 367 in 2007, surpassing the number of other countries and regions outside the five offices for the first time. The compound annual average growth rate grew slightly to 27.54% from 2007 to 2011 as shown in Table 5.4, and the compound yearly average growth rate declined slightly to 20.54% thereafter, or 74.58% of the previous 4-year CAGR from 2011 to 2015, as shown in Table 5.4; with the assumption that the compound yearly average growth rate declined at the same ratio of 74.58% of the 2011–2015 average yearly growth rate of 20.54% or 15.32% from 2015 to 2019. The number of patent families originated in China will grow to 2,842 in 2017, surpassing the corresponding number originated in Korea for the first time.

Table 5.5 shows that the patent globalization of 8.88% in China would surpass the internationalization of 7.78% of Korea for the first time in 2017, and it would surpass 10% to 10.48% in 2018. China's patent globalization is expected to surpass the Japanese patent internationalization in 2023 with the same declining accumulated average annual growth rate ratio of 74.58% assumption from 2019 to 2023. The steady growth of Chinese patent families is supported by the steady growth of R&D of Chinese companies in recent years, as shown in Chapter 12.

5.5.6 *Average quality of patent families*

Patent globalization results in Table 5.4 give us good estimations of the competitiveness of science and technology of various regions, yet they did not take into consideration a very vital issue — average quality of patent families of each bloc varies significantly across various patent blocs or patent originators. The results in Table 5.4 will be significantly different if we take the factor of average quality of patent families into consideration. Chapter 7 will analyze such issues using IP usage exports and imports data.

5.6 More on Distribution of Subsequent Filings

Table 5.4 gives us reasonably good results of the total number of patent families of foremost patent originators, yet all reports of five of the leading offices do not give us the exact distribution of how patent families of various patent originators distribute across other originators in the world, making it difficult for us to know how different blocs depend on other regions in patent families. However, reports of five offices give us specific data of first filings in blocs of origin leading to priority claims in filings in various offices, from which we can obtain critical information of how patent families of each bloc are distributed around the world.

Besides the flows to subsequent filings in any other blocs and any other five blocs given in Table 5.3, yearly reports of the chief five offices and WIPO also provide us with the subsequent filings in each of EPC states, Japan, Korea, US, China, and other countries and regions. Such data provide valuable information of how patent families are distributed in various blocs. Table 5.6 lists the main distribution of subsequent filings of each bloc from 2000 to 2015.

5.6.1 *Distribution of flows to subsequent filings from top four blocs*

Table 5.6 shows that flows to subsequent filings from EPC states, Japan, and the US to other blocs maintained average annual growth rates of 0.62%, −0.41%, and 1.36% from 2003 to 2015, like the average yearly growth rates of first filings, flows to subsequent filings of these three blocs, indicating the chief three blocs of patent originators reached stable growth stages.

It is worth noting that from 2003 to 2015, flows to subsequent filings of the Republic of Korea maintained higher average growth rates than the chief three patent originators with middle level single-digit average annual growth rates, implying that Korea also reached stable growth rates in flows to subsequent filings.

5.6.2 *Distribution of flows to subsequent filings from China*

Table 5.6 indicates that from 2003 to 2015, the number of flows to subsequent filings from China maintained a steady growth pattern with a two-digit average yearly growth rate. Yet, average annual growth rates declined steadily from middle two-digit to low two-digit rates from 2003 to 2015, indicating that growth rate decreases with high base filing number. Even with the declining growth pattern, average yearly growth rates of flows to subsequent filings may maintain low double-digit levels for another 4-year period from 2015 to 2019.

Table 5.6: More on the Distribution of Flows to Subsequent Filings of Each Bloc from Which Priority is Claimed of Patent Families (2000–2015) (Unit: %)

2000 Bloc	**EPC States**	**Japan**	**Korea**	**US**	**China**	**Others**	**Total**
EPC States	—	23,917	5,778	45,060	12,138	37,243	124,136
Japan	33,466	—	15,151	59,105	17,220	21,174	146,116
Korea	2,328	3,947	—	6,079	2,623	3,208	18,185
US	49,639	31,667	8,631	—	13,726	65,209	168,872
China	378	246	84	708	—	1,633	3,049
Others	4,013	2,348	468	8,012	1,295	—	16,136
Global	89,824	62,125	30,112	118,964	47,002	128,467	476,494
2001	**EPC States**	**Japan**	**Korea**	**US**	**China**	**Others**	**Total**
EPC States	—	22,867	7,946	45,522	13,580	25,324	115,239
Japan	31,501	—	18,120	57,992	22,618	18,523	148,754
Korea	2,688	4,396	—	7,425	3,411	2,179	20,099
US	50,359	31,583	11,029	—	16,209	55,313	164,493
China	480	308	120	934	—	432	2,274
Others	3,938	2,376	610	9,170	1,312	—	17,406
Global	88,966	61,530	37,825	121,043	57,130	101,771	468,265
2002	**EPC States**	**Japan**	**Korea**	**US**	**China**	**Others**	**Total**
EPC States	—	22,792	8,599	44,936	16,876	40,312	133,515
Japan	31,314	—	18,816	59,478	28,972	24,334	162,914
Korea	3,401	5,333	—	9,494	5,285	4,331	27,844
US	52,161	32,702	12,716	—	20,869	67,862	186,310
China	632	413	199	1,203	—	1,348	3,795
Others	4,052	2,606	697	10,701	1,572	—	19,628
Global	91,560	63,846	41,027	125,812	73,574	138,187	534,006
2003	**EPC States**	**Japan**	**Korea**	**US**	**China**	**Others**	**Total**
EPC States	—	22,634	9,624	44,340	19,140	22,011	117,749
Japan	32,076	—	20,510	62,049	33,122	19,744	167,501
Korea	4,863	6,915	—	13,168	7,571	3,677	36,194
US	53,327	34,209	15,117	—	24,386	48,440	175,479

Table 5.6: (*Continued*)

2003	EPC States	Japan	Korea	US	China	Others	Total
China	875	523	254	1,711	—	877	4,240
Others	4,050	2,619	839	12,051	1,600	—	21,159
Global	95,191	66,900	46,344	133,319	85,819	94,749	522,322

2004	EPC States	Japan	Korea	US	China	Others	Total
EPC States	—	23,072	9,523	45,119	22,004	20,330	120,048
Japan	33,411	—	21,087	67,539	35,919	19,204	177,160
Korea	6,302	8,182	—	16,426	9,875	3,444	44,229
US	56,793	36,406	16,412	—	29,128	46,876	185,615
China	1,161	676	279	2,498	—	491	5,105
Others	4,013	2,656	977	12,234	1,641	—	21,521
Global	101,681	70,993	48,278	143,819	98,567	90,345	553,683

2005	EPC States	Japan	Korea	US	China	Others	Total
EPC States	—	23,023	9,912	44,954	23,197	21,150	122,236
Japan	31,383	—	20,888	67,577	35,215	18,538	173,601
Korea	7,278	8,555	—	19,725	10,810	3,941	50,309
US	60,421	37,645	18,859	—	32,984	50,440	200,349
China	2,018	1,068	456	4,523	—	701	8,766
Others	4,447	2,883	1,106	13,674	1,817	—	23,927
Global	105,547	73,174	51,221	150,453	104,023	94,770	579,188

2006	EPC States	Japan	Korea	US	China	Others	Total
EPC States	—	21,060	9,132	44,295	23,325	21,124	118,936
Japan	30,421	—	20,481	66,674	35,332	17,789	170,697
Korea	6,987	7,257	—	19,715	9,501	3,381	46,841
US	59,147	34,476	18,158	—	33,447	50,669	195,897
China	2,240	1,175	496	4,955	—	796	9,662
Others	4,205	2,636	1,074	14,035	1,744	—	23,694
Global	103,000	66,604	49,341	149,674	103,349	93,759	565,727

(*Continued*)

Table 5.6: (*Continued*)

2007	**EPC States**	**Japan**	**Korea**	**US**	**China**	**Others**	**Total**
EPC States	—	18,637	8,522	43,451	23,384	20,901	114,895
Japan	28,510	—	18,608	65,054	36,025	17,319	165,516
Korea	6,290	6,054	—	19,023	8,355	3,148	42,870
US	57,728	31,409	17,304	—	34,923	49,427	190,791
China	2,536	1,407	722	6,761	—	1,023	12,449
Others	3,992	2,312	981	13,987	1,752	—	23,024
Global	99,056	59,819	46,137	148,276	104,439	91,818	549,545
2008	**EPC States**	**Japan**	**Korea**	**US**	**China**	**Others**	**Total**
EPC States	—	17,986	9,085	42,610	25,081	20,718	115,480
Japan	26,146	—	16,640	60,981	34,894	15,724	154,385
Korea	5,112	5,097	—	16,868	7,055	2,601	36,733
US	56,457	30,865	18,770	—	38,101	47,669	191,862
China	2,787	1,606	809	8,194	—	1,050	14,446
Others	4,164	2,240	997	14,683	1,946	—	24,030
Global	94,666	57,794	46,301	143,336	107,077	87,762	536,936
2009	**EPC States**	**Japan**	**Korea**	**US**	**China**	**Others**	**Total**
EPC States	—	17,416	9,862	42,358	27,172	21,517	118,325
Japan	26,777	—	16,733	57,618	37,949	16,096	155,173
Korea	5,865	5,124	—	17,252	7,826	2,598	38,665
US	57,188	30,690	19,932	—	40,366	47,903	196,079
China	4,343	2,378	1,177	10,162	—	1,745	19,805
Others	4,542	2,245	1,059	14,636	2,175	—	24,657
Global	98,715	57,853	48,763	142,026	115,488	89,859	552,704
2010	**EPC States**	**Japan**	**Korea**	**US**	**China**	**Others**	**Total**
EPC States	—	16,687	9,869	42,847	28,966	21,814	120,183
Japan	29,759	—	18,651	63,465	46,516	18,607	176,998
Korea	6,823	5,753	—	20,106	9,192	2,950	44,824
US	60,003	30,705	20,146	—	44,364	49,256	204,474

Table 5.6: (*Continued*)

2010	EPC States	Japan	Korea	US	China	Others	Total
China	5,089	2,641	1,369	11,198	—	2,234	22,531
Others	4,716	2,259	1,192	15,707	3,358	—	27,232
Global	106,390	58,045	51,227	153,323	132,396	94,861	596,242
2011	**EPC States**	**Japan**	**Korea**	**US**	**China**	**Others**	**Total**
EPC States	—	16,510	9,900	43,307	30,175	21,783	121,675
Japan	30,411	—	18,505	63,640	48,706	19,680	180,942
Korea	7,200	5,717	—	19,828	9,885	3,051	45,681
US	64,979	31,882	21,593	—	48,836	51,273	218,563
China	5,956	2,841	1,574	13,323	—	5,619	29,313
Others	4,893	2,385	1,266	16,352	6,455	—	31,351
Global	113,439	59,335	52,838	156,450	144,057	101,406	627,525
2012	**EPC States**	**Japan**	**Korea**	**US**	**China**	**Others**	**Total**
EPC States	—	15,996	10,022	43,844	30,788	20,012	120,662
Japan	30,296	—	18,164	62,237	47,256	18,997	176,950
Korea	7,783	6,057	—	22,583	11,674	3,415	51,512
US	68,621	32,455	22,595	—	52,715	52,631	229,017
China	7,796	3,504	2,096	16,567	—	6,363	36,326
Others	4,837	2,265	1,250	17,266	6,671	—	32,289
Global	119,333	60,277	54,127	162,497	149,104	101,418	646,756
2013	**EPC States**	**Japan**	**Korea**	**US**	**China**	**Others**	**Total**
EPC States	—	16,779	10,042	46,148	31,996	20,083	125,048
Japan	29,193	—	16,669	60,097	43,821	18,270	168,050
Korea	8,381	5,661	—	26,660	13,153	3,748	57,603
US	73,717	33,980	24,202	—	56,755	55,480	244,134
China	8,350	3,892	2,541	17,775	—	5,805	38,363
Others	4,643	2,359	1,176	16,692	6,421	—	31,291
Global	124,284	62,671	54,630	167,372	152,146	103,386	664,489

(*Continued*)

Table 5.6: (*Continued*)

2014	**EPC States**	**Japan**	**Korea**	**US**	**China**	**Others**	**Total**
EPC States	—	17,168	10,277	47,302	33,186	19,529	127,462
Japan	30,090	—	16,526	60,628	42,929	17,810	167,983
Korea	8,620	5,424	—	26,690	13,992	3,042	57,768
US	67,900	31,225	22,941	—	52,230	50,163	224,459
China	10,181	4,966	3,336	19,754	—	5,600	43,837
Others	4,925	3,321	1,246	16,144	6,472	—	32,108
Global	121,716	62,104	54,326	170,518	148,924	96,144	653,732
2015	**EPC States**	**Japan**	**Korea**	**US**	**China**	**Others**	**Total**
EPC States	—	16,750	10,172	45,637	33,521	20,738	126,818
Japan	28,795	—	15,152	57,141	41,400	17,035	159,523
Korea	8,635	5,530	—	26,253	14,738	3,147	58,303
US	66,990	30,773	3,288	—	54,195	51,060	206,306
China	9,222	4,929	22,009	20,647	—	6,734	63,541
Others	5,250	3,805	1,180	15,938	6,251	—	32,424
Global	118,892	61,787	51,801	165,616	150,105	98,714	646,915
2003–2007 CAGR	**EPC States**	**Japan**	**Korea**	**US**	**China**	**Others**	**Total**
EPC States	—	−4.74	−2.99	−0.51	5.13	−1.29	−0.61
Japan	−2.90	—	−2.40	1.19	2.12	−3.22	−0.30
Korea	6.64	−3.27	—	9.63	2.49	−3.81	4.32
US	2.00	−2.11	3.44	—	9.39	0.51	2.11
China	30.48	28.07	29.85	40.99	—	3.92	30.90
Others	−0.36	−3.07	3.99	3.79	2.29	—	2.13
Global	1.00	−2.76	−0.11	2.69	5.03	−0.78	1.28
2007–2011 CAGR	**EPC States**	**Japan**	**Korea**	**US**	**China**	**Others**	**Total**
EPC States	—	−2.98	3.82	−0.08	6.58	1.04	1.44
Japan	1.63	—	−0.14	−0.55	7.83	3.25	2.25
Korea	3.44	−1.42	—	1.04	4.29	−0.78	1.60

Table 5.6: (*Continued*)

2007–2011 CAGR	**EPC States**	**Japan**	**Korea**	**US**	**China**	**Others**	**Total**
US	3.00	0.37	5.69	—	8.74	0.92	3.46
China	23.79	19.20	21.51	18.48	—	53.09	23.87
Others	5.22	0.78	6.58	3.98	38.54	—	8.02
Global	3.45	−0.20	3.45	1.35	8.37	2.51	3.37
2011–2015 CAGR	**EPC States**	**Japan**	**Korea**	**US**	**China**	**Others**	**Total**
EPC States	—	0.36	0.68	1.32	2.66	−1.22	1.04
Japan	−1.36	—	−4.87	−2.66	−3.98	−3.54	−3.10
Korea	4.65	−0.83	—	7.27	10.50	0.78	6.29
US	0.76	−0.88	−37.53	—	2.64	−0.10	−1.43
China	11.55	14.77	93.37	11.57	—	4.63	21.34
Others	1.78	12.39	−1.74	−0.64	−0.80	—	0.84
Global	1.18	1.02	−0.49	1.43	1.03	−0.67	0.76
2003–2015 CAGR	**EPC States**	**Japan**	**Korea**	**US**	**China**	**Others**	**Total**
EPC States	—	−2.48	0.46	0.24	4.78	−0.50	0.62
Japan	−0.90	—	−2.49	−0.68	1.88	−1.22	−0.41
Korea	4.90	−1.85	—	5.92	5.71	−1.29	4.05
US	1.92	−0.88	−11.94	—	6.88	0.44	1.36
China	21.68	20.56	45.04	23.06	—	18.51	25.31
Others	2.19	3.16	2.88	2.36	12.03	—	3.62
Global	1.87	−0.66	0.93	1.82	4.77	0.34	1.80

Source: The 2019 reports of the top five offices, www.fiveipoffices.org.

5.6.3 *Flows to subsequent filings to China*

Table 5.6 indicates that flows to subsequent filings from Japan to China increased by 18,805 from 17,220 in 2000 to 36,025 in 2007 and flows to subsequent filings from the US to China increased by 21,197 from 13,726 in 2000 to 34,923 in 2007; flows from Japan remained higher than flows from the US in the same period, indicating that Japan was the foremost patent or technology provider to China before the 2008 global financial crisis; flows to subsequent filings from Japan to China increased by 5,375 from 36,025 in 2007 to 41,400 in 2015, and flows to subsequent filings from the US to China increased by 19,272 from 34,923 in 2007 to 54,195 in 2015. Flows from Japan remained less than flows from the US in the same period, indicating that the US replaced Japan as the major patent or technology provider to China after the 2008 global financial crisis; flows to subsequent filing from Japan, EPC states, Korea, and others to China were 41,400, 33,521, 14,738, and 6,251 in 2015, respectively.

Flows to subsequent filing from the US, Japan, and EPC states to China in 2015 consisted of 6.1%, 27.6%, and 22.3% of the total flows to subsequent filings to China, and the accumulated increased flows to subsequent filings from the US, Japan, and EPC states to China from 2001 to 2015 were 37,986, 18,782, and 19,941, representing 40.9%, 20.2%, and 21.4% of the total increased flows to China at 92,975 in the same period. The above data show that the US has played a leading role in providing technology to China, and this leading role is higher than the above percentages with higher weights of US patents than corresponding Japanese and EPC weights in Chapter 7.

5.6.4 *Flows to subsequent filings to other blocs from China*

Table 5.6 indicates that flows to subsequent filings from China to Korea, US, EPC states, Others, and Japan were 22,009, 20,647, 9,222, 6,734, and 4,929 in 2015; the increases in flows to subsequent filings from China to Korea, US, EPC states, others, and Japan were 2,421, 16,841, 7,870, 5,373, and 3,584 from 2001 to 2013; the increased flows to subsequent filings from China to Korea, US, EPC states, others, and Japan were 19,468, 2,872, 872, 929, and 1,037 from 2013 to 2015, indicating that Korea became the most vital receiver of flows to subsequent filings from China during 2013–2015.

5.7 Implications of Total Flows to Subsequent Filings in Major Blocs

Table 5.3 gives us the patent families of the chief five offices and others, but it does not give us patent families of the top five offices in others, yet the flows in subsequent filings of the chief five offices and others provide us with good information of patent families of the top five offices in others and better estimate of the total patent families of chief five offices and others in any other bloc. The purpose of this section is to estimate total patent families of chief five offices and others in any other bloc.

5.7.1 *Top position of the US in total flows to subsequent filings and implications*

Table 5.4 shows that the US has the highest number of patent families in the world, and it is the most attractive marketplace for all foreign patents to enter because of the US market size and its innovative environment of science and technology. Although the US share of total flows to subsequent filings to any other region fell from 35.66% in 2000 to 32.09% in 2015, the accumulative increment of US flows to subsequent filings to any other region increased by 15,039, or 21.00% of the total global accumulative incremental of 71,611, much higher than the corresponding share of Japan at 7.69%, and the accumulative incremental share of EPC states at −5.74% for the same period. This implies that the US, the world's largest importer and consumer market, is also a hotspot for global science and technology innovators. The inflow of many new international patents around the world has stimulated the US to further innovate and lead global science and technology innovation, forming a prosperous cycle of global science and technology innovation with the US at the center and a vital driving force for the US to lead and control global science and technology innovation.

5.7.2 *Second position of China of total flows to subsequent filings and implications*

Table A5.1 in the Appendix also shows that the total flows to subsequent filings to China from all other blocs surpassed Japan and EPC states in 2002 and 2006, respectively, to become the world's third and second largest receiving bloc of subsequent filings of patent families. The share difference between the US and China declined from 5.73% in 2000 to the lowest level of 0.68% in 2011, and the average yearly difference share remained less than 0.9% from 2012 to 2015. The above results imply that China has been viewed as a huge market for technology applications by foreign countries for many years, despite the significant GDP gap between the US, EPC states, and China before 2015 (the US and EPC states' share of world GDP of 24.34% and 22.90% were 9.51% and 8.06% higher than the Chinese share of world GDP of 14.83% in 2015). This not only indicates that China's science and technology level still has room for improvement but also shows the global recognition of China's potential in consumption and economic growth. Meanwhile, it also points out that China's science and technology has high dependence on overseas countries and regions.

It needs to be noted that the share of total flows to subsequent filings into China reached its highest level of 18.36% in 2015, and it remained at the average annual level of 18.31% without much change from 2011 to 2015. The implementation of further opening policies of China to the outside world will likely lead to more flows of subsequent filings of patent families into China in years to come. We may expect that the share of total flows of subsequent filings of patent families into China will surpass that of the US a few years before the Chinese GDP surpasses that of the US.

5.8 Distribution of Patent Families Based on Flows to Subsequent Filings in Major Blocs

The yearly distribution of total patent families of each bloc in Table 5.4 gives us the patent families of each bloc distributed in each of the five blocs and others resulting from flows to subsequent filings in any other of the five blocs, but we still do not know how the flows to subsequent filings in each individual five bloc and others in Table 5.6 affect the patent families in the five blocs and others. The purpose of this section is to estimate the distribution of patent families of each bloc in other blocs to gather necessary information for the mutual dependence of each bloc on other blocs so as to find a good way to measure patent internationalization.

5.8.1 *A simple assumption for estimation*

Table 5.3 shows that patent families of the US in chief five offices were 13,175 and flows of subsequent filings of the US to any other top five offices were 82,686. The ratio of former to latter was 15.93% in 2015. It is reasonable to assume that the ratios of patent families of the US in the chief five offices and others over flows of subsequent filings of the US to any other top five offices and others remain the same as the above at 15.93%, then we can estimate the additional patent families of the US in EPC states, Japan, Korea, China, and others by multiplying the ratio at 15.93% with flows to subsequent filings of the US to each bloc given in Table 5.6 as 10,674, 4,903, 524, 8,636, and 8,136. The sum of these additional patent families of the US and the patent families of the US in each of the chief five offices is 13,175. In Table 5.3, the estimated patent families of the US in EPC states, Japan, Korea, China, and others were 23,849, 18,078, 13,699, 21,811, and 21,311 in 2015, and the total number of patent families of the US is 98,747 in 2015.

5.8.2 *Estimation of patent families of each bloc*

With the same assumption from 2000 to 2014, we can obtain similar results for the US from 2000 to 2014, and we can obtain similar estimated results for other blocs from 2000 to 2015. Results from 2016 to 2020 are estimated using 2015 patent families of each bloc as a base and the compound yearly average growth rate of each bloc from 2003 to 2015 to find the corresponding patent families of each bloc and global total patent families. Table 5.7 gives the results.

5.8.3 *Patent families of the US and other major blocs in China*

Table 5.7 shows that patent families from the US in China was the highest at 24,876, or 47%, of all foreign patent families in China. It was 52,918 in 2013, much higher than the corresponding share of patent families from EPC states at 20.75% and Japan at 22.75% in the same year, or higher than the total share of EPC states and Japan at 43.5%, indicating the importance of the US technology in China. Despite the decline of the US patent families in China from 2013 to 2015, the US share in China remained above 43.5%, implying the deeper relationship between the two chief economies of the world.

5.8.4 *Patent families of China in other blocs*

Table 5.7 shows that patent families of other foremost blocs besides China changed at single-digit rates from 2000 to 2015. Patent families from China to other blocs grew at double-digit rates; What's more, total patent families of China continued growing at a faster average yearly growth rate of 28.09% in the 4-year period from 2007 to 2011 than the corresponding rate of 24.77% for the previous 4-year period from 2003 to 2007, yet the CAGR from 2011 to 2015 of 24.27% was lower than the CAGR of the previous 4-year period from 2007 to 2011, indicating the moderately deaccelerating growth of science and technology in China from 2001 onward.

5.9 Mutual Dependence of Patent Families among Blocs

The estimated results of patent families of each of the five chief offices and others are not only useful to find better measure of patent globalization but also useful to find mutual dependence of patent families among various blocs.

5.9.1 *Definition of dependence of patent families between two blocs*

Table 5.7 shows that the US patent families in Japan were 18,078 in 2015, and Japanese patent families in the US were 12,875 in the same year. Thus, we may define the US independence of patent families from the Japanese patent families or US self-reliance capacity (SRC) of patent families as 18,078/(18,078+12,875) = 58.40%. Put another way, US dependence of patent families on Japanese patent families as 100% − 58.40% = 41.60% or Japanese independence of patent families of US patent families as 12,875/(12,875+18,078) = 41.60%, and Japanese dependence of patent families on US patent families as 100% − 41.60% = 58.40%, indicating the dependence of patent families of Japan on US.

5.9.2 *Mutual dependence of patent families among blocs*

With the above definition of dependence of patent families of one bloc on another, we can find mutual dependence and independence of patent families among blocs from 2000 to 2015. Table 5.8 gives the results, where the x-axis from left to right represents the independence or SRC of one bloc of another bloc of patent families, and the y-axis represents the dependence of one bloc on another bloc of patent families.

Table 5.7: Distribution of Patent Families of Each Bloc in Other Blocs and Related CAGRs (2000–2015)

2000 Bloc	**EPC States**	**Japan**	**Korea**	**US**	**China**	**Others**	**Total**
EPC States	3,803	5,723	4,267	7,420	4,777	7,676	33,665
Japan	9,569	6,263	7,760	12,101	7,964	8,557	52,213
Korea	1,640	1,926	1,229	2,302	1,692	1,956	10,745
US	9,556	7,896	5,768	4,971	6,239	13,336	47,766
China	52	46	40	66	36	157	397
Others	407	355	297	532	322	282	2,196
Global	24,793	22,262	19,336	27,456	20,880	32,034	146,761
2001	**EPC States**	**Japan**	**Korea**	**US**	**China**	**Others**	**Total**
EPC States	5,470	8,087	6,379	10,679	7,024	8,908	37,639
Japan	13,095	8,711	11,233	16,781	11,859	11,437	61,678
Korea	1,979	2,289	1,491	2,838	2,110	1,939	10,707
US	14,234	11,692	8,910	7,417	9,611	17,446	51,864
China	113	101	87	147	78	118	526
Others	571	507	435	784	464	410	2,761
Global	34,946	31,440	28,410	39,045	30,877	39,774	164,718
2002	**EPC States**	**Japan**	**Korea**	**US**	**China**	**Others**	**Total**
EPC States	6,392	9,465	7,551	12,451	8,667	13,410	44,527
Japan	14,336	9,666	12,472	18,536	13,987	13,721	68,997
Korea	2,738	3,124	2,060	3,953	3,114	3,161	14,989
US	16,626	13,677	10,650	8,723	11,885	22,658	61,560
China	181	161	143	231	125	305	841
Others	535	486	421	761	451	397	2,654
Global	40,331	36,406	33,174	45,182	37,783	52,684	192,875
2003	**EPC States**	**Japan**	**Korea**	**US**	**China**	**Others**	**Total**
EPC States	6,928	10,240	8,336	13,417	9,729	10,584	48,651
Japan	14,700	10,013	13,010	19,079	14,852	13,129	71,653
Korea	3,828	4,235	2,863	5,477	4,366	3,700	20,769

(*Continued*)

Table 5.7: (*Continued*)

2003	**EPC States**	**Japan**	**Korea**	**US**	**China**	**Others**	**Total**
US	18,629	15,478	12,331	9,839	13,859	19,848	70,135
China	212	186	167	273	148	235	985
Others	535	490	435	784	459	409	2,703
Global	44,212	40,047	37,022	49,824	42,832	46,750	213,936
2004	**EPC States**	**Japan**	**Korea**	**US**	**China**	**Others**	**Total**
EPC States	6,841	10,074	8,175	13,163	9,924	9,921	48,177
Japan	14,130	9,747	12,513	18,607	14,459	12,413	69,457
Korea	4,184	4,498	3,130	5,876	4,781	3,725	22,469
US	20,503	17,048	13,661	10,880	15,815	20,539	77,907
China	212	188	167	281	153	182	1,001
Others	554	511	457	817	478	426	2,818
Global	45,433	41,130	37,946	51,340	44,996	45,679	220,845
2005	**EPC States**	**Japan**	**Korea**	**US**	**China**	**Others**	**Total**
EPC States	7,021	10,345	8,452	13,511	10,370	10,327	49,698
Japan	13,813	9,724	12,446	18,529	14,312	12,322	68,824
Korea	4,177	4,360	3,136	5,958	4,683	3,724	22,314
US	23,107	19,036	15,678	12,307	18,203	23,259	88,330
China	322	280	253	433	233	268	1,522
Others	597	549	494	883	516	460	3,039
Global	47,701	43,155	40,073	54,006	47,487	48,187	232,421
2006	**EPC States**	**Japan**	**Korea**	**US**	**China**	**Others**	**Total**
EPC States	6,438	9,251	7,658	12,354	9,553	9,540	45,253
Japan	13,466	9,533	12,181	18,153	14,101	12,020	67,434
Korea	3,818	3,854	2,881	5,525	4,155	3,360	20,234
US	21,524	17,348	14,586	11,513	17,174	22,182	82,145
China	374	325	293	500	270	315	1,762
Others	503	463	423	756	440	395	2,585
Global	44,770	39,915	37,612	50,997	44,817	45,710	218,111

Table 5.7: (*Continued*)

2007	**EPC States**	**Japan**	**Korea**	**US**	**China**	**Others**	**Total**
EPC States	6,085	8,477	7,179	11,662	9,087	9,064	42,490
Japan	11,516	8,278	10,391	15,667	12,370	10,428	58,222
Korea	3,078	3,051	2,366	4,519	3,312	2,745	16,326
US	20,262	16,001	13,717	10,916	16,570	20,952	77,466
China	490	435	402	694	367	427	2,388
Others	458	418	386	696	405	363	2,364
Global	40,520	35,709	34,032	46,554	41,180	41,703	197,994
2008	**EPC States**	**Japan**	**Korea**	**US**	**China**	**Others**	**Total**
EPC States	6,704	9,282	8,006	12,812	10,299	9,941	47,103
Japan	10,738	7,794	9,668	14,661	11,724	9,711	54,586
Korea	2,621	2,619	2,057	3,917	2,835	2,363	14,049
US	23,499	18,604	16,290	12,700	19,988	23,902	91,081
China	515	463	428	752	393	446	2,552
Others	528	478	445	805	470	419	2,726
Global	42,665	37,758	36,228	49,141	44,316	43,661	210,108
2009	**EPC States**	**Japan**	**Korea**	**US**	**China**	**Others**	**Total**
EPC States	7,113	9,755	8,609	13,538	11,235	10,711	50,249
Japan	11,894	8,477	10,612	15,829	13,320	10,696	60,132
Korea	3,063	2,972	2,343	4,462	3,304	2,692	16,144
US	25,177	19,794	17,609	13,560	21,760	25,436	97,901
China	980	856	780	1 347	706	832	4,669
Others	649	576	539	970	574	505	3,308
Global	46,973	41,066	39,752	53,233	49,397	47,796	230,422
2010	**EPC States**	**Japan**	**Korea**	**US**	**China**	**Others**	**Total**
EPC States	6,600	8,880	7,948	12,454	10,557	9,884	46,440
Japan	12,758	9,117	11,399	16,882	14,808	11,615	64,964
Korea	3,687	3,550	2,813	5,390	3,991	3,220	19,432
US	24,462	19,002	17,035	13,281	21,548	24,536	95,327

(*Continued*)

Table 5.7: (*Continued*)

2010	**EPC States**	**Japan**	**Korea**	**US**	**China**	**Others**	**Total**
China	1,134	976	894	1,527	806	974	5,337
Others	624	555	525	933	586	491	3,222
Global	47,427	40,920	40,003	53,743	50,927	47,999	233,020
2011	**EPC States**	**Japan**	**Korea**	**US**	**China**	**Others**	**Total**
EPC States	6,642	8,876	7,981	12,501	10,725	9,949	46,725
Japan	12,246	8,755	10,879	16,060	14,346	11,251	62,285
Korea	4,238	4,021	3,187	6,080	4,629	3,671	22,155
US	25,878	19,852	17,979	14,048	22,939	25,547	100,697
China	1,367	1,160	1,076	1,856	971	1,409	6,429
Others	808	723	686	1 194	861	643	4,272
Global	49,300	42,120	41,258	55,008	53,363	50,073	241,049
2012	**EPC States**	**Japan**	**Korea**	**US**	**China**	**Others**	**Total**
EPC States	6,659	8,794	7,996	12,510	10,767	9,598	46,726
Japan	11,678	8,322	10,334	15,217	13,557	10,665	59,109
Korea	4,180	3,959	3,183	6,075	4,678	3,650	22,074
US	25,717	19,534	17,848	13,985	22,997	25,098	100,080
China	1,689	1,409	1,318	2,261	1,181	1,674	7,859
Others	721	647	617	1 082	775	581	3,842
Global	48,909	41,487	40,714	54,334	52,651	48,915	238,096
2013	**EPC States**	**Japan**	**Korea**	**US**	**China**	**Others**	**Total**
EPC States	6,791	8,989	8,106	12,835	10,982	9,673	47,703
Japan	10,522	7,498	9,224	13,722	12,037	9,622	53,003
Korea	3,722	3,452	2,891	5,533	4,195	3,293	19,792
US	27,797	20,955	19,271	15,104	24,876	26,903	108,003
China	2,204	1,854	1,748	2,944	1,548	2,113	10,298
Others	583	528	499	874	626	471	3,110
Global	49,509	41,971	40,987	54,781	52,918	49,265	240,165

Table 5.7: (*Continued*)

2014	EPC States	Japan	Korea	US	China	Others	Total
EPC States	7,051	9,324	8,412	13,314	11,445	9,862	49,546
Japan	10,673	7,547	9,264	13,845	12,006	9,623	53,335
Korea	3,544	3,247	2,743	5,223	4,043	3,054	18,800
US	25,327	19,117	17,714	13,830	22,674	24,276	98,662
China	2,892	2,423	2,277	3,752	1,977	2,575	13,321
Others	710	663	602	1,038	755	566	3,768
Global	48,450	41,233	40,291	54,358	51,744	47,383	236,075
2015	**EPC States**	**Japan**	**Korea**	**US**	**China**	**Others**	**Total**
EPC States	6,964	9,223	8,336	13,119	11,485	10,119	49,128
Japan	9,974	7,027	8,578	12,875	11,264	9,005	49,717
Korea	3,498	3,212	2,703	5,120	4,060	3,018	18,593
US	23,849	18,078	13,699	13,175	21,810	23,150	90,612
China	2,875	2,491	4,019	3,897	2,050	2,848	15,332
Others	669	630	559	959	696	527	3,514
Global	46,489	39,744	38,564	52,008	50,176	46,344	226,980
2003–2007 CAGR	**EPC States**	**Japan**	**Korea**	**US**	**China**	**Others**	**Total**
EPC States	−3.19	−4.61	−3.67	−3.44	−1.69	−3.80	−3.33
Japan	−5.92	−4.65	−5.46	−4.81	−4.47	−5.60	−5.06
Korea	−5.31	−7.87	−4.65	−4.69	−6.67	−7.20	−5.84
US	2.12	0.83	2.70	2.63	4.57	1.36	2.52
China	23.30	23.64	24.64	26.29	25.49	16.13	24.77
Others	−3.80	−3.91	−2.92	−2.91	−3.08	−2.94	−3.30
Global	−2.16	−2.83	−2.08	−1.68	−0.98	−2.82	−1.92
2007–2011 CAGR	**EPC States**	**Japan**	**Korea**	**US**	**China**	**Others**	**Total**
EPC States	2.21	1.16	2.68	1.75	4.23	2.36	2.40
Japan	1.55	1.41	1.15	0.62	3.77	1.92	1.70
Korea	8.32	7.14	7.73	7.70	8.73	7.54	7.93

(*Continued*)

Table 5.7: (*Continued*)

2007–2011 CAGR	EPC States	Japan	Korea	US	China	Others	Total
US	6.31	5.54	7.00	6.51	8.47	5.08	6.78
China	29.25	27.77	27.90	27.87	27.54	34.81	28.09
Others	15.24	14.69	15.42	14.44	20.76	15.37	15.95
Global	5.03	4.21	4.93	4.26	6.69	4.68	5.04
2011–2015 CAGR	**EPC States**	**Japan**	**Korea**	**US**	**China**	**Others**	**Total**
EPC States	1.19	0.96	1.09	1.21	1.73	0.42	1.26
Japan	−5.00	−5.35	−5.77	−5.38	−5.87	−5.42	−5.48
Korea	−4.68	−5.46	−4.03	−4.21	−3.23	−4.78	−4.29
US	−2.02	−2.31	−6.57	−1.59	−1.25	−2.43	−2.60
China	20.43	21.06	39.03	20.38	20.54	19.24	24.27
Others	−4.60	−3.39	−4.98	−5.34	−5.16	−4.85	−4.77
Global	−1.46	−1.44	−1.67	−1.39	−1.53	−1.92	−1.49

Source: Calculated using the assumption that the ratio of patent families in each five chief office overflows to subsequent filings of each bloc in any other five blocs and remains the same as the patent families of each bloc over additional flows to subsequent filings of that bloc in other blocs, as explained in Section 5.8.1.

Table 5.8: Mutual Independence of One Bloc of Another and Dependence of One Bloc on Another of Patent Families (2000–2015)

2000 Bloc	EPC States (%)	Japan (%)	Korea (%)	US (%)	China (%)	Others (%)	Total (%)
EPC States	—	37.42	72.23	43.71	98.92	94.96	57.59
Japan	62.58	—	80.12	60.52	99.42	96.01	70.11
Korea	27.77	19.88	—	28.53	97.72	86.83	35.72
US	56.29	39.48	71.47	—	98.95	96.16	63.50
China	1.08	0.58	2.28	99.05	—	32.81	1.87
Others	5.04	3.99	13.17	3.84	67.19	—	6.41
Global	42.41	29.89	64.28	36.50	98.13	93.59	—

Table 5.8: (*Continued*)

2001	**EPC States**	**Japan**	**Korea**	**US**	**China**	**Others**	**Total**
EPC States	—	38.18	76.32	42.87	98.41	93.98	51.86
Japan	61.82	—	83.07	58.94	99.16	95.76	66.24
Korea	23.68	16.93	—	24.16	96.05	81.68	27.37
US	57.13	41.06	75.84	—	98.49	95.70	57.05
China	1.59	0.84	3.95	99.61	—	20.35	1.67
Others	6.02	4.24	18.32	4.30	79.65	—	6.49
Global	48.14	33.76	72.63	42.95	98.33	93.51	—
2002	**EPC States**	**Japan**	**Korea**	**US**	**China**	**Others**	**Total**
EPC States	—	39.77	73.39	42.82	97.96	96.16	52.47
Japan	60.23	—	79.97	57.54	98.86	96.58	65.46
Korea	26.61	20.03	—	27.07	95.62	88.25	31.12
US	57.18	42.46	72.93	—	98.09	96.75	57.67
China	2.04	1.14	4.38	99.75	—	40.36	2.18
Others	3.84	3.42	11.75	3.25	59.64	—	4.80
Global	47.53	34.54	68.88	42.33	97.82	95.20	—
2003	**EPC States**	**Japan**	**Korea**	**US**	**China**	**Others**	**Total**
EPC States	—	41.06	68.53	41.87	97.87	95.19	52.39
Japan	58.94	—	75.44	55.21	98.76	96.40	64.15
Korea	31.47	24.56	—	30.75	96.33	89.48	35.94
US	58.13	44.79	69.25	—	98.07	96.20	58.47
China	2.13	1.24	3.67	99.79	—	33.83	2.25
Others	4.81	3.60	10.52	3.80	66.17	—	5.47
Global	47.61	35.85	64.06	41.53	97.75	94.53	—
2004	**EPC States**	**Japan**	**Korea**	**US**	**China**	**Others**	**Total**
EPC States	—	41.62	66.15	39.10	97.90	94.71	51.47
Japan	58.38	—	73.56	52.19	98.72	96.05	62.81
Korea	33.85	26.44	—	30.08	96.62	89.07	37.19
US	60.90	47.81	69.92	—	98.26	96.17	60.28

(*Continued*)

Table 5.8: (*Continued*)

2004	**EPC States**	**Japan**	**Korea**	**US**	**China**	**Others**	**Total**
China	2.10	1.28	3.38	99.79	—	27.54	2.18
Others	5.29	3.95	10.93	3.83	72.46	—	5.81
Global	48.53	37.19	62.81	39.72	97.82	94.19	—

2005	**EPC States**	**Japan**	**Korea**	**US**	**China**	**Others**	**Total**
EPC States	—	42.82	66.92	36.90	96.98	94.53	51.03
Japan	57.18	—	74.06	49.33	98.08	95.73	61.46
Korea	33.08	25.94	—	27.54	94.87	88.29	35.77
US	63.10	50.67	72.46	—	97.67	96.34	62.06
China	3.02	1.92	5.13	99.86	—	34.18	3.11
Others	5.47	4.27	11.71	3.66	65.82	—	5.93
Global	48.97	38.54	64.23	37.94	96.89	94.07	—

2006	**EPC States**	**Japan**	**Korea**	**US**	**China**	**Others**	**Total**
EPC States	—	40.72	66.73	36.47	96.23	94.99	50.27
Japan	59.28	—	75.96	51.13	97.75	96.29	62.82
Korea	33.27	24.04	—	27.47	93.41	88.83	34.98
US	63.53	48.87	72.53	—	97.17	96.70	61.70
China	3.77	2.25	6.59	99.88	—	41.72	3.78
Others	5.01	3.71	11.17	3.30	58.28	—	5.35
Global	49.73	37.18	65.02	38.30	96.22	94.65	—

2007	**EPC States**	**Japan**	**Korea**	**US**	**China**	**Others**	**Total**
EPC States	—	42.40	69.99	36.53	94.89	95.19	51.19
Japan	57.60	—	77.30	49.47	96.60	96.15	61.98
Korea	30.01	22.70	—	24.78	89.18	87.66	32.42
US	63.47	50.53	75.22	—	95.98	96.78	62.46
China	5.11	3.40	10.82	99.91	—	51.31	5.48
Others	4.81	3.85	12.34	3.22	48.69	—	5.36
Global	48.81	38.02	67.58	37.54	94.52	94.64	—

Table 5.8: (*Continued*)

2008	**EPC States**	**Japan**	**Korea**	**US**	**China**	**Others**	**Total**
EPC States	—	46.36	75.34	35.28	95.24	94.95	52.47
Japan	53.64	—	78.68	44.07	96.20	95.31	59.11
Korea	24.66	21.32	—	19.39	86.87	84.15	27.94
US	64.72	55.93	80.61	—	96.37	96.74	64.95
China	4.76	3.80	13.13	99.91	—	48.69	5.45
Others	5.05	4.69	15.85	3.26	51.31	—	5.88
Global	47.53	40.89	72.06	35.05	94.55	94.12	—
2009	**EPC States**	**Japan**	**Korea**	**US**	**China**	**Others**	**Total**
EPC States	—	45.06	73.76	34.97	91.98	94.29	51.69
Japan	54.94	—	78.12	44.43	93.96	94.89	59.42
Korea	26.24	21.88	—	20.22	80.90	83.33	28.88
US	65.03	55.57	79.78	—	94.17	96.33	64.78
China	8.02	6.04	19.10	99.95	—	59.18	8.64
Others	5.71	5.11	16.67	3.67	40.82	—	6.47
Global	48.31	40.58	71.12	35.22	91.36	93.53	—
2010	**EPC States**	**Japan**	**Korea**	**US**	**China**	**Others**	**Total**
EPC States	—	41.04	68.31	33.74	90.30	94.06	49.47
Japan	58.96	—	76.25	47.05	93.82	95.44	61.35
Korea	31.69	23.75	—	24.04	81.70	85.99	32.69
US	66.26	52.95	75.96	—	93.38	96.34	63.95
China	9.70	6.18	18.30	99.96	—	62.45	9.49
Others	5.94	4.56	14.01	3.66	37.55	—	6.29
Global	50.53	38.65	67.31	36.05	90.51	93.71	—
2011	**EPC States**	**Japan**	**Korea**	**US**	**China**	**Others**	**Total**
EPC States	—	42.02	65.32	32.57	88.70	92.49	48.66
Japan	57.98	—	73.01	44.72	92.52	93.96	59.66
Korea	34.68	26.99	—	25.27	81.15	84.26	34.94
US	67.43	55.28	74.73	—	92.52	95.53	64.67

(*Continued*)

Table 5.8: (*Continued*)

2011	**EPC States**	**Japan**	**Korea**	**US**	**China**	**Others**	**Total**
China	11.30	7.48	18.85	99.97	—	62.08	10.75
Others	7.51	6.04	15.74	4.47	37.92	—	7.86
Global	51.34	40.34	65.06	35.33	89.25	92.14	—
2012	**EPC States**	**Japan**	**Korea**	**US**	**China**	**Others**	**Total**
EPC States	—	42.95	65.67	32.73	86.44	93.01	48.86
Japan	57.05	—	72.30	43.79	90.58	94.28	58.76
Korea	34.33	27.70	—	25.39	78.02	85.54	35.16
US	67.27	56.21	74.61	—	91.05	95.87	64.81
China	13.56	9.42	21.98	99.97	—	68.36	12.99
Others	6.99	5.72	14.46	4.13	31.64	—	7.28
Global	51.14	41.24	64.84	35.19	87.01	9272	—
2013	**EPC States**	**Japan**	**Korea**	**US**	**China**	**Others**	**Total**
EPC States	—	46.07	68.54	31.59	83.29	94.32	49.07
Japan	53.93	—	72.77	39.57	86.65	94.80	55.81
Korea	31.46	27.23	—	22.31	70.59	86.83	32.56
US	68.41	60.43	7.69	—	89.42	96.86	66.35
China	16.71	13.35	29.41	99.98	—	77.15	16.29
Others	5.68	5.20	13.17	3.14	22.85	—	5.94
Global	50.93	44.19	67.44	33.65	83.71	94.06	—
2014	**EPC States**	**Japan**	**Korea**	**US**	**China**	**Others**	**Total**
EPC States	—	46.63	70.36	34.46	79.83	93.28	50.56
Japan	53.37	—	74.05	42.00	83.21	93.55	56.40
Korea	29.64	25.95	—	22.77	63.97	83.52	31.82
US	65.54	58.00	77.23	—	85.80	95.90	64.48
China	20.17	16.79	36.03	99.98	—	77.32	20.47
Others	6.72	6.45	16.48	4.10	22.68	—	7.37
Global	49.44	43.60	68.18	35.52	79.53	92.63	—

Table 5.8: (*Continued*)

2015	EPC States	Japan	Korea	US	China	Others	Total
EPC States	—	48.04	70.44	35.49	79.98	93.80	51.38
Japan	51.96	—	72.76	41.59	81.89	93.46	55.57
Korea	29.56	27.24	—	27.21	50.25	84.37	32.53
US	64.51	58.41	72.79	—	84.84	96.02	63.53
China	20.02	18.11	49.75	99.98	—	80.35	23.40
Others	6.20	6.54	15.63	3.98	19.65	—	7.05
Global	48.62	44.43	67.47	36.47	76.60	92.95	—

Source: Calculated using data from Table 5.8 and the definition in Section 5.9.1.

5.9.3 *US independence of and dependence on other blocs*

Table 5.8 shows that the US had the lowest level of dependence on all other blocs in 2013, its dependence levels on EPC states, Japan, Korea, China, others, and the world were 31.59%, 39.57%, 22.31%, 99.98%, 3.14%, and 33.65% in 2013, and the US autonomy levels of patent families of the above blocs were 68.41%, 60.43%, 77.69%, 89.42%, 96.86%, and 66.35%, indicating the high autonomy of patent families of other blocs of the US in the same year or high technology SRC in the US.

5.9.4 *Independence of the top three blocs from other blocs*

Table 5.8 shows that the autonomy of the US, Japan, and EPC states from other blocs on average was largely above 50% from 2000 to 2015, implying the high technology SRC of the leading three blocs compared with other blocs.

5.9.5 *Independence of China of other blocs*

Table 5.8 shows that the dependence levels of China on EPC states, Japan, Korea, the US, and others were 98.92%, 99.42%, 97.72%, 98.95%, and 67.19% in 2000, and these dependence levels declined to 79.98%, 81.89%, 50.25%, 84.84%, and 53.62% in 2015, indicating the rapid progress of technology SRC in China from 2000 to 2015; the dependence of patent families of China on Korea and others was lower than 50% for the first time in 2016, or China should have won relative autonomy of patent families of Korea and others in 2016, and it would take another 10 years or so for China to win relative independence of patent families of EPC states and Japan in about 2026.

5.10 Key Changes and Causes in the Global Patent Field since 2013

Due to the time lag in statistics of patent families, the most updated report issued in 2020 by the top five offices only provided the global patent family statistics of 2015, which increases the difficulties for us to summarize the key changes in the global patent field and to estimate the future trend. According to the rules of statistics publishing by the top five offices, the data of 2019 would not be announced until 2024 and confirmed until 2025. The worldwide situation of patents will undergo even greater changes in the following 5 years. Timely and scientific research on the changes of global patent is important for working out strategies to methodically, reasonably, and steadily improve China's scientific and technological autonomy.

Although the most updated data of patent family numbers published by the top five offices are available only from 2015, the 2019 yearly report of the leading five offices provides the number of patent family applications in 2018 and the refreshed data of 2017. Based on these data and the number of patent family mutual applications among the top five offices of 2015 in the 2018 annual report of leading five offices, we can conclude the key changes in global patent field from 2014 to 2018.

5.10.1 *Key changes in first filings and flows to subsequent filings in any other region, any other five offices, and patent families of major blocs from 2013*

Although the Japanese first filings decreased almost every year from 2000 to 2015, with the only exception being 2004, and Japanese patent families decreased most of the years from 2004, the US decreases affect world patent families more. Table 5.3 shows that patent families of the US decreased by 1,929 from 2013 to 2015, more than the total decrease in global patent families of 1,857 for the same period, and more than the loss of 1,391 patent families from 2005 to 2007, or 30.9% of total decrease in global patent families of 4,506 for the same period. The significant decrease of US patent families from 2013 to 2015 was the direct result of related declines in first filings and flows to subsequent filings in any other five blocs of the US in the same period as shown in Table 5.3, particularly accumulative decrease of total flows to subsequent filings to other blocs, as shown in Table 5.6.

5.10.2 *Key changes in patent applications since 2013*

The most recent IP5 Statistical Report 2019 contains patent families information of leading blocs in 2015. We must wait for several years to obtain patent family information from 2016 to 2018. Though the PCT applications among the leading offices from 2016 to 2018 should contain implied information of patent families from 2016 to 2018, such information is crucial for us to forecast how patent families changed from 2015 to 2018. IP5 Statistical Report 2019 and earlier reports show that despite the total US PCT applications in other leading five offices increased at an average yearly growth rate of 9.15% from 110,177 in 2013 to 131,263 in 2015, US patent families decreased at an average annual rate of 6.6% from 15,104 to 13,175, as shown in Table 5.9. As the total US PCT applications in other chief five offices decreased at an average yearly rate of 0.54% from 131,263 in 2015 to 129,155 in 2018, US patent families should have decreased at a yearly rate much higher than 5.4%. Thus, yearly growth rates of US patent families from 2016 to 2018 cannot be as high as the average yearly growth rate from 2011 to 2015.

5.10.3 *Brief cause analysis on changes in global family patents since 2013*

In the second half of 2014, the US exited from four rounds of "quantitative easing policy" for more than 5 years, which had been discussed in the world since the second half of 2013. This action had a huge impact on worldwide finance, economy, and trade. The impact on the global patent family application number of the US since this withdrawal is unclear from 2014. At the same time, the number of applications the other four chief-five office countries filed with the US significantly increased (the financial crisis also has a significant negative impact on the technological innovation ability of the US). This withdrawal directly caused almost every currency, except the JPY, to depreciate against the USD. CNY's depreciation against USD caused a decrease in our foreign currency reserves of $823.5 billion from 2014 to 2016 and further caused a slowdown of our overseas patent applications from 2014 to 2017. The fact shows that the downward pressure of foreign exchange reserves also has a certain negative effect on overseas patent applications.

5.11 Relationship between "Patent Families" and "PCT" Patents

A patent family is a collection of patent applications covering the same or similar technical content. The applications in a family are related to each other through priority claims; PCT patent provides a good solution for applicants to apply the subsequent patent in many countries. Therefore, these two worldwide patents are greatly similar and correlated. Many patent families flowing among different regions prefer to use PCT patent system. If the patent family, which are related to each other through priority claims, includes at least one PCT patent application, the patent family is regarded as "using the PCT patent system". According to the 2019 IP5 Statistical Reports, the proportions of patent families using the PCT patent system were 91.4%, 93.0%, and 93.6% in EPC states, China, and US in 2015, and the global average proportion was 88.8%. The average proportions of patent families using the PCT patent system were 80.1%, 79.4%, and 81.7% in EPC states, China, and US from 2008 to 2015, and the global average ratio was 76.9%. The average percentage was over 72.1% in Japan and 60.4% in Korea from 2008 to 2015, respectively, and the corresponding ratios in Japan and Korea were up to 82.7% and 77.0% in 2015. The high proportion of patent families that use the PCT patent system indicate the high connections between patent families and PCT patents or that analytic results using detailed patent families data provide a good representation of patent globalization.

According to the number of global PCT patents and patent families shown in Tables 5.2 and 5.3, the latter is only 10–20% of the former. However, patent family always includes one or more than one PCT patent applications, which allows repeat applications and grants. If we assume that one patent family includes two to three PCT patent applications, the number of PCT patents included in patent families may account for over 30% or even 50% of the number of all PCT patents.

5.12 Estimate of Patent Families of Major Blocs Using PCT Applications

IP4 patent families represent highly internationalized applications, and proportions of PCT in IP5 patent families are over 90%, as shown in the previous section. Data on PCT applications from 2016 to 2018 contain useful information for patent families of the chief five from 2016 to 2018. Thus, we may use Interbloc Activity PCT applications data from 2011 to 2018 to forecast patent families of leading offices from 2016 to 2018.

5.12.1 *PCT applications and patent families*

Table 5.9 gives us the PCT applications among leading five offices and patent families/total PCT application ratios of each patent originator from 2011 to 2018. Ratios of patent families over total PCT applications are stable for most blocs, particularly for the top three blocs. We can calculate the average ratio change from 2011 to 2015 for five blocs as −0.00092, −0.00303, −0.00662, 0.00549, and −0.00758 for EPC states, Japan, Korea, China, and the US. Using the 2015 ratios as a base and the average yearly ratio change, we can obtain the estimated ratios of patent families over total PCT applications for each bloc from 2016 to 2018, and then we can estimate patent families with the estimated ratios and the total PCT applications in the same period. Table 5.9 gives the useful estimated results.

5.12.2 *Compound annual growth rates of patent families from 2015 to 2018*

Table 5.9 shows that patent families decreased with average yearly rates of 0.70%, 6.67%, 20.31%, and 8.70% in EPC states, Japan, Korea, and the US from 2015 to 2018, which were largely similar to the corresponding average yearly change rates of Japan and Korea, and almost the same as the corresponding average yearly growth rate of 25.44% for China from 2003 to 2015, indicating the reasonability of the estimated results. As Table 5.9 contains forward information for the period of 2016–2018, the estimated results in Table 5.10 should be useful for us to forecast patent families from 2016 to 2020.

Table 5.9: Patent Families and PCT Applications of Five Blocs (2011–2018)

2011 Bloc	EPC States	Japan	R. Korea	China	US	Total	Patent Families	Patent Families/ Total
EPC states	—	21,023	10,569	30,199	80,314	142,105	6,642	0.04674
Japan	24,577	—	15,234	39,231	85,184	164,226	8,755	0.05331
R. Korea	6,110	5,007	—	8,129	27,289	46,535	3,187	0.06849
P.R. China	2,893	1,401	752	—	10,545	15,591	971	0.06228
US	43,481	23,414	12,139	28,457	—	107,491	14,048	0.13069
2012 Bloc	**EPC States**	**Japan**	**R. Korea**	**China**	**US**	**Total**	**Patent Families**	**Patent Families/ Total**
EPC states	—	20,899	10,194	31,820	85,195	148,108	6,659	0.04496
Japan	27,526	—	16,004	42,278	88,686	174,494	8,322	0.04769
R. Korea	7,476	5,708	—	8,985	29,481	51,650	3,183	0.06163
P.R. China	4,211	2,022	982	—	13,273	20,488	1,181	0.05764
US	44,888	22,922	29,510	29,992	—	127,312	13,985	0.10985
2013 Bloc	**EPC States**	**Japan**	**R. Korea**	**China**	**US**	**Total**	**Patent Families**	**Patent families/ Total**
EPC states	—	20,604	11,738	33,287	88,904	154,533	6,791	0.04395
Japan	28,105	—	16,299	41,193	84,967	170,564	7,498	0.04396
R. Korea	7,995	6,134	—	10,866	33,499	58,494	2,891	0.04942
P.R. China	4,837	2,064	1,147	—	15,093	23,141	1,548	0.06689
US	43,713	23,481	12,991	29,992	—	110,177	15,104	0.13709
2014 Bloc	**EPC States**	**Japan**	**R. Korea**	**China**	**US**	**Total**	**Patent Families**	**Patent Families/ Total**
EPC states	—	21,150	12,299	34,994	91,679	160,122	7,051	0.04404
Japan	28,455	—	15,653	40,460	96,691	181,259	7,547	0.04164
R. Korea	7,756	5,082	—	11,528	36,744	61,110	2,743	0.04489
P.R. China	5,792	2,531	1,572	—	18,040	27,935	1,977	0.07077
US	46,787	25,998	13,952	33,963	—	120,700	13,830	0.11458
2015 Bloc	**EPC States**	**Japan**	**R. Korea**	**China**	**US**	**Total**	**Patent Families**	**Patent Families/ Total**
EPC states	—	20,784	12,027	35,653	93,203	161,667	6,964	0.04308
Japan	28,823	—	15,283	40,078	86,359	170,543	7,027	0.04120
R. Korea	8,010	5,222	—	12,907	38,205	64,344	2,703	0.04201

Table 5.9: (*Continued*)

2015 Bloc	**EPC States**	**Japan**	**R. Korea**	**China**	**US**	**Total**	**Patent Families**	**Patent Families/ Total**
P.R. China	7,194	2,840	1,947		21,386	33,367	2,050	0.06144
US	52,891	26,501	14,655	37,216		131,263	13,175	0.10037
2016 Bloc	**EPC States**	**Japan**	**R. Korea**	**China**	**US**	**Total**	**Patent Families**	**Patent Families/ Total**
EPC states	—	20,568	11,851	36,467	97,269	166,155	7,005	0.04216
Japan	28,837	—	14,773	39,207	86,021	168,838	6,446	0.03818
R. Korea	8,219	5,216	—	13,764	37,341	64,540	2,284	0.03539
P.R. China	8,819	3,810	2,829	—	26,026	41,484	2,540	0.06123
US	50,639	23,979	13,643	35,895	—	124,156	11,521	0.09279
2017 Bloc	**EPC States**	**Japan**	**R. Korea**	**China**	**US**	**Total**	**Patent Families**	**Patent Families/ Total**
EPC states	—	20,559	11,699	36,818	96,995	166,071	6,849	0.04124
Japan	30,181	—	15,043	40,908	86,113	172,245	6,054	0.03515
R. Korea	7,819	4,735	—	13,180	35,565	61,299	1,764	0.02877
P.R. China	11,080	4,172	3,015	—	29,674	47,941	2,925	0.06102
US	53,343	23,949	13,442	36,980	—	127,714	10,883	0.08521
2018 Bloc	**EPC States**	**Japan**	**R. Korea**	**China**	**US**	**Total**	**Patent Families**	**Patent Families/ Total**
EPC states	—	20,884	12,702	39,810	95,699	169,095	6,819	0.04033
Japan	31,605	—	15,595	45,284	85,322	177,806	5,712	0.03212
R. Korea	8,845	5,070	—	13,875	33,961	61,751	1,368	0.02215
P.R. China	11,327	5,325	3,140	—	32,615	52,407	3,187	0.06081
US	54,140	23,121	13,035	38,859	—	129,155	10,027	0.07763
CAGR 2015–2018	—	—	—	—	—	—	—	—
EPC states	—	—	—	—	—	—	−0.70%	—
Japan	—	—	—	—	—	—	−6.67%	—
R. Korea	—	—	—	—	—	—	−20.31%	—
P.R. China	—	—	—	—	—	—	15.84%	—
US	—	—	—	—	—	—	−8.70%	—

Source: PCT application data from Figure 3.14 of the IP5 Statistical Reports of 2019 and previous reports; patent families data from Table 5.3; patent families from 2016 to 2018 are estimated using the average annual changes of ratios of patent families/total PCT applications of each bloc from 2011 to 2015.

5.12.3 *Comparisons between CAGR of China from 2007 to 2015 and estimated CAGR of China from 2015 to 2018*

Table 5.3 shows that the CAGR of 20.54% of patent families of China from 2011 to 2015 was 74.59% of the CAGR of 27.54% of patent families of China from 2007 to 2011, indicating deaccelerating CAGR from 2007 to 2015. Assuming deaccelerating ratio of 74.59% remains the same for the ratio of CAGR from 2015 to 2019 to the CAGR of 20.54% from 2011 to 2015, we can estimate CAGR of China from 2015 to 2019 as 20.54% × 74.59% = 15.32%, which is so close to the estimated CAGR of 15.84% in Table 5.9 of patent families of China from 2015 to 2018, indicating the historical information in Table 5.3 for patent families of China was so consistent with the forward information for patent families of China from 2015 to 2018. Therefore, we can use CAGR of patent families of China from 2015 to 2019 with more certainty in Tables 5.10 and 5.11.

5.13 More on Patent Internationalization

The results in Table 5.5 give us a good estimate of patent internationalization of critical blocs from 2000 to 2015 and forecasting results for 2016 to 2020 based on the historical information. The results in Table 5.5 are reasonable because patent families of the top five offices represent more than 90% of world patent families. However, these results cannot represent the actual patent globalization as it misses patent families of countries outside the leading five offices, while the results in Table 5.7 give the estimated patent families of others comparable to results in Table 5.4. Thus, the corresponding patent families given in Table 5.7 can better represent global distribution of patent families of all blocs, and the corresponding patent globalization results are better than those given in Table 5.4. Table 5.10 gives the results.

Results in Table 5.10 are like those given in Table 5.5, but they are more reasonable because Table 5.8 is based on the estimated patent families of each bloc in others whereas such data are missing in Table 5.5. Another reason that results in Table 5.10 are more reasonable than those in Table 5.5 is that the results in Table 5.8 are not only based on the patent families and flows to subsequent filings of each bloc to any other five blocs but also based on the information of flows to subsequent filings of each bloc to other individual blocs, and it reflects the information from Table 5.9 which uses the PCT application data from 2016 to 2018.

Table 5.10: Patent Internationalization of Major Blocs (2000–2020)

Year/Bloc of Origin	EPC States (%)	Japan (%)	Korea (%)	US (%)	China (%)	Others (%)	Global Total (%)
2000	22.90	35.52	7.31	32.50	0.27	1.49	100.00
2001	22.66	35.59	6.16	33.74	0.31	1.54	100.00
2002	23.44	33.46	7.34	34.07	0.46	1.23	100.00
2003	22.54	32.26	9.31	34.24	0.46	1.18	100.00
2004	21.60	30.43	9.74	36.59	0.44	1.21	100.00
2005	21.13	28.56	9.17	39.28	0.63	1.23	100.00
2006	20.50	29.73	8.83	39.04	0.78	1.12	100.00
2007	21.20	28.22	7.84	40.46	1.16	1.12	100.00
2008	22.03	24.84	6.34	44.42	1.16	1.21	100.00
2009	21.52	25.00	6.65	43.54	1.94	1.35	100.00
2010	19.73	26.83	7.94	41.99	2.21	1.30	100.00
2011	19.21	24.92	8.75	42.79	2.66	1.67	100.00
2012	19.36	23.98	8.84	43.02	3.28	1.52	100.00
2013	19.52	21.30	7.85	45.89	4.22	1.22	100.00
2014	20.67	21.91	7.60	42.78	5.53	1.51	100.00
2015	21.50	21.31	7.84	41.28	6.60	1.47	100.00
2016*	23.02	16.73	7.48	42.96	8.31	1.49	100.00
2017*	24.25	12.93	7.65	43.99	10.33	1.49	100.00
2018*	25.16	9.84	6.49	44.37	12.67	1.46	100.00
2019*	25.74	7.39	5.92	44.15	15.38	1.42	100.00
2020*	25.99	5.48	5.34	43.37	18.47	1.36	100.00

Source: The results from 2000 to 2015 are calculated using data of patent families of each bloc in Table 5.7; the results from 2016 to 2020 are estimated using the 2015 patent families of each bloc as base and the arithmetic average of CAGR of EPC States, Japan, Korea, and US from 2011 to 2015 in Table 5.3 and the estimated CAGR of these four blocs from 2015 to 2018 in Table 5.9; the CAGR of China is obtained using the assumption that deaccelerating ratio of 74.59% (ratio of the CAGR of China from 2011 to 2015 to the CAGR of China from 2007 to 2011) remains unchanged, or CAGR of China at 15.32% from 2016 to 2020, which is lower than the estimated CAGR of 15.84% of China from 2015 to 2018.
*Data from 2016 to 2020 are estimated using related previous CAGRs from 2003 to 2015.

Thus, the information contents of the results in Table 5.10 are broader than those in Table 5.5.

Table 5.10 shows that Chinese patent internationalization should have surpassed Korean patent internationalization for the first time in

2016, it should have surpassed Japan in 2018, and it would take more than a decade to catch up with the EPC states. Yet, the results in Table 5.10 did not take the crucial issue of patent quality into consideration. We will discuss and analyze such issues in Chapter 7.

5.14 World Independence of Patent Families of Major Blocs

Table 5.8 gives us good results of mutual dependence of patent families of one bloc on another. We can use such results to concentrate on the total dependence of one bloc on world patent families and estimate future development of such dependence in this section.

5.14.1 *Estimation assumptions and results*

Dependence of one bloc on global patent families or on world patent families from 2000 to 2015 can be obtained from Table 5.9 directly, and dependence of one bloc on world patent families from 2016 to 2020 can be obtained with the same assumptions of Table 5.10. The results are given in Table 5.11.

5.14.2 *Estimation results*

Table 5.11 shows that the autonomy or SRC of China and EPC states grew from 2015 to 2020 simply because their CAGRs remained positive, and those of Japan and Korea declined as their CAGRs remained negative; the reason that independence of the US also grew from 2015 to 2020 is that its decreasing CAGR of −5.15% was less negative than those of Japan and Korea. Chinese autonomy surpassed others in independence of patent families of the world for the first time in 2009, and it should have surpassed Korea and Japan for the first time in 2017 and 2018, respectively. It would take more than a decade for China to surpass EPC states in autonomy of patent families after 2030.

It is noticeable that China should have achieved relative patent autonomy for the first time in 2020 with independence of 50.63%, yet her autonomy will still be lower than those of EPC states and the US in 2030. Thus, there is much more for China to do to catch up with EPC states and the US in the coming decades.

Table 5.11: Mutual Independence of and Mutual Dependence of One Bloc on Another Bloc (2000–2020)

Year/Bloc of Origin	EPC States (%)	Japan (%)	Korea (%)	US (%)	China (%)	Others (%)
2000	57.36	70.16	35.69	63.55	1.85	6.43
2001	56.76	69.97	30.71	64.20	2.03	7.30
2002	58.67	69.34	35.28	65.35	2.91	5.38
2003	56.92	67.60	39.72	64.81	2.73	6.10
2004	55.58	66.06	40.74	66.49	2.53	6.43
2005	55.04	64.69	39.16	68.37	3.57	6.50
2006	54.30	66.09	38.29	68.13	4.35	5.87
2007	55.17	65.19	35.64	69.03	6.26	5.84
2008	56.12	62.10	30.79	71.58	6.16	6.30
2009	55.50	62.54	31.75	71.28	9.75	6.97
2010	53.34	64.54	35.80	70.37	10.77	6.82
2011	52.55	62.89	38.20	70.93	12.58	8.57
2012	52.65	62.06	38.38	71.00	15.01	7.94
2013	52.64	59.14	35.61	72.56	18.61	6.43
2014	54.20	59.80	34.76	70.68	23.11	7.98
2015	55.33	59.09	36.32	69.83	26.14	7.67
2016*	56.94	52.95	35.22	70.85	30.94	7.74
2017*	58.22	46.41	35.44	71.49	35.87	7.73
2018*	59.23	39.72	31.25	71.80	40.83	7.64
2019*	59.97	33.18	28.50	71.81	45.77	7.48
2020*	60.49	27.06	25.36	71.58	50.63	7.26

Source: Results from 2000 to 2015 are from Table 5.8. *Results for 2016–2020 are obtained using the same assumptions as in Table 5.10.

5.14.3 *Average quality of patent families*

The results in Tables 5.10 and 5.11 all depend on one crucial assumption that the quality of all patent families of different blocs is the same as in Tables 5.4 and 5.8 for patent internationalization. As was argued in Section 5.5.6, the average quality of patent families cannot be of the same quality because the average IP export fees generated by patent families vary significantly across blocs. Thus, the autonomy results of patent families can be viewed as a good reference for changes in them, yet they need to be further refined with IP export and import data need to be more accurate in understanding technology originality capability of different blocs. We will leave the work to Chapter 7.

5.15 Summary

The IP5 reports include detailed data of patent families' regional distribution. The data of patent families of each bloc from which priority is claimed are very useful for us to identify patent internationalization and SRC. Such data make it possible to identify the origin of these high global patents and conclude the patent internationalization level and science and technology independence level of different countries. In this chapter, we estimate the patent internalization level of critical blocs of patent originality by using the leading five offices' patent data, especially the patent family data. It is very helpful to have a deep understanding of global exports of goods, international PCT patents are essential for the majority of global exports of goods. Only goods with low technology contents such as raw materials and crafts can be exported without sufficient international patents. The content of this chapter provides good reference to understand China's position in global trade. The high proportion of patent families which use the PCT patent system indicate the high globalization nature of patent families and thus the validity of our analysis in this chapter.

Science and technology are the backbone of the economy and trade worldwide, and the cornerstones for further upgrading of China's high-end value in the global trade chain. Patents are a crucial manifestation of science and technology progress and carry the complex market rules which promote the steady progress of China's scientific and technological innovation. How do we extend the road of international trade and protect intellectual property rights by applying global patents? How do we promote domestic independent innovation by leveraging overseas patent grants? These subjects are worthy of our deep thinking. On the one hand, we can start by establishing financial legal system rules, policy guidance, market environment, capital mobilization, etc., to promote domestic innovation and scientific research. On the other hand, further studies can be considered to effectively promote the use of patents by foreign and overseas institutions in China to supplement our science and technology capability.

Although the number of China's patent family increased from 367 to 2,050 (increased nearly six times) in the period from 2007 to 2015, the ratio of patent family number to the patent first filing number remained at 0.20% from 2011 to 2015, which is significantly lower than the ratios of EPC states, the US, Japan, and Republic of Korea at 5.50%, 5.06%, 2.96%, and 1.62% in 2015. It is also lower than the average ratio of countries other than the leading five offices at 0.59% in the same year. The lower ratio reflects that China's patent filings need to significantly improve in quality. Only when patent families or PCT patents of China increase to a higher level can exports be accepted aboard more with Chinese IP and yuan settlement of trade be improved to a higher level.

Although China's patent families increased significantly in the period from 2007 to 2015 with double-digit growth, and patent internationalization and patent SRC improved accordingly, patent internationalization and patent SRC should have reached levels closer to those EPC states and Japan in 2020, reflecting the results of steady growth in research and development in China in the past two decades. However, the significant progress in patent internationalization and SRC in the past two decades did not take into consideration the average quality of patent families of China compared to other blocs. With average quality of patent families, or IP export fee per patent family taken into consideration, patent internationalization and patent SRC will be obviously reduced. We will analyze such issues in Chapter 7.

Appendix

Table A5.1: Distribution of Flows to Subsequent Filings of Top Five Offices and Others (2000–2015)

2000 Bloc	EPC States	Japan	Korea	US	China	Others	Total
EPC States	47,383	71,300	53,161	92,443	59,521	95,642	419,450
Japan	96,872	63,406	78,557	122,511	80,626	86,629	528,601
Korea	9,289	10,908	6,961	13,040	9,584	11,080	60,862
US	103,462	85,490	62,454	53,823	67,549	144,399	517,177
China	1,230	1,098	936	1,560	852	3,726	9,402
Others	13,047	11,382	9,502	17,046	10,329	9,034	70,340
Global	271,283	243,584	211,571	300,423	228,461	350,510	1,605,832

(*Continued*)

Table A5.1: (*Continued*)

2001 Bloc	EPC States	Japan	Korea	US	China	Others	Total
EPC States	47,801	70,668	55,747	93,323	61,381	77,849	406,769
Japan	94,097	62,596	80,716	120,588	85,214	82,187	525,398
Korea	10,904	12,612	8,216	15,641	11,627	10,683	69,683
US	105,153	86,377	65,823	54,794	71,003	128,888	512,038
China	1,537	1,365	1,177	1,991	1,057	1,605	8,732
Others	13,978	12,416	10,650	19,210	11,352	10,040	77,646
Global	273,470	246,034	222,329	305,547	241,634	311,252	1,600,266
2002 Bloc	**EPC States**	**Japan**	**Korea**	**US**	**China**	**Others**	**Total**
EPC States	47,406	70,198	56,005	92,342	64,282	99,452	429,685
Japan	96,129	64,815	83,631	124,293	93,787	92,008	554,663
Korea	13,730	15,662	10,329	19,823	15,614	15,849	91,007
US	109,737	90,278	70,292	57,576	78,445	149,557	555,885
China	2,050	1,831	1,617	2,621	1,418	3,459	12,996
Others	15,708	14,262	12,353	22,357	13,228	11,656	89,564
Global	284,760	257,046	234,227	319,012	266,774	371,981	1,733,800
2003 Bloc	**EPC States**	**Japan**	**Korea**	**US**	**China**	**Others**	**Total**
EPC States	47,340	69,974	56,964	91,680	66,480	72,319	404,757
Japan	100,608	68,532	89,042	130,581	101,654	89,862	580,279
Korea	19,288	21,340	14,425	27,593	21,996	18,642	123,284
US	113,017	93,899	74,807	59,690	84,076	120,413	545,902
China	2,903	2,551	2,282	3,739	2,028	3,214	16,717
Others	17,207	15,776	13,996	25,208	14,757	13,157	100,101
Global	300,363	272,072	251,516	338,491	290,991	317,607	1,771,040
2004 Bloc	**EPC States**	**Japan**	**Korea**	**US**	**China**	**Others**	**Total**
EPC States	48,823	71,895	58,346	93,942	70,827	70,805	414,638
Japan	107,708	74,297	95,384	141,836	110,216	94,620	624,061
Korea	25,024	26,904	18,722	35,148	28,597	22,283	156,678
US	121,007	100,620	80,626	64,214	93,342	121,219	581,028
China	4,151	3,666	3,269	5,488	2,990	3,554	23,118
Others	17,338	15,981	14,302	25,559	14,966	13,325	101,471
Global	324,056	293,368	270,653	366,194	320,942	325,810	1,901,023

Table A5.1: (*Continued*)

2005 Bloc	**EPC States**	**Japan**	**Korea**	**US**	**China**	**Others**	**Total**
EPC States	48,634	71,657	58,546	93,588	71,831	71,531	415,787
Japan	106,014	74,631	95,519	142,208	109,846	94,569	622,787
Korea	29,198	30,475	21,920	41,645	32,730	26,032	182,000
US	129,275	106,499	87,713	68,854	101,838	130,126	624,305
China	7,276	6,326	5,714	9,781	5,258	6,048	40,403
Others	19,332	17,768	15,991	28,559	16,702	14,885	113,237
Global	339,729	307,356	285,403	384,635	338,205	343,191	1,998,519
2006 Bloc	**EPC States**	**Japan**	**Korea**	**US**	**China**	**Others**	**Total**
EPC States	48,206	69,266	57,338	92,501	71,531	71,432	410,274
Japan	104,156	73,735	94,216	140,409	109,067	92,968	614,551
Korea	28,468	28,738	21,481	41,196	30,982	25,055	175,920
US	127,170	102,499	86,181	68,023	101,470	131,062	616,405
China	8,055	6,990	6,311	10,770	5,815	6,783	44,724
Others	19,551	17,982	16,420	29,381	17,090	15,346	115,770
Global	335,606	299,210	281,947	382,280	335,955	342,646	1,977,644
2007 Bloc	**EPC States**	**Japan**	**Korea**	**US**	**China**	**Others**	**Total**
EPC States	47,406	66,043	55,928	90,857	70,790	70,616	401,640
Japan	101,395	72,885	91,493	137,939	108,910	91,814	604,436
Korea	27,194	26,958	20,904	39,927	29,259	24,249	168,491
US	125,155	98,836	84,731	67,427	102,350	129,419	607,918
China	10,121	8,992	8,307	14,346	7,585	8,817	58,168
Others	19,223	17,543	16,212	29,218	16,983	15,231	114,410
Global	330,494	291,257	277,575	379,714	335,877	340,146	1,955,063
2008 Bloc	**EPC States**	**Japan**	**Korea**	**US**	**China**	**Others**	**Total**
EPC States	46,771	64,757	55,856	89,381	71,852	69,353	397,970
Japan	95,354	69,208	85,848	130,189	104,102	86,233	570,934
Korea	23,764	23,749	18,652	35,520	25,707	21,425	148,817
US	122,853	97,261	85,166	66,396	104,497	124,961	601,134
China	11,754	10,573	9,776	17,161	8,967	10,179	68,410
Others	20,113	18,189	16,946	30,632	17,895	15,949	119,724
Global	320,609	283,737	272,244	369,279	333,020	328,100	1,906,989

(*Continued*)

Table A5.1: (*Continued*)

2009 Bloc	**EPC States**	**Japan**	**Korea**	**US**	**China**	**Others**	**Total**
EPC States	46,894	64,310	56,756	89,252	74,066	70,614	401,892
Japan	93,208	66,431	83,164	124,049	104,380	83,822	555,054
Korea	24,943	24,202	19,078	36,330	26,904	21,916	153,373
US	123,939	97,441	86,683	66,751	107,117	125,211	607,142
China	15,534	13,569	12,368	21,353	11,191	13,193	87,208
Others	20,453	18,156	16,970	30,547	18,086	15,911	120,123
Global	324,971	284,109	275,019	368,282	341,744	330,667	1,924,792
2010 Bloc	**EPC States**	**Japan**	**Korea**	**US**	**China**	**Others**	**Total**
EPC States	48,308	64,995	58,177	91,155	77,274	72,348	412,257
Japan	104,276	74,517	93,168	137,982	121,033	94,933	625,909
Korea	28,771	27,701	21,948	42,054	31,140	25,122	176,736
US	131,278	101,980	91,421	71,275	115,639	131,675	643,268
China	17,602	15,154	13,882	23,711	12,513	15,122	97,984
Others	22,150	19,693	18,626	33,141	20,792	17,434	131,836
Global	352,385	304,040	297,222	399,318	378,391	356,634	2,087,990
2011 Bloc	**EPC States**	**Japan**	**Korea**	**US**	**China**	**Others**	**Total**
EPC States	49,092	65,602	58,992	92,399	79,267	73,535	418,887
Japan	106,684	76,273	94,778	139,913	124,979	98,022	640,649
Korea	29,042	27,559	21,842	41,670	31,727	25,159	176,999
US	142,141	109,044	98,755	77,162	125,998	140,323	693,423
China	20,577	17,462	16,195	27,944	14,621	21,215	118,014
Others	23,961	21,453	20,334	35,420	25,523	19,068	145,759
Global	371,497	317,393	310,896	414,508	402,115	377,322	2,193,731
2012 Bloc	**EPC States**	**Japan**	**Korea**	**US**	**China**	**Others**	**Total**
EPC States	49,901	65,897	59,923	93,745	80,689	71,923	422,078
Japan	105,412	75,116	93,280	137,353	122,372	96,261	629,794
Korea	32,641	30,915	24,858	47,441	36,532	28,508	200,895
US	150,423	114,257	104,397	81,802	134,517	146,807	732,203
China	25,907	21,615	20,207	34,678	18,111	25,667	146,185
Others	24,859	22,287	21,272	37,288	26,693	20,022	152,421
Global	389,143	330,087	323,937	432,307	418,914	389,188	2,283,576

Table A5.1: (*Continued*)

2013 Bloc	**EPC States**	**Japan**	**Korea**	**US**	**China**	**Others**	**Total**
EPC States	51,849	68,628	61,891	97,997	83,845	73,855	438,065
Japan	101,587	72,394	89,063	132,491	116,215	92,902	604,652
Korea	37,552	34,832	29,171	55,831	42,324	33,232	232,942
US	161,438	121,701	111,923	87,721	144,476	156,249	783,508
China	28,056	23,598	22,247	37,481	19,706	26,894	157,982
Others	24,174	21,890	20,707	36,223	25,952	19,531	148,477
Global	404,656	343,043	335,002	447,744	432,518	402,663	2,365,626
2014 Bloc	**EPC States**	**Japan**	**Korea**	**US**	**China**	**Others**	**Total**
EPC States	53,253	70,421	63,530	100,555	86,439	74,481	448,679
Japan	102,741	72,651	89,177	133,279	115,580	92,633	606,061
Korea	38,142	34,946	29,522	56,212	43,514	32,870	235,206
US	149,578	112,903	104,619	81,678	133,908	143,372	726,058
China	32,184	26,969	25,339	41,757	22,003	28,654	176,906
Others	24,294	22,690	20,615	35,513	25,841	19,369	148,322
Global	400,192	340,580	332,802	448,994	427,400	391,379	2,341,347
2015 Bloc	**EPC States**	**Japan**	**Korea**	**US**	**China**	**Others**	**Total**
EPC States	51,632	68,382	61,804	97,269	85,153	75,023	439,263
Japan	97,457	68,662	83,814	125,803	110,062	87,992	573,790
Korea	37,997	34,892	29,362	55,615	44,100	32,781	234,747
US	149,676	113,459	85,974	82,686	136,881	145,289	713,965
China	32,138	27,845	44,925	43,563	22,916	31,841	203,228
Others	24,692	23,247	20,622	35,380	25,693	19,442	149,076
Global	393,592	336,487	326,501	440,316	424,805	392,368	2,314,069
2003–2007 CAGR	**EPC States**	**Japan**	**Korea**	**US**	**China**	**Others**	**Total**
EPC States	0.03	−1.44	−0.46	−0.23	1.58	−0.59	−0.19
Japan	0.19	1.55	0.68	1.38	1.74	0.54	1.02
Korea	8.97	6.02	9.72	9.68	7.39	6.79	8.12
US	2.58	1.29	3.16	3.09	5.04	1.82	2.73
China	36.65	37.02	38.13	39.96	39.07	28.70	36.58
Others	2.81	2.69	3.74	3.76	3.57	3.73	3.40
Global	2.42	1.72	2.50	2.91	3.65	1.73	2.50

(*Continued*)

Table A5.1: (*Continued*)

2007–2011 CAGR	**EPC States**	**Japan**	**Korea**	**US**	**China**	**Others**	**Total**
EPC States	0.88	−0.17	1.34	0.42	2.87	1.02	1.06
Japan	1.28	1.14	0.89	0.36	3.50	1.65	1.47
Korea	1.66	0.55	1.10	1.07	2.05	0.93	1.24
US	3.23	2.49	3.90	3.43	5.33	2.04	3.34
China	19.41	18.05	18.16	18.14	17.83	24.55	19.35
Others	5.66	5.16	5.83	4.93	10.72	5.78	6.24
Global	2.97	2.17	2.87	2.22	4.60	2.63	2.92
2011–2015 CAGR	**EPC States**	**Japan**	**Korea**	**US**	**China**	**Others**	**Total**
EPC States	1.27	1.04	1.17	1.29	1.81	0.50	1.19
Japan	−2.24	−2.59	−3.03	−2.62	−3.13	−2.66	−2.72
Korea	6.95	6.08	7.68	7.48	8.58	6.84	7.31
US	1.30	1.00	−3.41	1.74	2.09	0.87	0.73
China	11.79	12.37	29.06	11.74	11.89	10.68	14.55
Others	0.75	2.03	0.35	−0.03	0.17	0.49	0.56
Global	1.45	1.47	1.23	1.52	1.38	0.98	1.34
2003–2015 CAGR	**EPC States**	**Japan**	**Korea**	**US**	**China**	**Others**	**Total**
EPC States	0.73	−0.19	0.68	0.49	2.08	0.31	0.68
Japan	−0.26	0.02	−0.50	−0.31	0.66	−0.18	−0.09
Korea	5.81	4.18	6.10	6.01	5.97	4.82	5.51
US	2.37	1.59	1.17	2.75	4.15	1.58	2.26
China	22.18	22.04	28.19	22.71	22.39	21.06	23.14
Others	3.06	3.28	3.28	2.87	4.73	3.31	3.37
Global	2.28	1.79	2.20	2.22	3.20	1.78	2.25

Source: The data of any other top five office regions in Table 5.3 have been added to the data of top five offices in Table 5.6 in the same year and the data of any other region in Table 5.3 have been added to the data of others in Table 5.6 in the same year to get the result.

Bibliography

Results from 2011 to 2017: According to the 2018 annual reports of the top five offices from the website of CNIPA, http://www.cnipa.gov.cn/tjxx/index.htm or the website of the top five offices, https://www.fiveipoffices.org/statistics/statisticsreports.

IP5 Statistics Report 2019 Edition, European Patent Office, Japan Patent Office, Korean Intellectual Property Office, China National Intellectual Property Administration, United States Patent and Trademark Office Edited by KIPO, April 2020, https://www.fiveipoffices.org/statistics/statisticsreports.

Chapter 6

Development of Global Trade in Services and Charges for Use of Intellectual Property

When it comes to international trade, we usually focus more on trade in goods than on trade in services. As global commerce shifts from goods to services, trade in services will become increasingly prominent. Although small compared with that of commerce in goods, trade in services has a far more significant impact than we expected. Performance in business in intellectual property (IP), information and technology services, and financial services can well reflect the soft power of a country/region to an extent that other indicators cannot reach. China has achieved rapid development in its economy and commerce over the last few decades, but China is still lagging in trade in services. We should therefore take effective measures and initiate reforms to rectify this gap. Only by doing so can we effectively promote RMB internationalization.

Global commerce friction, especially the escalating tension between China and the US, has made us fully realize the necessity to improve scientific and technological innovations independently. Data on the commerce of charges for use of intellectual property services can inform us of the progress we have made in scientific and technological innovations. By comparing with other countries in terms of trade in different categories of services, we can develop a clearer understanding of the weak spots in intellectual property and information and technology services in China. Moreover, we can also realize the significant cause behind our huge deficits in trade in services — the loss of RMB pricing power and non-independent development of finance. By going into detail about the reasons for our services trade deficits, we will see that the independent development of our finance industry is as important as the independent development of science and technology.

6.1 Overview of Trade in Services

Trade in services records the value of services exchanged between residents and non-residents of an economy, including services provided through foreign affiliates established abroad. By category, services include global travel services, international transport services, charges for the use of intellectual property, financial services, insurance and pension services, telecommunications, computer and information services, construction services, maintenance and repair services, etc. Different economies may have significantly different contents for trade in services. Taking the US, for example, its travel services exports reduced slightly by 0.8% from $244.7 billion in 2016 to $242.8 billion in 2017, with contribution to the country's total services export share from 33.4% to 31.9% in the same period, still remaining the top contribution sector. The US's charges for the use of intellectual property rose by 2.7% from $124.5 billion to $127.9 billion over the same period, with the contribution to the country's total services exports decreasing to 16.8% from 17%, making it the second principal contributor and reflecting the leading position of the US in science and technology. The third and fourth contributors to the US's services trade are financial services and professional and management consulting services, which grew by 8.4% and 6.4%, respectively, in exports during 2016–2017, contributing 13.4% and 10.1% separately to US total services exports in 2017.

As for China, one of the leading countries by services imports in the world, the top three contributors to its services imports were travel, transport, and charges for the use of intellectual property in 2018, with import value of $254.8 billion, $92.9 billion and $28.6 billion, respectively, accounting for 54.5%, 19.9%, and 6.1% of the total. The top three sectors in China's services exports were travel, transport, and processing services in 2018, with the export value of $38.8 billion, $37.1 billion, and $17.9 billion, respectively, constituting 18.3%, 17.5%, and 8.4% of the total.

6.2 Growth of Global Trade in Services and Goods over the Last Decade and Forecasts for the Next Decade

Table 6.1 provides services exports, imports, net exports, and ratios of leading countries and regions during 2001–2020 according to the World Bank's latest World Development Indicators (WDI) data.

As shown in Table 6.1, global services exports increased to $6.09 trillion from $1.69 trillion during the period of 2001–2019, up 2.6 times accumulatively, with a compound annual growth rate (CAGR) of 7.40%, whereas global services imports rose by 2.25 times over the same period, with a CAGR of 7.23%. The percentage of the value of global commerce in services to that of global exchange in goods expanded from 26.3% in 2001 to 32% in 2019. Based on the annual average percentage of global exchange in services to global trade in goods during 2001–2019, we can estimate that the percentage will exceed one-third in the coming years. Clearly, global exchange is showing an increasing reliance on services over goods.

As we can see in Table 6.1, OECD member countries contributed more than 70% and 60%, respectively, to global services exports and imports on average, while their average contribution to global surplus in trade in services was strikingly 190%, showing their dominant position in global trade in services. Still, according to Table 6.1, China's average surplus in trade in services as a share of the world's total was −83.1% in 2016 and 2019, whereas that of OECD countries was 180.2% over the same period. The sum of the two nearly amounts to 100%, which means nearly all of China's services imports and exports served the OECD, whose members are mainly developed economies (OECD's balance of trade in services nearly amounts to that of over 100 economies apart from the Chinese mainland). This suggests that while China is contributing more to global trade in services, it is also in urgent need of increasing the net exports of its services commerce.

With the data provided in Table 6.1, we can calculate the percentage of the value of global trade in services to that of global trade in goods rose to 31.1% in 2019 from 21.1% in 2007, up by 10% in a decade, signifying a growing trend in trade in services. At this growth rate, the value of global commerce in services is expected to reach and even exceed that of global commerce in goods in more than two decades, resulting in higher reliance on services than on goods.

Table 6.1: Services Exports, Imports, Net Exports, and Ratios of Major Countries and Regions (Unit: USD billion, %)

Year / **Country/Region**	**2001**	**2007**	**2010**	**2011**	**2012**	**2013**	**2014**	**2016**	**2019**	**2001–2007 Annual Change**	**2007–2019 Annual Change**
US	274.3	488.4	562.8	627.1	655.7	700.5	741.1	758.9	845.2	10.1	4.7
UK	128.1	322.1	278.4	315.6	324.4	348.8	374	348.1	416.2	16.6	2.2
Germany	85.4	211.8	227.6	252.1	252.5	273.3	299.4	285.7	346.6	16.3	4.2
China	90.1	125.4	117.5	201	201.6	207	219.1	208.4	244.4	5.7	5.7
Japan	**64.7**	**121.6**	**134.6**	**140.7**	**137**	**135.4**	**163.8**	**175.7**	**207.4**	**11.1**	**4.5**
India	**17.3**	**86.6**	**117.1**	**138.5**	**145.5**	**149.2**	**157.2**	**161.8**	**214.4**	**30.7**	**7.8**
Eurozone	520	1,160.2	1,196.8	1,351.7	1,336.3	1,446.3	1,564.6	1,492.9	1,852.7	14.3	4
OECD	1,261.5	2,661.2	2,791.2	3,127.3	3,173.6	3,387	3,635	3,513.7	4,212.7	13.2	3.9
Global	1,686.4	3,033.1	3,920.6	4,475.4	4,602.2	4,896.2	5,211.1	5,045.5	6,093.7	10.3	6
Goods exports as % of global total	27	52.7	25.5	24.2	24.7	25.7	27.3	30.1	32.5		
US	213.5	372.6	409.3	435.8	452	461.1	480.8	509.8	595.4	9.7	4
UK	104.5	214.8	184.8	193.9	196.3	208.1	222.1	210.8	283.4	12.8	2.3
Germany	141.7	259.4	263	296.4	294.3	328.1	332.1	307.9	369.4	10.6	3
China	39.5	129.1	140.9	247.8	281.3	330.6	432.9	441.5	505.5	21.8	12
Japan	111.1	158.7	164.9	175.8	184.7	170.9	192.6	186.4	206.3	6.1	2.2
India	20.1	70.2	78.9	77.8	79.9	78.7	81.1	95.9	130.6	23.2	5.3
Eurozone	528.9	1,103.5	1,135.9	1,253	1,224.5	1,329.2	1,437.8	1,393.3	1,738.4	13	3.9

OECD	1,208.7	2,393.6	2,504.2	2,742.7	2,763.1	2,903.9	3,093.5	3,008.8	3,657.3	12.1	3.6
Global	1,640.5	2,916	3,739.1	4,230.3	4,378.7	4,649	5,014.7	4,774.6	5,767.5	10.1	5.8
Goods imports as % of global total	25.6	24	24.1	22.9	23.4	24.5	26.3	29.3	31.4		
% of services trade to goods trade	26.3	24.8	24.8	23.6	24.1	25.1	26.8	30.3	32		
US	60.9	115.8	153.4	191.3	203.7	239.4	260.3	249.1	249.8		
UK	23.7	107.3	93.6	121.6	128.2	140.7	151.9	137.3	132.8		
Germany	−56.2	−47.6	−35.4	−44.3	−41.8	−54.8	−32.6	−22.2	−22.8		
China	50.7	−3.7	−23.4	−46.8	−79.7	−123.6	−213.7	−233.1	−261.1		
Japan	−46.4	−37.1	−30.3	−35.1	−47.7	−35.5	−28.8	−10.7	1.1		
India	−2.8	16.4	38.2	60.8	65.6	70.4	76.1	65.9	83.7		
Eurozone	−8.9	56.7	60.9	98.7	111.8	117.1	126.8	99.7	114.2		
OECD	52.9	267.6	287	384.5	410.4	483.1	541.5	504.9	555.4		
Global	45.9	117	181.5	245.1	223.5	247.3	196.4	270.8	326.1		
	Services Trade Surplus as % of Global Total									**Annual Average % Over 2007–2019**	
US	132.5	99	84.5	78.1	91.2	96.8	132.5	92	76.6	93.8	
UK	51.5	91.6	51.6	49.6	57.4	56.9	77.3	50.7	40.7	59.5	

(*Continued*)

Table 6.1: *(Continued)*

Germany	−122.4	−40.7	−19.5	−18.1	−18.7	−22.2	−16.6	−8.2	−7	−18.9
China	110.3	−3.1	−12.9	−19.1	−35.7	−50	−108.8	−86.1	−80.1	−49.5
Japan	−101	−31.7	−16.7	−14.3	−21.4	−14.3	−14.7	−4	0.3	−14.6
India	−6	14	21	24.8	29.4	28.5	38.7	24.3	25.7	25.8
Eurozone	−19.4	48.4	33.5	40.3	50	47.4	64.5	36.8	35	44.5
OECD	−19.4	48.4	33.5	40.3	50	47.4	64.5	36.8	35	194.4
Global	100	100	100	100	100	100	100	100	100	100

Source: Calculated and compiled according to WDI data of the World Bank published in 2021.

6.3 Major Contributors to Trade in Services

Table 6.1 provides data on services trade of certain countries and regions, while Table 6.2 presents services imports, exports, and ratios of the world's top 20 contributors to commerce in services in 2019.

As we can see in Table 6.2, the US is the world's undisputed leader in trade in services as both its services imports and exports account for more than 10% of the world's total. The UK is behind the Chinese mainland and Germany in terms of total services imports and exports, but the percentage of its services exports and its net exports both came only after those of the US. Following the US and the UK are Germany, France, the Chinese mainland, Ireland, and India, ranking from No. 3 to No. 7. Notably, Singapore, Belgium, Luxembourg, Hong Kong, and Thailand, which are small in economic size, rank Nos. 9, 14, 15, 17, and 19, respectively, in terms of services exports; what's more, only 13 out of the world's top 20 economies rank among the world's top 20 trade in services contributors.

6.4 Overview of Countries and Regions Having Services Trade Surplus

6.4.1 *The absolute leading position of the US in global services trade*

As presented in Table 6.2, the US is the world's principal contributor to services trade as its contribution to global exchange in services constituted 12.1% of the world's total in 2019, larger than the Chinese mainland (ranking No. 2) and Germany (ranking No. 3) combined (11.9%). In 2019, the US's surplus in services trade recorded $249.82 billion, accounting for 76.6% of the world's total; besides, according to Table 6.1, from 2001 to 2016, the US saw its services trade surplus significantly higher than that (76.6%) in 2019 (the US's annual surplus in services trade occupied 93.8% of the world's total on average during 2007–2019), over twice the monopoly position of the US dollar in the global foreign exchange market (accounting for less than 45% of the global foreign exchange market on average). This proves the absolute monopoly position of the US in global trade in services. The huge surplus in services commerce of the US offsets roughly one-third of its deficit in goods trade, which is a strong demonstration of the country's soft power. We will later break down the US's services commerce surplus by category.

Table 6.2: Trade in Services by Major Country/Region in 2020 (Unit: billion USD, %)

Country/ Region	Exports	%	Imports	%	Imports and Exports	%	Net Exports	%
US	845.2	13.9	595.4	10.3	1,440.6	12.1	249.8	76.6
UK	416.2	6.8	283.4	4.9	699.6	5.9	132.8	40.7
Germany	346.6	5.7	369.4	6.4	715.9	6.0	−22.8	−7.0
France	287.3	4.7	262.8	4.6	550.1	4.6	24.6	7.5
Mainland China	244.4	4.0	505.5	8.8	749.9	6.3	−261.2	−80.1
Ireland	238.4	3.9	319.7	5.5	558.1	4.7	−81.2	−24.9
India	214.4	3.5	130.6	2.3	345.0	2.9	83.7	25.7
Japan	207.4	3.4	206.3	3.6	413.6	3.5	1.1	0.3
Singapore	204.8	3.4	199.1	3.5	403.9	3.4	5.8	1.8
Netherlands	196.1	3.2	176.0	3.1	372.1	3.1	20.0	6.1
Spain	157.0	2.6	86.3	1.5	243.3	2.1	70.8	21.7
Italy	121.7	2.0	124.1	2.2	245.8	2.1	−2.3	−0.7
Switzerland	121.6	2.0	104.0	1.8	225.7	1.9	17.6	5.4
Belgium	120.8	2.0	120.3	2.1	241.1	2.0	0.5	0.2
Luxembourg	110.6	1.8	84.0	1.5	194.6	1.6	26.5	8.1
South Korea	107.6	1.8	130.7	2.3	238.3	2.0	−23.0	−7.1
Hong Kong	101.3	1.7	79.0	1.4	180.3	1.5	22.3	6.8
Canada	100.8	1.7	116.2	2.0	217.1	1.8	−15.4	−4.7
Thailand	82.0	1.3	58.8	1.0	140.8	1.2	23.3	7.1
Sweden	76.2	1.2	74.5	1.3	150.7	1.3	1.7	0.5
Eurozone	1,852.7	30.4	1,738.4	30.1	3,591.1	30.3	114.3	35.0
OECD	4,212.7	69.1	3,657.3	63.4	7,870.0	66.4	555.4	170.3
Global	6,093.7	100	5,767.5	100	11,861.2	100	326.1	100

Source: Calculated and compiled according to WDI data of the World Bank.

6.4.2 *The unique position of the UK in global services trade*

As reported in Table 6.1, the UK has been far ahead of all the other countries except the US in terms of services exports; though services exports of the UK are only about one-fourth of those of the entire Eurozone, its surplus in services trade accounted for 59.5% of the world's total on average during 2007–2019, 15% higher than that of the Eurozone (44.5%)

over the same period, making the UK the world's second largest services exporter. This demonstrates the important position held by the UK in global trade in services.

Moreover, according to statistics published on the website of Office for National Statistics (https://www.ons.gov.uk/), the UK's CAGR in services exports and imports stood at 7.7% and 6.9%, respectively, during 1998–2018, and its CAGR in services trade surplus remained miraculously at 9.5% during the same period. Its surplus in trade in financial services as a percentage of the total jumped to 96.5% from 40.3% over 1998–2000, which reduced to 40.1% in 2018. During 1991–1994, the country's surplus in trade in insurance and pension services as a share of the total increased from 40.3% to 50.3%, which declined to 16.6% in 2018, though the UK's surplus in trade in financial and insurance and pension services as a percentage of total continued to decrease over the last two decades. Combined, they still amounted to over 50%, reflecting the UK's significant position in global trade in services, especially in financial services. Notably, as we can see in Table 6.4, the US recorded a trade deficit only in insurance, likely with the UK, lending further proof that the UK still takes a stronghold in the global insurance sector.

6.4.3 *Eurozone*

According to Table 6.1, the Eurozone's services trade surplus as a percentage of the world's total remained at 44.5% on average during 2007–2019, 15% lower than that of the UK (59.5%) over the same period, making it the world's third largest services exporter. As we can see in Tables 6.1 and 6.2, Germany, the largest member country of the Eurozone, has recorded services trade deficits for years; the Eurozone's surplus in services trade mainly came from Spain, France, Luxembourg, the Netherlands, and Belgium.

6.4.4 *India*

As reported in Table 6.1, India recorded a CAGR in services exports at a remarkable clip of 30.7% during 2001–2007, nearly three times that of the world (10.3%) and almost twice that of the UK (ranking No. 2) and that of Germany (ranking No. 3). India ranked first in terms of CAGR in services imports during 2001–2007, more than twice that of the world over the same period; India's services trade surplus as a share of the world's total continued to rise to 29.4% from 14% during 2007–2012, which slightly reduced to 25.7% during 2012–2019. From 2007 to 2019, India's services trade surplus as a percentage of the world's total stood at 25.8% on average, ranking No. 1 among developing countries and No. 4 around the world, only after the US, the UK, and the Eurozone.

6.4.5 *Other economies*

According to Table 6.2, Thailand's services trade surplus as a share of the world's total reached 7.1% in 2019, only after India among developing countries and exceeding that of Hong Kong China, Switzerland, and Sweden over the same period, demonstrating the unique position which Thailand occupies in the global trade in services.

6.5 Trade in Services by Category

Table 6.1 provides services trade volumes by leading country/region during the period 2001–2020, and Table 6.3 presents trade in services by category over the same period.

6.5.1 *Booming computer, communications, and related services*

As seen in Table 6.3, since 2001, trade in computer, communications and related services have maintained pole position in global services trade and imports and exports of this category rose by 5.4% and 6.9% cumulatively during 2001–2019, the highest growth among all service categories. In 1996, total imports and exports of computer, communications, and related services outnumbered that of travel, the largest contributor to global services trade back then; the exports and imports of this type continued to increase by 7.5% and 4%, respectively, during 1996–2001, greatly exceeding the annual growth rate during 2001–2019, showing an increasingly large influence of communications technology on global trade in services.

6.5.2 *Shrinking travel and transport services*

According to Table 6.3, the proportion of trade in travel and transport services as a share of the world's total continues to shrink, declining by 3%

Table 6.3: Trade in Services by Category (2001–2020) (Unit: %)

Year Exported Service Category	2001	2007	2010	2011	2012	2013	2014	2016	2019	Cumulative Change 2001–2019
Travel	29.0	27.6	27.8	26.3	26.4	26.6	26.2	26.7	25.5	−3.5
Transport	23.3	24.7	24.5	22.9	22.6	21.5	20.8	19.5	18.8	−4.6
Insurance and finance	6.4	8.3	8.7	8.5	8.4	8.7	8.7	8.6	8.4	1.9
Computer, communications, and related services	42.1	40.2	39.6	43.0	43.3	43.4	44.4	45.4	47.4	5.4
Other services	2.0	1.8	1.7	1.7	1.6	1.5	1.4	1.4	1.2	−0.8
Business services	98.0	98.2	98.3	98.3	98.4	98.5	98.6	98.6	98.8	0.8
Total	100	100	100	100	100	100	100	100	100	0.0
Year Imported Service Category	**2001**	**2007**	**2010**	**2011**	**2012**	**2013**	**2014**	**2016**	**2019**	**Cumulative Change 2001–2019**
Travel	29.0	24.7	25.3	24.0	24.6	24.7	26.1	26.8	26.6	−2.4
Transport	28.0	29.1	28.0	26.9	26.5	25.3	24.1	22.2	21.6	−6.4
Insurance and finance	7.1	8.7	9.5	8.9	8.5	8.7	8.4	8.1	7.9	0.7
Computer, communications, and related services	37.0	38.3	38.0	41.0	41.1	41.3	41.4	42.9	43.9	6.9
Other services	3.3	2.7	2.9	2.5	2.3	2.2	2.2	1.8	1.6	−1.7

(Continued)

Table 6.3: (*Continued*)

Year Exported Service Category	**2001**	**2007**	**2010**	**2011**	**2012**	**2013**	**2014**	**2016**	**2019**	**Cumulative Change 2001–2019**
Business services	96.7	97.3	97.1	97.5	97.7	97.8	97.8	98.2	98.4	1.7
Total	100	100	100	100	100	100	100	100	100	0.0
Year Service Category	**2001**	**2007**	**2010**	**2011**	**2012**	**2013**	**2014**	**2016**	**2019**	**Cumulative Change 2001–2019**
Travel	29.0	26.1	26.5	25.1	25.5	25.7	26.1	26.7	26.0	−3.0
Transport	25.7	26.9	26.3	24.9	24.6	23.4	22.4	20.9	20.2	−5.5
Insurance and finance	6.8	8.5	9.1	8.7	8.5	8.7	8.5	8.4	8.1	1.3
Computer, communications, and related services	39.5	39.2	38.8	42.0	42.2	42.3	42.9	44.1	45.7	6.1
Other services	2.7	2.2	2.3	2.1	2.0	1.9	1.8	1.6	1.4	−1.2
Business services	97.3	97.8	97.7	97.9	98.0	98.1	98.2	98.4	98.6	1.2
Total	100	100	100	100	100	100	100	100	100	0.0

Source: Calculated and compiled according to WDI data of the World Bank published in 2021.

and 5.5%, respectively, during 2001–2019. In 2019, imports and exports of travel and transport services as a percentage of the world's total added up to 46.2%, only slightly higher than that of computer, communications and related services (45.7%). Based on the annual changes in the three categories' trade volumes as a share of the world's total, the total share of travel and transport services is expected to be overtaken by that of computer, communications and related services for the first time in 2020, further proving the powerful impact of technology development on services trade.

6.5.3 *Diminishing insurance and financial services*

As presented in Table 6.3, imports and exports of insurance and financial services as a percentage of the world's total rose accumulatively by 1.7% during 2001–2007, while that of computer, communications and related services dropped by 0.3% over the same period; during 2007–2019, the former diminished by 0.4% while the latter rose by 6.4%, reflecting the lowering position of insurance and financial services in global services trade after the financial crisis.

6.6 Overview of US Advantages in Services Trade

Table 6.4 presents the exports, imports, balance, as well as annual changes in services trade over a given period since 1999.

6.6.1 *Main features of US trade in services before the financial crisis*

As reported in Table 6.8, the US registered CAGR of 11.1% and 10.3%, respectively, in exports and imports of services during 2002–2008, roughly twice that of 1999–2002; its CAGR in services trade surplus reached 14.1% during 2002–2007, a sharp contrast to −12.4% during 1999–2002, reflecting the country's rapid growth of services trade before the financial crisis; from 1999 to 2006, the US surplus in charges for the use of intellectual property as a percentage of its total services trade surplus surged to 64.9% from 33.3%, then plunged to 24.9% in 2018, less than one-fourth of that in 2006. This reveals that the contribution of US charges for the use of intellectual property to the country's total services

Table 6.4: US Net Exports of Trade in Services by Major Category and Changes (1999–2020) (Unit: billion USD, %)

Service Category Year	Maintenance and Repair Services	Transport	Travel	Construction	Insurance	Financial Services	Charges for the Use of Intellectual Property	Communications and Computer Services	Other Services	Personal, Cultural, and Recreational Services	Government Services	Total
1999	3.66	46.30	89.15	3.97	3.05	26.00	39.91	12.32	36.42	9.01	8.22	278.00
2000	4.42	49.46	96.87	1.99	3.63	29.19	43.48	12.25	38.22	9.35	9.16	298.02
2001	5.19	45.97	86.41	2.61	3.42	27.50	41.01	12.86	41.25	9.63	8.19	284.04
2002	5.37	45.95	79.63	3.13	4.42	29.90	48.82	12.40	44.63	10.09	7.65	288.06
2003	5.07	46.70	76.98	2.38	5.97	33.50	47.31	14.10	46.17	10.52	9.03	297.74
2004	5.18	54.42	85.65	2.25	7.31	42.77	56.94	15.01	51.61	11.41	11.99	344.54
2005	6.65	58.38	93.42	1.49	7.57	47.41	64.47	15.57	56.85	11.11	15.58	378.49
2006	7.11	64.03	96.15	1.86	9.45	56.52	71.00	17.24	65.99	14.53	19.22	423.09
2007	8.90	70.84	106.92	2.77	10.87	73.98	84.50	20.34	79.37	16.27	20.92	495.66
2008	9.36	78.24	117.03	4.07	13.49	79.90	89.67	23.89	89.98	16.08	19.08	540.79
2009	11.57	65.81	110.76	4.26	14.59	73.84	85.73	24.93	93.51	16.93	20.54	522.46
2010	13.11	76.36	130.32	2.95	14.85	86.51	94.97	26.56	99.60	17.61	19.21	582.04
2011	14.74	82.93	142.20	3.19	14.67	101.08	107.05	29.38	108.42	19.54	21.47	644.67
2012	14.94	88.24	153.92	3.23	15.98	105.42	107.87	33.52	118.45	21.10	22.15	684.82
2013	15.72	90.00	170.98	2.21	15.77	109.79	113.82	36.33	122.17	20.89	21.85	719.53
2014	17.98	90.69	180.27	2.07	16.28	119.93	116.38	38.63	132.24	22.55	19.69	756.71
2015	19.85	84.43	192.60	2.76	15.46	114.95	111.15	41.43	141.42	24.22	20.09	768.36
2016	21.59	81.78	192.87	1.69	16.25	114.76	112.98	43.12	153.09	23.63	18.78	780.53
2017	23.24	86.34	193.83	2.05	18.22	128.04	118.15	47.66	167.27	25.66	19.92	830.39
2018	27.95	93.25	196.47	2.95	17.90	132.42	118.88	49.65	177.26	23.76	21.95	862.43

2019	27.87	91.09	193.32	3.19	16.24	135.70	117.40	55.66	189.44	23.37	22.56	875.83
2020	13.59	56.81	71.75	2.27	16.66	137.03	114.05	54.77	184.74	17.62	22.84	692.13
CAGR 1999–2002	13.7	−0.3	−3.7	−7.7	13.1	4.8	3.9	0.4	7.0	3.9	−2.3	1.2
CAGR 2002–2008	9.7	9.3	6.6	4.5	20.5	17.8	12.3	11.4	12.4	8.1	16.5	11.1
CAGR 2009–2014	22.3	12.0	14.6	−6.6	24.3	26.0	17.2	20.7	19.8	14.3	17.1	17.5
CAGR 2014–2020	9.2	0.1	1.4	9.0	0.0	2.5	0.2	7.6	7.5	0.7	2.8	3.0
1999	1.19	49.89	58.86	1.52	9.39	12.49	12.85	14.66	20.00	1.67	14.21	196.74
2000	2.32	58.53	64.17	1.45	11.28	16.45	16.14	14.13	20.31	1.65	14.52	220.93
2001	1.82	56.57	60.53	1.87	16.71	15.98	16.21	14.01	21.20	1.82	15.32	223.04
2002	2.02	55.40	59.02	2.62	21.93	15.21	18.98	13.21	24.03	1.72	19.35	233.48
2003	2.04	61.08	61.24	1.97	25.23	15.77	18.65	14.93	25.75	2.05	23.62	252.34
2004	2.18	71.95	70.33	2.30	29.09	19.04	22.82	16.38	28.03	2.18	26.30	290.61
2005	2.73	78.80	74.11	1.30	28.71	21.97	24.13	18.40	32.08	2.55	27.45	312.23
2006	4.09	82.35	78.38	1.65	39.38	27.01	23.08	20.85	41.38	3.82	27.35	349.33
2007	4.59	86.10	82.61	2.57	47.17	33.77	24.62	23.66	48.46	3.68	28.26	385.46

(Continued)

Table 6.4: (*Continued*)

Service Category Year	Maintenance and Repair Services	Transport	Travel	Construction	Insurance	Financial Services	Charges for the Use of Intellectual Property	Communications and Computer Services	Other Services	Personal, Cultural, and Recreational Services	Government Services	Total
2008	5.13	92.84	84.32	3.53	58.44	29.52	27.76	26.14	59.68	4.42	28.88	420.65
2009	5.26	75.78	82.51	3.67	63.97	24.90	29.42	26.04	59.52	5.02	31.46	407.54
2010	5.86	88.39	85.17	2.58	63.45	27.22	31.12	29.42	65.90	5.39	31.96	436.46
2011	7.17	95.03	86.62	3.03	58.28	30.31	32.91	32.83	74.08	6.64	31.29	458.19
2012	7.08	99.32	90.34	3.34	58.75	28.74	35.06	33.29	78.68	7.16	27.86	469.61
2013	6.67	94.43	91.12	2.58	52.99	29.28	35.30	35.87	84.02	8.21	25.34	465.82
2014	**6.73**	**99.81**	**96.25**	**2.31**	**52.76**	**32.77**	**37.56**	**38.46**	**90.72**	**9.32**	**24.24**	**490.93**
2015	**8.08**	**99.56**	**102.66**	**3.01**	**49.84**	**32.59**	**35.18**	**38.82**	**95.12**	**11.36**	**21.53**	**497.76**
2016	7.60	92.39	109.16	1.77	52.07	32.67	41.97	39.72	100.51	12.54	21.50	511.90
2017	6.80	96.52	117.97	1.95	50.89	36.65	44.41	43.09	106.99	17.53	22.05	544.84
2018	7.13	106.30	126.01	3.15	43.74	39.25	43.93	42.56	107.83	19.19	22.98	562.07
2019	7.82	107.46	134.59	1.33	51.55	40.35	42.73	43.72	113.58	21.14	24.08	588.36
2020	6.03	71.59	35.78	1.09	61.55	38.80	40.68	38.17	115.79	24.21	24.57	458.26
CAGR 1999–2002	19.1	3.6	0.1	19.7	32.7	6.8	13.9	−3.4	6.3	1.0	10.8	5.9
CAGR 2002–2008	16.8	9.0	6.1	5.1	17.7	11.7	6.5	12.0	16.4	17.1	6.9	10.3
CAGR 2009–2014	22.3	10.3	8.5	−2.0	15.8	13.6	12.0	19.5	24.8	32.6	3.8	13.2
CAGR 2014–2020	3.0	1.5	6.9	−10.5	−0.5	4.2	2.6	2.6	4.6	17.8	−0.1	3.7

1999	2.46	−3.59	30.28	2.45	−6.34	13.51	27.07	−2.34	16.42	7.34	−5.99	81.26
2000	2.11	−9.06	32.70	0.55	−7.65	12.75	27.34	−1.88	17.91	7.71	−5.36	77.10
2001	3.37	−10.61	25.88	0.74	−13.28	11.52	24.80	−1.15	20.05	7.81	−7.13	62.00
2002	3.35	−9.44	20.61	0.51	−17.51	14.69	25.83	−0.73	20.60	8.37	−11.70	54.58
2003	3.03	−14.38	15.74	0.40	−19.26	17.73	28.66	−0.83	20.42	8.47	−14.59	45.40
2004	3.00	−17.54	15.32	−0.05	−21.78	23.72	34.13	−1.37	23.58	9.23	−14.31	53.93
2005	3.92	−20.42	19.31	0.19	−21.14	25.43	40.34	−2.84	24.77	8.56	−11.87	66.26
2006	3.02	−18.32	17.77	0.21	−29.94	29.52	47.92	−3.61	24.61	10.71	−8.13	73.76
2007	4.31	−15.26	24.31	0.20	−36.30	40.21	59.88	−3.32	30.91	12.59	−7.34	110.20
2008	4.23	−14.60	32.71	0.55	−44.95	50.38	61.91	−2.25	30.30	11.66	−9.80	120.14
2009	6.32	−9.98	28.25	0.59	−49.37	48.94	56.31	−1.11	33.99	11.91	−10.92	114.92
2010	7.25	−12.04	45.15	0.37	−48.60	59.30	63.85	−2.87	33.69	12.22	−12.75	145.59
2011	7.57	−12.10	55.57	0.16	−43.60	70.77	74.14	−3.46	34.34	12.90	−9.82	186.48
2012	7.87	−11.09	63.58	−0.11	−42.77	76.68	72.81	0.24	39.77	13.94	−5.71	215.21
2013	9.05	−4.44	79.86	−0.37	−37.23	80.51	78.53	0.46	38.14	12.68	−3.49	253.71
2014	11.25	−9.12	84.02	−0.24	−36.48	87.16	78.82	0.17	41.52	13.23	−4.54	265.77
2015	11.76	−15.12	89.94	−0.25	−34.38	82.36	75.97	2.61	46.30	12.86	−1.44	270.61
2016	13.99	−10.61	83.71	−0.08	−35.82	82.09	71.01	3.40	52.58	11.08	−2.73	268.63
2017	16.44	−10.17	75.86	0.10	−32.67	91.39	73.74	4.57	60.28	8.13	−2.12	285.55
2018	20.82	−13.05	70.46	−0.20	−25.83	93.17	74.94	7.10	69.43	4.57	−1.03	300.36
2019	20.05	−16.37	58.72	1.86	−35.31	95.35	74.67	11.94	75.86	2.23	−1.53	287.47
2020	7.57	−14.78	35.98	1.18	−44.89	98.24	73.37	16.59	68.95	−6.59	−1.73	233.87
CAGR 1999–2002	10.8	38.0	−12.0	−40.7	40.3	2.8	−1.5	−32.3	7.9	4.5	25.0	−12.4

(*Continued*)

Table 6.4: (*Continued*)

Service Category Year	Maintenance and Repair Services	Transport	Travel	Construction	Insurance	Financial Services	Charges for the Use of Intellectual Property	Communications and Computer Services	Other Services	Personal, Cultural, and Recreational Services	Government Services	Total
CAGR 2002–2008	4.0	7.5	8.0	1.1	17.0	22.8	15.7	20.7	6.6	5.7	−2.9	14.1
CAGR 2009–2014	22.4	−0.6	26.4	−11.6	13.0	34.6	20.4	21.7	12.4	7.9	−14.6	30.2
CAGR 2014–2020	−6.4	8.4	−13.2	34.5	3.5	2.0	−1.2	114.6	8.8	−6.5	−14.8	−2.1

Source: Data published by the US Bureau of Economic Analysis (BEA) on May 4, 2021.

trade volume has been declining sharply since the financial crisis. The surplus of services fell from $300.36 billion to $233.87 billion from 2018 to 2020 after the COVID-19 pandemic hit global trade.

6.6.2 *Main categories of US trade in services*

As shown in Table 6.8, travel is the largest category in US trade in services, but exports of this category as a share of the country's total were only slightly above 24% on average over the last two decades, lower than the world's figure in this regard (almost 30%) over the same period. Intellectual property and financial services are the second and third largest categories in the US trade in services, altogether accounting for nearly 30% of the country's total services exports. Transport services accounted for slightly over 10%; other categories of services made up less than 20% of the total. By comparing the distribution of US trade in services by category in Table 6.8 and the distribution of global trade in services in Table 6.3, we can see that the proportion of traditional service categories such as transport is relatively low in US trade in services, while intellectual property, financial services, computer and communications services are major contributors to the country's services trade, affirming its leading global position in technology, finance and knowledge.

6.6.3 *Charges for the use of IP of the US*

As we can see in Table 6.6, US imports of intellectual property decreased slightly by 4.80% during 2019–2020 and exports declined by 2.85% over the same period, resulting in a fall of 1.74% in its intellectual property surplus to $73.37 billion in 2020. In 2020, intellectual property services became the second largest source of the country's surplus in services trade (only after financial services), making up nearly 31.4% of the total. Since 2011, the US has recorded an annual net income of over $70 billion from commerce in intellectual property services, a reward from its years of huge investments in scientific research, as described in Chapter 3. This shows that while leading the world's scientific and technological advancement, the US has also started a positive cycle globally through the worldwide market with its huge input in science and technology. Nonetheless, in 2019, the US recorded far higher growth in imports of intellectual property than in exports, and the surplus in intellectual property commerce was also outnumbered by that in exchange in other services, providing evidence that the absolute superiority of US intellectual property may be waning.

According to the *World Investment Report* 2019 (Figure 1.16, p. 16) published by the United Nations Conference on Trade and Development (UNCTAD), from 2010 to 2018, the global patent and patent royalty index rose by over 60% cumulatively, exceeding the growth of services trade indicators (by about 50%) and commodity trade indicators (by nearly 20%) over the same period. This shows that trade in intellectual property has been growing faster than trade in services. R&D and intellectual property have been gaining more prominence in global trade and economic development; global competition in science and technology has become fiercer over the last 20 years.

6.6.4 *US insurance and financial services*

According to Table 6.4, US exports and imports of financial services grew by 0.98% and fell by 3.80%, respectively, in 2020, and trade in financial services generated a surplus of $98.24 billion, becoming the largest source of US surplus in services trade, which manifests the important role of financial services in US trade in services and the important position of US financial services in the global market. As provided in Table 6.8, the US insurance sector is the largest source of the country's deficit in services trade, but US exports and imports of insurance and financial services as a percentage of the world's total were 29.7% and 20.2% in 2019 and net exports of US insurance and financial services contributed 17.2% to the world's total, proving the global influence of US insurance and financial services.

6.6.5 *US travel services*

As we can see in Table 6.8, US net exports of travel services far outnumbered those of other categories of services, but the surplus generated from trade in travel services was smaller than that from trade in intellectual property and financial services in 2018. Nonetheless, trade in travel services still yielded a surplus of nearly $36 billion for the US in 2020. Even though the travel industry will continue to be important for the US, the imports, exports, and balance of this sector will inevitably decline as the case stands globally (as shown in Table 6.1).

By comparing trade services of the US against the world in Tables 6.4 and 6.3, we can find that US exports of intellectual property, science and technology, and financial services have accounted for over 30% of the country's total services trade volume, and net exports of these fields made up more than 70% of the country's total, both higher than the world's average. This reaffirms that the US is the world leader in knowledge, science and technology, and finance, having shifted toward a knowledge economy faster than others.

6.7 Overview of Countries and Regions Having Services Trade Deficit

6.7.1 *Germany and Japan*

Boasting strong technology strengths, Germany and Japan rank No. 3 and No. 4, respectively, in global trade in goods. However, according to Table 6.1, the services trade surplus of Germany and Japan accounted for −122.4% and −101% of the world's total in 2001; during 2007–2019, the two countries saw a continuous decline in their services trade deficits, and Japan even realized positive net exports for the first time in 2019; during 2007–2019, the services trade surplus of Germany and Japan as a percentage of the world's total were −18.9% and −14.6% on average, ranking No. 2 and No. 3 globally.

According to the data published on the website (www.jetro.go.jp) of Japan External Trade Organization (JETRO), from 2010 to 2018, the top two sources of Japan's services trade deficit were travel and transport, contributing 55.8% and 16%, respectively, to the country's total. Moreover, Japan continued to have deficits in insurance services, cultural and recreational services, as well as other business services, accounting for 7%, 2.7%, and 16.5%, respectively, of the total on average. The top three sources of services trade surplus for Japan are intellectual property, construction, and financial services, which only made up 7.1%, 5%, and 4.8%, respectively, of the country's total on average during 2010–2018.

6.7.2 *Mainland China*

From 2013 to 2018, except for 2016, the Mainland China ranked first globally in commerce in goods, but it only ranked fifth in services exports during 2013–2019, as displayed in Table 6.2, and ranked second only after the US in services imports. China has continued to have deficits in services trade since 2007 and it has been the world's largest source of services trade deficits since 2011; China's deficits in services trade as a share of the world's total skyrocketed to 108.8% from 3.1% during 2007–2014, which continued to decline during 2014–2019 but still accounted for 80.1% of the world's total.

In fact, as displayed in Table 6.2, China recorded a deficit in services trade at $261.15 billion in 2019, 80.3% higher than that of the other five sources of services trade deficit combined ($144.83 billion). China has become the world's largest source of services trade deficits, contributing greatly to global trade in services. Since 2014, an annual services trade deficits of over $200 billion has offset more than half of China's surplus in goods trade. China recorded a services trade deficit of $261.15 billion in 2019, offsetting 62% of its surplus in commodity trade ($421.21 billion). Such offsets put depreciation pressures on the RMB and cast negative impacts on cross-border capital flow and RMB internationalization. Reforming the current services trade system to effectively reduce services trade deficits has become an important task for China.

6.7.3 *Other countries having services trade deficits*

As we can see in Table 6.2, apart from the Chinese mainland, five countries ranking among the world's top 20 services exporters also had a deficit in services trade in 2019, and they are Germany, Canada, Ireland, Italy, and South Korea; services exchange deficits of varying degrees also occurred in developing countries such as Brazil, Russia, Saudi Arabia, and Mexico.

6.8 Services Trade of China in Recent Years and Relevant Issues

6.8.1 *Services trade development in China*

Table 6.5 provides an overview of the imports, exports, and balance of trade in services of China as well as a comparison with goods trade from 1982 to 2020. As we can see in Table 6.5, trade in services in China grew

Table 6.5: Imports, Exports, and Net Exports of Services of China as well as a Comparison with Commodity Trade (1982–2020) (Unit billion USD, %)

Year	Exports	Imports	Trade	Net Exports	% of Trade in Services to Commodity Trade	% of Net Exports of Trade in Services to Net Commodity Export
1982	2.67	2.02	4.69	0.65	13.2	15.5
1983	2.77	1.99	4.76	0.77	13.0	42.9
1984	3.09	2.86	5.95	0.23	13.7	−130.1
1985	3.10	2.52	5.62	0.58	9.6	−4.4
1986	3.86	2.28	6.14	1.58	11.4	−17.7
1987	4.08	2.49	6.57	1.60	10.7	−122.3
1988	5.10	3.60	8.70	1.49	10.2	−26.9
1989	6.20	3.91	10.11	2.29	13.1	−31.7
1990	8.06	4.35	12.42	3.71	16.5	53.4
1991	9.55	4.12	13.67	5.43	15.9	87.9
1992	12.58	9.43	22.01	3.15	20.6	169.7
1993	14.58	12.04	26.62	2.55	19.9	−17.8
1994	20.20	16.30	36.50	3.90	22.1	112.7
1995	24.42	25.22	49.64	−0.80	24.6	−6.3
1996	27.98	22.59	50.57	5.40	20.9	44.4
1997	34.24	27.97	62.20	6.27	23.1	17.2

(*Continued*)

Table 6.5: (*Continued*)

Year	Exports	Imports	Trade	Net Exports	% of Trade in Services to Commodity Trade	% of Net Exports of Trade in Services to Net Commodity Export
1998	25.05	26.84	51.89	−1.79	18.4	−3.9
1999	29.37	31.65	61.02	−2.28	20.0	−6.9
2000	35.03	36.16	71.19	−1.13	17.5	−3.8
2001	39.18	39.27	78.45	−0.10	17.9	−0.3
2002	46.23	46.53	92.76	−0.30	17.3	−0.8
2003	51.33	55.31	106.64	−3.98	14.2	−10.0
2004	72.51	72.72	145.23	−0.22	14.3	−0.4
2005	84.31	83.97	168.28	0.34	13.4	0.3
2006	102.98	100.84	203.82	2.14	13.0	1.0
2007	135.32	130.13	265.45	5.19	13.7	1.7
2008	163.31	158.95	322.26	4.36	13.9	1.3
2009	143.57	158.92	302.49	−15.35	15.1	−6.5
2010	178.34	193.40	371.74	−15.06	13.7	−6.3
2011	201.05	247.84	448.89	−46.80	13.3	−20.5
2012	201.58	281.30	482.88	−79.72	13.3	−25.6
2013	207.01	330.61	537.61	−123.60	13.7	−34.4
2014	219.14	432.88	652.02	−213.74	16.1	−49.1
2015	217.40	435.72	653.12	−218.32	17.6	−37.9

2016	208.40	441.55	649.95	−233.15	18.6	−47.7
2017	213.06	472.00	685.06	−258.93	17.3	−54.4
2018	233.57	525.74	759.30	−292.17	17.0	−76.9
2019	244.36	505.51	749.87	−261.15	17.1	−66.5
2020	235.21	380.54	615.75	−145.33	13.7	−28.2
2021*	98.43	126.00	224.43	−27.57	12.9	−17.5
CAGR from 1982 to 2001	15.18	16.89	15.98	−190.49		
CAGR from 2001 to 2020	9.89	12.70	11.45	46.96		

Source: Website of State Administration of Foreign Exchange of China: www.safe.gov.cn. *2021 data include data of the first four months in 2021.

at an average annual compound rate of 15.98%, and service trade over commodity trade ratio grew from 13.2% in 1982 to 17.9% in 2001; although trade in services continued to grow with an average annual compound rate of 11.45%, the rate of trade in service/commodity fell from 17.9% in 2001 to 13.7% in 2020, indicating faster growth of trade in goods in China.

Table 6.5 shows that net export of trade in services in China was positive from 1982 to 1997 most of the time; although with a brief period from 2005 to 2008 with a positive net export of services trade, deficits grew steadily in trade services in China from 2009 to 2020, offsetting a significant portion of trade surpluses in goods. The trade deficit in services in China was in stark contrast to India which has seen a fast expansion of services trade surplus since 2004 (India's services trade surplus soared by 29.4 times during 2004–2018 while China's services trade deficits skyrocketed by 46.5 times during 2005–2019); the ratio of China's services trade deficit to its goods trade surplus was only 3.7% in 2008 before ballooning to 83.3% in 2018. As a result, most of the surplus generated from goods trade was offset by the deficit from services trade.

6.8.2 *High imports and exports of travel services and high deficits generated therefrom*

Tables 6.1 and 6.9 present only an overview of services imports and exports of China, while Table 6.10 provides a detailed description of imports and exports of over 10 categories of services of China and their growth rates during 1997–2019 (since Tables 6.1 and 6.9 have different sources of data, there are certain small differences in the figures).

As we can see in Table 6.6, from 1997 to 2020, travel exports as a share of China's total services exports continued to decline to 7.5% from 49.3%, while the proportion of travel imports increased from 29.3% to 36.2% over the same period. Trade in travel services still generated a certain amount of surplus for China during 1997–2008, but the deficits of this category roared by 46.8 times from $4 billion in 2009 to $191.4 billion in 2015, recording a CAGR of 90.5%, and the deficit of this category as a share of China's total services trade deficits surged to 92.7% from 13.5%; though the deficit proportion of travel services declined to 81.4% during 2015–2018, it rallied to 83.5% in 2019, making travel the biggest source of services trade deficits for China. In

Table 6.6: Imports, Exports, and Net Exports of Services of China by Category and Changes (1997–2020) (Unit: billion, USD, %)

Exports	**1997**	**2002**	**2007**	**2015**	**2016**	**2017**	**2018**	**2019**	**2020**	**2015–2020 (%)**
Travel	12.1	20.4	37.2	58.0	44.4	38.8	39.5	34.5	18.9	−20.1
Transport	3.0	5.7	31.3	38.5	33.8	37.1	42.3	46.0	59.9	9.2
Processing	0.0	0.0	0.0	20.5	18.6	18.1	17.4	15.7	14.4	−6.8
Construction	0.6	1.3	5.4	16.3	12.5	12.2	13.6	14.3	13.5	−3.7
Telecommunications, computer, and information*	0.4	1.2	5.5	24.5	25.6	26.9	30.0	34.7	41.0	10.9
Charges for the use of intellectual property	0.1	0.1	0.3	1.1	1.2	4.8	5.6	6.7	9.2	52.8
Insurance and pension	0.2	0.2	0.9	5.0	4.2	4.0	4.9	4.8	5.6	2.3
Maintenance and repair	0.0	0.0	0.0	3.6	5.0	5.9	7.2	10.2	8.1	17.5
Financial services	0.0	0.1	0.2	2.2	3.2	3.7	3.5	3.9	4.5	15.2
Other business services	7.7	8.8	26.9	58.5	57.5	58.3	66.1	68.8	75.3	5.2
Personal, cultural, and recreational services	0.0	0.0	0.3	0.7	0.7	0.8	1.0	1.0	1.1	8.6
Government services	0.0	0.0	0.0	1.1	1.2	1.7	1.8	1.5	2.6	19.1
Total	24.5	39.4	121.7	229.9	208.0	212.2	232.7	242.1	254.0	2.0
Imports	**1997**	**2002**	**2007**	**2015**	**2016**	**2017**	**2018**	**2019**	**2020**	**2015–2020 (%)**
Travel	8.1	15.4	29.8	249.5	262.1	254.8	276.8	251.1	152.0	−9.4
Transport	9.9	13.6	43.3	87.3	80.9	92.9	108.3	104.9	102.5	3.3

(Continued)

Table 6.6: *(Continued)*

Imports	**1997**	**2002**	**2007**	**2015**	**2016**	**2017**	**2018**	**2019**	**2020**	**2015–2020 (%)**
Processing	0.0	0.0	0.0	0.2	0.2	0.2	0.3	0.3	0.5	22.1
Construction	1.2	1.0	2.9	10.1	8.4	8.6	8.6	9.3	8.8	−2.6
Telecommunications, computer, and information*	0.5	1.6	3.3	11.4	12.6	19.2	23.0	26.9	34.8	25.0
Charges for the use of intellectual property	0.5	3.1	8.2	22.0	23.9	28.6	35.6	34.4	39.9	12.7
Insurance and pension	**1.0**	**3.2**	**10.7**	**8.0**	**13.0**	**10.4**	**11.9**	**10.8**	**13.1**	**10.4**
Maintenance and repair	**0.0**	**0.0**	**0.0**	1.3	2.0	2.3	2.5	3.7	3.6	22.7
Financial services	0.3	0.1	0.6	2.6	2.0	1.6	2.1	2.5	3.3	5.0
Other business services	5.3	4.9	18.2	39.7	43.5	42.9	47.3	49.8	54.2	6.4
Personal, cultural, and recreational services	0.0	0.1	0.2	1.9	2.3	2.8	3.4	4.1	3.3	11.9
Government services	0.0	0.0	0.0	2.6	2.9	3.5	4.5	3.7	3.8	7.6
Total	27.7	46.1	129.3	436.4	453.5	467.7	524.2	501.4	419.9	−0.8
Net Exports	**1997**	**2002**	**2007**	**2015**	**2016**	**2017**	**2018**	**2019**	**2020**	**2015–2020 (%)**
Travel	3.9	5.0	7.4	−191.4	−217.7	−216.0	−237.4	−216.6	−133.0	−7.0
Transport	−7.0	−7.9	−12.0	−48.8	−47.1	−55.8	−66.0	−58.8	−42.7	−2.6
Processing	0.0	0.0	0.0	20.3	18.5	17.9	17.2	15.4	13.8	−7.4
Construction	−0.6	0.3	2.5	6.2	4.1	3.6	5.0	5.0	4.6	−5.7

Telecommunications, computer, and information*	−0.2	−0.4	2.2	13.1	13.0	7.6	7.0	7.8	6.2	−13.9
Charges for the use of intellectual property	−0.5	−3.0	−7.9	−20.9	−22.7	−23.8	−30.0	−27.7	−30.7	8.0
Insurance and pension	−0.9	−3.0	−9.8	−3.0	−8.8	−6.4	−7.0	−6.0	−7.5	20.2
Maintenance and repair	0.0	0.0	0.0	2.3	3.0	3.7	4.6	6.5	4.4	14.1
Financial services	−0.3	0.0	−0.3	−0.4	1.2	2.1	1.4	1.4	1.1	31.1
Other business services	2.4	3.8	8.7	18.8	14.1	15.4	18.8	19.0	21.2	2.4
Personal, cultural, and recreational services	0.0	−0.1	0.2	−1.2	−1.5	−2.0	−2.4	−3.1	−2.3	13.7
Government services	0.0	0.0	0.0	−1.5	−1.7	−1.8	−2.7	−2.2	−1.1	−5.7
Total	−3.2	−6.7	−7.6	−206.5	−245.5	−255.5	−291.6	−259.3	−165.9	−4.3

Source: Calculated and compiled based on the data published on the website (http://m.safe.gov.cn/) of the State Administration of Foreign Exchange (SAFE); data for 1997–2007 were taken from the website of the Ministry of Commerce (MOFCOM); data for 2015–2019 were calculated according to the data published on the SAFE website; *data of communication services was integrated with data of computer and information services for 1997, so as to be consistent with telecommunications, computer and information services for 2015–2019; data of "charges for the use of intellectual property" for 1997–2007 are the years' data on "royalties and licensing fees for propriety rights" which may have different definitions with "charges for the use of intellectual property" after 2015; data for processing, maintenance and government services are not displayed for 1997–2007.

2020, the deficit proportion of travel services slightly declined to 80.2% due to suppressed traveling activities after the COVID-19 pandemic. Since 2016, an annual deficit from travel services trade of more than $200 billion has taken a toll on the current account of China, thereby further impacting RMB exchange rates. We should closely monitor this situation and conduct further studies. The huge increase in the deficits from travel services trade is closely related to the growth of per capita income of China, increasing convenience in overseas travel, RMB appreciation, and the popularity of studying abroad at a younger age, among other factors, but we should also take into account the less advantageous international competitiveness of China's travel industry and two-way openness factors ("Analysis of Internal Factors Impacting the Services Trade Deficit of China", China Outsourcing Institute, MOFCOM website, December 13, 2018).

6.8.3 *High proportion of two traditional categories of services*

According to Table 6.6, the exports and imports of transport services as a percentage of China's total declined to around 24% from 25.7% and 33.5%, respectively, during 2007–2020, and transport has become the second largest source of services trade deficit for China, only after travel. The contribution of travel and transport to China's total services trade volume dropped to 49.5% from 65% during 2015–2020, and the deficit from these two categories also reduced to 105.9% from 116.3%, demonstrating the significant role these two categories play in China's services trade.

In fact, a 49.5% share of travel and transport as a proportion of total services trade of China in 2020 is only equivalent to the global level in the early 1980s, as shown in Table 6.3. This means that after 40 years of rapid growth, China has become a top player in terms of goods trade, but it still relies on travel and transport in services trade, with a performance only equivalent to the world's level 40 years ago, severely lagging its development in economy and trade, science and technology, and finance.

6.8.4 *Overview of services trade balance of China*

According to Table 6.6, China has deficits in almost all the other fields of services except for processing, maintenance and repair, and construction services where China has a small surplus. Though China has a surplus in other business services, this surplus is basically offset by the deficit in telecommunications and computer and information services, leaving a negligible surplus in business services; it also has a surplus in financial services, but such a small surplus is far from enough to offset the deficit in insurance and pension services. China has ranked among the top in the world in terms of R&D investment, but it still sees its deficit in intellectual property trade rising considerably.

6.8.5 *Steady growth in intellectual property trade deficit*

The usage of intellectual property is the best indicator for assessing the science and technology level and innovation capability of a country/region. It can also reveal the soft power of a country/region. As displayed in Table 6.6, following the two traditional fields of travel and transportation, intellectual property is the third principal contributor to the services trade deficit of China. From 2007 to 2015, China's intellectual property trade deficit surged to $20.9 billion from $7.9 billion, recording a CAGR of 12.9%. The CAGR for 2015–2018 slightly dropped to 12.8%; with deficit reaching $30 billion in 2018, it fell to $27.8 billion in 2019 and rose back slightly to $30.7 billion in 2020, demonstrating China's improvement in scientific and technological innovation in recent years, but not consistent with its soaring number of patents filed and research papers in those years. It may take some time for R&D investment to yield effective results, but a substantial growth of patents should have had a far more conspicuous impact on intellectual property. During 2009–2017, China recorded a 20.3% CAGR in the number of patents, 5.6 times higher than that of the US (3.6%) over the same period. The number of patents of China exceeded that of the US for the first time in 2011 and grew to a quantity 1.28 times larger than that of the US in 2017. However, China's surging growth of patents fails to show a conspicuous impact on the country's intellectual property trade. This raises questions about the practicability of the patents, the quality of the patents, or the number of the patents. China has lagged behind only the USA in terms of both total R&D and total R&D of companies entering world's top 2500 companies with highest R&D, the increased R&D has generated more and more patents both in China and outside China, indicating noticeable progress of China in technology innovation. However, the vast amount of Chinese patents has not generated comparable exports of charges for the use of IP, clearly showing that average quality of Chinese patents needs to be further improved in the future. We should study this issue further. It bears some resemblance to the issue we discussed in Chapter 3 — China's GDP per patent is significantly smaller than that of other countries.

6.8.6 *Shrinking surplus in information technology services trade*

As shown in Table 6.10, following other business services and processing services, telecommunications, computer, and information services are the third principal source of services trade surplus of China. From 2015 to 2019, China's imports of telecommunications, computer and information services jumped to $26.9 billion from $11.4 billion, with a CAGR of 23.9%, showing China's increasing demand for such services, whereas exports of this category increased to $34.7 billion from $24.5 billion, recording a CAGR of 9.15%. According to data as of 2017 published by the World Intellectual Property Organization (WIPO), China's number of telecommunication patents has overtaken that of the US since 2013 and became 78.8% larger than that of the US in 2017. China's number of computer technology patents has exceeded that of the US since 2015 and became 75.9% larger than that of the US in 2017. China's number of information technology patents surpassed that of the US for the first time in 2016 and became 147.9% larger than that of the US in 2017. China has overtaken the US in the total number of patents in the above three fields since 2015, becoming 84.9% larger than that of the US in 2017. However, as we can see in Table 6.6, China's surplus in these fields declined by 40.4% cumulatively during 2015–2019, contradicting China's rapid growth of patents in these fields over the same period.

6.8.7 *A big but not strong financial sector*

As seen in Table 6.6, China's financial services trade stopped having deficits and generated a surplus of $2.1 billion during 2015–2017, but the surplus reduced to $1.4 billion in 2019; the deficit in insurance and pension services trade rose to $6 billion in 2019 from $3 billion in 2015; the deficit in insurance and financial services trade grew to $4.56 billion in 2019 from $3.3 billion in 2015, recording a CAGR of 7.6%. These results seem to contradict the Chinese financial sector's rapid development in recent years. In fact, China saw a soaring capital growth in its banking sector after the financial crisis. China overtook the US in terms of bank capital for the first time in 2010, and China's bank capital grew to be

2.38 times that of the US in 2018. From 2016 to 2018, China had a financial services trade surplus of under $0.5 per USD one trillion bank capital (the US had a financial services trade surplus of $45.2 and $46.7 per one trillion USD bank capital, respectively, in 2016 and 2017). The banking-focused financial sector of China is big but not strong, clearly lacking international competitiveness.

6.9 Major Exporters of Charges for Use of IP in the World

Exports of charges for the use of intellectual property of different countries and regions represent levels or capacity of science and technology (sci-tech); the greater the export, the higher the sci-tech development of a region. Table 6.7 gives the exports of charges for the use of IP of major economies with export over $1 billion in 2019.

6.9.1 *Top exporters of charges for the use of IP compared with top economies*

The world's top 20 economies are well known to economists, researchers, and professionals worldwide, yet the top 20 exporters of charges for use of IP are not so well known. Table 6.7 shows that of the top 20 exporters of charges for the use of IP, only 12 are among the top 20 economies of 2019. Russian Federation was ranked 25th in Table 6.3, and India, Brazil, Australia, Mexico, Indonesia, Saudi Arab, and Turkey are not even in the top 25 list in Table 6.3. Of the above eight top 20 economies not in the top 20 list in Table 6.3, only Australia is a developed country, and only China in the top 20 list in Table 6.3 is a developing country. These results show that exports of charges/fees for the use of IP are almost exclusive rights for developed countries (as the share of export of charges for the use of IP of China over total top 20 exporters in Table 6.7 was merely from 0.30% to 1.72% from 2006 to 2019), and all developing countries and other developed countries have to rely on imports of charges for the use of IP from developed countries.

6.9.2 *Concentration of exports of charges for use of IP*

Table 6.7 shows that of the top 20 exporters of world charges for the use of IP from US to Luxembourg, 18 were developed countries, with China

Table 6.7: Major Exporters of Exports of Charges for the Use of IP (2008–2019) (Unit: $billion USD, %)

Year/Region	2008	2010	2012	2014	2016	2018	2019	CAGR
US	89.67	94.97	107.87	116.38	112.98	118.88	117.40	2.48
Netherlands*	0.00	0.00	0.00	46.15	43.55	57.19	66.45	7.56
Japan	25.69	26.68	31.89	37.39	39.27	45.48	46.73	5.59
UK	14.31	14.19	13.46	19.89	19.17	26.31	25.27	5.31
Germany	7.34	8.25	10.29	15.46	18.82	24.43	24.33	11.52
Switzerland	9.10	13.36	17.75	18.70	22.03	25.85	23.91	9.17
France	15.47	13.62	12.72	14.59	15.50	16.81	15.36	−0.07
Ireland	1.48	2.92	4.99	6.96	8.91	13.91	11.10	20.14
Singapore	1.21	1.93	2.81	3.91	7.04	8.37	8.47	19.32
Sweden	4.71	5.78	7.55	9.18	7.65	7.44	7.95	4.88
Korea	2.43	3.19	3.90	5.54	6.94	7.75	7.75	11.10
China	0.57	0.83	1.04	0.68	1.17	5.56	6.64	24.99
Canada	4.11	2.81	3.93	4.75	4.51	5.51	5.39	2.49
Italy	3.97	3.65	4.10	3.35	3.44	4.96	4.53	1.21
Belgium	1.52	2.49	2.66	3.31	3.80	4.39	3.98	9.16
Finland	1.49	2.32	3.33	2.63	3.03	3.47	3.56	8.24
UAE	0.00	0.00	0.00	3.27	3.49	3.70	3.84	3.27
Denmark	2.37	2.03	2.26	2.52	2.43	3.34	3.49	3.59
Spain*	0.00	0.00	1.36	1.44	1.93	2.54	3.42	14.03
Luxembourg	0.34	0.55	1.34	2.18	2.27	2.44	2.56	20.17
Israel*	0.96	0.38	1.02	1.27	1.61	2.20	2.39	8.69
Austria	1.17	0.93	1.10	1.28	1.17	1.40	1.52	1.84
Hungary	1.71	2.03	2.04	2.08	1.79	1.77	1.46	0.37
Taiwan China	0.19	0.46	0.93	0.87	1.24	1.54	1.41	23.22
Russian Federation	0.41	0.39	0.66	0.67	0.55	0.88	1.01	7.99
Sum	190.20	203.75	238.99	324.43	334.29	396.10	399.90	6.99
Top 10	168.97	181.70	209.32	288.60	294.93	344.65	346.97	6.76
Top 11–20	16.80	17.87	23.93	29.67	33.01	43.65	45.14	9.40
Rest of World	45.92	43.36	43.82	6.65	6.75	9.07	9.27	−13.53

Table 6.7: (*Continued*)

Year/Region	2008	2010	2012	2014	2016	2018	2019	CAGR
World	236.11	247.11	282.80	331.08	341.04	405.17	409.17	5.13
Sum/World	80.55%	82.45%	84.51%	97.99%	98.02%	97.76%	97.73%	
Top 10/ World	71.57%	73.53%	74.01%	87.17%	86.48%	85.07%	84.80%	
EPC States	93.44	98.27	111.64	132.38	138.91	173.48	177.33	6.00
Eurozone	74.56	73.67	80.64	98.05	103.07	132.70	137.99	5.76
Euro/EPC	79.79%	74.96%	72.23%	74.07%	74.20%	76.49%	77.81%	

Source: WTO website: http://www.wto.org/; *average annual growth rates are CAGRs from 2008 to 2019 for all countries and regions, from 2014 to 2019 for the Netherlands, from 2012 to 2019 for Spain, and from 2008 to 2018 for Israel; data for Israel in 2019 are estimated using Israel data in 2018 as base and the CAGR from 2008 to 2018.

ranked 12th and United Arab Emirates (UAE) ranked 17th as exceptions. The top 10 world share was from 71.57% to 84.80%, and the share of top 25/world was from 80.55% to 97.73%, the rest of the world (world other than the top 25 countries in Table 6.7) accounted for 19.45% to 0.227% of world exports of world charges for the use of IP, indicating that most exports of charges for the use of IP are from major developed countries, and the rest of the world simply relies on their IP.

6.9.3 *Growth rates of exports of charges for use of IP*

Table 6.7 shows that of the top 25 exporters of world charges for the use of IP, only France experienced a negative CAGR, all others had various degrees of growth. Particularly, the top 10 countries had a CAGR of 6.76%, 1.63% higher than the corresponding world CAGR of 5.13%, showing that major developed countries still grow significantly in exports of charges for the use of IP.

It should be noted that China had the highest CAGR of 24.99% from 2008 to 2019 of all the 25 top exporters in Table 6.3, followed by Taiwan China with a CAGR of 23.22% and Ireland with a CAGR of 20.14% in the same period. The next three economies with double-digit CAGR were 14.03%, 11.52%, and 11.10% for Spain, Germany, and Korea, respectively, in the same period. It should also be noted that the rest of the world other than the top 25 economies experienced a CAGR of −13.53%, indicating that exports of charges for the use of IP has been concentrated in the leading exporters of charges for use of IP.

6.9.4 *Exports of charges for use of IP in China*

Table 6.7 shows that export of charges for use of IP in China grew with the highest average annual compound rate of 24.99% among all the top 25 leading exporters from 2005 to 2019, and export of charges for use of IP of 6.64 was ranked 12th in 2019. Data updated by the SAFE of China in May 2021 showed that export of charges for the use of IP in China increased to $8.68 billion, indicating a much higher annual growth rate of 30.64% from 2019 to 2020 than the rate of 19.43% from 2018 to 2019. About $8.64 billion in export of charges for the IP of China in 2020 was ranked within the top 10 leading exporters of charges for the use of IP in Table 6.7, and total export of charges for the use of IP in China increased by 45.2% to $4.54 billion in the first four months of 2021 compared to the same period of 2020, indicating much higher growth rates recently.

6.9.5 *Exports of charges for use of IP/GDP of major blocs*

The exports of charges for the use of intellectual property of the top 25 economies reflect the magnitudes of exports of these economies, yet as various economies differ in scale, the ratios of exports of charges for the use of IP over GDP of various economies can better reflect the technology capability of these economies. Table 6.8 gives such ratios of major blocs of patents from 2005 to 2019.

Table 6.8 shows that the US had the highest exports of charges for use of IP/GDP ratio from 2005 to 2013, yet Japan and EPC States surpassed the US in the ratio in 2014 and 2015, respectively. EPC States, Japan, and the US all surpassed world exports of charges for the use of IP/GDP ratio from 2005 to 2019; the rest of five blocs ratio was about half of the world ratio for the same period, yet the Chinese ratio was less than 7% of the rest of the world ratio from 2005 to 2016, and it was around 20% of the rest of the world ratio, implying that China has much to do to catch up not only with the advanced countries but also with the rest of the world.

Table 6.8: Exports of Charges for the Use of IP/GDP of Major Blocs (2005–2019)

Year/ Bloc	EPC States (%)	Japan (%)	Korea (%)	US (%)	China (%)	Others (%)	World (%)
2005	0.41	0.36	0.22	0.49	0.01	0.19	0.36
2006	0.41	0.44	0.20	0.51	0.01	0.17	0.36
2007	0.42	0.51	0.16	0.58	0.01	0.16	0.37
2008	0.44	0.50	0.23	0.61	0.01	0.14	0.37
2009	0.49	0.41	0.34	0.59	0.01	0.15	0.37
2010	0.52	0.46	0.28	0.63	0.01	0.12	0.37
2011	0.55	0.47	0.35	0.69	0.01	0.12	0.38
2012	0.57	0.51	0.31	0.67	0.01	0.11	0.38
2013	0.60	0.61	0.32	0.68	0.01	0.14	0.40
2014	0.63	0.76	0.37	0.66	0.01	0.16	0.42
2015	0.69	0.82	0.45	0.61	0.01	0.21	0.44
2016	0.75	0.78	0.46	0.60	0.01	0.20	0.45
2017	0.79	0.85	0.45	0.60	0.04	0.21	0.46
2018	0.83	0.90	0.45	0.58	0.04	0.23	0.47
2019	0.87	0.91	0.47	0.55	0.05	0.22	0.47

Source: Calculated using data from Table 6.7 and GDP data of the International Monetary Fund released in April 2021.

6.10 Major Importers of Charges for the Use of IP

As science and technology is so diverse that no matter how advanced a country is in sci-tech, it is impossible for it to do extremely well in every area of sci-tech. Thus, every country or region must import a certain amount of charge for the use of IP for its economic and trade development and for sci-tech progress. Table 6.9 gives the imports of charges for the use of IP of leading economies with import value over $1 billion in 2019.

6.10.1 *Top importers of charges for the use of IP compared with top economies*

Table 6.9 shows that of the top 20 importers of charges for the use of IP, Ireland, Singapore, Sweden, Luxembourg, and Thailand were not in the

Table 6.9: Imports of Charges for the Use of IP of Major Economies (2005–2019) (Unit: USD billion)

Year/Region	2008	2010	2012	2014	2016	2018	2019	CAGR
Ireland	35.45	37.46	38.19	57.48	76.60	85.24	95.11	9.39
Netherlands*	0.00	0.00	0.00	56.87	50.40	64.75	66.24	3.10
US	27.76	31.12	35.06	37.56	41.97	43.93	42.73	4.00
China	10.32	13.04	17.75	22.61	23.98	35.60	34.33	11.55
Japan	18.29	18.77	19.90	20.87	20.25	21.74	25.85	3.19
UK	10.21	10.16	9.74	12.18	11.83	14.49	16.94	4.71
Singapore	13.60	17.03	23.11	20.88	15.47	16.81	16.15	1.57
Germany	8.63	7.10	6.39	10.75	11.32	15.63	15.71	5.60
France	10.43	10.02	8.76	12.76	14.76	15.93	13.57	2.42
Switzerland	4.98	8.03	11.48	14.07	12.25	13.65	11.92	8.26
Canada	8.93	9.73	10.90	11.69	11.56	11.80	11.40	2.24
Korea	5.82	9.18	8.62	10.55	9.43	9.88	10.02	5.06
India	1.53	2.44	3.99	4.85	5.47	7.91	7.89	16.09
Sweden	2.06	1.50	2.48	3.91	3.35	4.86	6.93	11.64
Russian Federation	4.48	4.84	7.63	8.02	5.00	6.29	6.87	3.96
Spain*	0.00	0.00	5.47	4.48	4.99	6.65	6.86	3.30
Luxembourg	0.70	0.73	2.60	5.01	4.19	5.01	6.23	22.03
Brazil	2.70	3.23	4.20	5.92	5.14	5.12	5.34	6.41
Thailand	2.57	3.08	3.61	3.97	3.98	5.27	5.31	6.83
Italy	7.23	6.54	5.59	5.18	4.69	5.15	5.25	−2.87
Poland	1.77	2.24	2.32	2.96	2.70	3.65	3.76	7.07
Australia	2.95	3.41	4.17	3.97	3.32	3.63	3.50	1.56
Taiwan China	3.02	4.94	5.68	5.28	5.29	3.61	3.26	0.72
Belgium	2.02	1.90	2.82	3.40	2.77	3.73	3.22	4.31
UAE*	0.00	0.00	0.00	2.18	2.48	2.78	2.89	5.79
Malaysia	1.27	1.32	1.54	1.42	1.35	2.01	2.21	5.20
Austria	2.09	1.61	1.96	1.78	1.47	2.00	2.18	0.35
Hong Kong China	1.61	1.98	2.02	1.94	1.88	1.99	1.94	1.70
Turkey	0.73	0.82	0.74	1.69	1.88	1.88	1.93	9.26

Table 6.9: (*Continued*)

Year/Region	2008	2010	2012	2014	2016	2018	2019	CAGR
Indonesia	1.33	1.62	1.80	1.86	1.73	1.47	1.80	2.82
Argentina	1.53	1.71	2.22	2.10	2.11	2.09	1.75	1.21
South Africa	1.68	1.94	2.02	1.73	1.98	1.82	1.65	−0.15
Denmark	1.20	1.33	1.39	1.70	1.63	1.57	1.65	2.98
Czech	0.86	0.94	1.04	1.34	1.19	1.50	1.52	5.31
Hungary	2.60	1.80	1.70	1.70	1.45	1.50	1.41	−5.37
Finland	2.25	1.51	1.77	1.17	0.88	1.07	1.13	−6.07
Sum	202.61	223.06	258.64	365.83	370.70	432.00	446.46	7.45
Rest of World	68.76	63.98	61.94	16.39	15.76	19.10	18.68	−11.17
World	271.37	287.03	320.58	382.22	386.46	451.10	465.15	5.02
Top 10	139.68	152.72	170.37	266.04	278.82	327.77	338.55	8.38
Top 11–20	36.02	41.27	55.07	63.58	57.79	67.95	72.11	6.51
Top 21–30	16.79	19.84	23.06	26.48	24.86	26.75	26.69	4.30
Top 25	186.74	207.81	241.99	348.82	354.50	415.11	429.50	7.87
Sum/World	74.66%	77.71%	80.68%	95.71%	95.92%	95.77%	95.98%	
Top 10/World	51.47%	53.21%	53.15%	69.60%	72.15%	72.66%	72.78%	
Top 25/World	68.81%	72.40%	75.48%	91.26%	91.73%	92.02%	92.34%	
EPC States	154.46	150.30	156.86	203.74	213.27	254.77	267.89	5.13
Eurozone	128.67	121.89	124.21	161.72	174.81	208.78	218.95	4.95
Euro/EPC	83.30%	81.10%	79.18%	79.37%	81.97%	81.95%	81.73%	

Source: WTO website: http://www.wto.org/; *average annual growth rates are CAGRs from 2008 to 2019 for all countries and regions, from 2014 to 2019 for the Netherlands, from 2012 to 2019 for Spain, and from 2008 to 2018 for Israel; data for Israel in 2019 are estimated using Israel data in 2018 as base and the CAGR from 2008 to 2018.

list of top 20 economies of the world in 2019. The other 15 top 20 importers of charges for the use of IP were in the top 20 list of economies, and Australia, Mexico, Indonesia, Saudi Arabia, and Turkey are not even in the top 20 list in Table 6.10, and Mexico and Saudi Arabia were not even in the top 36 list of importers of charges for the use of IP. Of the above five countries not in the top 20 list in Table 6.10, Australia again was the only developed country, and China, India, Russia, and Brazil were four leading developing countries in the top 20 list in Table 6.10. These results show that more developing countries rely on imports of charges for the use of IP for their economic and trade development than exports of charges for the use of IP.

6.10.2 *Top importers of charges for the use of IP*

Table 6.9 shows that Ireland, a country with a population of less than 5 million and GDP much less than USD half-trillion, GDP ranked 29th in the world in 2019, was ranked No.1 with the imports of charges for the use of IP of $95.11 billion or 22.71% of GDP of the country in 2019. The ratio was not only the highest in the world but also 44.83 times the world ratio of 0.53%. The second ranked importer of charges for the use of IP was the Netherlands, with the import of $66.24 billion, or 7.3% of its GDP in 2019, the ratio was 13.71 times the corresponding world ratio of 0.53%. The high imports and high import/GDP ratios in these two European countries indicate that they employ a large number of foreign IP to develop their economies and trade.

6.10.3 *Concentration of imports of charges for the use of IP*

Table 6.8 shows that the concentration of imports of charges for the use of IP was not as intensive as the concentration of exports of charges for the use of IP, as shown in Table 6.7. We can see the total share of top 10 importers of world imports changed from 51.47% to 72.78%, much lower than the corresponding share of 71.57% to 84.80% in Table 6.3. The top 25 importers' share of world imports increased from 68.81% to 92.34%, also much lower than the corresponding share of 88.55% to 97.73% in Table 6.7 (Table 6.7 lists top 25 exporters of charges for use of IP).

6.10.4 *Growth rates of imports of charges for the use of IP*

Table 6.9 shows that of the top 36 importers of charges for use of IP, only Italy experienced a negative CAGR, all others had various degrees of growth. The total imports of all 36 countries and regions had an average annual compound growth rate of 7.45%, 2.43% higher than the corresponding world annual compound growth rate of 5.02%, showing that developed countries still grow significantly in imports of charges for the use of IP.

It should be noted that Luxembourg had the highest CAGR 22.03% of all 36 top importers in Table 6.9 from 2008 to 2019, followed by India, Sweden, and China mainland with CAGRs of 16.09%, 11.64%, and 11.55% for the same period. The two near double-digit CAGRs of 9.39% and 9.26% of Ireland and Turkey in the same period are also notable. The above average CAGRs indicate fast economic and trade development of corresponding economies in the same period.

6.10.5 *Growth rates of importers in comparison*

It is worth noting that the average annual compound growth rate of imports of top 10 importers of charges for the use of IP was 8.38%, 3.36% higher than the corresponding world growth rate of 5.02%. The CAGR of imports of the top 11–20 importers of charges for the use of IP was 6.51%, 1.49% higher than the corresponding world growth rate of 5.02%. The CAGR of imports of the top 11–30 importers of charges for the use of IP was 4.30%, 0.73% lower than the corresponding world growth rate of 5.02%. The average CAGR of imports of the rest of the world (other than the top 36 importers in Table 6.8) was −11.17%, 16.19% lower than the corresponding world growth rate of 5.02%, indicating that the higher importers intend to import more charges for the use of IP.

6.11 Major Traders of Charges for the Use of IP of the World and Related Implications

Export of charges for the use of IP of any economy presents its technology capability for international usage, and certainly for its domestic usage, and import of charges for the use of IP of the economy reveals its reliance on technology from the global marketplace. Thus, both export and import of charges for the use of IP are necessary for economic development. We introduced exports and imports of charges for the use of IP of leading economies in the previous sections. We will introduce both exports and imports or trade of charges for the use of IP of leading economies in this section. Table 6.10 gives the trade of charges for the use of IP of major economies from 2008 to 2019. Table 6.10 gives the results.

Table 6.10: Exports and Imports of Charges for the Use of IP of Major Economies (2008–2019) (Unit: USD billion)

Year/ Country or Region	**2008**	**2010**	**2012**	**2014**	**2016**	**2018**	**2019**	**CAGR**
US	117.44	126.08	142.93	153.94	154.96	162.81	160.13	2.86
Netherlands*	0.00	0.00	0.00	103.03	93.95	121.94	132.69	5.19
Ireland	36.93	40.38	43.18	64.44	85.51	99.15	106.21	10.08
Japan	43.98	45.46	51.79	58.25	59.52	67.22	72.57	4.66
UK	24.52	24.35	23.19	32.07	31.01	40.80	42.21	5.06
China	10.89	13.87	18.79	23.29	25.15	41.16	40.97	12.80
Germany	15.97	15.35	16.68	26.21	30.14	40.06	40.04	8.72
Switzerland	14.08	21.38	29.23	32.77	34.27	39.50	35.83	8.86
France	25.91	23.64	21.48	27.35	30.26	32.73	28.93	1.01
Singapore	14.82	18.96	25.92	24.79	22.51	25.18	24.62	4.73
Canada	13.04	12.55	14.83	16.45	16.08	17.31	16.78	2.32
Korea	8.26	12.37	12.52	16.09	16.37	17.63	17.77	7.21
Sweden	6.77	7.27	10.02	13.08	11.00	12.30	14.88	7.42
Spain*	0.00	0.00	6.83	5.92	6.92	9.19	10.28	6.01
Italy	11.20	10.19	9.69	8.52	8.13	10.10	9.78	−1.23
Luxembourg	1.04	1.28	3.94	7.19	6.46	7.45	8.79	21.46
India	1.68	2.57	4.31	5.51	5.99	8.69	8.76	16.22
Russian Federation	4.89	5.23	8.29	8.69	5.55	7.16	7.88	4.44
Israel*	1.87	0.83	1.38	1.72	2.05	2.79	7.74	13.81
Belgium	3.54	4.39	5.48	6.71	6.56	8.12	7.20	6.66
UAE	0.00	0.00	0.00	5.45	5.96	6.48	6.73	4.31
Brazil	3.16	3.42	4.47	6.30	5.79	5.95	5.99	5.97
Thailand	2.67	3.12	3.72	4.03	4.05	5.44	5.51	6.81
Denmark	3.56	3.35	3.66	4.22	4.06	4.91	5.14	3.39
Finland	3.74	3.83	5.10	3.80	3.91	4.53	4.69	2.07
Taiwan China	3.21	5.40	6.61	6.14	6.53	5.15	4.67	3.48
Australia	3.68	4.39	5.03	4.82	4.14	4.60	4.46	1.77
Poland	1.98	2.48	2.55	3.30	3.14	4.27	4.42	7.56
Austria	3.26	2.54	3.05	3.07	2.64	3.41	3.70	1.15

Table 6.10: (*Continued*)

Year/ Country or Region	**2008**	**2010**	**2012**	**2014**	**2016**	**2018**	**2019**	**CAGR**
Hungary	4.30	3.83	3.73	3.78	3.24	3.27	2.87	−3.62
Sum	386.36	418.49	488.40	680.92	695.81	819.29	842.23	7.34
Rest of World	121.12	115.66	114.98	32.38	31.69	36.98	32.09	−11.37
World	507.48	534.14	603.38	713.30	727.50	856.27	874.32	5.07
Top 10	304.52	329.48	373.18	546.14	567.27	670.54	684.22	7.64
Top 11–20	52.28	56.67	77.29	89.88	85.09	100.75	109.85	6.98
Top 21–30	29.56	32.34	37.93	44.90	43.46	48.00	48.16	4.54
Sum/World	76.13%	78.35%	80.94%	95.46%	95.64%	95.68%	96.33%	
Top 10/ World	60.01%	61.68%	61.85%	76.57%	77.97%	78.31%	78.26%	
EPC States	237.51	257.92	269.11	328.52	365.07	412.42	444.27	5.86
Eurozone	203.23	195.56	204.85	259.76	277.89	341.48	356.94	5.25
Euro/EPC	85.57%	75.82%	76.12%	79.07%	76.12%	82.80%	80.34%	

Source: Addition of exports and imports of charges for use of IP from Tables 6.7 and 6.9.

6.11.1 *Top traders of charges for use of IP compared with top economies*

Table 6.10 shows that of the top 20 traders of charges for use of IP, only 14 are among the top 20 economies of 2019. Brazil, Australia, Mexico, Indonesia, Saudi Arabia, and Turkey are not in the top 20 list in Table 6.7, Brazil and Australia are ranked 22nd and 27th in Table 6.10, respectively, and Mexico, Indonesia, Saudi Arabia, and Turkey are not even in the top 30 list in Table 6.10. Of the above six top 20 economies not in the top 20 list in Table 6.9, Australia is the only developed country, and only China, India, and Russia are in the top 20 list in Table 6.10.

6.11.2 *Trade of charges for use of IP/GDP of major countries and regions*

The trade volumes of charges for the use of IP of leading economies are more meaningful if we compare them with their corresponding GDP magnitudes. The empirical results in Chapter 8 show the importance of trade of charges for use of IP in economic development, and thus IP sufficiency is a good measure of sci-tech sufficiency compared to GDP of any economy. Table 6.11 gives the ratios of trade of charges for the use of IP over GDP of leading countries and regions from 2005 to 2019.

Table 6.11 shows that Ireland's trade of charges for the use of IP/GDP increased from 13.38% in 2008 to 26.66% in 2019 as a result of high trade volume of charges for the use of IP compared to Ireland's GDP. The average annual growth of the ratio was also the highest of all economies at 120.69% in the same period, indicating high IP sufficiency in Ireland from 2008 to 2019. Ratios in the Netherlands and Luxembourg were above 10% in recent years, much higher than any other economy besides Ireland. Ratios in Singapore and Switzerland were ranked fourth and fifth of all economies in Table 6.11, yet average annual growth was negative in Singapore. Ratios of 22 developed economies in Table 6.11 increased from 0.90% to 1.22% from 2008 to 2018, steadily higher than the corresponding ratios of the world, and also with an average annual change of 2.95%, indicating sufficiency of IP in developed economies, yet ratios of eight leading developing economies in Table 6.11 only increased from 0.28% to 0.37% in the same period, with an average annual change of 0.82%, 2.13% lower than the corresponding average annual change, indicating relevant insufficiency of IP in leading developing countries.

6.11.3 *Degrees of IP Sufficiency of major economies*

Table 6.11 shows that trade of charges for the use of IP/GDP was generally very low for most developing countries in Table 6.12. Calculations with the same data source show that ratios were lowest in Mexico with an average annual ratio of merely 0.03% and average annual change of −0.06% from 2008 to 2019. Average annual ratios were 0.20% and 0.17% in Indonesia and Turkey (as both export and import of charges for the use of IP were missing in the WTO website for Saudi Arabia, we cannot find comparable ratios of Saudi Arabia). Table 6.7 also shows that the trade of charges for the use of IP/GDP grew from 0.24% to 0.29% in China from 2008 to 2019, steadily lower than the corresponding ratios for eight developing countries in Table 6.10 in the same period. The average annual change of 0.43% was also lower than the corresponding average annual change of 0.82% for eight developing countries, indicating that IP

Table 6.11: Trade of Charges for the Use of IP/GDP Ratios of Leading Economies (2005–2019)

Year/Country or Region	2008	2010	2012	2014	2016	2018	2019	CAGR
US	0.80	0.84	0.88	0.88	0.83	0.79	0.75	−0.46
Netherlands*	0.00	0.00	0.00	11.54	11.99	13.33	14.63	61.65
Ireland	13.38	18.13	19.17	24.89	28.59	25.64	26.66	120.69
Japan	0.86	0.79	0.83	1.19	1.19	1.33	1.41	4.98
UK	0.83	0.98	0.86	1.05	1.15	1.43	1.49	6.00
China	0.24	0.23	0.22	0.22	0.22	0.30	0.29	0.43
Germany	0.43	0.45	0.47	0.67	0.87	1.01	1.04	5.55
Switzerland	2.47	3.55	4.22	4.46	4.93	5.36	4.89	22.03
France	0.88	0.89	0.80	0.96	1.22	1.17	1.06	1.64
Singapore	7.65	7.91	8.78	7.87	7.06	6.70	6.58	−9.78
Canada	0.84	0.78	0.81	0.91	1.05	1.01	0.96	1.13
Korea	0.79	1.08	0.98	1.08	1.09	1.02	1.08	2.65
Sweden	1.31	1.47	1.81	2.25	2.13	2.21	2.80	13.57
Spain*	0.00	0.00	0.52	0.43	0.56	0.65	0.74	6.70
Italy	0.47	0.48	0.46	0.39	0.43	0.48	0.49	0.20
Luxembourg	1.85	2.41	6.94	10.86	10.64	10.50	12.36	95.56
India	0.14	0.15	0.24	0.27	0.26	0.32	0.31	1.53
Russian Federation	0.27	0.32	0.38	0.42	0.43	0.43	0.47	1.74
Israel*	0.86	0.35	0.54	0.55	0.64	0.75	1.96	9.99
Belgium	0.68	0.91	1.10	1.25	1.38	1.49	1.35	6.05
UAE	0.00	0.00	0.00	1.35	1.67	1.53	1.60	4.92
Brazil	0.19	0.15	0.18	0.26	0.32	0.31	0.32	1.20
Thailand	0.92	0.91	0.93	0.99	0.98	1.07	1.01	0.87
Denmark	1.01	1.04	1.12	1.19	1.30	1.37	1.47	4.18
Finland	1.31	1.53	1.97	1.38	1.62	1.64	1.74	3.94
Taiwan China	0.77	1.22	1.33	1.15	1.20	0.85	0.76	−0.07
Australia	0.35	0.35	0.32	0.33	0.33	0.32	0.32	−0.25
Poland	0.37	0.52	0.51	0.61	0.67	0.73	0.74	3.36
Austria	0.75	0.65	0.74	0.69	0.67	0.75	0.83	0.69
Hungary	2.72	2.90	2.91	2.68	2.52	2.04	1.76	−8.78

(*Continued*)

Table 6.11: (*Continued*)

Year/Country or Region	2008	2010	2012	2014	2016	2018	2019	CAGR
Sum	0.74	0.77	0.80	1.06	1.11	1.15	1.17	3.90
Rest of World	1.06	0.97	0.82	0.22	0.24	0.25	0.21	−7.70
World	0.79	0.81	0.81	0.90	0.96	1.00	1.00	1.88
Top 10	0.85	0.88	0.89	1.21	1.24	1.30	1.30	4.11
Top 11–20	0.48	0.52	0.65	0.72	0.77	0.78	0.85	3.42
Top 21–30	0.53	0.53	0.55	0.64	0.73	0.72	0.72	1.71
Sum/World	92.70	95.63	99.72	117.36	116.13	115.60	116.39	
Top 10/World	106.52	109.74	110.36	134.79	129.90	130.55	129.59	
EPC States	1.03	1.23	1.25	1.43	1.77	1.80	1.98	8.63
Eurozone	1.44	1.55	1.62	1.92	2.32	2.49	2.67	11.22
Euro/EPC	139.98	125.55	129.56	134.59	131.18	138.53	135.20	
Developed Economies**	0.90	0.94	0.95	1.08	1.15	1.21	1.22	2.95
Developing Economies**	0.28	0.27	0.28	0.33	0.33	0.38	0.37	0.82

Source: Calculated using data from Table 6.10 and GDP data of International Monetary Fund released in April 2021; **developed economies and developing economies include the major developed economies and developing economies in Table 6.11.

sufficiency still needs to be much improved in China despite significant progress in technology in recent years.

It is also worth noting that the trade of charges for the use of IP/GDP grew from 0.35% to 0.32% from 2008 to 2019 in Australia, not only lowest of all developed economies in Table 6.12 but also lower than ratios of eight major developing countries from 2016 to 2019, indicating severe IP insufficiency in Australia as a developed country.

6.12 Major Net Exporters of Charges for the Use of IP

Exports of charges for the use of IP of economies represent science and technology capacity of the economies, and imports of charges for the use of IP present the reliance of science and technology on global market.

Thus, net exports of charges for the use of IP of one economy represents its net originality capability rather than reliance on others. Table 6.12 gives the net exports of charges for the use of IP of leading economies.

6.12.1 *Top 10 net exporters of charges for the use of IP*

Table 6.12 shows that the US is by far the largest net exporter of charges for the use of IP in the world, with average net exports of over 60% of total net exporters of the world from 2008 to 2019, indicating the monopolistic power of the US in world science and technology. The next chief net exporter of charges for the use of IP is Japan, with net exports of charges for the use of IP of over 10% of total net exporters of the world from 2008 to 2019, showing the importance of Japanese science and technology in the world following the US.

The second tier of net exporters of charges for the use of IP are Switzerland, Germany, and the UK, with average annual net exports of charges for the use of IP around $10 billion in recent years. Total net exports for charges for the use of IP of these three net exporters had an average annual share of total net exports of top 10 net exporters of about 16%. The third tier of net exporters of charges for the use of IP are Finland, France, Denmark, Israel, and Sweden, with average annual net exports of charges for the use of IP between $0.5 billion and $2.5 billion from 2008 to 2019. Total net exports for charges for the use of IP of these five net exporters had an average annual share of total net exports of top 10 net exporters of less than 10%.

6.12.2 *Monopolistic power to control world IP*

All the top 10 net exporters of charges for the use of IP in Table 6.13 are developed countries. Only US, Japan, Switzerland, Germany, UK, and France are in the top 20 economies of the world, indicating that the majority of major developed countries are net exporters of IP in the world, and all developing countries are net importers of charges for the use of IP. In other words, the leading developed countries had the monopolistic power to control world IP with their resources in research and development.

6.12.3 *Net exports of developing countries*

Table 6.12 shows that net exports of eight developing countries grew from $22.36 billion in 2008 to $52.48 billion in 2019. The CAGR was 8.06% from

Table 6.12: Net Exports of Charges for the Use of IP of Major Economies (2008–2019), (Unit: USD billion)

Year/Country or Region	2008	2010	2012	2014	2016	2018	2019	CAGR
US	61.91	63.85	72.81	78.82	71.01	74.94	74.67	1.72
Japan	7.40	7.91	11.99	16.52	19.03	23.75	20.88	9.89
Switzerland	4.13	5.33	6.27	4.63	9.78	12.21	11.99	10.18
Germany	−1.30	1.16	3.89	4.71	7.50	8.80	8.62	18.79
UK	4.10	4.03	3.72	7.70	7.34	11.82	8.34	6.66
Finland	−0.76	0.81	1.55	1.46	2.16	2.40	2.43	11.08
France	5.04	3.61	3.97	1.82	0.73	0.88	1.79	−9.00
Denmark	1.17	0.70	0.87	0.83	0.81	1.78	1.84	4.17
Israel*	0.05	−0.07	0.65	0.82	1.17	1.61	1.83	38.97
Sweden	2.64	4.28	5.07	5.27	4.31	2.58	1.02	−8.32
UAE	0.00	0.00	0.00	1.09	1.01	0.93	0.95	−2.65
Belgium	−0.51	0.59	−0.17	−0.09	1.03	0.66	0.76	3.72
Netherlands*	1.11	−0.84	0.57	−10.72	−6.85	−7.56	0.21	54.42
Hungary	−0.89	0.24	0.34	0.38	0.35	0.27	0.04	164.20
Austria	−0.93	−0.69	−0.86	−0.50	−0.30	−0.60	−0.65	3.11
Italy	−3.27	−2.89	−1.48	−1.83	−1.25	−0.19	−0.72	12.85
Taiwan China	−2.82	−4.48	−4.75	−4.41	−4.06	−2.07	−1.86	3.73
Korea	−3.39	−6.00	−4.71	−5.00	−2.49	−2.13	−2.28	3.55
Australia	−2.23	−2.44	−3.31	−3.11	−2.50	−2.67	−2.55	1.22
Poland	−1.57	−2.01	−2.10	−2.61	−2.25	−3.04	−3.10	6.40

Spain	0.00	0.00	−4.11	−3.04	−3.07	−4.11	−3.45	−2.47
Luxembourg	−0.36	−0.18	−1.26	−2.83	−1.91	−2.58	−3.67	23.57
Brazil	−2.23	−3.04	−3.92	−5.55	−4.49	−4.30	−4.70	7.01
Thailand	−2.47	−3.05	−3.51	−3.91	−3.91	−5.11	−5.12	6.86
Russian Federation	−4.08	−4.46	−6.97	−7.36	−4.45	−5.41	−5.85	3.34
Canada	−4.82	−6.92	−6.97	−6.94	−7.05	−6.30	−6.01	2.03
India	−1.38	−2.31	−3.67	−4.19	−4.94	−7.12	−7.02	15.93
Singapore	−12.39	−15.10	−20.29	−16.97	−8.43	−8.45	−7.68	−4.26
China	−9.75	−12.21	−16.71	−21.94	−22.81	−30.04	−27.68	9.95
Ireland	−33.98	−34.54	−33.21	−50.52	−67.69	−71.33	−84.01	8.58
Sum	−2.67	−7.87	−6.85	−27.47	−22.21	−20.39	−31.00	24.96
Rest of World	−36.79	−41.64	−39.99	−53.24	−47.53	−48.03	−57.72	4.18
World	−35.26	−39.93	−37.77	−51.14	−45.42	−45.94	−55.97	4.29
Top 10	84.37	91.60	110.80	122.58	123.83	140.76	133.39	4.25
Top 11−20	−15.60	−17.67	−17.04	−26.82	−17.30	−16.40	−9.19	4.69
Top 21−30	−71.45	−81.80	−100.60	−123.24	−128.74	−144.75	−155.19	7.31
Sum/World	7.58%	19.70%	18.12%	53.72%	48.90%	44.37%	55.38%	
EPC States	−71.42	−42.68	−44.62	−78.97	−61.46	−97.12	−91.50	2.28
Eurozone	−54.11	−48.22	−43.57	−63.67	−71.74	−76.08	−80.97	3.73

(*Continued*)

Table 6.12: (*Continued*)

Year/Country or Region	2008	2010	2012	2014	2016	2018	2019	CAGR
Euro/EPC	75.8%	113.0%	97.7%	80.6%	116.7%	78.3%	88.5%	
Developed economies**	19.69	18.96	29.68	16.62	19.29	33.44	21.48	0.80
Other developed economies	−64.69	−72.64	−81.12	−105.97	−104.54	−107.32	−111.91	5.11
Developing economies**	−22.36	−26.83	−36.53	−44.09	−41.50	−53.82	−52.48	8.06

Source: Calculated using data from Tables 6.7 and 6.9; developed economies and developing economies include those economies in Table 6.12; **other developed economies are those developed economies other than the top 10 net positive exporters in Table 6.12. Israel remained net exporters of charges for the use of IP from 2012 to 2019, and the Netherlands changed from net importer of IP from 2014 to 2018 and became net exporter of IP again in 2019.

2008 to 2019, higher than the corresponding CAGR of 5.11% of developed economies, other than the top 10 net exporters, implying the worsening of technology dependence of leading developing countries in the past decade or so.

It is notable that the net import of charges for the use of IP of China as a share of the total of eight major developing countries grew steadily from 43.60% in 2008 to 55.82% in 2018 and then fell to 52.76% in 2019. These results indicate that recent progress in technology in China has not reflected clearly in the net exports of charges for the use of IP as the CAGR of net imports of charges for the use of IP was 9.95% from 2008 to 2019, 1.89% higher than the corresponding average annual compound growth rate of eight major developed countries in the same period.

6.13 Average Exports of Charges for the Use of IP per Patent Family of Major Blocs and Their Implications

Table 6.13 gives the total exports of charges for the use of IP of leading economies. We can find average export of charges for the use of IP per patent family of leading blocs.

The average export of charges for the use of IP per family patent given in Table 6.13 is a good measure of the competitiveness of patent families on average of one bloc, yet it is not good enough as it does not include the relative reliance of patent families on other blocs. Higher average exports of charges for the use of IP in "others" from 2000 to 2019 than average exports in all other blocs combined shown in Table 6.14 for the same period should indicate that the average patent family of others is higher in quality than patent families in other blocs. Higher average exports of charges for the use of IP of EPC States than average exports of Japan and the US shown in Table 6.13 should also indicate that average patent family of EPC States is higher in quality than average patent family in Japan and US; again, it is not whole story either.

6.14 Average Net Exports of Charges for the Use of IP of Major Blocs and Their Implications

Table 6.14 gives the total net exports of charges for the use of IP of leading patent blocs. We can find the average net export of charges for the use of IP per patent family of large blocs.

Table 6.13: Export of Charges for the Use of IP per Patent Family of Major Blocs (2000–2019) (Unit: USD billion)

Year/Bloc of Origin	EPC States	Japan	Korea	US	China	Others	World
2000	14.73	1.63	0.57	8.75	2.50	18.58	6.98
2001	10.98	1.20	0.64	5.53	1.41	13.52	5.01
2002	10.07	1.08	0.43	5.14	1.06	14.77	4.62
2003	9.96	1.23	0.47	4.81	0.72	15.17	4.51
2004	10.81	1.61	0.61	5.23	1.54	15.40	4.98
2005	11.30	1.81	0.65	5.24	0.67	15.09	5.19
2006	12.90	2.11	0.73	6.17	0.76	18.72	5.93
2007	16.10	2.81	0.77	7.74	0.93	24.03	7.63
2008	16.05	3.30	1.18	7.06	1.45	24.16	7.85
2009	14.86	2.56	1.39	6.32	0.61	19.24	6.92
2010	17.01	2.93	1.13	7.15	1.03	18.73	7.46
2011	19.14	3.32	1.38	7.62	0.77	18.59	8.18
2012	18.74	3.83	1.23	7.71	0.88	22.92	8.34
2013	20.49	4.21	1.51	7.54	0.57	31.92	8.89
2014	21.53	4.95	2.02	8.42	0.34	34.08	9.82
2015	21.37	5.19	2.42	8.44	0.53	45.09	10.10
2016*	22.37	5.90	2.67	8.71	0.48	45.93	10.60
2017*	24.74	6.63	2.93	9.26	1.68	54.36	11.70
2018*	27.62	7.63	3.25	9.47	1.66	62.13	12.69
2019*	27.65	8.28	3.38	9.50	1.69	66.56	12.80

Source: Calculated using data from Tables 6.10 and 5.4; data for Japan, US, Republic of Korea, and China from 2000 to 2004 are from their official websites; data for EPC States and others from 2000 to 2004 are estimated using 2005 data as bases and CAGRs.

The average net export of charges for the use of IP per patent family given in Table 6.14 is a better measure of the competitiveness of patent families of one bloc than the average export of charges for the use of IP because it includes the relative reliance of patent families of other blocs in its own bloc with the average import of charges for the use of IP. Average net export of charges for the use of IP of the US were all positive and higher than all other blocs from 2000 to 2019, indicating that US patent families are higher in quality than any other blocs. US patent families were also in

Table 6.14: Export of Charges for the Use of IP per Patent Family of Major Blocs (2000–2019) (Unit: USD million)

Year/Bloc of Origin	EPC States	Japan	Korea	US	China	Others	World
2000	−3.69	−0.13	−2.11	5.50	−35.83	−113.73	−1.41
2001	−2.77	−0.08	−1.47	3.34	−23.46	−77.49	−1.14
2002	−2.56	−0.06	−1.09	2.96	−23.84	−79.22	−1.02
2003	−2.55	0.13	−0.81	2.91	−23.24	−76.06	−0.82
2004	−2.79	0.21	−0.86	3.14	−27.84	−72.18	−0.66
2005	−2.94	0.31	−0.86	3.28	−22.16	−66.02	−0.47
2006	−5.06	0.48	−0.92	4.16	−23.81	−83.05	−0.71
2007	−6.15	0.79	−1.48	5.49	−21.39	−101.66	−0.68
2008	−6.99	0.95	−1.65	4.87	−24.81	−106.40	−1.17
2009	−5.57	0.57	−1.75	4.15	−15.07	−87.92	−1.15
2010	−5.77	0.87	−2.13	4.81	−15.15	−112.89	−1.21
2011	−5.85	1.13	−0.95	5.28	−14.38	−96.80	−0.99
2012	−4.82	1.44	−1.48	5.21	−14.14	−118.88	−1.11
2013	−5.15	1.83	−1.90	5.20	−13.01	−150.61	−1.14
2014	−7.37	2.19	−1.82	5.70	−11.10	−119.44	−1.52
2015	−8.83	2.76	−1.30	5.77	−10.21	−108.46	−1.47
2016*	−7.89	2.86	−0.96	5.48	−9.45	−108.75	−1.41
2017*	−7.40	3.23	−0.97	5.78	−8.38	−114.86	−1.24
2018*	−7.69	3.98	−0.89	5.97	−8.98	−125.51	−1.44
2019*	−9.04	3.70	−0.99	6.04	−7.03	−128.68	−1.75

Source: Calculated using data from Table 6.7 and 5.4; data for Japan, US, Republic of Korea, and China from 2000 to 2004 are from their official websites; data for EPC States and others from 2000 to 2004 are estimated using 2005 data as bases and CAGRs.

the top tier of quality of all blocs, consistent with the fact that US patent families are the highest in independence of all blocs most of the time in Table 5.11. Although the average net export of charges for the use of IP of Japan was negative from 2000 to 2002, it was higher than any other bloc other than the US, and it remained positive and in a growing pattern from 2003 to 2019, indicating that patent families of Japan were second only to the US in quality, consistent with the fact that average independence of patent families was higher than all other blocs other than the US in Table 5.11.

However, the average net export of charges for the use of IP of South Korea was significantly higher than (less negative) the corresponding average net export of charges for the use of IP of EPC States from 2000 to 2019. This should indicate that the quality of patent families are higher in South Korea than that of EPC States, yet it is inconsistent with the fact that independence of patent families of South Korea were significantly lower than that of EPC States in Table 5.11. Thus, the average net export of charges for the use of IP is a better-quality measure of patent families than average export of charges for the use of IP, yet it is not good enough as a quality measure of patent families as it cannot be used to distinguish between patent families of South Korea and those of EPC States. We will find a good measure of comparativeness or quality measure of patent families and science and technology internationalization measure comparable to currency internationalization in Chapter 7.

6.15 Summary

As displayed in Table 6.1, global trade has been increasingly transitioning from goods to services in the last 10 years as the proportion of services trade continues to grow. Based on data from 2007 to 2020, it is estimated that the services trade volume may outnumber the goods trade volume in about 20 years, and services trade will dominate global trade as a result.

Over the period of 2001–2019, China recorded a CAGR of 15.2% in services imports, more than twice the global CAGR (7.2%), whereas its CAGR in services exports was only 5.7%, less than 80% the global level (7.4%), resulting in a CAGR of 42.6% in services trade deficit. This reflects the fact that China's services trade has been seriously lagging its commodity trade since it joined the WTO in 2001. Though China became the world's fifth largest and then second largest services importer in 2019, it has faced a critical services trade deficit since 2011. Over the years, continuing services trade deficits roughly offset 50% of goods trade surpluses of China. For multiple months in 2018, China faced total deficits in goods and services trade, which severely affected the stability of RMB exchange rates, cross-border capital flows and the CNY internationalization process.

Years of growth in services trade deficit not only means that China needs to further improve the quality of its intellectual property, science and technology investment, and financial competitiveness but also reveals the severe issue that RMB appreciation and depreciation is not so much affected by the sizes of the Chinese GDP and commodity trade, but rather by worldwide factors. This issue is highly related to the relative lack of financial originality and especially the sci-tech originality capability in China, leading to RMB pricing power and RMB internationalization. The only way is for China to further deepen her reforms with systematic measures and speed up sci-tech progress, then RMB pricing power and RMB internationalization will follow naturally.

Last, but not the least, the CAGRs of world exports and imports of charges for the use of intellectual property were 5.44% and 5.82% from 2007 to 2019, respectively. These CAGRs have more than doubled the corresponding CAGRs of world commodity exports and imports in the same periods and much higher than the corresponding CAGR of world nominal GDP in the same period. These CAGRs clearly indicate the increasing importance and intensified competition of sci-tech globally. It is necessary to make R&D investment, which is manifested by the increase in the number of patents filed. However, the measurement of R&D investment effectiveness and patent quality evaluation should also consider the contribution of patents to the economy, especially to the balance of trade of charges for the use of intellectual property. China has remained in the top two positions of the world R&D investments and the number of patents filed since 2013 and 2014, respectively, yet CAGR of net exports of charges for use of IP was still as high as 10.56% from 2007 to 2020, comparable to the corresponding CAGR 11.56% of nominal GDP of China in the same period. As it takes time for R&D investments and patents to make contribution to trade and economy, the continuously increasing R&D investments and fast growth in the number of patents filed have not had enough energy to brake on the soaring deficit in charges for the use of intellectual property. Given that, China needs to review and improve R&D investment efficiency and patent quality management. The relatively low IP sufficiency in China reveals great potentiality for sci-tech to play in China.

The reason that so much time is spent on exports and imports of charges for use of IP and related issues in this chapter is to prepare us for a good quality measure or a good measure of global competitiveness of patents of various patent blocs so that we can find a good measure of sci-tech internationalization compared to the currency internationalization measure in Chapter 4. We leave this task to the following chapter.

Bibliography

UNCTAD, World Investment Report 2019, www.un.org./publications.

Zhang Guangping (Peter G.), RMB Internationalization & Products Innovation (10th Edition), China Financial Publishing House, 2021.

Chapter 7

Science and Technology Originality Capability and Internationalization Measures

Chapter 5 measured patent internationalization using family patent share of major countries and regions based on global distribution of patent families with priority claim origin published by the top five offices in 2020. The higher the international level of family patent, the more competitive the exports of both goods and services naturally will be. Based on the conclusions in Chapter 5, this chapter discusses another important concept closely related to patent internationalization — science and technology independence or originality capability (OC), that is, the proportion of the export of charges for intellectual property (IP) of a country or region to its import and export of IP charges. The lower the degree of science and technology OC, the higher the degree of external dependence of science and technology, and *vice versa*. Of course, the higher the degree of science and technology internationalization of a country or region, the higher the degree of science and technology OC, and the two are closely related. Based on results of science and technology independence or OC of major countries and regions in the past two decades, we will further assess the status of different countries and areas in the global science and technology chain by using the exports and imports data of IP charges. Such results will help find the optimal currency internationalization in Chapter 4 and prepare us for the interaction analysis between science and technology internationalization and currency internationalization hereinafter.

7.1 Definition and Measurement of Science and Technology OC

Chapter 5 defined patent internationalization as a proportion of family patents of one bloc of global family patents and Table 5.3 provided the results. Results in Table 5.5 are relatively reasonable measures of patent internationalization, yet their shortcoming is that they treat family patents of different blocs as the same, or the results are obtained with the assumption that family patents of various blocs are of the same quality, which is certainly not true.

7.1.1 *Definition of science and technology OC*

Since patent families are only one part of international patents, the number of patent families in each county or region and the global share cannot represent science and technology OC level. All family patents of each country or region have the same influence domestically and abroad. At the same time, each country or region benefits from family patents of its own and accepts foreign family patents. Therefore, the proportion of "the number of patent families of each country or region in the world" to "its own patent families plus the total number of foreign family patents within its jurisdiction" only reflects patent OC of this country or region.

As export and import of IP charges of any country or region contain most information about the relative competitiveness of science and technology, including all data of relative competitiveness of all family patents, proportion of export of IP charges to total export and import of IP charges of one country or region can better reflect science and technology independence or OC, or science and technology OC is a broader concept than patent OC.

For example, Tables 6.7 and 6.8 show that the US export and import charges for IP were \$117.40 billion and \$42.73 billion in 2019, respectively, thus US science and technology independence or OC was 117.40/(117.40 + 42.73) = 0.7331 = 73.31%, or US dependence on world science and technology was 1 − 0.7331 = 02669 = 26.69%. With this definition of science and technology OC and data in Tables 5.10 and 5.11, we can find sci-tech self-reliance capacity (SRC) or OC of major countries and regions from 2000 to 2019, and the results are given in Table 7.1.

Table 7.1: Science and Technology OC of Major Countries and Regions (2000–2019) (Unit: %)

Year/ Country or Region	2008	2010	2012	2014	2016	2018	2019	Average Annual Change
Israel	51.31	45.95	73.76	73.91	78.48	78.90	80.93	2.69
Finland	39.79	60.58	65.22	69.22	77.58	76.44	75.86	3.28
USA	76.36	75.32	75.47	75.60	72.91	73.02	73.31	−0.28
Denmark	66.47	60.45	61.94	59.82	59.97	68.10	67.89	0.13
Switzerland	64.65	62.47	60.72	57.06	64.27	65.45	66.73	0.19
Japan	58.41	58.70	61.58	64.18	65.98	67.66	64.38	0.54
Germany	45.94	53.76	61.68	58.99	62.45	60.99	60.76	1.35
UK	58.36	58.27	58.02	62.01	61.83	64.49	59.88	0.14
Sweden	69.52	79.43	75.30	70.14	69.57	60.47	53.42	−1.46
France	59.72	57.62	59.24	53.33	51.21	51.34	53.08	−0.60
UAE				60.01	58.44	57.15	57.09	−0.97
Belgium	42.84	56.72	48.48	49.31	57.86	54.09	55.27	1.13
Hungary	39.66	53.11	54.50	54.98	55.34	54.08	50.71	1.01
Netherlands	51.16	49.36	50.40	44.80	46.36	46.90	50.08	1.76
Italy	35.43	35.81	42.34	39.28	42.34	49.07	46.32	0.99
Korea	29.48	25.77	31.17	34.45	42.38	43.96	43.59	1.28
Austria	35.80	36.50	35.92	41.83	44.41	41.15	41.15	0.49
Singapore	8.19	10.19	10.85	15.77	31.27	33.23	34.41	2.38
Spain			19.95	24.34	27.84	27.61	33.24	1.90
Thailand	11.67	15.15	27.07	35.45	36.37	31.60	32.50	1.89
Canada	31.51	22.43	26.51	28.90	28.07	31.81	32.08	0.05
Taiwan China	5.96	8.51	14.09	14.10	18.93	29.92	30.09	2.19
Luxembourg	32.72	42.83	34.03	30.33	35.21	32.71	29.10	−0.33
Australia	19.71	22.18	17.08	17.72	19.80	21.00	21.43	0.16
China	5.24	5.98	5.56	2.90	4.64	13.51	16.22	1.00
Poland	10.50	9.49	8.97	10.47	14.20	14.44	14.92	0.40
Russian Federation	8.31	7.38	8.01	7.67	9.88	12.23	12.87	0.41
Brazil	14.71	5.56	6.17	5.95	11.24	13.87	10.71	−0.36
Ireland	3.99	7.23	11.54	10.81	10.42	14.03	10.45	0.59
India	8.83	4.95	7.45	11.96	8.76	9.03	9.95	0.10
Top 10	66.36	66.87	68.14	67.34	67.14	67.26	66.37	0.00
World	46.53	46.26	46.87	46.42	46.88	47.32	46.80	0.02

(*Continued*)

Table 7.1: (*Continued*)

Year/ Country or Region	2008	2010	2012	2014	2016	2018	2019	Average Annual Change
EPC States	41.06	42.75	44.30	42.70	42.50	43.89	42.98	0.17
Eurozone	36.69	37.67	39.36	37.74	37.09	38.86	38.66	0.18
Euro/EPC	89.3%	88.1%	88.9%	88.4%	87.3%	88.5%	89.9%	0.00
12 other developed economies	17.32	17.70	20.41	30.17	31.05	33.70	33.87	1.50
8 major developing economies	12.19	11.12	10.19	13.46	14.75	17.35	18.43	0.57

Source: Calculated using data of Tables 6.7 and 6.9; top 10 economies in Table 7.1 are the corresponding top 10 economies with highest net exports of charges for use of IP in Table 6.12; 12 other developed economies are those developed economies besides the top 10 economies in Table 7.1; eight major developing economies are those eight developing economies in Table 7.1.

7.1.2 *Top 10 countries with highest sci-tech OC*

Table 7.1 shows the average annual sci-tech independence or origination capability over 60% from 2008 to 2019; the average yearly change of sci-tech OC was the highest at 2.69% from 2008 to 2019 in Israel OC and the highest OC was 80.93% in 2019 in Israel; sci-tech OC was over 70% in Finland and USA; sci-tech OC of Denmark, Switzerland, Japan, and Germany was over 60% in 2019, indicating the relative competitiveness of sci-tech of these countries. It is noticeable that the average annual changes of sci-tech OC in Sweden, France and USA were −1.46%, −0.60%, and −0.28%, and average annual changes of sci-tech OC of Finland, Germany, and Japan were 3.28%, 1.35%, and 0.54%, indicating relative declines and progresses of sci-tech independence in these countries. Total sci-tech OC remained around 66.36% of top 10 countries without much change from 2008 to 2019.

7.1.3 *Sci-tech OC in other developed economies*

Table 7.1 also shows that the sci-tech OC of other 12 developed economies as a group grew from 17.32% in 2008 to 33.87% in 2019 with an average annual growth rate of 1.50%, slightly higher than the corresponding average annual growth rate of 1.35% of Germany in the same period, indicating significant progress of sci-tech independence or origination capability of these economies compared to the relative stagnant status of top 10 countries as a group. It is noticeable that sci-tech OC was lowest for Australia of all 12 top 20 advanced economies.

7.1.4 *Sci-tech origination capability of Eurozone and EPC States*

Table 7.1 also shows that the sci-tech OC of Eurozone 19 countries as a group grew from 36.69% in 2008 to 38.66% in 2019 with an average annual growth rate of 0.18%, much lower than the corresponding average yearly growth rate of eight major developing countries and 12 other developed economies in Table 7.1, indicating relative slow growth of sci-tech independence or origination capability of the Eurozone; the sci-tech OC of EPC States as a group grew from 41.06% in 2008 to 42.98% in 2019 with an average annual growth rate of 0.17%, almost the same as the corresponding average annual growth rate of 0.17% of Eurozone in the same period, indicating the sluggish progress of sci-tech independence of EPC States.

7.1.5 *Sci-tech OC of eight major developing countries*

Table 7.1 also shows that the sci-tech OC of eight major developing countries as a group grew from 12.19% in 2008 to 18.43% in 2019 with an average annual growth rate of 0.57%, slightly higher than the corresponding average annual growth rate of 0.43% of 38 EPC States, indicating relative slow growth of sci-tech independence of major developing countries, indicating that the sci-tech progress of major developing countries is not comparable to their economic progress in the same period; the sci-tech OC of eight major developing countries as a group were lower than that of Australia, the lowest of all major developed countries in top 20 economies.

7.1.6 *Sci-tech OC of China*

Table 7.1 shows that sci-tech OC remained almost unchanged from 2008 to 2016, yet it increased from 4.64% in 2016 to 16.22% in 2019, and new data from the State Administration of Foreign Exchange showed that sci-tech OC grew further to 18.75% in 2020, likely higher than the corresponding OC of eight major developing countries as a group in 2020 for the first time, showing significant progress of sci-tech in China in recent years, yet with much to catch up with 12 developed economies and Eurozone. We will forecast the progress of sci-tech in China in relation to the Eurozone, Japan, and the USA in Chapter 16 when we predict currency internationalization of top eight currencies.

7.2 Correlation between Science and Technology OC of Major Countries and Regions

Science and technology independence or OC, defined above using market data of charges for IP of major countries and regions, is not only more accurate than all kinds of patent data but also includes all information of IP, including patents. The higher the level of science and technology OC of any country or region, the more export of charges for IP and the lower import of charges for IP. Thus, we can conclude that if patents can neither generate export of charges for IP nor replace foreign patents to reduce import of costs for use of IP, they are of no actual benefit to the economy. The relationship between science and technology OC of major countries and regions given in this section has essential reference for us to understand science and technology cooperation between major countries. We can calculate the correlation of the science and technology OC among the top 10 net exporters of IP charges. Table 7.2 gives the results.

7.2.1 *Relationship of science and technology OC of the United States and other major net exporters of IP charges*

Table 7.2 shows that the US, the country with the highest net export of IP charges in the world, has the highest correlation of 61.43% with Sweden, showing the support of US science and technology for Sweden. In addition, the correlation between science and technology OC of the US and that of France was also 42.01%; the correlation coefficients between the US OC with that of Switzerland, Finland, Israel, Japan, Germany, Denmark, and UK were −62.36%, −39.95%, −35.66%, −25.17%,

Table 7.2: Correlation of Science and Technology OC among Top 10 Net Exporters of IP Charges (2005–2019) (Unit: %)

Country	Israel	Finland	USA	Denmark	Switzerland	Japan	Germany	UK	Sweden	France
Israel	100.00	87.67	−35.66	−4.16	−11.92	90.43	89.32	37.08	−49.43	−80.10
Finland	87.67	100.00	−39.95	−0.36	−16.13	89.22	94.23	32.65	−39.35	−82.08
USA	−35.66	−39.95	100.00	−21.74	−62.36	−25.17	−22.56	−21.14	61.43	42.01
Denmark	−4.16	−0.36	−21.74	100.00	56.68	1.16	−10.28	19.08	−55.75	8.51
Switzerland	−11.92	−16.13	−62.36	56.68	100.00	−19.37	−28.26	4.98	−52.36	8.93
Japan	90.43	89.22	−25.17	1.16	−19.37	100.00	85.65	53.24	−47.83	−92.47
Germany	89.32	94.23	−22.56	−10.28	−28.26	85.65	100.00	17.83	−21.49	−69.75
UK	37.08	32.65	−21.14	19.08	4.98	53.24	17.83	100.00	−47.66	−62.21
Sweden	−49.43	−39.35	61.43	−55.75	−52.36	−47.83	−21.49	−47.66	100.00	57.22
France	−80.10	−82.08	42.01	8.51	8.93	−92.47	−69.75	−62.21	57.22	100.00

Source: Calculated using results in Table 7.1.

−22.56%, −21.74%, and −21.14%, respectively, indicating various degrees of competition between the US science and technology OC with these countries.

It is noticeable that besides the positive correlation coefficients between the US science and technology OC and Sweden and France, all other correlation coefficients between the US sci-tech OC and other seven countries were negative to various degrees, indicating that the top net export of IP charges are in competition with most other major net exporters of IP charges, or squeezing effects with other net exporters of IP charges, particularly with Switzerland, the third net exporter.

7.2.2 *The relationship between science and technology OC of Japan and other major net IP charge exporters*

Table 7.2 also shows that the correlation coefficients of science and technology OC between Japan and those of Israel, Finland, Germany, and UK were 90.43%, 89.22%, 8565%, and 53.24%, indicating close cooperation or complementarities between Japan and these four countries; the correlation coefficients of science and technology OC between Japan and those of France, Sweden, USA, and Switzerland were −92.47%, −47.83%, −25.17%, and −19.37%, indicating various degrees of competition between Japan and these four countries in science and technology. It is noticeable that there were four negative correlation coefficients between Japanese sci-tech OC and those of other countries, three less than seven negative correlation coefficients, showing less competition between Japanese sci-tech and other countries.

7.2.3 *The relationship between science and technology OC of Switzerland, Germany, and UK with other major IP charge net exporters*

Tables 6.12 shows that Switzerland, Germany, and UK are the three countries with the highest net IP charge exports besides the US and Japan. Table 7.2 indicates that Switzerland sci-tech OC had the highest correlation with Denmark at 56.68%, and Swiss OC correlation with France and UK was at less than 10%, and its correlation with six other major net IP charge exporters was all negative, indicating competition with these six countries; German OC correlation with Israel, Finland, and Japan were 89.32%,

94.23%, and 85.65%, respectively, implying closer technology cooperation between German and these three countries; the negative correlation between German OC and other five major net IP exporters, particularly −69.76% with France, indicating competitive relationship between the countries in technology. The highest correlation between British OC and Japan of 53.24% and the highest negative correlation between British OC and France of −62.11% had similar implications explained earlier. Positive and negative correlation coefficients between two countries show cooperative and competitive relationship between the relating countries.

7.3 Correlation between US Sci-Tech OC and Sci-Tech OC of Major East Asian Economies

The correlation between the US sci-tech OC and those of significant East Asian economies gives us an excellent indication of sci-tech dependence of these economies on the US sci-tech. This section concentrates on such relationships.

7.3.1 *Reconsidering the correlation between Japan and US science and technology OC*

Statistics from the Japan External Trade Organization (JETRO) show that Japanese net export of IP charges grew from $−0.78 billion in 1977 to $1.28 billion in 2003, and Japan became the net IP charge exporter or was relatively self-dependent in sci-tech for the first time in 2003, and Japanese sci-tech OC grew from 17.50% to 52.75% in the same period. Table 7.2 also gives the correlation of science and technology OC between the US, and Japan was −25.17% between 2000 and 2019, showing mild competition between the top two sci-tech providers evidenced by the top two largest net exporters of IP charges. The relationship between the top two sci-tech providers needs further analysis and consideration with more data. Figure 7.1 shows the rolling correlation coefficients between US sci-tech OC and Japanese sci-tech OC from 1992 to 2020 on a 12-year rolling basis.

Figure 7.1 clearly shows that shortly after Japan became a net exporter of IP charges in 2003, correlation coefficients between the top two net IP charge exporters reached the lowest level of −93.51% in 2004, indicating that competition or squeezing between the two countries became severe;

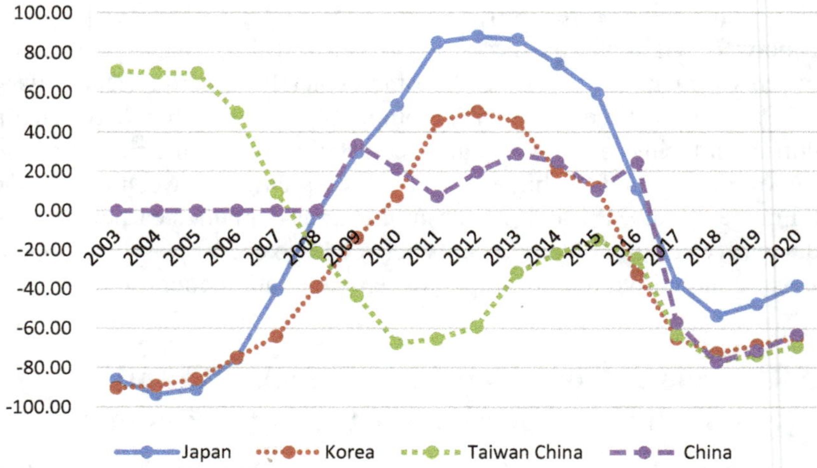

Figure 7.1: Correlation Coefficients between US Sci-Tech OC and Sci-Tech OC of Major East Asian Economies on 12-Year Rolling Basis (1992–2020) (Unit: %)

Source: The US Bureau of Economic Analysis: www.bea.gov and the JETRO: www.jetro.go.jp; correlation coefficients between US OC and OC of Mainland China was zero from 2003 to 2008 because both export and import of charges for use of IP were zero before 1997 as released by China Administration of Foreign Exchange.

yet the competition became milder from 2004 to 2008 as the correlation coefficient increased to −1.34% when Japanese sci-tech OC got closer from 60% to 58.42%; the relationship changed to a cooperation or compliment period from 2009 to 2016 as evidenced with positive correlation coefficients and with peak correlation coefficient of 88.22% in 2012, and Japanese sci-tech OC increased by 11.89% from 56.25% to a historical high of 68.14% in 2015; however, the relationship became competition again from 2017 to 2020 as the gap between US sci-tech OC and Japanese sci-tech OC reached a historical low of 6.55% evidenced with negative correlation coefficients in the same period. Japanese sci-tech OC declined by 5.44% from 2017 to 2020 because of competition between the countries and the only consecutive 3-year period with continuous annual decrease since 1977.

The above results between the top two countries show that the relationship between major sci-tech originators may change between competition and cooperation depending upon the relative levels of sci-tech OC of the originators, and the cooperation and competition may yield significant progresses or declines of sci-tech OC of related partner.

7.3.2 *Correlation between US sci-tech OC and other three major East Asian economies*

Figure 7.2 shows that the US sci-tech relationship with Korea and Mainland China were similar to that with Japan, despite the fact that similar cooperative relationship was not as high as with Japan from 2009 to 2015 and competitiveness was not as severe as with Japan from 2016 to 2020; the only exception was Taiwan China with steady US cooperation or help before 2008, and steady squeezing from 2009 to 2015, yet squeezing was similar with Korea and Mainland China from 2017. The relationships between US sci-tech OC and four major East Asian economies given in Figure 7.1 also revealed both the US sci-tech and USD influences on East Asian economies after the 2008 world financial crisis. We will further analyze the related effects of the 2008 world financial crisis in later chapters.

7.3.3 *Correlation between Japanese science and technology OC and other three major East Asian economies*

Table 7.3 gives the correlation coefficients among US sci-tech OC and those of the four major East Asian economies. Table 7.3 shows that the correlation coefficients between US sci-tech OC and those of all four

Table 7.3: Correlation Coefficients among US Sci-tech OC and the Four Major East Asian Economies and Four Asian Dragons (2005–2019)

Economies	**USA**	**Japan**	**China**	**Korea**	**Taiwan China**	**Singapore**	**Hong Kong China**
USA	100.00	−25.17	−55.60	−61.76	−64.08	−57.83	−43.18
Japan	−25.17	100.00	52.56	78.66	77.87	87.52	93.42
China	−55.60	52.56	100.00	68.80	86.48	74.45	66.59
Korea	−61.76	78.66	68.80	100.00	87.75	92.11	85.72
Taiwan China	−64.08	77.87	86.48	87.75	100.00	89.71	85.89
Singapore	−57.83	87.52	74.45	92.11	89.71	100.00	93.91
Hong Kong China	−43.18	93.42	66.59	85.72	85.89	93.91	100.00

Source: Calculated using results in Table 7.1.

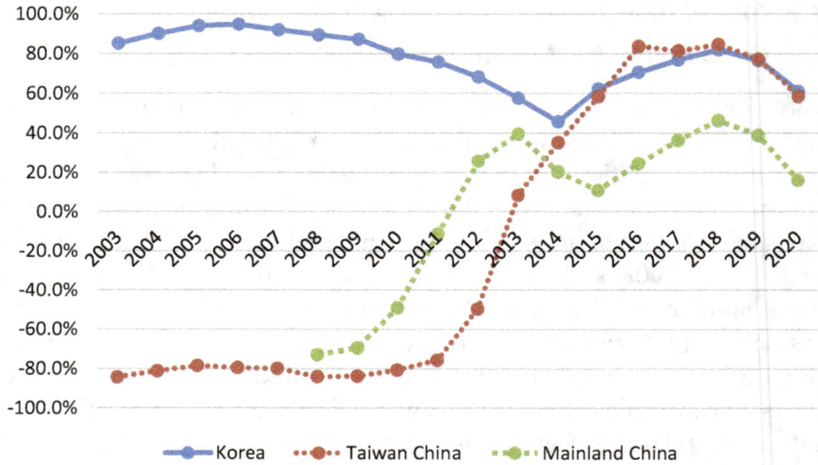

Figure 7.2: Correlation Coefficients between Japanese Sci-Tech OC and Sci-Tech OC of Three Other Major East Asian Economies on 12-Year Rolling Basis (1992–2020) (Unit: %)

Source: The US Bureau of Economic Analysis: www.bea.gov and the JETRO: www.jetro.go.jp; correlation coefficients between US OC and OC of Mainland China was zero from 2003 to 2008 because both export and import of charges for use of IP were zero before 1997 as released by China Administration of Foreign Exchange.

major East Asian economies were all negative, with Taiwan, China, and Korea above 60% in absolute terms, and correlation coefficients with China and Japan were −55.60% and −25.17%, indicating competition or squeezing of US sci-tech with these major East Asian economies to significant degrees; and correlation coefficients between Japanese sci-tech OC and Korea, Taiwan, and China were 78.66%, 77.87%, and 52.56%, indicating cooperation or compliment between Japanese sci-tech with these three major East Asian economies.

It is noticeable that the correlation coefficients between Japanese sci-tech OC and those of Korea and Taiwan China were above 77%, indicating close cooperation among these three East Asian economies. The relationship between Japanese sci-tech OC and the three other major East Asian economies can be better seen from Figure 7.2, which contains much more information than Table 7.3. Figure 7.2 shows that cooperation between Japanese sci-tech and Korean sci-tech was much higher before the 2008 world financial crisis, yet sci-tech between Japan and Taiwan China was squeezing severely before 2008 as evidenced with negative correlation coefficients between the two economies of about −80%; however, the relationship between Japan and Taiwan China improved dramatically from 2008 to 2016 when the US and Japan cooperation changed to competition, thus cooperation among major East Asian economies became necessary, and Japan–Taiwan sci-tech cooperation remained at the same level as Japan–Korea cooperation.

Figure 7.2 also shows that Japan and Mainland China were in sci-tech squeezing relationship from 2008 to 2011 to dramatically decreasing degrees; Japan and Mainland China entered mild cooperation relationship from 2012 to 2016 with an average correlation coefficient of about 20%, similar to those between US and Mainland China shown in Figure 7.1; although US–Mainland China entered into an increasing sci-tech squeezing relationship with more negative correlation coefficients shown in Figure 7.1, cooperation relationship continued and even strengthened between Japan and Mainland China from 2017 to 2020 with high average correlation coefficients.

7.3.4 *Close Cooperation between Mainland China and Taiwan China in science and technology*

Table 7.2 also shows that the correlation coefficient between Mainland China and Taiwan China was as high as 86.56% from 2005 to 2019, second only to the correlation coefficient of 87.75% between Taiwan China and Korea for the same period. Historical data show that the relationship between the two economies has become closer in sci-tech, and it increased to 86.98% from 2006 to 2020, and similar data show that correlation coefficients between science and technology OC of China and those of Japan, Switzerland, Germany, UK, Denmark, Israel, Finland, Korean, as well as Canada, Australia, and New Zealand were all positive, yet all these correlation coefficients were lower than the correlation coefficient between Mainland China and Taiwan China to various degrees, indicating specially closer sci-tech relationship between the two sides of Strait.

7.4 Correlation between US Sci-Tech OC and Those of "Four Asian Dragons"

South Korea, Taiwan China, Hong Kong China, and Singapore, the "Four Asian Dragons" are well known for their rapid economic growth from the 1970s to the 1990s in the world. Their export-oriented development model of leveraging US technology was of significant interest to Mainland in the initial stage of China's reform and opening-up, and thus these "Four Asian Dragons" somewhat stimulated China's economic reform process to some degree by their extreme successes or miracles, and sci-tech progresses of these dragons in the past should have clear indications for sci-tech progress in China.

Table 7.3 shows that the correlation pattern of the "Four Asian Dragons" with US are the natural extension of the correlation of the four major East Asian economies: with the only exception of correlations with US sci-tech negative, all the "Four Asian Tigers" are positively correlated with each other and also with the other two major Asian economies; Japanese sci-tech was more positively correlated with Hong Kong China and Singapore than with Korea and Taiwan China, indicating higher cooperation between Japan and the two Asian city economies or the two Asian financial centers; Korean correlation with Singapore, Taiwan China, and Hong Kong China was higher than with Japan; Taiwan China correlation of 89.71% with Singapore was also higher than with Korea, 87.75%, and with Japan, 77.87%; and Singapore correlation with Hong Kong China of 93.91% was higher than with Korea, 92.11%, and with Taiwan China, 89.71%; Hong Kong China correlation with Singapore and with Japan was both over 93%, close to the highest correlation between Germany and Finland 94.23% in Table 7.2; the Hong Kong China correlation with Mainland China of 66.59% was higher than most correlation among most top 10 net exporters of IP charges of the world in Table 7.2, yet the lowest of Hong Kong China correlation with other major East Asian economies or with any other Four Tigers. These high correlations show high degrees of cooperation among the major East Asian economies and among Asian Tigers.

It is noticeable that the correlation between US sci-tech with Singapore and Hong Kong China were somewhat higher or less negative than the correlation between US sci-tech with Korea and Taiwan China, indicating less squeezing influence of the US sci-tech on these two Asian financial centers.

7.5 Average Annual Change of Science and Technology OC of Major Economies and their Implications

Average annual changes of sci-tech OC of major economies tell us the speed of progress or backwardation in science and technology. We discuss the annual changes in this section.

7.5.1 *Annual change of science and technology OC of major economies of the world*

Table 7.1 shows that of the 30 major economies, only six economies with negative average annual change in sci-tech OC, notably −1.46%, −0.97%, and −0.60% average yearly change in Sweden from 2008 to 2019, UAE and France; of the 24 economies with positive average annual change, notably 3.28% average annual increase was noted in Finland, 2.69%, 2.38%, 2.19% average annual increase in Israel, Singapore, and Taiwan China for the same period, respectively, showing significant progress in sci-tech in these countries; average annual increase of sci-tech OC in Spain, Thailand, the Netherlands, Germany, Korea, Belgium, Hungary, and China were 1.90%, 1.89%, 1.76%, 1.35%, 1.28%, 1.13%, 1.01%, and 1.00% in the same period, respectively, indicating steady progress in sci-tech in these economies; average annual increase of sci-tech OC of other 12 significant economies was lower than 1.00%.

7.5.2 *Average annual change of science and technology OC in major East Asian economies and implications*

Since export and import of IP charges in Hong Kong were relatively low, Hong Kong was not included in Table 7.1, yet the corresponding average annual increase of sci-tech OC in Hong Kong was 0.75% from 2008 to 2019, lower than the corresponding average yearly increase of sci-tech OC of 2.38%, 2.19%, 1.28%, and 1.00% in Singapore, Taiwan China, Korea, and China for the same period, respectively, yet higher than the corresponding average annual increase of Japan 0.54%. The reason that the average annual growth of sci-tech OC was lowest in Japan from 2008 to 2019 was that Japan had passed its fast-growing period before 2008 (historical data show that average annual growth of sci-tech OC was 1.39% from 1997 to 2008 and 1.53% from 1984 to 1997).

South Korea's science and technology OC increased from 5.91% to 23.17% (exceeding one-fifth for the first time) from 1992 to 2001, with an average annual growth rate of 1.92%. From 2001 to 2018, the growth rate continued to increase to 43.96%, and the yearly average growth rate dropped to 1.22%. The continuous improvement of the Republic of Korea's science and technology OC in the past 20 years also provides some reference for the advancement of China's science and technology OC in the next 10 years or even longer.

Although the science and technology OC of Taiwan China in the past 30 years or so has a phenomenon rarely seen in other economies, the changing rhythm of the science and technology OC of Taiwan China in different periods should also be of significant reference to Mainland China. According to the relevant data above, Taiwan China's sci-tech OC increased from 1.63% to 24.07% (exceeding one-fifth for the first time) with an average annual growth rate of 2.80% from 1984 to 1992. However, the average annual growth rate was only 0.18% from 1992 to 2020, showing sluggish progress in the past 18 years.

7.5.3 *Science and technology progress in Singapore*

Table 7.1 shows that the average annual growth of sci-tech OC was 2.38%, the third highest average annual growth of the top 30 economies from 2008 to 2019 and the highest average growth rate of all Asian economies, showing significant progress of sci-tech in Singapore.

According to WIPO data, from 2000 to 2003, Singapore's science and technology OC was only slightly over 1%, and more than half of Singapore's import for IP charges were from the United States; from 2004 to 2005, Singapore's science and technology OC increased from 3.7% to 5.2%, but more than half of Singapore's import for IP charges were also from the United States; from 2005 to 2009, Singapore's science and technology OC remained 5–6%, but on average, more than half of Singapore's import for IP charges were from the United States; Singapore's science and technology OC exceeded 10–10.2% for the first time in 2010, and the proportion of import of IP charges from the United States in Singapore's total import of IP charges dropped to 26.6% in 2010; Singapore's science and technology OC increased to 15.77% in 2014 and import of IP charges from the United States accounted for about 30% of Singapore's total import of IP charges; Singapore's science and technology OC exceeded 30% for the first time to 30.84% in 2015 and Singapore's import of IP charges from the United States accounted for 33.9% in the same year; Singapore's science and technology OC increased to 34.41%, and the proportion of Singapore import for IP from the United States remained around 30% of Singapore's total import of IP in the same year.

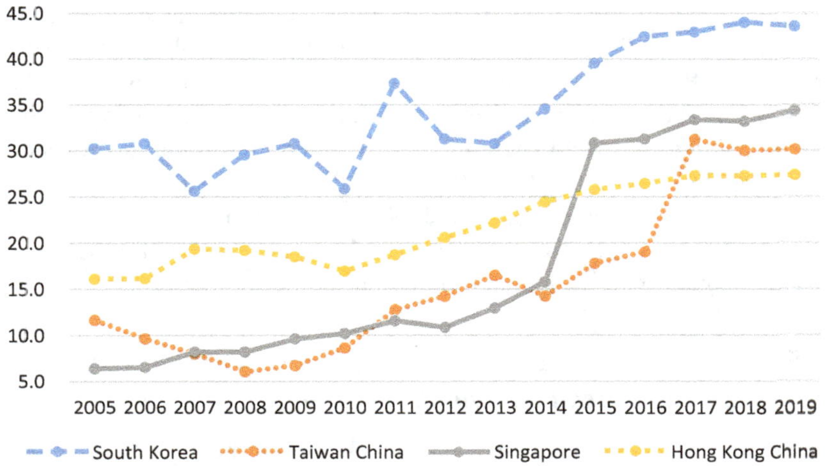

Figure 7.3: Science and Technology of "Four Asian Dragons" (2005–2019) (Unit: %)

Source: The US Bureau of Economic Analysis: www.bea.gov and the JETRO: www.jetro.go.jp; correlation coefficient between US OC and OC of Mainland China was zero from 2003 to 2008 because both export and import of charges for use of IP were zero before 1997 as released by China Administration of Foreign Exchange.

With steady help from the United States, Singapore made significant progress in sci-tech in the past two decades, leading to Singapore export and import of IP charges per unit of GDP or IP sufficiency to GDP to achieve the fourth highest in the world and the highest in Asia as shown in Table 6.11, indicating high competitiveness of Singapore in Asia and worldwide in science and technology.

7.5.4 *Science and technology progress in "Four Asian Dragons"*

Figure 7.3 shows the sci-tech OC of the "Four Asian Dragons". Figure 7.3 shows that sci-tech OC remained the highest of all Four Asian Dragons from 2005 to 2019, Singapore jumped from the lowest to the second position second only to Korea, Taiwan China remained at the third position in the same period, and Hong Kong China dropped from the second to the lowest position.

Results in Figure 7.3 indicate that although the "Four Asian Dragons" were in their middle stage of economic and trade take-off before reform and opening-up of Mainland China, and they had maintained the status of developed economies for many years, the overall science and technology OC of the "Four Asian Dragons" were not only much less than those of major net exporters of IP charges in Table 7.1 but also lower than the average of sci-tech OC of other 12 developed economies in Table 7.1. These results indicate that the export-oriented development model supported by technology-dependent policies of the "Four Asian Dragons" had suffered severe technology dependence on the US technology from the 1970s to the middle of 2010s, and the overall technology OC was still relatively low compared with other developed economies even with rapid progress in recent few years.

7.5.5 *Long-term average annual growth of sci-tech OC of major East Asian economies and their implications*

The average annual change rate of sci-tech OC of significant economies from 2008 to 2019 have good implications for China in the next decade or so, yet the time horizon from 2008 to 2019 was relatively too short for us to forecast how sci-tech OC will progress in China in the next two to three decades. We need longer historical horizons of OC changes of relevant economies.

Using data from JETRO, we can find that Japanese sci-tech OC increased from 32.14% in 1991 to 60.59% in 2020 with an average annual growth of 0.98% in 29 years; this yearly average growth rate is not as useful as Japanese sci-tech OC of 32.14% which was significantly higher than Chinese sci-tech OC of 18.75% in 2020, thus the most recent average annual growth 0.98% of Japan in the past 29 years is too low, and Japanese yearly average growth rate of 1.34% from 19.31% in 1978 to 58.27% in 2007 is useful for Chinese sci-tech OC in the coming 29 years until 2049 because the Japanese sci-tech OC of 19.31% in 1978 was closest to the Chinese sci-tech OC of 18.75% in 2020 and 2007 was the ending year of the 29-year period from 1978.

Similarly, we can find that Korean sci-tech OC increased from 5.91% in 1992 to 43.43% in 2020 with an average annual growth of 1.34%, almost the same as the average yearly growth rate of Japan from 1978 to 2007; Korean sci-tech OC increased from 17.53% in 2001, most comparable to the Chinese sci-tech OC of 18.76% in 2020, to 43.43% in 2040 if the 20-year average annual growth rate of 1.30% will maintain in China, and the corresponding Korean 29-year annual growth rate from 2001 to 2030 is very likely to be lower than the 20-year average annual growth rate of 1.30%. The average annual growth rate of sci-tech OC of Taiwan China was only 0.33% from 1991 to 2020, too low to be of any reference value.

Thus, the average annual growth rates of Japan and Korea in relevant past 29 years should have some implications for China, yet these historical average annual growth rates are likely to be proven too low for Chinese sci-tech OC in the coming 29 years.

7.6 Correlation of Science and Technology OC among Mainland China, Hong Kong China, and Taiwan China

We will introduce the relationship of science and technology OC among Mainland China, Hong Kong China, and Taiwan China, as well as the reasons for the "abnormality" in science and technology OC of Mainland China, Hong Kong China, and Taiwan China which had not increased but decreased in the decade or so before 2008.

7.6.1 *Science and technology OC and related issues of Hong Kong*

For many years, Hong Kong has played a unique role in the financial and trade sectors of Asia and the world at large. However, Hong Kong's position in the science and technology sector has been less prominent. According to the import and export IP charges of Hong Kong government from 1995 to 2018 published on the website of the Census and Statistics Department of Hong Kong Government, Hong Kong's trade deficit of charges for the use of IP continued to increase from HK$640 million to HK$12.26 billion, and its corresponding science and technology OC dropped from 38.0% to 16.8% from 1995 to 2010; the deficit dropped to HK$9.60 billion, and the science and technology OC rose to 27.59% in 2019.

Figure 7.4 shows the science and technology OC in Mainland China, Hong Kong China, Taiwan China, and China from 1997 to 2020; here "China" stands for the science and technology OC calculated using total exports and imports of charges for use of IP of above three regions together.

Figure 7.4 shows that from 1997 to 2005, Hong Kong's science and technology OC decreased from a historical peak of 39.40% to a historical low of 15.99%; Hong Kong's science and technology OC barely changed from its historic low from 2004 to 2006; it rose to 19.2% in 2007 but continued to fall to the low of 16.83% from 2007 to 2010; it rose steadily

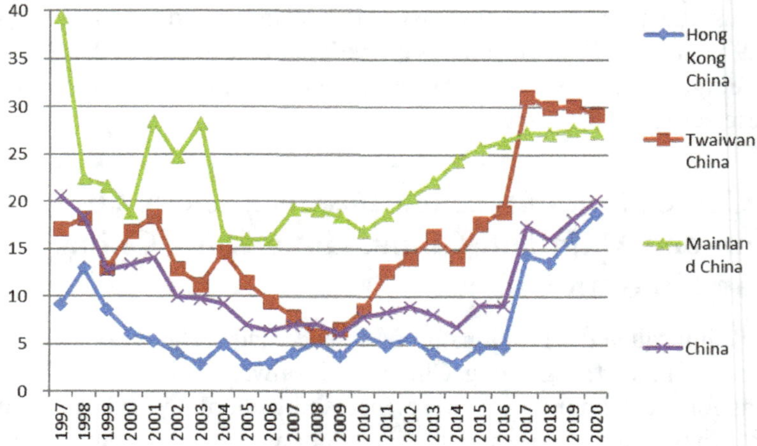

Figure 7.4: Science and technology OC in Mainland China, Hong Kong China, and Taiwan China (1997–2020) (Unit: %)

Source: Data for Mainland China from SAFE website: www.safe.gov.cn; Hong Kong China data from the website of the Census and Statistics Department of Hong Kong Government: www.censtatd.gov.hk; Taiwan China data source is the same as that of Figure 7.1; data for Hong Kong China 2020 are estimated with CAGR from 2016 to 2019.

to 27.59% in 2019, more than 12% lower than peak in 1997. These results show that in the 22 years from 1997 to 2019, the average of Hong Kong's science and technology OC was just over 20% annually, which was still a big gap from the relative autonomy of 50%. In 2019, Hong Kong's science and technology OC was 27.59%, 22.41 percentage point lower than its relative autonomy of 50%. These results indicate that Hong Kong, an international financial center, has been dependent on external technology for many years. Enhancing Hong Kong's independent innovation capability is one of the most critical tasks for Hong Kong's future development by virtue of its geographical advantages and talent accumulation, which is in line with Mainland China's goal of continuously improving its independent innovation capability in the future.

Hong Kong China was not in Table 6.11 because both imports and exports of IP charges were too low. Calculations using the same data source as that of Table 6.11 show that import and export/GDP ratio increased slightly from 0.91% in 2008 to 1.04% in 2010 and fell to 0.73% in 2019, lower than all ratios of developed economies in Table 6.11 with the only exceptions of Australia and Italy, and lower than the corresponding ratios of Thailand, UAE, Poland, and Hungary in Table 6.11, indicating severe IP insufficiency of Hong Kong compared to most developed economies. Particular attention should be paid to the imports and exports/GDP ratio of the other Asian financial center Singapore at 6.58% in 2019 in Table 6.11, eight times higher than 0.73% in Hong Kong, and corresponding ratios of the two European financial centers, 1.35% of Belgium and 12.36% of Luxembourg, in 2019 in Table 6.11 also show significant insufficiency of IP of Hong Kong.

7.6.2 *Correlation of science and technology OC among Mainland China, Hong Kong China, and Taiwan China*

By using the results of science and technology OC in Hong Kong China from 1997 to 2019 given in Figure 7.4 and the corresponding results of science and technology OC in Mainland China and Taiwan China in Table 7.1, we can calculate the correlations between Hong Kong's science and technology OC and that of the Mainland and Taiwan in the same period are 43.42% and 55.43%, respectively, indicating obvious mutual assistance and interaction between Hong Kong China and Mainland China and Taiwan China, yet the above two correlation coefficients were significantly lower than the correlation coefficient between Mainland China and Taiwan China of 83.00%, indicating close cooperation of science and technology between the two sides of the strait.

7.6.3 *The necessity of having Mainland China, Hong Kong, China and Taiwan China considered as a whole*

Due to "one country, two systems" rules, although more than 20 years have passed since Hong Kong's return to the motherland, statistics such as domestic output, foreign exchange reserves and foreign trade in Hong Kong Special Administration Region (SAR) are still calculated separately, this is an internationally acceptable practice. Taiwan China shall follow the same statistical rule. Nevertheless, given the high correlation and complementarity between Mainland China and Taiwan China in science and technology OC shown above and also the similar change patterns of science and technology OC of the three regions shown in Figure 7.4, it is necessary to calculate Mainland China, Hong Kong SAR, and Taiwan China together in the field of science and technology and measure the entire China (Macao SAR's magnitudes of population, GDP, trade and science and technology are relatively small, so we do not include Macao in our discussion) in order to assess the overall characteristics of China's science and technology, coordination, collaboration as well as economic and trade cooperation in science and technology in Mainland China, Hong Kong SAR, and Taiwan China. Figure 7.4 shows the results.

The similar change patterns of science and technology between Mainland China and Taiwan China shown in Figure 7.4 indicate close cooperation and complementarity between the two sides of the strait. Figure 7.4 shows that the science and technology of Mainland China will soon catch up with Hong Kong SAR and Taiwan China in a few years with higher annual progresses.

7.6.4 *Science and technology OC in Mainland China, Hong Kong China, and Taiwan China one decade before 2008*

Figure 7.4 clearly shows the decade before the outbreak of the international financial crisis from 1998 to 2008, the levels of science and technology OC in Mainland China, Hong Kong SAR, and Taiwan China all declined rather than increasing in Korea and Japan at the same time. Mainland China, Taiwan China, and Hong Kong SAR had cumulative declines of 3.93%, 11.15%, and 20.31%, respectively, and China's total had a cumulative decrease of 13.49% compared to incremental growth of 15.27% and 20.56% in Japan and Korea in the same period. Thus, it is clear that while the science and technology OC of Japan and Korea continued to improve, the science and technology OC of Mainland China, Hong Kong, and Taiwan all suffered considerable losses. Why did it decrease instead of increasing in China before the 2008 world financial crisis? This question deserves our further thought, and the conclusion will be of great significance to the improvement of science and technology OC in the future.

7.6.5 *Reasons for simultaneous declines of science and technology OC in Mainland China, Hong Kong SAR, and Taiwan China a decade before 2008*

Answers to the above questions would be considerably lengthy, which would be beyond the scope of this book. The course of economic and trade development in Mainland China, Hong Kong SAR, and Taiwan China over the past three decades should have the answers. The return of Hong Kong to the Mainland in 1997 brought the Mainland and Hong Kong closer together economically. Mainland China and Hong Kong SAR signed the Mainland and Hong Kong Closer Economic Partnership Arrangement (CEPA) in 2003, with Supplementary Agreement, Supplementary Agreement II, and Supplementary Agreement III signed in 2004, 2005, and 2006, respectively. The signing and implementation of these agreements have facilitated economic and trade cooperation between Hong Kong SAR and Mainland China. In addition, the Asian financial crisis that affected the whole East Asia broke out in 1997. From 1998 to 2002, Mainland China issued more than RMB 100 billion of long-term Treasury bonds each year for several consecutive years, directly driving investment of more than trillions of yuan. In the meantime, the loosening of monetary conditions, including the reduction of interest rates and reserve ratios, and the easing of lending policies, has further expanded the opportunities for domestic investment and development, and created greater room for Hong Kong SAR and Taiwan China investment to explore business opportunities in the Mainland.

In addition, with the encouragement and support of a series of policies adopted by the Central Government to promote cross-strait cooperation, especially from 1992 to 1996, cross-straits political dialogues were strengthened, and cross-straits economic and trade cooperation was rapidly deepened with the promulgation and implementation of "Law of the People's Republic of China on the Protection of Investment by Taiwan Compatriots" and "Regulations on Relations between the People in Taiwan and Mainland China". Mainland China's accession to the WTO in 2001 has also created better conditions for investment from Taiwan China in the Mainland. From 2002 to 2008, globalization accelerated, RMB continued to appreciate, and foreign capital flowed into Mainland China. With the unique relationship based on common language and culture ties among the Mainland, Hong Kong SAR, and Taiwan, which helped with special policy arrangements with Hong Kong and Taiwan from the Mainland, it is more convenient for Hong Kong SAR and Taiwan China to enter the Mainland than any other "foreign funds" and to take advantages of the Mainland market than additional "foreign funds". In this way, the development space of Mainland China market was vast, and there was a vast profit space for businesses and products without much technology content than those in the United States, Europe, and Japan. There were less incentives to take efforts and resources to improve science and technology OC. Broad market profit space squeezed or weakened the independent scientific and technological innovation that needs a lot of capital and energy, which to some extent provides a partial answer to the "abnormal" phenomenon that science and technology OC in Mainland China, Taiwan China, particularly Hong Kong SAR, declined instead of increasing in the decade before 2008. The average annual export of IP charges of $0.190 billion, compared to average import of IP charges of $4.196 in Mainland China from 1998 to 2008, showed the steady reliance on foreign IP.

7.7 Science and Technology OC in Japan

Japanese steady progresses in science and technology in the past three to four decades has set up a good model for the whole world, especially for China to learn. Introductions in previous chapters and above contents in this chapter have given us a lot of information of Japanese improvement in science and technology, yet the time span was not long enough, we will analyze science and technology progresses in the past four decades to find useful forward-looking information for Chinese progresses in science and

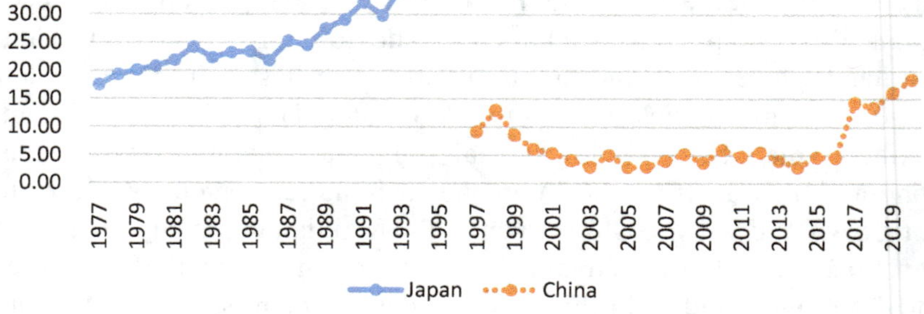

Figure 7.5: Science and technology OC of Japan and China (1977–2020) (Unit: %)

Source: Data of China from SAFE website: www.safe.gov.cn, both exports and imports of charges for use of IP in China were zero before 1997; and data of Japan from JETRO website: www.jetro.go.jp.

technology in the coming three decades or so. Figure 7.5 shows the science and technology OC of Japan and China from 1997 to 2020 which shows steady progress of Japanese science and technology OC from 1977 to 2015, a miracle in world history.

7.7.1 *Progress from 1977 to 1985*

Figure 7.5 shows that the Japanese science and technology OC grew from 17.50% in 1977 to 23.44% in 1985 with a moderate average annual growth of 0.74%, reflecting average annual growth rate of exports and imports of IP charges at 17.30% and 11.77% for the same period, indicating moderate improvement of science and technology of Japan before the Plaza Agreement was signed.

7.7.2 *Plaza Agreement and its impact*

The famous "Plaza Agreement" was signed between Japan and the United States at the Plaza Hotel in New York City in 1985. The implementation of this agreement in the next 3 years had important impacts on the Japanese economy and financial markets, leading to significant yen appreciation against the USD. The appreciation of yen, rises of Japanese stock market and real estate market naturally made imports of IP charges easier for Japan from 1985 to 1990, average annual growth of imports of IP charges in Japan rose to 21.20%, the highest of all 5-year periods from 1977 to 2020, and average annual growth of exports of IP charges in Japan rose to 28.15%, also the highest in the same period, leading to Japanese science and technology OC growth from 23.44% in 1985 to 29.10% in 1990 as shown in Figure 7.5 with an average annual growth rate of 1.13%, much higher than the average yearly growth rate of 0.74% from 1977 to 1985, indicating the implementation of Plaza Agreement somewhat accelerated science and technology progress in Japan.

7.7.3 *Financial bubble burst, yet science and technology progress continued*

The stock market crash in December 1989 marked the beginning of the burst of the Japanese stock market bubble and the real-estate market breaking up, which had significant impacts on the Japanese economy and financial markets in the following decades. Yet, statistics shows that the breaking of the Japanese bubble did interrupt the rising trend of Japanese science and technology progress. Data related to Figure 7.5 show that the bubble breaking up did reduce the Japanese average annual growth rate import of IP charges to single digit from 1990 to 1995, and it remained the single-digit growth since then for most of the time, yet average annual growth rate of exports of IP charges remained at two-digit level from 1990 to 2008 for most of the time, leading to Japanese science and technology OC growth from 29.10% in 1990 to 52.75% in 2003 with an average annual growth rate of 1.82%, and more than doubled the average annual growth rate in the previous 13-year period from 1977 to 1990, indicating that the breaking of the Japanese bubble not only did not interrupt the progress of science and technology in Japan but also accelerated the process.

It is noticeable that Japan achieved a surplus of $1.28 billion in trade of IP charges for the first time in 2003, with science and technology OC of 52.75%, surpassing 50% for the first time after 27 years of deficits from 1977.

7.7.4 *Growth from 2003 to 2015*

Data of Figure 7.5 show that Japanese export of IP charges continued two-digit annual growth from 2003 to 2008, yet the 2008 world financial crisis led both export and import of IP charges to two-digit declines of −15.58% and −7.74% from 2008 to 2009, both the highest annual decrease from 1977 to 2009; science and technology OC rose to the historical high of 68.14% in 2015 as shown in Figure 7.5, yet average annual growth reduced to 1.28% from 2003 to 2015.

7.7.5 *First declining period and the reason*

Figure 7.5 shows that Japan faced the first 5-year period decrease in science and technology OC from 2015 to 2020, with an average annual decline of 1.55%, the annual decline of 3.39% from 2019 to 2020 also marked the historical record of yearly decline since 1977. The rare steady decline in OC from 2015 to 2020 might be the result of severe competition with the US as Japanese science and technology OC got close to those of the US in recent years as the gap between the US and Japanese science and technology OC narrowed steadily from 50.32% in 1992 to 11.54% in

2014, and further to the one-digit level of 7.82% for the time in 2015, to the lowest level of only 2.17% in 2018, and back to 13.32% in 2020.

7.8 Analysis of Science and Technology OC in China and Related Issues

7.8.1 *Changes of science and technology OC in China from 1997 to 2020*

Using data of China's services trade from 1997 to 2020 updated by State Administration of Foreign Exchange on May 28, 2021, we can calculate China's science and technology OC from 1997 to 2020 (in the data of services trade since 1982 published by SAFE, both import and export data of China's intellectual property royalties from 1982 to 1996 are all zero). Figure 7.5 shows the results.

Figure 7.5 shows that science and technology OC increased rapidly from 9.17% to 13.0% from 1997 to 1998, however, it declined to 2.93% in 2003 and then to the lowest level of 2.87% in 2005; although it increased to 5.99% in 2010, it fell to 2.90% in 2014, almost back to the low level of 2003 to 2005; it grew slightly to 4.69% and 4.62% in 2015 and 2016. The average annual OC was merely 4.64% without much change from 1999 to 2016, indicating almost two decades of stagnation of science and technology OC.

Figure 7.5 also shows that science and technology OC increased from 9.67% to 14.28% from 2016 to 2017, the highest annual growth since 1997; it grew from 14.28% in 2017 to 18.75% in 2020 with an average yearly growth rate of 1.49% in the same period, and the average annual growth rate of 3.53% from 2016 to 2020, showing significant progress in science and technology in recent years.

7.8.2 *China's science and technology OC and the roles of foreign enterprises in China's trade*

Despite the gratifying improvement in China's science and technology autonomy in recent years, the level of China's science and technology OC has increased to 18.75% in 2020, indicating that more than 80% of China's economic and trade development relied on foreign science and technology over the past decades. These results are quite consistent with the results that about 70% of China's commodity exports as of 2018 were still dominated by foreign investment and consistent with the result that US-funded enterprises accounted for slightly more than a third of China's imports and exports during the same period (*Chinese Yuan Internalization and Product Innovation*, 9th Edition by Guangping (Peter G.) Zhang, published by China Finance Press in 2019) and also consistent with the updated results of the proportion of foreign investment in China's commodity exports by 2019 (10th Edition of *Chinese Yuan Internalization and Product Innovation*, the same published in March 2021 by the same publisher). These results of science and technology OC also explained well why China's deficits of IP charges have maintained steady growth until 2018. Its services trade deficit also claimed significant deficits. China's supply chain is indeed the most complete in the world, but most of the technologies or patents that supply chains rely on depend on foreign science and technology. If we do not strengthen our efforts to effectively improve science and technology OC, our economy and trade are likely to maintain the dependence when the international situation changes significantly.

7.8.3 *Inevitable deceleration in catching up and increasing difficulty for upgrading*

Table 5.3 shows that although compound annual growth rates of both first filings and family patents of China remained at two-digit levels, they went down in the period from 2011 to 2015 compared with rates in the period from 2007 to 2011, and Table 5.9 shows that the CAGR of family patents of China went down further to 15.84% from 2015 to 2018. Thus, it is inevitable that the growth of family patents of China will grow with a CAGR of about 10% for another 5 years or so, then it will fall to the one-digit level.

The above forecast was based on historical data before 2018 when trade tensions between China and the US just broke out. The pace of China's science and technology progress is likely to be affected over the next decade or so by US restrictions and sanctions on China's science and technology. At the same time, such restrictions and sanctions will push China to accelerate its innovation, as evidenced by the accelerated annual growth rates of export for IP charges in the past 2 years: 24.0% and

31.3%. Particularly, the growth rate was 45.4% in the first 4 months of 2021 over the same period of 2020.

7.8.4 *Indication of Japanese science and technology OC for China in coming decades*

The similarity between science and technology OC of 18.75% of China in 2020 and science and technology OC of 19.31% of Japan in 1978 shown in Figure 7.5 indicates that the near-to-four-decade science and technology OC of Japan might have some forward-looking reference for science and technology OC change for China in coming decades despite different international environments.

7.9 Problems Related to Patent Application and Authorization in China

According to WIPO updated data in October 2019, the number of patent applications in China increased from 19.6% to 24.4% from 2010 to 2011, surpassing Europe, Japan, and the United States for two consecutive years and becoming the country with the most significant number of patent applications in the world. From 2010 to 2015, China's cumulative patent application increment accounted for 77% of the global increment in the same period and further increased to 98.3% from 2016 to 2018, which is equivalent to almost all the new patent applications in the world in these 3 years.

However, according to the same data source of Figure 7.5, China's deficit of IP charges continued to grow, reaching a record high of \$30.03 billion in 2018; despite a slight decrease of \$2.35 billion to \$27.72 billion, it went up slightly to \$28.95 billion in 2020, indicating that the large number of domestic patent applications did not really reduce imports of IP charges, and China's reliance on foreign IP did not reduce accordingly with the vast application numbers.

The measure of intellectual property sufficiency in Table 6.11 also shows the insufficiency of intellectual property in China in relation to its GDP scales, particularly the trade of IP charges/GDP ratios of China from 2008 to 2019 were all lower than the average ratios of eight major developing countries in Table 6.11, indicating both exports and imports of IP charges are still too low in relation to GDP, and progresses in science and technology in China in the past few years were not significant enough to change the IP insufficiency problems, there is still much to catch up.

7.10 An Appropriate Quality Measure for Family Patents

Section 6.13 shows that average export of IP charges per family patents of any bloc is a good quality measure of family patent as it reflects the relative capacity of family patents on average to generate export fees, yet it is not good enough, as the average export of IP charges in other countries and regions, other than the top five blocs were higher than average exports for IP charges in any five blocs because the number of family patents of others was much fewer than that in five blocs. Section 6.14 shows that average net export of IP charges per family patent of any bloc is a better-quality measure of family patents as it reflects the relative capacity of family patents on average to generate net export fees. It can rank comparable quality of family patents between the US, Japan, Korea, and China, yet cannot rank quality of family patents between EPC States and Korea easily, as the average net exports of IP charges of EPC States were much lower than those of Korea. The purpose of this section is to find an appropriate quality measure of family patents among all five blocs and others.

7.10.1 *Definition of quality measure of family patents*

Since exports and imports of IP charges contain all information of science and technology qualities or usefulness, sci-tech independence or OC given in Table 7.1 is broader than patent internationalization defined in Table 5.10, thus the ratio of the former over the latter should be a good quality measure of family patents as it reflects all the good features of average export and average net export of IP charges. For example, the US sci-tech OC was 73.31% in 2019 as shown in Table 7.1, and the US patent OC was 20.33% in 2019 as shown in Table 5.10, the ratio of the former over the latter is 1.062.

Using this definition, we can find the ratios of sci-tech OC/patent OC, and Table 7.4 gives the results.

7.10.2 *Conditions for quality measures to be lower or higher than 100%*

We can prove that the quality measure in Table 7.4 is more significantly greater (lower) than 100% if the average export of IP charges per patent family of any bloc is greater (lower) than the average import of IP charges per foreign patent family in the bloc; interested readers may read the Appendix of this chapter for the proof.

Table 7.4: Quality Measures of Patent Families of Five Blocs and Others (2000–2020)

Year/ Bloc of Origin	EPC States (%)	Japan (%)	Korea (%)	USA (%)	China (%)	Others (%)
2000	77.5	68.6	49.1	114.7	330.2	191.6
2001	78.2	69.3	75.4	111.6	264.7	177.2
2002	75.6	70.1	62.3	107.5	140.8	252.4
2003	77.9	78.0	67.4	110.7	107.1	233.7
2004	79.7	80.9	72.2	107.4	197.3	232.6
2005	80.4	84.4	77.0	106.4	80.2	241.4
2006	77.0	85.4	80.1	110.8	69.0	264.9
2007	76.1	89.3	71.6	112.2	64.1	274.9
2008	73.2	94.1	95.7	106.7	85.2	247.9
2009	75.9	90.0	96.6	104.5	38.3	218.3
2010	80.1	91.0	72.0	107.0	55.6	182.6
2011	82.5	95.8	97.5	107.8	38.2	162.0
2012	84.1	99.2	81.2	106.3	37.0	175.2
2013	84.4	108.1	86.2	105.2	21.7	231.4
2014	78.8	107.3	99.1	107.0	12.6	227.6
2015	74.9	115.3	108.6	108.8	18.0	296.1
2016	76.1	113.6	117.8	104.7	16.5	303.9
2017	77.1	116.0	117.4	104.6	47.0	328.8
2018	77.1	120.9	125.7	105.4	41.4	343.1
2019	74.9	117.4	127.1	106.2	46.3	358.0
2020	75.6	113.1	129.8	107.3	49.4	389.7

Source: Calculated using results of sci-tech OC in Table 7.1 and patent OC results in Table 5.10.

7.10.3 *Extreme results in Table 7.4*

The extreme high values of quality measures of family patents from 2000 to 2004 in China and other results from 2000 to 2020 in Table 7.4 are due to relatively lower number of family patents, and high values from 2015 to 2020 of Korea and from 2013 to 2020 of Japan also resulted from decreasing numbers of family patents of these two countries.

7.10.4 *Leading roles of the US and Japan*

Table 7.4 shows that besides the extreme results of China from 2000 to 2004 and of others from 2000 to 2020, the quality measures of United States, remained above 100% despite general declining pattern, and the US results were higher than any other blocs from 2000 to 2012, indicating the highest quality of US family patents in the time span.

Table 7.4 shows that quality measure from 2000 to 2002 was lower than those of the US and of EPC States, and the Japanese quality measure increased steadily from 2002 to 2012, higher than those of EPC States in the same period and lower only than those of the US, indicating improving quality of family patents of Japan and its second position next to the US; the Japanese quality measure continued to rise from 2012 to 2018, surpassing the US quality measure during the same time period and indicating steady improvement of quality of family patents of Japan.

7.10.5 *Quality measures of EPC States and Korea*

Table 7.4 shows that quality measures of EPC States remained the third from 2003 to 2012, lower than those of both the US and Japan, and the quality measure of EPC States fell below those of Korea from 2013 to 2020, resulting from lower and decreasing family patents of Korea in the same period.

7.10.6 *Quality measures of China*

Table 7.4 shows that quality measures of China decreased dramatically from 2000 to 2014, resulting from increasing number of family patents and stagnant sci-tech OC at the same time, as shown in Table 7.1; yet it almost quadrupled from 12.6% in 2014 to 49.4% in 2020, indicating significant progress of quality of family patents of China from 2014.

7.11 Science and Technology Internationalization as Weighted Patent Internationalization

7.11.1 *Weighted family patents using quality measures as weights*

We can prove that the quality measure defined in Section 7.4 is proportional to the average export of IP (see the Appendix), thus it has the excellent characteristic of average export as shown in Section 6.13, and we can also prove the quality measure defined in Section 7.4 is also proportional to the average net export of IP (see the Appendix of this chapter). Thus, the quality measures can be used as "weights" to find weighted patent families shown in Table 5.7. Table 7.5 gives the weighted patent families of various blocs from 2000 to 2020.

7.11.2 *Science and technology internationalization*

Using the results in Table 7.5, we can obtain science and technology internationalization as patent internationalization of weighted family patents. Table 7.6 gives the results.

Comparing the results of science and technology internationalization of each patent office given in Table 7.6 with the patent internationalization results in Table 5.10, we find apparent differences. First, the overall levels of science and technology internationalization in the United States given in Table 7.6 are higher than the levels of patent internationalization shown in Table 5.10, which is due to the overall higher "weight" of US family patents. After reaching the historical peak of 48.88% in 2008, the science and technology internationalization in the United States was generally on a downward trend from 2008 to 2011, dropping to 47.02% in 2011, showing that the quantitative easing policy of the United States caused by the financial crisis has had a significant impact on US science and technology. However, science and technology internationalization of US returned to the upward trend to 49.12% in 2013, which was not only the highest in the top five offices and other regions in the same period but also higher than the total internationalization of EPC States, Japan, and Korea at 48.79%; the US science and technology internationalization declined steadily from 2013 to the low level of 42.44% in 2018 and rebounded slightly to 42.94% in 2020, back almost to the 2000 level of 42.98%, indicating relative

Table 7.5: Distribution of "Weighted" Patent Families of Various Blocs and Others (2000–2020)

Year/ Bloc of Origin	**EPC States**	**Japan**	**Korea**	**USA**	**China**	**Others**	**Global**
2000	26,077	35,829	5,277	54,811	1,312	4,206	127,512
2001	36,406	50,666	9,540	77,375	1,706	5,617	181,310
2002	43,798	58,007	11,300	90,531	1,613	7,700	212,949
2003	46,119	66,157	16,503	99,586	1,307	7,272	236,945
2004	46,282	66,259	18,918	105,710	2,334	7,545	247,048
2005	48,252	68,523	20,040	118,762	2,807	8,448	266,830
2006	42,182	67,893	18,908	115,567	1,432	7,893	253,875
2007	39,231	61,321	13,653	110,409	1,805	7,496	233,916
2008	41,741	60,473	15,714	122,654	2,554	7,797	250,933
2009	46,245	63,746	18,199	128,830	2,105	8,323	267,448
2010	45,142	69,652	16,303	128,295	3,507	6,780	269,680
2011	46,771	70,466	25,176	136,132	2,997	7,962	289,504
2012	47,391	69,238	20,893	133,060	3,527	7,750	281,859
2013	48,410	67,694	19,893	141,914	2,698	8,285	288,892
2014	46,797	67,568	21,656	131,499	1,997	9,863	279,380
2015	44,372	67,735	23,479	123,743	3,266	11,964	274,558
2016*	44,762	62,168	24,064	114,993	3,235	11,697	260,919
2017*	45,083	59,120	23,677	111,064	9,996	12,052	260,992
2018*	44,792	57,458	22,954	108,186	9,532	11,975	254,897
2019*	43,214	51,987	21,952	105,414	11,566	11,900	246,034
2020*	43,362	46,652	21,193	103,047	13,360	12,341	239,954

Source: Calculated using family patents given in Table 5.7 and quality measure in Table 7.2 as weights from 2000 to 2015; *family patents from 2016 to 2020 are based on estimated results with same assumptions in Table 5.10 and quality measures as weights in Table 7.4.

stable status of US sci-tech internationalization in the past two decades despite the international financial crisis in 2008, demonstrating the leading and monopoly position of the United States in global science and technology and also the strength of US science and technology to support the USD.

7.11.3 Science and technology internationalization

Table 7.6 shows that although Japan's science and technology OC continued to decline slightly from 2000 to 2020, the average annual level of science and technology internationalization in Japan is 24.83%, significantly higher than that of Europe of 17.70% in the same period. This is

Table 7.6: Science and Technology Internalization as "Weighted" Patent Internationalization (2000–2019) (Unit: case, %)

Year/ Bloc of Origin	EPC States	Japan	Korea	USA	China	Others
2000	20.45	28.10	4.14	42.98	1.03	3.30
2001	20.08	27.94	5.26	42.68	0.94	3.10
2002	20.57	27.24	5.31	42.51	0.76	3.62
2003	19.46	27.92	6.96	42.03	0.55	3.07
2004	18.73	26.82	7.66	42.79	0.94	3.05
2005	18.08	25.68	7.51	44.51	1.05	3.17
2006	16.62	26.74	7.45	45.52	0.56	3.11
2007	16.77	26.21	5.84	47.20	0.77	3.20
2008	16.63	24.10	6.26	48.88	1.02	3.11
2009	17.29	23.83	6.80	48.17	0.79	3.11
2010	16.74	25.83	6.05	47.57	1.30	2.51
2011	16.16	24.34	8.70	47.02	1.04	2.75
2012	16.81	24.56	7.41	47.21	1.25	2.75
2013	16.76	23.43	6.89	49.12	0.93	2.87
2014	16.75	24.19	7.75	47.07	0.71	3.53
2015	16.16	24.67	8.55	45.07	1.19	4.36
2016*	17.16	23.83	9.22	44.07	1.24	4.48
2017*	17.27	22.65	9.07	42.55	3.83	4.62
2018*	17.57	22.54	9.01	42.44	3.74	4.70
2019*	17.56	21.13	8.92	42.85	4.70	4.84
2020*	18.07	19.44	8.83	42.94	5.57	5.14

Source: Calculated using family patents given in Table 5.7 and quality measure in Table 7.2 as weights from 2000 to 2015; *family patents from 2016 to 2020 are based on estimated results with same assumptions of Table 5.10 and quality measures as weights in Table 7.4.

consistent with the above result that Japan is at the high end of the global science and technology chain. Republic of Korea's science and technology internationalization averaged 7.73% a year, second only to Europe, ranking the fourth in the top five offices.

It is worth noting that Table 7.6 also shows that the average annual growth rate of science and technology internationalization in China from 2014 to 2020 was the highest of all five blocs, with an average annual growth rate of 0.81%, indicating rapid progress of sci-tech in China in recent years. Science and technology internationalization of China first surpassed the other countries and regions outside the five blocs in 2020.

7.12 Summary

Patents are essential carriers and embodiment of science and technology, and science and technology is the pillar of economy and trade. Reports from the top five offices provide us with the most detailed data and regional distribution regarding patent families, and the data related to patent families are published according to the residence or bloc of origin of first filings and patent families. Therefore, data make it possible to determine the location of these highly international patents and then to determine the level of patent internationalization and the level of science and technology independence or OC in different regions. This chapter uses the patent data from the top five offices, especially patent family data, to calculate and estimate the level of science and technology independence or OC of major countries and regions in the world from 2000. Using data of imports and exports of IP charges of global services trade, differences between the average export fees and the average net export fees of each patent family in each patent office are calculated, which further indicates significant differences in the quality of patent families in each patent office.

Since exports and imports data of IP charges include essentially all information of all types of IP including patents, the ratio of export of costs for use of IP over export and import of charges for use of IP is a more accurate measure of science and technology OC. The ratios of science and technology OC over the patent independence or OC defined in Chapter 5 can be well taken as the quality measures of patent families of all blocs, and such measures are further taken as "weights" of patent families, then science and technology internationalization can be calculated as weighted patent families over total global weighted patent families.

Empirical results show that although China does have the most complete supply chain in the world, most of the technologies that these supply chains rely on are foreign technologies (the result that China's science and technology OC was still significantly lower than 20% before 2020 indicates that more than 80% of China's science and technology is still dependent on foreign countries). As a result, up to 70% of China's exports are exports of foreign-funded enterprises. Therefore, it is imperative to improve the internationalization level of China's science and technology, especially improving the level of China's science and technology OC is the top priority in the future.

In addition, the empirical results of correlation of science and technology OC among major countries and regions are calculated based on science and technology OC data of these countries and regions. The positive correlation of science and technology OC among some countries shows the relationship of science and technology mutual assistance or complementarity among these countries or regions to some extent. At the same time, the negative correlation of science and technology OC between some countries and regions shows the trend of squeezing science and technology among these countries or regions. These results reveal the profound relationship between scientific and technological development among countries or regions, providing new evidence for us to understand the deep connection between economic and trade activities of corresponding economies. What is particularly noteworthy is that from 1998 to 2008, the science and technology autonomy in major countries in the world has increased significantly and continuously, while a significant gap exists in the science and technology autonomy of Mainland China, Hong Kong SAR, and Taiwan China. Science and technology OC in Mainland China, Hong Kong, and Taiwan China shows a unique "abnormal" phenomenon of decreasing instead of increasing simultaneously. It is worth our deep thinking on the market factors, capital factors and other factors that influence the independence of science and technology.

Appendix

Let x stand for the average of export for charges of use of IP, then quality measure of Table 7.2 can be rewritten as follows:

$$\mathrm{QM} = x(1 + b)/(x + a)$$

where a = import of charges for use of IP of one bloc/family patents and b = foreign family patents in one bloc/family patents of the bloc. Thus, the first-order derivative of QM with respect to $x = a(1 + b)/(x + a)^2 > 0$ and the second-order derivative of QM with respect to $x = -2a(1 + b)/(x + a)^3 < 0$, and the first-order derivative of QM with respect to $x - a$ is the same as the first-order derivative of QM with respect to $x = a(1 + b)/(x + a)^2 > 0$.

QM $= x(1 + b)/(x + a) > 1$ implies that $xb > a$, or $x > a/b$ = import of charges for use of IP/number of foreign patent families in the bloc, similar procedure yields that when $x < a/b$, QM < 1.

Bibliography

IP5 Statistics Report 2018 Edition, European Patent Office, Japan Patent Office, Korea Intellectual Property Office, China National Intellectual Property Administration, United States Patent and Trademark Office Edited by KIPO, October 2019, https://www.fiveipoffies.org/statistics/statisticsreport.

Qiuju Zhou and Fuhai Leng, Research and Demonstration of Research Frontier Identification Method Based on the Perspective of Technology Media, *Journal of Modern Information*, 2018(2): 62–67.

Results for 2011–2017 are based on the 2018 annual report of the top five patent offices from CNIPA website: http://www.cnipa.gov.cn/tjxx/index.htm or website of the top five offices: https://www.fiveipoffies.org/statistics/statisticsreport.

Zunyi Liu, *The Sky Won't Fall — The Trade War between China and the United States and Future Economic Relations*, The Chinese University of Hong Kong Press, 2019.

Chapter 8

Impacts of Science and Technology on Trade, Current Accounts, and Others

International trade is a critical factor affecting world foreign exchange through trade settlement, current accounts and worldwide currency. Based on science and technology OC and science and technology internationalization, we briefly analyze the impacts of science and technology on both commodity and services exports and net exports influence on accounts of major count to obtain quantitative results on how science and technology affect currency valuation and currency internationalization. As a by-product, we also discuss and briefly analyze the impacts of science and technology on COVID-19 control and other issues.

8.1 Relationships between Commodity Exports, Imports, Net Exports and Science and Technology OC and Internationalization

Since commodity trade is still a critical part of international trade, we analyze the impacts of science and technology on commodity exports and net exports of major countries in this section.

8.1.1 *Impacts of science and technology on commodity exports and net exports in the US*

8.1.1.1 *Using import and export data of the US*

Using sci-tech internationalization of the US given in Table 7.6 and commodity exports data updated by the US BEA, we find the correlation coefficients between US commodity exports, imports and net trade and science and technology internationalization at 69.09%, 67.68%, and −50.17%. These results show that the higher the US science and technology OC or internationalization, the higher the US commodity export, yet the negative relationship between US science and technology and US commodity deficits appear contractionary to common intuition.

8.1.2 *Impacts of science and technology on commodity exports and net exports in Japan*

A significant name in the use of intellectual property and one of the world's major commodity exporters, Japan has a crucial position in world commodity trade. Using the results of science and technology OC of Japan given in Table 7.1 and commodity exports, imports, and net exports data updated by the Japan External Trade Organization (JETRO), we can find correlation coefficients between Japanese commodity exports, imports and net trade and science and technology OC at 77.14%, 82.29%, and −66.18% from 2000 to 2020; correlation coefficients between Japanese commodity exports, imports and net exports and science and technology internationalization given in Table 7.5 were −45.65%, −48.66%, and 39.08% in the same period. These results show that higher the Japanese science and technology OC, the higher the Japanese commodity exports, yet the lower the Japanese commodity surpluses.

8.1.2.1 *Commodity exports and net exports in China*

As the world's largest commodity since 2014, China has an important position in world commodity trade. Using the results of science and technology OC of China given in Table 7.1, commodity exports, imports, and net exports data updated by the State Administration of Foreign Exchange (SAFE), we can find the correlation coefficients between Chinese commodity exports, imports and net exports and science and technology OC were 56.11%, 57.31%, and 45.72% from 2000 to 2020; correlation coefficients between Chinese commodity exports, imports and net exports and science and technology internationalization given in Table 7.6 were 60.94%, 61.84%, and 51.17% in the same period. The above results show higher correlation coefficients between Chinese commodity exports, imports, and net exports with science and technology internationalization than with science and technology OC.

8.2 Relationships between Exports, Imports, Net Exports of Services Trade and Science and Technology OC and Internationalization of Major Services Traders

8.2.1 *Services exports, import, and net exports with science and technology in the USA*

Using the import and export data of the US services trade (cross-border US) released by the US BEA and the corresponding US science and technology OC in Table 7.1, we calculated the correlation coefficients between US services trade exports, imports and net exports and US science and technology OC as 10.14%, 11.40%, and 4.54%, respectively; similarly, correlation coefficients between US services trade exports, imports and net exports and US science and technology internationalization are given in Table 7.1 as −6 57.97%, 64.75%, and 47.45%, respectively. The above results indicate high correlation coefficients between US science and technology internationalization and US services exports, imports, and surpluses.

8.2.2 *Services exports, import, and net exports with science and technology of Japan*

Using the import and export data of JETRO and the corresponding Japanese science and technology OC in Table 7.1, we calculated the correlation coefficients between Japanese services trade exports, imports and net exports and Japanese science and technology OC as 93.30%, 91.74%, and −51.93%, respectively, from 2000 to 2020; correlation coefficients between Japanese services trade exports, imports and net exports and Japanese science and technology internationalization given in Table 7.6 were −80.49%, −77.98%, and 25.65% in the same period, respectively.

8.2.3 *Services exports, import, and net exports with science and technology of China*

Using the import and export data released by SAFE and the corresponding Japanese science and technology OC in Table 7.1, we calculated the correlation coefficients between Chinese services trade exports, imports and net exports and Chinese science and technology SRC as 51.71%, 59.41%, and −59.28%, respectively, from 2000 to 2020; correlation coefficients between Japanese services trade exports, imports and net exports and Chinese science and technology internationalization given in Table 7.6 were 56.39%, 63.02%, and −61.85% in the same period, respectively. The above results indicate a higher correlation between Chinese services exports, imports, and net exports with Chinese science and technology internationalization than with Chinese technology transactions.

8.3 Service and Commodity Trade of US-Owned Foreign Affiliates

Commodity and services trade of US-owned foreign affiliates (USOFA), or majority-owned foreign affiliates of US parent firms, play critical roles in international transactions. Data released by the US BEA show that the ratio of net services export or net sales of services of USOFA over net services export of US cross-border increased from 59.8% in 2000 to 105.3% in 2001, to the peak of 354.7% in 2009, and fell dramatically to merely 138.2% in 2020. This section analyzes the active roles of the USOFA externally rather than internally in the USA in the past two decades. Thus, we cannot calculate an accurate data of technology on total US trade in services. We analyzed the correlation coefficients between trade in services and commodity trade of USOFA with US science and technology and US science and technology internationalization in this section.

8.3.1 *Services exports, imports and net exports of USOFA with US science and technology*

Using the sales and purchases data of USOFA updated by the US BEA and US science and technology OC in Table 7.1, we can calculate correlation coefficients between US affiliate sales, purchases, and net sales of USOFA and US science and technology SRC as 22.03%, 5.15%, and 45.35% from 2000 to 2020. The correlation between sales of USOFA with US science and technology at 22.03% was more than twice as high as the corresponding correlation coefficient at 10.14% between US cross-border exports of trade in services and US science and technology OC, and the correlation coefficient between net sales of USOFA with US science and technology at 45.35% was nearly 10 times as high as the corresponding correlation coefficient at 4.54% between US cross-border net exports of trade in services and US science and technology OC, indicating that US science and technology are more effective to generate net services exports outside the US than in the US.

We can also obtain correlation coefficients between sales, purchases, and net sales of USOFA and US science and technology internationalization in Table 7.6 as 65.43%, 53.55%, and 75.47%, respectively, which were 7.46%, −1120%, and 28.02% higher than the corresponding correlation coefficients between exports, imports, and net exports of US cross-border data with US science and technology internationalization above, also indicating that it is much more effective for US enterprises to generate net sales outside the USA than in the USA.

The above results demonstrate that USOFA plays a critical role in international market place. The US cross-border data cannot give us the whole picture of the influence of US science and technology.

8.3.2 *Commodity exports, imports, and net exports of USOFA with US science and technology*

Although the US BEA regularly releases service sales and purchases of US majority-owned affiliates of parent firms, the US BEA does not release similar data of US exports and imports of goods. US exports and imports of goods shipped by US affiliates are far from accurate. For example, US exports and imports of goods shipped by US affiliates missed important data of US affiliates in China and Ireland most of time with the same reason quoting "suppressed to avoid disclosure of data of individual companies", and the rarely released exports data of US affiliates in China were merely \$0.8 billion in 2011 to \$3.475 billion in 2013. Thus, commodity trade data of USOFA released by the US BEA cannot be used because of too many "suppressed to avoid disclosure of data of individual companies". Using estimated exports and imports of USOFA from 2002 to 2019 of

Zhang (2020), based on estimated exports and imports more beneficial to foreign affiliates in China and the US science and technology OC in Table 7.1, we can find correlation coefficients between exports, imports, and net exports of USOFA and US science and technology OC at 41.28%, 18.42%, and 55.28%, which were much higher than the corresponding correlation coefficients of exports, imports, and net exports of US cross-border with US science and technology OC at 26.67%, 26.59%, and −20.82% obtained above, indicating that the US has more beneficial technology OC that is more useful for USOFA outside the US.

Similarly, we can find correlation coefficients between exports, imports criticality of USOFA, and US science and technology internationalization in Table 7.6, mainly at 77.60%, 61.16%, and 85.01%, which were much higher than the corresponding correlation coefficients of exports, imports, and net exports of US cross-border with US science and technology internationalization at 69.09%, 67.68%, and −50.17% obtained above, indicating again that the US science and technology OC is more beneficial for USOFA outside the US.

8.4 Relationship between Current Accounts and Science and Technology of Major Countries

Current accounts represent one of the critical factors to affect foreign exchange rates or currency valuation. Current accounts contain mainly commodity trade and trade in services of most monetary authorities, and transactions contain income elements of employees engaging in international trade. This section concentrates on relationships between current accounts and science and technology.

Using the current account data updated by the International Monetary Fund (IMF) in April 2021 and science and technology OC results of Table 7.1 from 2000 to 2020, we can find correlation coefficients between current account and science and technology OC of USA, Japan, China, and Korea at −12.23%, 10.20%, 0.35%, and 76.30%, respectively, indicating the higher the science and technology, the higher is the existing current accounts for most major countries; correlation coefficients between existing account and science and technology internationalization of USA, Japan, China, and Korea at 3.17%, −26.57%, 5.40%, and 69.99%, respectively, also indicate the higher the science and technology, the higher the current accounts for most countries.

8.5 Summary of Major Results of Major Traders

Results of the above sections are so broad that we cannot compare them easily. Table 8.1 summarizes the above results so that we can analyze them easily.

8.5.1 *Relationships between trade items with science and technology of USA much improved to reasonable levels*

Results in Table 8.1 clearly show that all correlation coefficients between trade items and two measures of science and technology become highly positive and thus become reasonable with the addition of US-owned foreign affiliates, indicating that the US-owned foreign affiliates or the offshore US make significant profits with US science and technology outside the US. Attention should be paid to the negative US current account, which becomes positive should net exports of US-owned foreign affiliates be added to the US cross-border current accounts, and the correlation coefficients between the adjusted US current account and US science and technology would become over 62%, indicating strong support of the US-owned foreign affiliates to the USD.

8.5.2 *Problematic relationships between trade items with science and technology of Japan and explanation*

Correlation coefficients of Japanese commodity trade items with Japanese science and technology in Table 8.1 are problematic as Japanese commodity import was more positively correlated with its science and technology at 82.29% than Japanese commodity export at 77.14%, leading to negative correlation coefficients of Japanese net export and its science and technology at −66.18%. A likely explanation for these complex correlation coefficients should be the same as the US case because net international investment position (IIP) of Japan or "offshore Japan" increased 1.64 times from 2000 to \$3.57 trillion in 2020, almost two-third of Japanese GDP \$5.05 trillion in 2020, or 88.46% of German GDP in the same year. Related to the most significant net IIP of the world, Japanese-owned foreign affiliates should have commodity commerce and trade in services like USOFA shown in Table 8.1, and correlation coefficients

Table 8.1: Correlation Coefficients between Trade Items and Current Accounts with Science and Technology OC and Science and Technology Internationalization (2000–2020) (Unit: %)

Correlation Coefficients with Science and Technology OC					
Items/Region	**USA (Cross-Border)**	**US-Owned FA**	**USA Total**	**Japan**	**China**
Commodity Export	54.56	63.64	61.09	77.14	56.11
Commodity Import	55.40	44.03	51.39	82.29	57.31
Commodity Net Export	−45.78	74.09	69.98	−66.18	45.72
Services Export	38.84	47.18	44.83	93.30	51.71
Services Import	44.47	33.54	37.28	91.74	59.41
Service Net Export	30.47	62.27	53.46	76.49	−59.28
Total Export	49.07	58.27	55.57	85.16	55.79
Total Import	53.63	39.60	47.12	85.11	58.37
Total Net Export	−32.75	71.54	65.50	−51.93	13.33
Current Account*	−12.23		62.75	10.20	0.35
Correlation Coefficients with Science and Technology Internationalization					
Items/Region	**USA (Cross-Border)**	**U.S.-Owned FA**	**USA Total**	**Japan**	**China**
Commodity Export	69.09	77.60	63.48	−46.65	60.93
Commodity Import	67.68	61.16	57.69	−48.66	61.84
Commodity Net Export	−50.17	85.01	68.51	39.08	51.17
Services Export	57.97	65.43	63.48	−80.49	56.39
Services Import	64.75	53.55	57.69	−77.98	63.02
Service Net Export	47.45	75.47	68.51	−68.52	−61.85
Total Export	65.41	74.13	71.68	−57.14	60.71
Total Import	67.59	58.41	63.69	−54.04	63.30
Total Net Export	−24.78	83.31	78.94	25.65	−1.39
Current Account*	3.17		76.96	−26.57	5.40

Source: Calculated with results of science and technology OC of Table 7.1, results of science and technology internationalization of Table 7.6, current account data from the International Monetary Fund website released in April 2021; trade data of three countries as specified above; USA cross-border stands for data released by the US Bureau of Economic Analysis for USA; US-owned FA stands for services and commodity trade of US majority-owned foreign affiliates of US parent firms; USA sum stands for the total of USA cross-border and US-owned FA; current account of USA total is calculated by adding the total net exports of both commodity and trade in services of US-owned FA to the original US cross-border current account; current account* of USA total is calculated by adding the total net exports of both commodity and trade in services of US-owned FA to the original US cross-border current account.

between trade items of the total Japanese economy and Japanese science and technology should be much higher than the correlation coefficients shown in Table 8.1.

8.5.3 *Relationships between trade items with science and technology of China*

Table 8.1 shows that the average correlation coefficients of Chinese commodity exports, commodity net exports, services exports and service net exports with science and technology OC at 23.57% are low to stimulate Chinese exports and net exports further and 45.19% of Japan, indicating that science and technology need to improve to further promote Chinese exports and net exports; the lowest correlation coefficients between Chinese current account and Chinese science and technology OC at 0.35% was less than 1% and 4% of the corresponding correlation coefficients of USA at 62.75% and of Japan at 10.20%, showing that the support of Chinese science and technology to Chinese yuan has great potentiality.

8.6 Impacts of Sci-tech on Gross Domestic Products

In previous sections, we studied the impacts of sci-tech on world trade, current accounts, and other factors. As foreign trade is part of gross domestic products (GDP), sci-tech should impact GDP and its major components. This section concentrates on the impacts of exports and imports of charges for the use of intellectual property (IP) on GDP and its major components. The contents of this section and Section 8.7 largely depend on Zhang and Lin (2021). Table 8.2 gives the correlation coefficients between nominal GDPs and exports, imports, net exports, trade (exports and imports) of charges for using IP in major world economies.

8.6.1 *Exports of charges for the use of IP*

Results in Table 8.2 are overwhelming as correlation coefficients between nominal GDP and exports and imports of charges for the use of IP are higher for major developed economies than correlation coefficients between sci-tech internationalization and currency internationalization, as shown in Tables 13.2 and 13.4. Table 8.2 shows that correlation

Table 8.2: Correlation Coefficients between Nominal GDP and Exports, Imports, Net Exports, Exports, and Imports of Charges for the Use of IP in Major World Economies (1992–2019)

Economy/IP Factor	Exports (%)	Imports (%)	Net Exports (%)	Exports and Imports (%)	Co (Imports)-Co (Exports) (%)	Co (Im)-MAX (Co (Im), Co (Ex)) (%)
USA	97.53	98.12	94.28	98.31	0.59	0.20
Japan	41.45	51.38	34.28	44.46	9.94	−6.92
Mainland China	17.64	37.50	−40.60	34.94	19.86	−2.57
UK	85.95	81.66	83.96	85.75	−4.29	−0.20
South Korea	95.77	95.64	−48.79	97.19	−0.12	1.42
Taiwan China	88.20	83.47	−70.82	89.44	−4.73	1.25
Japan (1980–2002)	80.99	94.08	−34.12	88.52	13.09	−5.56
Japan (2003–2020)	13.64	27.96	3.83	18.11	14.32	−9.85
USA (2003–2020)	91.74	93.55	82.28	94.11	1.81	0.56
Japan Net IIP (1996–2020)	90.22	89.01	86.44	90.80	−1.21	0.58
Japan GDP+Net IIP (1996–2020)	79.79	82.25	74.24	81.32	2.46	−0.93

Source: Calculated using exports and imports of charges for IP usages of Table 6.10 from 1992 to 2019 and corresponding nominal GDP data released by the IMF in April 2021 of related economies; Co (*x*) indicates correlation coefficient of *x*.

coefficients between nominal US GDP and exports and imports of charges for the use of IP of USA were all over 97% from 1992 to 2019. The correlation coefficients between nominal US GDP and net exports and trade (exports and imports) of charges for US IP use were 94.28% and 98.31% in the same period, respectively. These high correlation coefficients indicate significant impacts of science and technology on the US economy.

Table 8.2 also shows that correlation coefficients between nominal GDP and net exports and trade of charges for the use of IP of UK, South Korea, and Taiwan China were mainly close to 90%, indicating significant impacts of sci-tech on these economies.

8.6.2 *Imports of charges for the use of IP*

The correlation coefficient results between imports of charges for the use of IP and the nominal GDP of major economies are more overwhelming because they are not as consistent with a traditional understanding of dependence on foreign technology. Imports of charges for the use of IP represent the dependence of a particular economy on foreign intellectual property. They thus should have negative impacts on the economy, or at least their effects should not be as high as exports of charges for the use of IP. However, Table 8.2 shows that correlation coefficients between nominal GDP and imports of costs for the use of IP were all significantly higher than the corresponding correlation coefficients between nominal GDP and exports of charges for the use of IP for most economies. Only the correlation coefficients between two pairs of imports with GDP were 4.29% and 0.12% lower than the correlation coefficients in the UK and South Korea in the same period, respectively. The higher correlation coefficients between nominal GDP and imports of charges for the use of IP imply that imports for costs of the use of IP provide the necessary technology to support the development of GDP of the imported economy.

8.6.3 *Net exports of charges for the use of IP*

Net exports of charges for the use of IP represent sci-tech originality capability (OC), as discussed in Chapter 7. The fact that the highest correlation coefficient between nominal GDP and net exports of charges for the use of IP was 94.28% in the US from 1992 to 2019 of all economies provides the evidence that technology has strong positive impacts on GDP. However, both correlation coefficient between nominal GDP and exports of charges for the use of IP at 97.53% and the corresponding correlation coefficient between nominal GDP and imports of costs for the use of IP at 98.12% in the same period were higher than the correlation coefficient between nominal GDP and net exports of charges for the use of IP at 93.18%. The lower correlation coefficient between nominal GDP and net exports of charges for the service of IP results from more usefulness of imports of charges for IP use on GDP development.

8.6.4 *Trade of charges for the use of IP*

As exports of charges for the use of IP represent sci-tech OC of an economy and import of charges for the use of IP represent necessary sci-tech imported from foreign economies, both exports and imports of costs for the benefit of IP are essential for economic development. Table 8.2 shows that the correlation coefficient between nominal GDP and trade of charges for the use of IP at 98.31% from 1992 to 2019 was the highest in the USA of all corresponding correlation coefficients at the same time, followed by South Korea, Taiwan, China, and the UK with corresponding correlation coefficients at 97.19%, 89.44%, and 86.30% at the same time, respectively. The overall high correlation coefficients between nominal GDP and trade of charges for the use of IP demonstrate the usefulness of IP sufficiency defined in Chapter 6.

Generally, the correlation coefficient between the sum of two variables with another given variable lies between the two corresponding correlation coefficients between the two variables with the same given variable. However, Table 8.2 shows the correlation coefficient between nominal GDP and trade (sum of export and import) of charges for the use of IP at 98.31%, 97.19%, and 89.44% in the USA, South Korea, and Taiwan China, respectively. These three correlation coefficients were 0.20%, 1.42%, and 1.25% higher than the corresponding two correlation coefficients between nominal GDP and exports and imports of charges for the use of IP in the three economies, respectively. These "extra" correlation coefficients can be regarded as extra "synergy" generated by both exports and imports of charges for the use of IP to promote economic development. Additional "synergy" existed for overseas Japanese net IIPs from 1996 to 2020 in Table 8.2.

Zhang and Lin (2021) also found a condition under which exports and imports of charges for the use of IP together to generate extra synergy for nominal GDP in any economy. The condition is that correlation coefficient ratio between exports of charges for the use of IP with nominal GDP and correlation coefficient between imports of charges for the use of IP with nominal GDP should be within a certain range in order to generate the extra synergy. In other words, if exports of charges for the use of IP are too highly correlated with nominal GDP compared to imports of charges for the use of IP, no extra synergy exists because the economy does not take enough advantage of international IP or foreign IP. Similarly, if exports of charges for the use of IP are correlated with nominal GDP too lowly compared to imports of charges for the use of IP, no extra synergy exists because the economy relies on too much of international IP or foreign IP, exports of charges for the use of IP need to play more roles for the economy. Interested readers may refer to Zhang and Lin (2021) for more details.

8.6.5 *The special case of Japan*

Although correlation coefficients between nominal Japanese GDP and exports and imports of charges for the use of IP of Japan were merely about half of these of the corresponding US correlation coefficients in the same period, corresponding correlation coefficients of Japan from 1980 to 2002 were comparable to those of the US, the UK, South Korea, and Taiwan China. The low correlation coefficients of Japan from 1996 to 2019 are primarily the result of the Japanese GDP deflator during the time. The corresponding correlation coefficients between Japanese Net Investment Positions (IIP) and charges for the use of IP from 1996 to 2020 were also comparable to those of the US, the UK, South Korea, and Taiwan China. The above results indicate that sci-tech have significant impacts on overseas Japanese net assets, and they had substantial effects on Japanese GDP in the early stage of Japanese sci-tech progress when Japan had made dramatic progress in sci-tech from 1980 to 2002 before it entered a net surplus of charges for the use of IP for the first time in 2003. Various Japanese correlation coefficients in Table 8.2 indicate that Japanese exports and imports cost for the use of IP generated more growth of IIPs than domestic GDP as the CAGR of Japanese IIPs was as high as 5.33% from 1996 to 2020 compared to the CAGR of Japanese nominal GDP at 0.10% at the same time.

8.6.6 *The special case of Mainland China*

Table 8.2 shows that the coefficient between nominal GDP and exports of charges for the use of IP and the corresponding correlation coefficient between nominal GDP and imports of costs for the use of IP of Mainland China was the lowest of all economies. These lowest correlation coefficients demonstrate that the Chinese economy has been mainly propelled by economic system reforms, capital stock, and human resources. Science and technology still have great potential to drive the Chinese economy to develop further. The most significant difference of 19.86%, between the coefficient of 37.50% and between nominal GDP and imports of charges for the use of IP, and the corresponding correlation coefficient of 17.64% between nominal GDP and exports of charges for the use of IP indicate the long distance for China to catch up with all developed economies in sci-tech in Table 8.2.

8.7 Impacts of Sci-tech on Gross National Products and Their Major Components

Section 8.6 provides us with intuitive results of sci-tech impacts on nominal GDP. Following the same method in Section 8.6, this section studies the effects of exports, imports, net exports and trade of charges for the use of IP on capital stock at a constant price, human capital per person, total factor productivity (TFP), and GDP at a stable price of the US, Japan, South Korea, and Mainland China from 1992 to 2019 in this section. Table 8.3 gives the results.

8.7.1 *Impacts of sci-tech on capital stock*

Table 8.3 shows that correlation coefficients between exports, imports, net exports and trade of charges for using IP and capital stock at a constant price are highest in the US of the five major economies. Only exports and imports charges for the use of IP of the US and South Korea have extra "synergy" on capital stock, with additional synergy of 0.53% and 1.11%, respectively, implying that sci-tech have the most significant impacts on capital stock in the US and impacts of sci-tech on human capital in South Korea are second only to the US.

8.7.2 *Impacts of sci-tech on human capital*

Table 8.3 shows that correlation coefficients between exports, imports, net exports and trade of charges for the use of IP and human capital are also highest in the US of the five major economies. Exports and imports of charges for the use of IP of USA, Japan, UK, and South Korea have extra synergy on human capital, with synergy of 0.20%, 0.44%, 0.77%, and 1.09%, respectively, implying that sci-tech have the most significant impacts on human capital in the USA, and implications of sci-tech on human capital in Japan, UK, and South Korea are primarily comparable.

8.7.3 *Impacts of sci-tech on TFP*

Studies on the measurements of TFP are numerous, as illustrated in the reviews by Feenstra *et al.* (2009). Most studies on TFP are either on the measurements of TFP or factors influencing TFP; rare attention has been

Table 8.3: Correlation Coefficients of Exports, Imports, Net Exports and Trade of Charges for the Use of IP on Capital Stock at Constant Price, Human Capital per Person, TFP, GDP at Constant Price and Nominal GDP of Major Economies (1992–2019)

USA	**Capital Stock (%)**	**Human Capital (%)**	**TFP (%)**	**Real GDP (%)**	**Nominal GDP (%)**
Export	97.35	97.81	97.79	95.70	97.53
Import	97.02	96.29	94.08	97.01	98.12
Net Export	94.65	95.80	97.07	92.08	94.28
Trade	97.88	98.01	97.39	96.68	98.31
Co(Trade) — Max (Co (Ex), Co (Im))	0.53	0.20	−0.40	−0.34	0.20
Japan	**Capital Stock (%)**	**Human Capital (%)**	**TFP (%)**	**Real GDP (%)**	**Nominal GDP (%)**
Export	66.65	96.39	68.84	95.15	41.45
Import	75.35	95.84	67.62	93.93	51.38
Net Export	59.50	93.90	67.56	93.09	34.28
Trade	69.48	96.84	68.92	95.40	44.46
Co (Trade) — Max (Co (Ex), Co (Im))	−5.86	0.44	0.09	0.25	−6.92
UK	**Capital Stock (%)**	**Human Capital (%)**	**TFP (%)**	**Real GDP (%)**	**Nominal GDP (%)**
Export	88.61	95.37	1.02	96.95	90.01
Import	80.26	94.41	5.79	95.04	87.13
Net Export	88.96	89.91	−2.52	92.08	86.30
Trade	87.03	96.13	2.50	97.44	90.13
Co (Trade) — Max (Co (Ex), Co (Im))	−1.58	0.77	−3.30	0.49	0.11
South Korea	**Capital Stock (%)**	**Human Capital (%)**	**TFP (%)**	**Real GDP (%)**	**Nominal GDP (%)**
Export	96.50	94.71	48.56	95.02	95.77
Import	95.81	95.59	51.96	96.53	95.64
Net Export	−47.63	−50.97	−34.14	−52.85	−48.79
Trade	97.61	96.68	51.22	97.35	97.19
Co (Trade) — Max (Co (Ex), Co (Im))	1.11	1.09	−0.74	0.82	1.42

(Continued)

Table 8.3: (*Continued*)

Mainland China	Capital Stock (%)	Human Capital (%)	TFP (%)	Real GDP (%)	Nominal GDP (%)
Export	77.80	76.13	6.01	71.16	78.29
Import	98.99	97.24	30.93	97.21	99.15
Net Export	−99.39	−97.69	−34.59	−98.62	−99.48
Trade	97.95	96.17	27.93	95.42	98.16
Co (Trade) — Max (Co (Ex), Co (Im))	−1.04	−1.07	−3.00	−1.79	−0.99

Source: Zhang and Lin (2021); others are the same as Table 8.2.

paid to the impacts of sci-tech on TFP. We use real GDP, capital stock, and human capital data in Zhang and Lin (2021) to find the corresponding total factor GDP quantity and find correlation coefficients between exports, imports, net exports and trade of charges for the use of IP, and total factor GDP quantity, Table 8.3 gives the results.

The highest correlation coefficients between exports, imports, and trade of charges for the use of IP and total factor GDP quantity of US in Table 8.3 may indicate that TFP is mainly the contribution of sci-tech in the US. The contribution of sci-tech on TFP is just over two-thirds in Japan as a correlation coefficient of 68.92% between the trade of charges for the use of IP and TFP is slightly over two-thirds. The contribution of sci-tech on TFP is just over half in South Korea as a correlation coefficient of 51.22% between the trade of charges for the use of IP and TFP is slightly over half in South Korea. The contribution of sci-tech on TFP is marginal in the UK as a correlation coefficient of 2.50% between the trade of charges for the use of IP and TFP is just over zero in the UK. The extreme low contribution of sci-tech on TFP in the UK is somewhat questionable. We will explore related issues later on.

8.7.4 *Impacts of sci-tech on real GDP*

Results in Table 8.3 show that sci-tech impacts on real GDP are like effects on nominal GDP in Table 8.2 with the only exception of Japan. Table 8.3 shows that impacts of sci-tech on real GDP in Japan are like those in the US, UK, and South Korea. The corresponding low correlation coefficients of the nominal GDP of Japan are the results of the Japanese GDP deflator from 1996 to 2019 as explained earlier.

8.7.5 *The special case of Mainland China*

The highest correlation coefficients between imports of charges for the use of IP and capital stock, human capital, real GDP, and nominal GDP of Mainland China of five major economies in Table 8.3 indicate the importance or necessity of imports of charges for the use of IP in Chinese economic development from 1996 to 2019. Table 8.3 also shows at least three factors with extra "synergy" of all four developed economies in Table 8.3. However, there is no factor with extra synergy in Mainland China, implying coordination between exports and imports of charges for the use of IP has the excellent potentiality to improve for sci-tech to support the economic development more healthily in China.

Results in Tables 8.2 and 8.3 are intuitive and provide us with proper evidence of how sci-tech impacts GDP and its major components. However, correlation analysis is simplistic as it does not capture the critical nature of the time lag of sci-tech change over time. Since it takes time for sci-tech to function on GDP and its components, time-series analysis is likely to produce better results of impacts of sci-tech on GDP and its major components. We will return to related issues in Chapter 15.

8.8 Brief Introduction to Confirmed Cases, Cured Cases, Death Cases, and Relation Ratios of COVID-19

The COVID-19 epidemic has had a rare impact on world production and human life around the world in nearly a century. The epidemic has not been well controlled over 1 year as both total confirmed cases and death cases are more than doubled in less than half a year from the end of 2020 to June 20, 2021, indicating faster spreading of the epidemic and almost the same death rate. Although the impact of the epidemic on the global economy and people's lives is still difficult to estimate, the results of the epidemic control reflect not only the technological and medical levels of each region but also the overall level of governance in each region. The epidemic will prove to have significant impacts on the world economy, international politics, human life, and more. This section uses related data to find the relationships between global responses to COVID-19 epidemic and the overall level of science and technology and governance throughout the world. Table 8.4 gives cumulative confirmed cases, cured cases, death cases, and related ratios of 123 countries or regions with more than 30,000 cumulative confirmed cases as of June 10, 2021.

Table 8.4 shows that there are significant differences in positive rates in various sizes of countries. Table 8.4 shows that there are 13 countries with positive rates over 10% (Maldives, Bahrain, Montenegro, Czech, Hungary, Slovenia, Lebanon, Luxembourg, Sweden, the United States, Serbia, Lithuania, and Estonia with positive rates at 18.61%, 16.87%, 16.01%, 15.70%, 13.44%, 12.38%, 11.42%, 11.39%, 10.41%, 10.35%, 10.24%, 10.12%, and 10.02%, respectively), most of them small or mid-sized economies; there are nine countries with positive rates lower than 0.20% (Ivory Coast, Malawi, Madagascar, Uganda, Angola, Australia, Sudan, Congo, and China with positive rates at 0.18%, 0.17%, 0.15%, 0.14%, 0.12%, 0.12%, 0.08%, 0.04%, and 0.01%, respectively), again most of them are small and mid-sized economies. The positive rates of confirmed cases reflect an accurate level of control and governance in different countries. The time span of available data is still short, and the epidemic is still spreading at an accelerating pace around the world, so it is difficult to obtain specific analysis results.

8.9 Confirmed Cases, Cured Cases, and Death Cases Compared to Science and Technology Progress

The situation of epidemic control in different countries given in Table 8.4 still shows apparent differences in the development and management of science and technology in various countries. Indeed, death and cure ratios in some countries may be reliable indicators of technology and health care. Table 8.4 shows that the death rates of Israel, Denmark, Norway, Sweden, Finland, the Netherlands, Austria, Japan, Switzerland, the United States, France are all lower or slightly lower than the global death rate of 2.16%, which are consistent with the relative science and technology development status of these countries shown in Table 7.1; UK's death rate of 2.81% and Germany's death rate of 2.43% are significantly higher than the global death rate of 2.16%. Most of the above countries are

Table 8.4: Confirmed Cases, Cured Cases, and Death Cases from COVID-19 Epidemic in Major Countries and Regions and Their Relative Proportions (as of June 10, 2021) (Unit: 1,000 cases, %)

Country/ Region	Confirmed Cases	Cured Cases	Death Cases	Positive Rate	Cured Rate	Death Rate	Death Rate/ Cured Rate
USA	34,275.8	28,278.4	614.0	10.35	82.50	1.79	2.17
India	29,273.3	27,778.9	363.1	2.17	94.89	1.24	1.31
Brazil	17,215.2	15,670.8	482.1	8.17	91.03	2.80	3.08
France	5,730.0	5,471.1	110.3	8.76	95.48	1.92	2.02
Turkey	5,313.1	5,114.6	47.5	6.41	96.26	0.89	0.93
Russia	5,167.9	4,772.0	125.3	3.59	92.34	2.42	2.63
UK	4,543.0	4,283.3	127.9	6.80	94.28	2.81	2.99
Italy	4,239.9	3,943.7	126.9	6.98	93.01	2.99	3.22
Argentina	4,066.2	3,639.4	83.9	9.02	89.50	2.06	2.31
Spain	3,729.5	3,505.2	80.5	8.07	93.99	2.16	2.30
Germany	3,718.6	3,563.8	90.3	4.49	95.84	2.43	2.53
Columbia	3,665.1	3,409.1	94.0	7.28	93.01	2.57	2.76
Iran	2,990.7	2,590.7	81.5	3.59	86.62	2.73	3.15
Poland	2,876.7	2,647.1	74.4	7.58	92.02	2.59	2.81
Mexico	2,441.9	1,946.5	229.4	1.94	79.71	9.39	11.78
Ukraine	2,219.8	2,115.2	51.5	5.27	95.29	2.32	2.44
Peru	1,995.3	1,720.7	187.8	6.14	86.24	9.41	10.92
Indonesia	1,885.9	1,728.9	52.4	0.70	91.67	2.78	3.03
South Africa	1,722.1	1,593.1	57.4	2.95	92.51	3.33	3.60
Netherlands	1,669.1	1,553.7	17.7	9.72	93.08	1.06	1.14
Czech	1,664.6	1,628.2	30.2	15.70	97.81	1.81	1.86
Chile	1,453.5	1,376.3	30.3	7.74	94.69	2.09	2.20
Canada	1,398.3	1,353.1	25.9	3.73	96.77	1.85	1.91
Philippines	1,293.7	1,214.5	22.3	1.18	93.88	1.72	1.84
Iraq	1,242.5	1,160.0	16.6	3.04	93.35	1.34	1.44
Sweden	1,082.7	1,013.3	14.5	10.41	93.59	1.34	1.43
Romania	1,079.4	1,043.6	31.5	5.56	96.68	2.92	3.02
Belgium	1,073.4	991.6	25.1	9.36	92.38	2.33	2.53

(*Continued*)

Table 8.4: (*Continued*)

Country/ Region	**Confirmed Cases**	**Cured Cases**	**Death Cases**	**Positive Rate**	**Cured Rate**	**Death Rate**	**Death Rate/ Cured Rate**
Pakistan	937.4	871.7	21.5	0.46	92.98	2.30	2.47
Portugal	855.4	814.0	17.0	8.36	95.16	1.99	2.09
Israel	839.6	833.0	6.4	9.28	99.21	0.77	0.77
Bangladesh	820.4	759.6	13.0	0.49	92.59	1.58	1.71
Hungary	806.6	722.3	29.9	13.44	89.55	3.71	4.14
Japan	767.8	717.9	13.8	0.61	93.50	1.80	1.93
Jordan	742.2	724.5	9.6	9.96	97.61	1.29	1.32
Serbia	714.5	702.3	6.9	10.24	98.30	0.97	0.99
Switzerland	699.7	664.8	10.9	8.09	95.02	1.55	1.63
Austria	648.0	632.7	10.7	7.24	97.64	1.64	1.68
Malaysia	639.6	556.0	3.7	1.94	86.94	0.58	0.66
Nepal	601.7	515.6	8.2	2.00	85.69	1.37	1.60
UAE	591.6	571.0	1.7	5.50	96.51	0.29	0.30
Lebanon	525.1	7.8	7.7	11.42	1.48	1.47	99.34
Morocco	522.8	510.3	9.2	1.47	97.62	1.76	1.80
Saudi Arabia	462.5	444.8	7.5	1.37	96.17	1.62	1.69
Ecuador	436.0	398.6	20.9	2.53	91.43	4.80	5.26
Bulgaria	420.1	388.6	17.9	6.02	92.50	4.26	4.60
Belarus	402.8	395.5	2.9	4.31	98.17	0.73	0.75
Kazakhstan	398.0	372.4	4.1	2.12	93.58	1.04	1.11
Bolivia	396.8	313.4	15.2	3.47	78.99	3.84	4.86
Slovakia	390.8	376.9	12.4	7.18	96.44	3.18	3.30
Greece	388.0	12.4	12.1	3.63	3.19	3.12	97.78
Paraguay	385.0	316.9	10.4	5.38	82.30	2.70	3.29
Panama	384.5	369.9	5.4	9.11	96.19	1.41	1.46
Tunisia	362.7	317.8	13.3	3.08	87.62	3.67	4.19
Croatia	358.2	348.8	8.1	8.72	97.38	2.26	2.32
Georgia	352.0	337.0	5.0	9.53	95.76	1.42	1.48
Cost Rica	338.0	259.9	4.3	6.64	76.87	1.27	1.65
Azerbaijan	335.0	327.9	5.0	3.33	97.89	1.48	1.51

(*Continued*)

Table 8.4: (*Continued*)

Country/ Region	Confirmed Cases	Cured Cases	Death Cases	Positive Rate	Cured Rate	Death Rate	Death Rate/ Cured Rate
Uruguay	330.0	289.8	4.9	9.38	87.80	1.47	1.68
Kuwait	323.4	306.2	1.8	6.95	94.70	0.56	0.59
Palestine	311.0	302.9	3.5	6.64	97.40	1.13	1.16
Dominican Rep	305.6	249.0	3.7	2.95	81.48	1.21	1.48
Denmark	288.7	275.5	2.5	4.95	95.43	0.87	0.92
Lithuania	277.2	261.9	4.3	10.12	94.48	1.56	1.65
Ethiopia	273.7	249.0	4.2	0.29	90.99	1.55	1.70
Egypt	271.0	199.3	15.5	0.27	73.52	5.72	7.78
Guatemala	267.4	243.2	8.4	1.52	90.93	3.14	3.45
Ireland	265.8	248.6	4.8	5.51	93.55	1.82	1.95
Bahrain	254.9	211.0	1.0	16.87	82.78	0.38	0.46
Slovenia	256.1	248.5	4.4	12.38	97.02	1.72	1.77
Moldova	255.7	248.4	6.1	7.22	97.15	2.40	2.47
Venezuela	246.8	226.5	2.8	0.77	91.81	1.12	1.22
Honduras	243.5	86.5	6.6	2.85	35.55	2.69	7.58
Oman	230.2	207.8	2.5	5.24	90.26	1.07	1.19
Armenia	223.5	214.9	4.5	7.47	96.15	2.00	2.08
Qatar	219.3	216.3	0.6	7.80	98.64	0.26	0.27
Sri Lanka	216.1	182.2	1.9	0.99	84.32	0.88	1.05
Bosnia and Herzegovina	204.6	177.0	9.5	5.84	86.51	4.63	5.35
Libya	188.4	174.2	3.2	2.86	92.48	1.67	1.81
Thailand	187.5	139.3	1.4	0.27	74.27	0.73	0.99
Kenya	174.3	119.2	3.4	0.35	68.42	1.93	2.82
Nigeria	167.0	163.3	2.1	0.08	97.81	1.27	1.30
North Macedonia	155.5	149.6	5.5	7.47	96.20	3.52	3.66
Cuba	153.6	146.4	1.1	1.37	95.34	0.69	0.72
S. Korea	146.3	136.7	2.0	0.28	93.45	1.35	1.45

(*Continued*)

Table 8.4: (*Continued*)

Country/ Region	Confirmed Cases	Cured Cases	Death Cases	Positive Rate	Cured Rate	Death Rate	Death Rate/ Cured Rate
Myanmar	144.9	132.7	3.2	0.27	91.59	2.23	2.44
Latvia	135.6	129.9	2.4	7.00	95.81	1.80	1.88
Algeria	132.4	92.1	3.6	0.31	69.61	2.68	3.86
Albania	132.4	129.8	2.5	4.61	98.01	1.85	1.89
Estonia	130.4	125.4	1.3	10.02	96.16	0.97	1.01
Norway	127.7	89.0	0.8	2.36	69.67	0.62	0.89
Kyrgyzstan	108.7	101.7	1.9	1.67	93.60	1.72	1.84
Zambia	105.9	95.0	1.3	0.58	89.69	1.26	1.40
Uzbekistan	102.6	98.6	0.7	0.31	96.09	0.68	0.71
Montenegro	99.9	97.8	1.6	16.01	97.91	1.60	1.63
Ghana	94.4	92.5	0.8	0.32	98.01	0.84	0.85
Finland	93.6	46.0	1.0	1.69	49.14	1.03	2.10
China	91.3	86.3	4.6	0.01	94.47	5.08	5.37
Mongolia	70.5	55.6	0.3	2.24	78.84	0.47	0.60
Afghanistan	87.7	60.3	3.4	0.24	68.72	3.89	5.66
Cameroon	79.9	74.4	1.3	0.31	93.15	1.63	1.75
El Salvador	75.0	69.9	2.3	1.17	93.18	3.05	3.27
Cyprus	73.0	71.2	0.4	8.45	97.49	0.50	0.52
Mozambique	71.3	69.7	0.8	0.23	97.84	1.18	1.20
Luxembourg	70.4	68.9	0.8	11.39	97.84	1.16	1.19
Maldives	69.2	53.4	0.2	18.61	77.14	0.28	0.36
Singapore	62.2	61.8	0.0	1.09	99.24	0.05	0.06
Namibia	61.4	53.1	1.0	2.58	86.59	1.58	1.82
Botswana	59.5	55.6	0.9	2.66	93.51	1.51	1.61
Uganda	56.9	47.8	0.4	0.14	83.86	0.71	0.84
Jamaica	49.1	248.5	4.4	1.71	505.92	8.95	1.77
Ivory Coast	47.6	47.1	0.3	0.18	98.92	0.64	0.65
Senegal	41.9	40.4	1.2	0.25	96.54	2.75	2.85
Madagascar	41.8	40.2	0.9	0.15	95.98	2.09	2.18
Zimbabwe	39.5	36.9	1.6	0.25	93.53	4.12	4.40

(*Continued*)

Table 8.4: (*Continued*)

Country/ Region	Confirmed Cases	Cured Cases	Death Cases	Positive Rate	Cured Rate	Death Rate	Death Rate/ Cured Rate
Cambodia	36.7	29.8	0.3	0.22	81.29	0.82	1.01
Angola	36.3	30.0	0.8	0.12	82.48	2.24	2.72
Sudan	36.2	29.8	2.7	0.08	82.43	7.51	9.11
Malawi	34.4	32.7	1.2	0.17	94.95	3.36	3.54
DRC	34.3	27.8	0.8	0.04	81.19	2.41	2.97
Cabo Verde	31.4	30.1	0.3	5.70	95.90	0.86	0.90
Malta	30.6	30.1	0.4	6.46	98.41	1.37	1.39
Australia	30.2	28.7	0.9	0.12	94.99	3.01	3.17
Sum	174,813.6	158,074.6	3,774.6	3.06	90.42	2.16	2.39
America	70,346.5	60,544.0	1,837.8	6.92	86.07	2.61	3.04
Asia	53,062.0	49,359.8	728.8	1.17	93.02	1.37	1.48
East Asia	1,100.1	1,009.2	21.4	0.07	91.74	1.94	2.12
South Asia	31,920.0	30,162.9	408.0	1.80	94.50	1.28	1.35
ASEAN	4,262.5	3,868.7	83.4	0.65	90.76	1.96	2.16
Other Asia	15,779.5	14,319.0	216.1	3.36	90.74	1.37	1.51
Europe	47,067.4	43,965.6	1,083.5	6.37	93.41	2.30	2.46
West Europe	32,427.4	30,275.1	715.9	7.19	93.36	2.21	2.36
East Europe	14,640.1	13,690.5	367.6	5.09	93.51	2.51	2.68
Africa	5,043.3	4,522.8	134.2	0.39	89.68	2.66	2.97
Oceania	52.6	36.8	1.1	0.12	70.07	2.04	2.91
Global	175,622.4	159,172.0	3,788.7	2.33	90.63	2.16	2.38
Advanced economies	69,957.6	63,370.4	1,413.1	6.74	90.58	2.02	2.23

Source: World meters — coronavirus updates, www.worldometers.info.

among the top 10 net exports of charges for use of intellectual property in the world, as shown in Table 6.12, except for UK and Germany.

Thus, the overall level of science and technology of net exports of charges for use of intellectual property is high, and the vast majority (eight of the 10 top net surplus countries of charges for use of intellectual property have death rates below the global death rate) have done well in combating the epidemic. In the future, when we have sufficient data, we can conduct a more detailed analysis of the relationship between the anti-epidemic effect of other countries and the level of scientific and medical treatment.

The death rates of countries with intellectual property royalty deficits such as Singapore, Saudi Arabia, India, Turkey, and Qatar are significantly lower than the global conflict and are also inconsistent with the scientific and technological levels reflected by intellectual property royalty rates of these countries. These inconsistent results may be due to governance factors, or maybe due to insufficient epidemic data so far, which will be further analyzed later in this chapter.

8.10 Relationships between COVID-19 Positive Rates, Cured Rates, and Death Rates and Science and Technology OC

The relationship between death rates in countries with high levels of COVID-19 confirmed cases and of science and technology has been described previously. We will find the correlation coefficients between favorable rates, cured rates and death rates and science and technology OC in this section.

8.10.1 *Relationships between COVID-19 positive rates, cured rates, and death rates, and science and technology OC of major developed countries*

Of the 123 countries in Table 8.4, 33 are developed countries. The correlation coefficients between positive rates, cured rates, and death rates of the 33 developed countries with their science and technology OC in 2019 were 46.11%, 57.84, and 45.66%. Of the three correlation coefficients, only 57.84% is intuitively correct, indicating the higher the level of science and technology OC or medical treatment, the higher the cured rate of COVID-19. Yet, the other two correlation coefficients are accurate for both positive and death rates, respectively, and should be negatively correlated with science and technology OC, which indicate serious problems of COVID-19 data or related problems with controlling the epidemic. The unreasonable positive correlation coefficient between death rate and science and technology OC of major developed countries indicates that the major developed countries fail to give full play to their scientific and medical advantages to deal with the epidemic, which results in a high death rate.

8.10.2 *Relationships between COVID-19 positive rates, cured rates, and death rates and science and technology OC of major developing countries*

Of the 90 developing countries in Table 8.4, exports and imports of charges for use of IP are missing for 15 small or mid-sized developing countries. We can find the correlation coefficients between positive rates, cured rates, and death rates of other 75 major developing countries with their science and technology OC at 20.81%, −6.33%, and −1.87%. Of the three correlation coefficients, only −1.87% is intuitively correct, indicating the higher the level of science and technology OC or medical treatment, the lower the death rate of COVID-19. The other two correlation coefficients are not correct as positive rate should be negative with science and technology OC and cured rate should be positively correlated with technology SRR, indicating serious problems of COVID-19 data or related problems with controlling the epidemic in developing countries, yet the problems are not as serious with major developing countries as with major developed countries as a correlation between positive rate with science and technology SRC at 20.81% for major developing countries is less than half of 46.21% for major developed countries.

8.10.3 *Relationships between COVID-19 positive rates, cured rates, and death rates and science and technology OC*

Of the 123 countries in Table 8.4, data of exports and imports of charges for use of IP of 15 small and mid-sized developing countries are missing. We can find the correlation coefficients between positive rates, cured rates, and death rates of other 108 countries with their science and technology self-reliance capability (OC) at 26.18%, −6.12%, and −16.70%. Of the three correlation coefficients, only −16.7% is intuitive, indicating the higher the level of science and technology OC or medical treatment, the lower the death rate of COVID-19, the other two correlation coefficients are not correct as positive rates should be negatively correlated and cured rates should be positively correlated with science and technology OC.

8.11 Relationships between COVID-19 Cases, Cured Rates, and Death Rates and Government Effectiveness

COVID-19 epidemic positive rates and cured rates of each country should also be highly correlated with national governance or positively associated with government effectiveness measured by worldwide governance of the World Bank. We try to find the correlation coefficients between COVID-19 positive rates, cured rates, and death rates and government effectiveness estimated by worldwide governance of the World Bank of 2019 updated in 2020.

8.11.1 *Relationships between COVID-19 positive rates, cured rates, and death rates and science and technology OC of major developed countries*

Using the government effectiveness of 2019 estimated by the World Bank (www.worldbank.org/governance/wgi) updated in 2020 and COVID-19 positive rates, cured rates, and death rates, we can find correlation coefficients between government effectiveness and COVID-19 positive rates, cured rates, and death rates of 33 developed countries as 57.38%, 71.16%, and 57%. Of the three correlation coefficients, only 71.16% is intuitively correct, indicating the higher the government effectiveness, the higher the cured rate of COVID-19, yet the other two correlation coefficients are not as accurate as both positive rates and death rates should be negatively correlated with government effectiveness, indicating serious problems in COVID-19 data or related problems with government effectiveness estimations of the World Bank. The unreasonably high positive correlation coefficients between government effectiveness and positive rate of major developed countries indicate that the major developed countries have failed to control the epidemic, or their government effectiveness was estimated too high.

8.11.2 *Favorable relationships between government effectiveness and COVID-19 positive rates, cured rates, and death rates of major developing countries*

We can find similar correlation coefficients between government effectiveness of 2019 and positive rates, cured rates, and death rates of other 90 major developing countries in Table 8.2 at −13.87%, −45.38%, and −44.16%. Of these three correlation coefficients, only −45.38% is intuitively wrong because the cured rate should be positively correlated with government effectiveness, and the other two correlation coefficients are correct because both positive rate and death rate should be negatively correlated with government effectiveness. These results of major developing countries are mostly better than the results of major developed countries, indicating more problems with COVID-19 data and with government effectiveness estimation of major developed countries.

8.11.3 *Relationships between government effectiveness and COVID-19 positive rates, cured rates, and death rates*

We can similarly find the correlation coefficients between government effectiveness of 2019 and COVID-19 positive rates, cured rates, and death rates of 123 countries in Table 8.2 at 36.47%, 8.40%, and −20.17%. Of the three correlation coefficients, only −20.17% is intuitively correct, indicating the higher the level of government effectiveness, the lower the death rate of COVID-19. The two correlation coefficients are wrong because government effectiveness should be negatively correlated with COVID-19 positive rates and cured rates. The problems of these overall correlation coefficients are mainly due to the issues with major developed countries as analyzed above.

8.12 Summary

The correlation coefficients between science and technology OC and exports, net exports, and current accounts of the top three economies found in this chapter highlight the important roles of science and technology in international trade and current accounts and then in foreign exchange rates. Particular attention should be paid to the correlation coefficients between science and technology and trade items of the USA. With the addition of trade contribution of US-owned enterprises in foreign countries, the correlation coefficients of cross-border USA and overseas USA become reasonable, indicating necessary functionality of US-owned enterprises in foreign countries in international trade and international finance. These US-owned foreign enterprises provide significant support to USD worldwide.

Empirical results of impacts of science and technology represented by exports and imports of charges for the use of IP on GDP and its major components provide us with evidence of impacts of science and technology on economic development. Particularly, the generally higher correlation coefficients between GDP and imports of charges for use of IP than correlation coefficients between GDP and exports of charges for use of IP prove the necessity of imports of charges for the use of IP for economic development in both developed and developing economies. The extra synergy of exports and imports of charges for the use of IP found in this chapter also provides us evidence that efficient coordination between exports and imports of charges for the use of IP can produce additional GDP in major developed economies.

The empirical studies of science and technology OC with relation to COVID-19 show that world data of COVID-19 should improve in quality, and the unreasonable correlation coefficients between science and technology OC with COVID-19 positive rates and death rates of major developed countries show problems of major developed countries in combating COVID-19; the more unreasonable correlation coefficients between government effectiveness and COVID-19 positive rates and death rates of major developed countries show more serious problems of major developed countries in combating COVID-19. Studies of correlation coefficients between other governance measures such as rule of law, regulatory quality, control of corruption and COVID-19 ratios yield similar results. We leave these topics for future study with more data on COVID-19.

Bibliography

Feenstra, R.C., Heston, A., Timmer, M.P., and Deng, H., Estimating Real Production and Expenditures Across Countries: A Proposal for Improving the Penn World Tables, *Review of Economics and Statistics* 2009, 91(1): 201–212.

Zhang, Guangping (Peter G.) and Tan Ziyang, *Chinese Yuan Internationalization and Product Innovation*, 10th Edition, China Financial Press, 2021.

Zhang, Guangping (Peter G.) and Lin Ken, *Empirical Evidence of Impacts of Science and Technology on Gross Domestic Products and Their Major Components*, unpublished, 2021.

Part III

Chapter 9

Development and Current Status of Offshore CNY Centers

Hong Kong SAR (Hong Kong) was the first and the most important offshore CNY or Renminbi (RMB) center. Besides Hong Kong, the number of other offshore RMB centers has increased quickly in the past few years. These offshore RMB centers have become major driving forces of the internationalization of RMB. The primary purpose of this chapter is to introduce the recent developments and future trends of over 20 offshore RMB centers around the world, which will provide evidence to help us forecast the trends of future RMB internationalization development.

9.1 Global Distribution of Offshore RMB Centers with Clearing Agreements

CNY clearing is the basis of offshore CNY business. In July 2010, the People's Bank of China (PBOC), for the first time, signed the Settlement Agreement on the Clearing of Renminbi (RMB) Businesses with the Hong Kong Branch of Bank of China (BOC). After that, the PBOC has signed similar clearing agreements with more than 30 countries or regions, which lay the basis for the construction and development of RMB centers in these countries. Table 9.1 shows the schedule for RMB clearing in offshore RMB centers.

Table 9.1 shows that the Bank of China has 13 offshore RMB clearing banks. In contrast, the Industry Industrial and Commercial Bank of China (ICBC) has seven, China Construction Bank (CCB) has three, Bank of

Table 9.1: List of Offshore RMB Clearing Banks

Country/ Region	Clearing Center	Clearing Bank	Date
Hong Kong SAR	Clearing bank of RMB business in Hong Kong	Bank of China (Hong Kong) Limited	2010/7/19
Macao SAR	Clearing bank of RMB business in Macao	Bank of China Macao branch	2012/9/24
Taiwan China	Clearing bank of RMB business in Taiwan	Bank of China Taipei branch	2012/12/11
Singapore	Clearing bank of RMB business in Singapore	ICBC Singapore Branch	2013/2/8
Britain	Clearing bank for RMB business in London	China Construction Bank (London) Limited	2014/6/18
Germany	Clearing bank of RMB business in Frankfurt	Bank of China branch in Frankfurt	2014/6/19
South Korea	Clearing bank of RMB business in Seoul	Bank of Communications Seoul branch	2014/7/4
France	Clearing bank of RMB business in Paris	Bank of China Paris Branch	2014/9/15
Luxembourg	Luxembourg RMB business clearing bank	ICBC Luxembourg branch	2014/9/16
Qatar	Clearing bank of RMB business in Doha	ICBC Doha Branch	2014/11/4
Canada	Clearing bank of RMB business in Toronto	ICBC (Canada) Ltd	2014/11/9
Australia	Clearing bank of RMB business in Sydney	Bank of China Sydney Branch	2014/11/18
Malaysia	Clearing bank of RMB business in Kuala Lumpur	Bank of China (Malaysia) Limited	2015/1/5
Thailand	Clearing bank of RMB business in Bangkok	ICBC (Thailand) Co., Ltd.	2015/1/6
Chile	Clearing bank of RMB business in Chile	China Construction Bank Chile branch	2015/5/25
Hungary	Hungarian RMB business clearing bank	Bank of Hungary	2015/6/28

(*Continued*)

Table 9.1: (*Continued*)

Country/ Region	Clearing center	Clearing bank	Date
South Africa	Clearing bank for RMB business in South Africa	Bank of China Johannesburg branch	2015/7/7
Argentina	Clearing bank of RMB business in Argentina	ICBC (Argentina) Limited by Share Ltd	2015/9/18
Zambia	Clearing bank of RMB business in Zambia	Bank of China Zambia	2015/9/30
Switzerland	Swiss RMB clearing bank	China Construction Bank Zurich branch	2015/11/30
America	United States RMB clearing bank	Bank of China New Zealand branch	2016/9/21
Russia	Russian RMB clearing bank	ICBC (Moscow) branch	2016/9/23
The United Arab Emirates	United Arab Emirates RMB clearing bank	Agricultural Bank of China Dubai branch	2016/12/9
America	United States RMB clearing bank	JPMorgan Chase	2018/2/13
Japan	Japan RMB clearing bank	Bank of China Tokyo branch	2019/4/17
Japan	Japan RMB clearing bank	MUFG Bank	2019/6/27
Philippines	Philippines RMB clearing bank	Bank of China Manila branch	2019/9/17

Source: http://www.xinhua08.com.

Communications (BOCOM) and the Agricultural Bank of China (ABC) have 1 each, respectively. The other two non-Chinese RMB clearing banks are JPMorgan Chase and MUFG bank. With the future need for offshore RMB, the number of offshore clearing banks will increase in the next few years, and these centers will play an essential role in promoting the development of offshore RMB centers. Except for offshore deposit and clearing business, offshore RMB bond business is the main business of offshore

RMB centers. The PBOC issued a notice on June 3, 2015, that clearing banks and participating overseas banks were allowed to enter the interbank bond market and the offshore RMB business and conduct bond repurchase transactions, including bond collateral repo and outright bond repurchase transactions.

9.2 The Leading Role of Hong Kong RMB Center

Hong Kong is the offshore RMB center with the longest history and has kept its status as the largest offshore RMB center. Deposit is the most basic and straightforward financial service, also the foundation of other financial services. Before 2004, the amount of RMB flowing into Hong Kong has already reached tens of billions and even hundreds of billions. However, due to the lack of accurate statistics from authorities, different scholars have different opinions on the amount of the inflow. The publication titled RMB Exchange Rate System and RMB Internationalization, Jing Li (2009), can be used as a reference.

With the approval of the State Council, the People's Bank of China started to provide clearing arrangements for banks in Hong Kong engaged in personal RMB business including RMB deposit, exchange, RMB cards, and remittances to facilitate the economic, trade, and personnel exchanges between the Mainland and Hong Kong and to channel the RMB in Hong Kong back to the Mainland in an orderly manner. On November 18, 2003, People's Bank of China released Announcement of the People's Bank of China on Providing Clearing Arrangements for the Individual RMB Business of Hong Kong Banks, laying a solid foundation for the development of RMB business in Hong Kong.

9.2.1 *Changes of RMB deposit scale*

Table 9.2 shows both quarterly RMB deposit amount, and quarter-on-quarter growth rate after the banking industry in Hong Kong incorporated RMB deposit services since February 2004. The table indicates a continuous increase in RMB deposits since 2004, and reached a hike as of RMB 77.64 billion in June 2008 before the financial crisis. However, during the post-crisis period from 2008 to March 2009, the deposit went through a decrease to RMB 53.11 billion. From 2009 to 2014, the total RMB deposit in Hong Kong regained an increasing momentum, and reached a record high over one trillion to RMB 1.00356 trillion by the end of 2014, with a 5-year average compound growth rate of 74.1%. This was mainly due to the substantial growth of RMB deposit in Hong Kong after the trial practice of domestic RMB cross-border trade, and the increasing confidence in holding Renminbi on the RMB appreciation, as the US dollar fell against major global currencies after the launch of the quantitative easing policy in the United States.

With the RMB exchange rate reform in 2015 and the US's exit from the quantitative easing policy, the pressure of RMB depreciation against the USD started to increase. At the same time, China's regulatory authorities have stepped up efforts to combat false trade and cross-border arbitrage, which has led to the sharp decrease of offshore RMB settlement, and thus a downward trend in Hong Kong's RMB deposit. By March 2017, it dropped to the historical low of RMB 507.27 billion since March 2008, just over half of the peak at the end of 2014. Table 9.2 shows that RMB deposit in Hong Kong began a rebound trend since March 2017, period-to-period annual growth increased to the highest level of 16.3% in March 2021. The average compound annual growth rate was 11.09% in the 4 years from March 2017 to March 2021, reflecting both trade and economic growth in China the same period. With steady trade growth and RMB appreciation pressure, RMB deposit in Hong Kong is expected to rebound toward the peak in a couple of years.

9.2.2 *The relationship between the movement of RMB deposit in Hong Kong and offshore RMB appreciation/depreciation*

The RMB deposits from 2004 to Q1 2021 in Table 9.2 indicate offshore RMB appreciation and depreciation expectations. When the expectation of offshore RMB appreciation was high, the ratio of deposit increase went high. When the expectation of offshore RMB depreciation was high, the percentage of deposit dropped. This relationship showed its most robust connection during the financial crisis, from September 2008 to March 2009, and the reform of the RMB exchange rate from June 2015 to March 2017, during which the depreciation of the Renminbi has significantly reduced Hong Kong's Renminbi deposit, while from March 2009 to the end of 2014, RMB appreciation and cross-border RMB settlement jointly promoted rapid growth in RMB deposit.

Table 9.2: RMB Deposits and Allocation in Hong Kong Banking Industry (Unit: RMB billion)

Time	Current Deposit	Term Deposit	Total	Current Deposit Share (%)	Term Deposit Share (%)	Change of Total (%)	Banks
2004-02	0.70	0.19	0.90	78.7	21.3		32
2004-03	2.10	2.30	4.39	47.7	52.3		36
2004-06	2.85	3.95	6.80	41.9	58.1		39
2004-12	5.42	6.71	12.13	44.7	55.3		38
2005-06	9.36	11.54	20.90	44.8	55.2	207.2	39
2005-12	10.62	11.97	22.59	47.0	53.0	86.2	38
2006-06	11.29	11.43	22.71	49.7	50.3	8.7	39
2006-12	12.23	11.18	23.40	52.2	47.8	3.6	38
2007-06	17.23	10.39	27.62	62.4	37.6	21.6	38
2007-12	22.54	10.86	33.40	67.5	32.5	42.7	37
2008-06	51.24	26.40	77.64	66.0	34.0	181.1	40
2008-12	38.12	17.94	56.06	68.0	32.0	67.8	39
2009-06	35.92	18.46	54.38	66.1	33.9	−30.0	40
2009-12	40.66	22.06	62.72	64.8	35.2	11.9	60
2010-06	52.43	37.28	89.70	58.4	41.6	65.0	77
2010-12	117.57	197.37	314.94	37.3	62.7	402.1	111
2011-06	180.35	373.26	553.60	32.6	67.4	517.2	128
2011-12	176.40	412.13	588.53	30.0	70.0	86.9	133
2012-06	136.62	421.09	557.71	24.5	75.5	0.7	133
2012-12	123.54	479.45	603.00	20.5	79.5	2.5	139
2013-06	127.51	570.45	697.96	18.3	81.7	25.1	140
2013-12	151.06	709.42	860.47	17.6	82.4	42.7	146
2014-06	150.70	775.22	925.91	16.3	83.7	32.7	148
2014-12	176.97	826.59	1,003.56	17.6	82.4	16.6	149
2015-06	180.45	812.48	992.92	18.2	81.8	7.2	146
2015-12	160.91	690.20	851.11	18.9	81.1	−15.2	145
2016-06	204.28	507.27	711.55	28.7	71.3	−28.3	146
2016-12	135.52	411.19	546.71	24.8	75.2	−35.8	144
2017-06	142.52	383.56	526.08	27.1	72.9	−26.1	140
2017-12	159.70	399.44	559.14	28.6	71.4	2.3	137

(Continued)

Table 9.2: (*Continued*)

Time	Current deposit	Term deposit	Total	Current deposit share (%)	Term deposit share (%)	Change of total (%)	Banks
2018-06	167.02	417.50	584.52	28.6	71.4	11.1	137
2018-12	194.43	420.59	615.02	31.6	68.4	10.0	136
2019-06	214.54	389.70	604.24	35.5	64.5	3.4	136
2019-12	223.98	408.22	632.21	35.4	64.6	2.8	138
2020-06	241.11	398.80	639.91	37.7	62.3	5.9	140
2020-12	260.02	461.63	721.65	36.0	64.0	14.1	141
2021-03	265.40	507.08	772.48	34.4	65.6	16.3	143

Source: Hong Kong Monetary Authority: www.hkma.gov.hk; the change rate of March 2021 was change concerning March 2020.

9.2.3 *Comparison between current and term deposits of RMB in Hong Kong*

The amount of RMB current deposit in Hong Kong has largely exceeded that of term deposit during almost 5 years from September 2006 to the second quarter of 2010. (During this period, the total current deposit contributes over 60% of the total deposit.) Since the end of the third quarter of 2010, the increasing rate of the current deposit was significantly lower than that of the term deposit. The current deposit balance reached a historical low of 15.3% in September 2014 and then increased back to 37.7% in June 2020, still lower than that of the RMB term deposit.

9.2.4 *Certified institutions that hold licenses for RMB services in Hong Kong*

The number of certified institutions that held licenses for RMB services in Hong Kong was maintained within the interval of 30–40, with little variety from February 2004 to June 2009. However, the amount accelerated rapidly after June 2009. It reached a record high of 149 in December 2014, which was inconsistent with the historical high of RMB deposits in Hong Kong during the same period. From the second half of 2015 to the second quarter of 2019, with the decline of RMB deposit in Hong Kong, the number of certified institutions that held licenses for RMB services declined accordingly, dropping to 136. Yet, it increased steadily to 143 by March 2021.

9.2.5 *Proportion of RMB deposits to other deposits Hong Kong*

As indicated in Table 9.2, the RMB deposit amount in Hong Kong was only 12.13 billion at the end of 2004, which was 0.57%, 0.62%, and 0.29% of the HKD deposit, foreign currency deposit, and total deposit, respectively in Hong Kong. These proportions have increased to 19.40%, 18.83%, and 9.56% in 2011, and further increased to 26.09%, 23.75%, and 12.43% by the end of 2014. However, from 2014 to 2017, these proportions decreased to 10.34%, 10.69%, and 5.26%, falling back to less than half of the level at the end of 2014, and slightly lower than that in January 2011. The corresponding proportions rose slightly to 10.55%, 10.51%, and 5.26% at the end of March 2020, which were still less than half of the level at the end of 2014 and lower than the level at the end of January 2011. It shows that in the environment of RMB depreciation since 2014, deposits in Hong Kong have dropped significantly compared to the Hong Kong dollar and other foreign currencies. The decline is the same as Hong Kong RMB deposits plus Hong Kong RMB certificates of deposit during the same period.

9.2.6 *The ratio of RMB deposit in Hong Kong to that in Mainland China*

We can easily calculate the ratio of total RMB deposit in Hong Kong to that in Mainland China at any date based on the data in Table 9.2 and the data from the website of People's Bank of China. The result indicates that from 2006 to 2009, the ratio of total RMB deposit in Hong Kong to Mainland China was limited from 0.07% to 0.10%. However, from 2010 to 2014, this rate grew sharply to 0.86%. But it decreased to 0.33% in 2015–2019. These indicate that the ratio of Hong Kong's total Renminbi deposit to the Mainland's full Renminbi deposit has continuously dropped to less than 40% of the level at the end of 2014.

9.2.7 *Development of RMB certificate of deposit*

With the rising of RMB and the offshore RMB loan in Hong Kong, the certificate of deposit (CD) was initiated in Hong Kong since the second half of 2010. Citic International, a subsidiary of Citic Bank in Hong Kong, issued the first offshore RMB certificate of deposit in Hong Kong (First

Offshore RMB Certificate of Deposit issued in HK, English.xinhuanet.com, July 6, 2010). According to HKMA, from 2010 to 2012, the total amount of RMB certificate of deposit reached RMB 6.8 to 117.3 billion, respectively (Chan, 2013). At the end of 2013, the accumulated amount of RMB certificate of deposit rose to a historical high of RMB 192.5 billion. One year later, it dropped to RMB 154.7 billion at the end of 2014. The amount increased slightly to RMB 159.3 billion by the end of 2015 and decreased to RMB 59.3 billion at the end of 2017 (Hong Kong Monetary Authority Annual Report 2017), which was less than one-third of the peak at the end of 2013. At the end of 2019, this number had dropped to RMB 25.8 billion, only 14% of the peak value. By January 2021, it further increased to RMB 28.6 billion.

9.2.8 *The scale of RMB loans in Hong Kong*

Following the statistics provided by the HKMA, RMB loans in Hong Kong continuously increased from RMB 30.8 billion to 297.4 billion from 2011 to 2015 (refer to the 2015 Annual Report of HKMA), and the corresponding RMB loan-to-deposit ratio increased from 5.2% to 34.9%. The RMB loan decreased to RMB 294.8 billion and RMB 144.5 billion in 2016 and 2017; the correspondent loan-to-deposit ratios were 53.92% and 25.8%. By the end of 2018, the balance of RMB loan in Hong Kong was only RMB 105.6 billion, a decrease of 64.5% from the peak in 2015, and the ratio of RMB loan to RMB deposit was only 17.17%. In 2019, the balance of RMB loans in Hong Kong rebounded to 153.7 billion yuan. In recent years, Hong Kong's RMB loan business and deposit business have shown different trends of changes (Renminbi loan started to decline significantly only since 2016 and in 2017 alone, it had dropped more than half compared with the previous year). By the end of January 2021, the balance of RMB loan has slightly increased to RMB 159.2 billion.

9.2.9 *Changes in the proportion of RMB cross-border settlement in Hong Kong*

Hong Kong is the earliest established RMB center as well as the first offshore RMB clearing center. The RMB cross-border payment amount in Hong Kong gained as high as 86% in 2011. Nevertheless, with the arrival of other offshore RMB centers, the RMB cross-border payment in Hong

Kong decreased to about 80% in 2012. This rate further dropped below 70% for several times during 2013 and October 2016. After that, the rate has increased, and reached 75.07% in June 2020. Hong Kong has maintained its position as the largest offshore RMB payment center.

9.3 The Development of Offshore RMB Market in London

Table 9.1 shows that the UK is the fifth offshore RMB center that has RMB clearing arrangements. However, due to its position as the largest foreign exchange center globally and its positive attitudes toward offshore RMB business, London has become the second largest RMB settlement center following Hong Kong.

9.3.1 *Intercommunication and cooperation between the governments of China and UK*

The UK–China economic and financial dialogue was established based on the mutual perspectives by the prime minister (premier) of China and the UK. It is a bilateral dialogue mechanism in terms of economy, fiscal policies, and finance. Ten dialogues were held about this mechanism in April 2008, May 2009, November 2010, September 2011, October 2013, September 2014, September 2015, and November 2016, December 2017, and June 2019. This was very rare in China's bilateral relationships with other countries. It later proved an excellent drive in the China–UK bilateral relationship development and economic and financial development. Since August 2015, the seventh round of strategic dialogues between China and the UK, the third conference high-level cultural exchange mechanism between China and the UK, and the seventh China–UK economic and financial dialogue were held one after another. During the seventh China–UK economic and financial dialogue in Beijing, George Osborne, the Chancellor of the UK, said his country would like to be the best partner of China in the Western world (CCTV, 2015). The eighth China–UK economic and financial dialogue in November 2016 carried out gratifying achievements during which both sides reached an agreement on "establishment of Sino-UK comprehensive strategic partnership in 21st century", and developed cooperation on trade and investment, financial service, infrastructure, energy, and industry strategy fields. Concerning financial ices, both parties admit the success of the 3 billion offshore RMB sovereign bond and 5 billion short-term central bank bonds. This achievement shows the deepening cooperation on finance and economy and the China–UK bilateral economic relations. Both countries are welcome to the active issuance of RMB bonds in London to improve the liquidity of RMB, the products and services, to promote the development of offshore RMB markets. (The 8th Sino-UK Economic and Financial Dialogue, *Xinhua News Agency*, London, November 11).

Early in June 2013, both countries signed a foreign exchange swap deal of RMB 200 billion. In October 2015, the contract amount of this swap deal increased to RMB 350 billion. The UK has also become the first Western country to sign such an agreement with China. During Osborne's visit to China in October 2013, London was granted a quota of RMB 80 billion from RMB Qualified Foreign Institutional Investors (RQFII). Before this, Hong Kong was the only place that was awarded an RQFII quota. The UK became the first country outside Asia that was awarded an RQFII quota. At the end of May 2020, the United Kingdom received RMB 48.484 billion of RQFII quota. It is the country with the most significant amount approved in Western countries. The successful offering of the first Renminbi government bond in the United Kingdom on October 14, 2014, added a new highlight to the London Renminbi Center. The first issuance of Renminbi government bond for major developed countries will drive Renminbi business development in other offshore Renminbi centers in depth and breadth. It has taken a solid step toward RMB becoming an international reserve currency. In March 2015, the UK was the first to announce that it was joining the Asian Infrastructure Investment Bank, being the first from the Western countries. This was a significant lead for other Western countries joining in the Asian Infrastructure Investment Bank.

9.3.2 *The establishment and development of RMB center in London*

London has been closely monitoring the rise of RMB as a new international currency. Early in April 2012, the City of London announced the establishment of offshore RMB center. To become a truly global currency, RMB must first be used internationally. As the most important foreign exchange center in the world, London can be a significant contributor to this goal. On March 31, 2014, People's Bank of China and Bank of England signed a collaboration memo on establishing an RMB clearing center in London. On June 18 of the same year, People's Bank of China authorized China Construction Bank London Branch to be the clearing bank for RMB in London, the world's fifth and Europe's first offshore RMB clearing center authorized by People's Bank of China. These have brought vitality and motivation to the development of London RMB center.

Even though the RMB business in London started later than Singapore, statistics showed that the market share of offshore RMB center is growing at a fast pace. It is becoming a significant part of the offshore RMB market. The data from Society for Worldwide Interbank Financial Telecommunication (SWIFT) indicate that the RMB payment in UK exceeded that of Singapore for the first time since December 2012, being the most significant offshore RMB center other than Hong Kong. However, it did not last long. Singapore regained the top position in 2013. However, since the beginning of 2016, London has maintained its position as the largest RMB payment center besides Hong Kong. We will compare daily turnover of RMB foreign exchange of major offshore centers in Chapter 10.

In August 2014, China Construction Bank and London Securities Exchange signed a cooperative agreement to seek opportunities in product innovations actively. On March 25, 2015, the first money market exchange fund of RQFII was officially listed on the London Securities Exchange. This was another big breakthrough for the offshore RMB service in Europe after CCB was authorized as one of the first few RMB clearing banks in UK in June 2014 (Xinhuanet, March 26, 2015).

On June 17, 2019, the Shanghai–London Stock Connect was officially launched. The launch of the Shanghai–London Stock Connect will promote the development of cross-border securities industry by domestic securities companies and promote the two-way opening of the capital market and broaden the level of internationalization.

9.4 The Development of Offshore RMB Market in Singapore

Many years ago, Singapore started to prepare and push the offshore RMB service actively. As a significant strategy for offshore RMB, the Monetary

Authority of Singapore signed an RMB swap deal of RMB 150 billion with PBOC back in July 2010. Both governments of the two countries increased the deal to RMB 300 billion in March 2013; the amount was second only to Hong Kong, South Korea, United Kingdom, and Eurozone. According to Figure 9.1, on February 8, 2013, PBOC announced ICBC Singapore branch as the RMB clearing bank in Singapore, making Singapore the fourth RMB center with RMB clearing bank. On May 27, 2013, offshore RMB clearing service was initiated in Singapore. On the same day, RMB service in Singapore bank also started.

In recent years, the Singapore Renminbi Center has also experienced sustained and rapid growth in RMB deposit. Figure 9.1 gives the Renminbi deposit volume in Singapore from June 2003 to March 2021 released by the Monetary Authority of Singapore, as in April 2021. Figure 9.1 shows that from June 2012 to December 2014, Singapore's Renminbi deposit continued to grow. However, since June 2015, Singapore's Renminbi deposit has shown an overall downward trend till June 2020; and it has maintained a clear recovering trend since June 2020 and returned to the level of RMB 152 billion in December 2017. Still, Singapore has remained second only to Hong Kong China and Taiwan China, as the third largest Renminbi deposit center outside of the two largest offshore Renminbi centers.

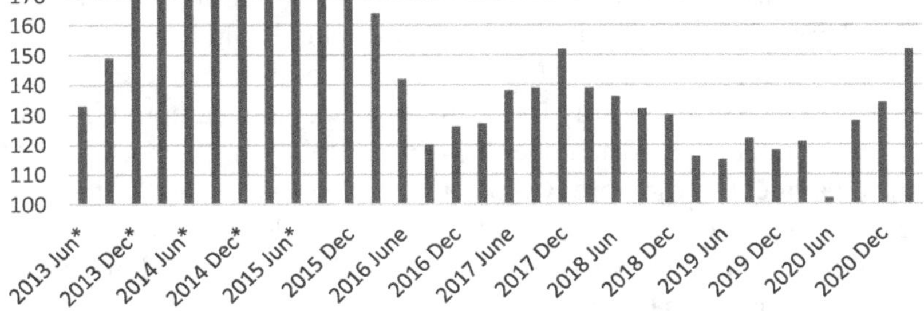

Figure 9.1: Renminbi Deposit Volume in Singapore (Unit: RMB billion)

Source: Singapore Monetary Authority, www.mas.gov.sg; *deposit data adjusted in December 2015 to reflect data re-submission by financial institution.

It is expected that RMB deposit in Singapore may surpass its historical high of June 2015 in the summer of 2022 if its recovering trend from June 2020 to March 2021 is maintained.

Singapore surpassed Japan for the first time in 2013 and became the third largest offshore RMB payment center following Hong Kong and UK since 2016. Singapore's Renminbi payment business has maintained its position as the third largest overseas Renminbi payment center after Hong Kong and the United Kingdom. As the third largest foreign exchange trading center in Asia-Pacific, and the largest trading and financial center in Southeast Asia, Singapore will play an essential role in promoting RMB internationalization in the Asia-Pacific region.

9.5 The Development of Other RMB Centers in Asia-Pacific Area

The Asia-Pacific region is the most critical region for China's trade, and it has naturally become the most active region for the overseas use of RMB in recent years. After introducing the two major offshore RMB centers in Hong Kong and Singapore, this section will introduce the business development of other major RMB centers in the Asia-Pacific region.

9.5.1 *The development of RMB center in South Korea*

South Korea signed an RMB 180 billion foreign exchange swap with the Bank of China in December 2008, being one of the first countries to sign a foreign exchange swap after the international financial crisis. In October 2011, both countries doubled the deal to RMB 360 billion, second only to the RMB 500 billion between Mainland China and Hong Kong, indicating a very active cooperation between China and South Korea. According to the statistics of SWIFT in July 2014, the RMB payment amount increased by 563% from June 2013 to June 2014, accounting for 2.5% of all RMB offshore payment in offshore RMB centers other than Hong Kong. South Korea became the eighth largest RMB center outside Hong Kong, indicating a rapid development of RMB services in South Korea. Even though the swap deal between China and South Korea was the earliest and almost near Hong Kong, the RMB center in South Korea grew relatively slower than other Asia-Pacific RMB centers several years ago. In October 2015, the People's Bank of China increased the RQFII quota for South Korean institutions to RMB 120 billion. As of May 31, 2020, the total RQFII approved for South Korean institutions reached RMB 73.187 billion.

In April 2017, South Korea accounted for 12.82% of offshore RMB payment other than Hong Kong China, surpassing the United States and Taiwan China, becoming the fourth largest offshore RMB payment center. South Korea has maintained this position till the end of June 2019. However, the proportion of South Korea's Renminbi payment has continued a downward trend since June 2019. By the end of 2020, South Korea's corresponding proportion declined to 4.7%, not only lower than the proportion in the United States and Taiwan China but also lower than that in France. Under the influence of Terminal High Altitude Area Defence (THAAD) in recent years, the RMB payment in South Korea has increased significantly, and this has potential for future cooperation between the two countries. Due to the close economic and trade relations between China and South Korea, it is believed that the proportion of Korean RMB payment may soon return to the proportion levels a few years ago.

9.5.2 *The development of RMB market in Taiwan China*

Although the cooperation between Mainland China and Taiwan China started later than Hong Kong China, it is still much earlier than other countries and areas. In June 2008, 14 financial institutions were officially authorized for the RMB business of cash trading. Monetary Authority in Taiwan gradually canceled the limitations of RMB services to banks and other financial institutions in Taiwan China. RMB businesses were further expanded to offshore banking units (OBU) and offshore banks in July 2011. Since the signing of "Memorandum of cooperation on currency clearing between Mainland China and Taiwan" in August 2012, the financial cooperation between the two parties speeded up. With the deregulation of RMB services, the innovation of RMB financial products is encouraged. This facilitates the offshore RMB market in Taiwan China to develop rapidly. On February 6, 2013, PBOC announced Bank of China Taipei Branch as the RMB clearing bank in Taiwan China, making Taiwan the third offshore RMB center with RMB clearing bank. In February 2013, Taiwan China initiated RMB services in domestic banking units (DBU). After that, the government further deregulated the RMB financial derivatives. In this way, the types and serving target audiences of RMB services have been expanded, providing good foundation for rapid development of RMB services in Taiwan China. On May 24, 2013, after Money Authority of Taiwan and Bank of China Taipei Branch signed the currency clearing deal, the RMB services in Taiwan China were initiated officially. By February 2014, the total amount of RMB deposit in Taiwan China was RMB 247.051 billion, with a year-on-year increasing rate of 533%. While the number was only RMB 6.598 billion in January 2012.

Figure 9.2 gives the RMB deposit amount in Taiwan China since January 2012. The figure shows a steady increase to 338.22 billion of RMB deposit in Taiwan RMB center from January 2012 to June 2015; it declined slightly and then increased again to a lower peak of RMB 322.25 billion by the end of 2017, and decreased steadily to RMB 244.49 billion in December 2020, fell below RMB 244 billion in April 2021. The change pattern of RMB deposits in Taiwan China in Figure 9.2 is similar to the trend of Hong Kong RMB deposit in Table 9.2 and of Singapore RMB deposits in Figure 9.1. Nevertheless, total RMB deposit in Taiwan China picked up to RMB 241.173 billion by June 2020. The RMB center of Taiwan has maintained its position as the second largest offshore RMB deposit center except for Hong Kong.

The RMB tracker report published by SWIFT in March 2013 indicated that RMB payment amount had increased by 120% in the past 6 months, exceeding America, and Australia to become the fourth RMB offshore center out of a total of 136 RMB payment countries and regions.

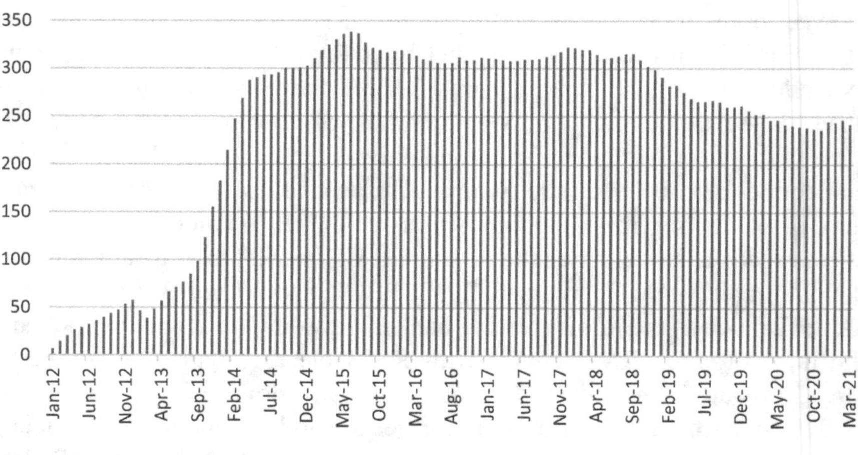

Figure 9.2: RMB Deposit Volume Taiwan China (Unit: RMB billion)

Source: Taiwan Monetary website, www.cbc.gov.tw.

A report of RMB published by SWIFT in August 2015 shows that the ranking of RMB payment in Taiwan China kept its fourth place after Singapore, UK, and America. However, the statistics of SWIFT in December 2015 shows that RMB payment percentage of Taiwan RMB center for November 2015 retains its fourth offshore place right next to Hong Kong, surpassing America RMB center while being lower than British and Singapore RMB center, as well as lower than Korea RMB center for the first time. Starting August 2016, the RMB payment percentage of Taiwan China surpassed that of South Korea again, even though it was significantly lower than the US, it kept its position as the fourth largest offshore RMB center. Taiwan's Renminbi payments accounted for 9.08–9.28% from September 2020 to December 2020 outside Hong Kong, ranked as the fourth largest Renminbi payment center outside Hong Kong; from December 2020 to April 2021, Taiwan China maintained its position as the fourth largest Renminbi payment center after the United Kingdom, Singapore, and the United States (excluding Hong Kong, China). This has shown the good advantages of cross-strait financial cooperation.

9.5.3 *The development of offshore RMB center in Australia*

Australia has kept its eighth position as a trading partner with China. In recent years, Australia increased the amount of trading with China. To enhance economy and finance cooperation between the two countries, both the countries signed an RMB swap deal of RMB 200 billion back in March 2012. Australia was one of the first developed countries that signed such agreement with China. After preparation for some time, RMB service in Australia grew at a fast pace. According to statistics from SWIFT on January 8, 2013, after an idle period, the RMB payment amount increased a lot from August to November in 2012. The ranking went from 12th to fourth (except Hong Kong, China). By the end of April 2014, the RMB payment increased by 2.5 times compared to the level a year ago. In June 2014, the RMB payment in Australia accounted for 4.8% of offshore RMB payment (not including Hong Kong), becoming the sixth largest RMB center after Singapore, UK, America, Taiwan China, and France. By the end of July 2015, Australia kept its position as the sixth largest RMB center. The proportion of RMB payment in Australia decreased from 4% in July 2015 to 3.4% in November 2015, ranking from sixth to eighth. Furthermore, by the end of June 2020, its RMB clearing proportion remained the seventh largest among all.

9.5.4 *The development of RMB center in Malaysia*

Malaysia's trading with China has grown rapidly in recent years. In addition, the cooperation in terms of other aspects between the two countries has also been close. In 2013, the trading volume between the two countries exceeded $100 billion for the first time. Malaysia has been the ninth largest trading partner with China (following Australia) since then. Early in February 2009, Malaysia signed an RMB foreign currency swap deal with China of RMB 80 billion, being a solid foundation for driving RMB service in Malaysia.

What's more, except the direct currency trading between RMB and USD, EUR, GBP, JPY, and Malaysian ringgit (MYR) were currencies that RMB traded with. Since August 19, 2010, the State Administration of Foreign Exchange started to publish the median price for MYR. Since then MYR has been the sixth foreign currency listed in China FX market, thus providing support for future tractions and settlement.

According to the data of SWIFT in September 2012, the RMB payment of Malaysia in August 2012 came only after London and Singapore, being the third largest offshore RMB center except Hong Kong, indicating an active RMB center in Malaysia in early years. In June 2014, the RMB payment accounted for 2.1% of all RMB centers outside Hong Kong, the 10th largest offshore RMB center except Hong Kong. Until July 2015, Malaysia kept its position as the 10th largest RMB center. Since August 2016, the proportion of RMB clearing in Malaysia fell out of the top 14, showing that the development of Malaysia's RMB business is relatively slow in recent years, and there is still tremendous room for growth.

9.5.5 *The RMB centers in Macau, China, and Mongolia*

Although the economy scale of Macau is relatively small, and the trading volume of Macau with Mainland China not significant, the development of RMB center in Macau kept a fast pace. Early in December 2009, Bank of China Macau Branch was appointed as the RMB clearing bank in Macau, making Macau the second RMB center with RMB clearing bank after Hong Kong. According to the data from SWIFT in September 2012, the RMB payment amount ranked the fifth (except Hong Kong) in August 2012, which is higher than Taiwan China being the eighth. In July 2015, the RMB payment in Macau accounted for 1.3%, ranking 10th, together with Malaysia and Japan. In November 2015, RMB payment in Macau slightly increased to 1.4%, and the offshore RMB business ranked 11th after Japan (9th) and Luxembourg (10th) and dropped to 12th in January 2017. Since January 2018, Macau's RMB center RMB payment ranked behind 12th place. At the end of June 2020, Macau returned to 10th place in this ranking; in September and October 2020, Macau's RMB clearing rankings rose to eighth and seventh, respectively.

Except for Macau, the development of RMB center in Mongolia in early days was relatively fast compared to its economy scale. Mongolia signed an RMB foreign exchange swap deal of RMB 5 billion with China on May 6, 2011 and increased it to RMB 10 billion in March 2012. According to the data from SWIFT, by August 2012, the RMB payment amount in Mongolia ranked seventh (except Hong Kong), which is higher than Taiwan's eighth, indicating a rapid business growth in the early stage. Since the development of RMB business size in Mongolia slowed down for the recent 2 years, the ranking fell beyond the 10th in June 2014 and July 2015, while it fell behind 14th since 2016.

9.5.6 *The RMB center in Japan*

Both governments of Japan and China made an agreement market between the two countries back in December 2011 (PBOC, December 25, 2011). Yet, there were neither official currency swap deals signed between the two countries nor such RMB clearing arrangements in Japan. On October 26, 2018, the People's Bank of China and the Bank of Japan signed a bilateral domestic currency swap agreement between China and Japan. The agreement was 200 billion yuan and was valid for 3 years. At the same time, the People's Bank of China authorized the Bank of China Tokyo Branch to act as the clearing bank for Japan's Renminbi business; on June 27, 2019, the People's Bank of China authorized Japan's Mitsubishi UFJ Bank to act as the clearing bank for Japan's Renminbi business. So far, Renminbi clearing business in Japan has been further expanded to promote bilateral trade and investment facilitation. The RMB payment amount in Japan ranked ninth of that of all offshore RMB centers (SWIFT, October 2012). The offshore RMB payment of Japan in July 2015 accounted for such a high ratio as 1.3%, ranking 10th along with Macau and Malaysia. In November 2015, the percentage doubled to 2.7% and became the ninth largest offshore RMB center again. From June to October 2020, RMB payment in Japan ranked eighth among other offshore RMB centers other than Hong Kong.

It should be noticed that average daily turnover of RMB in Tokyo increased from $4.06 billion in September 2019 to $5.00 billion in September 2020 (Tokyo Foreign Exchange Market Committee website:www.fxcomtky.com), with ranking from 10th to 8th of highest trading currency in Tokyo during the same period, signifying measurable growth of RMB trading in Japan. Since Mainland China surpassed the United States to become Japan's largest trading partner for the first time in 2007, China has maintained its status as Japan's largest trading partner. The trade volume between China and Japan far surpasses that of China and Australia, with that, Japan's Renminbi payment is expected to increase significantly with the implementation of the Regional Comprehensive Economic Partnership Agreement (RCEP).

9.5.7 *RMB centers in the State of Qatar and the United Arab Emirates* (*UAE*)

On November 3, 2014, People's Bank of China signed an RMB 35 billion bilateral currency swap agreement with Qatar Central Bank. At the same time, the two sides signed cooperation memorandum for establishing clearing arrangements in Doha. They agreed and expanded the RMB RQFII pilot areas to Qatar with the initial investment of RMB 30 billion ("new progress for the bilateral financial cooperation between China and Qatar", PBOC website, December 14, 2015). Table 9.1 shows that on November 4, 2014, the People's Bank of China signed an RMB clearing agreement with Qatar. The Qatar RMB Center held a launch ceremony on April 14, 2015, becoming the first RMB center in the Middle East. According to data released by the SWIFT in January 2016, 60% of the payments between Qatar, and Mainland China, and Hong Kong in 2015 were in Renminbi, and that is an increase of 247% over 2014. The Qatar RMB Center will play an essential leading role in promoting business throughout the Middle East.

United Arab Emirates (UAE) had signed an RMB 35 billion bilateral currency swap agreement with PBOC earlier before January 2012; however, the establishment of its center is later than Qatar's. PBOC has renewed the bilateral currency swap agreement with UAE central bank on December 14, 2015. This agreement maintains a scale of RMB 35 billion and has a validity period of 3 years. At the same time, the two sides signed cooperation memorandum for establishing RMB clearing arrangements in

UAE and agreed to expand the RMB. They agreed RQFII pilot areas for UAE with the initial investment of RMB 50 billion ("new progress for the bilateral financial cooperation between China and UAE", PBOC website, December 14, 2015). Although the pilot arrangement of RQFII in UAE is almost 1 year later than that of Qatar, the RMB 15 billion is greater than Qatar and the agreement is also signed earlier than Qatar. On December 9, 2016, the Dubai branch of the Agricultural Bank of China was designated as the UAE RMB Clearing Bank, marking the establishment of the UAE RMB Clearing Center. According to data published by SWIFT in January 2016, 74% of the payment made between UAE and Mainland China as well as Hong Kong uses RMB, showing an increase of 52% compared with 2014, becoming the second largest RMB payment country in the Middle East. From August 2014 and August 2015 to August 2016, UAE Renminbi payments increased by 210.8% and 44.6%, respectively, indicating a rapid growth of Renminbi payment in the UAE in recent years. Since UAE follows Saudi Arabia, maintaining its second place of trade between China and the Middle East country for so many years, the RMB center in UAE will lead to the development of RMB business in the Middle East area.

9.5.8 *Other RMB centers in Asia-Pacific*

In addition to the previously introduced RMB centers in Asia-Pacific, RMB centers in Thailand, Philippines, Indonesia, and Vietnam have also been developed to different levels in recent years. In particular, the Philippines's RMB payment with both Mainland China and Hong Kong increased from 53% to 73% from April 2012 to April 2015. During the same period, the rate in Indonesia, Thailand, and Vietnam went from 7%, 13%, and 6% to 26%, 25%, and 14%, indicating a rapid growth of RMB payment in the three countries. However, the overall proportion of the RMB settlement in these countries to the whole offshore RMB cross-border settlement is relatively low, which indicates vast room for further growth.

9.6 Development of RMB Centers in Europe

Other than the UK RMB center as discussed previously, Europe had also become the area with the most RMB centers in addition to the Asia-Pacific area in recent years. Central Bank of Europe signed an agreement of RMB swap with PBOC in October 2013 for an amount up to RMB 350 billion. This amount was second only to the swap amount signed with Hong Kong or South Korea. The swap deal between Central Bank of Europe and PBOC indicated an active attitude in the Eurozone to push forward the development of RMB service, being a solid foundation for the future of RMB in the Eurozone.

9.6.1 *The development of RMB center in France*

France has always been in the first place among the RMB centers in Eurozone for more than 8 years. According to the statistics of SWIFT in April 2012, the year after March 2012, the RMB payment amount in France increased by 249% year-on-year, making France the fourth largest offshore RMB center outside Hong Kong after UK, Singapore, and Taiwan China in March 2013. Later statistics from SWIFT showed that in July 2015, France dropped to seventh place of offshore RMB center, accounting for 1.1% of the offshore RMB payment amount. It kept its status as the seventh largest offshore RMB payment center from June 2015 to December 2016, and then became the sixth largest since January 2017. On March 26, 2014, a joint declaration of the People's Republic of China and the French Republic announced a distribution of RMB 80 billion RQFII distribution Paris, March 27, 2014). As of May 31, 2020, seven financial institutions in France received accumulative RQFII quota of RMB 24 billion, making France the second largest quota country in Europe. On June 28, 2014, the PBOC and Bank of France signed a memorandum of RMB clearing, and RMB clearing bank was soon confirmed.

For many years, GDP of France was at least 1% lower than that of Germany. The FX trading ratio of France was also 1% lower than that of Germany as shown in Table 4.3 from 1998 to 2004. However, FX trading ratio of France started to surpass Germany since 2007. Furthermore, the ratio exceeded that of Germany by 1.18% in 2013 and 0.98% in 2016, respectively. If we take a close look at Table 4.3, we will find out that from 2001 to 2013, the FX trading ratio of France kept around 2.8%. At the same time, the percentage of Germany was decreased by 3.7%, indicating a clear difference in the international FX trading market of the two countries after the global financial crisis. In the meantime, to a great extent, the ratio displayed a very energetic attitude in RMB foreign exchange market in France. It is believed that France will continuously lead RMB business in Europe.

9.6.2 *The RMB center in Germany*

Although Germany is the largest economy in Europe, the transaction ratio of global foreign exchange market in Germany dropped from 5.4% in 2001 to 1.7% in 2013. Though that ratio rose to 1.8% in 2016, the trend was moving downward, indicating that the fourth largest economy entity was paying more attention to economy, trading, and technology than to the foreign exchange market. According to data from SWIFT in June 2013, the RMB payment amount increased by 71% on a year-on-year basis in April and May 2013, making Germany the eighth largest offshore RMB center outside Hong Kong and later becoming the seventh largest in June 2014. Germany moved up to the eighth place in July 2015 in RMB payment ranking, and that proportion doubled to 4.1% from July 2015 to November 2015, surpassing that of France (3.7%) for the first time to become the sixth largest offshore RMB center except Hong Kong. However, its ranking declined to ninth in September 2016. Between December 2016 and April 2018, the RMB cross-border payment in Germany was lower than Australia or Japan, keeping it as the 10th largest RMB payment center. As of June 2020, that payment in Germany was second to Japan and made it as the ninth largest RMB payment center.

For many years, Germany has been regarded as the largest trading partner of China in Europe. On March 28, 2014, the PBOC and Deutsche Bundesbank signed a cooperation memorandum for establishing an RMB clearing center in Frankfurt. Later, PBOC assigned its Frankfurt branch as the RMB clearing bank in Frankfurt. As of May 31, 2020, only three institutions in Germany received RQFII quota, totaling only RMB 10.543 billion, which was less than half of that of France. This shows that France's cooperation between China and Germany needs to be significantly strengthened.

9.6.3 *The development of RMB center in Luxembourg*

As an important financial center in Europe, although the scale of Luxembourg GDP is small and the proportion of China's trade compared with the whole of Europe is low, the financial cooperation between the country and China is relatively high. Table 9.1 shows that Banque Centrale du Luxembourg signed the RMB clearing agreement with PBOC in September 2014 and appointed ICBC Luxembourg branch as Luxembourg's RMB clearing bank WIFT the same year, the year-on-year RMB payment ratio in Luxembourg increased by 86%, being the second largest RMB center after France in Eurozone (France ranked sixth and Luxembourg ranked eighth). In July 2013, over 58% of payment between Luxembourg and Mainland China or Hong Kong was in RMB, while the ratio was only 42% in July 2012. In June 2014, the RMB payment ratio in Luxembourg ranked ninth of all offshore RMB center outside Hong Kong. In July 2015, Luxembourg's RMB payment ranked the eighth, same as that of Germany. In August 2016, Luxembourg's ranking of RMB payments dropped to 11th place. As of June 2019, Luxembourg's Ranking of Renminbi payments dropped to 12th place. Although Luxembourg's population and economic scale are small, as of May 31, 2020, seven institutions in Luxembourg received a total of RMB 15.187 billion in RQFII, which exceeded the corresponding total quota in Germany (even after deducting the RMB 5 billion RQFII quota of Industrial and Commercial Bank of China and Bank of China, the rest of the five institutions received RMB 10.187 billion, which was close to RMB 10.543 billion received by institutions in Germany). The total quota of RQFII by institutions in Luxembourg also exceeded the total quota of RQFII in Canada and Switzerland. All these show the critical position of Luxembourg as offshore RMB center.

9.6.4 *Other RMB centers in Eurozone*

Besides the previous three RMB centers in Eurozone, there are also other RMB centers in Europe. Belgium was one of the earlier RMB centers and it made progress in early RMB business. In January 2012, the RMB payment amount in Belgium ranked the third largest in Eurozone and sixth most significant of all RMB centers except Hong Kong, after Singapore, UK, America, France, and Luxembourg. Due to the recent rapid developments of other RMB centers, the development in Germany surpassed Belgium, which became the fourth largest RMB center in Europe in 2014. By July 2015, the cross-border RMB payment ratio in Belgium ranked beyond the 12th place. In August 2016, its ranking was 14th. In 2017, it surpassed Macau and Luxembourg to become 11th. As of June 2020, its ranking was 14th. Given that there is no RMB clearing arrangement between China and Belgium so far, and Belgium is neither an RQFII pilot country nor a founding member of Asian Infrastructure Investment Bank, it is quite an outstanding achievement for Belgium to become the 13th ranking country in offshore RMB.

Although the Netherlands's GDP was only around one-third of the UK's, the Netherlands kept its position as the second or third most significant trading partner with China in Europe. Although the RMB center in the Netherlands started late, the cross-border RMB payment ratio accounted for 0.3% in July 2015, ranking 13th outside Hong Kong. The ratio exceeded that of Belgium. In November 2015, the RMB cross-border settlement ratio increased to 1.4%, with its ranking growing accordingly. It was tied for the 11th ranking along with Macau outside Hong Kong. The Netherlands ranked 13th in offshore RMB payment outside Hong Kong in August 2016. As of June 2020, the ranking remained at the 14th place. Due to the considerable trade volume between China and the Netherlands, the proportion of RMB center in the Netherlands will increase significantly in the future, and its ranking of RMB center in the world will be further improved.

9.6.5 *The comparison of RMB payment in Eurozone with other major RMB centers*

The previous sections have briefly introduced the five major RMB centers in the Eurozone. We can easily conclude the total RMB payment amount in the Eurozone by summing the amounts in respective countries. The number of RMB centers in the Eurozone grew from two in January 2012 to five in June 2013, and corresponding proportion of total RMB payments increased from 8.9% to 15.3% during the same time. The Eurozone can be regarded as the third largest RMB center following the UK and Singapore. In June 2014, the total proportion of RMB payment in Eurozone (outside Hong Kong) decreased to 10.2%, which was lower than that of 10.8% in the US, equivalent to the fourth largest offshore RMB center. In June 2015, the proportion of RMB payment in Eurozone increased to 10.3% (outside Hong Kong), which was lower than Taiwan's equivalent RMB center. In June 2016, its proportion rebounded back to 12.8% and exceeded US and Taiwan China, respectively. Its ranking returned to the third outside of Hong Kong. In June 2017, the total share of the Eurozone remained behind London, Singapore, and South Korea, ranking fourth; from February 2018 to April 2021, the total share of the Eurozone surpassed Singapore and the US, ranking as the second largest RMB center outside Hong Kong, second only to London.

9.6.6 *The development of RMB Center in Russia*

China is Russia's second largest trading partner after Europe. Since November 22, 2010, China State Administration of Foreign Exchange began to publish exchange rate of RMB to RUB, and RUB became the seventh RMB exchange rate in China after Malaysian Ringgit. The branch of Vneshtorgbank (VTB) in China already started RUB and RMB branch, which was vital to Sino-Russian bilateral trade. On October 13, 2014, PBOC and the Central Bank of the Russian Federation signed a bilateral currency swap agreement with a scale of RMB 150 billion, and aimed at facilitating bilateral trade and direct investment, and promoting the economic development of the two countries (www.pbc.gov.cn). Although there have been many reports on the economic and trade cooperation between China and Russia in recent years and the direct foreign exchange transactions between Russia and China have been launched as early as 2010, Russia's RMB clearing arrangements were established relatively late in September 2016. After Russia's RMB clearing arrangement was finalized, the Industrial and Commercial Bank of China acted as Russia's RMB clearing bank. In December 2016, Russia's RMB cross-border payments accounted for 0.35%, ranking 17th (outside Hong Kong). In February and April 2018, Russia's RMB payments, excluding Hong Kong, accounted for 1.16% and 1.08%. The ranking has risen to the 11th place, showing that Russia's RMB center had developed rapidly since 2018. However, as of June 2020, Russia's scale of RMB payment has decreased beyond the 14th place.

9.6.7 *RMB center in Switzerland*

On July 21, 2014, central bank of Switzerland signed a currency swap deal of RMB 150 billion with PBOC, being a liquidity support for economy and trade between two countries and the offshore RMB cash pool in Switzerland. In January 2015, PBOC announced an RQFII test region expansion to Switzerland, with a quota of RMB 50 billion. This expansion benefits foreign investors investing products of China capital market in Switzerland. In the meantime, it also enlarged the channels of RMB investment. As shown in Table 9.1, China Construction Bank was authorized with the license of banking industry in Switzerland in November 2015. The permit allowed China Construction Bank to establish its branch in Zurich to open the business of RMB clearing (www.gov.cn, October 20, 2015). In December 2016, Swiss RMB payment accounted for 0.35% of offshore RMB payment excluding Hong Kong, ranking 16th.

9.6.8 *Other European RMB centers*

As early as September 2013, Hungary signed a foreign exchange swap agreement of RMB 10 billion with the PBOC, indicating the country's enthusiasm for RMB business. On June 27, 2015, PBOC and central bank of Hungary signed a cooperation memorandum for establishing an RMB clearing center in Hungary. The next day, PBOC authorized Bank of China as the RMB clearing bank in Hungary, the first RMB clearing bank in the mid-east European area. This authorization made Hungary the first RMB center with RMB clearing arrangement in east Europe. At the same time, Hungary was included in the pilot area of RQFII with a quota of RMB 50 billion, which was the same as that of Australia, Switzerland, and Canada. China has now become the largest trading partner with Hungary outside Europe. Hungary is the most prominent investment target in the mid-east European area. Establishing an RMB clearing will further lower the cost of economy and trading between the two countries, enrich the options for both investment and fund-raising, and start a new chapter of deepening cooperation (China Economy Net, October 14, 2015).

9.7 The Development of RMB Center in USA

As the largest economy entity in the world, America has not signed RMB currency swap agreement with China, and RMB clearing was launched just in September 2016. In January 2012, the RMB payment amount in the America only accounted for 5.6% of other RMB centers outside Mainland China and Hong Kong, being the third largest RMB center after Singapore and London. In November 2012, the RMB payment amount ratio in USA counted to 6.6% of RMB centers outside Hong Kong. The ranking of RMB center in America dropped accordingly to sixth. An article "US Enterprises Prefer Settlement in RMB" was reported in the *Wall Street Journal* on July 10, 2014. It stated the number of transactions at the RMB level. Data from SWIFT showed that from April 2013 to April 2014, the RMB payment amount in America increased by 327%, becoming the third largest RMB center after Singapore and London except Hong Kong. This ranking had been kept until December 2014. Although from April 2017 to February 2018, South Korea's RMB center payment accounted for more than that of the United States, and from April to December 2018, the United States regained its share, surpassing Taiwan China and South Korea, returning to the place after Hong Kong, London and Singapore; in June 2020, the US once again was left behind by South Korea, ranking fourth among all excluding Hong Kong; in September and October 2020, the US continued to surpass South Korea in the proportion of RMB payments, maintaining the fourth largest RMB payment center after Hong Kong, UK, and Singapore.

PBOC announced on June 8, 2016 that it had recently signed a memorandum of cooperation to establish an RMB clearing arrangement in the United States with the Federal Reserve Board of the United States (China News Network, June 8, 2016). Figure 9.1 shows that in September 2016, PBOC designated Bank of China New York branch as RMB clearing bank in the US. The implementation of the US RMB clearing bank will play an essential role in promoting the development of US RMB cross-border payments and other RMB businesses. On February 13, 2018, JPMorgan Chase & Co. was approved by the PBOC and the US regulatory authorities to become the second RMB clearing bank in the US, and it was also one of the only two non-Chinese RMB clearing banks among a total of 27 RMB clearing banks overseas. With the promotion of RMB internationalization in the Asia-Pacific region and Europe, the market will promote the use of RMB in the United States, and the proportion of global cross-border payments of RMB in the United States will increase significantly, and the United States is expected to become one of the leading centers of RMB overseas.

It should be noticed that average daily turnover of RMB increased 63.3% from $8.54 billion in September 2019 to $13.95 billion in September 2020 in New York (New York Fed website: www.newyorkfed.org), with ranking from 14th to 12th highest trading currency in New York during the same period, signifying significant growth of RMB trading in New York and closer the financial cooperation with trade tension and other frictions between the two largest economies of the world in recent years.

9.8 The Development of Other Offshore RMB Centers

9.8.1 *The development of RMB centers in Canada*

On November 8, 2014, PBOC and Prime Minister's Office of Canada successively announced the establishment of the first offshore RMB center in North America. Both China and Canada agreed to increase the utilization of RMB in trading, commerce, and investment, promoting the stabilization and healthy development of RMB market in Canada the same day, Canada and China signed a bilateral domestic currency swap deal of RMB 200 billion. In this announcement, both parties signed a memorandum of

RMB clearing arrangement in Canada. In addition, both parties agreed on the expansion of RQFII test in Canada, with an initial quota of RMB 50 billion (http://wallstreetcn.com, November 9, 2014).

The RMB center in Canada was founded officially on March 23, 2015, appointing Industrial and Commercial Bank of China's Canada Subsidiary as the RMB clearing bank. After the establishment of the center, RMB transactions became more convenient for Western companies. Multiple corporations were able to make transactions over Bank of Canada ("Ontario home to first Renminbi trading hub in the Americas", China, March 2015). The total RMB cross-border payment ratio in Canada RMB center was 1% in November 2015 and surpassed other centers in Malaysia, for example, ranking 13th (excluding Hong Kong). The ranking indicated the promising result during the half year after the establishment of RMB center in Canada. In August 2016, the ranking of Canada RMB fell out of 14th and returned to 13th and 11th in December 2016 and December 2017, respectively. As of June 2020, RMB payment in Canada maintained the 12th place. As the 10th largest economy, the initiating and developing of RMB center in Canada will have a leading effect on the RMB business in North America as well as that in Canada.

9.8.2 *The RMB center in Chile*

During his official visit to Chile, Prime Minister of China, Li Keqiang, said, when meeting with journalists, that both countries will sign a currency swap deal (on May 25, 2015, both countries signed a currency swap deal of RMB 22 billion) and China Construction Bank will act as RMB clearing bank in Chile. At the same time, Chile became the first country with an RQFIII quota of RMB 50 billion in the Latin America. As of the end of May 2020, Chile had not yet been approved for any RQFII allocation. The launch of the Chilean RMB Center has certain demonstrative effect on the promotion of RMB business throughout Latin America.

9.8.3 *The development of RMB center in South Africa*

South Africa has been the largest trading partner of China in Africa for many years. Although its economy is ranked 33rd around the world, its financial system is relatively more open among developing countries. Tables 4.9–4.12 indicate that the internationalization of South Africa ZAR ranks first among the "BRICS" and surpassed currencies of many developed countries and those of the developing countries. On July 8, 2015, PBOC announced that according to the memorandum between itself and reserve bank in South Africa, PBOC authorized Johannesburg branch of Bank of China to be the clearing bank in South Africa (yicai.net, Xu Yanyan, July 9, 2015). As released by SWIFT, the RMB payment amount in South Africa increased by 65% during the 12 months before July 2016, and the increasing amount reached 112% during the past 2 years, increasing its rank from the 30th to the 24th in July 2014 in RMB payment. There is a vast room of cooperation in economy, trade, and finance between the two countries. The RMB center in South Africa will play a important role in promoting RMB business in Africa.

9.9 The Distribution and Ranking of RMB Deposits and Payment Amount among Offshore RMB Centers

9.9.1 *The distribution of RMB deposits among major offshore RMB centers*

Hong Kong, Taiwan China, and Singapore are the three sizable offshore RMB deposit centers. The RMB deposit amounts of other offshore RMB centers are relatively low compared to the three regions, so we will not discuss them herein.

9.9.2 *Comparison of the proportion of RMB cross-border payments in Overseas RMB centers*

According to data from SWIFT, the proportion of other RMB centers other than Hong Kong in overseas Renminbi payments remained at 14% from January to August 2012; from August 2012 to August 2016, it continued to rise to 29.7%. However, from August 2016 to April 2018, the proportion of offshore RMB payment (excluding Hong Kong) dropped to 25% in April 2018; as of April 2021, the balance was 24.7%, showing that the proportion of offshore RMB payments (excluding Hong Kong) from 2012 to 2016 has gradually increased, but in recent years has shown a slight decline. Table 9.3 shows the proportions of offshore RMB payments (excluding Hong Kong) from January 2012 to April 2021.

Table 9.3: Share and Ranking of RMB Payments in RMB Centers Outside Hong Kong (January 2012–April 2021)

Center/ Time	Jan-12 (%)	Dec-12 (%)	Jun-13 (%)	Jun-14 (%)	Dec-15 (%)	Dec-16 (%)	Dec-17 (%)	Dec-18 (%)	Dec-19 (%)	Dec-20 (%)	Mar-21 (%)
UK	23.7	28.3	30.9	22.5	20.8	25.4	23.0	24.7	25.9	24.5	24.5
Singapore	32.7	22.7	16.5	28.4	20.8	17.0	18.1	18.7	12.7	16.8	16.1
USA	5.6	4.1	8.5	10.8	10.8	13.2	10.6	10.5	10.3	12.2	11.5
Taiwan China			10.3	9.3	13.2	11.8	9.0	8.9	8.9	9.3	9.1
France	5.0	7.2	8.1	5.4	4.8	5.8	6.4	6.8	5.5	7.1	7.3
Korea			1.0	2.4	8.8	6.8	12.3	5.7	10.6	4.7	5.4
Australia		8.2	3.4	4.8	4.0	4.0	4.2	5.6	4.8	3.6	3.6
Japan					2.4	3.3		3.3	3.9	2.7	2.7
Germany			3.4	2.5	2.0	2.1	2.8	4.2	3.2	3.0	2.6
Luxembourg	3.9	4.3	3.8	2.3	2.4	1.7	1.4	2.0	1.8	1.8	1.5
Canada					1.6	1.3	0.9	1.4	1.6	2.0	2.6
Belgium					2.4	1.6		1.1	1.7	2.0	2.6
Netherlands					1.2	1.2			1.5	1.3	1.2
Russia							0.5	0.8			
Eurozone	8.9	11.5	15.3	10.2	12.8	12.3	10.6	14.1	13.7	14.9	16.1

Source: Calculated using monthly data released by RMB Tracker reporting and statistics on Renminbi (RMB) progress toward becoming an international currency.

9.9.3 *Ranking of major RMB payment centers outside Hong Kong*

Although more than 100 countries and regions have RMB payment services with Mainland China and Hong Kong, most countries have relatively small RMB payments. Hong Kong and dozens of major overseas RMB centers accounted for more than 90% of RMB payments. Singapore remained in the first position of the largest RMB payment outside Hong Kong from March 2014 to June 2015. From June 2014 to June 2015, the proportion of Singapore's RMB payment to overall amount, excluding Hong Kong, has exceeded that of London, making it the largest RMB payment center outside Hong Kong; however, in November 2015, London regained the first place for RMB payment center excluding Hong Kong, and has kept its position since July 2016. This shows that London and Singapore have competed fiercely for offshore RMB centers in recent years. The rankings of these centers have stabilized in recent years; except for London and Singapore that remained in the second and third positions following Hong Kong. It should be noticed that the United States remained in the fourth position following Singapore since the second half of 2019, Korean ranking fell significantly from 2020, and Eurozone came close to Singapore in total share.

9.10 Distributions of RQFII Quota and Authorized Quota among Offshore RMB Centers

The quota of different RQFII is the foundation to open the offshore RMB services and one of the critical indicators measuring offshore RMB centers. In the previous chapters, we introduced the quota for some RQFII in offshore RMB centers. In this section, we will systematically introduce and compare total allocation and RQFII quota of different offshore RMB centers. Table 9.4 shows total quota and approved quota of RQFII of major offshore RMB centers as of May 31, 2020.

9.10.1 *RQFII data based on the registration agency*

Figure 9.4 shows that the total amount of RQFII obtained by Hong Kong is up to highest RMB 500 billion, and 73.03% of the quota has been used

Table 9.4: Comparison of the Total Quota of RQFII Obtained by Offshore RMB Centers and the Approved Quota (Unit: RMB billion, %)

Country/ Region	Total Approved Quota	Accumulated Obtained Quota	Obtained Quota/ Approved Quota Ratio (%)
China Hong Kong	500	365.16	73.03
USA	250	39.17	15.67
Japan	200	9	4.50
ROK	120	73.19	60.99
Singapore	100	78.26	78.26
UK	80	48.49	60.61
France	80	24	30.00
Germany	80	10.54	13.18
Australia	50	32.01	64.02
Luxembourg	50	15.19	30.38
Switzerland	50	9.6	19.20
Canada	50	8.65	17.30
Thailand	50	2.1	4.20
Ireland	50	1.85	3.70
Malaysia	50	1.6	3.20
Holland	50	0	0.00
Hungary	50	0	0.00
Chile	50	0	0.00
UAE	50	0	0.00
Qatar	30	0	0.00
IMF	—	4.2	—
Total	1,990	722.99	36.33
Eurozone	310	51.58	16.64

Source: http://www.pbc.gov.cn/; http://www.safe.gov.cn/en/index.html.

in these years; the quota obtained by the United States was second to Hong Kong, which was RMB 250 billion, but as of May 31, 2020, only RMB 39.17 billion of quota was approved, accounting for 15.67% of its total quota; South Korea's quota ranked after Hong Kong, the United States, and Japan, reaching as high as RMB 120 billion. The approved quota of South Korea reached RMB 73.187 billion, ranking third after Hong Kong and Singapore, with a start-up rate of 60.99%, second only to 78.26% in Singapore and 73.03% in Hong Kong and 64.01% in Australia; Singapore's accumulative approved quota was as high as RMB 78.255 billion, ranking second only to Hong Kong. The United Kingdom, France, and Germany all had a quota of RMB 80 billion, but their accumulated approved quotas were RMB 48.484 billion, RMB 24.00 billion, and RMB 10.543 billion, respectively. The start-up rates were 60.61%, 30.00%, and 13.18%, respectively. Luxembourg, Canada, Switzerland, Malaysia, and Thailand all obtained quota for RMB 50 billion, and the accumulative approved quotas were RMB 15.187 billion, RMB 8.653 billion, RMB 9.60 billion, RMB 1.6 billion, and RMB 2.1 billion, respectively, and the start-up rates were 30.37%, 17.31%, 19.20%, 3.20% and 4.20%, respectively. The five centers in the Eurozone, France, Germany, Luxembourg, the Netherlands, and Ireland, had a total quota of RMB 310 billion, second only to Hong Kong and the United States, but the cumulative approved quota was only RMB 51.58 billion, and the start-up rate was only 16.64%; Chile, Hungary, and the United Arab Emirates all received RMB 50 billion as the quota, and Qatar received RMB 30 billion, but the four RMB centers have not yet obtained the approved quota. The RQFII quota or utilization rate of different centers given in Table 9.4 reflects their enthusiasm for promoting RMB business to a large extent, and reflects the activity of their RMB business, which corresponds to the RMB payment given in Table 9.3.

9.10.2 *RQFII quota distribution based on the country and region*

The distribution of RQFII quotas in different countries and regions given in Figure 9.4 is based on the investor's registration place. To a large extent, it shows the degree of support for the internationalization of the RMB in these countries or regions. However, this classification has certain limitations. For example, in Figure 29.4, Australia's 32.006-billion-yuan RQFII are given, respectively, to Vanguard Investment Australia Ltd., VanEck Investment Limited, and Russell Investment Management Limited. These three are companies in the United States. Using Australia's RQFII quota, it may seem to be Australia's support for the internationalization of RMB, but in fact it is the US funds' support for the internationalization of RMB to the country and region where the investors are located, we will get a new RQFII distribution, and combined with China's foreign securities investment data, the results are shown in Table 9.5.

Table 9.5 gives the RMB QFII quota distribution among major offshore RMB centers as of the end o May 2020. Most RQFII in Hong Kong are invested by Mainland investors, because Mainland investors conduct RMB transactions through Hong Kong, a major offshore RMB center. Regarding investment activities, the approved amount of Mainland RQFII investors in Hong Kong exceeds 70% of the total agreed amount in Hong Kong, and the total RQFII amount in the Mainland accounts for more than 40% of the total approved amount of RQFII in the world. The result shows that Mainland institutional investors are the leading promoters for RMB internationalization. At the same time, the Mainland's securities investment in Hong Kong also accounted for more than 30% of the total, showing the close relationship between Mainland and Hong Kong's financial markets.

9.10.3 *US funds are an essential promoter of RMB internationalization*

From the beginning of the RQFII pilot program in 2011 to the end of 2016, RQFII approved quotas were mainly distributed in overseas RMB centers such as Hong Kong, South Korea, Singapore, the Eurozone, the United Kingdom, and Australia. In early June 2016, Yi Gang, the then Deputy Governor of PBOC, stated at the China–US Strategic Economic Dialogue briefing that China had decided to give the US an RQFII investment quota of 250 billion yuan. However, it was not until February 2017 that the first investor in the United States, BlackRock Fund Advisors, applied for an RQFII quota of 11 billion yuan. In September and November 2017, the American Acadian Asset Management LLC, and BlackRock Institutional Trust Company, N.A. were approved for RQFII amounts of 1.6 billion and 4 billion yuan, respectively. In the second quarter of 2018, the US Wisdom Tree Management Limited was authorized for an RQFII quota of 1.22 billion yuan. The data show that as of the end of the second quarter of 2018, US funds have limited enthusiasm for RQFII. However, in the third quarter of 2018, Bridgewater Associates, LP, SSGA Funds Management, Inc. and State Street Global Advisors Trust Company were approved, respectively, for 2.6 billion yuan, 4.4 billion yuan and

Table 9.5: The Distribution of RQFII Quota in Different Countries and Regions and the Statistics of Security Investment from China in Corresponding Countries and Regions

RQFII Quota by Country/Region (Unit: RMB Billion)			China's Foreign Securities Investment Assets (Unit: USD billion)					
Country/ Region	**Cumulative Approved Quota**	**Percentage of Quota (%)**	**Total**	**Equity Securities**	**Debt Securities**	**Long-Term**	**Short-Term**	**Percentage of Total (%)**
Mainland China	331.25	45.80						
USA	142.68	19.70	162.83	110.87	67.56	61.54	6.02	19.83
ROK	74.99	10.40	7.3	2.87	2.6	0.66	1.94	0.61
UK	37.07	5.10	21.8	11.3	10.23	9.21	1.03	2.39
France	31.3	4.30	8.61	4.74	4.6	4.59	0.01	1.04
Switzerland	21.4	3.00	4.45	3.84	0.51	0.5	0.01	0.48
Japan	18.74	2.60	13.67	9.97	6.54	3.02	3.52	1.83
Singapore	18.37	2.50	7.49	1.1	5.45	4.17	1.27	0.73
Germany	12	1.70	12.57	4.47	9.93	9.41	0.53	1.60
Canada	10.15	1.40	4.7	3.08	2.46	2.46	0	0.62
China Hong Kong	6.4	0.90	226.43	341.62	67.48	57.05	10.43	45.46
Italy	5	0.70	2.41	2.33	1.73	0.61	0.61	0.26
International organizations	4.2	0.60	2.92	0	4.25	4.18	0.08	0.47

(*Continued*)

Table 9.5: (*Continued*)

RQFII Quota by Country/Region (Unit: RMB Billion)			**China's Foreign Securities Investment Assets (Unit: USD Billion)**					
Country/ Region	**Cumulative Approved Quota**	**Percentage of Quota (%)**	**Total**	**Equity Securities**	**Debt Securities**	**Long-Term**	**Short-Term**	**Percentage of Total (%)**
Holland	3	0.40	3.96	2.43	1.43	1.34	0.09	0.43
Thailand	2.1	0.30	0.69	0.27	0.11	0.07	0.03	0.04
Luxembourg	1.69	0.20	12.7	9.65	3.8	2.69	1.11	1.49
Australia	1.5	0.20	7.66	4.87	5.07	3.63	1.44	1.10
Taiwan China	1.16	0.20	1.15	1.05	0.24	0.24	0	0.14
Total	722.99	100.00	Total is USD899.9 billion					
Eurozone	52.99	7.30	40.25	6	5.23	5.07	0.16	12.48

Source: RQFII quota is calculated according to the statistics of the approved quota and the country and region where the investors are located as announced by the State Administration of Foreign Exchange as of May 31, 2020; the approved quota of Sino-foreign joint venture funds is calculated based on the country where the holding company is located; for some investors, especially those registered in Hong Kong, it is difficult to classify their countries or regions, which may result in some deviations. The data on China's foreign securities investment are taken from the data at the end of 2020 published on the SAFE website.

5 billion yuan, for a total of 12 billion yuan. The RQFII quota accounted for 66.3% of the total global RQFII increase of 18.1 billion yuan in the quarter, which significantly exceeded the total growth of 8.6 billion in the three RMB centers in Hong Kong and Ireland during the same period. In the third quarter of 2018, RMB depreciated 3.6% against the USD. The US funds significantly increased their holdings of the RQFII quota however, which clearly showed their support for RMB. As of the end of May 2020, investors had accumulated approved allocations of nearly 20%, showing that US investors' support for offshore RMB business and RMB globalization was significant. Around 25.2% of China's foreign securities investment went to the United States, and the high proportion also reflected the close connection and tacit relationship between China and the US financial economy. It is also worth noting that as of the end of June 2019, 425 US institutional investors had entered China's bond market, accounting for 23%, ranking at the first place, followed by Hong Kong and Singapore.

9.10.4 *A brief analysis of RQFII from other countries and regions*

Table 9.5 shows that the total amount of RQFII approved to South Korea is second only to China and the United States, accounting for over 10% of the total amount, indicating that South Korean investors have a high degree of support for the internationalization of RMB; investors in the UK, France, Switzerland, Japan, and Singapore accounted for 2–5% of the approved Renminbi quota, indicating that these RMB centers have a strong interest in RMB internationalization. Table 9.5 shows that the Swiss investors have been approved RQFII amount as high as 21.4 billion yuan at the end of May 2020, which is more than twice of 9.6 billion yuan given in Table 9.4 (this is due to the RQFII quota obtained by UBS through institutions registered in Hong Kong, Singapore, and South Korea). This shows the support of Swiss investors for the internationalization of RMB; the approved amounts in Germany and Canada also exceed the total amount given in Table 9.4 for the same reasons as above. As a regional financial center, Luxembourg is similar to Singapore and Hong Kong, with majority of the financial institutions as foreign financial institutions. The total approved RQFII amount given in Table 9.5 is significantly lower than the total amount shown in Table 9.4. It is worth noting that Taiwan China does not have the approved amount in Table 9.4, and the approved amount in Table 9.5 is obtained through institutions registered in other RMB centers.

9.11 The Distribution of RMB Rankings in the Top Five World Foreign Exchange Trading Centers

We have introduced the development of significant RMB centers around the world in the past few years; we will compare RMB rankings in the top five world foreign worldwide centers accordingly in this section.

9.11.1 *Hong Kong*

Hong Kong has been the most important offshore RMB center with about three-quarters of offshore RMB payments on average in the past few years. Hong Kong certainly is the most active offshore RMB trading center. Data from Hong Kong Treasury Markets Association (HKTMA, www.hktma.org.hk) show that average daily turnover of RMB was 16.8% of average daily turnover in Hong Kong, lower than the share of USD and Japanese yen at 95.4% and 23.9%; and it surpassed both HKD and Japanese yen to become the primarily second traded currency in Hong Kong in April 2020 and remained in the same ranking in September 2020, yet the daily turnover of RMB 93.6 billion was 22.9% of the corresponding US daily turn. Yet, in April 3, the share of RMB daily turnover in Hong Kong went up from 18% to 20.2% from April to October 2020, and the RMB/USD turnover ratio also increased to 26.2%, indicating the second position. The Hong Kong foreign exchange market was consolidated in 2020.

9.11.2 *Singapore*

According to data released by Singapore Monetary Authority (WWW.SFE), RMB daily average turnover of $23.86 was ranked seventh in Singapore in April 2013, lower than the corresponding daily average turnover of USD, Japanese yen, Euro, Australian dollar, British pound, and Singapore dollar; it increased significantly to $42.54 billion as ranked sixth in April 2016, lower than USD, Japanese yen, Euro, Australian dollar, and British pound; and RMB's average ranking remained sixth since 2017.

9.11.3 *London*

Data from Bank of England (www.bankofengland.co.uk) show that the daily average turnover of RMB was ranked eighth in London April 2016 and the average ranking remained eighth in the past few years until October 2020.

9.11.4 *Tokyo*

Data from Tokyo Foreign Exchange Market Committee (www.fxcomtky.com) show that RMB (including CNH) daily average turnover of $1.88 billion was ranked 11th in April 2017, it increased significantly to $3.08 billion in April 2020 and ranked 10th during the same period; and it increased further to $5.00 billion in October 2020 and ranked eighth during the same period, indicating the steady growth of ranking of RMB in Tokyo in the past few years.

9.11.5 *New York*

According to data released by New York Fed (www.newyorkfed.org), RMB daily average turnover of $7.08 billion was ranked 14th in April 2016 in New York, it increased to $8.23 billion in April 2020 and ranked 13th during the same period; and it increased significantly to $13.95 billion in October 2020 and ranked 12th during the same period. The tremendous growth rate of daily average turnover of RMB in New York was 633% from April to October 2020 indicating higher market acceptance of RMB in New York in 2020 despite trade friction between the two largest economies of the world.

The arithmetic average of RMB ranking in Singapore, London, Tokyo and New York 7.2 in October 2020 was not value-weighted, yet it was close to eighth position of RMB in April 2016 and April 2019 in Table 4.1, closer to seventh position of RMB in 2020 to be discussed in Chapter 12.

9.12 The Relation between the Rankings of Offshore RMB Center and the Distribution of Quotas Approved for QFII

The number and amount of applications for China QFII from different countries and regions can broadly reflect their interest in the development of China's capital market. Table 9.6 shows the distribution of developing countries and regions as of May 31, 2020.

Table 9.6: Distribution of Approved Quota of QFII among Different Offshore RMB Centers

Country/ Region	Number of Approved Organizations	Percentage of Approved Organizations to Total Approval Organizations (%)	Accumulated Approved Quota	Percentage of Accumulated Approved Quota (%)
China Hong Kong	72	24.41	26.06	22.41
UK	25	8.47	11.56	9.94
Taiwan China	37	12.54	10.86	9.34
USA	43	14.58	10.14	8.72
Singapore	22	7.46	7.92	6.81
ROK	16	5.42	7.75	6.66
China Macau	1	0.34	5.00	4.30
UAE	1	0.34	5.00	4.30
Canada	9	3.05	4.16	3.58
Switzerland	9	3.05	3.83	3.29
France	7	2.37	3.68	3.16
Japan	15	5.08	3.50	3.01
Australia	5	1.69	3.32	2.85
Norway	1	0.34	2.50	2.15
Malaysia	3	1.02	2.06	1.77
Kuwait	1	0.34	2.00	1.72
Germany	4	1.36	1.42	1.22
Portugal	2	0.68	1.20	1.03
Qatar	1	0.34	1.00	0.86
Holland	4	1.36	0.83	0.71
Luxembourg	4	1.36	0.40	0.34
Thailand	2	0.68	0.40	0.34
International organizations	1	0.34	0.28	0.24
Sweden	3	1.02	0.23	0.20
Lithuania	1	0.34	0.23	0.20
Belgium	1	0.34	0.21	0.18

(*Continued*)

Table 9.6: (*Continued*)

Country/ Region	Number of Approved Organizations	Percentage of Approved Organizations to Total Approval Organizations (%)	Accumulated Approved Quota	Percentage of Accumulated Approved Quota (%)
Brunei	1	0.34	0.20	0.17
Ireland	1	0.34	0.20	0.17
South Africa	1	0.34	0.15	0.13
Spain	1	0.34	0.10	0.09
Italy	1	0.34	0.08	0.07
Eurozone	26	8.81	8.35	7.18
Total	295	100.00	116.30	100.00

Source: Calculated based on the statistics of the approved quota and the place of registration of the institution as of May 31, 2020 announced by the State Administration of Foreign Exchange.

9.12.1 *The distribution of QFII in different RMB centers*

Table 9.6 shows the number of approved foreign institutional investors in Hong Kong ranking among the top, which accounts for close to one-fourth. It shows the vital position of the Hong Kong Special Administrative Region in China's financial opening-up. The amount of QFII approved for the United Kingdom is second only to Hong Kong, accounting for slightly less than 10%. The total amount of QFII approved for investors from Taiwan China is somewhat lower than that of the United Kingdom. It is consistent with Taiwan RMB Center's ranking of second place for overseas RMB deposits, showing close relationship between Taiwan and the Mainland China. The total QFII quotas applied for the United States, South Korea, and Singapore ranked fourth to sixth, accounting for around 7%; Macau, United Arab Emirates, Canada, Switzerland, France, Japan, Australia, and Norway ranked seventh to 14th, respectively, accounting for 2–5%; France, Germany and other 10 Eurozone countries account for 8.81% of the total approved QFII quota, slightly surpassing the United States, showing a growing trend of QFII quota in Eurozone. In addition, the total amount of QFII approved in Japan is less than \$3.5 billion, less than one-third of that of the United Kingdom, which is not commensurate with the international status of Japan's economic and trade and overseas assets. This shows that China–Japan financial cooperation still has vast potential.

9.12.2 *Comparison of QFII and RQFII quotas in different countries and regions*

Table 9.6 shows that, except for Taiwan China region, the QFII proportion and ranking of other RMB centers are basically the same as the proportion and order of the RQFII amount given in Table 9.5 show that the interest of different overseas RMB centers in the domestic capital market is basically the same as their interest in RMB.

9.12.3 *Enlightenment of QFII custodian bank related information*

The information of QFII's corresponding custodian bank given in Table 9.6 also has significant meanings. Table 9.6 shows that among the 295 QFII institutions, HSBC, Industrial and Commercial Bank of China, Citibank, China Construction Bank, and Bank of China as custodian banks managed 99, 51, 42, 32, and 25 institutions, respectively; in addition, Standard Chartered Bank and Deutsche Bank have 11 custodians. Agricultural Bank of China and the Bank of Communications have 10 each, and Industrial Bank, China Minsheng Bank and China CITIC Bank have 2, 1, and 1, respectively; the four foreign banks, HSBC, Citibank, Standard Chartered Bank, and Deutsche Bank have managed 163 institutions, accounting for 55.3% of the total number of institutions, demonstrating the vital influence of the four foreign banks in the domestic capital market.

In addition, among the 295 QFII institutions, HSBC, Citibank, Industrial and Commercial Bank of China, China Construction Bank, and Bank of China have custodian amounts of $42.906 billion, $19.193 billion, and $14.881 billion, $11.973 billion, and $10.278 billion, respectively. In addition, the three banks of Bank of Communications, Standard Chartered Bank, and Deutsche Bank have custodial amounts of $3.425 billion, $5.168 billion, and $2.802 billion, respectively. Agricultural Bank of China, Industrial Bank, and China CITIC Bank have custodian amounts of $4.814 billion, $700 million, and $100 million, respectively; HSBC, Citibank, Standard Chartered Bank, and Deutsche Bank have total custodian amount of $70.069 billion, accounting for as high as 60.3% of the total amount.

The total number of QFII custodians and the total amount of the four foreign banks, HSBC, Citibank, Standard Chartered Bank, and Deutsche

Bank exceed that of the total of the five largest domestic banks and two joint-stock banks, indicating that banks have advantages in cooperating with foreign institutional investors.

9.13 Main Problems for the Development of Offshore RMB Market

There are some problems for the development of offshore RMB market. In this section, we will briefly introduce some central issues in offshore RMB centers.

9.13.1 *Aspects to improve in offshore RMB centers*

Offshore RMB centers prospered from scratch and now are all over the world in only a few years. Such rapid development in a short time could not avoid problems. The only data source to reflect the business scale in RMB centers is the RMB payment amount and RMB trade financing data from SWIFT, while the deposits, transactions, etc., are challenging to obtain. Different degrees of errors still existed even if published by some centers themselves. It is believed that with further development of these offshore RMB centers, the primary data will gradually be comprehensive and disclosed in a timely basis.

9.13.2 *The progress of offshore RMB business is not synchronized with development of international trade*

First, in the previous context, we introduced the trade and financial cooperation between China and some major developing countries, i.e., Russia in BRICS. Although the collaboration of trade and finance started early between Russia, developing countries, and China, RMB in Russia is in the slow progress. Secondly, although China and Brazil signed exchange swap of RMB 190 billion as early as March 2013, and Brazil was China's largest trade partner in South America, the progress of RMB trade settlement in Brazil was relatively slow. Thirdly, India, or any country of BRICS and New Development Bank, has not yet signed any swap deal with China, and the RMB business is growing slowly in India. Last but now least, RMB centers have not yet been established in Italy or Spain, while these two Eurozone countries are essential to improve the degree of cooperation between China and the Eurozone as a whole.

9.13.3 *Basic business started up*

In the previous context, primary RMB business in offshore RMB centers, including Hong Kong, involves only RMB payments and RMB deposits. The RMB loan amount in Hong Kong, the most crucial RMB center, only accounted for one-fourth to one-third of total deposits in 2015 through 2017. In 2018, that statistics even dropped below one-fifth, though it rose back to one-fourth in 2019. The depth and width of offshore RMB market need to improve urgently.

With the approval of PBOC, offshore RMB clearing banks and participant banks are allowed to deal with offshore repurchase of China onshore interbank bond, which connects the two interbank bond markets together. Sovereigns and multilateral institutions may also issue RMB bonds in London. Along with the development of offshore RMB business, the business and products in these centers will be gradually enriched and active.

9.14 The Promotion of RMB Internationalization by Cross-Border Payment System

On October 8, 2015, Cross-border Interbank Payment System (CIPS) Phase 1 was officially launched. CIPS is a significant financial infrastructure providing clearing and settlement of RMB cross-border business and offshore RMB business of onshore and offshore institutions. The project of the system was planned into two phases. The first phase of the project was to facilitate cross-border RMB business, to support settlement of cross-border trade in goods and services, cross-border direct investment, cross-border financing, cross-border personal remittances and other services. Its main features include the following: firstly, CIPS (Phase 1) utilizes real-time gross settlement handling for both personal remittance and institution remittance. Secondly, all direct participants can access via a single point, and they are allowed to be part of central clearing to simplify the clearing operations, to improve the clearing efficiency. Thirdly, CIPS uses ISO20022 standard message to enable convenient processing of cross-border participants. Fourthly, operating time of CIPS covers main time zones, including Europe, Asia, Africa, Oceania, etc. Fifthly, onshore direct participants can connect to CIPS via dedicated lease lines.

To cultivate a fair competition environment, PBOC issued an "Interim Rules for Business Conducted through the Cross-Border Interbank Payment System", ruling the eligible participants, account management requirements and business processing to cultivate a fair competition environment requirement, being a foundation for the stable operation of CIPS. At the same time, the Cross-border Interbank Payment System (Shanghai) Co., Ltd. was established, which is responsible for the independent operation of CIPS. The company is supervised and managed by PBOC. First batch of direct CIPS participants includes top five banks in China (Industrial and Commercial Bank of China, Agricultural Bank of China, Bank of China, China Construction Bank, and Bank of Communications), six joint-stock banks (China Merchants Bank, Shanghai Pudong Development Bank, China Minsheng Bank, Industrial Bank, Ping An Bank, and Hua Xia Bank), and eight foreign banks with legal entities in China (HSBC, Citibank, Standard Chartered Bank, DBS Bank, Deutsche Bank, the BNP Paribas, ANZ, and Bank of East Asia). In addition, other indirect participants that joined at the same time include 38 domestic banks and 138 foreign banks in Asia, Europe, Oceania, Africa, and other regions.

After the entire demonstration and research, as well as the cooperation and support of domestic commercial banks, in 2012, PBOC established CIPS. CIPS is another milestone in China's financial market infrastructure, marking a substantial progress for the modern payment system of both domestic and international RMB payments. As a critical economic infrastructure, CIPS meets regulatory requirements such as "Principles for Financial Market." It plays an essential supporting role to promote the process of RMB internationalization (the contents of this section are directly quoted from www.pbc.gov.cn, October 8, 2015).

On March 26, 2018, the second phase of CIPS was put into trial operation. A total of 10 Chinese and foreign banks were simultaneously launched on a trial basis to improve further the clearing and settlement efficiency of RMB cross-border funds (Xinhuanet, March 26, 2018). By the end of December 2019, there had been 33 direct CIPS participants from onshore and offshore, and 903 indirect participants from onshore and offshore. The business scope extended to 167 countries and regions. The "Overall Operation of Payment System in 2019" published on PBOC website shows that in 2019, CIPS processed a total of 1.8843 million transactions with a total value 33.93 trillion yuan, a year-on-year in an increase of 30.64% and 28.28%, respectively. The continuous updates of CIPS promote the use of RMB in the world, and paved the way for RMB to be a global currency.

On January 16, 2019, SWIFT signed a letter of intent with CIPS Co., Ltd. (CIPS operating agency) to deepen further the cooperation between the two parties in the development of cross-border services. SWIFT will set up a wholly foreign developing-owned enterprise in Beijing to provide localized services to Chinese users. After the establishment of a wholly owned institution in China, SWIFT will establish the Payment and Clearing Association of China that will be supervised and managed by PBOC. SWIFT is jointly owned by about 2,400 banks around the world and serves more than 11,000 banks and financial in the world. By January 16, 2019, 141 Chinese banks joined SWIFT Global Payment Initiative (SWIFT GPI). Their cross-border payments accounted for more than 97% of all Chinese banks' cross-border payments.

9.15 The Promotion of Cross-Border Payment System of China UnionPay in RMB Internationalization

China UnionPay, an association of Chinese bank cards, realizes the communication and information shared among the commercial bank systems through UnionPay interbank transaction clearing system to ensure the cross-bank, cross-region, and cross-border use of bank cards. China UnionPay has had extensive cooperation with hundreds of domestic and overseas institutions, and the UnionPay network has spread throughout China's urban and rural areas. It has extended to 160 countries and regions in Asia, Europe, America, Oceania, and Africa. When China UnionPay expanded its cross-border business, it took advantages of network, product, and technology to take part in the financial infrastructure in overseas markets, so that it could innovate business models and accelerate localization of UnionPay card business. Thailand banking refers to standards of UnionPay chip cards. The local transit network, Thai Payment Network (TPN), built cooperatively by UnionPay and major banks in Thailand was launched, and UnionPay also took part in the construction of the national bank, card payment system in Laos UnionPay (*Financial Times*, October 13, 2016).

On October 12, 2016, China UnionPay signed a cooperation agreement with six international institutions, including National Interbank Transaction Management and Exchange (NITMX), Network for Electronic Transfers (NETS), Rintis (an ATM switch network in Indonesia), BancNet (a Philippine-based interbank network) and Malaysian Electronic Payment System (MEPS), and Korea Financial Telecommunications & Clearings Institute (KFTC). This agreement was of great significance for market parties. First, it marked the upgraded cooperation between China UnionPay and overseas payment industry from co-working business to products and standards. Second, it satisfied the requirements of the upgrade from magnetic cards to chip cards in the payment industry, which laid a foundation for the overseas extension of UnionPay innovative products like contactless payment, mobile payment, and electronic wallet products in the future, and expanded the room of cooperation. Third, it made full use of the Sino-foreign collaboration, such as the Belt and Road Initiative, and it raised international competitiveness of the Chinese payment industry via promoting infrastructure of payment and clearing, and technical standards. In fact, the above involves the five founding members and other members of ASEAN, indicating that they have reached a gratifying level in credit card payment technology and services, which actively promoted RMB internationalization in ASEAN and other regions.

9.16 Conclusion

This chapter introduced the development of more than 20 offshore RMB centers, including Hong Kong, in the past 7 years. Data from various sources showed that in recent years offshore RMB payment business had developed rapidly. More than 20 RMB centers across the four continents, Asia, Europe America, and Africa, are showing a sound momentum of such rapid development. Significantly, in the continued depreciation of RMB against USD in August 2015 with an expectation to depreciate significantly, the global cross-border RMB payment ratio still accounted for 2.79%. For the first time, it exceeded JPY, which was 2.76%, becoming the world's fourth largest payment currency. Offshore RMB payment service is still showing a gratifying momentum of development. The international market still has strong faith for the development RMB and China's economy in the future. However, since August 2015, the percentage of RMB offshore payment dropped to a lower ranking than that of Canadian dollars, which was in sixth place. The RMB depreciation had influence on

RMB offshore payment. As of June 2020, the global share of RMB cross-border payments reached 1.76%, making it the fifth largest payment currency.

We should have also see the uneven distribution between the offshore RMB centers and our country's international trade. There are some countries and regions to take note: India, the third largest economy in Asia and the largest in South Asia, Brazil, and the ninth largest economy across the world and the largest in Latin America, as well as Italy and Spain, the two main Eurozone countries. As to the leading developing countries, Mexico, Turkey, and Saudi Arabia, for example, RMB centers have not yet been established while there is tremendous growth potential of RMB cross-border payments. It is believed that in the next few years, RMB internationalization will go further along with RMB payments distributed to more countries and regions.

Bibliography

Chan, Norman T. L. Development of Offshore Renminbi Business in Hong Kong: Review and Outlook, *Insight*, February 21, 2013.

Chan, Norman T. L. *Hong Kong as Offshore Renminbi Centre — Past and Prospects*, Hong Kong Monetary Authority, 2014.

Hong Kong Monetary Authority, Briefing to the Legislative Council, Panel on Financial Affairs, May 5, 2014, www.hkma.gov.

Li, Jing, *The Impact and Strategies for Chinese Economy of RMB Regionalization*, China Financial Publishing House, 2009, pp. 57–58.

Lu, Ting, The Current Situation, Problems and Prospects of Offshore RMB Market in Taiwan, International Financial Research Center, Institute of International Economics and Politics, Chinese Academy of Social Sciences, dissertation 2014W13, 2014.

Mikeni, R. and Liu, Jianheng, *The Rising of RMB — International Status and Impacts*, China Citic Press, 2013.

Yue, Eddie, 2012, Hong Kong — Challenges and Opportunities Ahead, Deputy Chief Executive, Hong Kong Monetary Authority (Speech at the Hong Kong Institute of Bankers Annual Conference 2012, The Year of Transformation — Heading into a New Era) September 13, 2012.

Yue, Eddie, The Development and Future of the Offshore Renminbi Market, Deputy Chief Executive, Hong Kong Monetary Authority (Keynote address at Euromoney Global Offshore RMB Funding Forum 2013), May 8, 2013.

Zhang, Guangping (Peter G.), *RMB Internationalization & Products Innovation*, 7th Edition, China Financial Publishing House, 2017.

Chapter 10
Offshore CNY Markets

The offshore market is an integral part of the internationalization of currencies, and it is a more important part than the domestic market for most major international currencies. This chapter concentrates on the offshore CNY market.

People's Bank of China (PBOC) and Bank of China (Hong Kong) Limited, a clearing bank for RMB business in Hong Kong, signed a revised "Settlement Agreement on the Clearing of CNY Businesses" in Hong Kong on July 19, 2010. The agreement paved the way for launching the offshore CNY market. Relevant offshore institutions were allowed to perform pilot investment in China's domestic interbank bond market according to "Notice of the People's Bank of China on Issues concerning the Pilot Program of Investment in the Interbank Bond Market with RMB Funds by Three Types of institutions including Overseas RMB Clearing Banks" on August 17, 2010. The issuance of the notice marked the official launch of the offshore CNY market. Under the joint promotion of PBOC and Hong Kong Monetary Authority (HKMA), Hong Kong and Mainland China launched "Bond Connection" July 2017. In the early stage of the launch, "Northbound Trading" was opened, which means offshore investors can invest in Mainland China's interbank bond market via the interconnection of infrastructure between Mainland China and Hong Kong. It is under research whether Bond Connect will be extended to "Southbound Trading". "Bond Connect" is an essential milestone in the opening of the domestic interbank bond market. The scale of market participation grew steadily and a total of 2012 overseas institutions from 33 countries and regions participated, with an average daily trading volume of 21.1 billion yuan by the end of June 2020. In the context of CNY internationalization, to improve the status of CNY in international circulation and settlement, it is vital to carry out offshore CNY transactions and trade settlements under the condition that CNY is not fully convertible in capital account. The development of RMB settlement needs to solve problems regarding offshore CNY circulation and transaction. Offshore CNY market is expected to thrive, and to enable offshore CNY trading in offshore CNY market, leading to free exchange of CNY by enterprises according to its position.

10.1 Offshore CNY Bond Market

The degree of overseas participation in a country's bond market, and foreign investors' holdings of the country's bonds, is an essential indicator of the degree of that country's currency internationalization. The issuance and trading of CNY offshore bonds thus became one of the focuses of internal and external attention. PBOC announced that Mainland financial institutions could issue CNY bonds in Hong Kong upon approval on January 11, 2007, and PBOC will provide corresponding clearing arrangements for this business. By issuing CNY bonds in Hong Kong, Mainland financial institutions not only increased the number of bond issuers and bond currencies in the Hong Kong financial market but also helped Hong Kong banks expand their business scope and increase CNY investment options for Hong Kong residents and enterprises. Table 10.1 lists the significant events in the offshore CNY bond market since 2007.

10.1.1 *Regulations*

The "People's Bank of China Announcement [2007] No. 3" ("the Announcement") was issued on January 14, 2007, stipulating for the first time that domestic financial institutions may issue CNY bonds in Hong Kong upon approval. Subsequently, PBOC and the National Development and Reform Commission jointly issued the "Interim Measures for the Administration of the Issuance of CNY Bonds in Hong Kong Special Administrative Region by Financial Institutions within the Territory of China" on June 8, 2007 ("the Measures"). The Announcement and the Measures provided a policy basis for domestic institutions to issue CNY bonds overseas. Hong Kong Monetary Authority (HKMA) issued the "Elucidation of Supervisory Principles and

Table 10.1: Major Events in Offshore CNY Bond Market Since 2007

March 2020	The People's Bank of China, through the Hong Kong Monetary Authority, issues the third issue of Central Bank Notes 2020 in Hong Kong, with an issue volume of 10
February 2020	The People's Bank of China, through the Hong Kong Monetary Authority, issues the first and second issues of Central Bank Notes 2020 in Hong Kong, with a total issue volume of RMB 30 billion
December 2019	The People's Bank of China successfully issued RMB 10 billion central bank notes in Hong Kong
November 2019	First offshore RMB bond issued in both Hong Kong and Macau led by Standard Chartered
November 2019	PBOC issues RMB 30 billion central bank notes in Hong Kong
September 2019	State Ministry of Finance issues RMB 4.5 billion treasury bonds in Hong Kong
August 2019	PBOC issues RMB 30 billion central bank notes in Hong Kong
June 2019	People's Bank of China issues RMB 30 billion central bank notes in Hong Kong
June 2019	National Treasury issues RMB 5 billion treasury bills in Hong Kong
May 2019	People's Bank of China issues RMB 20 billion central bank notes in Hong Kong
February 2019	People's Bank of China issues RMB 20 billion central bank notes in Hong Kong
November 2018	PBOC issues RMB 10 billion each of 3-month and 1-year central bank notes in Hong Kong through HKMA
September 2018	China Agricultural Development Bank issues RMB 1.2 billion fixed rate bonds in Hong Kong
February 2018	Bank of China successfully priced a RMB 4 billion bond issue outside China, the largest single issue in the RMB market
May 2016	China's Ministry of Finance issued RMB 3 billion treasury bonds in London
June 2014	IFC issued the first RMB 500 million of green financial bonds in London
June 2014	HSBC and Standard Chartered Bank issued a total of RMB 1.5 billion bonds on the Singapore Exchange
June 2013	Ansett launched Asia's first offshore RMB bond ETF on the Hong Kong Stock Exchange

(*Continued*)

Table 10.1: (*Continued*)

March 2013	Taiwan's China Trust Commercial Bank issued RMB 1 billion bonds in Taiwan China, launching Taiwan's offshore RMB bond market
April 2012	HSBC issued RMB 2 billion bonds in London for the first time, launching the offshore RMB bond market in London
July 2010	Hopewell Highway issued RMB 13.8 billion of 2-year bonds, the first offshore RMB bond for a Chinese non-financial enterprise
July 2007	China Development Bank issued its first offshore RMB bond in Hong Kong

Source: The information is compiled from the official websites of People's Bank of China, Ministry of Finance, China Development Bank, Bank of China, and Sina Finance.

Operational Arrangements Regarding Renminbi Business in Hong Kong" on February 11, 2010, which for the first time explained matters related to the issuance of CNY bonds in Hong Kong from the perspective of Hong Kong regulators. As a result, Mainland China and Hong Kong had a policy basis for the issuance of CNY bonds in Hong Kong, laying a foundation for the development of the market.

PBOC issued "The Circular on Simplification of Crossborder CNY Business Process and Completion of Related Policies" on July 10, 2013. Cross-border CNY business and policies were significantly improved in the following perspectives: CNY settlement under current accounts, cross-border clearing of CNY accounts with bank cards, offshore CNY lending by domestic non-financial institutions, offshore issuance of CNY bonds by domestic non-financial institutions, offshore CNY guarantees by domestic non-financial institutions, and CNY account financing of offshore participating banks by domestic correspondent banks. All these played a positive role in further promoting cross-border RMB business.

10.1.2 *The situation of RMB bond issuance in Hong Kong by domestic banks*

China Development Bank issued the first offshore CNY bond in Hong Kong from June 27 to July 6, 2007. The target was for institutional and individual investors, with a tenor of 2 years and an annual coupon rate of 3%. The maximum bond issuance volume did not exceed CNY 5 billion, of which the minimum issuance volume of retail bonds was approximately

CNY 1 billion, and the minimum subscription amount for individual investors was CNY 20,000. The total subscription amount attracted at issuance exceeded 14 billion yuan, which was nearly three times the issuance amount, showing the enthusiasm of Hong Kong market for this business. After China Development Bank issued the first CNY offshore bond, Export-Import Bank of China, major domestic commercial banks, and other financial institutions were approved to issue CNY bonds in Hong Kong, London, and Luxembourg. Bank of China successfully completed the pricing and issuance of 4-billion-yuan offshore CNY bond in February 2018. This bond was issued by Macau branch of Bank of China, with a fixed interest rate and a maturity of 1 year and 3 years, respectively, and it was listed on the Hong Kong Stock Exchange. Agricultural Development Bank of China issued a 2-year fixed-rate CNY bond in Hong Kong with a bond size of 1.2 billion yuan in September 2018.

10.1.3 *The offshore institutions that issue RMB bonds*

HSBC Bank (China) and Bank of East Asia (China) were approved to issue CNY bonds in Hong Kong on June 19, 2009. These were the first batch of locally registered foreign banks to issue CNY bonds in Hong Kong. Since then, bond issuers gradually expanded to Hong Kong and Macau companies (Hopewell Highway Infrastructure Limited and Galaxy Entertainment), red chip companies, multinational companies (McDonald's and Caterpillar), and foreign banks (ANZ Bank and VTB Bank). YFY Cayman Co., Ltd., where Industrial Commercial Bank of China International and Sino Pac Securities (Asia) acted as joint lead underwriters and bookrunners on February 10, 2011, successfully issued 300-million-yuan CNY bonds in Hong Kong, marking the successful first issuer of Taiwan-funded enterprises in Hong Kong. In November 2019, Standard Chartered Bank, as the joint global coordinator, successfully priced and issued the first offshore RMB bond for an issuer as a non-financial institution and listed in Macau and Hong Kong at the same time.

Apart from Hong Kong, London became an important center for offshore CNY bond issuance. For example, HSBC issued a 3-year bond with size of CNY 2 billion in London as early as April 2012. Later, foreign banks such as ANZ Bank also issued CNY bonds in London. Japan's first domestic corporate bond denominated in CNY was officially issued on June 24, 2015, by MUFG Bank for domestic institutional investors such as banks and insurance companies to help Japanese companies raise CNY in China.

HSBC (Hong Kong) and Bank of China (Hong Kong) each issued 1 billion yuan of CNY financial bonds in China Interbank Bond Market on September 29, 2015. This was the first time that international commercial banks were approved to issue CNY bonds in China Interbank Bond Market. The initial "Panda Bond", i.e., CNY bonds issued by offshore institutions in China, are meant to explore and expand CNY financing channels for global issuers.

10.1.4 *CNY bond issued by international institutions*

Asian Development Bank issued a 10-year CNY 1 billion bond in early December 2009, with interest starting on December 8, 2009 and maturity on December 8, 2019. This was the first transaction conducted by an international institution, highlighting the Asian Development Bank's support for the CNY bond market. World Bank issued a 2-year 500-million-yuan CNY bond in Hong Kong on January 14, 2011, which was the first CNY bond issuance in 2011, with a credit rating of AAA. This was the first CNY bond issued by World Bank with iconic significance. The International Finance Corporation issued a 500-million-yuan green bond with a 3-year term in London in June 2014, with a yield of 2%. New Development Bank (NDB) first issued 3 billion yuan of green financial bonds in China Interbank Bond Market in July 2016. NDB announced to issue another 5-billion-yuan RMB bonds within this year at the third Annual Council Meeting held in Shanghai on May 28, 2018. Part of the bonds might be green financial bonds. On February 25, 2019, NDB once again issued 3 billion CNY bonds in China Interbank Bond Market. Then in July 2020, NDB issued 5-year 2-billion-yuan RMB bonds in China interbank market.

10.1.5 *"Dim Sum Bond" and "Panda Bond"*

CNY bonds in the offshore market started well and they are expected to continue to develop steadily in the future. In addition to continuing to promote the market construction of offshore CNY bond (Dim Sum Bond) market, the Chinese Government also needs to keep expanding the issuance scale of "Panda Bond" (the CNY bonds issued by offshore institutions or enterprises in China) to further promote CNY internationalization. "Dim Sum Bond" leads to "Going Out", and "Panda Bond" leads to "Bringing In". It is expected that "Dim Sum Bond" and "Panda Bond" would become dual engines to promote CNY internationalization in the long run.

10.1.6 *Issuance amount and outstanding amount of Hong Kong RMB bonds*

According to the annual report of HKMA, CNY bonds issued in Hong Kong increased by 69% from 116.6 billion yuan to 197 billion yuan from 2013 to 2014, showing high a growth trend; the total issuance fell to 75 billion yuan and 52.8 billion yuan, respectively, from 2015 to 2016 (HKMA did not announce the total amount of CNY bond issued in Hong Kong in 2017). In 2018, the amount of CNY bond issuance continued the previous trend and continued to fall to 41.9 billion yuan. The outstanding amount of Hong Kong RMB bonds increased from 166.7 billion yuan to 381 billion yuan from 2011 to 2014. The average annual compound growth rate was as high as 31.7%, but it continued to drop to 168.6 billion yuan from 2014 to 2019, a decrease of 55.7%, showing that the issuance and outstanding amounts of CNY bonds in Hong Kong fell significantly in recent years.

10.1.7 *The trading volume of Hong Kong RMB interest rate derivatives*

CNY deposits, introduced in Chapter 9, and CNY bonds issuances are highly related to CNY interest rate derivatives market in Hong Kong. According to the statistics published on the website of HKMA and Hong Kong Treasury Market Association (www.tma.gov.hk), the average Hong Kong CNY Interest Rate Derivatives trading volumes were $6.2 billion, $4.6 billion, $4.4 billion, $12.7 billion, $9.2 billion, and $8.8 billion from April 2016 to April 2021, respectively. These turnovers indicate upward trend of volume in CNY interest rate derivatives in the market from 2016 to 2019, while the degree of decline was less than that of Hong Kong RMB deposits, loans, and bond issuance amounts at the same time; yet the turnovers began to decrease from 2019 to 2021.

10.2 CNY Debt Securities and Money Market Securities in Hong Kong

10.2.1 *Outstanding amount of CNY debt securities under custody and settlement of Central Clearing and Settlement System (CCASS) in Hong Kong*

Hong Kong Securities Clearing Co., Ltd. (HKSCC) released data on the total outstanding amount and transaction volume of RMB, USD, and other foreign currency debt instruments of different maturities under custody and settlement of the company every month since 2011. These data reflect to a certain extent of CNY influence in Hong Kong market. Table 10.2 shows the total amount of fixed-rate and floating-rate bonds published by HKSCC for CNY, USD, HKD, and other currencies with different maturities from less than 1 year to more than 7 years from 2011 to the first half of 2021.

Table 10.2 shows that the total outstanding amount of CNY debt instruments under the custody and settlement of CCASS continued to grow to a high of $65.42 billion from 2011 to 2014, accounting for more than half of the entire market. However, it has continued to decline since 2014. At the end of 2018, the total RMB denominated outstanding was $23.86 billion, accounting for only 23.7% of the total. By 2019, it rebounded to $29.14 billion, accounting for 27.1% of the total. From 2011 to 2015, the outstanding amount of CNY bond instruments continued to exceed the amount of the HKD, USD, and other currencies. Since 2016, the CNY amount has been kept lower than the HKD's and slightly higher than the USD. From 2011 to 2014, the transaction volume of CNY debt instruments continued to grow to $118.89 billion, accounting for more than 60% of the entire market. From 2015 to 2018, the corresponding volume continued to drop significantly below the level of HKD and USD, accounting for only 19.4%, showing the shrinking of CNY denominated debt instruments in recent years. In 2019, the trading volume of CNY bond instruments rebounded sharply, but it was still in third place after that of USD debt instruments. The turnover of CNY denominated bonds in 2020 outpaced that of HKD denominated bonds and by the end of June 2021, the share of the turnover of CNY denominated bonds rebounded to 48.2%, with annualized turnover scaling up to $84.79 billion equivalent, which was first seen after 2015.

10.2.2 *Hong Kong CNY money market and international comparison*

The money market refers to the market in which financial assets have a maturity of less than 1 year. The Hong Kong money market is relatively small. Table 10.3 (including the custody/settlement amount of CNY and other currency debt instruments with a maturity of less than 1 year in Hong Kong) provides us with the necessary information to understand the

Table 10.2: Outstanding Amount of CNY, USD, and Other Foreign Currency Debt Instruments under Custody and Settlement of CCASS (from 2011 to 2021) (Unit: USD billion, %)

Currency Year	CNY	USD	HKD	Other Currencies	Total	Share of CNY
Year-End Balance						
2011	33.10	6.83	31.26	1.05	72.24	45.8
2012	50.41	13.57	40.77	0.42	10.52	47.9
2013	63.06	16.25	41.35	0.88	121.54	51.9
2014	65.42	16.16	42.61	1.30	125.49	52.1
2015	53.70	18.83	46.39	1.27	120.19	44.7
2016	40.07	23.16	52.20	1.47	116.90	34.3
2017	30.09	27.82	49.87	1.44	109.22	27.5
2018	23.86	21.93	53.41	1.56	100.76	23.7
2019	29.14	21.03	55.02	2.50	107.69	27.1
2020	32.32	17.96	61.99	2.30	114.57	28.2
2021*	33.66	14.89	58.00	2.05	108.59	31.0
Annual Turnover						
2011	61.69	21.42	31.16	2.47	116.74	52.8
2012	88.44	28.31	50.54	1.10	168.39	52.5
2013	103.51	28.00	41.42	1.62	174.55	59.3
2014	118.89	26.41	41.39	1.20	187.89	63.3
2015	67.90	27.15	42.97	0.27	138.29	49.1
2016	51.26	41.30	54.31	2.31	149.18	34.4
2017	31.39	50.42	66.16	3.22	151.19	20.8
2018	23.80	33.38	63.34	2.05	122.57	19.4
2019	33.53	35.51	57.05	1.83	127.92	26.2
2020	34.81	28.98	70.09	3.00	136.88	25.4
2021*	84.79	17.20	72.37	1.54	175.90	48.2

Source: Hong Kong Monetary Authority website: "http://www.hkma.gov.hk" www.hkma.gov.hk. *2021 data are an annualized number based on first half year.

CNY money market in Hong Kong. According to the data on various currency debt instruments with maturities of less than 1 year in Table 10.3, from 2012 to 2015, the amount of short-term CNY bonds in Hong Kong exceeded those amounts of HKD and USD, making it the most active

Table 10.3: Outstanding Amounts of Debt Instruments with No Longer than 1 Year Maturities in CNY, USD, HKD, and Other Currencies in Custodian of CCASS (2011–2021) (Unit: USD billion, %)

Year/ Currency	CNY	USD	HKD	Other Currencies	Total	Share of RMB
2011	10.82	4.95	14.03	0.89	30.69	35.3
2012	20.54	11.08	17.71	0.23	49.56	41.4
2013	34.13	12.07	15.59	0.20	61.99	55.1
2014	26.50	12.67	15.90	0.03	55.10	48.1
2015	22.21	14.62	19.79	0.47	57.09	38.9
2016	19.78	13.67	23.11	1.10	57.66	34.3
2017	11.98	17.83	23.20	1.19	54.20	22.1
2018	12.51	14.01	21.41	0.46	48.39	25.9
2019	18.04	14.50	19.12	1.41	53.07	34.0
2020	20.14	12.31	32.20	0.58	65.24	30.9
2021*	18.13	8.69	26.68	0.27	53.78	33.7

Source: Same as Table 10.2; *data for 2021 are based on the first half year.

currency in Hong Kong money market. However, during 2016–2018, the amount of short-term RMB bonds was surpassed by that of HKD and the USD one after another, becoming the third currency in the Hong Kong money market after the HKD and the USD. But by 2019, CNY amount once again surpassed that of USD, second only to the amount of HKD.

10.3 Size and Comparison of Major Currencies in the International Bond Market

The issuance amount, outstanding amount, and liquidity of different currencies in the international bond market also reflect the degree of internationalization of a currency to a certain extent. This section will briefly introduce the issuance size, proportion, and ranking of major international currencies to help understand the role of different currencies in the international bond market, and further to the role of CNY international bonds in the global market.

10.3.1 *Comparison of the size and proportion of Euro and USD in the international bond market*

The total amount of floating-rate, fixed-rate and equity-related international bonds issued in Euro exceeded the outstanding amount of global bonds issued in USD for the first time in the fifth year after the introduction of Euro, 2003. Then, international bonds in Euro had remained more significant over the outstanding international bonds of USD for 12 years from 2003 to 2014, demonstrating the importance of Euro in the global bond market. Table 10.4 gives the outstanding amounts of international bonds of 15 major currency issuers.

Table 10.4 shows that USD denominated international bonds have remained higher than Euro denominated international bonds since 2015, and the gap between USD denominated bonds and Euro denominated bonds has widened to 8.7% in 2019, indicating that Euro was severely impacted by USD in international bond market after US withdrew from its quantitative easing policies in 2014. The gap narrowed to 5.1% in 2020 when FED restarted a massive quantitative easing and credit stimulus when COVID-19 hit globally.

Table 10.4 shows that the share of international bonds of USD was significantly lower than the corresponding share of USD in global foreign exchange market shown in Table 4.1, and the percentage of international bonds of Euro was far higher than the share of Euro in global foreign exchange market before 2014. However, the share of international bonds of USD has remained slightly higher than the share of USD in world foreign exchange market since 2014, and the share of international bonds of Euro has remained significantly higher than the share of Euro in global foreign exchange market despite steady falls of share of international bonds of Euro. These results indicate the importance of the top two world currencies in international bond market.

10.3.2 *Comparison of share of international bonds of major international currencies*

Table 10.4 shows that, although there is a large gap between the international bonds in British pound and the international bonds in Euro and the USD, they are still much higher than other major global currencies, and indeed, have maintained the third largest international bond issuance

Table 10.4: Outstanding Amounts of International Bonds of Major Currencies (2007–2020) (Unit: USD billion, %)

Year / Currency	2007	2009	2011	2013	2015	2017	2018	2019	2020	2030*	CAGR 2011–2020
USD	5,679.6	6,226.5	6,905.1	8,173.8	9,211.3	10,672.7	11,144.3	11,737.6	12,155.5	22,785.8	6.49
EUR	8,807.7	10,307.9	9,580.2	10,105.9	8,070.9	9,293.7	9,269.2	9,565.6	10,798	12,333.5	1.34
GBP	1,855.9	2,174.3	2,021.6	2,202.5	2,005.7	1,962.9	1,910.7	2,091	2,131.4	2,260.4	0.59
JPY	611.8	693.1	759.3	494.6	399.9	426.1	444.3	451.3	448.1	249.4	−5.69
AUD	221.2	247	318.7	292.1	257.3	285.3	257.8	259.2	278.6	239.9	−1.48
CHF	319.5	378.8	392.4	360.6	258.9	209.5	191.3	189.7	203.1	97.7	−7.06
SEK	49.3	69.2	103.1	132.3	101.1	103	103.8	116.7	151.7	233.0	4.38
CAD	259.8	277.5	313	263	146.3	141.9	126.7	142	133.6	51.9	−9.03
HKD	81.2	70.5	65.5	63.4	69.3	89.5	108	112.7	120.5	237.2	7.01
CNY	5.2	11.5	39.1	89.5	125	102.3	107.3	96.6	112.8	366.1	12.49
NOK	28.9	51.2	86.3	96.3	59.4	58.3	56.5	73.6	83.9	81.3	−0.31
SGD	25.6	28.3	35.3	40.5	41.5	43	39.1	39.8	40.2	46.4	1.45
MXN	20.9	16.4	19.7	32.6	26.6	26	30.4	39	36.6	72.8	7.12
NZD	56	44.2	36.6	42.2	42.5	41.7	37.2	32.1	33.5	30.4	−0.98
BRL	24.5	24.5	46.4	47.9	29.6	28	24.5	20.6	14.1	3.8	−12.40
Total	18,047.1	20,621	20,722.4	22,437.2	20,845.2	23,483.8	23,851.2	24,967.2	26,969.8	39,089.7	2.97
Share of Top Eight Currencies	98.4	98.5	98.1	98	98.2	98.3	98.3	98.3	97.0	96.0	
USD Share	31.5	30.2	33.3	36.4	44.2	45.4	46.7	47.0	45.1	53.4	
EUR Share	48.8	50	46.2	45	38.7	39.6	38.9	38.3	40.0	30.9	
CNY Ranking	15	15	12	10	8	9	9	10	10	4	

Source: www.bis.org; *data and rankings of 2030 are estimated by accumulated average annual growth rate from 2011 to 2020 of each currency and the share of top eight currencies.

currencies for more than a decade. Japanese yen, Australian dollar, Swiss franc, and Swedish krona (replacing Canadian Dollar in 2020) rank from fourth to seventh, respectively. From 2001 to 2020, the ratio of the top seven international currencies plus RMB international bond issuance to the total global international bond issuance remained at a high level of 97%, which was much higher than the average share of these currencies in global FX transactions over the same period, 85%. It displays that the role of major international currencies in the international bond market is more important than that in the international FX market, highlighting the monopoly of the international bond market by major international currencies.

10.3.3 *Comparison of share of international bonds of major currencies*

Table 10.4 shows that the Canadian dollar fell to eighth position and replaced Swedish Krona in the ranking of largest international bond issuance currencies. HKD and Norwegian krone have maintained their positions as the world's ninth and 11th largest international bond issuance currencies in recent years, outstanding amounts of international bonds of Singapore Dollar, Mexican Peso, New Zealand Dollar, and Brazil Real rank from 12th to 15th, respectively.

10.4 Share of CNY International Bonds and Institutional Cooperation between Onshore and Offshore Bond Markets

10.4.1 *Comparison of the sizes and share of the CNY international bonds*

Table 10.4 shows that the ranking of CNY had continued to rise from 15th to eighth in the global international bond market from 2007 to 2015. However, the outstanding amount of CNY international bonds dropped 22.8% from 2015 to 2019, due to CNY depreciation against USD after United States' exit from the quantitative easing policy, and the ranking dropped to 10th behind the ninth ranking of HKD in 2019. CNY international bond issuance increased with CAGR of 12.49% to $112.8 billion from 2011 to 2020 and the gap of the global bond issuance of HKD and CNY narrowed from $26.4 billion in 2011 to $7.7 billion in 2020.

10.4.2 *Estimation of the size and share of CNY international bonds in 2030*

Table 10.4 shows that the compound annual growth rate of the outstanding RMB international bonds during this period was as high as 12.49% from 2011 to 2020, highest of the top 15 currencies the same period, the outstanding amount of CNY international bonds will reach $366.1 billion by the end of 2030, making it the fourth largest international bond issuance currency. The estimation matches the time points and corresponding rankings in Table 10.4 when CNY becomes number four as a major world currency in 2030.

China, however, is experiencing financial market opening fast pace and with great strength, and thus historical data may not correctly reflect the achievements of the new policies. From the perspective of the huge volume and demand of China market itself, considering the accelerating opening of capital accounts since 2019, overseas funds steadily flowed into China bond market and stock market. It is expected that in the future, around 2030, the outstanding amount of RMB international bonds will be in top three positions along with USD and Euro, much earlier than the estimated time in Table 10.4. This, in turn, confirms the urgency of adopting a combination of measures to deepen domestic reforms to ensure that the opening of the domestic capital market will continue to rapidly increase the process of RMB internationalization.

10.4.3 *PBOC allows foreign central banks to enter interbank FX market*

PBOC allowed foreign central banks to enter China interbank foreign exchange market through one or more of the three ways, via agent of PBOC or agent of members of China interbank FX market, or to be an offshore member of China interbank FX market to trade spot, forward, swap and FX Options (September 30, 2015, PBOC website: www.pbv.gov.cn). The admission for foreign central banks to enter the domestic interbank market can accelerate the growth of offshore RMB bond transaction volumes.

State Administration of Foreign Exchange (SAFE) issued "Circular of the State Administration of Foreign Exchange on Further Advancing Foreign Exchange Administration Reform to Enhance Authenticity and

Compliance Reviews" (No. 3 [2017]) in January 2017, which facilitated the FX risk management of offshore investors in interbank bond market and promoted the reform measures of the opening bond market and FX market. Offshore investors were able to conduct FX risk management in the offshore RMB market, and with the growth of China FX market, offshore investors were allowed to participate in domestic FX market under certain conditions, and they might manage bonds and FX in an integrated manner. In July 2017, PBOC and HKMA issued an announcement, deciding to approve the launch of "Bond Connect" between Hong Kong and Mainland China. "Northbound Trading" went live for trial operation on July 3, 2017. As of June 2020, the average daily trading volume of Bond Connect reached 21.1 billion yuan, and the total monthly trading volume reached 422.1 billion yuan. This is of positive significance for activating the domestic and offshore RMB bond markets and FX markets.

10.4.4 *Multiple offshore institutions allowed to enter China Interbank Bond Market*

According to data from PBOC, as of the end of June 2020, 456 offshore institutions were allowed to enter China Interbank Bond Market out of which 69 were foreign central banks and 387 were commercial institutions. The institutions include foreign central banks or monetary authorities, international financial institutions, sovereign wealth funds, foreign commercial banks, non-bank financial institutions, investment managers that take care of institutional financial products, etc. In addition, 561 foreign institutional investors entered China Interbank Bond Market through "Bond Connect". The entry of offshore institutions into the domestic interbank bond market will not only activate the domestic bond market but also have positive significance in promoting the connection of domestic and offshore CNY bond markets and the increase in the size of offshore CNY bonds.

10.4.5 *New measures to relax access to China Interbank Bond Market for offshore institutions*

PBOC Announcement [2016] No. 8 relaxed restrictions of entering interbank bond market on domestic qualified institutional investors of both legal person and non-legal person on May 6, 2016. The announcement clearly pointed out that the following investors were allowed to enter interbank bond market: the domestic qualified institutional investors of legal person approved by financial regulatory authorities, including but not limited to commercial banks, trusts, finance companies of enterprise groups, securities companies, fund management companies, futures companies, insurance companies, and other institutional investors taking care of products including but not limited to securities investment funds, bank wealth management products, trust plans, etc. Qualified institutional investors in the non-legal person category, including but not limited to insurance, private equity investment funds filed by the Fund Industry Association, housing provident funds, social security funds, corporate annuities, pension funds, charity funds, shall file electronically with the Shanghai Headquarters of PBOC in accordance with regulations. After account opening and network procedures in custody and settlement institutions are approved by PBOC, qualified institutional investors will become participants of interbank bond market (after completing the filing, account opening, and networking procedures). The announcement plays a very good role in activating the domestic bond market and promoting offshore CNY bond market.

10.4.6 *"Bond Connect" — Interconnection and cooperation between Mainland China and Hong Kong bond markets*

The "Northbound Trading" of Bond Connect was officially launched on July 3, 2017. Offshore investors could directly invest in the domestic interbank bond market through Bond Connect. "Bond Connect is an important milestone in deepening the interconnection between the Mainland China and Hong Kong's capital markets. This is the first time that Mainland China allows qualified offshore investors to invest domestic interbank bond market via infrastructure connection between Mainland and offshore bond markets. The Northbound Trading of Bond Connect has been operating smoothly since its launch, confirming that Hong Kong, as an international financial center, continuously plays a unique role in Mainland financial market opening," said Carrie Lam, the Chief Executive of Hong Kong Special Administrative Region, at the Bond Connect anniversary forum on July 3, 2018.

According to the data of Bond Connect, 2012 overseas institutions have obtained the central bank's approval to carry out investment businesses of the end of June 2020, covering 33 countries and regions. A total of 72 of the world's top 100 asset management companies have completed registration and entered the market. According to data from the website of China Bond, as of June 2020, the total amount of bonds in the interbank bond market held by offshore institutions reached CNY 2196 billion, accounting for 3.2% of the total interbank bond market holdings.

10.4.7 *Steady growth of CNY bonds held by foreign residents in recent years*

According to data released by PBOC, annual growth rates of CNY government bonds held by foreign residents were 40.61%, 42.77%, 32.21%, and 47.38% from 2016 to 2020, and the annual growth rate from June 2020 to 2021 was 49.19% to CNY 3.84 trillion or $0.59 trillion. The steady growth of CNY government bonds held by foreign residents should have positive impacts on CNY international bonds.

10.5 Offshore CNY FX Spot Rate and Volatilities

Offshore CNY foreign exchange market started its official operation in July 2010. The trading symbol of RMB foreign exchange in the international foreign exchange market is CNY, the abbreviation of "Chinese yuan". In the Hong Kong offshore market, the trading symbol of RMB is CNH. Many people may think the "H" in CNH means the first letter of Hong Kong, but the "insiders" think it means the first letter of Chinese phrase "Haiwai" meaning overseas or offshore (Minikin and Lau, 2013). It seems that the two explanations are both reasonable, and the latter one is more representative of offshore RMB exchange rate.

10.5.1 *USD/CNY (HK) base exchange rate*

In August 2010, spot USD/CNH formally made its debut in Hong Kong. After many years of practice, the Hong Kong offshore spot USD/CNY market has good liquidity, and the market quotation is continuous. With the constant improvement of the status of the RMB international settlement, offshore centers such as London, Singapore, and Taiwan China are more closely participating in the offshore RMB spot transactions. In June 2011, the Treasury Markets Association introduced TMA's Spot USD/RMB (HK) Fixing, and it became the USD/RMB (HK) base exchange rate. The base rate is calculated by first removing the two highest and two lowest quotations from 15 designated banks and then taking the average of the remaining quotations. The introduction has significant reference value to the development of offshore RMB spot market, forward market, future market, and other RMB foreign exchange market.

10.5.2 *Comparison of offshore USD/CNH spot exchange rate and onshore USD/CNY spot exchange rate*

Offshore CNH market has been playing a critical role in offshore CNH FX market since its launch in 2010. Figure 10.1 presents the onshore USD/CNY and offshore USD/CNH exchange rates from August 23, 2010 to August 26, 2021.

Figure 10.1 shows that at the beginning of the introduction of offshore CNH market from August 23, 2010 to October 18, 2010, there was a large gap between onshore and offshore CNY exchange rate, indicating a strong perception of CNY appreciation in offshore market then.

However, the gap narrowed rapidly from October to December 2010. The differences were −300 points to 0 most of the time from the beginning

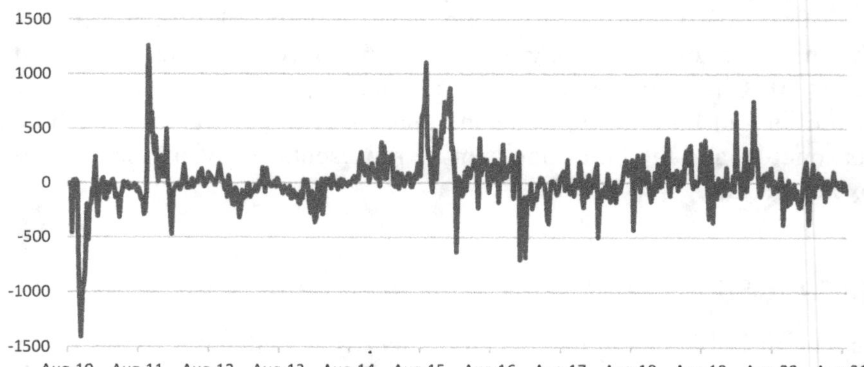

Figure 10.1: Onshore and offshore CNY Spot Exchange Rate Spread

Source: Using data from Bloomberg and calculated as 10,000* (offshore USD/CNY exchange rate-onshore USD/CNY exchange rate).

of 2011 to mid-September of 2011. Offshore CNH exchange rate was about 1,000 points higher than the corresponding onshore exchange rate in the second half of September 2011, reflecting the expectation of offshore CNH depreciation during the time. The differences began to narrow down from November 2011 to early August 2015. However, the differences widened again from early August of 2015, close to the level during the third quarter of 2010.

HKMA announced a relaxation on the requirements for RMB net position and the liquidity ratio to enhance the market liquidity on April 25, 2013. The authorized Hong Kong institutions were no longer required to maintain a minimum net position of USD against CNY, while USD against CNY could be managed as an ordinary foreign currency pair. At the same time, HKMA announced to cancel RMB liquidity ratio requirement issued on February 9, 2012 and June 14, 2012. The relaxation greatly improved the RMB liquidity in Hong Kong and paved the way for RMB internationalization and free convertibility.

PBOC announced to improve the USD/RMB middle price quotation to enhance its degree of market and benchmark qualification on August 11, 2015. Market makers refer to previous day's closing rate of interbank foreign exchange market before the market opening from August 11, 2015. Combining the factors like FX supply and demand and major currencies FX changes, the market makers provide to China Foreign Exchange Trade System (CFETS) the middle price quotation, and CFETS announces the CNY median price authorized by the PBOC. On August 11, 2015, USD/CNY exchange rate was 6.2298 in interbank foreign exchange market, and it was 1,136 base points higher than previous transaction day. The USD/CNY middle exchange rate devalued by 1.8%. The devaluation brought huge volatility to domestic exchange rates and offshore exchange rates. During that week, the domestic RMB exchange rate and offshore RMB exchange rate devalued by 2,000 base points and 2,500 base points, respectively, with the exchange rate spread expanded to 500 base points. CNY/USD exchange rate decreased by 4.7% in 2015. In 2016, with the rising trend of USD, the exchange rate of RMB/USD on domestic market devalued continuously, which accumulated a 5.7% decrease in the first 11 months in 2016. At the same time, the offshore CNY/USD exchange rate accumulated devaluation was up to 5.8%. The onshore and offshore exchange rate spread remained at +/−500 base points since 2016.

10.5.3 *Comparison of offshore CNY spot exchange rate volatilities*

Volatility is one of the essential parameters in foreign exchange market. Calculation of the data in Figure 10.1 shows that the volatility of offshore RMB spot exchange rates was higher than domestic CNY spot exchange rates during most of the time from October 2010 to March 2015. The former was 31.2% higher than the latter by average. High market volatility is an important reason for the active offshore RMB market. The volatility of offshore and that of domestic CNY spot exchange rates were very close from April 2015 to June 2015. However, volatility of offshore foreign exchange rate increased after July 2015, 118.2% higher than domestic exchange rates on average. The result shows that before the central bank reforming on the middle exchange rates, offshore and onshore CNY exchange rates spread, and volatility has largely increased.

10.6 Offshore RMB Spot Market Liquidity

Interbank market data are often difficult to be systematically collected, and it is more often the case on offshore CNY market with a shorter history. Since all types of international usage of any currency are reflected in its turnover in the global foreign exchange market, this foreign exchange turnover is the most straightforward and accurate indicator of currency internationalization. As a result, we make great efforts to do data excavation to judge the liquidity of offshore CNY market to find reasonable data and then determine the degree of RMB internationalization.

10.6.1 *Average daily turnover of CNY FX spot in London*

The London Foreign Exchange Joint Standing Committee (FXJSC, www.bankofengland.co.uk) began to release average daily turnovers of CNY FX spot against the USD in London every April and October since 2008 every year. Table 10.5 shows the average daily turnover of CNY/USD foreign exchange spot from April 2010 to April 2021. According to Table 10.5, the average daily turnover of London CNY/USD foreign exchange spot had increased 23 times to $19.40 billion from October 2010 to October 2016, the corresponding accumulative average annual growth rate was as high as 69.8%. The average daily turnover of CNY foreign exchange in London was $18.55 billion in April 2016, surpassing the average daily turnover of $16.27 billion of spot CNY/USD in Hong Kong in April 2016 for the first time, and London became the most active offshore CNY foreign exchange spot market then. It grew to $35.44 billion in April 2019, with an accumulative average annual growth rate 0f 24.1% from April 2016 to 2019, higher than the growth rates of CNY spot turnovers in any other offshore market. Affected by the COVID-19 in 2020, the daily average turnover fell to $21.50 billion in April 2020, still exceeding average daily turnover of the Hong Kong $17.18, showing the significance of the London CNY spot foreign exchange market.

10.6.2 *Average daily turnover of CNY FX spot in Hong Kong*

Although Hong Kong Monetary Authority released the average daily turnover of CNY foreign exchange in Hong Kong from April 2010 to April 2019 in its triennial foreign exchange reports, and Hong Kong Treasury Market Association (HKTMA) had released semi-annual CNY foreign exchange turnover data since October 2017, neither HHMA nor HKTMA released specific data of CNY foreign exchange spot turnover. Thus, we have to estimate CNY foreign exchange spot turnover using total CNY foreign exchange turnover and the overall spot turnover/total foreign exchange turnover ratios from April 2010 to 2019. For example, total spot daily average turnovers were $43.8 billion and $51.2 billion in April 2010 and April 2013 in Hong Kong foreign exchange market, respectively, and total foreign exchange daily turnovers were $237.6 billion and $274.2 billion in April 2010 and April 2013, respectively. Thus, the average ratio of sport daily average turnover/total foreign exchange daily average turnover was 18.43% and 18.67% in Hong Kong foreign exchange market in April 2010 and April 2013, respectively. Assuming that the spot turnover/foreign exchange turnover remained the same for all currencies in Hong Kong foreign exchange market, we can estimate spot daily turnover of CNY in Hong Kong using total CNY foreign exchange daily average turnover as 18.43% × 108 = $1.99 and 18.67% × 49.1 = $9.17 billion in April 2010 and April 2013. Semi-annual average daily turnover between April 2010 and April 2013 can be estimated using moderate semi-annual changes from April 2010 to April 2013. Table 10.5 gives the estimated average daily turnover of spot CNY foreign exchange trading.

Table 10.5 shows that the cumulated average annual growth rate (CAGR) of CNY spot daily turnover in Hong Kong was 41.67% from

Table 10.5: Average Daily Turnover of CNY Foreign Exchange Spot Markets in Major Offshore CNY Centers (2010–2021) (Unit: USD billion, %)

Time/ Currency	United Kingdom	Hong Kong	Singapore	New York	Tokyo	Sum
Apr-10	0.61	1.99	1.89		0.03	4.52
Oct-10	0.81	3.19	2.03		0.03	6.06
Apr-11	1.01	4.38	2.17		0.03	7.59
Oct-11	1.52	5.58	2.31		0.00	9.41
Apr-12	1.30	6.78	2.46		0.06	10.60
Oct-12	1.74	7.97	2.60		0.28	12.59
Apr-13	3.35	9.17	2.74		0.34	15.60
Oct-13	3.68	10.32	3.60		0.39	17.99
Apr-14	9.40	11.48	4.45		0.53	25.86
Oct-14	12.15	12.63	5.31		0.83	30.92
Apr-15	14.08	13.78	6.17		0.86	34.89
Oct-15	14.44	14.94	7.03		0.96	37.36
Apr-16	18.55	16.09	7.89	1.42	1.05	45.00
Oct-16	19.40	16.42	8.15	2.00	1.85	47.82
Apr-17	13.61	16.74	9.63	1.43	1.05	42.46
Oct-17	28.24	17.07	8.94	2.76	1.48	58.49
Apr-18	31.49	17.39	8.83	3.74	2.13	63.58
Oct-18	30.58	17.72	9.14	4.42	1.83	63.69
Apr-19	35.44	18.87	9.44	5.51	1.88	71.14
Oct-19	25.76	12.72	6.80	3.74	2.24	51.26
Apr-20	27.05	17.18	10.57	3.78	1.51	60.09
Oct-20	37.18	20.03	8.94	7.80	3.12	77.07
Apr-21	34.16	23.59	8.77	5.47	1.59	73.57
2010	0.61	1.99	1.89		0.03	4.52
2011	1.01	4.38	2.17		0.03	7.59
2012	1.30	6.78	2.46		0.06	10.60
2013	3.35	9.17	2.74		0.34	15.60
2014	9.40	11.48	4.45		0.53	25.86
2015	14.08	13.78	6.17		0.86	34.89
2016	18.55	16.09	7.89	1.42	1.05	45.00

(*Continued*)

Table 10.5: (*Continued*)

Time/ Currency	United Kingdom	Hong Kong	Singapore	New York	Tokyo	Sum
2017	13.61	16.74	9.63	1.43	1.05	42.46
2018	31.49	17.39	8.83	3.74	2.13	63.58
2019	35.44	18.87	9.44	5.51	1.88	71.14
2020	27.05	17.18	10.57	3.78	1.51	60.09
2021	34.16	23.59	8.77	5.47	1.59	73.57
2010–2016 CAGR	76.67	41.67	26.89		80.86	46.67
2016–2021 CAGR	12.99	7.95	2.13	30.96	8.65	10.33

Source: Data in United Kingdom are from the website of the London Foreign Exchange Joint Standing Committee (FXJSC) www.bankofengland.co.uk; data in Hong Kong are from the website of Hong Kong Monetary Authority (HKMA) www.hkma.gov.hk and the website of Hong Kong Treasury Market Association (HKTMA) www.tma.org.hk; data in Singapore are from the website of Singapore Monetary Authority www.mas.gov.sg; data in the United States are from the website of New York Fed www.newforkfed.org; data in Japan are from the website of Tokyo Foreign Exchange Market Committee www.fxcmtky.com.

April 2010 to April 2016, lower than the corresponding CAGR of 76.67% in London. CAGR of CNY spot daily turnover in Hong Kong was 7.95% from April 2016 to April 2021, also lower than the corresponding CAGR of 12.99% in London; yet the CAGR of CNY spot daily turnover in Hong Kong was 11.79% from April 2019 to April 2021, higher than the corresponding CAGR of −1.80% in London.

10.6.3 *Average daily turnover of CNY FX spot in Singapore, United States, and Japan*

Table 10.5 shows that Singapore had remained the second largest offshore CNY spot foreign exchange center from April 2010 to October 2013, yet its second position was replaced by London from April 2013 to April 2021. CNY spot daily average turnover of $1.42 billion surpassed that Japan's $1.03 billion from April 2016 and remained at the fourth position of offshore CNY spot trading since then. With the highest cumulated average annual growth rate of 30.96% from April 2016 to April 2021, the United States may replace Singapore as the third major offshore CNY spot trading center in 2–3 years.

Table 10.5 also shows that despite the high CAGR of 80.86% of CNY spot trading in Japan from April 2010 to April 2016, the corresponding CAGR decreased to 8.65% from April 2016 to April 2021, showing the potentiality of CNY spot trading in Japan in years to come.

10.6.4 *Problems with SWIFT RMB tracker monthly spot data*

The Society for Worldwide Interbank Financial Telecommunication (SWIFT) has been providing excellent monthly data for share of international payments and share of trade finance of significant currencies including CNY since January 2012. CNY monthly payment data of SWIFT in major offshore CNY centers are also beneficial. However, "Top economies doing FX Spot transactions in RMB FX confirmations" data of SWIFT can be misleading. For example, share of "Top economies doing FX Spot transactions in RMB FX confirmations" in United Kingdom, China, United States, and Hong Kong was 35.28%, 15.57%, 12.59%, and 10.92% in April 2021, respectively (RMB Tracker, May 2021). Thus, RMB Spot transactions based on value in United Kingdom should be 15.57%/12.57% = 2.27 times RMB Spot transactions in Mainland China. However, the average daily RMB spot turnover was $54.63 billion in Mainland China according to data released by the State Administration of Foreign Exchange (SAFE) of China, and daily average RMB spot turnover was merely $34.16 billion according to data released by the Foreign Exchange Joint Standing Committee (FXJSC) of the Bank of England in July 2021. RMB daily average turnover of $34.16 in UK was merely 62.5% of the corresponding daily average turnover of $54.93 billion in Mainland China in April 2021.

10.7 Liquidity of Offshore CNY Foreign Exchange Derivatives Markets

Section 10.6 introduced CNY spot trading in major CNY centers worldwide, this section will concentrate on average daily turnovers of CNY forwards, FX swaps, currency swaps and FX options in major CNY

Table 10.6: Daily Turnovers of CNY Foreign Exchange Derivatives in Major Offshore CNY Centers (2010–2021) (Unit: USD billion, %)

Time/ Currency	United Kingdom	Hong Kong	Singapore	New York	Tokyo	Sum
Apr-10	2.23	7.35	4.07		0.05	13.70
Oct-10	1.43	11.63	6.45		0.17	19.69
Apr-11	2.28	15.93	8.84		0.29	27.34
Oct-11	3.66	20.21	11.23		0.28	35.38
Apr-12	5.08	24.49	13.61		0.17	43.35
Oct-12	4.94	28.79	16.00		0.07	49.80
Apr-13	6.47	33.07	21.12		0.07	60.73
Oct-13	10.13	34.72	23.38		0.07	68.29
Apr-14	19.89	36.35	25.64		0.28	82.16
Oct-14	14.40	38.00	27.89		0.16	80.45
Apr-15	21.82	39.64	30.14		0.42	92.01
Oct-15	24.41	41.28	32.39		1.03	99.11
Apr-16	16.31	42.93	34.65	5.66	0.48	100.03
Oct-16	17.28	46.56	29.48	5.19	1.12	99.62
Apr-17	20.73	50.21	23.09	4.25	0.83	99.11
Oct-17	16.89	53.84	18.88	3.95	1.64	95.20
Apr-18	30.73	70.51	18.52	3.28	1.26	124.30
Oct-18	42.29	73.98	32.17	5.37	0.96	154.77
Apr-19	34.86	87.93	21.24	5.59	1.31	150.92
Oct-19	24.87	78.38	23.00	4.80	1.82	132.87
Apr-20	32.68	75.42	21.31	4.45	1.57	135.44
Oct-20	10.14	93.77	23.57	6.15	1.88	135.50
Apr-21	41.75	105.41	24.37	6.44	2.13	180.10
2010	2.23	7.35	4.07		0.05	13.70
2011	2.28	15.93	8.84		0.29	27.34
2012	5.08	24.49	13.61		0.17	43.35
2013	6.47	33.07	21.12		0.07	60.73
2014	19.89	36.35	25.64		0.28	82.16
2015	21.82	39.64	30.14		0.42	92.01
2016	16.31	42.93	34.65	5.66	0.48	100.03

(*Continued*)

Table 10.6: (*Continued*)

Time/ Currency	United Kingdom	Hong Kong	Singapore	New York	Tokyo	Sum
2017	20.73	50.21	23.09	4.25	0.83	99.11
2018	30.73	70.51	18.52	3.28	1.26	124.30
2019	34.86	87.93	21.24	5.59	1.31	150.92
2020	32.68	75.42	21.31	4.45	1.57	135.44
2021	41.75	105.41	24.37	6.44	2.13	180.10
2010–2016 CAGR	39.30	34.20	42.89		45.78	39.28
2016–2021 CAGR	20.68	19.68	−6.80	2.62	34.72	12.48

Source: Data in United Kingdom are from the website of the London Foreign Exchange Joint Standing Committee (FXJSC), www.bankofengland.co.uk; data in Hong Kong are from the website of Hong Kong Monetary Authority (HKMA), www.hkma.gov.hk and the website of Hong Kong Treasury Market Association (HKTMA), www.tma.org.hk; data in Singapore are from the website of Singapore Monetary Authority, www.mas.gov.sg; data in the United States are from the website of New York Fed, www.newforkfed.org; data in Japan are from the website of Tokyo Foreign Exchange Market Committee, www.fxcmtky.com.

offshore centers. Table 10.6 gives the average daily turnovers of CNY derivatives in major offshore CNY centers from April 2010 to April 2021.

Table 10.6 shows that the daily average turnover of CNY foreign exchange derivatives in Hong Kong has remained the highest of all five major CNY offshore centers with the share of sum growing from 53.6% in April 2010 to 58.5% in April 2021.

10.8 Average Daily Turnover of Offshore CNY Foreign Exchange Market

With average daily turnovers of CNY foreign exchange spot trading in major offshore CNY centers in Table 10.5 and corresponding average daily turnovers of CNY foreign exchange derivatives in Table 10.6, we can easily find average daily turnovers of CNY foreign exchange trading in major offshore CNY centers in Table 10.7.

Table 10.7: Average Daily Turnovers of CNY Foreign Exchange Trading in Major Offshore CNY Centers (2010–2021) (Unit: USD billion, %)

Time/ Currency	United Kingdom	Hong Kong	Singapore	United States	Tokyo	Sum
Apr-10	2.84	9.34	5.96		0.08	18.22
Oct-10	2.24	14.82	8.48		0.20	25.74
Apr-11	3.29	20.31	11.01		0.32	34.93
Oct-11	5.18	25.79	13.54		0.28	44.79
Apr-12	6.38	31.27	16.07		0.23	53.95
Oct-12	6.68	36.76	18.60		0.35	62.39
Apr-13	9.82	42.24	23.86		0.41	76.33
Oct-13	13.81	45.04	26.98		0.46	86.28
Apr-14	29.29	47.83	30.09		0.81	108.02
Oct-14	26.55	50.63	33.20		0.99	111.37
Apr-15	35.90	53.42	36.31		1.28	126.91
Oct-15	38.85	56.22	39.42		1.98	136.47
Apr-16	34.86	59.02	42.54	7.08	1.53	145.03
Oct-16	36.68	62.98	37.63	7.19	2.97	147.44
Apr-17	34.34	66.95	32.72	5.68	1.88	141.57
Oct-17	45.13	70.91	27.82	6.71	3.12	153.69
Apr-18	62.22	87.90	27.35	7.02	3.39	187.88
Oct-18	72.87	91.70	41.31	9.79	2.79	218.46
Apr-19	70.30	106.80	30.68	11.10	3.19	222.07
Oct-19	50.63	91.10	29.80	8.54	4.06	184.13
Apr-20	54.18	92.60	31.88	8.23	3.08	189.97
Oct-20	47.32	113.80	32.50	13.95	5.00	212.57
Apr-21	75.91	129.00	33.14	11.91	3.72	253.68
2010	2.84	9.34	5.96		0.08	18.22
2011	3.29	20.31	11.01		0.32	34.93
2012	6.38	31.27	16.07		0.23	53.95
2013	9.82	42.24	23.86		0.41	76.33
2014	29.29	47.83	30.09		0.81	108.02
2015	35.90	53.42	36.31		1.28	126.91
2016	34.86	59.02	42.54	7.08	1.53	145.03

(*Continued*)

Table 10.7: (*Continued*)

Time/ Currency	United Kingdom	Hong Kong	Singapore	United States	Tokyo	Sum
2017	34.34	66.95	32.72	5.68	1.88	141.57
2018	62.22	87.90	27.35	7.02	3.39	187.88
2019	70.30	106.80	30.68	11.10	3.19	222.07
2020	54.18	92.60	31.88	8.23	3.08	189.97
2021	75.91	129.00	33.14	11.91	3.72	253.68
2010–2016 CAGR	51.86	35.97	38.76		63.53	41.30
2016–2021 CAGR	16.84	16.93	−4.87	10.96	19.45	11.83

Source: Add the spot turnovers in Table 10.5 and turnovers of derivatives in Table 10.6.

10.8.1 *Average daily RMB foreign exchange turnover in Hong Kong*

Table 10.7 shows that Hong Kong has been the earliest and the most significant offshore CNY center for CNY settlement and trading even though Hong Kong has lost the top spot trading position since April 2015, it has maintained the most active CNY FX exchange trading with more than 50% of total turnover of all five major centers.

10.8.2 *Average CNY foreign exchange daily turnover in London*

Table 10.7 shows United Kingdom has replaced Singapore as the second largest CNY foreign exchange trading since April 2017. Share of CNY foreign exchange trading in United Kingdom of five major offshore CNY centers 29.9% almost doubled the share of 15.6% in 2010, indicating steady growth of CNY foreign exchange trading in United Kingdom.

10.8.3 *Average CNY foreign exchange daily turnover in Singapore*

Singapore has maintained Asia's largest foreign exchange center since 2013, as well as the third largest offshore CNY trading center after Hong

Kong and London. With the steady growth of Chinese trade with ASEAN and the third CNY offshore deposit center, Singapore has high potentiality to further grow in CNY foreign exchange trading in years to come.

10.9 Problems of Offshore CNY Foreign Exchange Trading Compared with Onshore Trading

With daily average turnovers of top five offshore CNY centers given in Table 10.7 and corresponding daily average CNY turnovers in Mainland China, we can find serious problems of global daily average turnovers of CNY released by the Bank for International Settlements (BIS). Table 10.8 gives average daily turnovers of CNY in Mainland China, CNY average daily turnovers in five major offshore CNY centers, global total average daily turnovers of CNY from April 2010 to April 2019.

10.9.1 *Offshore CNY foreign exchange turnovers compared to onshore*

Table 10.8 shows that the total average daily CNY foreign exchange turnover in Hong Kong, Singapore, London, and Japan was $18.22 billion in April 2010, about two-thirds of the average daily turnover of CNY in Mainland China $27.29 billion during the same time. However, total average daily CNY foreign exchange turnover increased with cumulated average annual growth rate (CAGR) of 61.20% from 2010 to 2013 to $76.33 billion, almost three times the corresponding CAGR of 21.41% in Mainland China at the same time, exceeding the onshore average daily turnover of $48.84 for the first time in April 2013. With CAGR of 23.86% from April 2013 to April 2016 in five major offshore CNY centers, higher than the corresponding CAGR of 15.27% during the same time, the total average daily turnover in five major offshore centers reached $145.03 billion in April 2016, 93.89% higher than the corresponding onshore average daily CNY turnover of $74.80 during the same time.

As CAGR of 11.83% from April 2016 to April 2021 in five major offshore CNY centers is lower than the corresponding CAGR of 13.20% during the same time, the total average daily turnover in five major offshore centers increased to $253.68 billion in April 2021, 82.42% higher than the corresponding onshore average daily CNY turnover of $139.06 during the same time.

Table 10.8: Average Daily Turnovers of Major Offshore CNY Centers Compared to Onshore Average Daily Turnovers (2010–2021) (Unit: USD billion)

CNY Centers/Year	2010	2013	2016	2017	2018	2019	2020	2021
Mainland China	27.29	48.84	74.80	88.81	110.93	134.65	109.63	139.06
Hong Kong SAR	9.34	42.24	59.02	66.95	87.90	106.80	92.60	129.00
Singapore	5.96	23.86	42.54	32.72	27.35	30.68	31.88	33.14
United Kingdom	2.84	9.82	34.86	34.34	62.22	70.30	54.18	75.91
USA	0.00	0.00	7.08	5.68	7.02	11.10	8.23	11.91
Japan	0.08	0.41	1.53	1.88	3.39	3.19	3.08	3.72
Sum of top five offshore centers	18.22	76.33	145.03	141.57	187.88	222.07	189.97	253.68
Offshore total (BIS)	6.97	71.16	127.22			50.38		
Global total (BIS)	34.26	120.00	202.02			285.03		
Other offshore than top five offshore	−11.25	−5.17	−17.81			−71.69		
Onshore and sum of five top offshore centers	45.51	125.17	219.83			356.72		
Mainland China/ Sum of Five Major Centers	1.50	0.64	0.52			0.61		

Source: Data for CNY daily average turnovers are calculated using data released by the State Administration of Foreign Exchange (SAFE) of China (www.safe.gove.cn); data of top five offshore CNY centers are from Table 10.7; data of global total CNY are from the BIS triennial survey for 2010, 2013, 2016, and 2019.

10.9.2 *Problems in offshore CNY FX turnover with BIS data*

The difference between global average daily CNY turnover was $33.26 billion in April 2010 as released by the BIS and the average daily CNY turnover was $27.29 billion in Mainland China during the same time; $6.97 billion should be the total average daily turnover of all offshore CNY centers. However, this total offshore CNY daily average turnover of $6.97 billion was $11.25 billion lower than the corresponding total average daily CNY turnover of $18.22 of five major offshore CNY centers, indicating a serious problem with the BIS data. Similar calculations show that the total average daily turnover of other offshore CNY centers was \$−5.17 billion, \$−17.81, and \$–71.69 in April 2013, April 2016, and April 2019, respectively, indicating ongoing problems with global CNY average daily turnovers released by the BIS.

10.10 Distribution of Offshore CNY Foreign Exchange Turnovers in Major Offshore CNY Centers

We introduced more than 20 offshore CNY centers in Chapter 9. We will briefly introduce the distribution of CNY foreign exchange turnovers in major CNY centers.

10.10.1 *Global distribution of offshore CNY foreign exchange turnovers from 2013 to 2019*

Table 10.9 gives the global distribution of CNY FX turnovers in 27 countries and regions worldwide released by the BIS from April 2013 to April 2019.

Comparing CNY daily turnovers in Tables 10.8 and 10.9, we can find serious problems. First, differences of CNY average daily turnovers in Tables 10.8 and 10.9 in Mainland China and five major offshore CNY centers in Table 10.9 can be found easily, the results are given in Table 10.10.

Despite the average daily turnovers in Table 10.9 not directly comparable to data in Table 10.8 because of survey methods, the huge differences in Mainland China and United States are obviously not errors but mistakes in the statistics.

10.10.2 *Distribution of offshore CNY foreign exchange turnovers in 2019*

Table 10.9 shows that although the share of Hong Kong's CNY FX turnover dropped slightly from 30.21% in 2016 to 29.87% in 2019, it still led the pack; the United Kingdom surpassed Singapore and became the second largest offshore CNY trading center in 2019; Singapore fell to the third place; the United States became the fourth largest offshore CNY trading center in 2016 and 2019 (Table 10.8). Switzerland, Taiwan

Table 10.9: Distribution of Average Daily CNY Foreign Exchange Turnover in 27 Countries and Regions (Unit: USD billion)

Time/ Change	13-Apr		16-Apr		19-Apr			
Countries/ Regions	**Turnover**	**Share (%)**	**Turnover**	**Share (%)**	**Turnover**	**Share (%)**	**Change**	**CAGR (%)**
Hong Kong China	49.47	33.52	77.09	30.21	107.62	29.78	58.15	13.83
Mainland China	33.52	22.71	55.35	21.69	101.23	28.01	67.71	20.23
Singapore	23.86	16.17	42.53	16.67	42.57	11.78	18.71	10.13
UK	24.28	16.45	39.15	15.34	56.67	15.68	32.39	15.17
US	8.62	5.84	24.24	9.50	29.86	8.26	21.24	23.01
Taiwan China	2.57	1.74	3.99	1.56	3.65	1.01	1.08	6.02
Japan	0.68	0.46	2.82	1.10	3.22	0.89	2.54	29.59
South Korea	0.20	0.13	2.64	1.03	3.12	0.86	2.92	58.07
Australia	0.92	0.63	2.16	0.85	2.22	0.62	1.30	15.81
Germany	0.49	0.33	1.58	0.62	0.81	0.23	0.32	8.74
France	1.19	0.81	1.04	0.41	1.93	0.53	0.74	8.39
Switzerland	0.29	0.19	0.68	0.26	4.44	1.23	4.15	57.58
Canada	0.04	0.03	0.61	0.24	0.98	0.27	0.94	70.42
Malaysia	0.15	0.10	0.23	0.09	0.24	0.07	0.09	8.15

Netherlands	0.39	0.27	0.16	0.06	1.20	0.33	0.81	20.60
Luxembourg	0.37	0.25	0.13	0.05	0.19	0.05	−0.18	−10.51
Russia	0.02	0.01	0.12	0.05	0.23	0.06	0.21	50.24
Indonesia	0.00	0.00	0.11	0.04	0.10	0.03	0.10	−3.13
Brazil	0.01	0.01	0.09	0.03	0.08	0.02	0.07	41.42
Thailand	0.16	0.11	0.08	0.03	0.18	0.05	0.02	1.98
Italy	0.01	0.00	0.08	0.03	0.16	0.04	0.15	58.74
Sweden	0.01	0.01	0.08	0.03	0.01	0.00	0.00	1.17
Spain	0.10	0.07	0.07	0.03	0.08	0.02	−0.02	−3.65
Belgium	0.13	0.09	0.03	0.01	0.05	0.01	−0.08	−14.72
Philippines	0.00	0.00	0.02	0.01	0.04	0.01	0.04	25.99
India	0.00	0.00	0.02	0.01	0.04	0.01	0.04	25.99
South Africa	0.00	0.00	0.02	0.01	0.10	0.03	0.10	71.00
Others	0.08	0.05	0.06	0.02	0.37	0.10	0.29	29.08
Total	147.57	100.00	255.19	100.00	361.39	100.00	213.82	16.10

(Continued)

Table 10.9: (*Continued*)

Time/ Change	13-Apr		16-Apr		19-Apr			
Countries/ Regions	**Turnover**	**Share (%)**	**Turnover**	**Share (%)**	**Turnover**	**Share (%)**	**Change**	**CAGR (%)**
Five major offshore CNY centers	**106.91**	**72.44**	**185.83**	**72.82**	**239.94**	**66.39**	**133.03**	**14.42**
Offshore total other than major five centers	7.14	4.84	14.01	5.49	20.22	5.60	13.08	18.95

Source: The average daily "net-gross" turnover data of the global interbank foreign exchange market by country and currency for April 2013, April 2016, and April 2019 by the BIS; "total" data refer to the average daily "net-net" turnover amount data of the global foreign exchange market by country and currency for April 2013, April 2016, and April 2019 by BIS.

Table 10.10: Differences of CNY Average Daily Turnovers of Major CNY Centers from April 2013 to April 2019 (Unit: USD billion)

Differences	Differences in Value			Differences in Percentages		
CNY Centers	Apr-13	Apr-16	Apr-19	Apr-13	Apr-16	Apr-19
Mainland China	−15.32	−19.45	−33.42	−45.70	−35.14	−33.01
Hong Kong SAR	7.23	18.07	0.82	14.61	23.44	0.76
Singapore	0.00	0.00	11.89	−0.01	−0.01	27.94
United Kingdom	14.46	4.29	−13.63	59.55	10.95	−24.05
USA	8.62	17.16	18.76	100.00	70.79	62.83
Japan	0.28	1.29	0.03	40.44	45.74	0.93
Sum	15.26	21.35	−15.55	10.87	8.85	−4.56

Source: Tables 10.8 and 10.9.

China, Japan, and South Korea were ranked fifth to eighth in offshore CNY trading in 2019; Australia, France, the Netherlands, Canada, and Germany were ranked from ninth to 12th in offshore CNY trading centers in 2019. Average daily turnover of CNY foreign exchange in other countries and regions is relatively small, less than $1 billion.

10.10.3 *Significant changes of offshore CNY foreign exchange transactions from 2013 to 2019*

Table 10.9 indicates that CAGRs of Canada, South Korea, and Switzerland reached 68.5%, 58.2%, and 58.0%, increasing the ranking of Canada, South Korea, and Switzerland from 18th, 13th, and 12th in 2013 to 12th, 8th, and 5th in 2019, respectively; the average daily growth rate of CNY foreign exchange daily average transactions of Japan, the United States, the Netherlands, and Australia reached a rapid growth rate of 29.7%, 23.0%, 20.4%, and 15.8%, respectively. The 6-year average annual growth rates of the three major offshore CNY centers, Hong Kong, UK, and Singapore were 13.8%, 15.2%, and 10.1%, which were all lower than the global average annual growth rate of 6.7% over the same period. This indicates the high base and a natural trend of downward growth rate of the three centers. In addition to the significant growth of CNY foreign exchange transactions in most of the countries and regions mentioned above, the RMB foreign exchange markets of Sweden, Belgium, Luxembourg, and Spain have declined to various degrees, with an average annual decline of 31.2%, 14.3%, 10.8%, and 4.6%.

10.10.4 *Problems with the data of the BIS*

Average daily turnovers of domestic CNY foreign exchanges given in Table 10.9 are, respectively, $15.32 billion, $19.45 billion, and $33.42 billion lower than the figures calculated using State Administration of Foreign Exchange (SAFE)'s data (Mainland China from Table 10.9) in April 2013, April 2016 and April 2019; the average difference was over 30%, and thus cannot be ignored. The total daily average turnover of global RMB foreign exchange in April 2013, April 2016, and April 2019 was $28.006 billion, $53.129 billion, and $76.285 billion higher than the combined figure given in Table 4.1. The apparent deviation will cause misjudgment on not only the development of different offshore CNY centers but also on the overall progress of CNY internationalization compared to other major currencies in recent years.

10.11 Potential Problems with FX Data Released by BIS

The only data of global foreign exchange turnovers are released by BIS triennially. However, the BIS global FX data may be problematic and related problems may affect internationalization of all currencies involved. We try to analyze such problems in this section.

10.11.1 *Data of BIS*

Observing data in Table 10.8, in April 2010, when Hong Kong's offshore RMB market was yet to start, the average daily turnover of RMB FX trade in Hong Kong, Singapore, and London had reached $10.91 billion, $7.85 billion, and $6.8 billion; and plus the domestic turnover as of

$27.29 billion during the same period, and that of Japan as of $110 million (see Table 10.8), the average daily turnover was 25% higher than the calculation using data released by BIS as $42.36 billion. However, Hong Kong only signed the new Hong Kong RMB clearing agreement in July 2010, which may indicate a limited average daily turnover in the RMB foreign exchange market in Hong Kong in April 2010, and a relatively smaller amount in London market. Under such background, the $6.8 billion average daily turnover of RMB FX trade in London seemed like an unconvincing data.

10.11.2 *A reasonable estimation of RMB foreign exchange transactions for BIS in April 2013*

Since many offshore RMB centers hope to improve their position in the RMB market, this goal could be achieved by exaggerating the RMB market transaction data. Among the three major functions of international currency, payment function, pricing function, and reserve function, the RMB has made the most remarkable progress in cross-border settlement payment in recent years, while improvement in the pricing function and reserve function has been relatively slow. The corresponding data in Figure 3.1 show that the RMB cross-border payment accounted for only 0.69% in April 2013, ranking only 13th in the world. Therefore, in April 2013 RMB internationalization, the overall ranking measured by FX proportion will not be as high as the ninth position given in Table 4.1, and the overall ranking cannot be higher than the cross-border payment ranking by four places.

According to Table 4.1, the RMB turnover accounted for 4% globally in April 2016, ranking the eighth in the world, lower than RMB's cross-border payment ranking in the sixth place by two places; in April 2013, the development of offshore RMB market was far less than that in 2016, and in April 2013 the RMB global cross-border payment ranked 13th, so in April 2013 the RMB foreign exchange market turnover should be at most 15th, and the average daily turnover during the corresponding period should be between that of 15th, TRY amounting to $70.66 billion and 14th, SGD amounting to $74.74 billion, accounting for 59.10–62.51% of the global RMB exchange daily turnover of $119.56 billion published by the BIS for April 2013, indicating that the overestimation of the RMB foreign exchange average daily turnover in April 2013 by BIS should be between 37.49% and 40.90%.

10.11.3 *Problems with data on CNY foreign exchange turnover for April 2016 and April 2019 by the BIS*

Table 4.1 shows that the average daily turnover of RMB foreign exchange trade in April 2016 and April 2019 announced by the BIS was $202.02 billion and $284.19 billion, accounting for 4.0% and 4.3% of the world's total, ranking 8th, and these were two and three places lower than RMB cross-border payment's ranking with the highest degree of RMB internationalization in the same period as shown in Table 3.1, which was sixth in April 2016 and fifth in April 2019. It shows that the average daily transaction value of domestic and offshore RMB and foreign exchange trade in April 2016 released by the BIS is reasonable, while the data in April 2019 were with much deviation. The main reason was that the BIS took low statistics on the amount of RMB and foreign exchange transactions for some regions. A detailed analysis will be given in Chapter 12. After adjustment, the actual ranking of the RMB in 2019 should be higher than the Canadian dollar, ranking sixth.

10.12 Changes of RMB Ranking in Major Offshore Centers in Recent Years

10.12.1 *Hong Kong*

According to data from April 2010 to April 2013 released by Hong Kong Monetary Authority (HKMA) and Hong Kong Treasury Market Association (HKTMA) the average daily turnover of RMB in the Hong Kong foreign exchange market rose from $10.8 billion, ranking seventh to $49.1 billion, ranking third; in April 2016, it grew to $76.7 billion, ranking third, only after the USD and HKD; in April 2017, it dropped slightly to $75.7 billion. The amount accounted for 16.8%, which was lower than the USD, Japanese yen, and HKD, which accounted for 79.1%, 21.5%, and 17.0%, respectively. The ranking dropped accordingly to fourth place after the USD, Japanese yen and HKD, becoming the second currency after the USD, but with huge gap compared to the USD share of 95.7%; in April and October 2019, CNY accounted for 16.9%, exceeding the Japanese yen's share of 15.8%, but was lower than the HKD's share of 23%, returning to the third place after the USD and the HKD; in April 2020, CNY's share reached 17.7%, exceeding the HKD's share of 17.5% and the Japanese yen's share of 15.8% again, returning to the place as the second largest currency after the USD, but there was still a considerable gap with the US dollar's share of 95.2% during the same period.

Data released by HHTMA show that CNY has remained the second currency in Hong Kong from April 2020 to April 2021. The gap between USD and CNY in Hong Kong FX market has also narrowed (USD share in Hong Kong FX market in April 2020 was 95.4%, 77.7% higher than the corresponding CNY share 17.7% during the same time, yet the difference narrowed to 74.6% in April 2021). As China's economy and trade continue to grow steadily in coming years, CNY will remain the second largest currency after the USD for many years to come, and the gap with the USD will gradually narrow down.

10.12.2 *Singapore*

According to the Singapore Monetary Authority's announcement on major currencies in Singapore's foreign exchange for April 2013 and April 2016, the RMB's average daily turnover data in 2013 ranked seventh after USD, Japanese yen, Euro, Australian dollar, British pound, and Singapore dollar, and raised to sixth place in April 2016 after the USD, Japanese yen, Euro, Australian dollar, and British pound. From 2013 to 2016, the cumulative increase of the average daily turnover of Singapore's CNY foreign exchange trade was 78%, surpassing the corresponding growth of all other currencies, indicating active trade of CNY in Singapore. During the 9 months from October 2017 to June 2018, the CNY ranked sixth in Singapore's foreign exchange market for 3 months and seventh for 5 months, and ranked fifth and seventh July and September, and ranked sixth by average for 6 months; from January 2019 to December 2019, the RMB ranked the sixth for 7 months, and ranked the fifth and seventh in January and February, respectively, and eighth for the rest of the 2 months, and ranked highest at fourth position (after USD, Euro and Japanese yen) for August. The 12-month average ranking was No. 6. During the 6 months from January to June 2020, RMB ranked sixth and seventh for 4 months and 2 months, respectively, and the 6-month average ranking was sixth position, and the gap between RMB's monthly average proportion with Australian dollar's average monthly proportion shrank to 1.70% from previous 3.25% during July 2019 to December 2019, but there was still a significant gap with Singaporean dollar's average monthly proportion (fourth place) (calculated by the monthly foreign exchange market data published by the Monetary Authority of Singapore since October 2017). As the trade between China and ASEAN continues to proliferate, CNY is expected to surpass Australian dollar in 2021 and become the fifth most largely traded currency in the Singapore market.

10.12.3 *London*

Table 10.8 shows that since October 2017, the average daily turnover of CNY in London has exceeded that of Singapore, becoming the second largest offshore CNY trading center. From April 2010 to April 2013, the ranking of average daily transaction value of RMB foreign exchange in London increased from 18th to 16th. It rose to 10th in April 2016 and fell to the 11th in April 2017, returned to eighth in October 2017 and April 2018, maintained eighth in April 2019; dropped to ninth place in October 2019, and back to eighth position in April 2020. CNY has maintained the eighth position in London most of the time from April 2017 to April 2021. The ranking was slightly lower to CNY's global ranking. With the continuous improvement of China's economic and trade status, especially the continuous improvement of China's technological ability, the status of the CNY in London, the world's largest foreign exchange trading center, will also continue to improve.

10.12.4 *Japan*

According to data released by the Tokyo Foreign Exchange Market Committee from April 2010 to April 2013, the ranking of CNY average daily transaction value in Japan's foreign exchange market increased from 13th to 12th; in April 2016, it was further increased to 10th; in April 2017 and April 2018, it dropped slightly and maintained at 11th; in April 2019, it dropped slightly to 12th place, and in April 2020 rose to 10th, and eighth and ninth in October 2020 and April 2021, respectively, showing a stable ranking growth of the CNY in Japan's foreign exchange market in recent years.

10.12.5 *USA*

According to data released by the Federal Reserve Bank of New York, the average daily turnover of RMB in New York foreign exchange market ranked 15th; in April 2017 and April 2018, it fell back to 17th, and in October 2018, it rose to 14th; it has remained 13th in the United States from April 2019 to April 2021, indicating that the CNYs ranking in the US foreign exchange market continues to rise.

The data of September to October of 2020 given in Table 9.7 show that the proportion of CNY payments in the US surpassed that of in ROK, indicating active RMB trading in US markets recently. CNY is expected to surpass Norwegian kroner, Swedish krona, and Brazilian real around 2021, and become the 10th largest trading currency in the US foreign exchange market.

10.12.6 *Conclusion on CNY rankings in offshore markets*

Overall, CNY has ranked as high as second in Hong Kong only after the USD in recent years, which is much higher than the CNY's ranking as seventh in the global foreign exchange market; CNYs ranking in Singapore as the sixth foreign currency is slightly higher than its ranking as seventh in the international foreign exchange market; CNY's ranking in London market as eighth is similar to its ranking as seventh in the global foreign exchange market; CNY's ranking in Japan's market as the 10th is slightly lower than its ranking as seventh in the international foreign exchange market; the ranking of CNY in the United States as 13th is significantly lower than its ranking as seventh in the global foreign exchange market, indicating that the CNY ranks the highest in East Asia, second in Europe, and lowest in the Americas, which is dominated by the United States. The average rankings were in line with the more accurate RMB internationalization ranking as calculated based on the average daily turnover of RMB transactions in major global RMB centers since 2019 as given in Chapter 12.

10.13 Mutual Influences between Domestic and Offshore CNY Foreign Exchange Rates and Forwards Exchange Rates

Compared with changes of domestic and offshore RMB Forwards exchange rates in Chapters 4 and 13, it can be found that it is illiquid in domestic buy/sell RMB Forwards, and the marketization of RMB exchange rate and interest rate needed to be improved. Around 1 year after 2002 offshore RMB appreciation pressure was generated, the pressure spread through the market of RMB Forwards buy/sell transactions to China. Guangping (Peter G.)

Zhang (2016) conducted an empirical study on domestic and offshore RMB FX rates and Forwards exchange rates in the recent 10 years. The result showed that before the establishment of offshore RMB FX market in 2010, offshore RMB non-deliverable exchange rates were always the main factor affecting domestic RMB FX Forwards rates. From 2010 to 2013, offshore RMB deliverable market was still in the early stage with relatively low liquidity. Offshore RMB non-deliverable Forwards still played an essential role in the pricing of the offshore RMB FX market. Since 2013, however, as offshore non-deliverable forwards market was replaced with offshore deliverable Forwards market which turned to be the mainstream of RMB FX market, offshore deliverable Forwards had better pricing function and thus it became the main pricing tool of offshore RMB FX Forwards. Interested readers may refer to Guangping (Peter G.) Zhang (2016) for details not described here.

Since the liquidity of domestic RMB FX Forwards market is much lower than that of offshore RMB deliverable FX Forwards market, the pricing function of domestic RMB FX Forwards is still far below that of offshore market. Only when the liquidity of domestic market reaches or exceeds that of offshore market, the pricing of RMB FX market products can be turned back to China's domestic market.

10.14 The Impetus and Future Trend of Offshore RMB Center Development

With the development of offshore RMB market, developing more products and services besides offshore RMB deposits and loan will be the trend of offshore RMB market. In order to make offshore RMB intermediary services become more common, especially to make non-Chinese residents more willing to borrow and lend RMB, there is still a lot of work to be prepared. Market efficiency needs to be improved through innovation and participation from different markets. The depth and width of the offshore RMB market also need to continue to explore.

10.14.1 *Impetus behind development of offshore CNY center*

In recent years, multiple factors have fostered the rapid development of Offshore RMB business. To begin, the government made great efforts to promote it. Soon after the outbreak of international financial crisis in 2008, PBOC started to sign FX agreements with a total amount over RMB 3 trillion with more than 20 countries and regions such as South Korea, Hong Kong, and other Asia-Pacific regions, Europe, and South America, laying a certain foundation for the RMB business in these countries and regions. In the meantime, PBOC relaxed some of the restrictions of FX control, which also gave impetus to the Offshore RMB business. Second, the PBOC has also signed RMB clearing agreement with several national and regional monetary authorities and designated the clearing banks, getting ready for the smooth development of the RMB business in these regions. Third, PBOC and State Administration of Foreign Exchange launched the RMB Qualified Domestic Institutional Investor program, opening the channel of RMB flowing back to China. Fourth, PBOC, HKMA, and other countries established specific technically related infrastructure platforms and systems for the flow of RMB after years of efforts, providing necessary technical support for the offshore RMB business. Fifth, HKMA carried out a lot of promoting, recommending, advertising, and training such as RMB-related roadshows, which played a critical role in facilitating RMB business around the world. Sixth, the HKMA set up a technical platform and system for RMB flow with RMB centers all over the world to provide technical support for global RMB business. Seventh, Bank of China, Industrial and Commercial Bank of China, China Construction Bank and other large domestic banks seized the strategic chance and commercial opportunity of RMB internationalization and actively pushed the offshore RMB business, especially the clearing business of RMB, which played a positive role in developing RMB business successfully. Eighth, the expansion using offshore RMB business for domestic and offshore enterprises was also the basis for the increase of RMB-related business.

10.14.2 *Radiation from Hong Kong to other offshore RMB centers*

The proportion of Hong Kong RMB cross-border payments to the total RMB cross-border payments is still up to about 80%. Such proportions of all the other offshore RMB centers are not even close to Hong Kong. Hong Kong has much more RMB deposits than other offshore RMB centers. Hong Kong keeps it as a most active offshore RMB transaction center, and furthermore, the daily average FX volume kept being higher than that in domestic market from 2013 to 2016. Hong Kong offshore RMB accounts payables and receivables were 19.6 billion yuan and 10.9 billion yuan, respectively, in 2010 and they grew to 121.7 billion yuan and 121.4 billion yuan, respectively, in 2011. In 2013, the amounts were further increased to 166 billion yuan and 164.5 billion yuan. In 2014, they were up to 145.2 billion yuan and 193.3 billion yuan. In 2015, the numbers decreased to 105.7 billion yuan and 132.1 billion yuan, respectively, and in 2016, the payables dropped to 69 billion yuan and the receivable was down to 91.6 billion yuan. Though the amounts were back to 87.8 billion yuan and 132.8 billion yuan in 2017, they were still lower than those in 2015. All these show that the RMB payables and receivables in Hong Kong experienced a significant increase first and a noticeable decrease later around 2015. From 2017 to 2019, the payables and receivables further went down to 83.9 billion yuan and 98.2 billion yuan. In 2020, those statistics of offshore RMB in Hong Kong rebounded back to 102.6 billion yuan and 107.2 billion yuan, respectively, while they still did not reach the peak amounts in 2013.

10.14.3 *More typologies of offshore CNY products*

Under the process of relaxing restrictions on capital account, offshore RMB products will rapidly increase within a year or two. Cross-border capital flow channels will be significantly widened such as Shanghai–Hong Kong Stock Connect, Shenzhen–Hong Kong Stock Connect and Mainland–Hong Kong Mutual Recognition of Funds. Domestic capital market is to relate to offshore capital market under the premise of maintaining a certain degree of risk control to achieve a global orderly circulation of RMB and enable RMB to able to "Going Out" and "Bringing In". Offshore RMB capital market will have new models and products, and the market is going to have more typologies and be more active.

10.15 Development Needs of Offshore CNY Capital Market

Further development of offshore RMB market is based on its capital development. Dim Sum Bonds in Hong Kong have made great achievements and further development requires efforts from issuers and investors to broaden the channels. In addition, bond maturities and types need to be enriched to meet the financing demands of issuers and investment purposes of buyers. Periodical issuance of offshore RMB bonds by the Ministry of Finance will positively affect the construction of RMB interest rate curve (Yue, 2013).

The establishment of a joint venture exchange can also further develop the offshore RMB market. According to the agreement, the joint venture company will be named "China Europe International Exchange AG". Shanghai Stock Exchange, China Financial Futures Exchange and Deutsche Börse AG will hold 40%, 20%, and 40% of the share, respectively, in the new company. The joint venture company's main responsibility is to research, develop and trade RMB denominated securities and derivatives. The new company will be registered in Frankfurt, Germany, and it was formally established on November 11, 2015.

10.16 Conclusion

In recent years, there was rapid development in the offshore RMB market and that became the main strength to promote RMB internationalization. The rapid development of the RMB market in recent years, of course, is closely related to the continuous growth of domestic economic and trade, and financial opening. A series of measures aiming to relax regulations about RMB issued by HKMA also contributed a lot toward activating RMB market in Hong Kong. The gradual exit of RMB related regulatory restrictions makes supervision of RMB business close to that of other currencies. It provides more room and flexibility for banks in Hong Kong to conduct RMB business (Chan, 2013).

Exchange of RMB and the mature and liquid domestic financial markets are the foundation of the development of offshore RMB market. Domestic RMB FX businesses showed a growing trend in recent years as well, contributing its effort to RMB internationalization. It is estimated that growing offshore RMB FX business will lead to, and in turn to a great extent, developing domestic RMB FX market and capital market for the long term from now on. Then it is expected to thrive both internally and externally for RMB markets. In the end the healthy market will be formed by the interactivity of domestic and offshore markets, and they will further promote RMB internationalization.

Bibliography

Chan, Norman T. L., *Development of Offshore RMB Business in Hong Kong: Review and Outlook*, Hong Kong Monetary Authority, February 21, 2013, http://www.hkma.gov.hk.

Chan, Norman T. L., *Remarks by Norman T. L. Chan, Chief Executive of the Hong Kong Monetary Authority*, April 25, 2013.

Chan, Norman T. L., *Opening Remarks at the Second Hong Kong–Australia RMB Trade and Investment Dialogue*, Hong Kong Monetary Authority, May 22, 2014.

China/HK: The Allure of Dim Sum Bond, DBS Group Research, March 31, 2011, www.bsrvresearch.com.

CNH: Eclipsing the NDF Market, DBS Group Research, February 4, 2013, www.bsrvresearch.com.

CNH: Singapore and Taiwan Style, DBS Group Research, February 19, 2013, www.bsrvresearch.com.

CNH: Qianhai to Offer CNH Trust Products, DBS Group Research, May 16, 2013, www.bsrvresearch.com.

Hong Kong Monetary Authority, *Briefing to the Legislative Council, Panel on Financial Affairs*, May 5, 2014, www.hkma.gov.

Minikin, R. and K. Lau, *The Offshore RMB: The Rise of the Chinese Currency and Its Global Future*, Citic Publishing House, 2013.

Ministry of Economic Development, City of London, *London: The Center of RMB Business*, April 2012, www.cityoflondon.gov.uk/economic research.

Ministry of Economic Development, City of London, *The Data of London RMB Business January to June 2012*, January 2013, www.cityoflondon.gov.uk/economic research.

Ministry of Economic Development, City of London: *The Data of London RMB Business January to December 2012*, June 2013, www.cityoflondon.gov.uk/economic research.

Ministry of Economic Development, City of London, *The Data of London RMB Business January to June 2013*, January 2014, www.cityoflondon.gov.uk/economic research.

Ministry of Economic Development, City of London, *The Data of London RMB Business January to December 2013*, June 2014, www.cityoflondon.gov.uk/economic research.

Yue, Eddie, *Welcome Remarks at the Third Meeting of the Hong Kong–London RMB Forum*, Acting Chief Executive, Hong Kong Monetary Authority, September 26, 2013.

Zhang, Guangping (Peter G.), *RMB Derivative*, 4th Edition, Beijing, Financial Publishing House, 2016.

Chapter 11

Overseas Assets and Bank Internationalization of Major Currency Issuers

The international foreign exchange market is essentially an interbank market, and thus, banks play essential roles in currency internationalization. This chapter will first compare the sizes of cross-border assets of major currency issuers and sizes of cross-border holdings of the bank sectors of major currency issuers, and finally compare the international holdings of top multinational firms and the internationalization of banks of major currency issuers.

11.1 Distribution of Cross-Border Assets and Liabilities of Major Currency Issuers

Sizes of the cross-border assets and liabilities of major world currency issuers give us the underlying strengths of currency issuers as international financial centers and currency internationalization. There are different definitions of cross-border assets and corresponding liabilities. We follow the definition and data of cross-border positions of the Bank for International Settlements (BIS) or holdings of foreign institutions in residence of major currency issuers. Table 11.1 gives us the assets, liabilities, and net assets of major world currency issuers from 2007 to 2021.

Table 11.1: Distribution of Cross-Border Assets, Liabilities, and Net Assets of Major World Currency Issuers (2007–2020) (Unit: USD trillion, %)

Cross-Border Assets of Major Currency Issuers									
Currency Issuer/Year	**2007**	**2009**	**2011**	**2013**	**2015**	**2017**	**2019**	**2020**	**CAGR**
USA	5.59	5.01	5.43	4.92	4.74	4.99	5.28	6.13	0.7
Eurozone	11.57	10.68	9.03	8.38	7.26	7.77	8.14	9.48	(1.5)
Japan	0.66	0.68	0.90	1.00	1.18	1.33	1.47	1.75	7.8
United Kingdom	5.72	4.70	4.91	4.17	3.61	3.65	3.90	5.23	(0.7)
Australia	0.35	0.37	0.40	0.38	0.40	0.44	0.47	0.55	3.6
Canada	0.36	0.39	0.39	0.42	0.47	0.48	0.58	0.72	5.6
Switzerland	1.05	0.61	0.65	0.63	0.61	0.65	0.62	0.66	(3.5)
China	0.19	0.18	0.48	0.90	0.76	0.96	0.94	1.00	13.7
Others	7.42	6.89	7.62	7.67	8.11	8.96	9.64	10.19	2.5
World	32.91	29.52	29.80	28.48	27.12	29.22	31.05	35.71	0.6
Cross-Border Liabilities of Major Currency Issuers									
Currency Issuer/Year	**2007**	**2009**	**2011**	**2013**	**2015**	**2017**	**2019**	**2020**	**CAGR**
USA	4.16	4.31	4.45	3.84	3.34	3.54	3.71	4.41	0.4
Eurozone	7.86	6.93	6.85	6.74	5.78	6.22	6.82	8.10	0.2
Japan	0.76	0.56	0.76	0.76	0.77	0.84	0.86	0.93	1.6
United Kingdom	5.21	4.44	4.86	4.34	3.86	4.15	4.11	5.40	0.3
Australia	0.11	0.13	0.18	0.19	0.24	0.23	0.24	0.32	8.6
Canada	0.15	0.20	0.26	0.26	0.29	0.33	0.38	0.49	9.3
Switzerland	1.68	1.00	0.92	0.83	0.66	0.68	0.71	0.70	(6.5)
China	0.28	0.20	0.30	0.36	0.59	0.68	0.78	0.96	9.9
Others	8.85	7.67	7.79	8.11	9.16	9.75	9.86	10.37	1.2
World	29.07	25.45	26.38	25.43	24.69	26.41	27.48	31.68	0.7
Cross-Border Net Assets of Major Currency Issuers									
Currency Issuer/Year	**2007**	**2009**	**2011**	**2013**	**2015**	**2017**	**2019**	**2020**	**CAGR**
USA	1.42	0.71	0.97	1.08	1.40	1.45	1.57	1.72	1.5
Eurozone	3.70	3.75	2.18	1.64	1.48	1.55	1.32	1.38	(7.3)

Table 11.1: (Continued)

Cross-Border Net Assets of Major Currency Issuers									
Currency Issuer/Year	**2007**	**2009**	**2011**	**2013**	**2015**	**2017**	**2019**	**2020**	**CAGR**
Japan	−0.10	0.12	0.14	0.24	0.41	0.49	0.61	0.82	17.7
United Kingdom	0.51	0.26	0.05	−0.17	−0.26	−0.50	−0.21	−0.17	(192.0)
Australia	0.24	0.24	0.21	0.20	0.16	0.20	0.23	0.23	(0.3)
Canada	0.20	0.19	0.13	0.16	0.18	0.15	0.20	0.24	1.2
Switzerland	−0.62	−0.39	−0.27	−0.19	−0.05	−0.03	−0.09	−0.04	(19.8)
China	−0.09	−0.02	0.17	0.53	0.16	0.28	0.17	0.05	5.4
Others	−1.43	−0.79	−0.17	−0.44	−1.05	−0.79	−0.22	−0.18	14.6
World	3.84	4.07	3.42	3.05	2.43	2.81	3.58	4.04	0.4

Source: Cross-border positions by residence and counterparty, website of the BIS: www.bis.org.

11.1.1 *Changes of world cross-border assets, liabilities, and their implications*

Changes in world cross-border assets and liabilities reflect changes in globalization and currency internationalization. Table 11.1 shows that the cumulative average annual growth rates of the total world cross-border assets, liabilities, and net assets were merely 0.6%, 0.7%, and 0.4% from 2007 to 2020, respectively, implying that world cross-border businesses just returned to the pre-2008 world financial crisis level after 13 years.

11.1.2 *Sizes of cross-border assets and world financial centers*

Table 11.1 shows that Eurozone, United States, and United Kingdom were by far the top holders of cross-border assets from 2007 to 2020. As more than half of the cross-border assets in Eurozone are assets within 19 Eurozone countries, the actual Eurozone cross-border assets should be less than half of the cross-border assets shown in Table 11.1. The above estimation is based on the fact that intra-EU commodity exports and imports data released by the World Trade Organization (WTO) were less than 40% of the total EU commodity trade value from 2007 to 2020. Thus, the cross-border assets of Eurozone should be less than the cross-border assets of both United States and United Kingdom, and thus more consistent with the fact that non-Eurozone country has been among the top two world financial centers in the past two decades.

The biggest decrease of cross-border assets in Switzerland from 2007 to 2019 is consistent with the largest declines of ranking of Switzerland as an international foreign exchange trading center from third in 2007 to sixth in 2019. The magnitudes of cross-border assets in Japan, Singapore, Hong Kong, and Luxembourg are largely comparable to international rankings of these economies in international foreign exchange trading.

11.1.3 *Changes of cross-border assets and liabilities of major currency issuers*

Table 11.1 shows that cross-border assets in Switzerland, Eurozone, and United Kingdom decreased with compound average annual rates (CAGRs) of 3.5%, 1.5%, and 0.7% from 2007 to 2020, respectively, indicating the relative declines of these three regions as world foreign exchange centers. Increases of cross-border assets in China, Japan, Canada, and Australia with CAGRs greater than 3% from 2007 to 2020 indicate the relative increases of their international positions in the global foreign exchange market.

11.1.4 *Cross-border net assets and international financial centers*

Besides magnitudes of cross-border assets as representations of international financial centers or global foreign exchange centers, net assets are also good references for international financial centers or global foreign exchange centers. For example, Table 11.1 shows that the net cross-border assets of United Kingdom were negative from 2013 to 2020, consistent with the top global foreign exchange center in United Kingdom, and those of Switzerland were all negative from 2007 to 2020, consistent with the third to sixth positions of Switzerland in the global foreign exchange market. The negative net cross-border assets of Hong Kong, Singapore, Belgium are also consistent with their high positions in global foreign exchange markets.

11.2 Distribution of Cross-Border Banking Assets and Liabilities of Major Currency Issuers

Banks play important roles in global foreign exchange market. Magnitudes of the cross-border bank-sector assets and liabilities of major world currency issuers give us underlying support of bank-sector of currency issuers. Table 11.2 gives us the bank-sector assets, liabilities, and net assets of major world currency issuers from 2007 to 2020.

11.2.1 *Distribution of bank-sector cross-border assets and liabilities of major world currency issuers*

Table 11.2 shows that bank-sector cross-border assets holdings of world decreased by CAGR of 1.60% compared to corresponding CAGR of 0.60% of total cross-border assets of world, indicating decreased role of the world bank sector in globalization after the 2008 world financial crisis. It is noticeable that bank-sector cross-border assets decreased with CAGR of 1.24%, 3.23%, 3.99%, and 4.70% in the United States, Eurozone, United Kingdom, and Switzerland from 2007 to 2020, all higher than the corresponding CAGR of total cross-border assets of these regions for the same period. Bank-sector cross-border assets of China, Japan, Canada, and Australia increased with CAGR of 12.57%, 8.05, 4.85%, and 3.38% from 2007 to 2020.

Table 11.2 also shows that the bank-sector cross-border liabilities follow similar patterns as cross-border assets with United States, Eurozone, United Kingdom, and Switzerland are decreasing, and China, Japan, Canada, and Australia are increasing.

The ratio of total banking assets over total world assets dropped from more than 60% from 2007 to 2011 to 50–60% from 2012 to 2018, and fell to less than half in 2019, with a cumulative decrease of more than 10%. However, the cross-border assets of the global banking industry remain in the dominant position, indicating the importance of the global banking industry in the global financial market. In the meantime, the proportion of cross-border liabilities of the global banking industry in the global financial market has been higher than the assets proportion, and the cross-border equity (the difference between total assets and total liabilities) of the global banking industry was less than 1/3 on average, indicating that the efficiency of overseas investment and operation of the global banking industry

Table 11.2: Distribution of Bank-Sector Cross-Border Assets, Liabilities, and Net Assets of Major World Currency Issuers (2007–2020) (Unit: USD trillion, %)

Cross-Border Assets of Major Currency Issuers									
Currency Issuer/Year	**2007**	**2009**	**2011**	**2013**	**2015**	**2017**	**2019**	**2020**	**CAGR**
USA	2.60	2.62	2.90	2.44	2.15	2.02	2.01	2.21	−1.24
Eurozone	7.58	6.79	5.63	4.65	3.91	4.37	4.39	4.95	−3.23
Japan	0.39	0.50	0.60	0.71	0.80	0.90	0.95	1.07	8.05
United Kingdom	4.59	3.69	3.84	2.90	2.47	2.30	2.23	2.70	−3.99
Australia	0.21	0.24	0.25	0.25	0.27	0.27	0.29	0.32	3.38
Canada	0.24	0.26	0.25	0.28	0.30	0.28	0.37	0.45	4.85
Switzerland	0.86	0.44	0.47	0.46	0.46	0.48	0.44	0.46	−4.70
China	0.12	0.12	0.33	0.61	0.45	0.62	0.55	0.57	12.57
Others	4.37	4.05	4.54	4.11	3.88	4.21	4.19	4.27	−0.17
World	20.97	18.69	18.82	16.41	14.68	15.45	15.42	17.01	−1.60
Cross-Border Liabilities of Major Currency Issuers									
Currency Issuer/Year	**2007**	**2009**	**2011**	**2013**	**2015**	**2017**	**2019**	**2020**	**CAGR**
USA	2.27	2.51	2.68	2.01	1.88	1.69	1.80	2.00	−0.97
Eurozone	7.58	4.92	4.59	4.02	3.41	3.59	4.02	4.44	−4.03
Japan	0.55	0.40	0.56	0.59	0.55	0.61	0.59	0.62	0.92
United Kingdom	3.85	3.42	3.48	2.95	2.59	2.68	2.48	2.89	−2.18
Australia	0.06	0.08	0.12	0.12	0.18	0.17	0.18	0.22	10.40
Canada	0.10	0.13	0.18	0.16	0.19	0.21	0.27	0.34	9.97
Switzerland	1.37	0.77	0.70	0.61	0.48	0.47	0.51	0.45	−8.19
China	0.20	0.13	0.20	0.23	0.39	0.45	0.52	0.65	9.25
Others	4.03	4.92	4.93	4.28	4.27	4.47	4.26	4.44	0.76
World	20.01	17.29	17.44	14.98	13.95	14.34	14.64	16.05	−1.68
Cross-Border Net Assets of Major Currency Issuers									
Currency Issuer/Year	**2007**	**2009**	**2011**	**2013**	**2015**	**2017**	**2019**	**2020**	**CAGR**
USA	0.34	0.11	0.23	0.43	0.27	0.33	0.21	0.22	−3.34
Eurozone	7.58	1.87	1.04	0.63	0.49	0.78	0.37	0.51	−18.77

Table 11.2: (*Continued*)

	Cross-Border Assets of Major Currency Issuers								
Currency Issuer/Year	**2007**	**2009**	**2011**	**2013**	**2015**	**2017**	**2019**	**2020**	**CAGR**
Japan	−0.16	0.09	0.04	0.12	0.25	0.29	0.36	0.45	8.43
United Kingdom	0.74	0.27	0.36	−0.04	−0.12	−0.37	−0.25	−0.19	−10.09
Australia	0.15	0.16	0.12	0.13	0.08	0.10	0.12	0.10	−3.06
Canada	0.15	0.12	0.07	0.11	0.11	0.07	0.10	0.11	−1.99
Switzerland	−0.51	−0.33	−0.23	−0.15	−0.01	0.01	−0.07	0.01	27.09
China	−0.08	−0.01	0.13	0.37	0.06	0.17	0.03	−0.08	−0.21
Others	0.34	−0.88	−0.38	−0.17	−0.38	−0.26	−0.07	−0.17	−5.31
World	0.96	1.40	1.38	1.44	0.74	1.11	0.79	0.96	−0.03

Source: Cross-border positions by residence and counterparty, website of the BIS: www.bis.org.

indeed was lower than that of other industries. In addition, since 2015, the leverage (the ratio of total assets to total equity) of various industries in the world has been at a level slightly higher than 10, and the leverage of global banking industry is significantly higher than that of all industries.

11.2.2 *Bank-sector cross-border net assets of major currency issuers*

Table 11.2 shows that although bank-sector cross-border net assets of all major currency issuers decreased from 2007 to 2020, bank-sector cross-border net asset of Eurozone and United Kingdom decreased with CAGR of 18.77% and 10.09%, which is higher than decreasing CAGRs of other major currency issuers.

11.2.3 *Bank-sector cross-border assets, liabilities, and net assets compared to total assets, liabilities, and net assets of major currency issuers*

We cannot see the relative importance of bank-sectors directly from data in Tables 11.1 and 11.2. Table 11.3 gives the share of bank-sector cross-border assets, liabilities, and net assets of the corresponding total cross-border assets, liabilities, and net assets of major currency issuers.

Table 11.3: Distribution of Share of Bank-Sector Cross-Border Assets, Liabilities, and Net Assets of Total Cross-Border Assets, Liabilities, and Net Assets of Major World Currency Issuers (2007–2020)

Cross-Border Assets of Major Currency Issuers									
Currency Issuer/Year	**2007 (%)**	**2009 (%)**	**2011 (%)**	**2013 (%)**	**2015 (%)**	**2017 (%)**	**2019 (%)**	**2020 (%)**	**Change from 2007 to 2020 (%)**
USA	46.6	52.3	53.5	49.6	45.3	40.5	38.2	36.1	−10.5
Eurozone	65.5	63.5	62.3	55.5	53.9	56.2	53.9	52.2	−13.3
Japan	59.1	72.6	66.4	71.0	67.9	67.6	64.7	61.2	2.1
United Kingdom	80.3	78.5	78.2	69.6	68.5	63.1	57.1	51.7	−28.5
Australia	60.0	64.1	62.1	65.4	66.4	61.9	62.4	58.7	−1.4
Canada	68.6	65.1	65.3	65.6	63.9	58.0	63.3	62.4	−6.2
Switzerland	81.8	72.1	72.3	73.1	76.0	73.8	70.5	69.4	−12.4
China	64.2	66.9	69.8	67.5	59.4	64.6	58.6	56.3	−7.9
Others	58.9	58.8	59.7	53.6	47.9	47.0	43.5	42.0	−16.9
World	63.7	63.3	63.2	57.6	54.1	52.9	49.7	47.6	−16.1
Cross-Border Liabilities of Major Currency Issuers									
Currency Issuer/Year	**2007**	**2009**	**2011**	**2013**	**2015**	**2017**	**2019**	**2020**	**Change from 2007 to 2020**
USA	54.5	58.3	60.1	52.3	56.3	47.7	48.7	45.3	−9.2
Eurozone	96.3	70.9	67.0	59.6	59.1	57.7	58.9	54.8	−41.5
Japan	72.3	71.4	73.8	77.5	71.5	72.8	68.5	66.3	−6.0
United Kingdom	73.9	77.1	71.6	67.9	67.2	64.5	60.3	53.5	−20.3
Australia	57.2	60.7	67.1	66.6	76.8	72.3	72.7	70.6	13.4
Canada	64.3	64.9	70.4	61.7	65.5	64.2	70.1	69.8	5.5
Switzerland	81.8	77.3	75.7	73.7	72.9	69.2	71.8	64.7	−17.1
China	72.6	65.2	65.8	64.2	66.4	66.4	67.2	67.5	−5.2
Others	45.5	64.2	63.3	52.8	46.6	45.9	43.3	42.9	−2.7
World	68.8	67.9	66.1	58.9	56.5	54.3	53.3	50.7	−18.1

Table 11.3: *(Continued)*

Cross-Border Net Assets of Major Currency Issuers									
Currency Issuer/Year	**2007**	**2009**	**2011**	**2013**	**2015**	**2017**	**2019**	**2020**	**Change from 2007 to 2020**
USA	23.7	15.7	23.2	40.1	19.0	23.0	13.4	12.6	−11.1
Eurozone	204.6	49.8	47.5	38.6	33.4	50.1	28.0	36.9	−167.7
Japan	161.8	78.4	26.4	50.3	61.2	58.7	59.2	55.4	−106.3
United Kingdom	145.6	103.8	678.8	25.4	48.4	75.3	119.6	107.7	−37.9
Australia	61.3	66.1	57.9	64.2	50.7	49.8	51.2	42.3	−19.0
Canada	71.8	65.3	55.3	71.9	61.2	44.8	50.1	47.2	−24.6
Switzerland	81.7	85.6	84.0	75.9	30.9	-34.4	81.2	−23.7	−105.4
China	89.7	52.8	76.7	69.8	33.9	60.1	18.1	−179.2	−268.9
Others	−24.0	111.4	224.8	39.4	36.3	32.6	34.2	92.4	116.4
World	25.1	34.5	40.3	47.1	30.2	39.6	22.0	23.8	−1.3

Source: Calculated with data in Tables 11.1 and 11.2.

Table 11.3 shows that bank-sector cross-border assets as share of total cross-border assets of all major currency issuers declined with the only exception of Japan with slight increase of 2.1% from 2007 to 2020. Total bank-sector cross-border assets as a share of total cross-border assets of world declined to 16.1% from 2007 to 2020. Bank-sector cross-border liabilities as share of total cross-border assets of all major currency issuers declined with exceptions of Australia and Canada with increases of 13.4% and 5.5%, respectively, from 2007 to 2020. Total bank-sector cross-border liabilities as a share of total cross-border liabilities of world declined to 18.1% from 2007 to 2020, and total bank-sector cross-border net assets as share of total cross-border net assets of all major currency issuers declined from 2007 to 2020.

It is noticeable that bank-sector cross-border assets, liabilities, and net assets as share of total cross-border assets, liabilities, and net assets of the United States were the lowest of all major world currency issuers from 2007 to 2020, indicating the importance of non-bank-sector of the United States. It is a complicated question that why the world banking industry has declined in its roles in world globalization. The tremendous steady growth of world equity market, particularly the faster growth of US equity market compared to the banking industry might be one of the most vital answers as evidenced by the world securitization ratio (world year-end equity market capitalization/world GDP), which more than doubled from 56% in 2008 to 125.2% in 2020.

11.3 Currency Distribution of All Sectors Claims, Liabilities, and Net Claims

Corresponding to Table 11.1, the Bank of International Settlements periodically publishes all sectors claims and liabilities of world's top five currencies. Table 11.4 gives such data from 2007 to 2020.

Table 11.4 shows that all sectors' claim and liabilities of the world decreased with CAGR of 1.60% and 1.68%. However, all sectors' claim of other currencies and unallocated increased with CAGR of 9.50% and 2.71%, indicating that the dominance of top five world currencies has decreased, consistent with the decreases of the same top five world currencies in currency internationalization shown in Table 4.1.

Calculations using data in Table 11.4 show that share of all sectors' claim of major currencies is like currency share of average daily turnovers of major currencies. In order words, share of all sectors claim of each currency can be considered as "substitute" of currency internationalization because more claims in a currency mean more international trading and risk management related to the currency.

11.4 Distribution of Cross-Border Assets, Liabilities, and Net Assets by Countries and Bank Internationalization of Major Currency Issuers

11.4.1 *Distribution of cross-border assets, liabilities, and net assets by countries*

Table 11.5 gives the cross-border assets, liabilities, and net assets by countries from 2007 to 2021 released by the Bank of International Settlements. Table 11.5 shows that total world cross-border assets in 2020 just returned to the pre-crisis level in 2007. Of all eight major world currency issuers,

Table 11.4: All Sectors Claims, Liabilities, and Net Claims of Major International Currencies (2007–2020) (Unit: %)

All Sectors Claims of Major Currencies									
Year/ Currency	**2007**	**2010**	**2011**	**2013**	**2015**	**2016**	**2019**	**2020**	**Change from 2007 to 2020**
USD	8.23	8.37	8.62	7.37	7.25	7.37	7.33	7.53	−0.68
Euro	8.40	6.90	6.81	5.59	4.28	4.10	4.74	5.56	−3.12
Yen	0.99	0.96	0.96	0.69	0.56	0.62	0.63	0.73	−2.32
Pound sterling	1.81	1.02	0.81	0.81	0.74	0.61	0.64	0.75	−6.57
Swiss franc	0.37	0.32	0.36	0.40	0.32	0.27	0.35	0.32	−1.07
Other Currencies	0.26	0.28	0.30	0.46	0.57	0.56	0.64	0.83	9.50
Unallocated	0.91	0.94	0.94	1.09	0.96	0.93	1.08	1.29	2.71
World	20.97	18.79	18.82	16.41	14.69	14.46	15.42	17.01	−1.60
All Sectors Liabilities of Major Currencies									
Year/ Currency	**2007**	**2009**	**2011**	**2013**	**2015**	**2017**	**2019**	**2020**	**Change from 2007 to 2020**
USD	8.99	8.45	8.82	7.67	7.52	7.47	7.57	7.86	−1.03
Euro	7.11	5.94	5.70	4.56	3.56	3.53	4.08	4.69	−3.16
Yen	0.76	0.76	0.71	0.48	0.46	0.51	0.57	0.61	−1.76
Pound sterling	1.85	1.05	0.81	0.84	0.83	0.67	0.66	0.77	−6.53
Swiss franc	0.29	0.24	0.32	0.29	0.24	0.21	0.27	0.27	−0.34
Other Currencies	0.33	0.44	0.44	0.55	0.78	0.71	0.92	1.17	10.31
Unallocated	0.69	0.61	0.64	0.59	0.55	0.57	0.56	0.69	0.09
World	20.01	17.48	17.44	14.98	13.95	13.67	14.64	16.05	−1.68

(*Continued*)

Table 11.4: (*Continued*)

All Sectors Net Claims of Major Currencies									
Year/ Currency	**2007**	**2009**	**2011**	**2013**	**2015**	**2017**	**2019**	**2020**	**Change from 2007 to 2020**
USD	−0.76	−0.07	−0.19	−0.30	−0.27	−0.10	−0.24	−0.33	−6.22
Euro	1.29	0.96	1.11	1.03	0.72	0.57	0.66	0.88	−2.92
Yen	0.22	0.20	0.26	0.21	0.10	0.11	0.06	0.12	−4.61
Pound sterling	−0.03	−0.04	0.00	−0.03	−0.09	−0.07	−0.02	−0.02	−4.38
Swiss franc	0.08	0.09	0.04	0.11	0.08	0.06	0.07	0.04	−4.44
Other Currencies	−0.07	−0.16	−0.14	−0.09	−0.21	−0.15	−0.28	−0.33	12.78
Unallocated	0.23	0.33	0.30	0.50	0.41	0.36	0.52	0.60	7.77
World	0.96	1.31	1.38	1.44	0.74	0.79	0.79	0.96	−0.03

Source: Summary of locational statistics by currency, website of the Bank of International Settlements: www.bis.org.

only Eurozone and Switzerland experienced decreases of both cross-border assets and liabilities, and only China has growth in both cross-border assets and liabilities with double digits.

It is noticeable in Table 11.5 that net cross-border assets of Japan as a percentage of total world cross-border net assets increased from 40.14% in 2007 to the highest level of 91.08% in 2016 and declined slightly to 87.64% in the first quarter of 2021. The high share of Japanese cross-border net assets indicated the strength of Japanese banking industry worldwide to support Japanese yen.

11.4.2 *Bank internationalization of major currency issuers*

Using cross-border assets of major currency issuers and corresponding GDP released by the International Monetary Fund (IMF) in April 2021, we can find bank internationalization, or cross-border assets/GDP of major currency issuers. Table 11.6 shows the results. Table 11.6 shows that despite the biggest declines of bank internationalization of Switzerland from 2007 to 2020, bank internationalization of 274.9% was still the highest for

Table 11.5: Cross-Border Assets, Liabilities, and Net Assets by Country (2007–2021) (Unit: USD billion, %)

Cross-Border Assets by Nationality of Reporting Bank											
Year/ Country	**2007**	**2008**	**2010**	**2011**	**2013**	**2015**	**2016**	**2019**	**2020**	**2020Q1**	**Change from 2007 to 2020**
USA	3.10	3.62	3.80	4.13	2.95	2.87	2.93	3.42	4.12	4.44	2.21
Eurozone	16.61	15.07	12.70	11.38	10.75	9.19	8.95	9.93	11.76	10.72	−2.62
Japan	2.67	2.89	3.41	3.66	4.09	4.14	4.44	4.93	5.44	5.49	5.62
UK	3.40	3.24	3.86	4.02	3.15	2.63	2.44	3.09	3.86	3.82	0.96
Australia	0.24	0.29	0.37	0.48	0.48	0.57	0.57	0.66	0.77	0.64	9.45
Canada	0.69	0.68	0.84	0.90	0.95	0.99	1.02	1.55	1.89	1.73	8.09
Switzerland	3.70	2.50	2.12	2.13	2.25	1.92	1.78	2.06	2.05	2.11	−4.41
China						1.45	1.73	2.26	2.47	2.60	11.18
Others	2.50	2.35	2.66	3.10	3.86	3.36	3.22	3.16	3.36	4.08	2.30
World	32.91	30.64	29.76	29.80	28.48	27.12	27.08	31.05	35.71	35.63	0.63
Cross-Border Liabilities by Nationality of Reporting Bank											
Year/ Country	**2007**	**2008**	**2010**	**2011**	**2013**	**2015**	**2016**	**2019**	**2020**	**2020Q1**	**Change from 2007 to 2020**
USA	3.94	4.43	4.43	4.72	3.68	3.51	3.43	3.85	4.65	5.01	1.27
Eurozone	14.66	13.16	11.66	10.47	9.67	8.20	8.09	8.96	10.45	10.40	−2.57
Japan	1.13	1.41	1.60	1.86	2.14	1.97	2.08	2.16	2.38	2.24	5.91
UK	3.31	3.05	3.48	3.74	2.84	2.58	2.46	3.07	3.97	3.98	1.41

(Continued)

Table 11.5: (*Continued*)

Cross-Border Assets by Nationality of Reporting Bank											
Year/ Country	**2007**	**2008**	**2010**	**2011**	**2013**	**2015**	**2016**	**2019**	**2020**	**2020Q1**	**Change from 2007 to 2020**
Australia	0.47	0.47	0.68	0.79	0.81	0.85	0.83	0.86	0.92	0.80	5.41
Canada	0.54	0.52	0.63	0.71	0.72	0.80	0.84	1.15	1.53	1.42	8.30
Switzerland	3.52	2.65	2.20	2.18	2.05	1.83	1.74	1.89	1.93	1.99	−4.52
China						1.40	1.57	2.08	2.27	2.41	10.14
Others	1.50	1.14	1.49	1.91	3.52	3.54	3.45	3.46	3.56	3.67	6.89
World	29.07	26.83	26.17	26.38	25.43	24.69	24.48	27.48	31.68	31.91	0.66
Cross-Border Net Assets by Nationality of Reporting Bank											
Year/ Country	**2007**	**2008**	**2010**	**2011**	**2013**	**2015**	**2016**	**2019**	**2020**	**2020Q1**	**Change from 2007 to 2020**
USA	−0.84	−0.81	−0.63	−0.59	−0.73	−0.64	−0.51	−0.43	−0.52	−0.58	−3.56
Eurozone	1.95	1.91	1.04	0.90	1.07	1.00	0.86	0.97	1.30	0.32	−3.06
Japan	1.54	1.48	1.82	1.80	1.95	2.16	2.36	2.77	3.05	3.26	5.40
UK	0.09	0.19	0.38	0.28	0.31	0.05	−0.02	0.01	−0.12	−0.16	−201.67
Australia	−0.23	−0.19	−0.32	−0.31	−0.32	−0.28	−0.26	−0.20	−0.16	−0.17	−2.89
Canada	0.14	0.16	0.21	0.19	0.22	0.19	0.18	0.40	0.36	0.31	7.27
Switzerland	0.17	−0.14	−0.08	−0.05	0.19	0.09	0.04	0.18	0.12	0.12	−2.54
China						0.05	0.16	0.18	0.20	0.20	30.53
Others	1.00	1.21	1.17	1.19	0.34	−0.19	−0.23	−0.30	−0.21	0.41	−188.54
World	3.84	3.81	3.59	3.42	3.05	2.43	2.60	3.58	4.04	3.72	0.39

Source: Cross-border positions by summary of locational statistics by currency, website of the Bank of International Settlements: www.bis.org; CAGR of China was from 2015 to 2020.

Table 11.6: Bank Internationalization of Major Currency Issuers (2007–2020) (Unit: %)

Currency Issuer/Year	2007	2008	2010	2011	2013	2015	2016	2019	2020	Change from 2007 to 2020
USA	21.5	24.6	25.3	26.6	17.6	15.7	15.6	15.9	19.7	−1.79
Eurozone	129.1	106.5	100.4	83.5	81.5	78.8	74.8	74.3	91.0	−38.04
Japan	58.3	56.6	59.3	58.8	78.5	93.0	88.7	95.7	107.7	49.38
UK	110.0	109.6	155.3	151.2	113.1	89.7	90.4	109.0	142.2	32.22
Australia	25.0	27.1	29.3	31.6	31.9	45.8	45.1	47.2	56.5	31.47
Canada	46.8	44.1	51.7	50.1	51.2	63.9	66.7	89.0	115.1	68.24
Switzerland	748.3	439.3	352.4	294.5	314.8	273.0	255.3	281.9	274.9	−473.32
China						13.1	15.4	15.8	16.8	3.69
Others	14.8	12.2	12.8	13.0	15.2	14.6	14.0	12.0	13.7	−1.12
World	56.5	47.9	44.9	40.5	36.9	36.2	35.6	35.6	42.2	−14.21

Source: Calculated using data in Table 11.5 and corresponding GDP data updated by the IMF (www.imf.org) in April 2021; bank internationalization change of China was from 2015 to 2020.

Switzerland in 2020, indicating the severest impacts of 2008 world financial crisis on Swiss banking industry and on Swiss franc. The second position of Eurozone bank internationalization in 2007 fell to fifth position in 2020. Bank internationalization of Japan remained in the fourth position from 2007 to 2020 despite of increase in the Japanese internationalization from 58.3% in 2007 to 107.7% in 2020; bank internationalization of UK rose from the third position in 2007 to the second position in 2020. Bank internationalization of Canada experienced the highest accumulated increase of 68.24% from 2007 to 2020 with ranking from the fifth to the third in 2020.

It is somewhat surprising that bank internationalization of USA has remained lower than those of all other six major world currency issuers from 2007 to 2020, with the only exception of bank internationalization of China.

11.5 Chinese and Japanese Cross-Border Assets and Net Assets

Although China's economic and trade sizes have surpassed those of Japan years ago, and China's foreign exchange reserves have also been significantly larger than Japanese foreign reserves, there is still a big gap between Chinese international investment positions (IIP) and net IIPs from those of Japan, and larger gap between cross-border net assets of the two neighboring countries. Due to the great comparability between China and Japan in many aspects, and the internationalization process of the Japanese yen is a great reference for CNY internationalization in many years to come, we compare the total cross-border assets, bank assets, bank sector cross-border assets and bank internationalization between the two countries in this section.

11.5.1 *Bank internationalization of China and Japan*

Table 11.5 shows that despite high CAGR of 11.18% of cross-border assets of China from 2015 to 2020, Chinese cross-border assets of $2.60 trillion and net assets of $0.20 trillion in 2021Q1 were merely 47.4% and 6.0% of the corresponding Japanese cross-border asset of $5.49 trillion and net asset of $3.26 trillion, respectively. Bank internationalization of China was merely 16.8% in 2020, 90.9% lower than the corresponding bank internationalization of Japan at 107.7%, during the same time as shown in Table 11.6. A gap of $3.06 trillion between Chinese cross-border net asset of $0.20 trillion and Japanese cross-border net asset of $3.26 trillion was much larger than the gap of $1.21 trillion between Chinese net IIP of $2.15 trillion in 2020 and Japanese net IIP of $3.36 trillion in the same year. All these data imply a significant gap between Chinese bank internationalization and Japanese bank internationalization despite larger Chinese GDP, and the acceleration of Chinese bank internationalization will help accelerate CNY internationalization.

11.5.2 *Assets of China and Japan in the United States, United Kingdom, and Hong Kong*

Data from BIS indicated that total Japanese assets and liabilities in the United States were $494.61 billion and $221.27 billion by the end of the first quarter of 2021, respectively, much higher than the corresponding Chinese assets and liabilities in the United States at $34.86 billion and $113.46 billion for the same time, respectively. Total Japanese assets and liabilities in United Kingdom were $363.26 billion and $139.31 billion by the end of the first quarter of 2021, respectively, much higher than the corresponding Chinese assets and liabilities in United Kingdom at $83.67 billion and $117.64 billion for the same time, respectively. The significant gaps between Chinese assets and Japanese assets in the United States and United Kingdom are consistent with the ranking gaps of CNY and Japanese yen in the United States and United Kingdom as discussed in Chapter 10.

Similar data from the BIS indicated that total Japanese assets and liabilities in Hong Kong China were $194.53 billion and $118.62 billion by the end of the first quarter of 2021, respectively, much lower than the corresponding Chinese assets and liabilities in Hong Kong China at $411.84 billion and $380.37 billion for the same time, respectively. The gaps between Japanese assets and Chinese assets in Kong Hong are consistent with the ranking gap of CNY and Japanese yen in Hong Kong as discussed in Chapter 10 (CNY has replaced both yen and Hong dollar as the second currency in Hong Kong since April 2020).

Therefore, the total asset of one currency issuer in a country or region is the underlying force to support its currency in the foreign exchange market in the country or region. As it would take many years for China to catch up with Japan in total assets in United States and United Kingdom, it would take almost the same time for CNY to catch up with Japanese yen in the foreign exchange markets in the United States and United Kingdom accordingly.

11.6 Internationalization of World's Major Banks in Recent Years

Global trade internationalization is the foundation of global financial internationalization. More specifically, international banks support international financial centers and international currencies. Bank internationalization results in Table 11.6 are aggregate bank internationalization of major currency issuers. They should be the aggregate results or weighted results of all banks of each currency issuers. We concentrate on internationalization of major global banks in recent years to understand better the internationalization of banks of major currency issuers. The main results of this section are from Ben *et al.* (2020).

11.6.1 *Overseas assets of major international banks*

According to Ben Shenglin *et al.* (2020), the top 10 banks in terms of overseas assets sizes in the world were HSBC, Banco Santander, MUFG, Citigroup, Bank of China, Deutsche Bank, ING Bank, Mizuho FG, JPMorgan Chase and Barclays in 2019, five of which were European banks. Measured by the share of overseas assets of total assets of a bank, the list includes Ahli United Bank, Banco Santander, Nordea Bank, HSBC Holdings, ING Bank, Standard Chartered Bank, Credit Suisse, Arab Bank, UniCredit Group, and Citi Group. All the top seven were European banks' overseas assets accounted for 69.59% of the total assets on average. The share of overseas assets of Bank of China accounted for 27.58%, ranking 20th. These results indicate that the degree of internationalization of European banks is not only significantly higher than that of China's banks but also significantly higher than the banks from the USA and Japan. These results are consistent with the country results of bank internationalization in Table 11.6.

11.6.2 *Share and ranking of overseas revenue and profits of major international banks*

Overseas revenue and its share of total revenue of a bank is a better measurement of its internationalization. Ben *et al.* (2020) showed that the top 10 banks measured by global overseas revenue in 2019 were Banco Santander, Citigroup, HSBC, MUFG, BNP Paribas, JPMorgan Chase, UBS, Bank of China, ICBC, and Mizuho FG, and similarly, four of the top 10 were European banks. Measured by the share of overseas revenue, the top 10 banks in the world were Standard Chartered Bank, Banco Santander, UBS, HSBC, Nordea Bank, MUFG, Arab Bank, ING Bank, BNP Paribas and Credit Suisse, eight of which were European banks, and overseas revenues of eight European banks accounted for 74.28% on average. It is noticeable that share of revenue of Bank of China was ranked out of the top 30 international banks. These results again indicate that the degree of internationalization of Europe banks is much higher in terms of revenue and share of revenue than in terms of overseas assets size and corresponding share. The results also indicate that there is much more work for Chinese banks to do to improve their internationalization levels, and to support CNY internationalization accordingly.

11.6.3 *Ranking of internationalization indexes of major international banks*

In addition to measurement of bank internationalization using overseas assets and share, overseas revenues and share introduced above, overseas profit and share, proportions of overseas deposit size, loan size and business outlets numbers are also important embodiments of the bank's degree of internationalization (readers may refer to the relevant results of Ben *et al.* (2020) for details). Ben *et al.* (2020) proposed an index for bank internationalization based on eight sub-indexes: the proportion of bank's overseas assets, the proportion of overseas customers' deposits, the proportion of overseas customers' loans, the proportion of overseas revenues, the proportion of overseas profits, the number of operating locations, the proportion of overseas branches, and the proportion of overseas employees. Such index can measure the degree of the internationalization of a bank more comprehensively. According to Ben *et al.* (2020), nine of the top 12 banks in terms of internationalization were all European banks in 2019, other three banks were Citibank from the USA, which was ranked fourth, Mitsubishi UFJ FG from Japan, ranked eighth, and Scotiabank from Canada, ranked 12th in 2019.There were two banks from France and two from Canada, one from the USA, the UK, Netherlands, and Japan, respectively, with total eight banks ranked from 13th to 20th for the same time. The highest-ranked Chinese bank was Bank of China with corresponding ranking of 23rd, followed by ICBC and Bank of Communications (BOC) ranked 30th and the 37th, respectively (refer to the relevant detailed ranking and internationalization indicators in the Appendix). The results indicated that the grade of internationalization of China's banking industry was not only significantly lower than that of European banks and American banks but also significantly lower than that of the banks from Canada and Singapore.

11.6.4 *Changes in bank internationalization indexes of major international banks from 2016 to 2019*

Comparing bank internationalization indexes (BII) of Ben *et al.* (2018, 2020), we can find changes of BII of major international banks from 2016 to 2019. The comparing results are given in Appendix Table A11.1. Appendix Table A11.1 shows that, despite a decrease in BII of the Standard Chartered Bank from 67.46 to 62.71 during 2016–2019, BII of this bank was still ranked No. 1 of all major international banks in 2019. Besides Standard Chartered, only BIIs of Deutsche Bank and UBS Group decreased among all other top 12 banks in 2019, indicating that most major European banks increased in BIIs from 2016 to 2019. Most major American banks experienced improvement in BII with the exceptions of JPMorgan Chase and Bank of America. Two major Japanese banks, Mitsubishi UFJ FG and Mizuho FG improved significantly in BIIs from 2016 to 2019. Four Chinese banks, Bank of China, ICBC, and Bank of Communications improved by about 1% on average, while BII of China Construction Bank decreased slightly from 8.25% to 7.92% during the same time.

11.7 Bank Internationalization of China and Internationalization of Major Banks in China in Recent Years

Table 11.5 shows that the CAGR of cross-border assets was 11.18% from 2015 to 2020, much higher than the corresponding CAGRs of commodity trade and nominal GDP of China at 3.28% and 5.78% for the same period, yet only slightly higher than the CAGR of assets of banking industry of 9.90% for the same period. The slightly higher CAGR of cross-border assets than the corresponding total assets of banking industry implies that banking internationalization of China increased slightly during the same period.

Table 11.6 shows that bank internationalization of China increased from 13.1% in 2015 to 16.8% in 2020 with an accumulated growth of 3.7% in 5 years from 2015 to 2020. To be more comparable with bank internationalization measured with overseas assets/totals asset of a particular bank, we can find bank internationalization of China using total cross-border assets in Table 11.5 and total assets of banking industry in China. Calculation results show that bank internationalization in China increased from 4.9% to 5.2% during 2015–2020 with accumulated growth of 0.3% over the same period.

11.8 Internationalization of Major Banks in China in Recent Years

Table 11.7 presents the total overseas assets, overseas loan balance, overseas pretax profit, and the ratio of overseas pretax profit to overseas assets of banks in China from 2015 to 2010.

Table 11.7: Total Overseas Assets, Balance of Overseas Loans, Overseas Pretax Profits, and Proportion of Overseas Pretax Profits to Overseas Assets of Major Chinese Banks (2013–2019) (Unit: USD billion, %)

Year Banks	2013	2014	2015	2016	2017	2018	2019
	Total Overseas Assets						
Industrial and Commercial Bank of China (ICBC)	262.33	313.69	377.38	451.18	517.59	538.48	569.26
China Construction Bank (CCB)	120.04	152.89	177.03	240.22	264.16	246.90	246.97
Agricultural Bank of China (ABC)	58.08	85.37	109.79	109.31	122.27	132.97	170.16
Bank of China (BOC)	630.80	683.18	699.18	730.73	833.33	904.35	900.16
Bank of Communications (BOC)	85.27	100.92	107.99	123.38	147.63	155.79	166.86
CITIC Bank	28.06	32.60	36.97	41.15	47.11	49.33	48.52
China Merchants Bank (CMB)	16.33	20.74	21.90	25.55	30.58	34.98	34.26
China Guangfa Bank	3.67	3.63	3.51	2.96	2.90	3.23	4.00
Total	1,204.58	1,393.02	1,533.75	1,724.48	1,965.57	2,066.03	2,140.17
Total bank assets	24,824.86	28,164.00	30,698.75	33,480.35	38,628.14	38,088.08	41,570.27
Proportion in banking industry	0.49	0.49	0.50	0.52	0.51	0.54	0.51

(Continued)

Table 11.7: (*Continued*)

Year Banks	2013	2014	2015	2016	2017	2018	2019
			Balance of Overseas Loans				
Industrial and Commercial Bank of China (ICBC)	108.12	130.98	144.06	175.87	216.36	207.59	
China Construction Bank (CCB)	88.26	92.16	105.53	129.41	153.27	1292.90	
Agricultural Bank of China (ABC)	50.80	64.83	68.78	63.51	58.96	56.74	
Bank of China (BOC)	306.81	303.66	295.77	308.59	351.29	365.28	
Bank of Communications (BOC)	45.80	45.27	50.26	55.41	64.57	51.82	
CITIC Bank	15.28	19.06	21.46	24.42	25.43	26.08	
China Merchants Bank (CMB)	8.37	11.36	8.90	14.29	16.76	17.97	
China Guangfa Bank	2.52	1.97	2.27	1.80	2.06	1.83	
Total	625.96	669.29	697.03	773.30	888.70	856.60	
Overseas Pretax Profits							
Industrial and Commercial Bank of China (ICBC)	2.23	3.02	3.17	3.25	3.92	4.12	4.98
China Construction Bank (CCB)	0.64	1.04	0.82	0.98	1.86	1.50	0.82
Agricultural Bank of China (ABC)	0.36	0.52	0.60	0.28	0.50	0.66	1.48

Bank of China (BOC)	6.66	8.66	8.78	12.23	10.19	9.95	10.53
Bank of Communications (BOC)	0.63	0.85	0.93	0.88	1.06	1.15	1.30
CITIC Bank	0.34	0.46	0.34	0.40	0.57	0.48	0.48
China Merchants Bank (CMB)	0.15	0.34	0.28	0.22	0.32	0.44	0.39
China Guangfa Bank	0.03	0.04	0.04	0.02	−0.01	0.04	0.03
Total	11.04	14.93	14.96	18.26	18.41	18.34	20.00
Overseas Pretax Profit/Overseas Assets							
Industrial and Commercial Bank of China (ICBC)	0.09	0.10	0.08	0.07	0.08	0.08	0.09
China Construction Bank (CCB)	0.05	0.07	0.05	0.04	0.07	0.06	0.03
Agricultural Bank of China (ABC)	0.06	0.06	0.06	0.03	0.04	0.05	0.09
Bank of China (BOC)	0.11	0.13	0.13	0.17	0.12	0.11	0.12
Bank of Communications (BOC)	0.07	0.08	0.09	0.07	0.07	0.07	0.08
CITIC Bank	0.12	0.14	0.09	0.10	0.12	0.10	0.10
China Merchants Bank (CMB)	0.09	0.16	0.13	0.09	0.11	0.13	0.11
China Guangfa Bank	0.08	0.11	0.11	0.07	−0.03	0.12	0.08
Total	0.09	0.11	0.10	0.11	0.09	0.09	0.09

Source: Sorted out from the annual reports of each bank.

11.8.1 *Overseas assets of major banks*

Table 11.7 indicates that Bank of China was the bank with the largest overseas assets and the leader in "go global" of China's banking industry, which was consistent with the result given in Table 11.1 that Bank of China is the bank with the most functions of overseas CNY settlements. The proportion of overseas assets of Bank of China in the overseas assets of China's banking industry remained about half, but the proportion kept declining. In recent years, the growth rate of overseas assets of ICBC has exceeded that of Bank of China on average, and in 2016, the proportion of the overseas assets of ICBC in those of China's banking industry exceeded 1/5 for the first time. In 2019, the overseas assets of China Construction Bank and Agricultural Bank of China ranked third and fourth, respectively, and those of Bank of Communications ranked the last among the "Big Fives".

11.8.2 *The proportion of overseas assets of major banks in China*

Table 11.7 indicates that from 2013 to 2019, the proportion of overseas assets of Chinese banks in the total assets of China's banking industry has increased contagiously from 4.9% to 5.1%, indicating that the pace of "go global" of China's banking industry has been steady since 2013.

11.8.3 *Overseas profitability of major banks in China*

Table 11.7 indicates that from 2013 to 2019, the ratio of overseas pretax profit to overseas assets (return on Assets, ROA) of China's banking industry was kept at around 1%, not only lower than the domestic ROA of these banks but also lower than the ROA of major international banks. The result indicates that China's major banks were still in the initial stage of overseas growth, and the operation efficiency needs improvement greatly.

11.8.4 *Brief introduction to "go global" of China's banking industry*

With the total overseas assets of ICBC, CCB, ABC, BOCOM, and CMB from 2013 to 2019 given in Table 11.4, we can calculate that the average annual compound growth rates were 13.8%, 12.8%, 19.6%, 11.8%, and 13.1%, respectively, all of which were "double-digit" growth, and the average annual compound growth rates of CITIC Bank and Bank of China were 9.6% and 7.5%. The results reflected the encouraging momentum of overseas development of China's major banks.

11.9 Introduction to Overseas Distribution and Development of Overseas Businesses of Bank of China

Bank of China is the leader of "go global" in China's banking industry. Both of its overseas assets and profits rank far ahead all other Chinese banks, and it has occupied a certain position in the international banking industry. This section will introduce overseas operations and international rankings of Bank of China.

11.9.1 *Overseas distribution and development of Bank of China in recent years*

The number of overseas entities of Bank of China had grown from 20 in 1978 to 559 in 2000, and those entities were distributed in Hong Kong Special Administrative Region (SAR), Macao SAR and 22 countries in five continents, with total assets of $155.1 billion, accounting for 42% of the total assets of the Bank of China. By the end of 2019, there were 557 overseas entities distributed in 61 countries and regions globally with total overseas assets of CNY6.28 trillion or $0.90 trillion, accounting for 27.58% of the total assets of Bank of China for the same time. Revenue from overseas was CNY131.7 billion accounting for 23.99% of the total revenues of Bank of China in that year (Ben Shenglin *et al.*, 2020).

11.9.2 *Overseas operations of Bank of China in recent years*

The pretax profits of overseas entities of Bank of China (including Hong Kong, Macao, and Taiwan) accounted for 37.72% in 2006 and 42.25% in 2007 of the Group's total profits. However, due to the severe impact of the international financial crisis in 2008, the contribution of overseas profit dropped rapidly to 8.09% in 2009, and then gradually recovered in the next few years. Since 2013, the growth of the overseas assets and profits of Bank of China has accelerated significantly. Overseas assets were about CNY3.1 trillion in 2012, and further went up to more than CNY5 trillion in 2016. The overseas pretax profits also increased contagiously from $6.65 billion to $12.2 billion from 2013 to 2016, leading to the improvement of the proportion in the Group's profits from 19.37% to 36.3% over the same period. However, in 2016–2017, the overseas pretax profits decreased to $10.24 billion which accounted for 29.5% (Table 11.4 and Annual Report of Bank of China, 2018). Overseas pretax profits were $9.95 billion and $10.53 billion in 2018 and 2019, respectively, and the proportion increased to 27.3% and 29.3%, respectively.

11.9.3 *Rankings of overseas assets and profits of Bank of China in recent years*

According to Ben *et al.* (2018), overseas assets, deposits, and loans of Bank of China ranked at fifth, sixth, and sixth in the world in 2016, respectively. Rankings of proportions of above indexes were, respectively, the 23rd, 24th, and 27th in the world in 2016. Overseas operating income and profits ranked, respectively, at ninth and second in the world for the same year, while the proportions of those two indexes only ranked at 30th and 20th, respectively. These data indicated that Bank of China can enter the top 10 global banks by assets and profits. However, in terms of the proportions of those indicators in the whole bank, Bank of China ranked 20th or even lower. Ben *et al.* (2020) measured the overall degree of internationalization of different banks by the weighted proportion of eight sub-indexes namely overseas assets, overseas deposits, overseas loans, overseas revenues, overseas profits, overseas outlets, and overseas employees. Bank of China ranked 23rd in 2019 (see Appendix Table A11.1), indicating that the degree of internationalization of the Chinese bank with the highest ranking was still lower than 20th in the world.

11.9.4 *Ranking of internationalization of other major Chinese banks*

According to Ben *et al.* (2020), Industry and Commercial Bank of China (ICBC), Bank of Communications (BOCOM), China Construction Bank (CCB), and Agricultural Bank of China (ABC)were ranked 30th, 37th,

40th, and 41st in 2019, respectively, in terms of BII. While China CITIC Bank, China Minsheng Bank, Shanghai Pudong Development Bank, China Everbright Bank, China Merchants Bank, and China Industrial Bank ranked 43rd, 44th, 45th, 46th, 47th, and 49th for the same year, respectively. Although the internationalization ranking of other banks in China was relatively low, the internationalization ranking has been rising relatively faster than that of most foreign banks in recent years. However, there is still a significant gap between the overall internationalization of China's banking industry and China's international worldwide trade and the international level of CNY internationalization.

11.10 Main Challenges in the "Go Global" Strategy of China's Banking Industry

Ben Shenglin and Yu Jiefang (2020) made a good summary and comment on the achievements and challenges of "go global" strategy of China's banks in recent years. Main achievements have already been summarized above and will not be repeated here. This section will briefly introduce the issues facing the "go global" progress of China's banking industry, so that we can have a reasonable judgment on the follow-up pace of "go global" of China's banks.

11.10.1 *Huge gap of internationalization of banking industry remain between China and major developed economies*

According to Ben *et al.* (2020), the average BII index of China's "Big Five" banks was only 13.71 in 2019, and that of joint-stock banks was merely 3.43 the same year. The average BII index of top 20 global banks was 43.52 in 2019, which was 3.17 times of the average of the "Big Five" and 12.69 times of that of the joint-stock commercial banks. The results indicate a huge gap of internationalization between Chinese banks and foreign banks.

11.10.2 *Risk management needs improvement*

Ben Shenglin and Yu Jiefang (2016) listed and analyzed the risk events in "go global" progress of China's banking industry since 2000 (see Ben

Shenglin and Yu Jiefang (2016), Section 5.2, and Table 5.4). These risk events involved market risks, such as the failure of Minsheng Bank's merger and the loss of 50% within 1 year after the China Development Bank's acquisition of 3.1% share of Barclays Bank; and operational risks such as the loan fraud case of Bank of China New York branch, which was fined for $10 million, etc. Refer to Ben Shenglin and Yu Jiefang (2016) for a detailed introduction and analysis of these cases. "In just over a decade, the 'go global' risk events of China's banks occurred frequently and caused huge losses. What a pity."

11.10.3 *Overseas legal compliance awareness and ability need to be strengthened*

In addition to the market risk and operational risk involved in the overseas risk cases of China's banks, the legal risk and compliance risk involved in the overseas risk cases of China's banks should not be ignored. The lawsuit case of ICBC Madrid branch involved the legal risks arising from the political and cultural differences of the host country. In addition, the case that ABC New York branch was fined more than $200 million due to its violation of the anti-money laundering statute of the United States is another vital case of overseas legal risks of China's banks. "The DFS released an announcement on November 11, 2016, declaring that the ABC New York branch will be fined $215 million for violating anti-money laundering statute, and will be required to set up an independent third-party supervision for rectification." "The ABC is fined USD 215 million by New York State for suspected money laundering in the United States" (Foreign Exchange News, November 7, 2016). About $215 million is equivalent to one-third of ABC's overall overseas profit in 2015.

In addition to the above risks and problems, overseas operations of China's banking industry also face other issues and risks. According to statistics, after the international financial crisis in 2008, the US regulatory authorities punished several US-funded financial institutions, with a cumulative amount of more than $100 billion, and punished several foreign financial institutions, with a cumulative amount of more than $40 billion. Several banks from China were in the list. With the enhancement of the depth and breadth of "go global" of Chinese enterprises and banks, China's total overseas assets and net assets will increase significantly.

Overseas market risk management, credit risk management, country risk management, and compliance management will become more and more important. To improve the management capacity of the above risks, China's banking industry needs to strengthen the professional skills by training of overseas executives in local laws and regulations.

11.11 Prospect of Internationalization of China's Banking Industry

As the CNY was enlisted as a SDR (Special Drawing Rights of the IMF) currency, there will be higher demand of CNY in years to come. The proportion of international reserves of CNY shall surpass those of British pound and Japanese yen according to share of CNY, pound, and yen in SDR. The status of internationalization of major Chinese banks cannot meet such demand and Chinese banking industry needs to accelerate internationalization process accordingly.

CNY's share in IMF SDR basket of 10.92% is 2.59% higher than Japanese yen's share of 8.33%, yet CNY's share in international reserves of 1.86% in 2019 was just over one-third of the corresponding share of Japanese yen of 5.52%, and CNY's share in global foreign exchange market of 2.16% was just over one-fourth of the corresponding share of Japanese yen at 8.40%. For CNY to catch up with Japanese yen in internationalization, cross-border assets, IIPs and many other aspects, there is a need to catch up with Japan.

11.12 Summary

Amounts of cross-border assets in certain countries or regions reflect positions of international financial centers or foreign exchange centers of the target country or region and amounts of total cross-border assets of currency issuers reflect the international support to the currency. We introduced cross-border assets in certain countries and regions, and cross-border assets of major currency issuers in this chapter. These data help us better understand the underlying drivers of currency internationalization. Results of this chapter show that world cross-border assets reversed in 2020 to the pre-2008 world financial crisis level in 2007 after 12 years, indicating the severe impacts of the crisis on globalization process and international financial markets.

With the steady growth of cross-border assets in China in recent years, total cross-border assets in China increased from $0.19 trillion in 2007 to $1.06 trillion in the first quarter of 2021, the corresponding ranking increased from eighth to fifth of eight major world currency issuers during the same time. These results reflect the steady improvement in business environment in the same period. Cross-border assets of China grew faster than most other countries to $2.60 trillion and ranked fifth of eight currency issuers in the first quarter 2021, indicating fifth or sixth position of CNY internationalization in 2021. However, cross-border assets of China at $2.60 trillion in the first quarter of 2021 was less than cross-border assets of Japan of $5.49 trillion for the same time, implying much for CNY to catch up Japanese yen in internationalization.

Despite the steady progresses of major Chinese banks in internationalization in recent years, bank internationalization is still too low to support CNY internationalization in general as evidenced by the fact that Bank of China, the Chinese bank with highest internationalization level, has ranked beyond 20th of the major world international banks in internationalization indexes from 2016 to 2019.

Appendix

Table A11.1: Rankings of Major Global Banks in BII 2019 and 2016

BII index Ranking	Bank Name	Country	Index in 2019	Index in 2016	Index Change from 2016 to 2019
1	Standard Chartered	UK	62.71	67.46	−4.75
2	HSBC Holdings	UK	59.16	55.37	3.79
3	Banco Santander	Spain	57.92	56.36	1.56
4	Citigroup	USA	54.92	51.77	3.15
5	ING Bank	Netherlands	53.23	49.97	3.26
6	Credit Suisse	Switzerland	51.83	51.38	0.45
7	Deutsche Bank	Germany	46.28	54.47	−8.19
8	Mitsubishi UFJ FG	Japan	45.1	36.69	8.41
9	UBS Group	Switzerland	43.43	54.71	−11.28
10	UniCredit Group	Italy	42.04	39.92	2.12
11	BNP Paribas	France	41.66	40.18	1.48
12	Bank of Bova Scotia	Canada	39.45	39.01	0.44
13	Société Générale	France	39.19	42.93	−3.74
14	Barclays Bank	UK	36.73		
15	Mizuho FG	Japan	35.2	27.79	7.41
16	Royal Bank of Canada	Canada	34.6		
17	Rabobank Group	Netherlands	33.41		
18	Goldman Sachs	USA	32.33	31.59	0.74
19	TD Canada Trust	Canada	30.58		
20	Groupe Crédit Agricole	France	30.53	31.07	−0.54
21	State Street Corp	USA	30.48		
22	ANZ Group	Australia	28.66		
23	Bank of China	China	27.68	26.62	1.06
24	Bank of New York Mellon	USA	27.44	20.63	6.81
25	SMBC	Japan	26.61		
26	Morgan Stanley	USA	25.07	23.00	2.07
27	Groupe BPCE	France	21.73		
28	JPMorgan Chase	USA	21.15	25.95	−4.80
29	Intesa Sanpaolo	Italy	19.74		

(*Continued*)

Table A11.1: (*Continued*)

BII Index Ranking	Bank Name	Country	Index in 2019	Index in 2016	Index Change from 2016 to 2019
30	ICBC	China	17.79	15.96	1.83
31	Credit Mutuel	France	14.12		
32	Bank of America	USA	13.84	15.08	−1.24
33	Commonwealth Bank of Australia	Australia	12.13	14.25	−2.12
34	Westpac Banking Corporation	Australia	12.08		
35	Wells Fargo	USA	10.8		
36	Banco Bilbao Vizcaya Argentaria	Argentina	10.44		
37	Bank of Communications	China	8.83	8.12	0.71
38	Royal Bank of Scotland	UK	8.55	8.51	0.04
39	Sberbank	Russia	8.39		
40	China Construction Bank	China	7.92	8.25	−0.33
41	Agricultural Bank of China	China	6.33		
42	Capital One Financial Corp	USA	5.51		
43	China Citic Bank	China	4.28		
44	China Minsheng Bank	China	4.23		
45	Shanghai Pudong Development Bank	China	4.21		
46	China Everbright Bank	China	2.89		
47	China Merchants Bank	China	2.89		
48	The Norinchukin Bank	Japan	2.71		
49	Industrial Bank	China	2.12		

Source: Ben *et al*. (2018, 2020).

Bibliography

Ben Shenglin and Yu Jiefang, *Report on Internationalization of China's Banks*, China Financial Publishing House, 2016.

Ben Shenglin, Yu Jiefang, Gu Yue *et al*., *Racing: Chinese and Foreign Banks Galloping in International Market*, Zhejiang University Press, 2018.

Ben Shenglin, Yu Jiefang, Gu Yue *et al*., *Will De-globalization Disrupt Banks' International Expansion? Report on Internationalization of China's Banks*, Zhejiang University Press, 2020.

Chapter 12

Current Status of Major International Currencies

After introducing offshore CNY centers and their developments in previous chapters, this chapter will use both domestic and foreign data to estimate international status of major world currencies in recent years. This will make it possible to judge systematically changes about the progress of CNY internationalization since 2016 compared to other major currencies.

12.1 Brief Review of CNY Internationalization in the Early Stage

CNY was mainly used inside Mainland China before 2004. The Hong Kong Monetary Authority (HKMA) put forward an idea about conducting personal CNY business in Hong Kong with the People's Bank of China (PBOC) early in November 2001, and discussions began early in February 2002. However, the outbreak of SARS in March 2003 delayed the discussion to a certain extent. In June 2003, the HKMA and the PBOC reached an agreement on the application of CNY in Hong Kong, and the State Council approved to conduct retail CNY business in Hong Kong in November. After about 3 months' preparation, banks in Hong Kong began to provide retail CNY deposits, foreign exchange, debit cards and credit card services from February 25, 2004 (Chan, 2014).

Since the 1990s, China has increasingly converged with the global economy, with the proportion of trade commodity imports and exports compared to its GDP soaring from around 38.2% in 2001 to a record high of 63.9% in 2006. Influenced by the world financial crisis in 2008, China's trade dependence declined to 43.4% in 2009. Although there was a slight increase to 49.3% in 2010, it declined steadily to 31.6% in 2020, the lowest level since 1990 and less than half of 63.9% in 2006. In addition, as part of its foreign exchange management reform, China undertook obligations under Articles 2, 3, and 4 of Section 8 of the International Monetary Fund (IMF) accord, with a view to free convertibility of the CNY under the current account. In the wake of the 1997 Asian financial crisis, the world's economics scholars have thoroughly studied the risk arising from global capital flows. When emerging markets come under speculative raids, capital restrictions can temporarily play the role of a firewall. Therefore, China has also been discreet in the free convertibility of the CNY. Since the outbreak of the world financial crisis in 2008, notably after the US exited the strategy of a fourth round of quantitative easing, cross-border capital flows caused a severe shock to many developing countries' economies and finances.

12.2 Basic Conditions of CNY Usage in the Offshore Market

Following China's reform and opening, Hong Kong has become China's bond to the world, the most critical source of its foreign direct investment, and one of its most important trading partners. According to the Ministry of Commerce's foreign investment statistics, 65% of direct foreign investment in Mainland China came from Hong Kong in 2016. Thanks to its unique status and particularly the implementation of the Mainland and Hong Kong Closer Economic Partnership Arrangement (CEPA) on January 1, 2004, Hong Kong has become the most active offshore CNY market. Leveraging its close relationship with Mainland China, Hong Kong, one of the major financial centers in East Asia, will play a pivotal role in the process of CNY internationalization.

12.2.1 *Implementation and changes of related policies*

At the end of 2003, as approved by the State Council, the PBOC agreed to arrange settlement for retail CNY business in Hong Kong. Following the official launch of CNY business in Hong Kong on January 18, 2004, local shops and automatic teller machines started to accept debit cards and credit cards issued by Mainland banks. Furthermore, banks in Hong Kong have been able to provide CNY deposits, exchange, and remittance services since February 25, 2004, and to dispense CNY debit cards and credit cards for Hong Kong residents' use in Mainland China since April 30, 2004.

On November 1, 2005, the PBOC stated its intention to widen the scope of closing positions and settlements for Hong Kong banks involved in CNY business, and to further improve and expand local CNY business by the following five-pronged approach: (1) allowing the PBOC Shenzhen Central Sub-Branch to accept deposits from clearing banks for CNY business in Hong Kong; (2) relaxing requirements for closing positions between the CNY and the HKD by increasing the limit on personal CNY exchanges per person each time from the equivalent of no more than CNY 6,000 to the equivalent of no more than CNY 20,000, expanding the list of designated local CNY exchange operators to cover those engaged in transportations, communications, medical and education industries, and allowing designated shops to convert their CNY deposits maintained in participating banks into HKD; (3) increasing the maximum amount of Hong Kong residents' CNY remittance accepted by eligible Mainland banks per person per day from CNY 50,000 to CNY 80,000; (4) clearing Hong Kong residents' personal CNY checks issued by clearing banks, these non-transferable personal checks can be used to draw up to CNY 80,000 from each account per day to pay for consumer expenditures in the Guangdong province; and (5) canceling the credit limit of CNY 100,000 for each CNY card distributed by Hong Kong banks. On July 19, 2010, the PBOC, and Bank of China (Hong Kong) Limited, as the Clearing Bank of CNY business, signed a revised Settlement Agreement on the CNY Business of Hong Kong Banks in Hong Kong. On the same day, a supplementary cooperation Memorandum on the expansion of the CNY trade settlement scheme was also signed by the PBOC and the HKMA. The revised agreement loosened restrictions on CNY exchange and opening institutions' account not involving cross-border capital flows, to stimulate the need of offshore CNY markets, promote the self-cycling of market supply and demand, and created a necessary foundation for the start of the Hong Kong offshore CNY market. The HKMA stated that, effective November in 2014, the CNY 20,000 per person per day conversion limit was no longer applicable for Hong Kong residents.

12.2.2 *Remittance*

Since customers prefer remittance to carrying cash to Mainland China, remittance services have expanded steadily. From the information published by the HKMA in 2010, the maximum remittance amount available for Hong Kong residents was CNY 80,000 per day in 2010. Since July 2009, enterprises have been able to use CNY checks to transfer funds from accounts opened in different banks and collect money for trade settlement. However, remittance is limited between overseas enterprises and pilot enterprises in Mainland China. Participating banks can transfer funds in Hong Kong, but only among the same enterprise's accounts opened in different banks. In 2011, the maximum remittance amount for Hong Kong residents was still CNY 80,000 per day. For check payments, CNY checks drawn by account holders from participating banks could be used in Hong Kong and Mainland China. Individuals and enterprises can freely make CNY payments and transfers through banks in Hong Kong since November 2014.

With the rapid growth of the cross-border CNY trade settlement business, the amount of receipts and payments between banks in Hong Kong and outside also increased rapidly. According to data from the HKMA, the accounts of receipts and payments from Hong Kong banks' offshore CNY business increased from 19.6 billion and 10.9 billion with a net balance of 8.7 billion in 2010 to 164.5 billion and 166.0 billion with a net balance of −1.5 billion in 2013, to 193.3 billion and 145.2 billion with a balance of 48.1 billion in 2014. These amounts show the continuously increasing effect of Hong Kong, as the most prominent global CNY center, on global CNY capital flows.

Following the "8.11" RMB Exchange Rate Regime Reform, the data above in 2015 dropped to CNY 105.7 billion and CNY 132.1 billion with the difference of CNY −27.4 billion. During 2016, receipts and payments declined further to CNY 91.6 billion and CNY 69 billion, respectively, with a net balance of CNY 22.6 billion. In 2017, due to the stable CNY exchange rate, these figures increased to CNY 132.8 billion and CNY 87.8 billion, respectively, with a net balance of CNY 45 billion.

12.2.3 *Rapid growth of credit card consumption overseas*

The usage of UnionPay cards overseas also reflects the internationalization of CNY to a certain extent. The overseas transaction volume of China

UnionPay cards increased from 363.4 billion RMB in 2012 to 520.3 billion RMB in 2014 with a compound annual growth rate of 19.7%. In addition, overseas transactions from UnionPay cards grew from 5.08 billion to 6.42 billion with a yearly growth rate of 26.4%. In 2015, Chinese residents spent $133 billion overseas by credit card (SAFE, March 31, 2016), equivalent to CNY 828.2 billion (estimated at CNY/USD 6.2269 in 2015). In 2016, the amount of overseas consumption conducted by domestic individuals using credit cards decreased to $109.1 billion compared with 2015. In 2017, the number of overseas transactions conducted by domestic using credit card holders decreased from 144 million in 2016 to 124 million, but the consumption amount increased to $114.6 billion. Although the State Administration of Foreign Exchange (SAFE) no longer publishes detailed data regarding residents' overseas credit card expenditures, overseas consumption amounted to nearly $200 million in 2019. As the acceptance of CNY overseas further improves, the usage of UnionPay cards overseas will continuously increase, which will also enhance CNY internationalization.

12.2.4 *Continuously increasing daily transactions of Hong Kong CNY RTGS system*

A Hong Kong CNY settlement system was launched in March 2006 in Hong Kong to improve the efficiency of settlements for interbank transactions. In June 2007, the HKMA upgraded the system to become a general CNY Real Time Gross Settlement system (RTGS). The Bank of China (Hong Kong) Limited was the clearing bank and Hong Kong Interbank Clearing Limited (HKICL) was responsible for operating the system. Since June 2007, CNY RTGS along with HKD, USD, and EUR RTGS and the Central Money Markets Unit (CMU) was transferred to the open platform of Society of Worldwide Interbank Financial Telecommunications (SWIFT) from the original dedicated operational platform. In recent years, CNY RTGS's average daily transactions increased continuously, which has been a primary indicator on the activity of the offshore CNY market. The average amount of CNY transactions conducted through Hong Kong's RTGS system on a daily basis was CNY 5 billion in 2010. The total amount increased from 213.7 billion in 2012 to 395.4 billion in 2013, which represented a growth rate of 85%. Between 2014 and 2015, the amount grew from CNY 734.1 billion to CNY 947 billion, before declining to \$863.6 billion in 2016. In 2017, the amount rose to \$903.6 billion. In 2018, the amount increased further to \$1,010.1 billion, before reaching \$1,133.9 billion in 2019 (HKMA Annual Report 2015). These figures indicate that the level of activity in the overseas CNY market has been generally trending upward in recent years.

12.3 Introduction to Offshore CNY Transactions

12.3.1 *Introduction to CNY overseas transactions*

Shortly after the start of the offshore CNY market in 2010, the *Wall Street Journal* reported that, "It may just need a few years that 20%–30% of China's imports and exports will use CNY instead of USD." "Soon afterwards, CNY trading volumes will rival JPY to be the third active currency following USD and EUR (*CNY offshore transaction rises significantly*, WSJ.com, 2010-12-14)". Data about CNY cross-border trading settlements and the proportion introduced in Chapter 3 show that the proportion of cross-border trading settlements conducted in CNY had already reached 26.8% in 2015. CNY cross-border settlements fell to 21.1% in 2016 and 15.7% in 2017, and then rose to 16.8% in 2018 and 19.1% in 2019. In August 2015, the CNY surpassed the JPY for the first time to become the world's fourth chief payment currency. The CNY was ranked fifth and sixth in 2016 and 2019, respectively. In September 2020, the CNY accounted for 1.97% of the world's cross-border payments, ranking fifth globally. Meanwhile, the JPY notched a proportion of 3.43% and the GBP accounted for 7.04%, ranking fourth and third for the corresponding time period (data from SWIFT).

12.3.2 *Overseas CNY securities products*

The first CNY-denominated security, Hui Xian Real Estate Investment Trust, on April 29, 2011, began trading in Hong Kong. As the first CNY-denominated security, Hui Xian was the touchstone of CNY business, which will promote the development of CNY securities in Hong Kong.

The Hong Kong Stock Exchange's (HKEx) first CNY-traded equity securities, the CNY-traded shares of Hopewell Highway Infrastructure Limited, were listed for trading on October 29, 2012. These were the first CNY-traded equity shares to be listed in an overseas market and the first dual counter equity securities. Xiaojia Li, as the CEO of HKEx, said that the first CNY equity security listed offshore with the HKEx and the first dual counter equity security were both crucial milestones for developing CNY products, which further strengthened the leading position of Hong Kong as a CNY offshore center. Li Xiaojia expressed that CNY equity securities would be another vital product besides CNY bonds, Exchange Traded Funds (ETFs), Real Estate Investment Trusts (REITs) and CNY currency Futures. Li Xiaojia predicted that investors would have more interest in CNY products due to CNY internationalization. It is believed that more and more CNY-denominated security products will be launched in Hong Kong in the future.

CSOP Asset Management Limited and Source, the provider of the London Exchange's Exchange Traded Fund (ETF) announced on January 9, 2014 that the ETF launched by both would officially begin trading that day on the London Exchange. The ETF was named "South Source FTSE China A50 UCCITS ETF". It is the first RMB Qualified Foreign Institutional Investors (RQFII) ETF in the European markets, providing a new channel for European investors to enter China's A-share market. On March 25, 2015, the first European RQFII ETF officially began trading on the London Exchange, with CCB International Asset Management Limited as the fund manager.

12.3.3 *General introduction of Eurodollar market*

The offshore CNY business has only been in existence for a relatively short period of time; however, it has quite a lot of similarity with the Eurodollar market, which has existed for half a century and is already quite mature. There is a good reference for the development of offshore CNY market in the future to compare these two markets.

The Eurodollar boomed in the early 1960s thanks to the control of the American capital account and tax restrictions. Not subject to the regulation of Federal Reserve Bank and American Taxation authorities, the Eurodollar market based in London could not only provide lower interest rates than the US domestic market but also offer higher rates for saving dollars overseas. Despite the further spread of the regulation of American capital account and tax restrictions in the 1980s and 1990s, the Eurodollar market had quietly developed. By the end of 2008, dollar bonds in offshore markets amounted to $8,396 billion, covering 30.6% of all the dollar bonds with a scale of $27,430 billion within and outside of the US for the same period (Standard Chartered, Special Report, 2010).

At the end of 2017, the US treasury bonds had a scale of $10.78 trillion, more than 70% higher than $6.28 trillion, the amount of global dollar reserves at the same period. There are many factors to the success of Eurodollar market, but one of the main reasons is that the American government never interfered with Eurodollar settlement in America (He and McCauley, 2010). In other words, institutions in the offshore Eurodollar market can do business settlement freely with domestic institutions in America. Available for free settlement with the onshore market, offshore banks can establish their foreign exchange positions according to their own needs. It plays a crucial role in developing US dollars harmoniously inside and outside foreign exchange market (Standard Chartered, Special Report, 2010).

12.4 Direct Trade between CNY and Other Currencies

The higher the level of direct trading between the CNY and other currencies, the lower the transaction costs will be, which would directly reflect a higher degree of currency internationalization. The PBC authorized the China Foreign Exchange Trade System (CFETS) to publish the central parity rate of the CNY compared to USD, EUR, JPY, and HKD on 9:15 am every weekday since January 4, 2006, as the middle rate of the interbank foreign exchange market (including OTC and deal-making) and the over-the-counter transaction rate. From 2010 onward, the CNY began to trade directly with the Malaysian Ringgit (MYR), Russian Ruble (RUB), Australian Dollar (AUD), and Canadian Dollar (CAD), respectively, in addition to the USD, EUR, JPY and GBP, the four major international reserve currencies, as well as HKD. Here we will briefly introduce FX spot turnover between the CNY and these currencies in this section.

12.4.1 *Commencement of FX trading with the MYR*

Although the size of the Malaysian economy is just a little more than 1/3 of Indonesian in recent years, it was the largest trading partner of China in the Association of Southeast Asian Nations (ASEAN) with the transactions first exceeding $100 billion in 2013. Therefore, the MYR is one of the earliest currencies to trade with CNY. Since August 19, 2010, the SAFE published the central parity rate of CNY toward MYR for trading and clearing. It used an indirect quotation system, namely the price of MYR per 100 CNY. From 2014 to 2017, the total value of the CNY–MYR trading in the domestic foreign exchange market steadily grew from CNY 1.2 billion to CNY 3.8 billion before declining to CNY 3.5 billion in 2018 and CNY 2.64 billion in 2019. The value declined to CNY 504 million in 2020 and amounted to only CNY 88 million in the first quarter of 2021.

12.4.2 *Commencement of FX trading with the RUB*

Since November 22, 2010, the SAFE published the central parity rate of CNY toward RUB. It used an indirect quotation system, namely the price of RUB per 100 CNY. On November 24, Mr. Wen Jiabao, the Prime Minster, and Mr. Vladimir Putin, the Russian President, stated that they planned to use domestic currency for the settlement of bilateral trade. RUB is the seventh currency for listing trade in the domestic market following USD, HKD, JPY, EUR, GBP, and MYR. It is also the first direct trade currency between China and other developing countries. However, data indicate that the total transaction amount of RUB against CNY in domestic and offshore market decreased from CNY 25.5 billion to CNY 9.8 billion from 2014 to 2017.The ranking has fallen from ninth to 12th (see Table 12.1). In 2018, the total transaction amount rose to CNY 14.83 billion, ranking 13th among currencies in the domestic market. The amount dropped to CNY 13.41 billion and 14.37 billion in 2019 and 2020, respectively, retaining the 11th ranking. During the first quarter of 2021, the trading amounted to CNY 5.24 billion, and the ranking returned to 13th. Going forward, the close cooperation between China and Russia provides significant prospects for the development of RUB–CNY trading in the domestic foreign exchange market.

12.4.3 *Commencement of FX trading with the AUD and CAD*

Canada's economy remained world's ninth since 2009, while the Australian economy remained the 13th for the same period. Table 4.1 shows that from 2013 to 2019, in terms of transaction amounts, CAD and AUD ranked sixth and fifth, respectively, in the global foreign exchange market. These results show that the position of AUD and CAD in the global FX market was higher than their rankings in the world economy, which means that AUD and CAD play more essential roles in the international FX market than their positions in world economy. The SAFE published the central parity rate of CNY toward AUD and CAD since November 28, 2011 and CNY has been trading with AUD and CAD since then. Data indicate that total transaction amounts of CAD against CNY in both domestic foreign exchange markets increased more than 40.5 times from CNY 1.4 billion to CNY 58.1 billion between 2014 and 2018, rising from a ranking of 10th to sixth in the same period, the biggest increase among all foreign currencies. Yet, CAD–CNY transactions declined almost half to CNY 29.03 billion and ranked eighth in 2019, and it rose to CNY 33.7 billion and ranked ninth in 2020; the CAD–CNY turnover reached CNY 34.22 billion and ranked the fourth foreign currency in the first quarter of 2021. Direct trade between CNY and CAD will certainly strengthen cooperation between China and Canada.

12.4.4 *Direct trade with the Japanese yen (JPY)*

The CFETS authorized by the PBC stated on May 29, 2012, that it planned to improve trading between CNY and JPY in the interbank foreign exchange markets to develop direct trade with Japan. China and Japan are both major economic and trading entities in the world. The cooperation between the two countries in the field of economics and trade, finance and foreign exchange will not only reduce trade costs, improve the international competence and the internationalization of both countries' currencies but also play an active role in the Asian-Pacific region and even the whole world. However, data indicate that the total transaction amount of JPY against CNY in domestic foreign exchange markets decreased from CNY 451.1 billion in 2014 to CNY 278.4 billion and CNY 355.0 billion in 2018 and 2019, respectively. It decreased to CNY 273.4 billion in 2020, slightly lower than the amount CNY 278.4 billion in 2018. JPY's ranking fell from second to third place among foreign currencies in Mainland China from 2014 to 2020.

12.4.5 *Direct trade with the British pound (GBP)*

CFETS was authorized by the PBC to start to trade CNY vs. GBP in the interbank foreign exchange market on June 18, 2014. Based on market principles, developing direct trade between CNY and GBP is an essential step for both countries to mutually push the further development of their economic and commercial relationship. Direct trade in GBP will benefit the direct quotation against GBP, reduce currency conversion costs, and facilitate the usage of CNY and GBP in bilateral trade and investments. It will also help enhance both countries' financial cooperation and support the evolving economic and financial relationship between China and the UK. Although direct trading between GBP and CNY was accepted in 2014, the total transaction amount of GBP against CNY in domestic foreign exchange markets decreased from CNY 137.7 billion to 51.6 billion in 2018, and the GBP's ranking fell from sixth down to eighth among foreign currencies. These results were similar to CNY turnover in the London foreign exchange market; CNY–GBP turnover rose to CNY 77.7 billion in 2019 and dropped to CNY 58.7 billion in 2020, ranking as sixth and seventh in 2019 and 2020 respectively; it increased by 34.2% from CNY 48.7 billion in the first quarter of 2020 to CNY 85.7 billion in the first quarter of 2020.

12.4.6 *Direct trade with the EUR*

CEFTS was authorized to trade CNY vs. EUR directly in the interbank foreign exchange market in September 2014. Based on market principles, developing direct trade between CNY and EUR is a crucial step for China and EU to mutually push the further development of their economic and commercial relationship. The Eurozone is an important trade partner with China. Direct trade with EUR will benefit the direct quotation against EUR to reduce currency conversion costs and facilitate the usage of CNY and EUR in bilateral trade and investments. It also helps to enhance financial cooperation and support the evolving economic and financial relationship between China and the Eurozone. Total turnover of EUR against CNY in domestic foreign exchange spot market was CNY 315.5 billion in 2014, accounting for 1.24% of total spot foreign exchange market, and ranked third following USD and JPY. It rose to CNY 425.7 billion, 459.8 billion, 580.5 billion, and 754.7 billion from 2015 to 2018, respectively, exceeding the amount of JPY, ranking second only to USD, comparable to EUR's international status globally. It increased to CNY 1363.8 billion and CNY 1419.4 in 2019 and 2020, respectively, second only to USD; the turnover increased 34.2% from the first quarter of 2020 to CNY 473.8 billion in the first quarter of 2021. Table 4.1 indicates that EUR turnover share in global foreign exchange market accounted for about 17% from 2001 to 2019, yet the turnover of EUR and CNY accounted for only about 2.5% in the domestic CNY spot foreign exchange market from 2019, indicating greater role for the second world currency to play in China.

12.4.7 *Direct trade with the Singapore dollar (SGD)*

Singapore has been the world's third and Asia's most prominent foreign exchange trading center since 2013. It is the main commercial and financial center in ASEAN. Moreover, it is also CNY's principal overseas center besides Hong Kong and London. Spot trading between CNY and SGD benefits the development of Singapore's CNY center and the economic, commercial, and financial cooperation between China and ASEAN. In the 11th meeting of China–Singapore Bilateral Cooperation Joint Committee, held in Suzhou, Jiangsu province on October 27, 2014, Vice Premier Zhang Gaoli, announced trade agreement directly between CNY and SGD in the interbank foreign exchange market on October 28, 2014. Based on market principles, developing direct trade between CNY and SGD is an essential step for China and Singapore to strengthen the relationship both China and Singapore.

Total turnover of SGD against CNY in Mainland Chinese spot foreign exchange market was CNY 83.8 billion, ranked seventh in 2014, and it increased to CNY 380.1 billion and ranked fourth following USD, EUR, and JPY in 2015. Yet, it decreased to CNY 108.8 billion and CNY 12.9 billion in 2016 and 2017, respectively, with the ranking dropped to 11th in 2017. It increased to CNY 55.4 billion and CNY 133.2 billion in 2018 and 2019, ranking rose to fifth in 2019; however, it decreased by 36.9% to CNY 84.0 billion in 2020 with ranking remaining fifth, and it decreased 10.4% in the first half of 2021 to CNY 20.5 billion compared to the first quarter of 2020, and its ranking dropped down to seventh in the first quarter of 2021. With CNY deposits steadily increasing from June 2020 to June 2021 as shown in Table 9.1 and increasing commodity trade between China and ASEAN countries, CNY foreign exchange turnover should increase accordingly. We will discuss similar implications later in this chapter.

12.4.8 *Launch of Spot auction between CNY and New Zealand dollar (NZD)*

CFETS launched a spot auction between CNY and NZD on January 12, 2015. It uses centralized settlement cleared by the Shanghai Clearing

House. Spot foreign exchange turnover between CNY and NZD with market makers continuously providing two-way pricing provides liquidity to the market and the limit of auction liquidity is NZD 5 million. Direct trade between NZD and CNY was officially launched later, the total turnover of NZD/CNY trading in Mainland market was as high as CNY 28.1 billion in 2014, higher than that of RUB (CNY 25.5 billion) and ranked eighth. It dropped to CNY 19.6 billion in 2018, resulting in NZD's ranking dropping to 11th; it rose to CNY 21.4 billion and ranking 10th in 2020. With close relationship between China and New Zealand, trading between CNY and NZD will grow steadily in the coming years.

12.4.9 *Direct trade between CNY and Swiss franc (CHF)*

The China Foreign Exchange Trading System authorized by PBOC announced direct trade between CNY and CHF in the interbank foreign exchange market following market principles on December 9, 2015. Total turnover of CHF against CNY in Mainland Chinese spot foreign exchange market reached CNY 14.9 billion and CNY18.0 billion in 2015 and 2016, respectively, and CHF was ranked 10th in 2015 and 2016. It dropped slightly to CNY 16 billion in 2017 and significantly to CNY 7.3 in 2019, respectively, and its ranking was down to 13th in 2019; it increased to CNY 13.5 billion in 2020 ranked as 12th the same year. It is noticeable that CHF/CNY trading in the Mainland spot market increased 15.13 times to CNY 13.8 billion from the first half of 2020 to the same period in 2021, slightly more than the annual turnover in 2020. With high correlation coefficient between sci-tech originality capacity of the two countries, potential cooperation between China and Switzerland will strengthen, and foreign exchange turnover between these two currencies will grow accordingly.

12.4.10 *Direct trade between CNY and South African rand (ZAR)*

South Africa has been China's biggest trading partner in Africa for many years and is the only African country in the BRICS. Tables 4.9–4.12 show that the Rand was not only the currency with the highest degree of internationalization in BRICS but also a currency more international than many currencies of developed economies before 2010. On June 17, 2016, upon authorization of the PBOC, the China Foreign Exchange Trading

Center announced that the CNY was directly traded with the ZAR in the interbank foreign exchange market. In 2017, ZAR–CNY turnover of ZAR against CNY amounted to CNY 0.98 billion, ranking 17th among foreign currencies. The amount then fell to CNY 0.6 billion in 2018, ranking 20th. In 2019, the ZAR dropped again to CNY 0.1 billion, ranking 23rd; and in the first half of 2020, these transactions amounted to CNY 94 million, ranking 20th.

12.4.11 *Direct trade between CNY and South-Korean Won* (*SKW*)

SKW started to trade against CNY between banks in China and South Korea on December 1, 2014, a symbolic event for the development of the South Korean offshore CNY market. Shinhan Bank, Woori Bank, Industrial Bank of Korea (IBK), Korea Development Bank (KDB), Standard Chartered Bank, Citibank, and the Korean Exchange Bank (KEB), along with the South Korean branches of the Communication Bank of China (CCB), Industrial and Commercial Bank of China (ICBC), Deutsche Bank, JPMorgan Chase, and the Hong Kong and Shanghai Banking Corporation (HSBC) Limited were appointed as market makers in the interbank foreign exchange market in South Korea. SKW–CNY turnover amounted to CNY 31.3 billion in 2016, and it rose to CNY 39.4 billion in 2017, it yet fell to CNY 21.9 billion and CNY 11.9 billion in 2018 and 2019, respectively, with ranking from eighth to 12th from 2016 to 2019. Turnover of CNY/SKW shrank to CNY 6.2 billion in 2020, causing SKW ranking further down to 13th in 2020.

12.4.12 *Direct trade between CNY and the Saudi Riyal* (*SAR*)/*the UAE Dirham* (*AED*)

Authorized by the PBOC, the China Foreign Exchange Trading Center began to carry out direct transactions of CNY against the SAR and the AED in the interbank market in China on September 26, 2016. Saudi Arabia is the largest economy in the Middle East, ranked 19th of the world economy from 2012 to 2014, 20th from 2015 to 2017, 18th from 2018 to 2019, yet back to 20th in 2020. Over the years, it has been a principal trading partner of China in West Asia. Although UAE's economy scale is smaller, it was still China's second largest trading partner in West Asia.

Furthermore, the UAE has had the most extraordinary improvement in financial opening and reform during recent years. Direct transactions of CNY against the SAR and the AED will reduce the cost of trading, which is of great significance to promote cooperation between China and West Asia countries as well as the "One Belt, One Road" strategy. In 2016, SAR–CNY transactions and AED–CNY transactions amounted to CNY 47 million and CNY 57 million, respectively; and in 2017, they increased to CNY 769 million and CNY 102 million, respectively. In 2018, they notched even larger increases, rising to CNY 7.441 billion and CNY 8.589 billion, respectively. In 2019, SAR–CNY transactions and AED–CNY transactions fell to CNY 2.642 billion and CNY 1.088 billion, ranking 14th and 16th, respectively; and during the first half of 2020, these transactions amounted to CNY 802 million and CNY 631 million, ranking 15th and 16th, respectively.

In addition to the above-mentioned currencies that are directly traded with the CNY, as of June 2020, the CNY was also exchanged directly with the Hungarian Forint (HUF), Polish Zloty (PLN), Danish Krone (DKK), Swedish Krona (SEK), Norwegian Krone (NOK), Turkish Lira (TRY), Mexican Peso (MXN), and Thai Baht (THB). However, these currencies accounted for a small share of the transactions in China's foreign exchange market, and it will take time for these markets to be further cultivated and developed.

12.5 Overview of Domestic CNY Spot Foreign Exchange Turnover since 2014

12.5.1 *Distribution of foreign exchange transaction amount in domestic market since 2014*

Table 12.1 provides turnover of CNY spot foreign exchange in Mainland China since 2014. Table 12.1 shows that the USD maintained its top position as CNY's biggest currency pairing domestically from 2014 to the first quarter of 2021. The USD/CNY turnover accounted for over 94% of the entire market during the period from 2014 to 2021Q1 with the highest share 96.81 in 2018, which represented an increase of 2.64% compared to 2014, and its share was higher than the corresponding USD share in the world foreign exchange market given in Table 4.1. For the CNY's second biggest currency pairing, the EUR, its share increased steadily from

Table 12.1: Turnover of CNY Spot Trading against Other Countries (2014–2021Q1) (Unit: CNY billion, %)

Currency/ Year	**2014**	**Share**	**2016**	**Share**	**2018**	**Share**	**2020**	**Share**	**2021Q1**	**Share**	**Share Change from 2018 to 2020**
USD	23,994.2	94.17	38,261.5	96.77	49,190.7	96.81	55,320.5	96.20	14,484.6	95.20	−0.07
EUR	315.5	1.24	459.8	1.16	754.7	1.49	1,419.4	2.47	473.8	3.11	0.14
JPY	451.1	1.77	327.5	0.83	278.4	0.55	273.4	0.48	85.7	0.56	−0.13
CAD	1.4	0.01	25.2	0.06	58.1	0.11	33.7	0.06	34.2	0.22	0.04
HKD	293.1	1.15	149.3	0.38	192.0	0.38	145.7	0.25	27.0	0.18	0.12
AUD	148.6	0.58	79.3	0.20	87.9	0.17	58.9	0.10	22.0	0.14	0.00
SGD	83.8	0.33	108.8	0.28	55.4	0.11	84.0	0.15	20.5	0.13	−0.28
GBP	**137.7**	**0.54**	**49.0**	**0.12**	**51.6**	**0.10**	**58.7**	**0.10**	**14.5**	**0.10**	**−0.02**
CHF			**18.0**	**0.05**	**29.6**	**0.06**	**13.5**	**0.02**	**13.9**	**0.09**	**−0.05**
NZD	28.1	0.11	13.8	0.03	19.6	0.04	21.4	0.04	11.8	0.08	0.07
THB				0.00	18.1	0.04	35.9	0.06	11.7	0.08	0.00
RUB	25.5	0.10	11.8	0.03	14.8	0.03	14.4	0.02	5.2	0.03	−0.03
DKK				0.00	4.7	0.01	5.5	0.01	3.2	0.02	0.00
SKW		0.00	31.3	0.08	21.8	0.04	6.2	0.01	1.9	0.01	0.02
ZAR			0.9	0.00	0.6	0.00	1.1	0.00	1.8	0.01	0.00
SEK	0.0	0.00	0.0	0.00	10.0	0.02	2.8	0.00	1.7	0.01	0.00
MYR	1.2	0.00	3.4	0.01	3.5	0.01	0.5	0.00	0.1	0.00	−0.01
NOK				0.00	2.1	0.00	1.6	0.00	0.0	0.00	0.00
Others		0.00	0.3	0.00	17.9	0.04	6.7	0.01	0.9	0.01	0.00
Total	25,480.2	100.00	39,539.9	100.00	50,811.4	100.00	57,503.7	100.00	15,214.5	100.00	0.00

Source: China Monetary Policy Reports for 2014Q4–2020Q1.

1.24% in 2014 to 3.11% in the first quarter of 2021, yet still much lower than share of EUR in world foreign exchange market in Table 4.1; the JPY remained as the third biggest foreign currency in Mainland China since 2015, yet its share declined from 1.77% in 2014 to 0.56% in the first quarter of 2021, much lower than the corresponding share of yen in world foreign exchange market from 2014 to 2019 in Table 4.1. Share of other currencies, particularly the GBP, the fourth world currency, is relatively low compared with the top three foreign currencies in Table 12.1.

12.6 Development of CNY-Denominated Funds and Other CNY-Denominated Products in Offshore Market

12.6.1 *Development of CNY-denominated funds in offshore market*

With the rapid promotion of CNY cross-border trade settlement, overseas offshore CNY funds drew more and more attention in the second half of 2010. On August 31, 2010, Haitong Securities in Hong Kong issued the first CNY-denominated fund overseas — Haitong Global CNY Income Fund with an upper limit of CNY 5 billion. By February 28, 2017, the fund's total assets amounted to about CNY 526 million. Besides Haitong Global Fund, offshore CNY-denominated funds already launched include Hang Seng CNY bond fund issued by Hang Seng Bank (public bond fund and the scale about 300 million in February 2010), ICBC Asia Global CNY Fixed-income Fund distributed by ICBC Asia (public bond fund) and CCB International Income Fund issued by CCB International (public bond fund). Except these public bond funds, Guoxin Securities (Hong Kong), Schroder and UBS plan to issue offshore CNY-denominated Private Equity Fund and other PE. Pharo Management, with total assets of about $4 billion, plans to issue the first CNY-denominated Hedge Fund.

Apart from these funds, HSBC Global Asset Management, Alliance Bernstein, Amundi, Barclays, BNP Paribas, Manulife, and Allianz Global Investors also launched CNY bond funds.

The first global CNY golden ETF (Exchange Traded Fund) started to trade in Hong Kong and provided a new way for Hong Kong offshore CNY capital on February 15, 2012. This fund was issued by Hang Seng Bank and its return was denominated in CNY and aimed at offering new investment choices for CNY in Hong Kong to keep CNY stay in Hong Kong instead of flowing back to Mainland.

Not only Hong Kong CNY-denominated fund, Taiwan CNY-denominated fund also developed very fast. The first Taiwan CNY-denominated fund, Fuhua Umbrella CNY Fund, was approved by the competent authority in early April 2013 and raised funds from CNY 20 billion up to CNY 28 billion.

Citadel LLC under hedge fund manager Kenneth C. Griffin became the first foreign company based on a pilot plan to raise CNY fund. Accordingly, the statement released by the Shanghai Government on May 21, Citadel, based in Chicago, could use all CNY raised to convert into USD for investment. In September 2013, China's foreign exchange regulator granted Citadel and other five offshore hedge funds the qualification of "Qualified Domestic Limited Partner Program" (QDLP), with each one raising maximum of $50 million. This trial plan allowed China's high net-worth individuals to invest in overseas markets through offshore hedge funds.

On May 22, 2015, the spokesman of China Securities Regulatory Commission (CSRC), Deng Ge announced that CSRC and the Hong Kong Securities and Futures Commission signed the Memorandum of Regulatory Co-operation on Mutual Recognition of Mainland and Hong Kong funds between CRSC and HKSFC and issued the Provisional Regulation of Hong Kong Mutual-recognition Fund Management, implemented on July 1, 2015. CRSC said mutual-recognition would help to attract foreign capital into Mainland capital market, broaden cross-border investment channels to improve the competitiveness of two markets. It would lay a foundation for regulators to build fund supervision standards and provide more diversified investment products for investors in Mainland and Hong Kong.

12.6.2 *Breakthrough of CNY denomination for commodities*

On November 19, 2012, the Hong Kong Exchange and Clearing Limited (HKEx) acquisition of London Metal Exchange (LME) was approved by the Financial Service Authority (FSA). It issued the first Aluminum, Zinc and Copper small-sized futures contract, denominated in CNY, in December 2014. On July 28, 2015, London Metal Exchange (LME) announced the acceptance of CNY as collateral, which was a milestone for China to enter the London Commodities market and laid a foundation for the LME to issue CNY-denominated products in future. It is expected that there are more CNY-denominated products issued in the LME.

On March 26, 2018, CNY-denominated crude oil futures were listed for trading at the Shanghai International Energy Exchange, a subsidiary of the Shanghai Futures Exchange. The experience gained in the oil futures market in various areas, including open paths, tax management, foreign exchange management, bonded delivery, and cross-border regulatory cooperation, can gradually be applied to the trading of other commodity futures, such as iron ore and non-ferrous metals, thereby promoting the opening-up of China's CNY-denominated commodity futures market.

12.7 Progress of Liberalization of CNY Capital Account and Its Development in Future

The Chinese government's CNY internationalization initiatives can be traced back to 2003 when the following measures were proposed at the third session of the 16th Central Committee of the Communist Party of China to broaden the limits on cross-border capital transactions selectively and incrementally, gradually realize capital account convertibility, and expedite trial trade settlements in CNY for Hong Kong and Macao. The report of the 18th national congress of the Communists' Party put "gradually realizing capital account convertibility" as one of the goals of financial reforms from now on. Over decades, China has taken a series of essential steps in capital account liberalization. This section will introduce the progress of liberalization of CNY capital items.

12.7.1 *Two-way orderly opening of capital items*

During the 11th Five-Year Plan, the liberalization of CNY capital items has made significant progress.

Firstly, financial channels of foreign investments broadened. On April 2006, Qualified Domestic Institutional Investor (QDII) was implemented to orderly broaden financial channels for institutions and individual foreign investments. Secondly, the domestic securities market was further opened. After introducing Qualified Foreign Institutional Investor (QFII) in 2002, increased total QFII quotas and single QFII quota helped encourage foreign investors to invest in domestic market since 2007 (Yi Gang, 2011). According to the data from SAFE website, as of July 31, 2020, 152 QDIIs have been approved with the quota of $116.259 billion; there were 295 QFIIs with $116.259 billion by May 28, 2020. To broaden the investment channels of CNY flown into Hong Kong, the China Securities Regulatory Commission, the PBOC, and SAFE jointly published "Trial Measures of domestic securities investment for RQFIIs of Fund Management Companies and Securities Companies" on December 16, 2011, laying a foundation for the pilot of CNY Qualified Institutional Investors. By May 28, 2020, 230 RQFIIs had been approved, which amounted to a cumulative quota of CNY 722.992 billion (equivalent to $104.79 billion); this amount accounted for almost 90% of the total authorized QFII amount. On September 18, 2019, the SAFE officially abolished the investment quota restrictions for QFII/RQFII, including the total investment quota restrictions for QFII and RQFII, the filing and approval requirements for single foreign institutional investors, and the restrictions on RQFII pilot countries and regions. These changes marked an advancement in the CNY's internationalization.

Thirdly, domestic and foreign capital markets have been further integrated, and trading among Mainland China, Hong Kong SAR, and the London stock markets has started. On November 17, 2014, the stock trading between the Shanghai Stock Exchange and the Hong Kong Stock Exchange (hereinafter referred to as the Shanghai–Hong Kong Stock Connect) was officially launched. This mechanism represents a major institutional innovation in the opening-up of the capital market, and it represents a new model for cross-border securities investment. Through specific technology and cross-border settlement arrangements, investors from Mainland China and Hong Kong SAR can directly buy and sell stocks listed on each other's exchanges. On December 5, 2016, the Shenzhen–Hong Kong Stock Connect was officially opened, and the bilateral control over the total quota was canceled, together with that of the Shanghai–Hong Kong Stock Connect. In April 2018, the daily quotas of the Shanghai–Hong Kong Stock Connect and Shenzhen–Hong Kong Stock Connect were expanded four times to CNY 52 billion and CNY 42 billion, respectively. On August 31, 2018, the China Securities Regulatory Commission publicly solicited opinions on the *Shanghai-London Stock Connect Depository Receipt Business Regulatory Rules* and clarified the Shanghai–London Stock Connect China Depository Receipt (CDR) issuance review system and the CDR cross-border conversion system arrangements, among other matters. The Regulatory Rules provide important principled provisions on matters such as the issuance of public offerings, cross-border conversion, continuous regulatory requirements, regulatory enforcement, and investor protection for the Shanghai–London Stock Connects east-bound and west-bound business. On October 12, 2018, the Regulatory Rules were officially released. Compared with the draft for comments, the final version clarified multiple issues. For example, the final version detailed the limit on the withdrawal period for domestic listed companies that dispense CDRs overseas, and clarified the allotment of shares for issuers of overseas underlying securities that distribute domestic CDRs. On June 17, 2019, the Shanghai–London Stock Connect officially launched trading. The launch of the Shanghai–London Stock Connect promoted the development of cross-border securities business in domestic securities firms while also promoting the two-way opening-up and globalization of China's capital market.

Fourthly, the interbank bond market has been fully liberalized, attracting overseas institutions to participate in domestic financial transactions. Since 2010, foreign central banks and monetary authorities, CNY clearing banks in Hong Kong and Macau, banks participating in overseas cross-border CNY exchange settlement, and other "Tier 3 institutions" have been able to invest in the interbank bond market within the approved (approval later changed to filing) quota. This change marked the opening-up of the domestic bond market. In May 2016, the interbank bond market was fully opened to foreign investors and investment was not subject to administrative licenses, single institution limits or total limits. Foreign institutional investors do not need to receive approval for remittances or inflows of funds. Furthermore, investments in the interbank bond market are not subject to lock-up periods, remittance ratios or quota restrictions. Only the filing and foreign exchange registration requirements have been retained, which greatly facilitates foreign institutional investors' investment in the interbank bond market. The Bond Connect officially, launched in July 2017, has effectively promoted the integration of the capital markets in Mainland China and Hong Kong SAR. The Bond Connect also provided more convenient investment channels for foreign investors and promoted the opening-up of the country's financial market. As of June 2020, the scale of CNY bonds held by foreign institutions in the interbank bond market amounted to CNY 2,196.011 billion.

12.7.2 *CNY cross-border settlement and direct investment under the capital account*

In 2007, the People's Bank of China and the National Development and Reform Commission decided to allow qualified domestic financial institutions to distribute CNY bonds in Hong Kong. The pilot of cross-border capital items, including CNY offshore direct investment, foreign lending and guarantees, was carried out in 2010. The People's Bank of China published "trial measures on CNY settlement of offshore direct investment" on January 13, 2011. According to the measures, banks, and enterprises in the pilot area of cross-border trading CNY settlement could develop pilot settlement of offshore direct investment. It meant that offshore direct investment settlement trialed in Xinjiang in the end of October 2010 has been extended.

In 2010, all the pilot areas dealt with 386 business of CNY cross-border investment and financing, amounting to CNY 70.17 billion. From 2011 to 2016, banks cumulatively handled offshore direct investment settlement in CNY of 20.15 billion, CNY 29.2 billion, CNY 85.61 billion, CNY 186.56 billion, CNY 736.2 billion, and CNY 1,061.9 billion, respectively, and foreign direct investment settlement of CNY 90.72 billion, CNY 251 billion, CNY 448.13 billion, CNY 862.02 billion, CNY 1,587.1 billion, and CNY 1,398.8 trillion. With the continuous growth of CNY cross-border direct investment, foreign direct investment in CNY also increased in 2016. In 2017, the total CNY transactions under the capital account amounted to CNY 4,830 billion. In 2018, this figure reached CNY 10,740 billion, an increase of 122.4% from 2017 indicating strong growth from the previous year. In 2019, total CNY transactions under the capital account amounted to CNY 1,360 billion, which represented an increase of 26.7% from the previous year.

12.7.3 *Liberalization of IMF categories*

By early 2011, there were seven categories and 40 capital items by IMF reference. China maintains strict controls mainly in cross-border financial derivatives trading. The convertibility of CNY capital items was liberalized obviously. With the continuous opening-up of the domestic interbank bond market, foreign exchange risk hedging tools for investment in the bond market are being fully liberalized. Foreign investors can flexibly use foreign exchange derivatives to avoid risk, which has greatly promoted the opening-up of the capital account (Yigang, 2011).

It needs to meet many criteria to realize capital items convertibility: whether macro-economy is stable, whether financial system is comprehensive, whether enterprises and financial institutions have the awareness of risk management and management skills, whether the balance of international payments is stable, whether the path and means of domestic macro-control are mature, and whether cross-border capital flow can be monitored effectively and so on.

12.7.4 *Cancellation of obligatory foreign exchange-selling mechanism*

In December 1996, China announced to realize convertibility of current account items: there was no limit on foreign payment and transferring of current items, but foreign exchange currencies like firm's export, in principle, still should sell to designated banks. In 2002, the quota was 20% of previous year's foreign exchange earnings of current items. In 2004, it raised to 30% or 50%, and further 50% or 80% in 2005. In 2006, changing the way of verifying the quota by earnings, it was verified by the sum of 80% of previous year's foreign exchange earnings of current items and 50% of foreign exchange expenditure to further improve enterprises' reserves for foreign exchange. In 2007, the quota management was canceled, and enterprises could retain foreign exchange independently based on operation's needs. In 2008, the revised "Regulations on Foreign Exchange Control" specified that enterprises and individuals could retain foreign exchange or sell to banks. Since 2009, to further facilitate trading and investing and improve policy transparency, foreign exchange regulation authorities have vigorously cleared regulations and many normative documents related to obligatory foreign exchange-selling mechanism have been abolished, expired, or revised. Now obligatory foreign exchange-selling mechanism has lost effect and not executed in practice anymore.

12.7.5 *Liberalization of capital items and currency internationalization*

The IMF, especially the American government, repeatedly emphasized free capital flow as the necessary condition for CNY becoming a basket of currencies of IMF SDR. It makes sense, but in fact is arbitrary. It is quite different from other currencies. Japan's capital items were liberalized in December 1998, after the implementation of "Programs of Financial System Reform". JPY already covered 0.5% of internationally recognized foreign currency reserve assets in 1975, it increased to 2.5% and 3.3% in 1977 to 1978, respectively, and it exceeded 4% in 1980. In fact, from early July 1974 to December 1980, JPY became one of the basket currencies of IMF SDR, with weight up to 7.5%. In other words, the JPY was included in the IMF's SDR basket of currencies 24 years before the liberalization of Japan's capital account. Although time has passed, the IMF should not apply a double standard regarding this issue.

12.7.6 *Schedule of China capital items liberalization*

For years, the process and schedule of CNY capital items liberalization have drawn much attention inside and outside China, but competent authorities have not yet made declaration. On February 27, 2012, the People's Daily Online published an article titled "The People's Bank of China" which outlined the path to capital account liberalization for the first time, indicating that the time is ripe. This article referred to the report introduced in *Economic Information Daily*. The report was written by the research group under the lead of Sheng Songcheng, Director of Financial Survey and Statistics Department of the PBOC. It specified that the condition of China's capital items liberalization was mature, and it had three phases: short term, mid term, and long term. "Short-term arrangement (1–3 years): relaxing the control of direct investment with real transaction background and encouraging enterprises to 'go out'. Direct investment itself is stable and less affected by economy; Mid-term arrangement (3–5 years): relaxing the control of commercial credit and improving CNY internationalization; Long-term arrangement (5–10 years): enhancing the construction of financial market and first opening inflow and then outflow. Real estate, stocks and bonds transactions will be opened successively and prudently, and price-oriented management will replace quantity-oriented management." This is the first time the PBOC in an official report described a more specific path of China capital items liberalization and gave a comparatively detailed schedule.

"Central Committee of the Communist Party of China: Recommendations for the 13th Five-year plan for Economic and Social

Development", published in early November 2015, specified to broaden finance two-way opening, orderly promote CNY capital items convertibility, and make CNY become freely convertible and application through being part of SDR. On October 1, 2016, the CNY was officially added to the Special Drawing Rights (SDR) basket. Since 2014, the Shanghai–Hong Kong Stock Connect, the Shenzhen–Hong Kong Stock Connect, and the Bond Connect have been launched one after another. These developments have signified that China's stock market and bond market are opening and that the country's capital account is opening up in an orderly manner.

12.8 CNY Currency Swaps Signed between China and Other Monetary Authorities

Before the full liberalization of the CNY capital account, signing CNY currency swap agreements with other countries and regions will further promote CNY cross-border trade settlement and CNY investment, as well as bilateral trade and investment and financial stability, which are all critical parts of CNY internationalization.

12.8.1 *Overview of currency swap agreements between CNY and foreign currencies*

Since 2008, the PBOC has signed CNY currency swap agreements with almost 40 countries and regions, including Hong Kong SAR, Malaysia, South Korea, Singapore, Australia, Brazil, the UK, the Eurozone, Swiss, Russia, and Canada, with the amount exceeding CNY 3 trillion. Table 12.2 outlines the dates, CNY amounts of the agreements that had been signed as of November 25, 2020.

12.8.2 *Distribution of CNY currency swaps*

As shown in Table 12.2, most of the countries and regions that have signed CNY currency swap agreements with China are concentrated in the Asia-Pacific region, which accounts for 57.71% of the total amount of the arrangements. Meanwhile, Europe and the Americas account for 28.81% and 8.55%, respectively. These figures appear to coincide with

Table 12.2: CNY Currency Swaps Signed between the People's Bank of China and Other Monetary Authorities (Unit: CNY billion, %)

Date of Signing	Country/ Region	Contractual Amount	Date of Signing	Country/ Region	Contractual Amount
25/11/2020	Hong Kong SAR	500	30/03/2018	Australia	200
05/12/2019	Macau SAR	30	22/12/2017	Thailand	70
23/11/2020	Russia	150	02/11/2017	Qatar	35
11/10/2020	Korea	400	21/07/2017	Switzerland	150
17/09/2020	Hungary	40	18/07/2017	Argentina	70
25/10/2019	Chile	50	06/07/2017	Mongolia	15
12/01/2020	Canada	200	19/05/2017	New Zealand	25
13/05/2019	European Central Bank	350	21/12/2016	Iceland	3.5
10/12/2018	Singapore	300	06/12/2016	Egypt	18
19/11/2018	Ukraine	15	17/06/2016	Serbia	1.5
12/11/2018	Indonesia	200	11/05/2016	Morocco	10
26/10/2018	Britain	350	14/12/2015	UAE	35
20/08/2018	Japan	200	26/09/2015	Turkey	12
28/05/2018	Malaysia	180	03/09/2015	Tajikistan	3
25/05/2018	Kazakhstan	7	15/05/2015	Ukraine	15
24/05/2018	Pakistan	30	25/03/2015	Armenia	1
03/05/2018	Nigeria	15	18/03/2015	Suriname	1
27/04/2018	Belarus	15	16/09/2014	Sri Lanka	10
11/04/2018	South Africa	30	26/03/2013	Brazil	190
03/04/2018	Albania	2	19/04/2011	Uzbekistan	0.7
	Total	3929.7			
Region	Asia-Pacific	2267.7	Share	57.71	
	Europe	1132		28.81	
	America	336		8.55	
	Others	194		4.94	
	Developed economies	2708.5		68.92	
	Developing countries and regions	1221.2		31.08	

Source: The website of the People's Bank of China.

the activeness of offshore CNY centers and the acceptance of CNY in these regions. In addition, in Table 32.2, the developed economies that have signed agreements with China account for close to 70% of all the agreements, while developing countries account for just over 30%, which does not quite align with the distribution of bilateral commerce.

12.8.3 *Usage of CNY currency swap agreements*

Most of the funds in the CNY swap agreements outlined in Table 12.2 were not actually used initially. Taking South Korea as an example, early on April 20, 2009, it signed a nominal value of CNY 180 billion swap agreement with the PBOC, and the amount in the agreement doubled on October 26, 2011. For quite some time, the Bank of Korea did not use the currency swap funds. In January 2013, the Bank of Korea used CNY in currency swaps for the first time when it granted a loan of CNY 62 million to the Korea Exchange Bank. On May 30, 2014, the PBOC used KRW 400 million (about CNY 2.4 million) within the currency swap to support trade finance. It is the first time for the PBOC to use counterpart's currency within currency swaps.

According to the data in the Monetary Policy Implementation Report issued by the PBOC, the monetary authorities that had signed currency swap agreements with China had used CNY 22.149 billion as of the end of 2016 and CNY 22.150 billion as of the end of 2017; and the PBOC had used $1.118 billion of foreign currencies in 2016 and $1.614 billion of foreign currencies in 2017. At the end of 2018, the monetary authorities that had signed currency swap agreements with China had used CNY 32.786 billion, and the balance of foreign currency used by the People's Bank of China was $471 million. In 2019, the ratio of CNY used by foreign monetary authorities was CNY 32.922 billion, and the balance of foreign currency used by the People's Bank of China amounted to $323 million. In recent years, the amount of CNY currency swap agreements has trended upward, but the amount utilized as a proportion of the total contracted amount is still only slightly more than 1%. Therefore, there is still room for these currency swap agreements to play a greater role in promoting the use of CNY abroad. If the used amount accounted for 10–50% of the total contracted amount, these CNY currency swap agreements would more effectively promote the internationalization of the CNY.

12.8.4 *Relationship between CNY currency swap agreements and offshore CNY centers*

Comparing the dates and amounts of the currency swap agreements in Table 12.2 with the overseas CNY payment ratios in different overseas CNY centers in Table 9.3, it is clear that countries that signed CNY currency swap agreements earlier and in larger amounts have higher ratios of CNY payments. For instance, offshore CNY centers such as Hong Kong SAR, Singapore, London, and South Korea have each engaged in CNY currency swaps of more than CNY 300 billion.

12.9 Average Daily Turnover of CNY Foreign Exchange Market Since 2010

To measure the internationalization of currencies using data provided by Bank for International Settlements (BIS), calculation and comparison of internationalization from 2007 to 2019 of main currencies were made in Chapter 4. With the same method and updated data, this chapter will calculate the average daily turnover of domestic CNY since 2010, reflecting the situation in the domestic CNY foreign exchange market.

12.9.1 *Turnover of CNY foreign exchange market in Mainland China in recent years*

Table 12.3 gives the turnover of CNY foreign exchange market from 2010 to the first half of 2021.

Table 4.1 includes the global foreign exchange market data released by the BIS for April every 3 years. The data show the average daily turnover in April every 3 years, and the semi-annual data of the five major international foreign exchange centers in London, New York, Singapore, Hong Kong, and Tokyo. The average daily turnover for these five centers is broadcasted in April and October each year, like the announcements of the BIS. Although the SAFE has continued to announce the monthly transaction value in the domestic foreign exchange market since 2015, the total transaction value in April and October each year and the corresponding number of working days are used to calculate the average daily transaction value, so it is difficult to directly compare the domestic figures with the average daily transaction value in the international market. However,

Table 12.3: Turnover of CNY Foreign Exchange Market in Mainland China (2010–2021) (Unit: USD billion)

Time/ Markets	Spots		Forwards		Foreign Exchange Swaps	Currency Swaps	Foreign Exchange Options		Total Foreign Exchange Turnover	
Period	Inter Banks	Banks to Clients	Inter Banks	Banks to Clients	Inter Banks	Inter Banks	Inter Banks	Banks to Clients		
2010H1	1,546.6	1,037.5	5.5		630.6				3,220.2	27.3
2010H2	1,498.6	1,257.1	27.3		669.3				3,452.2	27.8
2011H1	1,750.8	1,302.4	115.9		792.6	5.8	0.3	0.2	3,968.0	33.3
2011H2	1,803.0	1,525.2	98.7		978.4	8.6	0.7	0.6	4,415.2	35.3
2012H1	1,730.0	1,460.6	64.5	173.1	1,140.0	12.8	1.4	5.9	4,588.4	39.6
2012H2	1,630.0	1,594.4	22.1	191.0	1,380.0	20.3	2.3	22.6	4,862.7	38.6
2013H1	1,909.0	1,684.4	7.2	289.1	1,517.3	28.3	3.9	31.2	5,470.4	48.8
2013H2	2,191.1	1,811.3	25.1	283.0	1,883.4	51.7	17.8	20.2	6,283.6	50.3
2014H1	2,070.0	1,740.9	25.9	316.3	2,040.0	98.0	13.2	23.3	6,327.6	53.2
2014H2	2,050.0	1,925.0	27.0	250.4	2,450.0	128.8	135.5	39.6	7,006.2	56.1
2015H1	2,062.9	1,567.6	17.3	251.1	3,100.0	170.2	120.8	65.0	7,354.9	61.8
2015H2	2,799.4	1,830.2	19.9	206.7	5,251.4	81.7	168.0	50.9	10,408.2	84.6
2016H1	2,531.8	1,459.5	44.2	108.4	4,426.8	62.8	183.7	84.2	8,901.3	74.8
2016H2	3,395.1	1,449.0	108.8	117.1	5,578.2	61.7	563.4	123.7	11,396.9	91.9
2017H1	2,902.5	1,492.4	40.4	129.1	5,560.1	203.0	159.3	121.4	10,486.3	88.1
2017H2	3,495.5	1,599.0	63.0	193.5	7,856.6	69.4	211.9	109.4	13,598.2	112.4
2018H1	3,253.0	1,654.5	38.4	289.4	7,550.6	58.3	246.1	109.7	13,200.1	105.2
2018H2	4,380.2	1,776.9	49.1	165.0	8,911.7	96.5	365.0	126.5	15,871.0	137.7
2019H1	4,002.4	1,640.3	42.8	150.3	8,900.6	81.8	318.4	133.7	15,270.2	128.5
2019H2	3,935.0	1,778.5	33.2	154.4	7,477.8	72.6	262.8	135.2	13,849.5	104.2
2020H1	3,430.6	1,676.9	51.3	170.4	7,353.2	129.8	227.0	133.4	13,172.5	104.7
2020H2	4,947.7	1,940.8	53.1	289.6	9,017.9	85.3	339.6	141.2	16,814.9	130.7
2021H1	4,953.8	1,994.5	52.3	414.3	9,301.4	87.9	424.8	176.3	17,405.3	139.1

Source: Data for 2011–2014 are based on the monetary policy implementation reports of the PBOC and data from Chinamoney.com.cn; data for 2010 are calculated based on the data from the same period in 2011; data for 2015–2021 are based on the monthly foreign exchange data released by the SAFE. Since 2015, SAFE's foreign exchange data have only included the total amount of foreign exchange swaps and currency swaps, so the currency swap data since 2015 are calculated using the Monetary Policy Implementation Reports issued by the PBOC. The currency swap data have been obtained by subtracting foreign exchange swaps from the total amount of foreign exchange swaps and currency swaps announced by the SAFE; the semi-annual turnover is actual total semi-annual turnover, and the average daily turnover from 2015 to 2021 is the average daily turnover of April and October of the year to be more comparable with international data.

the domestic semi-annual average daily transaction value is more stable and has better comparability. Therefore, it is appropriate to use the average daily data in April and October of the year in Table 12.3 since 2015 for the domestic data to be more comparable to the international data.

As shown in Table 12.3, the domestic foreign exchange market experienced significant growth from 2010H1 to 2016H1. The average daily transaction value in the domestic market increased 1.74 times from $27.3 billion to $74.8 billion, and the accumulated annual increase rate was 18.3%, which was more than three times higher than the 4.1% rate achieved by the global exchange market during the same period; growth continued from 2016H1 to 2019H1 with the average daily turnover increasing from $74.8 billion to $128.5 billion, which represented an accumulated annual increase rate of 19.8%, 10.6 percentage points higher than the 9.2% rate achieved by the global exchange market during the same period. In addition, the 19.8% rate was 11.3 percentage points higher than the compound annual growth rate of 8.5% notched by the average daily foreign exchange turnover of the world's top seven currencies in the world's nine major foreign exchange centers during the same period. The data indicate that the domestic CNY foreign exchange market caught up from 2010 to 2019. However, the domestic foreign exchange market fell steadily from the second half of 2018 to the second half of 2019 with annual average turnover down by 24.3%. This was due primarily to the US–China trade tensions during the period.

Table 12.3 also shows that the domestic CNY foreign exchange transaction volume recovered significantly from the first half of 2020 to the same period in 2021 with annual growth rate of 32.9%, and the average daily turnover reached the historical high of $139.1 billion in April 2021.

12.9.2 *Product distribution in domestic CNY foreign exchange market since 2010*

With the data provided in Table 12.3, we can calculate domestic spot exchange, forward exchange, swap, and option transactions as a ratio of the total transaction amount from 2010 to 2015, the results are given in Table 12.4. According to Table 12.4, the balance of CNY foreign exchange spot transactions has continued to decline from more than 80% in 2010H1 to 49.4% in 2015H1, indicating that the domestic CNY market changed from the traditional spot trading to derivatives dominating in the

Table 12.4: Product Distribution in CNY Foreign Exchange Market (2010–2021) (Unit: %)

Time/ Products	Spots	Forwards	Swaps	Currency Swaps	Options
2010H1	80.2	0.2	19.6		
2010H2	79.8	0.8	19.4		
2011H1	76.9	2.9	20.0	0.1	0.0
2011H2	75.4	2.2	22.2	0.2	0.0
2012H1	69.5	5.2	24.8	0.3	0.2
2012H2	66.3	4.4	28.4	0.4	0.5
2013H1	65.7	5.4	27.7	0.5	0.6
2013H2	63.7	4.9	30.0	0.8	0.6
2014H1	60.2	5.4	32.2	1.5	0.6
2014H2	56.7	4.0	35.0	1.8	2.5
2015H1	49.4	3.6	42.1	2.3	2.5
2015H2	44.5	2.2	50.5	0.8	2.1
2016H1	44.8	1.7	49.7	0.7	3.0
2016H2	42.5	2.0	48.9	0.5	6.0
2017H1	41.9	1.6	53.0	1.9	2.7
2017H2	37.5	1.9	57.8	0.5	2.4
2018H1	37.2	2.5	57.2	0.4	2.7
2018H2	38.8	1.3	56.2	0.6	3.1
2019H1	37.0	1.3	58.3	0.5	3.0
2019H2	41.3	1.4	54.0	0.5	2.9
2020H1	38.8	1.7	55.8	1.0	2.7
2020H2	41.0	2.0	53.6	0.5	2.9
2021H1	39.9	2.7	53.4	0.5	3.5

Source: Calculations based on data in Table 12.3.

period. In the first half of 2015, the percentage of spot transactions fell below 50% for the first time, and the proportion fell further to the lowest level of 37% in the first half of 2019. This trend aligns with the ratios of spot transactions in global market; meanwhile, the proportion of foreign exchange swap transactions has continued to increase from merely 19.6% in 2010H1 to the historical high of 58.3% in the first half of 2019. After fast growth in the initial stage of market development from 2012 to 2016, the ratio of foreign exchange options trading began to decline from 2016 and has remained at about 3%, about half of the global share of 6% of options turnover.

It is noticeable that share of CNY forwards turnover reached its highest level of 5.4% in the first half of 2014, and fell to below 3% since 2016, much lower than the global share of forwards turnover over 10% since 2001.

12.10 Ranking of Internationalization of Major World Currencies in 2020 and 2021

The purpose of this section is to find internationalization or foreign exchange turnover changes of the world's top eight currencies from 2019 to 2021.

12.10.1 *Inconsistence of CNY turnover ranking and other rankings from 2016 to 2019*

Table 4.1 includes the average daily trading value of foreign exchange in major currencies in the world from April 1998 to 2019 released by the BIS in 2019. The data show that the global share of CNY increased from 2.23% to 4.32% during April 2013–April 2019. Meanwhile, the average annual compound growth rate (CAGR) of the average daily turnover of CNY foreign exchange was 15.6% during the same period; this rate was two times higher than CAGR of 5.2% posted for the CAD for the same period, which notched the highest compound annual growth rate among the top seven currencies other than CNY in the same period. In addition, the average daily turnover of the CNY from 2013 to 2016 increased and its global ranking dropped from ninth to eighth from 2013 to 2016, and then retained the eighth ranking from 2016 to 2019. The corresponding data in Table 3.2 show that the global share accounted for by CNY cross-border clearing was only ranked at 13th in April 2013, while Table 12.1 shows that the share accounted for by CNY foreign exchange turnover in the same period ranked at ninth — a ranking difference of four places. In April 2016, the ratio accounted for by CNY cross-border settlements ranked sixth in the world, while the proportion of CNY turnover in the same period ranked eighth — a ranking difference of two places. In April

2019, the ratio of CNY cross-border payments ranked fifth, while the proportion of CNY foreign exchange turnover was ranked eighth during the same period — a difference of three places. IMF COFER (Currency Composition of Official Foreign Exchange Reserves) data show that the global share of CNY foreign exchange reserves increased from 1.1% (ranking of seventh) in 2016 to 2.0% (ranking of fifth) in the second quarter of 2019, and to 2.4% in the first quarter of 2021. These data show that both CNY cross-border payments and COFER had increased significantly by 2019 compared with 2016, but it is surprising that there was no change in the CNY foreign exchange turnover rankings from 2016 to 2019.

12.10.2 *The data from the BIS are significantly lower than the average daily turnover of domestic CNY foreign exchange*

According to the latest data from the BIS, the average daily turnover of domestic CNY foreign exchange market in April 2019 amounted to only $101.23 billion, which was $27.3 billion lower than the average daily turnover of CNY 128.5 in Table 12.3 for the same period. This difference is equivalent to a reduction of 21.2% of onshore average daily turnover of CNY foreign exchange in April 2019, which clearly shows that the BIS has drastically reduced onshore CNY foreign exchange turnover, as a result, it reduced CNY's actual turnover share worldwide.

12.10.3 *BIS local currency turnover compared with data release by local monetary authority*

According to data released by Reserve Bank of Australia (www.rba.gov.au), average daily turnover of AUD against all foreign currencies in Australia was $58.82 billion, which was exactly the same as data released by BIS in December 2019; yet, the average daily turnover of CAD against all foreign currencies in Canada was $55.30 in April 2019 (www.bankofcanada.ca), which was $5.74 billion lower than the daily average turnover of CAD against all other currencies in April 2019 released by BIS in December 2019. Thus, BIS lowered CNY daily turnover by $27.3 billion in China for April 2019, yet it raised $5.74 billion in Canada for the same period, leading to significant errors for ranking of globalization of the two currencies.

12.10.4 *Significant differences and serious problems in the data released by BIS and the UK*

Table 12.5 shows the average daily foreign exchange turnover of major currencies in the UK in April 2019, as announced by the BIS in September 2019 and the London Foreign Exchange Joint Standing Committee (FXJSC) under the Bank of England in July 2019. These data show the average daily foreign exchange transaction values of 18 major currencies in the UK in April 2019. As shown in Table 32.5, in April 2019, the average daily foreign exchange turnover in the UK of the 18 currencies announced by the BIS, excluding the CNY, ranged from 5% to 38% higher than the data broadcasted by the FXJSC. The CNY amount published by the BIS was 29% lower than that announced by the FXJSC, which shows that the FXJSC has a certain preference for the CNY. By observing the data in Table 12.5 carefully, we find that the top eight currencies for which the BIS data are higher than the FXJSC data include the CAD and the AUD, which are 38% and 35% higher, respectively. While drastically decreasing CNY transactions, the BIS also substantially increases transactions involving the CAD and AUD, with the obvious goal of causing the two currencies to exceed the CNY in foreign exchange transactions.

12.10.5 *Global ranking of CNY in 2019*

Table 12.5 shows that only the daily turnover of CNY was suppressed in the BIS format, and turnovers of all other currencies were increased. It is natural to use the FXJSC CNY turnover $80.02 billion as the actual turnover of CNY in UK for April 2019 as it was neither suppressed nor increased. Then the total CNY average daily turnover would be 285.03 + 80.02 + 56.67 + 27.30 = $335.7 billion, which was $8.70 billion and $3.60 billion higher than the corresponding average daily equivalent turnover of $327 billion and $332.1 of CHF and CAD in April 2019, respectively, making CNY the world's sixth global currency in 2019. The sixth ranking of CNY in 2019 was more consistent with the fifth place of CNY share of global payments and global foreign exchange reserves.

Table 12.5: Average Daily Turnover of Major Currencies in April 2019 According to the BIS and the FXJSC (Unit: USD billion)

Currency	US Dollar	Euro	Japanese Yen	British Pound	Australian Dollar	Canadian Dollar	Swiss Franc	Chinese Yuan	Swedish Krona
BIS	3,201.53	1,286.93	552.32	592.68	232.80	162.05	174.37	56.67	82.83
FXJSC	2,557.91	1,060.32	408.69	477.29	171.48	117.18	142.90	80.02	68.59
BIS/FXJSC	1.25	1.21	1.35	1.24	1.36	1.38	1.22	0.71	1.21
Currency	**Norwegian Franc**	**New Zealand Dollar**	**South Korean Won**	**Singapore Dollar**	**South African Guilder**	**Mexican Peso**	**Russian Ruble**	**Brazilian Real**	**Polish Zloty**
BIS	70.27	70.66	53.17	46.73	44.54	53.94	29.87	34.11	23.45
FXJSC	60.02	51.44	42.87	37.15	34.30	31.44	28.58	25.72	20.01
BIS/FXJSC	1.17	1.37	1.24	1.26	1.30	1.72	1.05	1.33	1.17

Source: BIS website and FXJSC website.

12.11 Global Ranking of Major World Currencies Since 2019

12.11.1 *Estimation of average daily turnover in the global foreign exchange market in non-announced years*

Since the BIS only publishes data regarding average daily turnovers of world foreign exchange market every 3 years, it is difficult to know the corresponding average daily foreign exchange turnovers between two consecutive triennial data. Two methods are usually used to estimate the turnovers between the two-triennial data. One is to calculate the linear difference of the data between two consecutives triennial data, and the other is to calculate the compound annual growth rate between two consecutive triennial data, and assume that the annual compound growth rate is the average annual growth rate of the next 2 years based on the previous published data. The data of 2 years in the middle years are estimated using the data of the starting year and the compound growth rate.

Zhang and Ma Jun (2015) used the average daily turnover in the 2 publication years, the amount of foreign exchange derivatives in the first half of the year, and the amount of foreign exchange derivatives in the first half of the non-announced year to estimate the average daily transaction amount for the first half of the non-announced year between the 2 publication years. Their results show that average daily turnover in the global foreign exchange market in the first half of 2008 and the first half of 2009 was $4.428 trillion and $3.530 trillion, respectively. These results represent differences of positive $0.901 trillion and negative $0.213 trillion, respectively, compared with the results estimated by the compound growth rate method, which were $3.527 trillion and $3.743 trillion. Zhang and Ma's results are 25.5% higher and 5.7% lower, respectively, than the results obtained under the compound growth rate method.

In the first half of 2008, the financial crisis had not yet occurred, and the average daily transaction value at that time should have been higher than in 2007, while the average daily turnover in the first half of 2009 after the outbreak of the financial crisis should have been lower than the estimate provided by the average annual compound growth rate method. After using the data regarding derivatives in the global foreign exchange market for the first half of the year, the results of the new method are more accurate than the previous simple methods, and they are also more consistent with the intuitive logic of market changes. These global market estimates have made judgments regarding the progress of CNY Internationalization in different years more accurate. Due to the strong technical nature of this method, the specific details have been provided in the Appendix (the Appendix includes the relevant updated results for recent years), so we will not repeat them here. In what follows, we will use this method to estimate the results of the CNY foreign exchange market in 2011, 2012, 2014, 2015, 2017, and 2018. In the same way, we can also estimate the average daily foreign exchange turnover in the first half of the year for the USD, EUR, JPY, GBP, CHF, and CAD. Appendix Tables A12.1 and A12.2 outline the corresponding updated results. The updated method provides us with more accurate and useful information for assessing the degree of CNY Internationalization in recent years.

12.11.2 *Ranking of foreign exchange turnovers of major world currencies in recent years*

According to the data on the value of domestic CNY foreign exchange market transactions in recent years in Table 12.3, the average daily turnover of the overseas CNY foreign exchange market in recent years provided in Chapter 9, and the data on transactions involving the USD, EUR, JPY, GBP, CHF, and CAD in the non-announced years provided in Appendix Tables A12.1 and A12.2, we can calculate the market share of CNY foreign exchange transactions in recent years. Table 12.6 shows the results of these calculations.

According to the results in Table 12.6, the CNY became the world's sixth rather than eighth biggest trading currency in 2019 as CNY turnover share rose to 5.09%, higher than the corresponding share of 5.03% and 4.98% of CAD and CHF.

12.12 Ranking of Major World Currencies in 2020 and 2021

12.12.1 *Semi-annual Turnovers of the top eight currencies in major foreign exchange markets*

The above data show the changes in the globalization rankings of major world currencies from 2007 to 2019. However, the next set of worldwide

Table 12.6: Distribution of Daily Turnovers of Major World Currencies (2007–2019)

Currency/Year	2007	2010	2013	2014	2015	2016	2017	2018	2019
USD	85.60	84.86	87.04	80.70	76.30	87.58	87.28	92.35	88.30
EUR	37.04	39.05	33.41	32.90	32.30	31.39	31.67	34.21	32.28
JPY	17.25	18.99	23.05	17.90	17.40	21.62	18.11	17.42	16.81
GBP	14.87	12.88	11.82	12.40	12.30	12.80	12.71	12.99	12.79
AUD	6.62	7.59	8.64	8.10	7.50	6.88	6.84	6.81	6.77
CAD	4.29	5.28	4.56	3.70	3.80	5.14	5.08	4.85	5.03
CHF	6.82	6.31	5.16	5.20	4.90	4.80	5.09	4.96	4.96
CNY	0.45	0.86	2.23	2.80	3.40	3.99	4.10	4.21	4.32
SEK	2.70	2.19	1.76	1.90	2.10	2.22	2.16	2.09	2.03
MXN	1.31	1.26	2.53	2.40	2.30	1.92	1.85	1.79	1.72
NZD	1.90	1.59	1.96	2.00	2.00	2.05	2.06	2.07	2.07
SGD	1.17	1.42	1.40	1.50	1.70	1.81	1.81	1.81	1.81
HKD	2.70	2.37	1.45	1.50	1.60	1.73	2.33	2.93	3.53
NOK	2.10	1.32	1.44	1.50	1.60	1.67	1.71	1.76	1.80
KRW	1.16	1.52	1.20	1.30	1.50	1.65	1.77	1.88	2.00
TRY	0.18	0.74	1.32	1.30	1.40	1.44	1.32	1.20	1.08
INR	0.71	0.95	0.99	1.00	1.10	1.14	1.34	1.53	1.72
RUB	0.75	0.90	1.60	1.40	1.30	1.15	1.13	1.11	1.09
BRL	0.39	0.69	1.10	1.10	1.00	1.00	1.02	1.05	1.07
ZAR	0.91	0.72	1.11	1.10	1.00	0.97	1.01	1.05	1.09
CNY*	0.45	0.86	2.23	2.80	3.40	3.99	4.36	4.72	5.09
CNY (domestic)	0.39	0.69	0.91	1.01	1.20	1.48	1.63	1.79	1.95
Ranking of CNY*	20	17	9	8	8	8	8	8	6
Ranking of CNY (domestic)	22	21	20	20	17	16	15	12	12
Foreign CNY*/ Domestic Transaction	0.15	0.25	1.45	1.77	1.83	1.70	1.67	1.64	1.61

Source: The BIS share of major currencies in the global markets updated by the BIS in December 2019. For the years 2011, 2012, 2014, 2015, 2017, and 2018, the proportions of USD, EUR, JPY, GBP, CHF, and CAD are from Appendix Table A12.2; data for other currencies in the corresponding years are calculated using the linear interpolation method based on the proportions in 2010 and 2013, 2013 and 2016, and 2016 and 2019; the percentage of the global average daily turnover of domestic CNY* from 2017 to 2019 was calculated based on the total turnover of the CNY foreign exchange in April of those years released by SAFE foreign exchange market in April of those years as shown in Appendix Table A12.1.

foreign exchange data will not be released by the BIS until the second half of 2022, Thus, we do not the change of globalization of major world currencies in 2020 and 2021 until late 2022.

The average daily turnover of world foreign exchange and average turnovers of major world currencies in the first half of 2020 can be estimated using the global foreign exchange derivatives market data as shown in Appendix Table A12.1. The results in Appendix Table A12.1 can be used to rank turnover share of USD, EUR, JPY, GBP, CHF, and CAD, yet the corresponding data are missing for AUD and CNY. Therefore, we will encounter difficulties in judging the changes in the internationalization rankings of the major global currencies in the first half of 2021. However, the semi-annual average daily foreign exchange turnovers of the world's top eight currencies in major foreign exchange markets provide us extremely useful information to judge the trend of internationalization of major currencies after 2019.

London and Tokyo have published foreign exchange market data (including the CNY) for the months of April and October every year since 2008. In addition, the Monetary Authority of Singapore and the Federal Reserve Bank of USA have also published average daily turnovers of foreign exchange market (including the CNY) for the months of April and October every year since April 2016. Meanwhile, the Treasury Markets Association of Hong Kong (www.tma.org.hk) has released the average daily transaction data in the foreign exchange market (including the CNY) in April and October every year for the Hong Kong market since October 2017. Furthermore, similar semi-annual data are released by monetary authorities of Australia and Canada. SAFE of China releases monthly foreign exchange turnover of the Mainland Chinese foreign exchange market since January 2015. Thus, we have semi-annual foreign exchange turnovers of major world currencies in eight major world foreign exchange centers since 2017. These eight foreign exchange centers represent 81.54–83.83% of world foreign exchange turnover from April 2016 to April 2019. The majority share of these eight foreign exchange markets in world foreign exchange market turnover indicate they can represent world foreign exchange market well enough, and we can use related semi-annual data to judge the globalization of world major currencies from 2020 to 2021. Table 12.7 gives the average turnovers of top eight world currencies in eight foreign exchange centers from April 2020 to April 2021.

Table 12.7: Average Turnovers of Major World Currencies (April 2019–April 2021) (Unit: USD billion, %)

Currency/ Time	Apr-19	Apr-20	Apr-21	Change from 2019 to 2020	Change from 2020 to 2021	Change from 2019 to 2021
USD	5,110.3	4,586.6	5,473.6	−10.2	19.3	7.1
EUR	1,674.5	1,491.8	1,782.3	−10.9	19.5	6.4
JPY	1,081.6	1,062.7	1,114.8	−1.8	4.9	3.1
GBP	696.4	596.3	793.4	−14.4	33.1	13.9
AUD	366.4	352.8	404.5	−3.7	14.7	10.4
CAD	290.0	284.9	369.3	−1.8	29.6	27.3
CHF	286.2	306.3	385.7	7.0	25.9	34.8
CNY	377.7	301.3	399.6	−20.2	32.6	5.8
Sum	9,883.1	8,982.7	10,723.2	−9.1	19.4	8.5

Source: Summarized semi-annual foreign exchange turnovers from FXJSC (www.bankofengland.com.uk), the New York Federal Reserve (www.forex.com), Monetary Authority of Singapore (www.mas.gov.sg), Hong Kong Treasury Market Association (www.tma.org.hk), Tokyo Foreign Exchange Market Committee (www.fxcomtky.com), the Australian Foreign Exchange Commission (afxc.rba.gov.au), Canadian Foreign Exchange Commission (www.cfec.ca), and SAFE (www.safe.org.cn) of China. The average daily turnovers CHF in Switzerland in April 2020 and April 2021 are estimated using data of turnovers of major currencies in Switzerland in April 2019 and related accumulated annual growth rates from April 2016 to April 2019.

12.12.2 *The positions of top four world currencies in the nine major foreign exchange markets*

Table 12.7 shows that the world's top four currencies remained their monopolistic positions from 2019 to 2021 without much change. The accumulated growth of average daily turnover of USD was 7.1% from 2019 to 2020, only 1.4% lower than the accumulated change of top eight currencies, indicating that the internationalization position of USD had not weakened as much despite the COVID-19 epidemic and around $6 trillion US national debt issuance from 2020 to the first half of 2021. The accumulated growth rates of average daily turnovers of EUR, JPY, and GPB were 6.4%, 3.1%, and 13.9%, respectively, from 2019 to 2020, indicating that the internationalization positions of EUR and JPY were weakened slightly and GPB was slightly strengthened from 2019 to 2021 as the accumulated growth rates of EUR and JPY were lower than the corresponding accumulated growth rate of eight currencies of 8.5%.

12.12.3 *Rankings of CNY in nine major world foreign exchange markets*

Table 12.7 shows that the average daily turnover of the CNY was $377.7 billion in April 2019, $11.3 billion higher than the corresponding average daily turnover of AUD at $366.4 billion for the same period, and $87.7 billion and $91.6 billion higher than the corresponding average daily turnovers of CAD and CHF. These results confirmed the sixth ranking of CNY in April 2019. However, as the average daily turnover of CNY in foreign exchange markets other than the nine foreign exchange markets in Table 12.7 was lower than the corresponding average turnover of AUD, CNY was ranked sixth in 2019. Since the average daily turnover of CNY declined by 20.2%, more than any other currency in Table 12.7, this led to the drop of CNY's ranking to seventh in 2020.

Table 12.7 also shows that average daily turnover of CNY increased by 32.6% from April 2020–2021, the highest annual growth rate of all eight currencies in Table 12.7, yet the accumulated growth rate from April 2019–2021 was only 5.4%, lower than the corresponding rates of AUD, CAD and CHF 10.4%, 27.3%, and 34.8%. Therefore, it is reasonable to estimate CNY's ranking in April 2021 as sixth as it was in 2019.

12.13 Conclusion

With semi-annual turnover data of eight major world foreign exchange centers, we can find relatively reliable changes of worldwide positions of top eight world currencies from 2020 to 2021 even before the release of the next BIS world foreign exchange data in 2022. Our results show that the COVID-19 epidemic had significant impacts on global foreign exchange markets, and in turn on global positions of major world currencies.

The release of semi-annual turnovers of major currencies in foreign exchange market by Hong Kong Treasury Market Association since 2017 has given us a more reliable market basis for understanding the changes of globalization of major world currencies including CNY. These data have also helped us conduct better forecasts of the CNY's future trends. The data in this chapter show that from 2016 to 2019 the CNY improved its world ranking from eighth to sixth, which is a remarkable result. Especially in recent years, the depreciation of the CNY against the USD has led to the stagnation of indicators such as CNY cross-border payments, overseas CNY savings, and CNY global debt issuance. However, the domestic and offshore CNY foreign exchange markets have maintained considerable growth despite these challenges. The significant increase in the CNY's activity in the global foreign exchange market shows that the acceptance of the CNY in the global foreign exchange market is still increasing. In recent years, the overseas environment for CNY internalization has improved significantly. Considering the favorable global environment and deepening domestic reforms, CNY internationalization is expected to return to the steady improvements it was making before 2015 and effectively promote the implementation of the Belt and Road Initiative.

However, due to the obvious impacts of US–China trade friction and the COVID-19 epidemic, turnover of domestic foreign exchange market declined significantly from the first half of 2019 to the first half of 2020, and the corresponding decreasing rate of worldwide CNY of 20.2% was higher than all other major currencies in the same period. This steep decrease was a sign that the country's insufficiency of technology originality capacity has led to restrictions on bilateral commerce, which in turn resulted in a decline in CNY cross-border settlement and related derivatives product transactions within the context of CNY depreciation, ultimately leading to a decline in the domestic CNY foreign exchange market. These results show that China must improve its technology originality capability to increase its trade, the proportion of CNY settlements, and other vital indicators.

Currency internationalization takes relatively long processes. Although foreign experience can be used as useful references, it is still necessary to explore and move forward in many areas to steadily promote CNY internationalization based on China's current situation. Exploration is indispensable and must be carried out in a planned or orderly manner. In other words, there should be a road map and timetable for promoting CNY internationalization. Efforts to promote CNY internationalization should mainly focus on domestic medium- and long-term strategic development and the steady and continuous improvement of national living standards.

At the same time, the promotion of CNY's internationalization should also be coordinated with the development of Asia's regional economy as well as the region's trade and financial markets. Ultimately, the reform of the worldwide monetary and financial system should be linked to the peaceful development of the world. Going forward, we should explore the route and timetable for CNY internationalization and the corresponding implementation details based on judgments regarding the future development of China's and the world's economy, trade conditions, and science and technology, while also making appropriate and necessary adjustments in accordance with changes in the domestic and foreign economies, trade conditions and markets. In the next few years, CNY internationalization is expected to achieve more significant results as China's technological originality capacity improves, gradually approaching and even reaching a status equivalent to the country's worldwide economic and trade status.

Appendix (Guangping (Peter G.) Zhang and Ma Jun (2015))

Since the total transaction amounts of foreign exchange currencies is the concentrated expression of all global applications of currencies, and foreign exchange currency transactions were recorded on a regular basis to form unified worldwide data, the ratio of currency trading in the international foreign exchange market is the best measure of its globalization (Zhang Guangping (Peter G.), 2014). Unfortunately, however, data about turnover of different currencies in the global foreign exchange market are only published by the BIS, and the institution published worldwide foreign exchange transaction data only once every 3 years. So, for 2 years between them (the non-publication of the years), we can only use simple linear interpolation method or CAGR between them to estimate the average daily turnover of the worldwide foreign exchange market data (Zhang Guangping (Peter G.), 2014). Although these methods are simple, they did not take full advantage of stock data for non-publication years of the foreign exchange derivatives market, so the results of estimation have room for improvement.

The purpose of this section is to apply data about stock of foreign exchange derivatives in the first half of non-published years and the average daily turnover of foreign exchange in domestic and offshore markets published by BIS every 3 years to estimate average daily turnover of foreign exchange derivatives in non-publication years and further estimate average daily foreign exchange amount in global market and major worldwide currencies in non-published years. With more accurate estimation of average daily turnover in global foreign exchange market and major global currencies, we can calculate the ratio of different currencies in global foreign exchange market during these years more accurately to have better judgment and command of CNY globalization progress in different years.

A12.1 *Turnover of international foreign exchange derivative products in published years*

Although the BIS publishes data of average daily turnover in global foreign exchange market in April of that year once every 3 years, the institution has published stock data of the global foreign exchange derivatives market in every 6 months. Over recent years, the trading of global foreign exchange derivatives is a major part of the global foreign exchange market and the retained amount of foreign exchange derivative products is equivalent to positions of the product published by the Exchange. Average daily turnover of global foreign exchange derivatives markets published by the BIS in April every 3 years can be seen as the corresponding average daily turnover in the first half of this year. Thus, we can easily calculate the total daily turnover of foreign exchange derivatives (an average of 125 days every 6 months, so the turnover of derivatives in foreign exchange markets in the first half of this year can be estimated by multiplying the average daily turnover in April 125 times). The total turnover in the first half of years (HY) divided by the corresponding retained amount of total foreign exchange derivatives can generate these turnovers of foreign exchange derivatives in the first half of years. Figure A12.1 shows the turnovers of foreign exchange derivatives in global market from the first half of 1998 to the first half of 2016.

Figure A12.1 indicates that although there was a global financial crisis from 2007 to 2010, the turnover rate in the global foreign exchange derivatives market among the top eight currencies in the first half of the year every 3 years has changed steadily.

A12.2 *Estimation of average daily turnover of foreign exchange derivatives in global market in non-published years*

Since the turnover of foreign exchange derivatives in global market has kept decreasing steadily in published years, we can take the turnover of foreign exchange derivatives in the published years and apply the linear

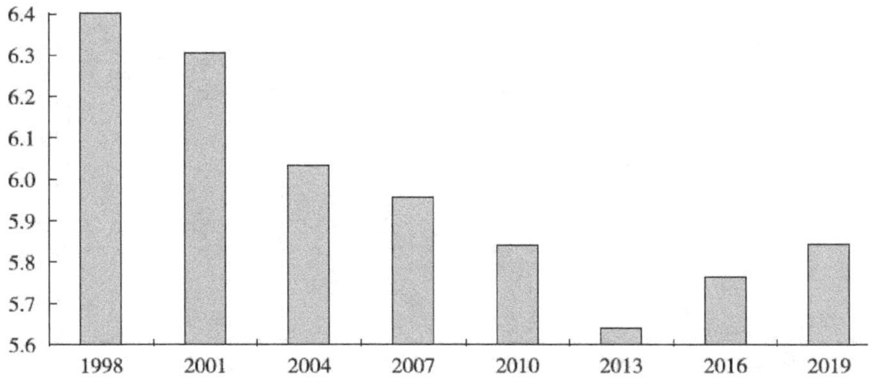

Figure A12.1: Turnover Rates of Foreign Exchange Derivatives in Global Market in the First Halves of Years

Source: Calculated by Triennial Central Bank Survey Global foreign exchange market turnover from 1998 to 2019 according to www.bis.org.

interpolation method to calculate the figures in the non-published years (such as 2014 and 2015, and 2017 and 2018). Moreover, the estimated turnover in the first half of the non-published years and the corresponding retained amount of foreign exchange derivatives in the first half of these years are used to estimate the average daily transaction amount of foreign exchange derivatives in these years. Appendix Table A12.1 lists the corresponding results.

A12.3 *Estimation of average daily transaction amount in foreign exchange market in non-published years*

With the estimation of average daily foreign exchange derivatives in non-published years without a corresponding average daily spot transaction of foreign exchange, we still have difficulty to obtain the appropriate total daily turnover of the global foreign exchange market. However, with the average daily turnover of spot and derivatives products published by the BIS every 3 years since 1998, we can calculate the percentage of average daily amount of spot market in total foreign exchange market from April 1998 to April 2016. We can obtain the proportion of average daily amount of spot market in total foreign exchange market in non-published years by

Table A12.1: Derivatives and Estimation of Average Daily Transaction Amount in Domestic and Offshore Foreign Exchange Market (1998–2019) (Unit: $1 trillion, %)

Year	Notional Amount Outstanding	Turnover/ Notional Amount Outstanding	Average Daily Turnover in 1st HY	Average Daily Turnover of Derivatives in 1st HY	Share of Spot Market (%)	Share of Spot Market (%)	Average Daily Turnover of Spot Market	Average Daily Turnover of the Currency	Share of Average Daily Turnover of Total
1998	18.70	6.40	6.40	0.96	37.20	37.20	0.57	1.53	1.527
1999	14.90		6.37	0.76		35.20	0.41	1.17	1.424
2000	15.50		6.34	0.79		33.20	0.39	1.18	1.328
2001	16.90	6.31	6.31	0.85	31.20	31.20	0.39	1.24	1.239
2002	18.10		6.21	0.90		31.60	0.42	1.31	1.437
2003	22.10		6.12	1.08		32.10	0.51	1.59	1.667
2004	27.00	6.03	6.03	1.30	32.60	32.60	0.63	1.93	1.934
2005	31.10		6.01	1.49		31.80	0.70	2.19	2.317
2006	38.10		5.98	1.83		31.00	0.82	2.65	2.775
2007	48.60	5.96	5.96	2.32	30.20	30.20	1.01	3.32	3.324
2008	63.00		5.92	2.98		32.60	1.45	4.43	3.527
2009	48.70		5.88	2.29		35.10	1.24	3.53	3.743
2010	53.20	5.84	5.84	2.48	37.50	37.50	1.49	3.97	3.972
2011	64.70		5.77	2.99		37.70	1.81	4.80	4.385
2012	66.70		5.71	3.04		38.00	1.87	4.91	4.841
2013	73.10	5.64	5.64	3.30	38.30	38.30	2.05	5.35	5.345
2014	75.00		5.69	3.42		38.60	2.14	5.56	5.258

2015	73.60		5.75	3.38		38.80	2.15	5.53	5.172
2016	74.00	5.80	5.80	3.43	32.50	32.50	1.65	5.09	5.088
2017	88.40		5.79	4.10		30.70	1.91	6.01	5.533
2018	95.80		5.82	4.46		28.10	2.00	6.46	6.041
2019	98.60	5.84	5.84	4.61	30.10	30.10	1.99	6.60	6.595

Source: Stock in the first half of years come from www.bis.org; turnovers in the first half of years calculated by daily transaction amount in the first halves of published years and Stock of foreign exchange derivatives in the first half of years (suppose April as the first half year); turnovers in the first half of non-published years calculated by linear interpolation method; spot transaction proportion in April of published years calculated by average daily transaction amount of foreign exchange derivatives in the first half of years; spot transaction in the first half of years in 2014 and 2015 is calculated by that in 2013 and annual change from 2010 to 2013; FX spot = a*FXD/(1 − a) FX spot represents average daily spot foreign exchange transaction; a represents spot transaction proportion in total foreign exchange transaction; FXD represents average daily transaction amount in foreign exchange derivatives.

applying those in published years and liner interpolation method. Since we have obtained "a" and FXD, it is easy to get FX spot.

Since a = FX spot/(FX spot+ FXD), so FX spot = $a \times$ FXD/(1 − a). Applying this formula, we can obtain total average daily transaction amount in the first half of these years (FX spot + FXD), i.e., average daily transaction amount in April of non-published years, as listed in Appendix Table A12.1.

Appendix Table A12.1 indicated that there are huge differences between estimations of average daily transaction amount in foreign exchange market in non-published years by using average daily transaction amounts in foreign exchange market published by BIS and stock data or using CAGR in every 3 years. To be specific, Appendix Table A12.1 indicated that the estimation by using the second one will be smoother than the first one since the second one assumes an equal growth rate in every year instead of fluctuation caused by foreign exchange derivatives in non-published years. Although the first one fluctuated a lot, it is closer to the reality. Since global financial crisis did not break out in the first half of 2008, the estimation by the first one is $4.428 trillion, which is higher than the second one $3.527 trillion by $901.1 billion or 25.5%. Meanwhile, the estimation by the first one in the first half of 2009 is $3.530 trillion, which is lower than the second one $3.743 trillion by $213 billion or 5.7%.

The above results show that the results estimated by the new method using the global foreign exchange derivatives data are more consistent with the changes in market activities before and after the financial crisis than the results estimated by the average annual growth rate method. Thus, estimations of average daily transaction amount in foreign exchange market in non-published years by using average daily transaction amount in foreign exchange market published by BIS and stock data are more accurate and reliable than that by using CAGR in every 3 years.

A12.4 *Estimation of average daily transaction amount of major world currencies in foreign exchange market in non-published years*

Since we obtained a more accurate estimation of average daily transaction amounts in foreign exchange market in non-published years, it is easy to calculate the ratio in domestic and offshore market, which contributes to a

Table A12.2: Estimation of Average Daily Transaction Amount of Major World Currencies in Domestic and Offshore Foreign Exchange Market in Non-published Years (Unit: $1 trillion, %)

Year	Notional Amount Outstanding	Turnover/ Notional Amount Outstanding	Average Daily Turnover in first HY	Average Daily Turnover of Derivatives in first HY	Share of Spot Market (%)	Share of Spot Market (%)	Average Daily Turnover of Spot Market	Average Daily Turnover of the Currency	Share of Average Daily Turnover of Total (%)
USD									
2007	33.76	7.468	7.468	2.017	35.16	29.70	0.845	2.862	86.09
2010	45.13	6.066	6.066	2.185	35.20	35.20	1.187	3.371	84.90
2011	54.04		5.957	2.575		35.58	1.423	3.998	91.16
2012	57.38		5.848	2.684		35.97	1.508	4.192	86.60
2013	64.48	5.74	5.74	2.961	36.35	36.35	1.691	4.652	87.03
2014	65.13		5.798	2.934		34.60	1.553	4.487	80.68
2015	64.1		5.856	2.832		32.85	1.386	4.217	76.26
2016	64.9	5.915	5.915	3.071	31.11	31.11	1.387	4.458	87.61
2017	77.04		5.921	3.649		30.39	1.594	5.243	87.28
2018	88.45		5.928	4.194		29.68	1.77	5.965	92.35
2019	87.14	5.934	5.934	4.137	28.97	28.97	1.687	5.824	88.30
EUR									
2007	18.28	5.315	5.315	0.777	44.45	36.90	0.454	1.231	37.04
2010	20.11	5.378	5.378	0.863	44.40	44.40	0.689	1.553	39.10
2011	24.97		5.407	1.08		43.68	0.838	1.918	43.74
2012	23.8		5.436	1.035		42.96	0.779	1.814	37.48
2013	24.37	5.291	5.291	1.032	42.24	42.24	0.754	1.786	33.41
2014	26.45		5.386	1.113		39.05	0.714	1.827	32.85
2015	27.34		5.48	1.145		35.87	0.64	1.785	32.27

(Continued)

Table A12.2: (*Continued*)

Year	Notional Amount Outstanding	Turnover/ Notional Amount Outstanding	Average Daily Turnover in first HY	Average Daily Turnover of Derivatives in first HY	Share of Spot Market (%)	Share of Spot Market (%)	Average Daily Turnover of Spot Market	Average Daily Turnover of the Currency	Share of Average Daily Turnover of Total (%)
2016	24.02	5.575	5.575	1.071	32.68	32.68	0.52	1.591	31.28
2017	27.83		5.862	1.305		31.42	0.598	1.903	31.67
2018	31.37		6.148	1.543		30.17	0.666	2.209	34.21
2019	29.4	6.435	6.435	1.514	28.91	28.91	0.616	2.129	32.28
JPY									
2007	10.6	3.854	3.854	0.327	39.75	40.40	0.231	0.558	16.78
2010	11.82	4.822	4.822	0.455	39.70	39.70	0.3	0.754	19.00
2011	13.07		4.913	0.514		43.04	0.388	0.902	20.57
2012	13.67		5.005	0.547		46.39	0.473	1.021	21.08
2013	15.18	5.096	5.096	0.619	49.73	49.73	0.612	1.231	23.03
2014	13.18		5.37	0.547		45.17	0.451	0.998	17.94
2015	13.5		5.643	0.57		40.61	0.39	0.96	17.35
2016	14.82	5.916	5.916	0.701	36.05	36.05	0.395	1.097	21.56
2017	14.9		5.942	0.708		34.87	0.379	1.088	18.11
2018	15.63		5.968	0.746		33.68	0.379	1.125	17.42
2019	15.61	5.993	5.993	0.748	32.50	32.50	0.36	1.108	16.81
GBP									
2007	7.77	5.406	5.406	0.336	41.55	32.50	0.161	0.497	14.95
2010	6.62	5.659	5.659	0.299	46.10	46.10	0.236	0.535	13.48
2011	7.01		5.771	0.324		42.71	0.241	0.565	12.88
2012	7.59		5.882	0.357		39.32	0.231	0.589	12.16
2013	8.43	5.994	5.994	0.404	35.92	35.92	0.227	0.631	11.81
2014	9.18		5.856	0.449		34.82	0.24	0.688	12.37

2015	9.03		5.719	0.449		33.71	0.228	0.678	12.26
2016	9.8	5.582	5.582	0.438	32.61	32.61	0.212	0.65	12.77
2017	11.07		5.932	0.525		31.21	0.238	0.764	12.71
2018	11.72		6.282	0.589		29.81	0.25	0.839	12.99
2019	11.38	6.631	6.631	0.604	28.42	28.42	0.24	0.844	12.79
CHF									
2007	3.06	5.342	5.342	0.131	36.35	42.20	0.095	0.226	6.80
2010	3.86	5.249	5.249	0.191	36.40	36.40	0.091	0.282	7.10
2011	4.88		5.405	0.211		38.42	0.131	0.342	7.81
2012	4.05		5.56	0.18		40.43	0.122	0.303	6.25
2013	4.18	5.716	5.716	0.191	42.45	42.45	0.084	0.275	5.14
2014	3.94		6.108	0.185		36.15	0.105	0.29	5.22
2015	3.93		6.501	0.189		29.86	0.081	0.27	4.88
2016	3.37	6.894	6.894	0.186	23.56	23.56	0.057	0.243	4.78
2017	4.12		7.014	0.231		24.44	0.075	0.306	5.09
2018	4.2		7.134	0.239		25.32	0.081	0.321	4.96
2019	4.16	7.254	7.254	0.241	26.20	26.20	0.086	0.327	4.96
CAD									
2007	2.24	5.487	5.487	0.098	37.04	29.70	0.042	0.141	4.23
2010	2.24	7.431	7.431	0.162	37.00	37.00	0.078	0.24	6.03
2011	3.07		6.867	0.168		34.88	0.09	0.259	5.90
2012	3		6.303	0.151		32.75	0.074	0.225	4.65
2013	3.28	5.74	5.74	0.151	30.63	30.63	0.093	0.244	4.57
2014	3.25		5.831	0.135		33.80	0.069	0.203	3.66
2015	3.58		5.922	0.132		36.98	0.078	0.21	3.79
2016	3.24	6.013	6.013	0.156	40.16	40.16	0.105	0.261	5.12
2017	4.07		5.718	0.186		39.00	0.119	0.305	5.08
2018	4.48		5.424	0.195		37.84	0.118	0.313	4.85
2019	5.12	5.129	5.129	0.21	36.68	36.68	0.122	0.332	5.03

Source: Data and calculation method are derived from Appendix Table A12.1.

better understanding of CNY internationalization in non-published years. However, it is hard for us to know the accurate rank in non-published years without main currencies and estimation of proportion of those that ranked before CNY in average daily transaction amount in foreign exchange market in non-published years. The good news is that we can estimate average daily transaction amounts of the USD, EUR, JPY, GBP, CHF, and CAD in the foreign exchange market in non-published years and the corresponding ratios by applying the data from Appendix Table A12.1 and the above method. Appendix Table A12.2 lists the estimated results.

Appendix Table A12.2 indicates that average daily transaction amounts of USD in the foreign exchange market in 2014 accounted for 80.68% and decreased by 6.35% when compared to 87.03% in 2013 and in 2015 accounted for 76.26% and decreased by 4.42% in 2015 compared to 2014. However, the accounting for USD in 2016 has a significant rebound to 87.16%, it not only exceeded 86.09% in 2007 before the financial crisis but also exceeded 87.03% in 2013. The average daily turnover of EUR foreign exchange between 2014 and 2016 continued to decline, as it did between 2010 and 2013, although the decline between 2014 and 2016 was not as steep. This movement pointed to the EUR's continuing downward trend.

The global average daily turnover of JPY continuous declined in 2014 and 2015 compared with 2013. However, the percentage returned to 21.56% in 2016, which was only 1.47% less than in 2013, and 2.56% more than 19.0% in 2015 at the same time, indicating that the position of JPY in global foreign exchange market is rising. The global average daily turnover of GBP didn't change a lot, with a slight increase in 2016 compared with 2013 though the situation of GBP's decline did not change overall. The global average daily turnover of CAD returned obviously, with a distance between 5.12% in 2015 and 6.03% in 2013. These conclusions showed that the average daily turnover of the USD and GBP as a percentage of the global total increased significantly, while the proportion of JPY, EUR, and CHF dropped from 2013 to 2019, with the CAD recovering slightly.

A12.5 *Estimation of proportion of average daily transaction amount in CNY foreign exchange market in non-published years*

Since we have obtained an accurate estimation of average daily transaction amount in global foreign exchange market in non-published years, we can get global percentages according to average daily transaction amount of CNY. Appendix Table A12.3 lists the average daily transaction amounts in the domestic foreign exchange market by quarter from 2010 to 2019, as well as the average daily transaction amounts in April and the corresponding percentages. Appendix Table A12.1 indicates that the estimates of average daily transaction amounts that were obtained by applying the published years' data and foreign exchange derivatives data in the first half of the year were higher than those obtained by applying the CAGR method. The ratios of CNY's average daily transaction amount in the global market as listed in Appendix Table A12.3 were lower than those estimated using the traditional method. The gap was 0.06% and 0.01%. The ratio figures about average daily transaction in the first half of 2014 and 2015 by applying stock data of foreign exchange derivatives were a little bit lower than those by applying traditional CAGR. As listed in Appendix Table A12.3, the proportions in recent years were 0.91% and 1.11%; these amounts were 0.05 percentage points and 0.08 percentage points lower than the figures of 0.96% and 1.19% obtained using the traditional method. Since our estimation of different currencies' average daily transaction amounts directly affects the ranking of globalization, a new evaluation method helps explain CNY internationalization in different years.

Appendix Table A12.3 indicates that the ratio of average daily transaction amount of CNY in global market increased relatively low from 0.66% to 1.42% (0.76% in 6 years) and ranked from 21st in 2010 to 15th in 2016 and remained unchanged from then, indicating relatively low growth in domestic foreign exchange market when compared to offshore foreign exchange market. Appendix Table A12.1 indicates that the CNY's ranking climbed from 21st in 2010 to eighth in 2016, which is much higher than the ranking of 16th obtained by the domestic CNY foreign exchange market. From 2016 to 2017, the average daily turnover of domestic CNY foreign exchange increased slightly, but the CNY's global shares did not change significantly. From 2017 to 2019, the CNY's percentage increased to 2.04%; and the domestic CNY's ranking increased from 15th to 12th. These results indicate that, during this period, the offshore CNY market was the main contributor to the CNY's globalization. For this reason, accelerating the development of the domestic CNY foreign exchange market is a critical part of balancing both the domestic and offshore CNY market.

Table A12.3: Average Daily Turnover in Domestic CNY Foreign Exchange Market by Quarter and in April and Corresponding Global Proportion (2010–2019) (Unit: $1 trillion, %)

Quarter/ Year	Spot	Forward	Foreign Exchange Swap and Currency Swap	Option	Amount	Quarterly Average Daily	Total Average Daily Turnover in April	Total Average Daily Turnover Proportion in April (%)
2010Q1	12,503.0	30.4	2,849.8	0.0	15,383.2	240.4		
2010Q2	13,338.4	24.4	3,455.7	0.0	16,818.5	275.7	263.9	0.66
2010Q3	13,584.7	17.5	3,199.9	0.0	16,802.1	271.0		
2010Q4	13,972.3	255.0	3,493.0	0.0	17,720.3	281.3		
2011Q1	14,305.0	595.0	3,402.7	0.0	18,302.7	286.0		
2011Q2	16,227.0	564.0	4,580.8	5.5	21,377.4	350.4	329.0	0.69
2011Q3	17,550.0	608.0	5,278.5	7.2	23,443.6	378.1		
2011Q4	15,732.0	379.0	4,591.0	6.1	20,708.1	328.7		
2012Q1	15,809.0	1,385.0	5,502.1	32.8	22,728.9	355.1		
2012Q2	16,097.0	991.0	6,025.9	40.7	23,154.6	379.6	371.4	0.76
2012Q3	16,550.0	947.0	6,690.6	114.4	24,302.0	392.0		
2012Q4	15,694.0	1,184.0	7,312.4	134.2	24,324.6	386.1		
2013Q1	17,534.0	1,411.0	7,379.1	160.0	26,484.1	413.8		
2013Q2	18,399.5	1,552.3	8,076.9	191.5	28,220.2	462.6	446.4	0.84
2013Q3	19,622.9	1,377.1	9,228.8	111.9	30,340.7	489.4		
2013Q4	20,400.6	1,704.5	10,122.2	268.2	32,495.4	515.8		
2014Q1	19,799.0	2,169.2	10,457.4	169.4	32,595.0	509.3		
2014Q2	18,310.0	1,252.9	10,922.6	195.6	30,681.1	503.0	505.1	0.91
2014Q3	19,121.0	1,509.9	12,952.6	535.5	34,119.0	550.3		
2014Q4	20,629.0	1,263.8	12,835.4	1,215.2	35,943.4	570.5		
2015Q1	19,339.7	1,376.7	13,742.0	941.8	35,400.3	553.1		
2015Q2	16,965.9	1,306.4	18,960.4	915.9	38,148.6	625.4	616.6	1.11
2015Q3	25,769.5	1,682.0	24,668.7	971.2	53,091.5	856.3		
2015Q4	20,526.6	584.4	28,662.0	1,217.8	50,990.8	809.4		
2016Q1	19,206.1	753.7	21,107.5	1,295.0	42,362.3	672.4		
2016Q2	20,707.3	771.3	23,790.2	1,383.5	46,652.3	764.8	719.8	1.41
2016Q3	21,538.2	975.5	25,913.9	3,211.9	51,639.6	832.9		

Table A12.3: (*Continued*)

Quarter/ Year	Spot	Forward	Foreign Exchange Swap and Currency Swap	Option	Amount	Quarterly Average Daily	Total Average Daily Turnover in April	Total Average Daily Turnover Proportion in April (%)
2016Q4	26,368.4	1,279.4	30,489.1	3,881.7	62,018.7	992.3		
2017Q1	20,369.1	980.4	26,247.0	1,526.7	49,123.3	786.0		
2017Q2	23,579.8	714.1	30,165.0	1,280.7	55,739.6	891.8	787.1	1.42
2017Q3	25,588.0	1,086.3	36,172.1	1,498.2	64,344.5	1,029.5		
2017Q4	25,357.0	1,478.1	43,087.7	1,715.0	71,637.7	1,146.2		
2018Q1	22,971.8	1,531.0	35,117.4	1,632.6	61,252.8	980.0		
2018Q2	26,103.6	1,747.3	40,971.7	1,925.5	70,748.2	1,132.0	1,052.1	1.74
2018Q3	29,436.9	1,417.8	39,669.1	2,222.7	72,746.4	1,163.9		
2018Q4	32,134.6	722.7	50,413.1	2,693.0	85,963.4	1,375.4		
2019Q1	27,740.3	907.0	45,784.4	2,349.9	76,781.7	1,228.5		
2019Q2	28,686.1	1,024.3	44,039.5	2,170.4	75,920.2	1,214.7	1,346.5	2.04
2019Q3	29,158.9	1,001.9	39,807.5	2,041.1	72,009.5	1,152.2		
2019Q4	27,975.9	873.2	35,697.1	1,938.8	66,485.1	1,063.8		
2020Q1	25,482.4	1,237.5	33,297.8	1,638.3	61,656.0	986.5		
2020Q2	25,592.1	979.2	41,531.3	1,966.2	70,068.9	1,121.1	1,096.3	1.87

Source: The data from 2015 to April 2020 are the average daily data calculated based on the monthly data published by the State Foreign Exchange Administration. Prior to 2015, the central bank and the SAFE did not publish domestic average daily foreign exchange data, so we can only estimate the average daily foreign exchange turnover from April 2010 to April 2014 using the quarterly data contained in the PBOC's quarterly Monetary Policy Implementation Report. The figures in the first quarter of each year represent the average daily transaction amount in February. The figures in the second quarter were considered as average daily transaction amount in May. Then, average daily transaction amount in April could be calculated by linear interpolation method using the figures in February and May. The global proportions in April are calculated by applying average daily transaction amount in Appendix Table A12.3 divided by corresponding average daily transaction amount of global market in April in Appendix Table A12.1. The global proportions in April 2020 as shown in Table 12.6 were derived as follows: the average daily transaction value of the world's eighth largest foreign exchange markets in April 2020 of $590.42 billion was divided by the estimated average daily transaction value of the global foreign exchange market in April 2020 of $586.05 billion. (In April 2019, the average daily transaction value of the eight major foreign exchange markets accounted for 85.63% of the world's total. Assuming that the global average daily transaction value of the eight major foreign exchange markets in April 2020 remained unchanged from 2019, the estimated average daily trading value of global foreign exchange in April 2020 was $586.05 billion.)

Appendix Table A12.3 also indicates that the CNY's average daily transaction amount as a percentage of the global total from April 2015 to 2016 increased by 3% from 1.12% to 1.42%, which exceeded the increase of 0.25% from 2010 to 2014 and the increase of 0.07% from 2013 to 2014. In addition, from 2016 to 2019, the average daily turnover of the CNY foreign exchange market notched a cumulative increase of 0.62% globally, which indicates that the domestic CNY foreign exchange market has grown rapidly since 2014.

However, in April 2020, the average daily turnover in the domestic CNY foreign exchange market fell by 18.6% on year-on-year basis, which was only 1% lower than the 18.7% drop in the total average daily turnover of the five major foreign exchange markets during this period. (The five major foreign exchange markets of Hong Kong, London, Singapore, New York, and Tokyo have accurate CNY data. CNY transactions in the foreign exchange markets of Australia and Canada are still not sufficiently active, and the average daily turnover there is lower than the top five overseas markets. Australia's and Canada's foreign exchange statistics do not include detailed CNY data.) However, during the same period, this drop was 9.1% higher than the 9.5% drop experienced by the world's top seven foreign exchange markets (the top seven above), indicating a significant decline in the activities of domestic and offshore CNY foreign exchange markets due to the dual impact of US–China trade friction and COVID-19.

As shown in Table 10.6, during the 4 years following the commencement of the offshore CNY market, from 2010 to 2014, the offshore CNY market developed rapidly. During this time, the compound annual growth rate of the offshore CNY market's average daily transaction amount was 70.2%. However, the growth rate calculated from the data in Appendix Table A12.3 is only 17.6%, which is only about one-fourth of the growth rate. The offshore CNY market has become the major driver of CNY internationalization in the global market in recent years.

The growth rate of the overseas market slowed from 2014 to 2019, with the average annual growth rate declining to 12.2%. During the same period, the domestic market's compound annual growth rate of 15.1% slightly exceeded that of the overseas market, which indicated that the domestic market was catching up with the overseas markets. In 2020, the domestic CNY foreign exchange market dropped 18.6%, which nearly doubled the 9.5% drop recorded for the total average daily turnover of the world's seven major foreign exchange markets. This discrepancy indicates that China has accelerated the improvement of its technology autonomy, thereby enhancing exchange autonomy and financial autonomy; these developments are necessary conditions for reducing constraints on CNY foreign exchange markets at home and abroad, and are also necessary conditions for the CNY internationalization process as a whole.

Bibliography

Chan, Norman T. L., 2014, Opening Remarks at the Second Hong Kong — Australia RMB Trade and Investment Dialogue, May 22, 2014, Hong Kong Monetary Authority.

Part IV

Chapter 13

Mutually Supportive Relationship between Science & Technology Internationalization and Currency Internationalization and Better Currency Internationalization Measure

Science and technology originality capability (OC) is the driving force of economic and trade development, while economy and trade are the foundations of currency internationalization. Therefore, sci-tech OC or level of sci-tech internationalization of any currency issuer should have a high correlation relationship with currency internationalization. This chapter uses sci-tech internationalization results of Table 7.6 of major international currency issuers and the currency internationalization results of major currencies given in Chapter 4 to explore the relationship between the two internationalization measures. Noticeable problems of correlation coefficients between the two international measures of specific years lead us to obtain a better currency internationalization measure through overcoming correlation problems between sci-tech internationalization measure and traditional currency internationalization measure.

13.1 Science and Technology Internationalization of Major Currency Issuers

13.1.1 *Science and technology internationalization major of currency issuers*

Table 7.6 gives the sci-tech internationalization of five major blocs and other countries and regions, yet we still do not know the corresponding sci-tech internationalization of Euro, British pound, and other major international currency issuers as IP5 reports do not have patent family data of these currency issuers. However, as exports of charges for the use of intellectual property are highly correlated with the number of international patents, or sci-tech internationalization, we can use weights of exports of charges for the use of intellectual property of Eurozone, UK, and Switzerland of EPC States total exports of charges for the use of intellectual property to multiply the sci-tech internationalization of EPC States in Table 7.6 to find the corresponding sci-tech internationalization of Eurozone, UK, and Switzerland. Similarly, we can estimate sci-tech internationalization of Australia and Canada by multiplying weights of exports of charges for the use of intellectual property of these two countries of total exports of charges for the use of intellectual property with sci-tech internationalization of "others" in Table 7.6. The results of sci-tech internationalization of all eight major international currency issuers are given in Table 13.1.

13.1.2 *Comparing sci-tech internationalization of major currency issuers*

Table 13.1 shows that the US sci-tech was not only by far the highest of all eight major currency issuers from 2000 to 2019, it was higher than the total internationalization of other seven major world currency issuers on average as the average annual US internationalization at 45.67% was higher than the yearly average internationalization of other seven major currency issuers at 42.98%, indicating the near monopolistic role of US internationalization to support the USD; although Japanese yen was ranked third, yet the average annual Japanese sci-tech internationalization at 24.18% was more than twice the corresponding sci-tech internationalization of Eurozone at 11.37% in the same period; the average yearly

Table 13.1: Comparisons of Sci-technology Internationalization of Major Currency Issuers with Currency Internationalization (2000–2019) (Unit: %)

Science & Technology Internationalization of Major Currency Issuers									
Currency Issuer/ Year	**USA**	**Eurozone**	**Japan**	**UK**	**Australia**	**Canada**	**Switzerland**	**China**	**Others**
2000	42.98	11.51	28.10	4.68	0.36	1.81	1.17	1.03	8.36
2001	42.68	11.34	27.94	4.27	0.36	1.60	1.22	0.94	9.66
2002	42.51	11.66	27.24	4.06	0.44	1.76	1.32	0.76	10.26
2003	42.03	11.08	27.92	3.56	0.39	1.40	1.33	0.55	11.74
2004	42.79	10.71	26.82	3.18	0.41	1.32	1.35	0.94	12.48
2005	44.74	11.90	25.81	3.27	0.26	1.32	1.59	0.54	10.58
2006	45.52	11.09	26.74	2.90	0.27	1.41	1.29	0.56	10.22
2007	47.20	11.39	26.21	2.75	0.26	1.40	1.28	0.77	8.72
2008	48.88	11.52	24.10	2.21	0.22	1.26	1.41	1.02	9.38
2009	48.17	11.50	23.83	2.26	0.25	1.15	1.98	0.79	10.07
2010	47.57	10.99	25.83	2.12	0.27	0.77	1.99	1.30	9.17
2011	47.02	10.70	24.34	1.89	0.22	0.77	2.00	1.04	12.03
2012	47.21	10.87	24.56	1.81	0.18	0.81	2.39	1.25	10.92
2013	49.12	10.73	23.43	2.13	0.15	0.87	2.30	0.93	10.33
2014	47.07	10.82	24.19	2.19	0.16	0.87	2.06	0.71	11.93
2015	45.07	10.49	24.67	2.25	0.14	0.75	1.89	1.19	13.54
2016*	45.63	11.60	21.52	2.16	0.16	0.89	2.48	1.29	14.28
2017*	45.04	12.03	18.55	2.36	0.17	0.89	2.38	4.14	14.45
2018*	45.76	12.59	17.00	2.50	0.17	0.94	2.45	4.25	14.35
2019*	46.38	12.97	14.75	2.38	0.16	0.93	2.25	5.61	14.57
Average	45.67	11.37	24.18	2.75	0.25	1.15	1.81	1.48	11.35
Currency Internationalization of Major Currencies									
Currency/ Year	**US Dollar**	**Euro**	**Japanese Yen**	**British Pound**	**Australian Dollar**	**Canadian Dollar**	**Swiss Franc**	**Chinese Yuan**	**Others**
2001	44.93	18.96	11.77	6.52	2.16	2.24	2.99	0.00	10.42
2004	44.00	18.70	10.42	8.25	3.01	2.10	3.01	0.05	10.45
2007	42.80	18.52	8.62	7.43	3.31	2.14	3.41	0.23	13.53
2010	42.43	19.52	9.49	6.44	3.79	2.64	3.15	0.43	12.10
2013	43.52	16.70	11.52	5.91	4.32	2.28	2.58	1.12	12.05
2016	43.79	15.70	10.81	6.40	3.44	2.57	2.40	1.99	12.89

(*Continued*)

Table 13.1: (*Continued*)

Currency/ Year	US Dollar	Euro	Japanese Yen	British Pound	Australian Dollar	Canadian Dollar	Swiss Franc	Chinese Yuan	Others
Currency Internationalization of Major Currencies									
2019	44.15	16.14	8.40	6.40	3.38	2.52	2.48	2.16	14.37
Average	43.66	17.75	10.15	6.76	3.35	2.36	2.86	0.85	12.26
Science & Technology Internationalization of Currency Issuers/Currency Internationalization									
Currency/ Year	**US Dollar**	**Euro**	**Japanese Yen**	**British Pound**	**Australian Dollar**	**Canadian Dollar**	**Swiss Franc**	**Chinese Yuan**	**Others**
2001	−2.26	−7.62	16.18	−2.26	−1.81	−0.65	−1.77	0.94	−0.76
2004	−1.21	−8.00	16.41	−5.07	−2.60	−0.78	−1.66	0.90	2.03
2007	4.40	−7.13	17.59	−4.69	−3.05	−0.74	−2.13	0.55	−4.81
2010	5.14	−8.54	16.33	−4.32	−3.53	−1.87	−1.16	0.87	−2.93
2013	5.60	−5.98	11.91	−3.78	−4.16	−1.41	−0.28	−0.18	−1.72
2016	1.84	−4.10	10.71	−4.24	−3.28	−1.68	0.08	−0.71	1.39
2019	2.23	−3.17	6.35	−4.02	−3.22	−1.59	−0.23	3.44	0.21
Average	2.25	−6.36	13.64	−4.05	−3.09	−1.25	−1.02	0.63	−0.91
Science & Technology Internationalization of Currency Issuers/Currency Internationalization									
Currency/ Year	**US Dollar**	**Euro**	**Japanese Yen**	**British Pound**	**Australian Dollar**	**Canadian Dollar**	**Swiss Franc**	**Chinese Yuan**	**Others**
2001	0.95	0.60	2.37	0.65	0.16	0.71	0.41	245.46	0.93
2004	0.97	0.57	2.58	0.39	0.14	0.63	0.45	19.70	1.19
2007	1.10	0.62	3.04	0.37	0.08	0.65	0.38	3.42	0.64
2010	1.12	0.56	2.72	0.33	0.07	0.29	0.63	3.02	0.76
2013	1.13	0.64	2.03	0.36	0.04	0.38	0.89	0.84	0.86
2016	1.04	0.74	1.99	0.34	0.05	0.35	1.03	0.65	1.11
2019	1.05	0.80	1.76	0.37	0.05	0.37	0.91	2.59	1.01
Average	1.05	0.6	2.36	0.4	0.08	0.48	0.67	38.28	0.93

Source: Sci-tech internationalization of USA, Japan, and China is from Table 7.6; sci-tech internationalization of Eurozone, the United Kingdom and Switzerland is estimated by multiplying the weights of exports of charges for the use of intellectual property of these three regions of total exports of charges for the use of intellectual property and sci-tech internationalization of EPC States in Table 7.6, respectively; sci-tech internationalization of Australia and Canada is estimated by multiplying the weights of exports of charges for the use of intellectual property of total exports of charges for the use of intellectual property of "others" and sci-tech internationalization of "others" in Table 7.6.

sci-tech of United Kingdom was 2.75% in the same period, consistent with world ranking of British pound at fourth; although Australian dollar and Canadian have been ranked fifth and sixth, the average annual sci-tech internationalization of Australia and Canada at 0.25% and 1.15% was lower than that of Switzerland and China, indicating that the currency rankings of Australian dollar and Canadian dollar did not have enough supports of sci-technology of their issuers.

13.1.3 *Comparing sci-tech internationalization of major currency issuers and currency internationalization*

Table 13.1 shows that sci-tech internationalization of the USA was on average higher than corresponding internationalization of USD, indicating USA has enough sci-tech to support the USD. Japanese sci-tech was on average more than twice the internationalization of Japanese yen, indicating that yen's internationalization has been insufficient compared to Japanese science and technology, or Japanese yen should have played a more important role in international foreign exchange market. Euro's science and technology were not sufficient to support its position as world's second currency as annual average sci-tech internationalization of Eurozone was less than two-thirds of the average annual internationalization of Euro, yet Euro's ratio 0.64 was more than 50% higher the corresponding ratio of British pound 0.41, indicating that the internationalization of British pound was less supportive of British science and technology than Euro. The ratio of average annual sci-tech internationalization to yearly average of Swiss Franc ratio 0.63 was similar to that of Euro 0.64, indicating sci-tech internationalization of Switzerland had similar supportive capability to Swiss Franc internationalization as sci-tech internationalization of Eurozone to Euro internationalization.

It is noticeable that the ratio 0.07 of average annual Australian sci-tech internationalization to internationalization of Australian dollar was the lowest of all eight major international currencies, indicating that Australian sci-tech had the weakest supportive capability to Australian Dollar internationalization of all eight currencies. The second lowest ratio was that of Canada 0.49, implying that Canadian sci-tech supportive capability to Canadian dollar internationalization was also the weakest besides Australia. Of the eight major currencies, only USD, Japan yen, and Chinese yuan had more than enough supportive capability of sci-tech internationalization to the corresponding currency internationalization.

13.2 Correlation Coefficients between Sci-tech Internationalization of Major Currency Issuers and Corresponding Currency Internationalization

Based on the results given in Table 13.1, we can calculate the correlation coefficients between the internationalization of the eight major currencies and the internationalization of the corresponding currency issuers from 2000 to 2019. Table 13.2 shows the results.

Table 13.2: Distribution of Correlation Coefficients between Sci-tech Internationalization of Major Currency Issuers and Currency Internationalization (2000–2019) (Unit: %)

Year	2001	2004	2007	2010	2013	2016	2019
2000	89.88	88.15	85.43	86.45	89.96	89.39	85.96
2001	89.89	88.13	85.70	86.61	90.14	89.62	86.32
2002	90.57	88.82	86.59	87.45	90.85	90.35	87.18
2003	89.47	87.63	85.66	86.40	89.97	89.52	86.37
2004	90.33	88.55	86.87	87.48	91.02	90.71	87.80
2005	92.47	90.84	88.92	89.68	92.84	92.43	89.59
2006	91.64	89.94	87.90	88.69	92.10	91.69	88.74
2007	92.48	90.86	88.63	89.52	92.82	92.39	89.46
2008	94.08	92.60	90.75	91.49	94.56	94.27	91.73
2009	94.15	92.67	90.96	91.63	94.66	94.38	91.90
2010	92.51	90.86	88.80	89.62	92.98	92.61	89.78
2011	93.13	91.55	90.16	90.66	93.91	93.73	91.30
2012	93.11	91.50	89.88	90.50	93.75	93.51	90.97
2013	94.14	92.70	91.10	91.65	94.77	94.59	92.20
2014	93.39	91.84	90.44	90.93	94.11	93.93	91.50
2015	92.19	90.56	89.39	89.77	93.10	92.99	90.56
2016*	94.49	93.07	92.39	92.61	95.39	95.39	93.51
2017*	95.34	94.08	93.73	93.82	96.35	96.63	95.22
2018*	96.21	95.10	94.90	94.94	97.17	97.50	96.34
2019*	96.40	95.46	95.54	95.48	97.45	97.96	97.20
Average	92.79	91.24	89.69	90.27	93.40	93.18	90.68

Source: The horizontal axis corresponds to the data on the internationalization level of the world's top eight currencies every 3 years from 2000 to 2019; the vertical axis corresponds to the level of science and technology internationalization of the eight major international currency issuers in the same time span. *stands that data from 2016 to 2019 are estimated using related previous CAGRs from 2003 to 2015.

Table 13.2 shows that correlation coefficients between science and technology internationalization of major currency issuers and currency internationalization have been on average over 90%, indicating very high mutual dependence and mutual supporting relations between the two, consistent with our intuition that science and technology and currency support each other.

13.3 Problems with Correlation Coefficients between Science and Technology Internationalization of Major Currency Issuers and Currency Internationalization

13.3.1 *Problematic correlation coefficients*

The high correlation coefficients in Table 13.2 are intuitively correct, yet it is difficult to directly see the relationship between currency internationalization and sci-tech internationalization in different years from such similar data. Figure 13.1 shows the relationship between the two more intuitively.

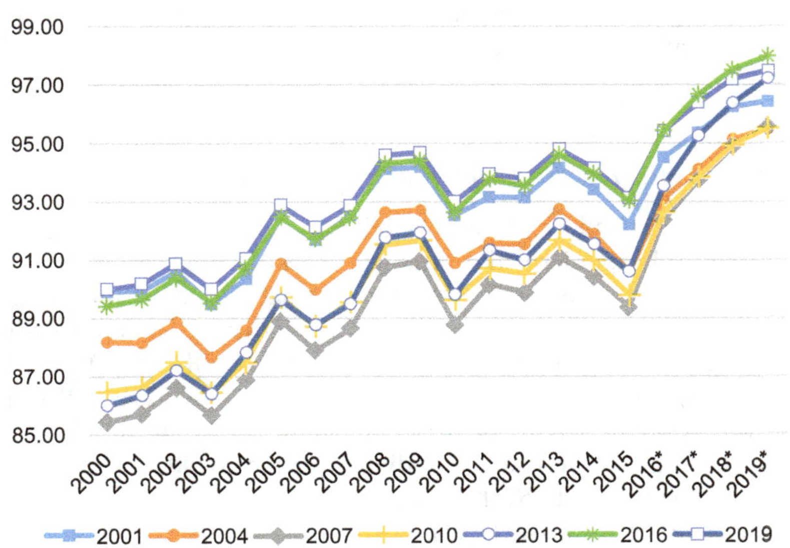

Figure 13.1: Correlation Coefficient between Sci-tech Internationalization and Currency Internationalization (2000–2019) (Unit: %)

Source: Table 13.2.

Figure 13.1 shows that correlation coefficients between sci-tech internationalization and currency internationalization in 2010 mainly were higher than those of 2007, as evidenced by the higher average annual correlation coefficient 93.4% of 2010 than the average annual correlation 89.69% of 2007. These results are somewhat counter-intuitive because 2007 was the year before the 2008 world financial crisis, world financial condition in 2007 was better than that in 2010 for financial market to support currency. Thus, financial supportive capability to sci-tech internationalization should be more robust in 2007 than in 2010, the second year after the 2008 world financial crisis when the United States was in the early stage of implementing the quantitative easing policies. Therefore, relationship between currency internationalization and sci-tech internationalization should be higher in 2007 than in 2010.

The year 2010 was the second year into quantitative easing policies, where the daily average of USD was only 82.2. The USD internationalization index, the share of average daily turnover of USD of global foreign exchange turnover shown in Table 4.1, was 42.43%, the lowest since 1998. USD supportive capability to US sci-tech internationalization should be lower than that of 2007 before the financial crisis. However, Figure 14.1 shows that the correlation between technology and currency in 2010 was generally higher than the corresponding correlation in 2007, indicating that the relevant results in Figure 13.1 or Table 13.2 are highly questionable.

13.3.2 *Reasons for the problematic correlation coefficients*

The complex correlation coefficients in Figure 13.1 are the results of overall foreign exchange derivatives trading in total foreign exchange daily turnover. Statistics from the Bank for International Settlements (BIS) show that the ratio of foreign exchange derivatives daily turnover over total foreign exchange daily turnover increased steadily from 68.85% in 2001 to 69.77% in 2007. It decreased significantly to 62.53% in 2010 and decreased further to 61.72% in 2013, indicating significant slowing down of foreign exchange derivatives trading after the world financial crisis. However, it recovered to 67.49% and 69.87% in 2016 and 2019, respectively, back to the pre-crisis levels.

The lowest ratio of foreign exchange derivatives daily turnover 61.72% in 2013 and the highest average annual correlation coefficient

93.40% in Table 13.2 tell us the source of the problematic correlation coefficients of Figure 13.1. The problem arises from foreign exchange derivatives turnover in Table 4.1 because foreign exchange derivatives turnover is not based on the actual money-changing hands of traditional trading, but rather on the nominal trading value of foreign exchange derivatives.

For example, the option fee of a 1 billion notional amount of foreign exchange option is usually a few percentages of the notional amount, and the actual money changing hands of a 1 billion notional amount of foreign exchange swap is also a few percentages of the notional amount. Thus, about two-thirds of foreign exchange daily average turnover is not real money changing hands, they exaggerate actual foreign exchange turnover. Therefore, actual correlation coefficients between sci-tech internationalization and currency internationalization must wrongly be calculated because of the exaggerated foreign exchange derivatives turnover.

13.4 Reassessment of the Relationship between Sci-tech Internationalization and Currency Internationalization with Discounted Foreign Exchange Derivatives Turnover

13.4.1 *Currency internationalization with actual foreign exchange turnover*

Problems of the relationship between sci-tech internationalization and currency internationalization in 2007 and 2010 using the data shown in Table 4.1 based on the average daily transaction value of traditional foreign exchange turnover or nominal foreign exchange turnover can be overcome using "actual" or discounted foreign exchange derivatives turnover. The BIS foreign exchange derivatives turnover data in Tables 4.4 and 4.5 are turnover data of nominal values of foreign exchange derivatives turnovers, and there are no corresponding actual money-changing turnover data. We have to assume that 5% of all derivatives nominal daily turnover is actual daily turnover and estimated actual daily turnover of foreign exchange daily turnover of eight currencies. This section uses the daily turnover of foreign exchange turnover of major international currencies released by the BIS to estimate the actual average daily transaction value of foreign exchange data. The corresponding results of the relationship between technology and currency internationalization are different from the results in Table 13.3.

Comparing currency internationalization results in Tables 13.1 and in 13.3, we find the average annual USD internationalization and British pound internationalization declined 1.96% and 0.32%, respectively, and

Table 13.3: Comparisons of Sci-tech Internationalization of Major Currency Issuers with Currency Internationalization (2000–2019) (Unit: %)

Year/ Currency	US Dollar	Euro	Japanese Yen	British Pound	Australian Dollar	Canadian Dollar	Swiss Franc	Chinese Yuan	Others
2001	42.61	21.17	12.85	5.59	1.84	2.06	3.42	0.00	10.47
2004	42.81	21.34	10.43	6.94	2.63	1.92	3.22	0.07	10.64
2007	39.84	20.55	10.01	7.46	2.73	1.95	4.24	0.41	12.83
2010	40.17	22.72	10.00	7.06	3.74	2.62	3.09	0.29	10.32
2013	41.59	18.22	14.54	5.58	4.73	2.28	2.12	0.86	10.06
2016	42.18	15.71	11.79	6.39	4.20	3.08	1.83	2.04	12.77
2019	42.70	15.58	8.96	6.09	4.14	2.98	2.20	2.40	14.94
Average	41.70	19.33	11.23	6.44	3.43	2.41	2.87	0.87	11.72

Science & Technology Internationalization of Currency Issuers/Currency Internationalization

Year/ Currency	US Dollar	Euro	Japanese Yen	British Pound	Australian Dollar	Canadian Dollar	Swiss Franc	Chinese Yuan	Others
2001	0.07	−9.83	15.10	−1.32	−1.48	−0.46	−2.20	0.94	−0.81
2004	−0.02	−10.63	16.39	−3.76	−2.23	−0.60	−1.87	0.88	1.84
2007	7.36	−9.15	16.21	−4.71	−2.46	−0.55	−2.95	0.36	−4.11
2010	7.40	−11.74	15.83	−4.94	−3.47	−1.85	−1.10	1.01	−1.15
2013	7.53	−7.49	8.89	−3.46	−4.58	−1.41	0.17	0.07	0.28
2016	3.45	−4.12	9.73	−4.23	−4.04	−2.19	0.65	−0.75	1.51
2019	3.68	−2.61	5.79	−3.71	−3.98	−2.05	0.04	3.21	−0.37
Average	4.21	−7.94	12.56	−3.73	−3.18	−1.30	−1.04	0.82	−0.40

Science & Technology Internationalization of Currency Issuers/Currency Internationalization

Year/ Currency	US Dollar	Euro	Japanese Yen	British Pound	Australian Dollar	Canadian Dollar	Swiss Franc	Chinese Yuan	Others
2001	1.00	0.54	2.18	0.76	0.19	0.78	0.36	193.05	0.92
2004	1.00	0.50	2.57	0.46	0.15	0.69	0.42	13.95	1.17
2007	1.18	0.55	2.62	0.37	0.10	0.72	0.30	1.86	0.68

Table 13.3: (*Continued*)

Science & Technology Internationalization of Currency Issuers/Currency Internationalization									
Year/ Currency	**US Dollar**	**Euro**	**Japanese Yen**	**British Pound**	**Australian Dollar**	**Canadian Dollar**	**Swiss Franc**	**Chinese Yuan**	**Others**
2010	1.18	0.48	2.58	0.30	0.07	0.29	0.65	4.45	0.89
2013	1.18	0.59	1.61	0.38	0.03	0.38	1.08	1.08	1.03
2016	1.08	0.74	1.82	0.34	0.04	0.29	1.36	0.63	1.12
2019	1.09	0.83	1.65	0.39	0.04	0.31	1.02	2.34	0.98
Average	1.10	0.60	2.15	0.43	0.09	0.49	0.74	31.05	0.97

Source: Sci-tech internationalization is the same as in Table 13.1; currency internationalization is calculated with the assumption of 5% of foreign exchange derivatives nominal turnover as the actual daily turnover of foreign exchange derivatives plus actual daily turnover of spot foreign exchange daily turnover.

annual average internationalization of Euro and Japanese yen increased 1.58% and 1.08%, respectively. These changes of average internationalization of the top four currencies indicate the exaggerated contribution of high foreign exchange derivatives trading of USD and British pound were stripped off and internationalization of Euro and Japanese yen restored to their reasonable levels because of relative low foreign exchange derivatives trading.

13.4.2 *Currency internationalization with actual foreign exchange turnover*

Using the sci-tech internationalization results in Table 13.1 and the top eight international currency internationalization data given in Table 13.3, we can calculate the internationalization level of the top eight major currencies and the internationalization of currency issuers from 2001–2019. Table 13.4 and Figure 13.2 give the corresponding results.

Table 13.4 shows that the average annual correlation coefficients with 2010 currency internationalization at 88.08% were 1.43% lower than the yearly average correlation coefficients with currency internationalization at 89.61%. Thus, the problems with counter-intuitive higher correlation coefficients of 2010 than 2007 are resolved. Apart from these 2 years before and after year 2008, the average annual correlation coefficients between currency internationalization and sci-tech internationalization in Table 13.4 increased by 1.31%, 0.66%, and 0.41% from the corresponding annual average correlation coefficients in Table 13.1.

Table 13.4: Distribution of Correlation Coefficients between Sci-tech Internationalization of Major Currency Issuers and Corresponding Currency Internationalization (2000–2019) (Unit: %)

Year	2001	2004	2007	2010	2013	2016	2019
2000	89.83	87.03	85.86	85.02	92.64	90.41	86.35
2001	89.86	87.04	86.08	85.00	92.66	90.64	86.78
2002	90.57	87.82	86.96	85.82	93.23	91.34	87.66
2003	89.51	86.62	86.00	84.53	92.28	90.55	86.97
2004	90.20	87.48	86.96	85.30	92.91	91.64	88.41
2005	92.32	89.85	89.07	87.85	94.73	93.25	90.01
2006	91.39	88.82	87.94	86.73	94.05	92.55	89.19
2007	92.13	89.71	88.60	87.66	94.73	93.18	89.81
2008	93.54	91.44	90.45	89.40	95.89	94.88	92.03
2009	93.64	91.54	90.68	89.47	95.90	94.97	92.22
2010	92.10	89.69	88.67	87.55	94.66	93.30	90.12
2011	92.64	90.40	89.82	88.19	95.02	94.35	91.75
2012	92.65	90.36	89.62	88.17	95.02	94.12	91.35
2013	93.45	91.43	90.62	89.24	95.74	95.09	92.50
2014	92.89	90.69	90.11	88.50	95.21	94.54	91.93
2015	91.81	89.44	89.12	87.19	94.22	93.67	91.12
2016*	94.02	92.11	91.97	89.99	95.85	95.85	93.96
2017*	94.67	93.16	93.06	91.07	96.19	96.87	95.57
2018*	95.45	94.22	94.13	92.22	96.71	97.63	96.62
2019*	95.48	94.61	94.55	92.67	96.47	97.91	97.40
Average	92.41	90.17	89.51	88.08	94.70	93.84	91.09

Source: Calculated using sci-tech internationalization data in Table 13.1 and currency internationalization data in Table 14.3, others are the same as in Table 13.1. *stands that data from 2016 to 2019 are estimated using related previous CAGRs from 2003 to 2015.

The lowest average annual correlation coefficient with 2010 currency internationalization, the first full year of the implementation of the quantitative easing policy in the United States, is consistent with the weakest financial support to sci-tech in 2010 right after the 2008 world financial crisis. Results in Table 13.4 compared to those in Table 13.2 show that the USD's support for sci-tech steadily restored from 2013 to 2019, which is consistent with the recovering of the US financial system from 2013, the last full year of US quantitative easing policy. The more likely results in

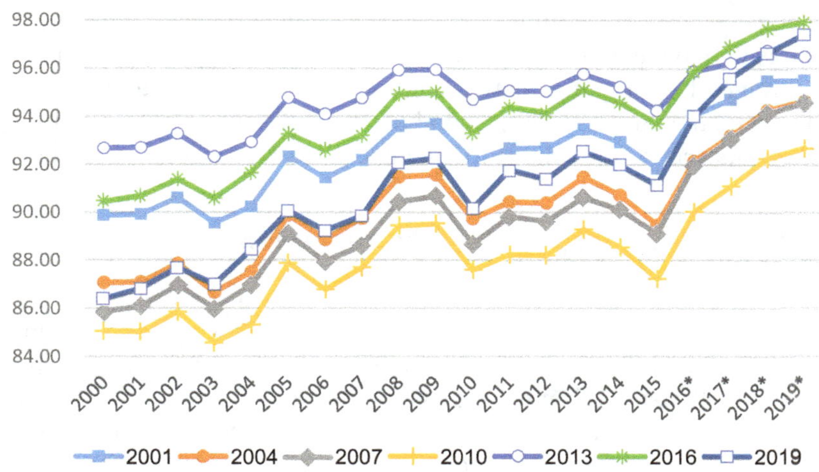

Figure 13.2: Correlation Coefficient between Sci-tech Internationalization and Corresponding Currency Internationalization (2000–2019) (Unit: %)

Source: Table 13.3.

Table 13.4 show the rationality of using actual or discounted foreign exchange derivatives turnover.

13.5 The Better Measure of Currency Internationalization

Table 13.3 gives the average daily foreign exchange turnover (actual foreign exchange turnover) of different currencies calculated based on the assumption that 5% of the nominal amount of foreign exchange derivatives is counted as foreign exchange transactions as a measure of currency internationalization. The results shown in Figure 13.2 are significantly better than those shown in Figure 13.1, i.e., the nominal daily trading value of foreign exchange based on the nominal trading value of foreign exchange derivatives given in Table 4.1 is not regarded as a good trading value measure of currency internationalization. The main reason is that the nominal foreign exchange derivatives trading does not represent actual transfer transactions. The results in Table 13.4 are significantly better than those in Table 13.1, showing that our method of "discounting" the nominal transaction amount of foreign exchange derivatives is rational. Yet, a new problem arises: is 95% "discount" of foreign exchange derivatives, or foreign exchange derivatives' nominal amount of 5% the best result? This section attempts to find the best measurement method of currency internationalization through the correlation between currency internationalization and sci-tech internationalization corresponding to different discounts on the nominal transaction amount of foreign exchange derivatives.

13.5.1 *Searching the better measure of currency internationalization*

The mutual support of sci-tech internationalization and currency internationalization is logical, and we have found evidence in this chapter. Currency internationalization results of the average daily transaction amount of foreign exchange turnover calculated according to different "discount" rates for foreign exchange derivatives are different, leading to different correlation coefficients between the corresponding currency internationalization and sci-tech internationalization. However, the criterion for judging which discount method is the best should be that the overall average correlation coefficients between before and after the international financial crisis in 2008 and before and after the US withdrew from its easing policy in 2014 are reasonable, and the corresponding overall average correlation is the highest in all years.

Use the same method above to calculate different currency internationalization measurement combinations with different "discount" rates for foreign exchange derivatives turnover in other years, and then calculate the correlation between sci-tech internationalization and currency internationalization. Table 13.5 gives the corresponding results.

Table 13.5 shows that correlation coefficients between sci-tech internationalization and 2010 currency internationalization surpass correlation coefficients with 2007 currency internationalization when 50% or more than 50% of foreign exchange derivatives turnover is considered as actual foreign exchange turnover, indicating that too much weight given to foreign exchange derivatives turnover leads to incorrect results. Overall average correlation coefficients with 2007–2019 five currency internationalization increase with the percentage of foreign exchange derivatives turnover as actual foreign exchange derivative turnover to the point of 30.6% with highest overall average correlation coefficient of 91.526576, and the overall average correlation coefficients decline with the percentage of foreign exchange derivatives turnover as actual foreign exchange derivative turnover after 30.6%.

Table 13.5: Comparison of Average Correlation Coefficients between Different Measurement Results of Currency Internationalization and Sci-tech Internationalization (2000–2019) (Unit: %)

% Of FX Derivatives Turnover as Real FX Turnover/Year	2007	2010	2013	2016	2019	Overall Annual Average Correlation Coefficient
2.00	89.45	87.84	94.75	93.89	91.12	91.411904
3.00	89.47	87.92	94.74	93.87	91.11	91.423699
4.00	89.49	88.00	94.72	93.86	91.10	91.434454
5.00	89.51	88.08	94.70	93.84	91.09	91.444258
6.00	89.53	88.15	94.69	93.82	91.08	91.453191
7.00	89.55	88.22	94.67	93.80	91.07	91.461327
8.00	89.56	88.29	94.65	93.79	91.06	91.468731
9.00	89.58	88.35	94.63	93.77	91.05	91.475463
10.00	89.59	88.41	94.61	93.76	91.04	91.481578
15.00	89.64	88.69	94.52	93.69	90.99	91.504463
20.00	89.67	88.92	94.43	93.62	90.95	91.517705
25.00	89.69	89.11	94.33	93.57	90.92	91.524387
28.00	89.70	89.21	94.28	93.54	90.90	91.526127
30.00	89.70	89.27	94.25	93.52	90.89	91.526549
30.50	89.70	89.28	94.24	93.52	90.89	91.526575
30.60	89.70	89.29	94.24	93.52	90.89	91.526576
31.00	89.71	89.30	94.23	93.51	90.88	91.526570
31.50	89.71	89.31	94.22	93.51	90.88	91.526536
32.00	89.71	89.33	94.21	93.51	90.88	91.526475
35.00	89.71	89.41	94.16	93.48	90.86	91.525575
45.00	89.72	89.64	94.01	93.41	90.82	91.517752
48.00	89.72	89.69	93.96	93.39	90.81	91.514431
49.00	89.72	89.71	93.95	93.38	90.80	91.513255
50.00	89.72	89.73	93.93	93.38	90.80	91.512050
60.00	89.71	89.89	93.80	93.32	90.77	91.498812
80.00	89.70	90.11	93.58	93.24	90.72	91.469927
100.00	89.69	90.27	93.40	93.18	90.68	91.442045

Source: Calculated using foreign exchange derivatives turnovers of eight major international currencies released by the BIS from 2007 to 2019 and various "discount" rates of foreign exchange derivatives.

It is noticeable that the overall average correlation coefficient between sci-tech internalization and currency internationalization reaches the peak of 91.526567% when 30.6% of nominal foreign exchange derivatives turnover is regarded as the actual foreign exchange turnover.

13.5.2 *Currency internationalization corresponding to the better currency internationalization*

Using the best currency internationalization point of 30.6% of foreign exchange derivatives turnover as actual foreign exchange turnover in Table 13.5, we can find eight central internationalizations, the results are given in Table 13.6. Table 13.6 shows that the support of US sci-tech internationalization to USD internationalization becomes stronger as the difference of the two increases from 2.01% in Table 13.1 to 2.98% in Table 13.6 resulting from stripping off USD foreign exchange derivatives turnover and lower USD internationalization in Table 13.5. We will discuss related issues further in Section 13.7.

Table 13.6: Comparison of Sci-tech Internationalization of Major Currency Issuers with Corresponding Currency Internationalization (2000–2019) (Unit: %)

Currency Internationalization of Major Currencies									
Year/ Currency	**US Dollar**	**Euro**	**Japanese Yen**	**British Pound**	**Australian Dollar**	**Canadian Dollar**	**Swiss Franc**	**Chinese Yuan**	**Others**
2001	43.81	20.03	12.29	6.07	2.00	2.15	3.20	0.00	10.45
2004	43.41	20.01	10.42	7.60	2.82	2.01	3.12	0.06	10.55
2007	41.38	19.49	9.29	7.44	3.03	2.05	3.81	0.32	13.20
2010	41.25	21.20	9.76	6.76	3.76	2.63	3.12	0.36	11.16
2013	42.50	17.50	13.12	5.74	4.54	2.28	2.34	0.98	11.00
2016	43.00	15.70	11.30	6.40	3.82	2.82	2.12	2.02	12.84
2019	43.46	15.87	8.67	6.25	3.75	2.74	2.35	2.27	14.64
Average	42.69	18.54	10.69	6.61	3.39	2.38	2.86	0.86	11.97
Science & Technology Internationalization of Currency Issuers/Currency Internationalization									
Year/ Currency	**US Dollar**	**Euro**	**Japanese Yen**	**British Pound**	**Australian Dollar**	**Canadian Dollar**	**Swiss Franc**	**Chinese Yuan**	**Others**
2001	−1.13	−8.69	15.66	−1.80	−1.65	−0.56	−1.98	0.94	−0.79
2004	−0.62	−9.30	16.40	−4.42	−2.42	−0.69	−1.76	0.89	1.94

Table 13.6: (*Continued*)

Science & Technology Internationalization of Currency Issuers/Currency Internationalization									
Year/ Currency	**US Dollar**	**Euro**	**Japanese Yen**	**British Pound**	**Australian Dollar**	**Canadian Dollar**	**Swiss Franc**	**Chinese Yuan**	**Others**
2007	5.82	−8.09	16.93	−4.70	−2.77	−0.65	−2.52	0.46	−4.47
2010	6.33	−10.21	16.07	−4.65	−3.50	−1.86	−1.13	0.94	−1.99
2013	6.62	−6.78	10.31	−3.61	−4.38	−1.41	−0.04	−0.05	−0.66
2016	2.63	−4.11	10.22	−4.24	−3.66	−1.93	0.36	−0.73	1.45
2019	2.92	−2.90	6.08	−3.87	−3.58	−1.81	−0.10	3.33	−0.07
Average	3.22	−7.16	13.10	−3.90	−3.14	−1.27	−1.02	0.83	−0.66

Science & Technology Internationalization of Currency Issuers/Currency Internationalization									
Year/ Currency	**US Dollar**	**Euro**	**Japanese Yen**	**British Pound**	**Australian Dollar**	**Canadian Dollar**	**Swiss Franc**	**Chinese Yuan**	**Others**
2001	0.97	0.57	2.27	0.70	0.18	0.74	0.38	216.96	0.92
2004	0.99	0.54	2.57	0.42	0.14	0.65	0.43	16.37	1.18
2007	1.14	0.58	2.82	0.37	0.09	0.68	0.34	2.44	0.66
2010	1.15	0.52	2.65	0.31	0.07	0.29	0.64	3.63	0.82
2013	1.16	0.61	1.79	0.37	0.03	0.38	0.98	0.95	0.94
2016	1.06	0.74	1.90	0.34	0.04	0.32	1.17	0.64	1.11
2019	1.07	0.82	1.70	0.38	0.04	0.34	0.96	2.47	1.00
Average	1.08	0.62	2.24	0.41	0.09	0.49	0.70	34.78	0.95

Source: Sci-tech internationalization is the same as in Table 13.1; currency internationalization is calculated with 30.6% of foreign exchange derivatives nominal turnover as the actual daily turnover of foreign exchange derivatives plus actual daily turnover of spot foreign exchange daily turnover.

13.6 Function of Foreign Exchange Derivatives Trading Implied in the Best Measure of Currency Internationalization

Since most of the notional amounts involved in foreign exchange derivatives transactions only have less than 5% of the cash transfer or actual trading, the best currency internationalization point should occur lower than 5% intuitively. Yet, Table 13.5 shows the result of the best currency internationalization point of 30.6%, which is not only puzzling but also a little strange. However, after careful analysis of the relevant results, we will find the answer from the functions of foreign exchange derivatives trading. Foreign exchange derivatives transactions are not only the cash that changes hands but also more importantly, it provides traders with the necessary exchange rate "safe haven", which reduces the risk of corporate investment or cross-border R&D investment, thereby promoting the internationalization of technology development. Therefore, the best point of currency internationalization is 30.6%, which clearly exceeds 5%. The result reflects the investment function of currency as well as the hedging function of foreign exchange derivatives transactions. If the overall average correlation of 5% corresponding to 91.444258% is regarded as the investment function of currency, then the corresponding increase of percentage from 5% to 30.6% or 25.6% should reflect the degree of support of the currency's hedging function to technology.

Since the global foreign exchange derivatives are mainly traded between banks, most of their types and maturities are different, so it is indeed challenging amounts of foreign exchange derivatives with average daily nominal turnover as high as tens of thousands of billion-dollar value. If we assume that an average of 4% of foreign exchange derivatives is the real turnover, or 4% of foreign exchange derivatives turnover is cash functionality, then 30.6 − 4.0 = 24.4% belongs to the hedging functionality of foreign exchange derivatives. The latter is more than six times as much as the former, indicating that the hedging functionality of foreign exchange derivatives significantly exceeds its corresponding cash functionality. Therefore, this section also deepens our understanding of the trading functions of foreign exchange derivatives through the analysis results of better measurement of currency internationalization.

13.7 Overestimation and Underestimation of Internationalization of Major Eight Currencies Compared with their Sci-tech Internationalization

13.7.1 *Under measurement of internationalization of three major international currencies*

The high correlation coefficient between currency internationalization and currency issuer's sci-tech internationalization indicates that the interaction between the two is considerable. Table 13.1 shows that the internationalization level of US sci-tech is significantly higher than that of the

USD, the former is 5% higher than the latter on average from 2000 to 2019, indicating that the US sci-tech has sufficient supporting role for the dollar. The sci-tech internationalization of Japan are 136% higher than that of Japanese yen on average from 2000 to 2019. The sci-tech internationalization/yen internationalization ratio is the highest among the eight major international currencies, indicating that the internationalization of the yen is the lowest compared to the internationalization of Japanese sci-tech among eight currencies.

Results of Table 13.6 show that the ratio of the US sci-tech internationalization over USD internationalization increases from 1.05 in Table 13.1 to 1.08 with better measurement of currency internationalization, indicating the USD is more under measured internationally. The ratio of Japanese sci-tech internationalization over internationalization of Japanese yen decreases from 2.36 in Table 13.1 to 2.24 with the best measure of currency internationalization, indicating that Japanese yen is less over-measured internationally with the better measurement of currency internationalization. The total extra sci-tech internationalization (sci-tech internationalization — currency internationalization) of USD and Japanese yen increases from 2.25% + 13.64% = 15.89% to 3.22% + 13.10% = 17.14%.

13.7.2 *Over-measurement of internationalization of five major international currencies*

Table 13.1 shows that the ratios of average annual sci-tech internationalization of Eurozone, United Kingdom, Australia, Canada, and Switzerland over the corresponding average annual currency internationalization of Euro, British pound, Australian dollar, Canadian dollar, and Swiss franc are 65%, 40%, 8%, 48%, and 67%, respectively. Or sci-tech internationalization of Eurozone, United Kingdom, Australia, Canada, and Switzerland is 35%, 60%, 92%, 52%, and 33% lower than the corresponding internationalization of Euro, British pound, Australian dollar, Canadian dollar, and Swiss franc, respectively. In other words, the sci-tech internationalization of Eurozone, United Kingdom, Australia, Canada, and Switzerland is not sufficient to support the internationalization of their currencies, or their internationalization levels are mainly funded by Japanese sci-tech and US sci-tech internationalization.

Table 13.6 shows that the proportion of average annual sci-tech internationalization over the corresponding average annual currency internationalization of Eurozone decreases from 65% in Table 14.1 to 62% with the best measure of currency internationalization, and the ratios of average annual sci-tech internationalization/average annual currency internationalization of United Kingdom, Australia, Canada, and Switzerland increase from 40%, 8%, 49%, and 70% in Table 14.1 slightly to 41%, 9%, 49%, and 70%, respectively, with the best measure of currency internationalization, indicating that with the exception of Euro, British pound, Australian dollar, Canadian dollar, and Swiss franc are slightly less over-measured internationally with the best measure of currency internationalization.

The total insufficiency of sci-tech internationalization (sci-tech internationalization — currency internationalization) of the above five major international currencies decreases from 6.36% + 4.05% + 3.09% + 1.25% + 1.02% = 15.78% to 7.16% + 3.90% + 3.14% + 1.27% + 1.02% = 16.49%.

13.7.3 *Under-measurement of Chinese yuan internationalization*

Tables 13.1 and 13.6 show that ratios of sci-tech internationalization over yuan internationalization were extremely high due to the extremely low Chinese yuan foreign exchange turnover in 2000 and 2004. Regardless of the extremely high ratios of these 2 years, the ratios of average annual sci-tech internationalization over average annual yuan internationalization decrease slightly from 2.10 in Table 13.1 from 2007 to 2019 to 2.03 during the same period. These results indicate that Chinese yuan was under-measured internationally from 2007 to 2019, and the degree of under-measurement of Chinese yuan was second only to Japanese.

Calculations with Korean sci-tech internationalization and Korean won internationalization data show that Korean won has been under-measured internationally, the degree of under-measurement of Korean won is between Japanese yen and Chinese yuan, indicating that all three major Asian currencies are under-measured internationally compared to the over-measured three major European currencies in Table 13.6.

13.8 Mutual Support of Major International Currency Issuers

Differences between sci-tech internationalization of major currency issuers and currency internationalization of major currencies shown in Tables 13.1 and 13.6 can be better understood from mutual holding of long-term securities among the major currency issuers. In other words, mutual holdings of long-term securities reflect mutual supports of one currency with another. Specifically, holdings of US long-term securities by other currency issuers compared to US holding of long-term securities of other currency issuers reflect support to the USD by other currency issuers, at the same time, extra US holding of long-term securities of other currency issuers reflects US support to other currencies. Extra holdings of US holdings of long-term securities of other currency issuers also reflect dependence of other currencies on the USD. Table 13.7 gives the

Table 13.7: Distribution of US Long-Term Securities Held by Major Currency Issuers and US Holdings of Long-Term Securities Issued by Other Major Currency Issuers (2011–2021) (Unit: USD trillion, %)

Total US Long-Term US Securities Held by Foreign Residents									
Year/Region	**2012**	**2013**	**2014**	**2016**	**2019**	**2020**	**Jun-21**	**Average**	**Share of Average**
Eurozone	2.58	3.20	3.67	3.92	5.00	5.76	6.32	4.69	23.47
Japan	1.80	1.82	1.87	1.90	2.31	2.61	2.69	2.31	11.56
China	1.65	1.80	1.80	1.44	1.52	1.53	1.57	1.74	8.71
UK	1.03	1.22	1.40	1.42	1.84	2.19	2.40	1.77	8.86
Canada	0.73	0.91	1.01	0.98	1.38	1.61	1.84	1.30	6.51
Australia	0.17	0.22	0.23	0.24	0.34	0.39	0.45	0.31	1.58
Switzerland	0.54	0.58	0.64	0.73	0.81	0.99	1.12	0.83	4.17
Korea	0.23	0.30	0.32	0.39	0.40	0.49	0.56	0.41	2.07
UKCanAustra	1.93	2.35	2.64	2.64	3.56	4.19	4.69	3.38	16.95
Total Asia	5.11	5.37	5.71	5.60	6.97	7.73	8.11	6.86	34.37
Total Europe	4.89	5.81	6.55	6.94	8.71	10.16	11.24	8.35	41.85
Total	13.22	14.72	16.08	16.46	20.50	23.37	25.40	19.96	100.00
Total Foreign Long-Term Securities Held by US Residents									
Year/Region	**2012**	**2013**	**2014**	**2016**	**2019**	**2020**	**Jun-21**	**Average**	**Share of Average**
Eurozone	1.57	1.99	2.08	2.19	2.91	3.12	3.47	2.67	22.61
Japan	0.49	0.67	0.67	0.79	1.09	1.20	1.20	0.94	7.98
China	0.13	0.10	0.13	0.10	0.22	0.29	0.31	0.20	1.67
UK	1.05	1.26	1.22	1.15	1.43	1.36	1.47	1.38	11.67

(*Continued*)

Table 13.7: (*Continued*)

Total Foreign Long-Term Securities Held by US Residents

Year/Region	2012	2013	2014	2016	2019	2020	Jun-21	Average	Share of Average
Canada	0.77	0.78	0.79	0.75	0.98	1.08	1.22	0.98	8.32
Australia	0.29	0.28	0.27	0.27	0.32	0.35	0.37	0.33	2.81
Switzerland	0.35	0.45	0.43	0.42	0.60	0.63	0.68	0.55	4.63
Korea	0.17	0.18	0.18	0.18	0.23	0.30	0.31	0.24	2.02
UKCanAustra	2.12	2.33	2.28	2.18	2.73	2.79	3.07	2.69	22.79
Total Asia	1.38	1.57	1.71	1.81	2.55	2.94	3.10	2.32	19.62
Total Europe	3.45	4.26	4.26	4.31	5.58	5.87	6.46	5.26	44.55
Total	7.66	8.84	9.19	9.49	12.58	13.86	15.11	11.80	100.00

Total US Long-Term US Securities Held by Foreign Residents/Total Foreign Long-Term Securities Held by US Residents

Year/Region	2012	2013	2014	2016	2019	2020	Jun-21	Average	Share of Average
Eurozone	1.01	1.20	1.59	1.73	2.09	2.63	2.85	2.02	24.73
Japan	1.30	1.14	1.20	1.11	1.22	1.41	1.49	1.37	16.74
China	1.52	1.69	1.67	1.34	1.30	1.24	1.26	1.54	18.90
UK	−0.03	−0.04	0.18	0.27	0.42	0.82	0.93	0.39	4.80
Canada	−0.04	0.13	0.22	0.22	0.40	0.53	0.61	0.32	3.90
Australia	−0.12	−0.07	−0.03	−0.03	0.02	0.05	0.08	−0.02	−0.20
Switzerland	0.19	0.14	0.21	0.30	0.21	0.36	0.44	0.29	3.50
Korea	0.05	0.12	0.15	0.21	0.17	0.19	0.24	0.17	2.13
UKCanAustra	−0.19	0.02	0.36	0.46	0.83	1.40	1.62	0.69	8.50
Total Asia	3.72	3.80	4.00	3.79	4.42	4.79	5.02	4.54	55.71
Total Europe	1.43	1.56	2.29	2.63	3.12	4.29	4.78	3.09	37.94
Total	5.55	5.88	6.89	6.97	7.92	9.51	10.29	8.16	100.00

Total Foreign Long-Term Securities Held by US Residents/Total US Long-Term US Securities Held by Foreign Residents

Year/Region	2012	2013	2014	2016	2019	2020	Jun-21	Average
Eurozone	163.9	160.4	176.3	179.1	171.8	184.3	182.2	172.7
Japan	365.4	269.9	277.2	241.4	211.3	217.9	223.9	263.8
China	1,250.6	1,717.3	1,430.4	1,390.9	683.7	532.8	509.4	1,167.6

Table 13.7: (*Continued*)

Total Foreign Long-Term Securities Held by US Residents/Total US Long-Term US Securities Held by Foreign Residents								
Year/Region	**2012**	**2013**	**2014**	**2016**	**2019**	**2020**	**Jun-21**	**Average**
UK	97.5	96.7	114.4	123.5	129.4	160.2	162.9	120.3
Canada	94.2	116.8	127.9	130.0	140.2	149.2	150.1	126.4
Australia	58.4	76.7	87.0	87.9	106.0	113.4	122.0	88.2
Switzerland	155.4	130.2	147.7	172.1	136.1	157.9	164.5	149.9
Korea	130.8	164.2	183.3	221.7	171.8	162.9	178.0	172.5
UKCanAustra	90.9	101.0	115.8	121.3	130.5	150.1	152.8	118.3
Total Asia	369.4	342.0	334.3	309.9	273.0	262.7	262.1	315.2
Total Europe	141.5	136.6	153.8	161.2	155.9	173.2	174.1	153.7
Total	172.5	166.5	175.0	173.4	163.0	168.6	168.1	169.8
Total US Long-Term US Securities Held by Foreign Residents/Total Foreign Long-Term Securities Held by US Residents								
Year/Region	**2012**	**2013**	**2014**	**2016**	**2019**	**2020**	**Jun-21**	**Average**
Eurozone	61.0	62.3	56.7	55.8	58.2	54.3	54.9	58.1
Japan	27.4	37.0	36.1	41.4	47.3	45.9	44.7	39.2
China	8.0	5.8	7.0	7.2	14.6	18.8	19.6	10.2
UK	102.6	103.4	87.4	81.0	77.3	62.4	61.4	85.7
Canada	106.1	85.6	78.2	76.9	71.3	67.0	66.6	80.9
Australia	171.2	130.4	115.0	113.8	94.3	88.2	82.0	118.8
Switzerland	64.4	76.8	67.7	58.1	73.5	63.3	60.8	67.3
Korea	76.4	60.9	54.6	45.1	58.2	61.4	56.2	59.4
UKCanAustra	110.0	99.0	86.3	82.5	76.6	66.6	65.4	86.8
Total Asia	27.1	29.2	29.9	32.3	36.6	38.1	38.1	32.2
Total Europe	70.7	73.2	65.0	62.0	64.1	57.8	57.5	65.5
Total	58.0	60.1	57.1	57.7	61.4	59.3	59.5	58.9

Source: Calculated according to data updated by the US Treasury website www.treasury.gov; the data in 2021 are data as of end of June 2021; UKCanAustra stands for United Kingdom, Canada and Australia together.

distribution of US long-term securities held by major international currency issuers, US holdings of long-term securities of other currency issuers from the end of 2011 to the end of 2020 and the end of June 2021 and the corresponding asset size of the seven major international currency issuers held by the United States.

13.8.1 *Mutual support and measurement of major international currencies*

Table 13.7 shows that although the US long-term securities held by the Eurozone and Japan continued to exceed China in April 2011–2020, but during 2011–2015, 1 year after the United States had withdrawn from the quantitative easing monetary policy, China maintained as the largest net holding country of US long-term securities, and accounting dropped slightly from 28.68% of the world's share of net USD assets to 23.56%, showing China's strong support for USD in the primary implementation period of the US quantitative easing monetary policy.

The net number of US long-term securities held by the Eurozone surpassed China for the first time in 2016, becoming the largest net holding area of US long-term securities. Japan also surpassed China to become the second largest net holder of US long-term securities in April 2020, and China's net amount of US long-term securities ranked third. The net holdings of the top three US long-term securities account for more than 60% of the net US long-term securities. After the US withdrew from the quantitative easing monetary policy in 2014, the net amount of long-term securities held by the UK continued to grow significantly, but the total amount was less than half of that of Japan and China. The amount of US long-term securities held by Switzerland has decreased substantially, which is lower than the net amount held by Canada in recent years.

Table 13.7 shows that during 2011–2019, although the USD assets held by Japan continued to grow, the proportion continued to decline from 15.68% to 11.36%. Meanwhile, the Japanese yen assets held by the United States also continued to grow. In particular, the proportion of Japanese long-term securities held by the United States has increased significantly since 2015, indicating the mutual support between the Japanese yen and the USD in the same period. From 2011 to 2019, the cumulative growth rates of long-term securities held by the European zone and Japan are 27.1% and −27.4%, respectively, which shows that the Euro's support for the USD is significantly higher than that of the Japanese yen. Judging from the growth rates of long-term securities held by the US in the two places in the same period of 19.9% and 29.7%, the US's support for the

Japanese yen is significantly higher than that of the Euro. The results show that during 2011–2019, while the three major international currencies of USD, Euro, and yen support each other, the support of USD to the two major international currencies of Euro and yen is obviously different.

13.8.2 *Inequality of mutual support between major international currencies*

Table 13.7 shows that in 2012, the net dollar assets held by the UK, Canada, and Australia were all negative. From 2011 to 2013, the accumulated net dollar assets held by the three countries were \$−49.4 billion, \$−6 billion, and \$−191.6 billion, respectively. In other words, the US was the net holder of the three countries' long-term securities in the 3 years before the US withdrew from the quantitative easing policy in 2014. It shows that the United States received substantial support from China during the implementation of quantitative easing policy, the Eurozone and Japan, but at the same time, it strongly supported the currencies of the three "five-eye allies". From 2014 to 2020, although the net dollar assets held by the UK and Canada turn to be positive, the net share is meager compared with the Eurozone, China, and Japan, and the net dollar assets held by Australia in the same period still reach \$−269.7 billion, which shows the unique and sustainable support of the United States for the Australian dollar, and there is apparent inequality between the main currencies. In addition, from 2011 to 2015, the proportion of net US long-term securities assets held by Switzerland continued to decline from 8.03% to −6.04%. Although the proportion returned to a positive value in 2016, by the end of April 2020, the proportion of net US long-term securities assets held by Switzerland was 2.42%, less than one-third of that in 2011.

13.8.3 *The amount of China's long-term securities held by the United States shows great inequality*

Table 13.2 shows that, although Mainland China has maintained the largest holding country in the US long-term securities from 2011 to 2015, the US holding Mainland China's long-term securities remained at a low level of 1 percentage point over the same period. The securities amount held by US are lower than that of all the countries or areas as shown in Table 13.7, and less than half of the US holding Australian assets. At the same time, it is less than one-twelfth of the Euro assets held by the United States in the same period. Moreover, the proportion of Chinese long-term bonds held by the United States did not increase from 2011 to 2015, but decreased from 1.36% to 1.21%, and further decreased to 1.05% in 2016. Although the proportion rose slightly to 2.0% during 2016–2020, there is still a considerable gap in the proportion of long-term securities held by China in the United States, which shows that while China has dramatically supported the USD, it has received little equivalent support from the United States. These data indicate that while China is the leading supporter of the USD, the US has the lowest degree of support for China's equity and bonds, or for the RMB. The inequality is evident and needs to be considered and concerned.

13.9 Summary

We have found high correlation coefficients between currency internationalization and sci-tech internationalization of eight major international currency issuers, indicating a mutually supporting relationship between sci-tech internationalization and currency internationalization. The unusually higher correlation coefficients between sci-tech internationalization and currency internationalization of 2010 than correlation coefficients between sci-tech internationalization and currency internationalization of 2007 help us to find problems of using foreign exchange derivatives nominal turnover directly as foreign exchange turnover. We find the best currency internationalization measure by stripping off most of the nominal turnover of foreign exchange derivative, and corresponding currency internationalization results are more reasonable than currency internationalization results using foreign exchange derivatives nominal turnover directly. The best currency internationalization measure of currency internationalization helps us to understand the functionality of foreign exchange derivatives trading, the hedging functionality of foreign exchange derivatives is much more critical than their cash functionality.

Chapter 14

Mutual Impacts of Sci-tech Internationalization and Currency Internationalization

Chapter 13 finds that sci-tech internationalization of currency issuers and currency internationalization are highly correlated, indicating the two internationalization measures support each other strongly. Yet, it is difficult to see the degrees of the interaction between the two internationalization measures. Chapter 14 focuses on the mutual impacts of these internationalization measures.

14.1 Time Lag of Impacts of Sci-tech Internationalization on Currency Internationalization

The influence of sci-tech on economy and trade has unavoidable delay in time, as the influence of sci-tech on the currency is through the economy and business in the global market, it also takes time for sci-tech to influence currency. Since research and development (R&D) of science and technology take time to generate valuable patents, often taking several years for a valuable patent to complete the examination and pass the patent application, therefore, it takes sci-tech time to influence currency valuation and currency internationalization. The above intuition is correct, yet we still do not know precisely the time lag for sci-tech internationalization to affect currency internationalization. The purpose of this section is to find the appropriate length of time or time lag for sci-tech to influence currency internationalization using sci-tech internationalization and currency internationalization results.

14.1.1 *An example to show influence of sci-tech internationalization on currency internationalization*

Although we know that there is a time lag of the influence of sci-tech internationalization on currency internationalization, yet we still do not know exactly if the lag is 2, 4, or 7 years. Only empirical results can give us reliable results. Using sci-tech internationalization and currency internationalization results in Table 13.1, we can find the influence of sci-tech internationalization on currency internationalization. For example, using sci-tech internationalization of 2004, 2007, and 2010 as independent variables and 2010 currency internationalization as a dependent variable, we can find the simple regression results in Table 14.1.

Table 14.1 shows that sci-tech internationalization of 2004 and 2010 has a positive contribution in influencing currency internationalization in 2010 as their regression coefficients 2.42973709 and 5.1763959 are positive, and sci-tech internationalization of 2007 has a negative contribution to 2010 currency internationalization as the corresponding coefficient is −6.8345615. Total regression effectiveness or R-Squared is 93.72%, high enough to indicate that sci-tech internalization from 2004 to 2010 together has an influence on 2010 currency internationalization.

14.1.2 *Time lag of influence of sci-tech internationalization on currency internationalization*

The regression results in Table 14.1 are results of sci-tech internationalization of 5 sequential years to influence currency internationalization. We have sci-tech internationalization results of 20 successive years from 2000 to 2019. Corresponding to the 20 successive years of sci-tech internationalization measures, there are 70 simple regressions with sci-tech internationalization in 2 successive years to influence the currency internationalization, such as sci-tech internationalization from 2000 to 2001 to influence currency internationalization in 2001, 2004, 2007, 2010, 2013, 2016, and 2019, respectively; sci-tech internationalization from 2001 to

Table 14.1: Regression Results for Sci-tech Internationalization from 2004 to 2010 as Independent Variables to Influence Currency Internationalization in 2010

5.1763959	−6.8345615	2.42973709	2.53809439
2.04512872	4.33588726	2.55132161	2.120033017
0.9372273	4.16213031	N/A	N/A
24.8841514	5	N/A	N/A
1,293.22901	86.6166437	N/A	N/A

Source: Simple regression using data in Table 13.1.

2002 to influence currency internationalization in 2004, 2007, 2010, 2013, 2016, and 2019, respectively; sci-tech internationalization from 2002 to 2003 to influence currency internationalization in 2004, 2007, 2010, 2013, 2016, and 2019, respectively; sci-tech internationalization from 2003 to 2004 to influence currency internationalization in 2004, 2007, 2010, 2013, 2016, and 2019, respectively; sci-tech internationalization from 2004 to 2005 to influence currency internationalization in 2007, 2010, 2013, 2016, and 2019, and so on. The average regression effectiveness of these 70 regressions is 86.95%.

Similarly, there are 63 simple regressions with sci-tech internationalization in 3 successive years to influence the currency internationalization, such as sci-tech internationalization from 2000 to 2002 to influence currency internationalization in 2004, 2007, 2010, 2013, 2016, and 2019, respectively; sci-tech internationalization from 2001 to 2003 to influence currency internationalization in 2004, 2007, 2010, 2013, 2016, and 2019, respectively; sci-tech internationalization from 2002 to 2004 to influence currency internationalization in 2004, 2007, 2010, 2013, 2016, and 2019, respectively; sci-tech internationalization from 2003 to 2005 to influence currency internationalization in 2007, 2010, 2013, 2016, and 2019, respectively; sci-tech internationalization from 2005 to 2007 to influence currency internationalization in 2007, 2010, 2013, 2016, and 2019, and so on. The simple regression effectiveness of these 63 regressions is 83.40%. There are 57, 51, 45, 40, and 35 regressions with sci-tech internationalization in 4, 5, 6, 7, and 8 successive years to influence currency internationalization. Appendix Table A14.1 gives the list of 45 simple regression with six consecutive sci-tech internationalization influencing currency internationalization.

Table 14.2: Average Regression Effectiveness of Sci-tech Internationalization Influencing Currency Internationalization with Various

Number of Consecutive Years of Sci-tech Internationalization	Degree of Freedom	Number of Regressions	Average Regression Effectiveness (%)
2	6	70	86.95
3	5	63	93.40
4	4	57	97.27
5	3	51	98.53
6	2	45	98.99
7	1	40	99.39

Source: Summarizing regression results following the example results in Table 11.1 and results in Appendix A14.1.

14.1.3 *Optimal time lag of influence of sci-tech internationalization on currency internationalization*

We can summarize the average regression effectiveness (R-Squared) of sci-tech internationalization with 2–8 successive years in Table 14.1.

Table 14.2 shows that the average regression effectiveness (R-Squared) increases strictly with the number of successive years of sci-tech internationalization, showing that influence of sci-tech internationalization on currency internationalization increases with more successive years of sci-tech internationalization. The average regression effectiveness is merely 86.95% with 2 successive years of sci-tech internationalization and 93.40% with 3 successive years of sci-tech internationalization, implying 2 and 3 consecutive years are not enough for sci-tech internationalization to influence currency internationalization.

14.2 Time Lag of Influence of Currency Internationalization on Sci-tech Internationalization

Similarly, the influence of currency internationalization on sci-tech internationalization should also have some time lag simply because it takes time for investment in research and development to generate useful patents, and it takes time for patents to generate charges for the use of intellectual property. Again, we do not know the time lag specifically. Similar empirical tests can give us an estimation of the time lag.

14.2.1 *An example of currency internationalization to influence sci-tech internationalization*

Table 14.3 gives us regression results of one example of currency internationalization of 2007, 2010, 2013, and 2016 as independent variables and sci-tech internationalization of 2016 as a dependent variable.

Table 14.3 shows that currency internationalization of 2010 and 2016 has a positive influence on sci-tech internationalization of 2016 as their regression coefficients are 7.78524492 and 2.65979857, yet currency internationalization of 2007 and 2013 has a negative influence on sci-tech internationalization of 2016 as their regression coefficients are −2.336988246 and −7.3539411. The total regression effectiveness is 99.586112%, which implies that currency internationalization from 2007 to 2016 together has a high influence on sci-tech internationalization of 2016.

14.2.2 *Time lag of influence of currency internationalization on sci-tech internationalization*

Following the example given in Table 14.3, we can find regression results using currency internationalization of 2–7 uninterrupted data as independent variables and sci-tech internationalization as dependent variables. Appendix A14.2 gives the results with four consecutive currency internationalization as independent variables and sci-tech internationalization as dependent variables.

Table 14.3: Regression Results for Sci-tech Internationalization from 2007 to 2016 As Independent Variables to Influence Currency Internationalization in 2016

2.65979857	−7.3539411	7.78524492	−2.336988246	2.7320655
0.50906778	1.29811107	0.89199273	0.371815953	0.5308273
0.99586112	1.20577652	N/A	N/A	N/A
240.611327	4	N/A	N/A	N/A
1,399.29637	5.81558808	N/A	N/A	N/A

Source: Standard multiple linear regression using data in Table 13.1.

Table 14.4: Average Regression Effectiveness of Currency Internationalization to Influence Sci-tech Internationalization with Various Currency Internationalization Observations

Number of Consecutive Data of Currency Internationalization	Degree of Freedom	Number of Years Corresponding to Data	Number of Regressions	Average Regression Effectiveness (%)
2	6	4	51	89.79
3	5	7	35	92.58
4	4	10	22	96.79
5	3	13	12	98.28
6	2	16	5	99.42
7	1	19	1	99.66

Source: Summarizing regression results following the example results in Table 14.3 and results in Appendix A14.2.

Table 14.4 summarizes regression results of currency internationalization to influence sci-tech internationalization with successive currency internationalization from 2–7 consecutive observations.

Table 14.4 shows that the typical regression effectiveness (R-Squared) increases strictly with the number of uninterrupted observations of currency internationalization, showing that the influence of currency internationalization on sci-tech internationalization increases with more repeated observations of currency internationalization. The typical regression effectiveness is merely 89.79% with two repeated data of currency internationalization and 92.58% with three consecutive data of currency internationalization, implying two and three sequential observations of currency internationalization may not be enough for currency internationalization to influence sci-tech globalization.

14.3 Optimal Time Lag for Sci-tech Internationalization and Currency Internationalization to Influence Each Other

Results in Tables 14.2 and 14.4 show that regressions become more effective with more sequential years or data, thus the more consecutive years of data imply more effectiveness of sci-tech internationalization and currency internationalization influencing one another. However, careful observation of Appendices A14.1 and A14.2 tells us that influence effectiveness or corresponding regression effectiveness of sci-tech internationalization on currency internationalization increases with more sequential years of sci-tech internationalization, yet the regression degree of freedom (DF) declines with more uninterrupted years of sci-tech internationalization.

The same is true for currency internationalization to influence sci-tech internationalization: more consecutive data of currency internationalization with higher regression effectiveness, yet with a lower degree of freedom. Since we have only 7 uninterrupted 3-year currency internationalization data from 2000 to 2019, and the degree of freedom of regressions with 5–7 uninterrupted currency internationalization is only 3 to 1, it is too low for the results to be reliable. Thus, we may use currency internationalization with four uninterrupted data to compromise high regression effectiveness with a low degree of freedom when we find a specific influence of currency internationalization on sci-tech internationalization, and *vice versa*.

14.4 Optimal Continuous Number of Independent Variables Using Hypothesis Tests

The results in Tables 14.2 and 14.4 are useful for us to judge an optimal number of repeated independent variables to forecast or influence dependent variables, yet they have limitations not to balance the higher regression effectiveness with a lower degree of freedom of regressions, and we cannot be sure of the optimal repeated number of years of independent variables. We use statistical hypothesis tests to find the optimal number of consecutive years of independent variables in this section.

14.4.1 *Hypothesis testing examples*

Hypothesis tests are employed in statistics to test an assumption regarding a population parameter. We use this method to test the null hypothesis that any regression coefficient is zero. The testing results of the regression in Table 14.1 are given in Table 14.5. Table 14.5 shows that one coefficient of sci-tech 2010 passed the null hypothesis tests with probability 5.25% < 10%.

Table 14.5: Coefficients, Standard Errors, *t* Value and Probability That *t* is Greater Than the Absolute Value of *t* (alpha =10%)

Parameters	Coefficient Estimated	Standard Error	*t* Value	Pr(>|*t*|) (%)
Sci-tech 2004	2.430	2.551	0.952	38.47
Sci-tech 2007	–6.835	4.336	–1.576	17.56
Sci-tech 2010	5.176	2.045	2.531	5.25

Source: *t* tests for standard multiple regression coefficients.

Table 14.6: Coefficients, Standard Errors, *t* Value and Probability That *t* is Greater Than the Absolute Value of *t* (alpha =10%)

Parameters	Coefficient Estimated	Standard Error	Value	Pr(>|*t*|)(%)
Sci-tech 2007	–2.3370	0.3718	–6.285	0.327
Sci-tech 2010	7.7852	0.8920	8.728	0.095
Sci-tech 2013	–7.3539	1.2981	–5.665	0.4787
Sci-tech 2016	2.6598	0.5091	5.225	0.6406

Source: *t* tests for standard multiple regression coefficients.

Similarly, the testing results of the regression in Table 14.3 are given in Table 14.6. Table 14.6 shows that one coefficient of sci-tech 2010 passed the null hypothesis with a probability 5.25% < 10%. Table 14.6 shows that all four coefficients of the regression passed the null hypothesis tests with probabilities all below 10%.

14.4.2 *Summarized testing results*

Using the same methods of the two examples in Section 14.4.1, we can obtain similar testing results of 15 standard multiple regressions with three repeated sci-tech internationalization measures as independent variables and corresponding currency internationalization as a dependent variable. The results are summarized in Table 14.7. Similarly, testing results for 10 standard multiple regressions with four consecutive sci-tech internationalization measures as independent variables are also summarized in Table 14.7, and

Table 14.7: Summarizing Results of Hypothesis Tests with Consecutive Number of Years from 3 to 6

Categories	Consecutive Number of Independent Variables	Number of Models All Coefficients Passed Tests and Proportion (%)	Number of Total Coefficients Passed Tests and Proportion (%)
Sci-tech leads currency	3	0 /15 = 0.0	20/45 = 44.4
	4	5/10 = 50.0	27/40 = 67.5
	5	0/6 = 0.0	17/30 = 56.7
	6	0/3 = 0.0	6/18 = 33.3
Currency leads sci-tech	3	0/15 = 0.0	12/45 = 26.7
	4	0/10 = 0.0	12/40 = 30.0
	5	1/6 = 16.7	12/30 = 40.0
	6	0/3 = 0.0	3/18 = 16.7
Total proportion	3	0.00	71.11
	4	50.00	97.50
	5	16.67	96.67
	6	0.00	50.00

Source: Summarized coefficient tests for related standard multiple regressions with a consecutive number of years from 3 to 6.

testing results for six standard multiple regressions with five repeated sci-tech internationalization measures as independent variables and three standard multiple regressions with six repeated sci-tech internationalization measures as independent variables are also summarized in Table 14.7.

Using the same methods of Sections 14.4.1 and 14.4.2, we can obtain similar testing results of tests for standard multiple regression with currency internationalization measures as independent variables and sci-tech internationalization measures as dependent variables. The results are shown in Table 14.7.

Table 14.7 shows that not only the total proportion 50% of the number of models that all coefficients passed tests are the highest with four consecutive number of years independent variables but also the total proportion 67.5% of the number of total coefficients passed tests are also highest with four consecutive number of years independent variables. Therefore, the optimal consecutive number of independent variables is four.

14.5 Mutual Influence of Currency Internationalization and Sci-tech Internationalization on Each Other

14.5.1 *Empirical results of currency internationalization influencing sci-tech internationalization*

Using four consecutive currency internationalization measures as independent variables and sci-tech internationalization as dependent variables, we can find influence of currency internationalization on sci-tech internationalization. The results are given in Table 14.8.

Table 14.8: Regression Results of the Influence of Currency Internationalization on Sci-tech Internationalization (2001–2019)

Currency Internationalization from 2001 to 2010 as Independent Variables and Sci-tech Internationalization of 2010 as Dependent Variable				
–4.7376945	2.0335471	–4.038273	7.4906422	2.797554769
2.26867759	1.7918529	2.0140499	1.8818842	1.841027263
0.97485778	3.5650928	N/A	N/A	N/A
38.7737284	4	N/A	N/A	N/A
1,971.2388	50.839547	N/A	N/A	N/A
Currency Internationalization from 2001 to 2010 as Independent Variables and Sci-tech Internationalization of 2013 as Dependent Variable				
–5.1942935	2.5030733	–4.694817	8.0867743	3.325168472
2.42625185	1.9163086	2.1539387	2.0125932	1.968898455
0.97047482	3.8127115	N/A	N/A	N/A
32.8693937	4	N/A	N/A	N/A
1,911.2591	58.147075	N/A	N/A	N/A
Currency Internationalization from 2001 to 2010 as Independent Variables and Sci-tech Internationalization of 2016 as Dependent Variable				
–5.6720996	3.3855253	–5.35395	8.2973648	3.812902012
2.7098308	2.1402857	2.4056898	2.2478239	2.199022198
0.96042859	4.258339	N/A	N/A	N/A
24.2707729	4	N/A	N/A	N/A
1,760.45152	72.533805	N/A	N/A	N/A

Table 14.8: (*Continued*)

Currency Internationalization from 2001 to 2010 as Independent Variables and Sci-tech Internationalization of 2019 as Dependent Variable				
−3.9820139	3.275666	−4.374427	5.8708633	2.332369644
1.8696596	1.4766995	1.6598162	1.5508959	1.517224977
0.97929014	2.9380596	N/A	N/A	N/A
47.2861754	4	N/A	N/A	N/A
1,632.73383	34.528778	N/A	N/A	N/A
Currency Internationalization from 2004 to 2013 as Independent Variables and Sci-tech Internationalization of 2013 as Dependent Variable				
4.12835771	−1.80536	−1.734369	0.4704158	−0.656045658
1.23620173	2.410204	1.882693	1.5408021	2.048595875
0.96074696	4.3961683	N/A	N/A	N/A
24.4757328	4	N/A	N/A	N/A
1,892.10099	77.305182	N/A	N/A	N/A
Currency Internationalization from 2004 to 2013 as Independent Variables and Sci-tech Internationalization of 2016 as Dependent Variable				
4.19459538	−2.175214	−0.960251	−0.035126	−0.266711483
1.38548191	2.7012534	2.1100416	1.7268649	2.29597844
0.9470248	4.927037	N/A	N/A	N/A
17.8767557	4	N/A	N/A	N/A
1,735.88255	97.102773	N/A	N/A	N/A
Currency Internationalization from 2004 to 2013 as Independent Variables and Sci-tech Internationalization of 2019 as Dependent Variable				
3.03110426	−1.537927	0.1976939	−0.640267	−0.562270761
0.91157316	1.7772806	1.3882948	1.136185	1.510631284
0.9747879	3.2417274	N/A	N/A	N/A
38.6635006	4	N/A	N/A	N/A
1,625.22743	42.035186	N/A	N/A	N/A
Currency Internationalization from 2007 to 2016 as Independent Variables and Sci-tech Internationalization of 2016 as Dependent Variable				
−0.6600339	4.9003544	−2.679687	−0.542847	−0.197624199
3.6243541	4.1363316	3.5807571	3.1156954	2.225554499
0.94745497	4.9069916	N/A	N/A	N/A

(*Continued*)

Table 14.8: (*Continued*)

Currency Internationalization from 2007 to 2016 as Independent Variables and Sci-tech Internationalization of 2016 as Dependent Variable				
18.0312958	4	N/A	N/A	N/A
1,736.67105	96.314268	N/A	N/A	N/A
Currency Internationalization from 2007 to 2016 as Independent Variables and Sci-tech Internationalization of 2019 as Dependent Variable				
2.13250843	0.5265377	−0.4224	−1.19002	−0.518067792
2.24750231	2.5649853	2.2204673	1.9320774	1.380091108
0.97778606	3.0428801	N/A	N/A	N/A
44.0167706	4	N/A	N/A	N/A
1,630.22613	37.036478	N/A	N/A	N/A
Currency Internationalization from 2010 to 2019 as Independent Variables and Sci-tech Internationalization of 2019 as Dependent Variable				
−1.33802	3.5892241	−0.173267	−1.017949	−0.666528889
1.77397359	3.606314	2.9895679	1.2018172	1.384977785
0.97870753	2.9790994	N/A	N/A	N/A
45.9649673	4	N/A	N/A	N/A
1,631.76248	35.500134	N/A	N/A	N/A
Average Regression Effectiveness (R-Squared)				96.72%
1/ (1 − Average R-Squared)				30.45

Source: Standard multiple linear regression using data in Table 13.1.

Table 14.8 shows that regression effectiveness (R-Squared) of currency internationalization influencing sci-tech internationalization is above 94%, and the typical regression effectiveness of all 10 regressions is 96.72%, indicating high influence of currency internationalization on sci-tech internationalization.

14.5.2 *Empirical results of sci-tech internationalization influencing currency internationalization*

We can follow the same method to find empirical results of sci-tech internationalization influencing currency internationalization in Table 14.9. As we have many more sequential annual data of sci-tech internationalization than currency internationalization (only every 3-year annual data), we

Table 14.9: Regression Results of the Influence of Sci-tech Internationalization on Currency Internationalization (2001–2019)

Sci-tech Internationalization from 2001 to 2010 as Independent Variables and Currency Internationalization of 2010 as Dependent Variable				
9.04878103	−16.490551	5.44710819	2.985996909	0.0962728
3.42612511	8.17405261	3.24448401	2.202222537	2.6631293
0.95699372	3.85168877	N/A	N/A	N/A
22.2524191	4	N/A	N/A	N/A
1,320.50363	59.3420257	N/A	N/A	N/A
Sci-tech Internationalization from 2001 to 2010 as Independent Variables and Currency Internationalization of 2013 as Dependent Variable				
6.77880521	−11.362024	3.67889371	1.830545657	0.8197664
2.79521988	6.6688383	2.64702716	1.796693356	2.1727263
0.97191738	3.14241795	N/A	N/A	N/A
34.6092151	4	N/A	N/A	N/A
1,367.035	39.4991623	N/A	N/A	N/A
Sci-tech Internationalization from 2001 to 2010 as Independent Variables and Currency Internationalization of 2016 as Dependent Variable				
6.86596066	−11.363396	3.77303902	1.641458442	0.9215359
2.63469767	6.28586424	2.49501526	1.693513924	2.0479522
0.97502494	2.96195705	N/A	N/A	N/A
39.0399405	4	N/A	N/A	N/A
1,370.0192	35.0927583	N/A	N/A	N/A
Sci-tech Internationalization from 2001 to 2010 as Independent Variables and Currency Internationalization of 2019 as Dependent Variable				
7.97570511	−13.263286	4.63928259	1.57150964	0.8532083
2.967179	7.07909854	2.80986961	1.907224127	2.3063902
0.96920501	3.33573635	N/A	N/A	N/A
31.4728182	4	N/A	N/A	N/A
1,400.80944	44.5085479	N/A	N/A	N/A
Sci-tech Internationalization from 2004 to 2013 as Independent Variables and Currency Internationalization of 2013 as Dependent Variable				
−5.4443181	10.368516	−8.5375042	4.477521011	1.5087254
1.05657036	1.31629435	1.45875091	0.935965503	0.6686337

(*Continued*)

Table 14.9: (*Continued*)

Sci-tech Internationalization from 2004 to 2013 as Independent Variables and Currency Internationalization of 2013 as Dependent Variable				
0.9953691	1.27608007	N/A	N/A	N/A
214.94067	4	N/A	N/A	N/A
1,400.02065	6.51352137	N/A	N/A	N/A
Sci-tech Internationalization from 2004 to 2013 as Independent Variables and Currency Internationalization of 2016 as Dependent Variable				
−4.9663724	10.1773521	−8.8786335	4.530242014	1.5267987
1.1228879	1.39891393	1.55031203	0.994713059	0.7106017
0.99476423	1.35617553	N/A	N/A	N/A
189.99374	4	N/A	N/A	N/A
1,397.75511	7.35684823	N/A	N/A	N/A
Sci-tech Internationalization from 2004 to 2013 as Independent Variables and Currency Internationalization of 2019 as Dependent Variable				
−5.3077001	11.7516964	−11.198761	5.633209366	1.350614
1.37116684	1.7082243	1.89309766	1.214651585	0.8677211
0.9924101	1.65603612	N/A	N/A	N/A
130.753999	4	N/A	N/A	N/A
1,434.34816	10.9698225	N/A	N/A	N/A
Sci-tech Internationalization from 2007 to 2016 as Independent Variables and Currency Internationalization of 2016 as Dependent Variable				
2.65979857	−7.3539411	7.78524492	−2.336988246	2.7320655
0.50906778	1.29811107	0.89199273	0.371815953	0.5308273
0.99586112	1.20577652	N/A	N/A	N/A
240.611327	4	N/A	N/A	N/A
1,399.29637	5.81558808	N/A	N/A	N/A
Sci-tech Internationalization from 2007 to 2016 as Independent Variables and Currency Internationalization of 2019 as Dependent Variable				
3.36170826	−8.3827062	8.83557761	−3.069790801	2.835679
0.54041079	1.37803503	0.94691221	0.39470845	0.56351
0.99546552	1.2800155	N/A	N/A	N/A
219.532682	4	N/A	N/A	N/A
1,438.76423	6.5537587	N/A	N/A	N/A

Table 14.9: (*Continued*)

Sci-tech Internationalization from 2010 to 2019 as Independent Variables and Currency Internationalization of 2019 as Dependent Variable				
1.36913458	0.99783935	−6.6534395	5.172585729	1.2653318
0.23720159	0.76968145	1.90728872	1.397699789	0.7698018
0.99216385	1.68268617	N/A	N/A	N/A
126.61366	4	N/A	N/A	N/A
1,433.99225	11.325731	N/A	N/A	N/A
Average Regression Effectiveness (R-Squared)				98.39%
1/ (1 − Average R-Squared)				62.18

Source: Summarized coefficient tests for related standard multiple regressions with a consecutive number of years from 3 to 6.

must use the same time span as in Table 14.1 to use similar four consecutive data in Table 14.5. For example, the first regression in Table 14.8 is the standard multiple regression with four sequential currency internationalization measures of 2001, 2004, 2007 and 2010 as four independent variables and 2010 sci-tech internationalization as a dependent variable. In order to obtain comparable data on the influence of sci-tech internationalization on currency internationalization, we have to use four similar sequential sci-tech internationalization measures of 2001, 2004, 2007, and 2010 as four independent variables and currency internationalization of 2010 as dependent variable. Table 14.9 gives the corresponding results.

Table 14.9 shows that regression effectiveness (R-Squared) of the first four regressions of currency internationalization influencing sci-tech internationalization is between 95% and 98%, and regression effectiveness of the other six regressions is above 99%, and the typical regression effectiveness of all 10 regressions is 98.26%, indicating a high influence of currency internationalization on sci-tech internationalization.

14.5.3 *Mutual influence of currency internationalization and sci-tech internationalization on each other*

Average regression effectiveness of influence of currency internationalization on sci-tech internationalization in Table 14.8 at 96.72% is slightly lower than the corresponding usual regression effectiveness of influence of sci-tech internationalization on currency internationalization in Table 15.5 at 98.39%, implying sci-tech internationalization has more influence than currency internationalization on the other. The share of mutual average regression effectiveness 96.72%/(96.72% + 98.39%) = 49.57% and 98.39%/(96.72% + 98.39%) = 50.43% can be considered as the relative mutual influence of each other, again implying that sci-tech internationalization has more impacts on currency internationalization, indicating sci-tech internationalization has higher influence on currency internationalization.

As the difference of mutual influence of sci-tech internationalization and currency internationalization 50.43% and 49.57% is not significantly large enough, we may use 1/(1 − R-Squared) to convert the average regression effectiveness R-Squared into a more significantly different measure. Table 15.5 shows that the influence of currency internationalization on sci-tech internationalization 1/(1 − R-Squared) = 30.45. Table 15.6 shows that the influence of sci-tech internationalization on currency internationalization 1/(1 − R Squared) = 62.18. Thus, the mutual influence of the currency internationalization on sci-tech internationalization 30.45/(30.45 + 62.18) = 32.87%, and sci-tech internationalization on currency internationalization 62.18/(30.45 + 62.18) = 67.13%, shows that sci-tech internationalization has much more influence on currency internationalization.

The summarized results in Table 14.5 also contain useful information regarding mutual influence of sci-tech internationalization and currency internationalization. It is interesting to notice that the mutual influence measures 67.13% and 32.87% using 1/(1 − Average R-Squared) are actually very similar to the total number of share of coefficients that passed the tests of 10% confidence interval 67.5% and 30.0% in Table 14.5. Thus, the method to convert average regression effectiveness R-Squared into 1/(1 – Average R-Squared) is a good method to find a better mutual influence of sci-tech internationalization and currency internationalization.

14.6 Mutual Influence of Better Currency Internationalization and Sci-tech Internationalization on Each Other

The above results of mutual influence of sci-tech internationalization and currency internationalization use the traditional currency internationalization results given in Table 4.1 (the currency internationalization with a nominal turnover of foreign exchange derivatives turnover) and sci-tech internationalization results to analyze the empirical results of the interaction between technology internationalization and currency internationalization. These results provide specific quantitative support for our understanding of the degree of mutual influence of sci-tech internationalization and currency internationalization. However, as shown in Chapter 13, the nominal daily typical turnover of foreign exchange derivatives over the past 10 years has accounted for about 70% of the traditional foreign exchange daily turnover given in Table 4.1, thus a large portion of foreign exchange daily turnover is not the actual turnover of "money changing hands". The traditional measure of currency internationalization has caused a problem as the nominal typical daily transaction value of foreign exchange derivatives exaggerated actual foreign exchange turnover. This section uses the same method as Section 14.4 to analyze the degree of mutual influence between sci-tech internationalization and better currency internationalization in Table 13.6.

14.6.1 *Empirical results of better currency internationalization influencing sci-tech internationalization*

Using the better currency internationalization results in Table 13.6 and sci-tech internationalization in Table 13.1 and following the same method in Section 14.4, we can find regression results of influence of currency internationalization on sci-tech internationalization in Table 14.10.

Comparing the results in Tables 14.5 and 14.7, we find that the typical regression effectiveness of 97.67% (R-Squared) in Table 14.7 is higher than the corresponding normal regression effectiveness of 96.79%, implying that better currency internationalization has a higher influence on sci-tech internationalization than traditional currency internationalization results in Table 14.5.

14.6.2 *Empirical results of sci-tech internationalization influencing better currency internationalization*

We can follow the same method to find empirical results of sci-tech internationalization influencing currency internationalization in Table 14.6 to find the influence of sci-tech globalization on currency internationalization. The results are shown in Table 14.11.

Table 14.10: Regression Results of the Influence of Better Currency Internationalization on Sci-tech Internationalization (2001–2019)

Currency Internationalization from 2001 to 2010 as Independent Variables and Sci-tech Internationalization of 2010 as Dependent Variable				
–3.9258469	0.510613	–1.15129	5.397377	1.879148362
1.39472611	1.116113	1.985376	1.226344	1.548753139
0.98224899	2.995577	N/A	N/A	N/A
55.33483	4	N/A	N/A	N/A
1,986.18442	35.89393	N/A	N/A	N/A
Currency Internationalization from 2001 to 2010 as Independent Variables and Sci-tech Internationalization of 2013 as Dependent Variable				
–4.1486213	0.879139	–1.76196	5.836957	2.160602792
1.4640267	1.17157	2.084025	1.287278	1.62570697
0.97991805	3.14442	N/A	N/A	N/A
48.7959666	4	N/A	N/A	N/A
1,929.85666	39.54951	N/A	N/A	N/A
Currency Internationalization from 2001 to 2010 as Independent Variables and Sci-tech Internationalization of 2016 as Dependent Variable				
–4.2081067	1.72844	–2.71656	5.995445	2.230567216
1.64560013	1.316872	2.342492	1.446931	1.82733252
0.97273957	3.534402	N/A	N/A	N/A
35.6832013	4	N/A	N/A	N/A
1,783.01735	49.96798	N/A	N/A	N/A
Currency Internationalization from 2001 to 2010 as Independent Variables and Sci-tech Internationalization of 2019 as Dependent Variable				
–3.1094802	2.066164	–1.91151	3.862771	1.022576166
1.44222526	1.154123	2.052991	1.268109	1.601497874
0.97698	3.097595	N/A	N/A	N/A
42.4404871	4	N/A	N/A	N/A
1,628.88223	38.38038	N/A	N/A	N/A
Currency Internationalization from 2004 to 2013 as Independent Variables and Sci-tech Internationalization of 2013 as Dependent Variable				
3.22640099	–2.8375	0.044081	0.629752	-0.697043979
0.8483112	1.715579	1.317474	2.020311	1.989587936
0.97328944	3.626428	N/A	N/A	N/A

Table 14.10: (*Continued*)

Currency Internationalization from 2004 to 2013 as Independent Variables and Sci-tech Internationalization of 2013 as Dependent Variable				
36.4383823	4	N/A	N/A	N/A
1,916.80224	52.60393	N/A	N/A	N/A
Currency Internationalization from 2004 to 2013 as Independent Variables and Sci-tech Internationalization of 2016 as Dependent Variable				
3.34352574	−2.85073	0.874567	−0.30184	−0.727997496
0.90711416	1.834499	1.408798	2.160354	2.127501549
0.96718498	3.877804	N/A	N/A	N/A
29.4738465	4	N/A	N/A	N/A
1,772.83587	60.14946	N/A	N/A	N/A
Currency Internationalization from 2004 to 2013 as Independent Variables and Sci-tech Internationalization of 2019 as Dependent Variable				
2.25418897	−2.19885	1.529102	−0.49781	−0.962603591
0.68749567	1.390354	1.067718	1.637318	1.612419009
0.97927742	2.938961	N/A	N/A	N/A
47.2565479	4	N/A	N/A	N/A
1,632.71264	34.54998	N/A	N/A	N/A
Currency Internationalization from 2007 to 2016 as Independent Variables and Sci-tech Internationalization of 2016 as Dependent Variable				
−1.7610005	4.87925	−4.50739	2.435394	−0.513970641
1.51571804	1.523725	1.749757	1.807484	1.519755232
0.97534493	3.361264	N/A	N/A	N/A
39.559602	4	N/A	N/A	N/A
1,787.79293	45.19239	N/A	N/A	N/A
Currency Internationalization from 2007 to 2016 as Independent Variables and Sci-tech Internationalization of 2019 as Dependent Variable				
0.42419107	1.741374	−2.12011	1.017159	−0.695694557
1.32362704	1.330619	1.528006	1.578416	1.327152589
0.97932927	2.935282	N/A	N/A	N/A
47.3775964	4	N/A	N/A	N/A
1,632.79908	34.46353	N/A	N/A	N/A

(*Continued*)

Table 14.10: (*Continued*)

Currency Internationalization from 2010 to 2019 as Independent Variables and Sci-tech Internationalization of 2019 as Dependent Variable				
−0.0699871	1.204468	1.105559	−1.17759	−0.693902819
2.22220074	3.818999	2.428738	0.93316	1.462592036
0.97718893	3.083506	N/A	N/A	N/A
42.8383638	4	N/A	N/A	N/A
1,629.23057	38.03204	N/A	N/A	N/A
Average regression effectiveness (R-Squared)				97.64%
1/(1 − Average R-Squared)				42.28

Source: Regressions using sci-tech internationalization data in Table 13.1 and better currency internationalization data in Table 13.6.

Table 14.11: Regression Results of the Influence of Sci-tech Internationalization on Better Currency Internationalization (2001–2019)

Sci-tech Internationalization from 2001 to 2010 as Independent Variables and Currency Internationalization of 2010 as Dependent Variable				
9.80510985	−18.645	6.05485538	3.812203078	−0.30186
3.80361952	9.07467914	3.60196499	2.444865953	2.956556
0.94525999	4.27607228	N/A	N/A	N/A
17.2681746	4	N/A	N/A	N/A
1,262.98007	73.1391766	N/A	N/A	N/A
Sci-tech Internationalization from 2001 to 2010 as Independent Variables and Currency Internationalization of 2013 as Dependent Variable				
6.42073896	−11.146575	3.50954894	2.152566183	0.708011
2.9166817	6.95862202	2.7620495	1.874765797	2.267139
0.96837653	3.2789667	N/A	N/A	N/A
30.6220784	4	N/A	N/A	N/A
1,316.94813	43.0064906	N/A	N/A	N/A
Sci-tech Internationalization from 2001 to 2010 as Independent Variables and Currency Internationalization of 2016 as Dependent Variable				
6.43936472	−10.621299	3.55168996	1.52696919	1.147506
2.74006606	6.53725227	2.5947974	1.76124194	2.129855
0.97185304	3.0804134	N/A	N/A	N/A

Table 14.11: (*Continued*)

Sci-tech Internationalization from 2001 to 2010 as Independent Variables and Currency Internationalization of 2016 as Dependent Variable				
34.5278104	4	N/A	N/A	N/A
1,310.53021	37.9557868	N/A	N/A	N/A
Sci-tech Internationalization from 2001 to 2010 as Independent Variables and Currency Internationalization of 2019 as Dependent Variable				
7.49485232	−12.282396	4.40137375	1.280745893	1.171378
3.00362134	7.16604269	2.8443799	1.930648294	2.334717
0.96719684	3.37670523	N/A	N/A	N/A
29.484872	4	N/A	N/A	N/A
1,344.76234	45.6085529	N/A	N/A	N/A
Sci-tech Internationalization from 2004 to 2013 as Independent Variables and Currency Internationalization of 2013 as Dependent Variable				
−5.7279631	9.90353989	−7.4419679	4.120752277	1.61821
1.26399213	1.57470412	1.7451272	1.119710601	0.799897
0.99314538	1.52659513	N/A	N/A	N/A
144.887029	4	N/A	N/A	N/A
1,350.63265	9.32197078	N/A	N/A	N/A
Sci-tech Internationalization from 2004 to 2013 as Independent Variables and Currency Internationalization of 2016 as Dependent Variable				
−5.019342	9.9572537	−8.5368796	4.450352417	1.651283
1.1954705	1.48933864	1.65052299	1.059010539	0.756534
0.99381627	1.44383766	N/A	N/A	N/A
160.714782	4	N/A	N/A	N/A
1,340.14733	8.33866874	N/A	N/A	N/A
Sci-tech Internationalization from 2004 to 2013 as Independent Variables and Currency Internationalization of 2019 as Dependent Variable				
−5.0916245	11.4112331	−11.035294	5.584008639	1.463077
1.48175116	1.84599224	2.04577559	1.312612984	0.937703
0.9907862	1.78959509	N/A	N/A	N/A
107.532828	4	N/A	N/A	N/A
1,377.56029	12.8106023	N/A	N/A	N/A

(*Continued*)

Table 14.11: (*Continued*)

Sci-tech Internationalization from 2007 to 2016 as Independent Variables and Currency Internationalization of 2016 as Dependent Variable				
2.64296559	−7.4235512	7.63964639	−2.113557719	2.827744
0.51554708	1.31463315	0.90334581	0.376548346	0.537584
0.99557684	1.22112338	N/A	N/A	N/A
225.082713	4	N/A	N/A	N/A
1,342.52143	5.96456926	N/A	N/A	N/A
Sci-tech Internationalization from 2007 to 2016 as Independent Variables and Currency Internationalization of 2019 as Dependent Variable				
3.40326263	−8.2783052	8.59679082	−2.984310873	2.917362
0.50801445	1.29542509	0.89014706	0.371046612	0.529729
0.99583453	1.2032816	N/A	N/A	N/A
239.069025	4	N/A	N/A	N/A
1,384.57935	5.79154639	N/A	N/A	N/A
Sci-tech Internationalization from 2010 to 2019 as Independent Variables and Currency Internationalization of 2019 as Dependent Variable				
1.32591118	1.11190888	−6.6128669	5.049461492	1.395392
0.23358762	0.75795471	1.87822958	1.376404664	0.758073
0.99210049	1.65704904	N/A	N/A	N/A
125.590161	4	N/A	N/A	N/A
1,379.38765	10.9832461	N/A	N/A	N/A
Average regression effectiveness (R-Squared)				98.14%
1/ (1 − Average R-Squared)				53.75

Source: Summarized coefficient tests for related standard multiple regressions with a consecutive number of years from 3 to 6.

Comparing the results in Tables 14.9 and 14.10, we find that the average regression effectiveness of 97.64% (R-Squared) in Table 14.10 is lower than the corresponding typical regression effectiveness of 98.14%, implying sci-tech globalization has a higher influence on better currency internationalization than on traditional currency internationalization. Results are shown in Table 14.6.

14.6.3 *Mutual influence of the better currency internationalization and sci-tech internationalization on each other*

Average regression effectiveness of influence of the better currency internationalization on sci-tech internationalization at 97.67% in Table 14.7 is slightly lower than the corresponding typical regression effectiveness of influence of sci-tech internationalization on currency internationalization at 98.01% in Table 14.8, implying sci-tech internationalization has more impacts than currency internationalization as in Section 14.4. However, the difference of the typical regression effectiveness of sci-tech internationalization on the better currency internationalization 98.14% – 97.64% = 0.50% is much lower than the corresponding difference 98.39% – 96.72% = 1.68% in Section 14.4, indicating that sci-tech internationalization has less impact on better currency internationalization than on traditional currency internationalization.

The converted measures of above two average R-Squared are 1/(1 – 98.14%) = 53.75 and 1/(1 – 97.64%) = 42.28, the corresponding share is 53.75/(53.75 + 42.28) = 55.97% and 42.28/(53.75 + 42.28) = 44.03%, also implying relatively lower influence of sci-tech internationalization on better currency internationalization 55.97% than the corresponding 67.13% on traditional currency internationalization in Section 14.5.

14.7 Mutual Influence of Sci-tech and Currency Internationalization

Chapter 8 shows that not only exports of charges for the use of intellectual property have high correlation coefficients with GDP, but imports of charges for the use of IP also have similarly high correlation coefficients with GDP for most major economies.

14.7.1 *Unique relationship between the US sci-tech internationalization and the USD internationalization*

Table 13.1 shows that the US sci-tech internationalization is not only ranked No. 1 in the world steadily but also continues to surpass the sum of sci-tech internationalization of the next three major global currency issuers: Euro, yen, and pound from 2005 to 2019. What's more vital is that the typical annual difference of the US sci-tech internationalization and the total sci-tech internationalization of Eurozone, Japan, and UK remained as high as 11.46% from 2009 to 2019. That indicates the relative monopoly of USA's science and technology in the world, and the degree of internationalization of US science and technology provides great support for the USD. Therefore, after introducing and analyzing the relationship between sci-tech internationalization and currency internationalization, we specifically discuss the close relationship between the US sci-tech internationalization and the USD internationalization in this section.

Comparing the degree of sci-tech internationalization in the United States and the USD internationalization in Table 13.1, we find that when the USD was vulnerable (2007–2014), the US technology internationalization tended to be high, and when the USD was strong (2015–2019), the internationalization of the USD became weak. When the USD is vulnerable or USD internationalization is low, the USD capital flows to the rest of the world with increased US charges for the use of intellectual property surpluses, thus witnessed by significant US sci-tech internationalization; and when the USD is significant or USD internationalization high, the return of USD capital to the United States causes the US charges for the use of intellectual property surplus to decrease. Therefore, there is a negative correlation between the USD internationalization and US sci-tech internationalization.

US sci-tech internationalization has been in a relatively worldwide monopoly for many years, the relatively small increase or decrease does not reflect changes in the US scientific and technological strength, while US scientific and technological strength or intellectual property rights serve the overall monetary policy of the United States and the general strategy of world investment. When the USD was vulnerable (before the 2003–2008 worldwide financial crisis and the period when the USD withdrew from the quantitative easing policy in 2009), it was precisely the flow of USD funds to worldwide investment which often requires related technology or intellectual property services. Therefore, the export of intellectual property royalties and surpluses increase with the outflow of USD funds; when the USD is robust, funds return to the United States. The decline in demand for charges for use of intellectual property has led to a decline in the surplus of US intellectual property rights. We will analyze in more detail the different contributions of US sci-tech and the USD in the US intellectual property royalty's surplus in different years in the last chapter of this book, which will provide us with a deeper understanding of the coordination function of US sci-tech and the USD.

14.8 The Special Role of Overseas US-Funded Enterprises in the Internationalization of US Technology and the Internationalization of the Dollar

When we compare and analyze major world currencies, we mainly consider the economy and trade issues of currency issuers as in Table 1.1. All factors in Table 1.1 are essentially cross-border data, and overseas activities of most currency issuers are not included. These cross-border factors can largely reflect supporting backgrounds of most currencies, yet they cannot reflect supporting backgrounds enough for the USA, the world's largest economy and the most technologically advanced country. It is difficult to understand the relationship between the maintenance of the USD's worldwide status and the United States' scientific and technological innovation capabilities without considering the worldwide trade activities of US-owned foreign affiliates outside the United States. In other words, we cannot ignore the colossal roles of US-owned foreign affiliates in the world to explain the relationship between the internationalization of the USD and the internationalization of US technology.

Table 8.1 shows that both commodity export and services export of US-owned foreign affiliates are more highly related to the US sci-tech originality capability and the US sci-tech internationalization than the corresponding US cross-border commodity export and services exports, showing that US sci-tech supports exports of US-owned foreign affiliates more than cross-border US exports.

14.8.1 *US-owned foreign affiliates have huge overseas services trade surplus*

Data in Tables 8.1 and 8.2 show that the compound annual growth rates (CAGRs) of the sales and net purchases of US-owned foreign affiliates are significantly higher than the corresponding growth rates of US cross-border services trade exports and imports. Higher growth rates of sales of US-owned foreign affiliates lead to the "surplus" of US-owned foreign affiliates services trade outside the US which grows faster than US cross-border. The surplus of US-owned foreign affiliates exceeded the corresponding surplus of US cross-border services trade surplus (the difference between services sales and purchases). The US cross-border services trade surplus was $3.3 billion or 5.3% for the first time in 2001; the former surpassed the latter by 2.547 times in 2009, showing that US-owned foreign affiliates made substantial profits in the worldwide scope shortly after world financial crisis in 2008. However, when the world financial crisis broke out in 2008, US-owned foreign affiliates had to slow down their foreign businesses significantly and returned to their related income from services trade outside the US to the US to "escort the US dollar". The "surplus" growth rate of US-owned foreign affiliates in services trade outside the US has slowed significantly since 2009, and the ratio of their net sales to domestic US net services export fell to 138.2% in 2019, the lowest level since 2002.

The results in Table 8.2 show that total services trade of US-owned foreign affiliates grew from $2.09 trillion to $2.2.72 trillion, steadily higher than the total Japanese commodity trade and services trade from $1.93 trillion to $1.81 trillion in the same period, indicating the importance of US-owned foreign affiliates in supporting the USD.

14.8.2 *Investments of US-owned foreign affiliates*

When the USD is relatively weak (2002–2008), US-owned foreign affiliates bring USD capital to the world for investments and speculation, which accompany US science and technology and other services. These investments lead to significant increases in the US net exports of charges for use of intellectual property. When the United States experienced a crisis (2009–2014), the US-owned foreign affiliates returned high profits they obtained abroad back to the US to protect the USD and kept the USD relatively stable (the US quantitative easing policy was implemented in 2009 and the USD index remained at 80.1 per year for more than 5 years). The US-owned foreign affiliates have successfully played the role of a dollar stabilizer and made a substantial contribution to maintaining the relative worldwide monopoly of the USD.

14.8.3 *R&D investments of US-owned foreign affiliates*

Part of the large overseas services trade surplus and other profits of US-owned foreign affiliates is used for overseas R&D investment to further support their technological progress in cooperation with overseas partners. According to data published on the US Bureau of Economic Analysis (BEA) website under the US Department of Commerce, the total worldwide R&D investment by US-owned foreign affiliates outside the United States increased from $45.38 billion to $68.11 billion from 2007 to 2017. The total R&D investment of US-owned foreign affiliates at $68.11 billion was higher than the total R&D investment of South Korea, the fifth largest R&D investment country during the same year.

Total overseas R&D investments of US-owned foreign affiliates at $68.11 billion were close to total R&D investments at $69.07 billion of 134 major UK companies (in the list of the world's top 2,500 companies with highest R&D investments, the 2016/2017 European Commission's Industrial R&D Investment Report) at $34.93 billion, and total R&D investments of 52 major Swiss companies (in the list of the world's top 2,500 companies with highest R&D investment) at $34.14 billion. The $68.11 billion R&D investment surpassed total R&D investments at $62.47 billion of 71 major French companies (in the list of the world's top 2,500 companies with highest R&D investments) at $30.53 billion, and total R&D investments of 50 Korean companies (in the list of the world's top 2,500 companies with highest R&D investment) at $31.93 billion. The above data show that the total R&D investments of US-owned foreign affiliates were comparable to total R&D investments of major companies of major countries.

14.9 Global M&A Activities and Indications of Companies with Most R&D Investment in the World

The 2019 European Commission's Industrial R&D Investment Report also provides information on the distribution of worldwide mergers and procurements data among different countries and regions of the 2,500 companies that have invested the most in R&D in the world in recent years. Table 14.12 gives the relevant results.

14.9.1 *Comparison of the proportions of internal mergers and acquisitions in major countries and regions*

Table 14.12 shows that the US had the largest number of 4,087 mergers and procurements from the world to the US, and 4,697 mergers and

Table 14.12: Cases of Mergers and Acquisition and Share of the World's Top R&D Investment Companies (2007–2016)

From to (%)	China	Japan	India	EU	USA	Other Asian Countries or Regions	Other Countries or Regions	Total
China	615	1	0	59	24	16	53	768
Japan	43	711	54	156	117	71	122	1,274
India	0	1	39	15	13	2	11	81
EU	59	16	56	1,769	642	43	691	3,276
USA	75	19	52	865	2,990	47	649	4,697
Other Asian Countries or Regions	4	5	2	18	14	184	152	379
Other Countries or Regions	26	10	21	378	287	22	632	1376
Total	823	763	222	3,259	4,087	385	2,310	11,852
From to (%)	**China**	**Japan**	**India**	**EU**	**USA**	**Other Asian Countries or Regions**	**Other Countries or Regions**	
China	80.1	0.1	0.0	7.7	3.1	2.1	6.9	100.0
Japan	3.4	55.8	4.2	12.2	9.2	5.6	9.6	100.0
India	0.0	1.2	48.1	18.5	16.0	2.5	13.6	100.0
EU	1.8	0.5	1.7	54.0	19.6	1.3	21.1	100.0
USA	1.6	0.4	1.1	18.4	63.6	1.0	13.8	100.0
Other Asian Countries or Regions	1.1	1.3	0.5	4.7	3.7	48.5	40.1	100.0
Other Countries or Regions	1.9	0.7	1.5	27.5	20.9	1.6	46.0	100.0

Source: The 2019 EU Industrial R&D Investment Scoreboard, www.ijr.ire.europa.Eu. The results in the table are based on the Zephyr company, Merger and Acquisitions database of 11,852 procurements and merger case data collated with the 2,500 companies with the largest R&D investment by the European Commission.

acquisitions from the US to the world from 2007 to 2016; besides the US domestic mergers and procurements with 2,990 cases or a share of 63.6%, EU and Japan were the largest and second largest targets for US mergers and purchases with 642 cases and 117 cases or share of 19.6% and 9.2%, indicating USA, EU and Japan are three regions with most mergers and purchases led by the USA.

China had 615 mergers and purchases within China, accounting for 80.1% of the total number of 768 mergers and purchases in China, which was the highest ratio in Table 14.12, showing that China's R&D investment is mainly domestic and international cooperation in science and technology needs to be strengthened.

14.9.2 *Comparison of the proportion of mergers and acquisitions outside the jurisdiction of major countries and regions*

Table 14.12 also shows that the proportion of companies outside the jurisdiction of mergers and purchases with the largest R&D investment in China is the lowest, only 19.9%, of which mergers and purchases from China to the EU accounted for only 7.7%, followed by 6.9% from China to other countries and regions, and mergers and mergers from China to the United States accounted for 3.1%, ranking No. 3; mergers and procurements from the United States to outside the United States accounted for 36.4% of the total US mergers and procurements, of which 865 were mergers and acquisitions from the United States to the EU, surpassing all the 768 mergers and procurements in China during the same period, and accounted for 18.4%, followed by 649 mergers and acquisitions from the United States to other countries and regions around the world, accounting for 13.8%. The total number of mergers and procurements from the United States to the EU and the United States to other countries and regions in the world was 1,514, second only to the EU, with a total of 3,275 mergers and purchases, showing the important position of the United States in the world's most researched and developed corporate mergers and purchases, or the ability of the United States to transfer technology to the world through purchases and mergers; mergers and procurements outside the EU account for 46.0%. Among them, the proportion with the United States and other countries and regions around the world is as high as 19.6% and 21.1%, respectively. The EU has a total of 1,333 mergers and procurements with these two countries and regions, showing that the activity of mergers and procurements outside the EU is second only to the United States. The number of mergers and procurements outside the jurisdiction of Japan, China, and other countries and regions around the world is smaller than that of the United States and EU.

14.9.3 *Technical of comparison of internal and external judicial M&A in major countries and regions*

Table 14.12 shows that, although the proportion of mergers and procurements from the United States to the EU accounted for 18.4% of the total mergers and procurements in the United States, which was lower than the proportion of the latter to the former at 19.6%, the total number of mergers and purchases in the United States was higher than that of the European Union, and from the United States to the EU the number of mergers and purchases of 865 was 223 more than the total of 642 from the latter to the former, showing the result of the inflow and acceptance of American technology into the EU; the total number of mergers and purchases from the United States and the European Union to other countries and regions around the world was 649 and 691, respectively, the latter slightly more than the former by 42; the total number of mergers and purchases from the United States and the European Union to China, Japan, India, and other Asian countries and regions was 193 and 174, respectively, and the former was slightly higher than the latter with 19. These data show that the United States is still the world's largest exporter of technology, followed by the European Union.

14.9.4 *International comparison and inspiration of internal mergers and acquisitions outside China*

Table 14.12 shows that the maximum number of mergers and acquisitions from China to the EU was 59, which is the same as the number of mergers and acquisitions from the EU to China. It shows that China and the EU have a relatively high degree of cooperation in technology and the cooperation is relatively equal. The number of mergers and acquisitions from China to other countries and regions in the world and other Asian countries and regions was 53 and 16, respectively, which was slightly higher than the number of mergers and acquisitions from these two regions to China, 26 and 4, respectively, signaling the higher level of export of Chinese technology to these two regions. The number of mergers and acquisitions from China to the United States and Japan was 24 and 1, which is significantly lower than the 75 and 43 mergers and acquisitions from the United States and Japan to China, showing the extent to which the United States and Japan are exporting technology to China.

14.9.5 *Taking advantage of mergers and acquisitions to promote research and development*

Mergers and acquisitions are a vital channel for companies to use their technology and other advantages to increase innovation. Cross-border acquisitions are an important method for companies to optimize the allocation of technology and other resources on a worldwide scale to accelerate innovation and development. In today's world of rapid worldwide technological innovation, various fields have accumulated technology patents to varying degrees. Renewal innovation is not only too late but also difficult to approach the worldwide technological frontier. In this way, accelerating the catching up, and maintaining existing advantages through cross-border mergers and acquisitions, has become the only way for global technological innovation in the future. The data in Table 14.12 show that the number of mergers and acquisitions within and outside the jurisdiction of China's enterprises with a large investment in scientific research ranks behind the United States, the European Union, and Japan, and the number of mergers and acquisitions outside the jurisdiction of China ranks behind other countries and regions in Asia and other countries and regions around the world. China's worldwide scientific and technological cooperation needs to be significantly improved. Making full use of the current and future national policy of further opening to the outside world, increasing international scientific research cooperation to improve China's R&D capabilities, and actively exporting advanced technologies such as 5G to accelerate technology applications will become another direction of China's technological innovation.

14.10 Summary

This chapter uses the results of sci-tech internationalization in Chapter 8 and results of currency internationalization in Chapter 4 to find empirical results of mutual influence between the internationalization of the world's top eight world currencies and the technology internationalization of currency issuers. The results show that currency internationalization and sci-tech internationalization have high correlation coefficients, showing high degrees of mutual influence between the two, the impact of sci-tech internationalization on currency internationalization is higher than the latter's impact on the former. These results provide a good basis for sci-tech to influence economy and trade, and economy and trade in turn to influence currency. At the same time, higher currency internationalization corresponds to higher global financing capabilities, and higher worldwide financing capabilities are the foundation of technology R&D investments. Therefore, currency internationalization has a positive impact on sci-tech internationalization.

The United States has been the leader in world science and technology innovation. The degree of internationalization of American science and technology not only ranks among the top in the world but also the degree of internationalization of US science and technology has exceeded the sum of the three global currency issuers Euro, Japan yen, and the British pound, indicating the monopolistic status and effective support for the USD's monopolistic status in the worldwide foreign exchange market. In contrast, the global status of the Japanese yen is significantly lower than Japan's second position in the global ranking of sci-tech internationalization and the level of technology internationalization in the Eurozone, the United Kingdom, Australia, and Canada all are in varying degrees lower than the worldwide status of global currencies such as Euro, pound sterling, Australian dollar, and Canadian dollar. In particular, sci-tech internationalization of Australia and the internationalization level of the Australian dollar are seriously mismatched.

With statistical hypothesis analysis, we find optional sequential number of years first, and then find the mutual influence of sci-tech globalization and currency internationalization on each other. The typical impact of science and technology internationalization on currency internationalization is about two-third, and the normal influence of the latter on the former is around one-third corresponding to the traditional currency internationalization for sci-tech internationalization and currency internationalization measures from 2001 to 2019. With better currency internationalization measurement, the normal impact of sci-tech internationalization on currency internationalization is reduced to 55.97%, while the influence of better currency internationalization on sci-tech internationalization is raised to 44.03. These results provide a direct empirical basis for us to understand sci-technology internationalization and currency internationalization.

Although China has made significant progress in sci-tech innovation with significant R&D investments in recent years, there is still a considerable gap in sci-tech technology internationalization compared to United States, Japan, and Europe. The sci-tech internationalization measure of China was only 4.9%, 13.4%, and 25.7% of the internationalization measures of USA, Eurozone, and Japan, respectively, in 2019, indicating much for China to catch up with the top three world currency issuers.

Appendix

Table A14.1: Regressions with 6 Consecutive Years of Sci-tech Internationalization as Independent Variables and Currency Internationalization as Dependent Variables (2000–2019)

Sci-tech Inter from 2000 to 2005 to Influence Currency Inter in 2007						
−0.72487	−18.969	21.56017	23.69282	−24.6046	0	0.505115
4.024263	10.30327	4.92754	34.86799	22.74913	0	1.411794
0.980675	3.006942	N/A	N/A	N/A	N/A	N/A
30.44836	3	N/A	N/A	N/A	N/A	N/A
1,376.525	27.12511	N/A	N/A	N/A	N/A	N/A
Sci-tech Inter from 2000 to 2005 to Influence Currency Inter in 2010						
−1.34955	−17.8172	22.1429	20.962	−22.9788	0	0.45174
3.092654	7.918079	3.786824	26.79612	17.48275	0	1.084967
0.98839	2.310841	N/A	N/A	N/A	N/A	N/A
51.07975	3	N/A	N/A	N/A	N/A	N/A
1,363.826	16.01996	N/A	N/A	N/A	N/A	N/A
Sci-tech Inter from 2000 to 2005 to Influence Currency Inter in 2013						
1.195464	−14.4123	16.60465	12.05312	−14.4977	0	0.631168
3.215472	8.23253	3.937211	27.86028	18.17705	0	1.128054
0.987688	2.402611	N/A	N/A	N/A	N/A	N/A
48.13188	3	N/A	N/A	N/A	N/A	N/A
1,389.217	17.31763	N/A	N/A	N/A	N/A	N/A

(*Continued*)

Table A14.1: (*Continued*)

Sci-tech Inter from 2000 to 2005 to Influence Currency Inter in 2016						
2.103933	–15.9648	15.39256	15.38938	–15.9949	0	0.819967
2.99455	7.666907	3.666701	25.94611	16.92818	0	1.05055
0.989311	2.237538	N/A	N/A	N/A	N/A	N/A
55.53066	3	N/A	N/A	N/A	N/A	N/A
1,390.092	15.01973	N/A	N/A	N/A	N/A	N/A
Sci-tech Inter from 2000 to 2005 to Influence Currency Inter in 2019						
2.389674	–18.797	17.50002	19.82984	–19.9947	0	0.802403
3.29727	8.441957	4.037369	28.56901	18.63945	0	1.15675
0.987401	2.463731	N/A	N/A	N/A	N/A	N/A
47.02191	3	N/A	N/A	N/A	N/A	N/A
1,427.108	18.20991	N/A	N/A	N/A	N/A	N/A
Sci-tech Inter from 2001 to 2006 to Influence Currency Inter in 2007						
1.498243	–2.36193	–17.0414	17.93673	26.34042	–25.4784	1.181608
5.200774	7.457662	14.05931	13.89865	42.84241	27.4692	2.895692
0.981445	3.608628	N/A	N/A	N/A	N/A	N/A
17.63151	2	N/A	N/A	N/A	N/A	N/A
1,377.606	26.04439	N/A	N/A	N/A	N/A	N/A
Sci-tech Inter from 2001 to 2006 to Influence Currency Inter in 2010						
1.709335	–3.21726	–15.618	18.00894	23.98264	–23.9758	1.223547
3.89569	5.586234	10.53126	10.41092	32.09152	20.57607	2.169046
0.98941	2.703077	N/A	N/A	N/A	N/A	N/A
31.14142	2	N/A	N/A	N/A	N/A	N/A
1,365.232	14.61325	N/A	N/A	N/A	N/A	N/A
Sci-tech Inter from 2001 to 2006 to Influence Currency Inter in 2013						
1.413446	–0.34894	–12.5938	13.18629	14.55088	–15.3221	1.269373
4.121417	5.909915	11.14147	11.01415	33.95099	21.7683	2.294726
0.988372	2.859701	N/A	N/A	N/A	N/A	N/A
28.33206	2	N/A	N/A	N/A	N/A	N/A
1,390.178	16.35578	N/A	N/A	N/A	N/A	N/A
Sci-tech Inter from 2001 to 2006 to Influence Currency Inter in 2016						
0.146717	1.943622	–15.776	15.03773	15.64865	–16.0804	0.886213
3.948136	5.661438	10.67304	10.55107	32.52355	20.85307	2.198247

Table A14.1: (*Continued*)

Sci-tech Inter from 2001 to 2006 to Influence Currency Inter in 2016						
0.989318	2.739467	N/A	N/A	N/A	N/A	N/A
30.8719	2	N/A	N/A	N/A	N/A	N/A
1,390.103	15.00936	N/A	N/A	N/A	N/A	N/A
Sci-tech Inter from 2001 to 2006 to Influence Currency Inter in 2019						
−0.08471	2.482237	−18.906	17.7049	19.68014	−19.9453	0.764152
4.348342	6.235315	11.75492	11.62059	35.82033	22.96686	2.421074
0.987403	3.017156	N/A	N/A	N/A	N/A	N/A
26.1283	2	N/A	N/A	N/A	N/A	N/A
1,427.112	18.20646	N/A	N/A	N/A	N/A	N/A
Sci-tech Inter from 2002 to 2007 to Influence Currency Inter in 2007						
−6.65012	7.095606	4.278751	−8.27074	9.898677	−5.35901	0.075897
3.863214	5.298976	4.7033	6.611208	11.48721	6.708499	2.302371
0.989307	2.739475	N/A	N/A	N/A	N/A	N/A
30.83927	2	N/A	N/A	N/A	N/A	N/A
1,388.641	15.00944	N/A	N/A	N/A	N/A	N/A
Sci-tech Inter from 2002 to 2007 to Influence Currency Inter in 2010						
−5.31273	6.105318	2.687313	−7.14803	11.55705	−6.92053	0.351251
3.206605	4.398338	3.903907	5.487538	9.534793	5.568293	1.91105
0.992506	2.273861	N/A	N/A	N/A	N/A	N/A
44.14529	2	N/A	N/A	N/A	N/A	N/A
1,369.505	10.34089	N/A	N/A	N/A	N/A	N/A
Sci-tech Inter from 2002 to 2007 to Influence Currency Inter in 2013						
−3.58342	4.396282	3.493072	−7.22405	8.841626	−4.98457	0.678421
3.724428	5.10861	4.534335	6.373701	11.07453	6.467497	2.219658
0.990082	2.641059	N/A	N/A	N/A	N/A	N/A
33.27468	2	N/A	N/A	N/A	N/A	N/A
1,392.584	13.95039	N/A	N/A	N/A	N/A	N/A
Sci-tech Inter from 2002 to 2007 to Influence Currency Inter in 2016						
−4.19708	3.679371	6.134795	−10.2405	9.964681	−4.35819	0.188367
3.248677	4.456046	3.955128	5.559537	9.659893	5.641351	1.936124
0.992446	2.303695	N/A	N/A	N/A	N/A	N/A

(*Continued*)

Table A14.1: (*Continued*)

Sci-tech Inter from 2002 to 2007 to Influence Currency Inter in 2016						
43.79419	2	N/A	N/A	N/A	N/A	N/A
1,394.498	10.61402	N/A	N/A	N/A	N/A	N/A
Sci-tech Inter from 2002 to 2007 to Influence Currency Inter in 2019						
−5.13905	4.235439	7.656407	−12.0247	11.49113	−5.21113	−0.08953
3.424184	4.69678	4.168799	5.859885	10.18176	5.946119	2.040721
0.991841	2.42815	N/A	N/A	N/A	N/A	N/A
40.52316	2	N/A	N/A	N/A	N/A	N/A
1,433.526	11.79183	N/A	N/A	N/A	N/A	N/A
Sci-tech Inter from 2003 to 2008 to Influence Currency Inter in 2010						
−8.09716	4.57129	10.04988	0.741872	−10.463	4.084962	1.245616
8.895354	13.98743	2.877563	4.678474	8.296672	5.961477	2.035865
0.990609	2.545462	N/A	N/A	N/A	N/A	N/A
35.15993	2	N/A	N/A	N/A	N/A	N/A
1,366.887	12.95876	N/A	N/A	N/A	N/A	N/A
Sci-tech Inter from 2003 to 2008 to Influence Currency Inter in 2013						
−6.53621	4.621822	7.19045	1.956723	−10.0761	3.723194	1.335109
9.440349	14.8444	3.053864	4.965113	8.804988	6.326722	2.160597
0.989623	2.701416	N/A	N/A	N/A	N/A	N/A
31.78966	2	N/A	N/A	N/A	N/A	N/A
1,391.939	14.5953	N/A	N/A	N/A	N/A	N/A
Sci-tech Inter from 2003 to 2008 to Influence Currency Inter in 2016						
−7.58587	5.863134	5.997698	4.432466	−13.9684	6.189334	0.795784
7.441614	11.70151	2.407292	3.913886	6.940774	4.987212	1.70315
0.993546	2.129466	N/A	N/A	N/A	N/A	N/A
51.3105	2	N/A	N/A	N/A	N/A	N/A
1,396.043	9.069247	N/A	N/A	N/A	N/A	N/A
Sci-tech Inter from 2003 to 2008 to Influence Currency Inter in 2019						
−8.92805	6.670318	7.01698	5.648251	−16.3882	6.92363	0.63423
7.732913	12.15956	2.501524	4.067094	7.212467	5.182434	1.769819
0.993224	2.212823	N/A	N/A	N/A	N/A	N/A
48.86144	2	N/A	N/A	N/A	N/A	N/A
1,435.525	9.793167	N/A	N/A	N/A	N/A	N/A

Table A14.1: (*Continued*)

Sci-tech Inter from 2004 to 2009 to Influence Currency Inter in 2010						
19.15535	−15.8663	−6.34548	−1.88306	−18.8822	24.5805	2.679869
20.19106	13.60321	13.32289	13.9942	19.36516	31.26026	1.669956
0.992003	2.348942	N/A	N/A	N/A	N/A	N/A
41.34734	2	N/A	N/A	N/A	N/A	N/A
1,368.811	11.03505	N/A	N/A	N/A	N/A	N/A
Sci-tech Inter from 2004 to 2009 to Influence Currency Inter in 2013						
15.09233	−12.2371	−4.52779	−2.06429	−13.7024	18.20846	2.564754
22.77472	15.34388	15.0277	15.78491	21.84313	35.26034	1.883644
0.990018	2.649514	N/A	N/A	N/A	N/A	N/A
33.06053	2	N/A	N/A	N/A	N/A	N/A
1,392.494	14.03985	N/A	N/A	N/A	N/A	N/A
Sci-tech Inter from 2004 to 2009 to Influence Currency Inter in 2016						
7.225423	−6.64491	−3.30568	2.851537	−4.78885	5.459597	2.254255
23.81119	16.04218	15.7116	16.50328	22.83721	36.86504	1.969368
0.989078	2.770093	N/A	N/A	N/A	N/A	N/A
30.18572	2	N/A	N/A	N/A	N/A	N/A
1,389.765	15.34683	N/A	N/A	N/A	N/A	N/A
Sci-tech Inter from 2004 to 2009 to Influence Currency Inter in 2019						
8.084846	−7.87674	−3.58702	3.496051	−4.66915	5.348094	2.265805
25.53415	17.20298	16.84848	17.69745	24.4897	39.53257	2.111871
0.987789	2.970535	N/A	N/A	N/A	N/A	N/A
26.96542	2	N/A	N/A	N/A	N/A	N/A
1,427.67	17.64815	N/A	N/A	N/A	N/A	N/A
Sci-tech Inter from 2005 to 2010 to Influence Currency Inter in 2010						
−6.08819	10.62842	−14.3644	7.093892	10.28628	−6.82549	2.994372
3.732462	4.601847	7.200909	9.525836	1.921573	3.725788	1.263223
0.995507	1.760594	N/A	N/A	N/A	N/A	N/A
73.85933	2	N/A	N/A	N/A	N/A	N/A
1,373.646	6.19938	N/A	N/A	N/A	N/A	N/A
Sci-tech Inter from 2005 to 2010 to Influence Currency Inter in 2013						
−5.1724	9.571487	−11.9368	6.256616	7.09383	−5.07231	2.883727

(*Continued*)

Table A14.1: (*Continued*)

Sci-tech Inter from 2005 to 2010 to Influence Currency Inter in 2013						
4.730784	5.832703	9.126936	12.07371	2.435536	4.722324	1.601097
0.992919	2.2315	N/A	N/A	N/A	N/A	N/A
46.74329	2	N/A	N/A	N/A	N/A	N/A
1,396.575	9.959183	N/A	N/A	N/A	N/A	N/A
Sci-tech Inter from 2005 to 2010 to Influence Currency Inter in 2016						
−5.57598	10.40434	−11.4897	4.964537	6.469186	−4.03089	2.87242
4.395441	5.419251	8.479971	11.21786	2.262893	4.387581	1.487603
0.993881	2.073319	N/A	N/A	N/A	N/A	N/A
54.14543	2	N/A	N/A	N/A	N/A	N/A
1,396.515	8.597307	N/A	N/A	N/A	N/A	N/A
Sci-tech Inter from 2005 to 2010 to Influence Currency Inter in 2019						
−6.14543	12.01955	−13.4604	5.369349	7.1878	−4.23728	2.960052
4.597693	5.668613	8.87017	11.73404	2.367018	4.589472	1.556054
0.993492	2.168721	N/A	N/A	N/A	N/A	N/A
50.88254	2	N/A	N/A	N/A	N/A	N/A
1,435.911	9.406705	N/A	N/A	N/A	N/A	N/A
Sci-tech Inter from 2006 to 2011 to Influence Currency Inter in 2013						
−2.83561	0.662131	3.355548	0.02909	−5.00639	4.628264	1.855223
2.344985	4.963362	5.066425	3.491296	2.89816	2.86002	1.113898
0.99355	2.129761	N/A	N/A	N/A	N/A	N/A
51.34845	2	N/A	N/A	N/A	N/A	N/A
1,397.462	9.07176	N/A	N/A	N/A	N/A	N/A
Sci-tech Inter from 2006 to 2011 to Influence Currency Inter in 2016						
−2.72891	−0.34901	5.021772	−1.53602	−3.75937	4.164201	2.081567
1.920184	4.064236	4.148629	2.858839	2.373151	2.34192	0.912113
0.995671	1.743949	N/A	N/A	N/A	N/A	N/A
76.66693	2	N/A	N/A	N/A	N/A	N/A
1,399.029	6.082715	N/A	N/A	N/A	N/A	N/A
Sci-tech Inter from 2006 to 2011 to Influence Currency Inter in 2019						
−2.90525	−0.60537	6.327271	−2.96278	−3.78381	4.73818	2.130743
1.977867	4.186327	4.273255	2.944719	2.444441	2.412272	0.939513
0.995535	1.796337	N/A	N/A	N/A	N/A	N/A

Table A14.1: (*Continued*)

Sci-tech Inter from 2006 to 2011 to Influence Currency Inter in 2019						
74.31778	2	N/A	N/A	N/A	N/A	N/A
1,438.864	6.453657	N/A	N/A	N/A	N/A	N/A
Sci-tech Inter from 2007 to 2012 to Influence Currency Inter in 2013						
−22.0181	11.38224	8.546748	21.198	−48.4795	30.23077	1.553546
20.8373	15.76334	5.570463	21.22983	48.19195	30.09996	1.581451
0.990441	2.592731	N/A	N/A	N/A	N/A	N/A
34.53925	2	N/A	N/A	N/A	N/A	N/A
1,393.09	13.44451	N/A	N/A	N/A	N/A	N/A
Sci-tech Inter from 2007 to 2012 to Influence Currency Inter in 2016						
−17.1776	8.092801	6.386722	18.48269	−39.1116	24.15285	1.934723
18.95925	14.34261	5.068402	19.3164	43.84845	27.38707	1.438916
0.992079	2.359051	N/A	N/A	N/A	N/A	N/A
41.74758	2	N/A	N/A	N/A	N/A	N/A
1,393.982	11.13024	N/A	N/A	N/A	N/A	N/A
Sci-tech Inter from 2007 to 2012 to Influence Currency Inter in 2019						
−19.9435	9.70616	7.112994	22.03574	−46.6357	28.54929	1.944814
20.28804	15.34783	5.423627	20.67022	46.92163	29.30653	1.539764
0.991182	2.524388	N/A	N/A	N/A	N/A	N/A
37.46739	2	N/A	N/A	N/A	N/A	N/A
1,432.573	12.74507	N/A	N/A	N/A	N/A	N/A
Sci-tech Inter from 2008 to 2013 to Influence Currency Inter in 2013						
−14.5919	5.460491	4.985179	11.8551	−2.82659	−4.17581	3.261275
11.41953	5.378955	7.570548	6.433502	4.571124	3.645641	1.269345
0.992083	2.359546	N/A	N/A	N/A	N/A	N/A
41.77249	2	N/A	N/A	N/A	N/A	N/A
1,395.399	11.13491	N/A	N/A	N/A	N/A	N/A
Sci-tech Inter from 2008 to 2013 to Influence Currency Inter in 2016						
−13.1906	5.470966	3.95235	9.645531	−1.04068	−4.14133	3.375712
9.697691	4.567914	6.429058	5.463456	3.881888	3.09595	1.077953
0.994285	2.003773	N/A	N/A	N/A	N/A	N/A
57.99273	2	N/A	N/A	N/A	N/A	N/A
1,397.082	8.030212	N/A	N/A	N/A	N/A	N/A

(*Continued*)

Table A14.1: (*Continued*)

Sci-tech Inter from 2008 to 2013 to Influence Currency Inter in 2019						
−13.6244	5.936046	3.566231	10.17474	−0.61912	−4.75293	3.549768
11.28161	5.31399	7.479114	6.3558	4.515916	3.601611	1.254015
0.992481	2.331048	N/A	N/A	N/A	N/A	N/A
43.99788	2	N/A	N/A	N/A	N/A	N/A
1,434.45	10.86757	N/A	N/A	N/A	N/A	N/A
Sci-tech Inter from 2009 to 2014 to Influence Currency Inter in 2016						
0.114042	−2.06788	0.562099	−4.18978	5.402801	0.936435	2.691981
3.032911	8.050128	4.10428	3.39013	6.193005	5.201809	1.425746
0.98918	2.757159	N/A	N/A	N/A	N/A	N/A
30.47273	2	N/A	N/A	N/A	N/A	N/A
1,389.908	15.20385	N/A	N/A	N/A	N/A	N/A
Sci-tech Inter from 2009 to 2014 to Influence Currency Inter in 2019						
0.166133	−0.91332	0.324221	−5.75285	5.296278	1.630052	2.772041
3.505217	9.303749	4.743427	3.918064	7.157421	6.01187	1.647773
0.985949	3.186522	N/A	N/A	N/A	N/A	N/A
23.39014	2	N/A	N/A	N/A	N/A	N/A
1,425.01	20.30784	N/A	N/A	N/A	N/A	N/A
Sci-tech Inter from 2010 to 2015 to Influence Currency Inter in 2016						
−4.12464	0.125925	−4.03526	5.150629	−3.81962	7.454733	2.758123
7.302116	2.697152	6.780999	8.69404	2.39582	3.553535	1.328748
0.990517	2.581137	N/A	N/A	N/A	N/A	N/A
34.81766	2	N/A	N/A	N/A	N/A	N/A
1,391.787	13.32454	N/A	N/A	N/A	N/A	N/A
Sci-tech Inter from 2010 to 2015 to Influence Currency Inter in 2019						
−5.38056	0.260116	−3.80913	6.37914	−5.09533	8.390274	2.838726
8.353326	3.085433	7.757188	9.945631	2.740722	4.0651	1.520034
0.987935	2.952716	N/A	N/A	N/A	N/A	N/A
27.29589	2	N/A	N/A	N/A	N/A	N/A
1,427.881	17.43707	N/A	N/A	N/A	N/A	N/A

Table A14.1: (*Continued*)

Sci-tech Inter from 2011 to 2016 to Influence Currency Inter in 2016						
−5.14731	6.487114	0.939205	−5.91144	5.914995	−1.65225	4.107515
9.484727	11.03067	7.091984	11.82522	20.05792	3.6187	2.588669
0.973546	4.311084	N/A	N/A	N/A	N/A	N/A
12.26714	2	N/A	N/A	N/A	N/A	N/A
1,367.941	37.17088	N/A	N/A	N/A	N/A	N/A
Sci-tech Inter from 2011 to 2016 to Influence Currency Inter in 2019						
−5.4308	6.404318	1.42271	−5.79081	6.664722	−2.65746	4.303527
10.83243	12.59805	8.099701	13.50549	22.908	4.132889	2.9565
0.966454	4.923656	N/A	N/A	N/A	N/A	N/A
9.603243	2	N/A	N/A	N/A	N/A	N/A
1,396.833	48.48478	N/A	N/A	N/A	N/A	N/A
Sci-tech Inter from 2012 to 2017 to Influence Currency Inter in 2019						
3.116846	−4.63928	4.288533	0.824342	−4.44997	1.6228	2.630345
1.300773	6.058752	6.804482	4.492151	5.242034	12.55345	1.827853
0.989542	2.749121	N/A	N/A	N/A	N/A	N/A
31.53978	2	N/A	N/A	N/A	N/A	N/A
1,430.203	15.11533	N/A	N/A	N/A	N/A	N/A
Sci-tech Inter from 2013 to 2018 to Influence Currency Inter in 2019						
2.420724	−1.09527	−8.53937	18.09201	−4.62521	−5.42994	1.967317
1.041238	1.943739	2.771231	6.838868	3.167786	1.938508	0.756157
0.997152	1.43468	N/A	N/A	N/A	N/A	N/A
116.698	2	N/A	N/A	N/A	N/A	N/A
1,441.201	4.116612	N/A	N/A	N/A	N/A	N/A
Sci-tech Inter from 2014 to 2019 to Influence Currency Inter in 2019						
18.98544	−20.4944	−1.57308	7.201755	−3.12105	−0.19777	2.212279
4.46371	5.207582	1.39879	4.165181	5.561876	2.480878	0.54384
0.998604	1.004368	N/A	N/A	N/A	N/A	N/A
238.4622	2	N/A	N/A	N/A	N/A	N/A
1,443.3	2.017511	N/A	N/A	N/A	N/A	N/A

Table A14.2: Regressions with four Consecutive Data of Currency Internationalization as Independent Variables and Sci-tech Internationalization as Dependent Variables (2001–2019)

Currency Inter from 2001 to 2010 to Influence Sci-tech Inter in 2010				
–4.73769	2.033547	–4.03827	7.490642	2.797555
2.268678	1.791853	2.01405	1.881884	1.841027
0.974858	3.565093	N/A	N/A	N/A
38.77373	4	N/A	N/A	N/A
1,971.239	50.83955	N/A	N/A	N/A
Currency Inter from 2001 to 2010 to Influence Sci-tech Inter in 2011				
–5.06695	1.837023	–4.18746	8.110927	3.405124
2.528213	1.99684	2.244456	2.09717	2.05164
0.96897	3.972937	N/A	N/A	N/A
31.22709	4	N/A	N/A	N/A
1,971.582	63.13691	N/A	N/A	N/A
Currency Inter from 2001 to 2010 to Influence Sci-tech Inter in 2012				
–5.3448	2.873398	–4.92026	8.096427	3.280406
2.549085	2.013325	2.262986	2.114484	2.068578
0.967267	4.005737	N/A	N/A	N/A
29.55023	4	N/A	N/A	N/A
1,896.643	64.18371	N/A	N/A	N/A
Currency Inter from 2001 to 2010 to Influence Sci-tech Inter in 2013				
–5.19429	2.503073	–4.69482	8.086774	3.325168
2.426252	1.916309	2.153939	2.012593	1.968898
0.970475	3.812711	N/A	N/A	N/A
32.86939	4	N/A	N/A	N/A
1,911.259	58.14707	N/A	N/A	N/A
Currency Inter from 2001 to 2010 to Influence Sci-tech Inter in 2014				
–5.19085	2.44213	–4.15267	7.657241	2.71279
2.341564	1.84942	2.078756	1.942344	1.900174
0.974016	3.679629	N/A	N/A	N/A
37.48485	4	N/A	N/A	N/A
2,030.131	54.15869	N/A	N/A	N/A

Table A14.2: (*Continued*)

Currency Inter from 2001 to 2010 to Influence Sci-tech Inter in 2015				
−5.34186	2.840557	−4.74035	7.952552	3.212206
2.481176	1.959689	2.202698	2.058153	2.013469
0.968958	3.899022	N/A	N/A	N/A
31.21443	4	N/A	N/A	N/A
1,898.133	60.80948	N/A	N/A	N/A
Currency Inter from 2001 to 2010 to Influence Sci-tech Inter in 2016				
−5.6721	3.385525	−5.35395	8.297365	3.812902
2.709831	2.140286	2.40569	2.247824	2.199022
0.960429	4.258339	N/A	N/A	N/A
24.27077	4	N/A	N/A	N/A
1,760.452	72.53381	N/A	N/A	N/A
Currency Inter from 2001 to 2010 to Influence Sci-tech Inter in 2017				
−4.93832	3.439257	−5.0994	7.32775	3.007975
2.140368	1.690511	1.900141	1.77545	1.736904
0.974657	3.363461	N/A	N/A	N/A
38.4587	4	N/A	N/A	N/A
1,740.313	45.25149	N/A	N/A	N/A
Currency Inter from 2001 to 2010 to Influence Sci-tech Inter in 2018				
−4.37473	3.40208	−4.73803	6.455031	2.840535
1.992419	1.573657	1.768797	1.652725	1.616844
0.97615	3.130968	N/A	N/A	N/A
40.92932	4	N/A	N/A	N/A
1,604.914	39.21185	N/A	N/A	N/A
Currency Inter from 2001 to 2010 to Influence Sci-tech Inter in 2019				
−3.98201	3.275666	−4.37443	5.870863	2.33237
1.86966	1.476699	1.659816	1.550896	1.517225
0.97929	2.93806	N/A	N/A	N/A
47.28618	4	N/A	N/A	N/A
1,632.734	34.52878	N/A	N/A	N/A

(*Continued*)

Table A14.2: (*Continued*)

Currency Inter from 2004 to 2013 to Influence Sci-tech Inter in 2013				
4.128358	−1.80536	−1.73437	0.470416	-0.65605
1.236202	2.410204	1.882693	1.540802	2.048596
0.960747	4.396168	N/A	N/A	N/A
24.47573	4	N/A	N/A	N/A
1,892.101	77.30518	N/A	N/A	N/A
Currency Inter from 2004 to 2013 to Influence Sci-tech Inter in 2014				
4.030866	−2.04006	−1.57618	0.681904	−1.07253
1.080944	2.107499	1.64624	1.347288	1.791307
0.971642	3.844041	N/A	N/A	N/A
34.26323	4	N/A	N/A	N/A
2,025.183	59.10659	N/A	N/A	N/A
Currency Inter from 2004 to 2013 to Influence Sci-tech Inter in 2015				
4.070249	−2.01415	−1.32706	0.334342	−0.70426
1.243863	2.425141	1.89436	1.550351	2.061291
0.960047	4.423412	N/A	N/A	N/A
24.0292	4	N/A	N/A	N/A
1,880.676	78.2663	N/A	N/A	N/A
Currency Inter from 2004 to 2013 to Influence Sci-tech Inter in 2016				
4.194595	−2.17521	−0.96025	−0.03513	−0.26671
1.385482	2.701253	2.110042	1.726865	2.295978
0.947025	4.927037	N/A	N/A	N/A
17.87676	4	N/A	N/A	N/A
1,735.883	97.10277	N/A	N/A	N/A
Currency Inter from 2004 to 2013 to Influence Sci-tech Inter in 2017				
3.645518	−1.82196	−0.3958	−0.3749	−0.58737
1.17541	2.29168	1.79011	1.465032	1.947854
0.960859	4.179983	N/A	N/A	N/A
24.54857	4	N/A	N/A	N/A
1,715.676	69.88903	N/A	N/A	N/A
Currency Inter from 2004 to 2013 to Influence Sci-tech Inter in 2018				
3.311002	−1.67709	0.018901	−0.62227	−0.33935
0.995286	1.940494	1.515786	1.240524	1.649357

Table A14.2: (*Continued*)

Currency Inter from 2004 to 2013 to Influence Sci-tech Inter in 2018				
0.969522	3.539425	N/A	N/A	N/A
31.81026	4	N/A	N/A	N/A
1,594.016	50.11012	N/A	N/A	N/A
Currency Inter from 2004 to 2013 to Influence Sci-tech Inter in 2019				
3.031104	−1.53793	0.197694	−0.64027	−0.56227
0.911573	1.777281	1.388295	1.136185	1.510631
0.974788	3.241727	N/A	N/A	N/A
38.6635	4	N/A	N/A	N/A
1,625.227	42.03519	N/A	N/A	N/A
Currency Inter from 2007 to 2016 to Influence Sci-tech Inter in 2016				
−0.66003	4.900354	−2.67969	−0.54285	−0.19762
3.624354	4.136332	3.580757	3.115695	2.225554
0.947455	4.906992	N/A	N/A	N/A
18.0313	4	N/A	N/A	N/A
1,736.671	96.31427	N/A	N/A	N/A
Currency Inter from 2007 to 2016 to Influence Sci-tech Inter in 2017				
-0.09498	3.63701	−2.14694	−0.35493	−0.44622
3.112184	3.551813	3.074748	2.675406	1.911054
0.960227	4.213568	N/A	N/A	N/A
24.14291	4	N/A	N/A	N/A
1,714.548	71.01662	N/A	N/A	N/A
Currency Inter from 2007 to 2016 to Influence Sci-tech Inter in 2018				
1.737349	1.240585	−0.83696	−1.11689	−0.26764
2.551402	2.911814	2.520711	2.193326	1.566702
0.97097	3.454328	N/A	N/A	N/A
33.44672	4	N/A	N/A	N/A
1,596.396	47.72953	N/A	N/A	N/A
Currency Inter from 2007 to 2016 to Influence Sci-tech Inter in 2019				
2.132508	0.526538	−0.4224	−1.19002	−0.51807
2.247502	2.564985	2.220467	1.932077	1.380091
0.977786	3.04288	N/A	N/A	N/A

(*Continued*)

Table A14.2: (*Continued*)

Currency Inter from 2007 to 2016 to Influence Sci-tech Inter in 2019				
44.01677	4	N/A	N/A	N/A
1,630.226	37.03648	N/A	N/A	N/A
Currency Inter from 2010 to 2019 to Influence Sci-tech Inter in 2019				
−1.33802	3.589224	−0.17327	−1.01795	−0.66653
1.773974	3.606314	2.989568	1.201817	1.384978
0.978708	2.979099	N/A	N/A	N/A
45.96497	4	N/A	N/A	N/A
1,631.762	35.50013	N/A	N/A	N/A

Chapter 15

Currency Originating Capability and Relationships among Currency Originality Capability, Currency Internationalization, and Sci-tech Originality Capability

Science and technology are the basis for economic development; thus, science and technology originality capability (OC) determines economic progress. Furthermore, economy and trade development are the basis for currency usage; thus, economy and trade OC determines the monetary OC. Based on data of trade settlements of major world currencies, we define currency OC first in this chapter in line with sci-tech OC discussed and analyzed in Chapter 7, we explore the relationship between currency OC and sci-tech OC in this chapter, and then find empirical evidence among currency OC, sci-tech OC, and currency internationalization. Empirical evidence on mutual relationships among sci-tech OC, currency OC, sci-tech internationalization, and currency internationalization will help us better understand the relationship between sci-tech internationalization and currency internationalization.

15.1 Major Factors Affecting Currency Originality Capacity

15.1.1 *Interest rate determination*

As interest rate is the most critical factor affecting and determining the prices of all assets, it is not only the most critical factor of the whole financial market and the whole economy but also the most important source of market risk, as well as the most significant factor affecting currency originating capacity. All monetary authorities have the power as to what extent to raise and lower interest rates in their economic domains, yet different monetary authorities have different degrees of freedom to raise or lower their interests depending on their concerns for cross-border capital flows, foreign exchange rates, and so on. Taking USD as an example, the rise and fall of USD interest rates are determined mainly by the economic conditions of the United States with little regard for changes in current accounts, foreign currency reserves, or capital flows. Changes of US interest rate under the Federal Reserve Board before the international financial crisis in 2008 and after withdrawal from the quantitative easing policies in 2014 fully reflect the independence of the USD from 2007 to 2020. Other monetary authorities, including those of the Eurozone, Japan, the United Kingdom, Switzerland, and other countries, often need to consider capital flow and other issues to adjust their interest rates according to the interest rate of USD. Under similar circumstances, the interest rate policy of the People's Bank of China (PBC) also takes factors such as the stability of RMB exchange rate and cross-border capital flows into consideration. Thus, the lower the degree of monetary autonomy or OC, the more restrictive factors of interest rate policies, and the lower the degree of freedom.

15.1.2 *Currency issuance*

The right of currency issuance is the connotation within the scope of national sovereign rights, but the currency issuance with a low degree of monetary autonomy must be subject to changes in the current account and other factors, and the constraints of international factors often exceed the domestic economic factors. Studies show that trade surplus as a share of money supply change (M1 change) averaged around 20.4% from 2002 to 2004 in China, and it jumped to 75.5% from 2005 to 2007. The share jumped to 152.3% in 2008 because of world financial crisis, and the average share returned to 77.4% from 2009 to 2012, slightly higher than the pre-crisis average share of 75.5% from 2005 to 2007 (Zhang, 2021). Although the share fell steadily to below 50% from 2013 to 2020, it is still significantly higher than most other major economies in the world. These data indicate that CNY issuance has been largely determined by commodity exports that are significantly affected by foreign-funded enterprises in China over the years. As the currency issuance is affected by external factors, the excess deposit margin ratio in China is a passive way to redraw the excess currency back to the monetary authority, which is a clear sign of low monetary autonomy.

15.1.3 *Gold reserves*

The share of gold reserves in foreign exchange reserves of various monetary authorities also reflects their degrees of financial freedom to a certain degree. Although the monetary function of gold has weakened significantly since the 1970s, the steady amounts of gold reserves of the United States and the Eurozone indicate that the monetary functionality of gold has not been eliminated. A lower share of gold reserves in foreign exchange reserves of an economy means a higher percentage of foreign currency reserves in foreign exchange reserves or higher dependence on foreign currencies of a monetary authority.

15.1.4 *Currency pricing power*

In addition to interest rates and economic growth rates, the most critical factor in determining the currency price or foreign exchange rate is the change in the current account balance, which is mainly affected by trade in goods and services. Therefore, when an economy's exports are largely determined by foreign enterprises, its currency pricing power is actually in the hands of foreign enterprises or investors. Currencies without enough independent pricing power are in fact only dependent currencies or derivative currencies of major world currencies, and derivative currencies are not qualified to become major international currencies.

15.1.5 *Overseas listing*

Overseas listing is another reflection of the enterprises' reliance on the overseas capital markets or technology, as well as the currencies of the object listing country. Overseas listing brings dividends of the listed company to overseas investors. As a result, overseas listing increases the financial wealth of the investors in object overseas country, thus increasing the consumption and investments, and ultimately supporting the currency of the object listing country or region. Therefore, the more companies listed abroad, the higher the reliance of the listed company on the target listed country or region. Since the United States is the country with the most significant number of listed foreign companies, the USD is the most independent currency in world capital market.

15.2 Concept of Currency Originality Capacity

The ability or degree of monetary autonomy involves various aspects such as currency issuance, circulation, pricing, and reserves. The higher the monetary autonomy, the lower the degree of influence of other currencies on essential decisions such as currency issuance, circulation, and pricing except for the domestic economic and trade factors. Conversely, the lower the monetary autonomy or currency OC, the higher the degree of influence of other currencies on currency issuance due to factors such as current account balance and foreign exchange reserves changes. In other words, the higher the degree of currency OC, the more flexible the monetary policy. Otherwise, the lower the currency OC, the higher the degree of reliance on other currencies. Therefore, a currency with low OC is a derivative currency of other currencies with high OC, it does not have a necessary qualification to become a major international currency.

Zhang (2021) also shows that the ratio of China's commodity trade surplus to China's currency issuance (M1) increased from 22.8% in 2002 to 151.2% in 2008. Affected by the 2008 world financial crisis, China's commodity trade surplus accounted for 24.3% of China's currency issuance in 2009, yet it continued to increase to an average of 77.5% from 2009 to 2012. The ratio dropped slightly to 56.2% in 2013 and surged to a historical high of 218.2% in 2014, accounting for 74.5% of the total from 2009 to 2014, the average ratio declined slightly to 72.3% from 2015 to 2020, and it rose to 128.7% in the first half of 2021. The high proportions of commodity trade surpluses over money issuances imply high dependence of money supply on foreign capital through foreign trade.

The exchange rate of CNY against the USD is mainly affected by the current account balance, which is dominated by the commodity trade, while the balance of trade in commodity and trade in services is also heavily affected by foreign enterprises, so that the initiative of RMB exchange rate is also heavily influenced by foreign enterprises. In this way, due to the low currency OC, the CNY issuing right and pricing power, which originally belong to the scope of national sovereign, cannot be controlled independently to some extent.

15.3 Definition and Measurement of Currency OC

Corresponding to sci-tech OC measure defined and measured in Chapter 7 and analyzed in Chapter 14, currency autonomy or currency OC refers to the ratio of the total settlements of trade and capital accounts with its own currency over the total settlements of trade and capital accounts with its own currency and all foreign currencies. The higher the ratio, the lower the dependence of the currency issuer on other currencies, and the higher the originality capacity of the currency. Conversely, the higher the reliance of the currency issuer on foreign currencies, the lower the currency OC.

15.3.1 *Rationality of negligence of capital market daily turnover*

Data from the world federation of exchanges show that the average daily turnover of world stock market was \$27.8 billion, \$22.4 billion, \$28.9 billion, and \$34.2 billion in April 2010, April 2013, April 2016, and April 2019, respectively, representing merely 1.40%, 0.84%, 1.14%, and 1.04% of the corresponding average daily turnover of global foreign exchange market given in Table 4.1, respectively. What's more, most of world stock turnover is domestic rather than international. There, the average daily turnover of world stock market can be neglected comparing to the average daily turnover of global foreign exchange market. The similar scale of world bond market average daily turnover with world stock market turnover and the majority domestic trading nature of world bond market make similar negligence of world bond market turnover of not much influence on currency OC.

15.3.2 *Calculation of currency OC of CNY and USD*

Table 4.1 shows that the average daily turnover of CNY in the global foreign exchange market accounted for 4.32% of the world's total average daily turnover, or \$285.03 billion in 2019. The average daily commodity and services trade was \$20.491 billion in China during the same time. Table 3.13 shows that the proportion of CNY trade settlement was 19.1% in 2019. Therefore, China's trade settlement depended on 20.491 × (1 − 0.191) = \$16.577 billion on foreign currencies. The average daily turnover of world foreign exchange cannot be directly compared with daily world trade value because the former was 28.49 times, 30.05 times, and 33.58 times of the latter in 2013, 2016, and 2019, respectively, and a different currency has different similar ratios. For simplicity, we use the world ratio 33.58 to convert daily average trade of \$16.577 billion in China in 2019, or \$556.726 as China's dependence on foreign currencies for her trade settlement in 2019. Therefore, CNY OC was 0.285/(0.285 + 556.726) = 33.86% in 2019. Using the same method, we can obtain CNY OC as 1.00%, 2.31%, 8.04%, 12.15%, 22.21%, 34.09%, and 33.86% in 2001, 2007, 2010, and 2016, respectively.

Similarly, we can obtain USD OC from 2001 to 2019 using the above definition and the proportion of USD exports and imports in USD settlement in corresponding years given in Sato (1998). Ratios of US exports settled in USD in 1980, 1988, 1992–1996 were 97%, 96%, and 98%, with accumulated change merely at 1% from 1980 to 1996; and US imports settled in USD in 1980, 1988, 1992–1996 were 85%, 85%, and 88.8%, with accumulated change merely at 3.8% from 1980 to 1996. Thus, USD settlement of US exports and imports reached stable levels up to 1996. Therefore, we assume that the ratio of USD exports and imports settled in USD remained at an average annual growth rate of 1%/16 = 0.06% and 3.8%/16 = 0.24% from 1980 to 1996. Then we can estimate US exports and imports settled in USD from 2001 to 2019 with ratios 98.0% and 88.8% in 1996 and the assumed average increase accordingly. Therefore, we can obtain USD OC in 2001, 2004, 2007, 2010, 2013, 2016, and 2019 following the same procedure above to find CNY originality capacity, the results are shown in Table 15.1.

15.3.3 *Calculation assumptions to obtain originality capabilities of other major world currencies*

Using exports and imports data of goods and services of Japan, the average annual changes of Japanese exports and imports settled in Japanese yen from 1988 to 1996 were 0.32% and 1.64% (calculated using Table 3 of Sato (1998)). Assume the average annual change remained the same from

Table 15.1: Distribution of Currency Originating Capacity of Major International Currencies (2001–2019) (Unit: %)

Currency/Year	2001	2004	2007	2010	2013	2016	2019
USD	99.21	99.28	99.39	99.46	99.47	99.48	99.56
Euro	79.14	76.89	77.66	80.29	76.43	75.20	74.42
JPY	88.62	87.55	87.40	88.49	90.38	90.36	88.64
GBP	88.58	90.22	90.20	90.40	88.46	89.00	89.17
AUD	89.04	88.19	88.20	87.65	87.24	85.56	84.37
CAD	66.09	66.08	68.89	74.44	68.94	72.19	71.64
CHF	91.47	91.17	92.30	90.10	85.28	84.38	85.74
CNY	0.32	2.31	8.04	12.15	22.21	34.09	33.86
Euro 2	87.94	84.95	91.28	91.91	89.59	89.47	88.88
Others	44.72	28.90	52.53	47.74	42.51	44.51	54.97

Source: Summarized results using various assumptions in Section 15.3.3.

1996 to 2019, we can obtain Japanese exports and imports settled in Japanese yen, and then find yen originating capacity in Table 15.1. Similarly, we can obtain results for British pound using British exports and imports of both goods and services from World Development Indicators of the World Bank, and the average annual changes of British exports and imports settled in British pound from 1980 to 1996 were −0.88% and 0.86% (calculated using Table 3 of Sato (1998)). Assume the average annual change remained the same from 1996 to 2019, we can obtain British exports and imports settled in pound, and then find pound originating capacity in Table 15.1.

As Sato (1998) did not have exports and imports settlement data for Euro, we use the arithmetic average exports and imports settlements ratios of Germany, France, and Italy to stand for corresponding settlement ratios for Euro. The average annual changes of Euro exports and imports settled in Euro from 1980 to 1996 were −0.33% and 0.90% (calculated using Table 3 of Sato (1998)). Following the same above procedures to calculate yen and pound originality capacity, we can obtain Euro originality capacity in Table 15.1. The Euro results in Table 15.1 are not directly comparable with others because exports and imports of Eurozone released by WTO include intra-Euro trading, thus Euro exports and import values are significantly larger than those of other currency issuers. We use intra-EU exports and imports ratios to exclude the intra-Euro exports and imports and estimate comparable exports and imports data for

Eurozone and find corresponding Euro originality capacity results in Table 15.1 as Euro 2.

As related comparable settlement ratios of exports and imports of Switzerland, Australia, and Canada with Swiss franc, Australian dollar, and Canadian dollar were absent in Sato (1998), we must use exports and imports data of charges for use of intellectual property of these three countries compared with UK and USA. Table 6.7 shows that the average ratio of exports of costs for use of intellectual property of Switzerland over exports of charges for use of intellectual property of UK was 94.80% from 2008 to 2019, and the average ratio of imports of charges for use of intellectual property of Switzerland over imports of charges for use of intellectual property of UK was 98.57% during the same period. Both average ratios were close to 100%, implying that sci-tech internationalization of the two countries was similar. Thus, we assume that proportion of Swiss exports and imports settled with Swiss franc was 94.80% of the proportions of British exports settled with British pound and 98.57% of the British imports paid with British pound from 2001 to 2019, and similarly obtain Swiss franc originality capacity from 2001 to 2019 given in Table 15.1.

We use average ratios of Australian exports and import of charges for the use of intellectual property over US exports and imports of charges for the use of intellectual property at 1.13% and 9.48% from 2008 to 2019, and assume Australian proportions of exports and imports settled in Australian dollar as the multiplications of the corresponding US proportions with average ratios of exports and imports at 1.13% and 9.48%. Australian originality capacity from 2001 to 2019 can be obtained accordingly by following similar procedures above, and the results are given in Table 15.1. Canadian dollar originality capacity from 2001 to 2019 can be similarly calculated in Table 15.1.

15.3.4 *Distribution of currency originality of major world currencies*

Table 15.1 shows that USD had the highest OC of all eight currencies, with OC over 99% from 2001 to 2019. Euro, JP, and BP, the three second-tier world currencies had currency OC about 10% lower than the USD OC, their OC was close to 90%; AUD and CHF had OC slightly lower than the three second-tier currencies Euro, JY, and BP; and CAD and CNY were ranked seventh and eighth in OC, respectively.

It is noticeable that CNY OC increased over 100 times from 0.32% in 2001 to 33.86% in 2019, yet CNY OC as a percentage of SD OC was from 0.3% in 2001 to 34.0% in 2019, indicating much to catch in years or decades to come.

15.4 Currency OC with Better Currency Internationalization Measures

Currency OC measures in Table 15.1 were based on the currency internationalization data corresponding to the nominal turnovers of global foreign exchange markets. The results in Chapter 13 show that the currency internationalization corresponding to the nominal foreign exchange turnovers is not accurate because most of the nominal amounts of foreign exchange derivatives are not actual cash transactions or cash exchanged. Thus, the corresponding currency internationalization results are not accurate enough. We measure currency OC of major world currencies using the corresponding daily average turnovers corresponding to the better currency internationalization in Chapter 13, and the results are shown in Table 15.2.

Table 15.2: Distribution of Currency OC of Major International Currencies Corresponding to the Better Currency Internationalization Measures (2001–2019) (Unit: %)

Currency/Year	2001	2004	2007	2010	2013	2016	2019
USD	98.46	98.64	93.58	99.02	99.05	99.01	99.13
Euro	67.67	65.45	65.36	71.47	65.99	61.76	59.58
JPY	80.94	78.94	79.38	81.74	85.93	83.90	80.58
GBP	79.03	81.91	82.62	84.84	80.95	81.14	80.56
AUD	73.99	78.84	77.94	79.94	80.40	77.77	75.48
CAD	49.42	49.81	52.20	62.12	55.92	60.28	58.61
CHF	85.69	85.04	87.34	83.60	75.00	71.71	74.58
CNY	0.19	1.49	5.93	6.11	12.56	17.93	21.72
Euro 2	86.64	85.23	85.03	87.48	83.74	81.90	80.20
Others	29.75	17.92	35.76	32.31	27.82	44.51	39.05

(Continued)

Table 15.2: (*Continued*)

Changes from Table 15.1							
Currency/Year	**2001**	**2004**	**2007**	**2010**	**2013**	**2016**	**2019**
USD	−0.75	−0.64	−5.81	−0.44	−0.42	−0.47	−0.43
Euro	−11.47	−11.44	−12.30	−8.83	−10.44	−13.44	−14.84
JPY	−7.68	−8.61	−8.01	−6.76	−4.45	−6.46	−8.06
GBP	−9.55	−8.31	−7.58	−5.55	−7.50	−7.86	−8.61
AUD	−15.05	−9.35	−10.26	−7.71	−6.84	−7.78	−8.89
CAD	−16.66	−16.26	−16.68	−12.32	−13.02	−11.91	−13.03
CHF	−5.78	−6.13	−4.96	−6.50	−10.28	−12.67	−11.16
CNY	−0.13	−0.82	−2.11	−6.04	−9.65	−16.16	−12.14
Euro 2	−1.31	0.28	−6.25	−4.43	−5.85	−7.57	−8.68
Others	−14.97	−10.98	−16.77	−15.43	−14.69	0.00	−15.91

Source: Using the currency internationalization data in Table 13.5 and the same method in Table 15.1.

Currency OC results in Table 15.2 are all lower than Table 15.1 because many foreign exchange derivatives turnovers are eliminated. Table 15.2 shows that the OC of USD remained at the level around 90% from 2001 to 2019 with the slightest changes, which are still significantly higher than the originality capacities of any other currencies, indicating that the USD is still far ahead of other currencies in originality capability. OCs of Euro 2, Japanese yen, British pound, and Australian dollar were 8% to 9% lower with better currency internationalization measures than with nominal currency internationalization measures in Table 15.1; and those of Canadian dollar, Swiss franc, and Chinese yuan were 11–13% lower than those in Table 15.1. The ratio of Chinese yuan originality capacity over that of USD increased over 100 times from 0.2% in 2001 to 21.72%, showing a more significant gap between the two currencies.

15.5 The Relationship between Currency OC and Sci-tech OC

With the above estimation results of major currency OC and the corresponding sci-tech OC measures of major currency issuers given in

Table 7.1, we can easily calculate the relationship between currency OC and its issuers' sci-tech OC. The results are shown in Table 15.3.

Table 15.3 shows that average correlations coefficients between currency OC using traditional nominal foreign exchange turnovers and sci-tech OC is 37.61% from 2000 to 2019, indicating a relatively mutual supporting relationship between sci-tech OC and currency OC. Average correlation coefficients between currency OC using better currency internationalization and sci-tech OC are 43.71% from 2000 to 2019, indicating a higher mutual supportive relationship between sci-tech OC and currency OC.

Table 15.3: Distribution of Correlation Coefficients between Currency OC and Sci-tech OC of Major Currency Issuers (2001–2019) (Unit: %)

	Results Corresponding to COC Measures in Table 15.1							
Year	**2001**	**2004**	**2007**	**2010**	**2013**	**2016**	**2019**	**Average**
2000	36.35	34.12	36.33	36.33	41.54	43.48	45.82	39.14
2001	36.90	34.50	36.87	36.83	41.93	43.76	46.17	39.56
2002	37.98	35.35	37.98	37.86	42.77	44.44	47.00	40.48
2003	39.07	36.42	38.93	38.83	43.76	45.34	47.81	41.45
2004	36.81	34.32	36.59	36.55	41.74	43.45	45.71	39.31
2005	40.19	37.49	40.12	40.04	44.98	46.54	48.92	42.61
2006	39.60	37.16	39.39	39.48	44.56	46.24	48.40	42.12
2007	38.33	35.92	38.10	38.18	43.37	45.08	47.19	40.88
2008	36.44	33.99	36.19	36.22	41.50	43.23	45.29	38.98
2009	37.67	34.75	37.58	37.28	42.14	43.59	46.16	39.88
2010	36.00	33.55	35.74	35.52	41.00	42.69	44.81	38.47
2011	36.74	33.98	36.53	36.18	41.40	42.90	45.27	39.00
2012	36.41	33.81	36.11	35.84	41.19	42.76	44.93	38.72
2013	38.12	35.50	37.77	37.53	42.80	44.29	46.47	40.36
2014	37.42	34.10	37.18	36.60	41.41	42.52	45.30	39.22
2015	34.34	30.68	34.05	33.22	38.03	38.97	41.94	35.89
2016	34.13	30.16	33.96	33.02	37.55	38.35	41.54	35.53
2017	24.84	21.61	24.54	23.82	29.39	30.80	33.20	26.89
2018	26.19	23.02	25.83	25.20	30.79	32.20	34.50	28.25
2019	23.14	20.22	22.84	22.28	28.14	29.79	31.91	25.47
Average	35.33	32.53	35.13	34.84	40.00	41.52	43.92	37.61

(Continued)

Table 15.3: (*Continued*)

	Results Corresponding to COC Measures in Table 15.2							
Year	**2001**	**2004**	**2007**	**2010**	**2013**	**2016**	**2019**	**Average**
2000	44.65	39.82	38.53	40.95	48.08	54.35	52.93	45.61
2001	45.04	40.07	38.93	41.28	48.35	54.66	53.11	45.92
2002	45.89	40.73	39.83	42.09	49.03	55.42	53.70	46.67
2003	46.66	41.46	40.65	42.84	49.88	56.12	54.25	47.41
2004	44.70	39.56	38.58	40.73	48.06	54.08	52.32	45.43
2005	48.08	42.79	42.02	44.09	51.07	57.08	55.22	48.62
2006	47.39	42.31	41.29	43.57	50.73	56.60	54.84	48.10
2007	46.24	41.17	40.09	42.34	49.62	55.44	53.70	46.94
2008	44.58	39.42	38.34	40.44	47.85	53.56	51.85	45.15
2009	45.62	40.09	39.50	41.27	48.26	54.32	52.47	45.93
2010	44.55	39.30	38.35	39.94	47.45	52.93	51.40	44.85
2011	45.00	39.53	38.87	40.35	47.67	53.36	51.63	45.20
2012	44.77	39.35	38.60	40.04	47.48	52.89	51.25	44.91
2013	46.08	40.67	40.02	41.52	48.94	54.39	52.60	46.32
2014	44.70	38.85	38.79	40.10	47.31	53.43	51.13	44.90
2015	41.27	35.19	35.44	36.48	43.95	50.29	47.66	41.47
2016	41.07	34.70	35.22	36.11	43.31	49.78	47.05	41.03
2017	33.08	27.17	26.86	27.79	36.01	41.85	39.61	33.20
2018	34.31	28.45	28.12	29.11	37.34	43.07	40.80	34.46
2019	31.86	26.20	25.50	26.62	35.03	40.68	38.68	32.08
Average	43.28	37.84	37.18	38.88	46.27	52.22	50.31	43.71

Source: Calculated with sci-tech OC results in Table 7.1, currency OC in Tables 15.1 and 15.2, respectively.

15.6 Mutual Influence between Currency OC and Sci-tech OC

The relatively high degree of correlation between currency OC and sci-tech OC indicates that the two OC measures are mutually supportive to each other, but we do not know the degree of mutual influence between the two. We use the same method in Chapter 14 to analyze the difference in the degree of mutual leverage between the two.

15.6.1 *Sci-tech OC to influence currency OC*

Since we have continuous annual data on sci-tech OC from 2001 to 2019, and only data on currency OC are triennial data every 3 years during the same period, it is difficult for us to match sci-tech OC and currency OC. For the annual impact results, we can only obtain the regression results of the impact of currency OC on sci-tech OC like Table 14.6, as shown in Table 15.4.

Table 15.4: Regression Results of the Influence of Currency OC on Sci-tech OC with Currency OC in Table 15.1 (2001–2019)

Sci-tech OC 2001 to 2010 as Independent Variables and COC of 2010 as Dependent Variable				
−434.069	2,306.151	−2,097.14	82.149768	77.5502
689.6401	1,259.611	1,879.011	714.98125	14.6699
0.541809	27.03124	N/A	N/A	N/A
1.182498	4	N/A	N/A	N/A
3,456.149	2,922.753	N/A	N/A	N/A
Sci-tech OC 2001 to 2010 as Independent Variables and COC of 2013 as Dependent Variable				
−305.666	2,078.934	−2009.7	107.77883	75.6148
622.0903	1,136.233	1,694.963	644.94934	13.233
0.556607	24.38355	N/A	N/A	N/A
1.255336	4	N/A	N/A	N/A
2,985.478	2,378.23	N/A	N/A	N/A
Sci-tech OC 2001 to 2010 as Independent Variables and COC of 2016 as Dependent Variable				
−250.4	1,820.534	−1810.6	128.73119	76.9118
525.421	959.6688	1431.576	544.72781	11.1767
0.578931	20.59448	N/A	N/A	N/A
1.374906	4	N/A	N/A	N/A
2,332.57	1,696.531	N/A	N/A	N/A
Sci-tech OC 2001 to 2010 as Independent Variables and COC of 2019 as Dependent Variable				
−235.569	1,548.034	−1,532.64	132.63104	76.4235

(*Continued*)

Table 15.4: (*Continued*)

503.8583	920.285	1,372.825	522.37278	10.718
0.546219	19.74931	N/A	N/A	N/A
1.203708	4	N/A	N/A	N/A
1,877.953	1,560.141	N/A	N/A	N/A
Sci-tech OC 2004 to 2013 as Independent Variables and COC of 2013 as Dependent Variable				
399.7946	–819.318	1,857.342	–1,556.435	74.1435
560.3643	806.0734	1,100.452	1,229.9468	12.6434
0.603915	23.04606	N/A	N/A	N/A
1.524711	4	N/A	N/A	N/A
3,239.225	2,124.484	N/A	N/A	N/A
Sci-tech OC 2004 to 2013 as Independent Variables and COC of 2016 as Dependent Variable				
286.4368	–645.803	1,650.186	–1393.78	75.8121
483.4711	695.464	949.4482	1,061.1735	10.9085
0.607495	19.88368	N/A	N/A	N/A
1.547737	4	N/A	N/A	N/A
2,447.658	1,581.443	N/A	N/A	N/A
Sci-tech OC 2004 to 2013 as Independent Variables and COC of 2019 as Dependent Variable				
305.7299	–655.067	1,367.285	–1,096.277	75.2538
459.2868	660.6754	901.9547	1,008.0913	10.3628
0.58489	18.88906	N/A	N/A	N/A
1.409002	4	N/A	N/A	N/A
2,010.908	1,427.186	N/A	N/A	N/A
Sci-tech OC 2007 to 2016 as Independent Variables and COC of 2016 as Dependent Variable				
–496.628	1,284.069	–1,062.59	265.05082	74.5543
206.7931	488.2678	494.9561	329.5717	7.43749
0.769939	15.22285	N/A	N/A	N/A
3.346666	4	N/A	N/A	N/A
3,102.161	926.9406	N/A	N/A	N/A

Table 15.4: (*Continued*)

Sci-tech OC 2007 to 2016 as Independent Variables and COC of 2019 as Dependent Variable				
−376.295	1,067.076	−980.707	285.26304	74.0648
223.4021	527.484	534.7094	356.04191	8.03484
0.685344	16.4455	N/A	N/A	N/A
2.17807	4	N/A	N/A	N/A
2,356.276	1,081.818	N/A	N/A	N/A
Sci-tech OC 2010 to 2019 as Independent Variables and COC of 2019 as Dependent Variable				
−405.315	12.88745	390.6593	11.372957	83.3515
98.60101	147.5197	305.872	267.61304	4.18433
0.930106	7.750856	N/A	N/A	N/A
13.30733	4	N/A	N/A	N/A
3,197.791	240.303	N/A	N/A	N/A
Average Regression Effectiveness (R-Squared)				64.05%
1/(1-Average R-Squared)				2.78

Source: Standard multiple regressions with currency OC data in Table 15.1 as independent variables and sci-tech OC in Table 7.1 as dependent variables.

Table 15.4 shows that in the first four regressions of the influence of sci-tech OC of the 4 years of 2001, 2004, 2007, and 2010 on currency OC of the 4 years of 2010, 2013, 2016, and 2019, all had the regression effectiveness (R-Squared) over 54%. Five of the other six standard multiple regressions all had regression effectiveness more significant than 60%, and the average regression effectiveness of all 10 regressions is 64.05%, implying that sci-tech OC has a considerable influence on currency OC.

15.6.2 *Influence of currency OC on sci-tech OC*

Table 15.5 shows the regression results of the influence of currency OC on sci-tech OC from 2001 to 2019. Table 15.5 indicates that currency OC has a positive impact on sci-tech OC like that of Table 15.4, while the influence of currency OC on sci-tech OC is lower than that of the latter on the former.

Table 15.5: Regression Results of Influence of Currency OC on Sci-tech OC with Currency OC Table 15.1 (2001–2019)

Currency OC 2001 to 2010 as Independent Variables and Sci-tech OC of 2010 as Dependent Variable				
0.019172	−0.05232	−0.021579	0.0559321	0.171826336
0.064493	0.115437	0.0413223	0.1141868	0.876528516
0.187267	0.3429	N/A	N/A	N/A
0.230417	4	N/A	N/A	N/A
0.10837	0.470321	N/A	N/A	N/A
Currency OC 2001 to 2010 as Independent Variables and Sci-tech OC of 2013 as Dependent Variable				
0.021407	−0.06239	−0.024943	0.0668961	0.209434126
0.065891	0.117939	0.042218	0.1166621	0.895529936
0.217982	0.350333	N/A	N/A	N/A
0.278743	4	N/A	N/A	N/A
0.136844	0.490934	N/A	N/A	N/A
Currency OC 2001 to 2010 as Independent Variables and Sci-tech OC of 2016 as Dependent Variable				
0.020711	−0.06861	−0.030524	0.078521	0.286866131
0.064258	0.115016	0.0411717	0.1137706	0.873334038
0.233288	0.34165	N/A	N/A	N/A
0.304271	4	N/A	N/A	N/A
0.142064	0.4669	N/A	N/A	N/A
Currency OC 2001 to 2010 as Independent Variables and Sci-tech OC of 2019 as Dependent Variable				
0.018063	−0.06143	−0.025219	0.0678456	0.361676854
0.065663	0.117532	0.0420724	0.1162596	0.892440208
0.139496	0.349125	N/A	N/A	N/A
0.16211	4	N/A	N/A	N/A
0.079037	0.487552	N/A	N/A	N/A
Currency OC 2004 to 2013 as Independent Variables and Sci-tech OC of 2013 as Dependent Variable				
0.071463	−0.02068	0.0148852	−0.047642	−1.288461152
0.032337	0.046431	0.0312394	0.0266739	0.672577842
0.618946	0.244549	N/A	N/A	N/A

Table 15.5: (*Continued*)

Currency OC 2004 to 2013 as Independent Variables and Sci-tech OC of 2013 as Dependent Variable				
1.624298	4	N/A	N/A	N/A
0.388561	0.239218	N/A	N/A	N/A
Currency OC 2004 to 2013 as Independent Variables and Sci-tech OC of 2016 as Dependent Variable				
0.070331	−0.0227	0.0193493	−0.049368	−1.256973811
0.032364	0.046469	0.0312649	0.0266956	0.673126473
0.606532	0.244749	N/A	N/A	N/A
1.5415	4	N/A	N/A	N/A
0.369356	0.239608	N/A	N/A	N/A
Currency OC 2004 to 2013 as Independent Variables and Sci-tech OC of 2019 as Dependent Variable				
0.073585	−0.02511	0.0171593	−0.048877	−1.174993898
0.030968	0.044465	0.0299168	0.0255445	0.644101971
0.612788	0.234196	N/A	N/A	N/A
1.582564	4	N/A	N/A	N/A
0.347199	0.21939	N/A	N/A	N/A
Currency OC 2007 to 2016 as Independent Variables and Sci-tech OC of 2016 as Dependent Variable				
0.045695	−0.02206	−0.056847	0.0437216	−0.587329292
0.139034	0.157163	0.0657821	0.0717077	1.455596481
0.289313	0.328931	N/A	N/A	N/A
0.40709	4	N/A	N/A	N/A
0.176181	0.432782	N/A	N/A	N/A
Currency OC 2007 to 2016 as Independent Variables and Sci-tech OC of 2019 as Dependent Variable				
0.054218	−0.02783	−0.060694	0.0450488	−0.602802646
0.134288	0.151798	0.0635365	0.0692598	1.405906645
0.287422	0.317702	N/A	N/A	N/A
0.403356	4	N/A	N/A	N/A
0.16285	0.403739	N/A	N/A	N/A

(*Continued*)

Table 15.5: (*Continued*)

Currency OC 2010 to 2019 as Independent Variables and Sci-tech OC of 2019 as Dependent Variable				
0.090849	−0.01739	−0.006245	−0.044792	−1.581803651
0.047114	0.059324	0.0805493	0.0293267	1.102623514
0.591653	0.240502	N/A	N/A	N/A
1.448898	4	N/A	N/A	N/A
0.335224	0.231365	N/A	N/A	N/A
Average regression effectiveness (R-Squared)				37.85%
1/(1 − Average R-Squared)				1.61

Source: Standard multiple regressions with currency OC data in Table 15.1 as independent variables and sci-tech OC in Table 7.1 as dependent variables.

15.6.3 *Mutual influence of sci-tech OC and currency OC on each other*

Table 15.5 shows that the average regression effectiveness of 10 regressions of currency OC influencing sci-tech OC is merely 37.85%, 26.21% lower than the corresponding average 10 regressions of sci-tech OC influencing currency OC 64.05% in Table 15.4. The share of the average regression effectiveness of sci-tech OC 65.05% in Table 15.4 over the sum of two average regression effectiveness 65.05% and 37.85%, or 64.05%/(65.05% + 37.85%) = 62.86%, is 25.72% higher than the share of the average regression effectiveness 37.85% in Table 15.5 over the sum of two moderate regression effectiveness 37.14%. The higher percentage of sci-tech OC implies it has a higher influence on currency OC.

It is noticeable that the results in Tables 15.4 and 15.5 are results corresponding to currency OC in Table 15.1 with nominal foreign exchange turnover. The mutual influence of sci-tech OC and currency OC is quite different with corresponding currency OC in Table 15.2. Regression results show that average regression R-Squared of sci-tech OC influencing currency OC with currency OC in Table 15.2 is 65.07%; and average regression R-Squared of currency OC influencing sci-tech OC with currency OC in Table 15.2 is 70.66%, much higher than the corresponding average regression R-Squared 37.85% in Table 15.5. The share of the average regression effectiveness of sci-tech OC 65.07% in Table 15.4 over the sum of two average regression effectiveness 65.05% and 37.85%, or

64.07%/ (65.07% + 70.66%) = 47.94%, is 4.12% lower than the share of the average regression effectiveness 70.66% in Table 15.5 over the sum of two moderate regression effectiveness 52.06%. The slightly lower percentage of sci-tech OC implies sci-tech OC has a lower influence on currency OC.

15.7 Relationship between Currency OC and Currency Internationalization

The positive correlation between currency OC and currency internationalization is obvious. This section briefly discusses the degree of mutual influence between these two.

15.7.1 *Correlation between currency OC and currency internationalization*

Using the data of currency internationalization of the world's top eight international currencies from 2007 to 2019 given in Table 4.1 (the currency internationalization measured by the corresponding daily average foreign exchange turnover based on the nominal foreign exchange turnover) and Table 15.1 of corresponding currency OC, we can calculate that correlation coefficients between currency internationalization and currency OC in Table 15.1 are 43.0%, 41.4%, 42.2%, 42.2%, 43.4%, 41.0%, and 42.4% from 2001 to 2019, respectively; and correlation coefficients between currency internationalization and currency OC in Table 15.2 are 52.8%, 48.9%, 45.3%, 49.2%, 52.0%, 63.7%, and 49.3% from 2001 to 2019, respectively. These results indicate currency internationalization and currency OC have a higher mutual influence each with better currency internationalization measures.

15.7.2 *Mutual influence between currency OC and currency internationalization with nominal foreign exchange turnover*

Following the same procedures as in Chapter 14 to find mutual influence between sci-tech internationalization and currency internationalization, we can find mutual influencing results between currency OC and currency internationalization. Regression results show that average regression R-Squared of currency OC influencing currency internationalization (currency OC in Table 15.1 and currency internationalization in Table 4.1) is 39.88%; and average regression R-Squared of currency internationalization influencing currency OC (Table 15.1) is 56.95%. The share of the average regression R-Squared of currency originality 39.88% over the sum of two moderate regression effectiveness 39.88% and 56.95%, or 39.88%/ (39.88% + 56.95%) = 41.18%, is 17.63% lower than the share of the average regression effectiveness 56.95% over the sum of two average regression effectiveness 58.82%. The lower percentage of currency OC implies currency OC has a lower influence on currency internationalization.

15.7.3 *Mutual influence between currency OC and currency internationalization with better currency internationalization measures*

Similarly, we can find mutual influencing results between currency OC and currency internationalization. Regression results show that average regression R-Squared of currency OC influencing currency internationalization (currency OC in Table 15.2 and currency internationalization in Table 13.6) is 56.40%; and average regression R-Squared of currency internationalization influencing currency OC (Table 15.2) is 55.11%. The share of the average regression R-Squared of currency OC 56.40% over the sum of two average regression effectiveness 56.40% and 55.11%, or 56.40%/(56.40% + 55.11%) = 50.58%, is 1.16% higher than the share of the average regression effectiveness of 55.11% over the sum of two average regression effectiveness of 49.42%. The higher percentage of currency OC implies currency OC has a lower influence on better currency internationalization.

15.7.4 *Reasonable results of mutual influence between currency OC and currency internationalization*

The above results of mutual influence between currency OC and currency internationalization appear conflicting, yet they are in fact not conflicting at all. The higher impact of currency internationalization on currency OC corresponding to nominal foreign exchange turnover clearly means the over-valued nominal foreign exchange turnover exaggerates the function of currency internationalization. The influence of better currency internationalization on related currency OC is higher because better currency internationalization eliminates the majority (69.4%) of foreign exchange nominal derivatives turnover, thus a higher influence of currency OC corresponding to better currency internationalization is reasonable.

15.8 Mutual Influence between Sci-tech OC and Sci-tech Internationalization

We have studied mutual influencing relationships between sci-tech internationalization and currency internationalization in Chapter 14, relationships between currency OC and sci-tech OC in Section 15.6, and relationships between currency OC and currency internationalization in Section 15.7. Only the relationships between sci-tech OC and sci-tech internationalization need further exploring before we can know the relationships among two internationalization measures of sci-tech and currency and two OC measures of sci-tech and currencies.

15.8.1 *Influence of sci-tech OC and sci-tech internationalization on each other*

Using the same procedures to find the mutual influence of sci-tech internationalization and currency internationalization in Chapter 14, we can find the mutual impact of sci-tech OC and sci-tech internationalization. Regression results show that the average regression R-Squared of sci-tech OC influencing sci-tech internationalization is 97.42%; and the average regression R-Squared of sci-tech internationalization influencing sci-tech OC is 98.90%. The share of the average regression R-Squared of sci-tech OC of 97.42% over the sum of two moderate regression effectiveness 97.42% and 98.90%, or 97.42%/(97.42% + 98.90%) = 49.62%, is 0.75% lower than the share of the average regression effectiveness R-Squared of 98.90% over the sum of two average regression effectiveness of 50.38%. The lower percentage of sci-tech originality capacity implies sci-tech OC has a lower influence on sci-tech internationalization.

15.8.2 *More evidence of mutual influence of sci-tech OC and sci-tech internationalization*

Above results of mutual influence between sci-tech OC and sci-tech internationalization are obtained using the same method to find the mutual influence of sci-tech internationalization and currency internationalization using four consecutive currency internationalization data and corresponding sci-tech internationalization data in Chapter 14. To a high degree, the results are reasonable because we have made the best use of existing data of currency internationalization based on triennial foreign exchange turnover data from 2001 to 2019.

However, the situation is different when we study relationships between sci-tech OC and sci-tech internationalization as we have continuous annual data of both sci-tech OC and sci-tech internationalization from 2000 to 2019, thus we can have more regressions of mutual influence of sci-tech OC and sci-tech internationalization without considering triennial data of currency internationalization.

Results of 15 standard multiple regressions with five consecutive annual sci-tech OC data from 2001 to 2019 as independent variables and related sci-tech internationalization as dependent variables show that the average regression R-Squared of these 15 regressions is 98.38%. The average regression R-Squared of corresponding 15 standard multiple regressions of five consecutive annual sci-tech internationalization data from 2001 to 2019 as independent variables and related sci-tech OC as dependent variables is 98.66%. The share of the former average R-Squared 98.38% of the two average R-Squared is 49.93%, and the percentage of the later average R-Squared 98.66% of the two average R-Squared is 50.07%, indicating that sci-tech internationalization has higher influence on sci-tech OC as in Section 15.8.1.

Similarly, results of 14 standard multiple regressions with six consecutive annual sci-tech OC data from 2001 to 2019 as independent variables and related sci-tech internationalization as dependent variables show that the average regression R-Squared of these 14 regressions is 98.55%. The average regression R-Squared of corresponding 14 standard multiple regressions with six consecutive annual sci-tech internationalization data from 2001 to 2019 as independent variables and related sci-tech OC as dependent variables is 98.64%. The share of the former average R-Squared 98.55% of the two average R-Squared is 49.98%, and the share of the latter average R-Squared 98.64% of the two average R-Squared is

50.02%, also indicating that sci-tech internationalization has a higher influence on sci-tech OC as in Section 15.8.1. Therefore, sci-tech internationalization has a higher influence on sci-tech OC with consecutive annual data as with consecutive triennial data.

15.8.3 *Rationality of higher influence of sci-tech internationalization on sci-tech OC*

The additional evidence of the higher influence of sci-tech internationalization on sci-tech OC with 5–6 consecutive annual data is consistent with the same result with four consecutive triennial data. The rationality of higher influence of sci-tech internationalization on sci-tech OC lies in the fact that the former reflects the accumulation of weighted international patents, or more specifically accumulation of weighted patent families as shown in Chapter 7, and sci-tech OC is the measure of annual exports and imports of charges for the use of intellectual property. Thus, the accumulated measure of patent families in previous years should possess inertia of sci-tech innovation to influence current measure of sci-tech OC.

15.9 Summary of Mutual Influence of Sci-tech and Currency OC and Sci-tech and Currency Internationalization

Mutual influencing relationships between sci-tech internationalization and currency internationalization in Chapter 14, relationships between currency OC and sci-tech OC in Section 15.6, relationships between currency OC and currency internationalization in Section 15.7, and relationships between sci-tech OC and sci-tech internationalization of Section 15.8 are interactive and somewhat complicated. We summarize the relationships of mutual influence of the above four symmetric concepts of sci-tech OC, currency OC, sci-tech internationalization, and currency internationalization. In addition, currency internationalization and currency OC have two related concepts: traditional currency internationalization and better currency internationalization are related to conventional currency OC and better currency OC using the different ways of currency internationalization. Thus, it is difficult to grasp the results of the interaction between the concepts and metrics. Figure 15.1 shows the mutual

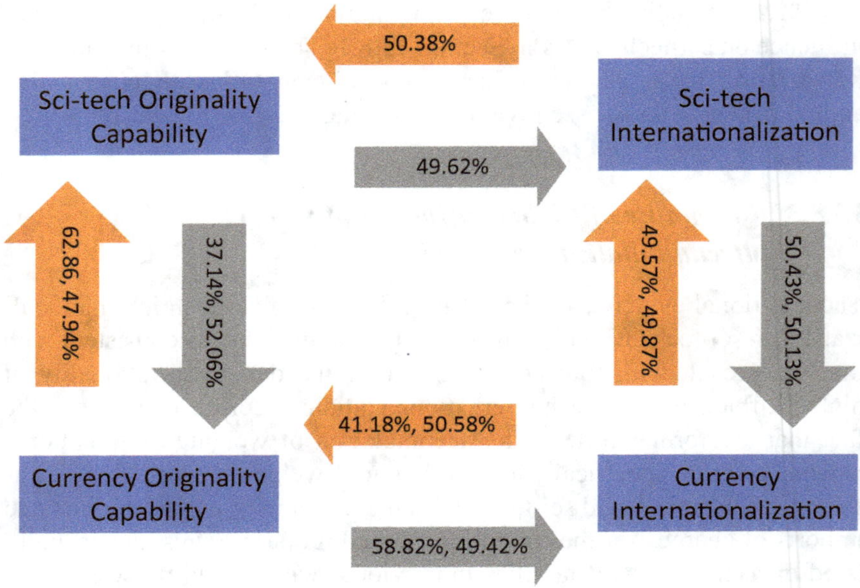

Figure 15.1: Summary of the Mutual Influence between Sci-tech OC, Sci-tech Internationalization, Currency OC, and Currency Internationalization (2001–2019)

Source: Tables 14.8, 14.9, 15.4, 15.5, and results from Sections 15.7 and 15.8. The first number following each arrow represents the result with traditional currency internationalization using nominal foreign exchange average daily turnovers, and the second number following each arrow represents the result with better currency internationalization using 30.6% of foreign exchange derivatives average daily turnovers. The results between sci-tech OC and sci-tech internationalization are corresponding to Section 15.8.1 for consistency.

relationships among sci-tech OC, sci-tech internationalization, currency OC, and currency internationalization.

Figure 15.1 shows that the influence of sci-tech internationalization has more impact on currency internationalization on whatever currency internationalization measure is used; sci-tech internationalization also has more influence on sci-tech OC, implying the importance of sci-tech internationalization. Currency internationalization has more impact on currency OC with better currency internationalization measures as it is more reasonable with discounted foreign exchange derivatives turnovers, sci-tech OC has more influence on currency OC with better currency internationalization measures. All the above results show the importance of sci-tech internationalization and sci-tech OC.

15.10 Summary

We defined and measured currency OC following the sci-tech OC definition in Chapter 13. With the definition and measurements of currency OC of major international currencies, we find the mutual influence of currency OC and sci-tech OC using the same method in Chapter 13, and mutual impact of currency OC and currency internationalization using the same process in Chapter 13. With the mutual influence of sci-tech OC and sci-tech internationalization using the same method in Chapter 13, we find mutual influences among two pairs of OC of sci-tech and currency, two pairs of internationalization of sci-tech and currency. The importance of sci-tech internationalization lies in the fact that it represents accumulated qualified patent families or it contains inertia of sci-tech innovation.

Results of this chapter show that sci-tech internationalization has more influence on both currency internationalization and sci-tech OC. These results indicate the critical roles of sci-tech internationalization. Currency OC is influenced by both sci-tech OC and currency internationalization, implying the influence of sci-tech internationalization on currency OC through both currency internationalization and sci-tech OC, which implies the importance of sci-tech internationalization.

Attention should be paid to the importance of better currency internationalization, as our understanding of mutual influence between currency internationalization and currency OC can be misleading without it, and our understanding of mutual influence between sci-tech OC and currency OC can also be misleading without it.

Bibliography

Sato, K., *The International Use of the Japanese Yen: The Case of Japan's Trade with East Asia*, Research Associate, ICSEAD Working Paper Series Vol. 98-16, August 1998.

Chapter 16

Future Changes of Major Currency Internationalization and Market Development

We focus on future changes of internationalization of major world currencies in line with sci-tech internationalization of these currency issuers in the next two to three decades after a brief introduction of interest rate liberalization in China in this last chapter. Then we introduce three key circles of world currencies, and finally we analyze the contribution of sci-tech and currency to net exports of charges for the use of intellectual property of major currency issuers in this chapter.

16.1 Coordination of Exchange-Traded Market and OTC Market

The experience of the worldwide market development in the past decades shows that the coordinated development of the exchange-traded market and OTC markets (exchange traded market refers to organized exchange marketplace, and the OTC market mainly refers to the inter-bank OTC market) is a vital feature of the development of the entire world market. Due to the unique business needs of customers, the OTC market has strong personalization, low standardization, and relatively low transparency, but the flexibility of product innovation is preferable; the exchange market is necessary because products in exchange-traded market are mostly standardized products, and the market liquidity is relatively high.

Exchanges as central counterparties, effectively reduce the credit risk of most transactions. At the same time, exchanges have high liquidity and an especially high degree of transparency. Thus, exchanges have naturally become hedging places for trading positions in the OTC market. Therefore, it can be said that without the massive demand of the OTC market, the exchange market is problematic to become active; at the same time, if there are no necessary hedging tools provided by the exchanges, risks of OTC market would be problematic to be effectively hedged, and therefore it is difficult to develop. These two markets promote each other and develop in a coordinated manner, and neither is indispensable. Of course, due to the existence of excessive leverage and excessive speculation in the worldwide market before the worldwide financial crisis, the excessive growth of derivatives transactions has contributed to the international financial crisis to some degree.

Without exchange-traded products such as interest rates and stock index options, many fiscal products will lack a reliable basis for pricing, and relevant market risks are also problematic to be effectively hedged and managed because of the implied information as implied volatility in such products is highly useful. The advancement of interest rate liberalization will change the degree of marketization of China's entire economic system, and the corresponding interest rate risk will also need to be hedged. This will create a good policy environment for the launch of interest rate options, and it will create an active creation of OTC interest rate risk management tools. It is believed that products such as exchange futures and options in China will gradually be launched and developed steadily. The exchange and OTC markets will further improve and develop. The mutual coordination and mutual promotion of the two markets will eventually form, which will continue to stabilize the national economy.

16.2 Orderly Promotion of Interest Rate Liberalization and Its Impacts in China

Interest rate is the opportunity cost of capital, and it is the most vital market factor that affects the whole economy and every corner of the fiscal market. The liberalization of interest rates is also a necessary measure to increase the degree of marketization of the economy as a whole and every part of the financial market. Since interest rates are the basis for the pricing of various foreign exchange products, interest rate liberalization is one of the necessary conditions for CNY pricing in the worldwide foreign exchange market. It is the main driving force to activate both domestic and foreign CNY products, and it is also the source of motivation for the innovation of fiscal institutions. The People's Bank of China canceled the upper limit of inter-bank lending rates on June 1, 1996, as a sign of the beginning of China's interest rate liberalization, it has been over quarter of a century since the first sign of CNY interest rate liberalization. The time span surpassed US's 16 years, and Japan and South Korea's 17 years to complete the liberalization of interest rates. If the implementation of the upper and lower limits of deposit and loan interest rates in June 2012 is taken as the starting time for China's interest rate liberalization, the time for China's interest rate liberalization has passed 9 years, and interest rate liberalization is getting close to its end.

16.2.1 *The importance of interest rate risk in global financial market*

Interest rate is not only the main pricing factor for fixed income products but also an important factor for the pricing of other fiscal products. The pivotal position of interest rates in the entire international financial system can be seen from the proportion of worldwide interest rate futures and options in the global exchanges: the average of the yearly share of interest rate futures turnover in the total worldwide exchange-traded futures turnover was as high as 90.8% for 25 years from 1995 to 2019. The proportion of the corresponding interest rate options and the trading value of worldwide on-the-spot options is 82.8% on average in the same period. (The 1995–2014 result is calculated based on the data released by the Bank for International Settlements. The 2015–2019 foreign exchange and interest rate futures and options data are based on the average daily transaction value of the global foreign exchange and interest rate market published on the website of the Bank for International Settlements and the website of the Global Exchange Alliance Association. Global stock index futures and options and stock futures and options data calculated.) These data show that interest rate risk is the top priority of financial risks in the global market. In other words, only with the increase of interest rate liberalization, interest rate risk can be gradually released, activities of various fiscal markets such as fixed income, foreign exchange, asset mergers and acquisitions will increase accordingly, and the pricing functionality of products in these markets will be enhanced accordingly.

16.2.2 *Major measures for interest rate liberalization in China*

The People's Bank of China (PBC) decided on June 7, 2012, to adjust the upper limit of the floating range of deposit interest rates of fiscal institutions to 1.1 times the benchmark interest rate from June 8, 2012. At the same time, the lower limit of the floating range of loan interest rates of fiscal institutions was adjusted to the benchmark 0.8 times the interest rate. Financial institutions were permitted to adjust the deposit and loan interest rates within a certain range as the official start of interest rate liberalization. With the approval of the State Council, the "Notice of the People's Bank of China on Further Promoting the Reform of Interest Rate Marketization" was released on July 19, 2013. The PBC decided to abolish the lower limit of 0.7 times the loan interest rate of fiscal institutions from July 20, 2013. Fiscal institutions can determine the level of loan interest rates independently according to commercial principles and cancel the upper limit of 2.3 times the loan interest rate of rural credit cooperatives. The principle is to independently determine the loan interest rate to customers, and comprehensively liberalize the loan interest rate control of financial institutions. This is another chief move of China's interest rate liberalization, which will have a significant impact on transforming China's fiscal institutions' business model, product innovation, market activity, and risk control.

The PBC decided to lower the benchmark interest rates for CNY loans and deposits of fiscal institutions from October 24, 2015, to further reduce the cost of financing. The benchmark of 1-year loan interest rate of financial institutions was reduced by 0.25 percentage points to 4.35%; the benchmark of 1-year deposit interest rate was reduced by 0.25 percentage points to 1.5%. At the same time, commercial banks and rural cooperative fiscal institutions would no longer set floating ceilings on deposit interest rates, and step up efforts to improve the market-oriented formation and control mechanism of interest rates, strengthen the central bank's regulation and supervision of the interest rate system, and improve the efficiency of monetary policy transmission ("China's the People's Bank of China Decided to Lower the Benchmark Deposit and Loan Interest Rates and Lower the Deposit Reserve Ratio", the People's Bank of China website, October 23, 2015).

To deepen the reform of interest rate liberalization, improve the efficiency of interest rate transmission, and promote the reduction of the financing cost of the real economy, the People's Bank of China decided to reform and improve the formation mechanism of the loan market quoted interest rate (LPR) (the website of the People's Bank of China) on August 17, 2019. The central bank announced and soon many domestic media reported that the domestic interest rate marketization is nearing its end. From the perspective of the upper and lower limits of deposit and loan interest rates, China's interest rate liberalization is indeed nearing an end, but the mechanism of interest rate liberalization still has a long way to go.

16.2.3 *Interest rate liberalization is the major source for financial innovation*

Interest rate risk is the most vital market risk in the entire fiscal market. Managing interest rate risk has a huge impact on the innovation and development of the entire financial market. When the author began to work in the fiscal industry in New York in the early 1990s, it was at the climax of global economic innovation. Various fiscal derivative products, especially bizarre derivatives, emerged one after another. Working while learning, the author compiled and derived structures and pricing formulas for nearly a hundred types of exotic options that were popular in the inter-bank market in the early 1990s of the last century in New York. Based on compiling and derivations efforts, in a few years, the first edition of the book *Exotic Options — A Guide to Second Generation Options* came into being in 1997 (Zhang 1997) began to be used in the international financial market and academic field for product structuring in the past two decades. Later, a group of young financial professionals in China spent a few years translating the 700-page English monograph of *Exotic Options* (2nd Edition, 1998) into Chinese (see Zhang (Peter G.) (2014) and Ma Xiaojuan) which was published by China Machinery Industry Press in 2014. The translators invited me to write a foreword for the Chinese edition. When I prepared the foreword, I recalled the endless emergence of fiscal products in the worldwide market at the beginning of my financial career in the global financial community. I remembered in the mid-1980s, when the US interest rate liberalization and the Japanese interest rate liberalization were close to completion, the international interest rate risk was fully released, and hedging instruments were in great need during the 1980s and 1990s of the last century. The need to hedge risks of bonds, exchange rates, stocks, and other assets due to interest rate risk was the fundamental driving force for the emergence of various types of fiscal derivatives during that time. Interest rate liberalization in the United States was the main source of power for the climax of worldwide financial innovation in the mid-1980s to the mid-1990s. As CNY interest rate liberalization gets into its final stage, the trading and hedging activities of CNY bonds, foreign exchange, stocks, futures, options, and other markets will increase significantly, and the climax of CNY product innovation should also happen accordingly.

16.2.4 *Necessity of interest rate risk management*

China's interest rate risk management market has maintained rapid growth as evidenced in the compound yearly growth rate of 174.1% from 2014 to 2018 of interest rate swaps, compared with the CAPR of 28.1% from 2010 to 2014. Yet, the CAPR of −4.6% from 2018 to 2020 implies slowing down of interest rate risk management recently. The ratio of turnover of bond futures to China's GDP increased from 8.7% in 2015 increase to 15.0% in 2019, and it increased further to 26.0% in 2020. Despite of the significant growth of bond futures trading, the ratio of bond future turnover over GDP is far below the corresponding worldwide ratio of 1500% in 2019. The ratio difference indicates great room for interest risk management in China in years to come, and that interest risk awareness of fiscal institutions needs to be much improved.

16.3 Latest Measures to Open the Domestic Foreign Exchange Market

Shortly after the release of the "Notice of the People's Bank of China on Issues Concerning the use of RMB to invest in the Interbank Market by Foreign Central Banks, International Financial Organizations, and Sovereign Wealth Funds" in July 2015, the PBC announced that the first batch of foreign central bank institutions was allowed to enter the domestic foreign exchange market, extending foreign exchange trading hours and further introducing qualified foreign entities into the domestic foreign exchange market, etc., which will play an crucial role in further activating the domestic foreign exchange market.

16.3.1 *Foreign central bank institutions enter the domestic foreign exchange market*

The PBC completed the filing of the first batch of foreign central bank institutions with the China Foreign Exchange Trading Center on November 25, 2015, indicating they are officially entering the Chinese interbank foreign exchange market. The entry of foreign central bank institutions into the domestic foreign exchange market is conducive to steadily promoting the opening of China's foreign exchange market. These foreign central bank institutions include the Hong Kong Monetary Authority, the Reserve Bank of Australia, the National Bank of Hungary, the International Bank for Reconstruction and Development, the International Development Association, the World Bank Trust Fund, and the Singapore Government Investment Corporation. The foreign central banks (monetary authorities) and other official reserves are of three kinds: management institutions, worldwide fiscal organizations, and sovereign wealth funds. These foreign central bank institutions have chosen to become overseas members of China's interbank foreign exchange market directly, or be represented by China's interbank foreign exchange market members, and be represented by the People's Bank of China. Foreign central bank institutions may choose one or more than one of foreign exchange swaps, money swaps, and options to trade in domestic foreign exchange market (The First Batch of Foreign Central Bank Institutions Enters the Chinese Interbank Foreign Exchange Market, The People's Bank of China website, November 25, 2015). The entry of these institutions into the domestic foreign exchange market will not only help to activate the domestic foreign exchange spot market but will also play a critical role in promoting the market for foreign exchange derivatives trading.

The second batch of foreign central bank institutions completed the filing at the China Foreign Exchange Trade System on January 12, 2016, and officially entered the Chinese interbank foreign exchange market. These foreign central bank institutions include the Reserve Bank of India, Bank of Korea, Singapore Monetary Authority, Bank of Indonesia, Bank of Thailand, the Bank for International Settlements, and International Finance Corporation. As of the end of August 2019, a total of 41 overseas central bank institutions have completed the filing and officially entered the Chinese inter-bank foreign exchange market.[1]

---

[1] *Source*: China Foreign Exchange Trade Center.

16.3.2 *Extending foreign exchange trading hours and further introducing qualified foreign entities*

In addition to approving foreign central bank-like institutions to participate in the domestic foreign exchange market, the PBC took measures to extend foreign exchange trading hours and further introduced qualified foreign entities in December 2015. These measures further activated the domestic foreign exchange market and promoted the formation of a consistent RMB exchange rate domestically and abroad, thereby promoting the globalization of the RMB.

"With the acceleration of the liberalization of CNY exchange rate, convertibility, and internationalization of the RMB exchange rate, the demand for accelerating the development of the domestic foreign exchange market, especially promoting the opening of the market to the outside world, is increasing. The time extension of foreign exchange trading time and further introduction of qualified foreign entities mainly focus on enriching the participants in the domestic foreign exchange market. These measures broadening the trading channels of domestic and foreign market participants, and promoting the formation of a consistent RMB exchange rate in domestic and overseas market are reform measures to deepen the development of the foreign exchange market" (The relevant person in charge of the People's Bank of China answers questions from reporters on the extension of foreign exchange trading hours and the further introduction of qualified foreign entities," the website of the People's Bank of China, December 23, 2015).

16.4 Changes of GDP World Share of Major Currency Issuers

It is a problematic task to forecast changes of GDP share of major currency issuers in the next two decades or so. However, this forecast is an important basis for forecasting changes in globalization levels of chief world currencies. Using the updated GDP data from 1980 to 2020, and forecast data of chief world money issuers from 2021 to 2025 by the International Monetary Fund (IMF) in April 2021, we can make reasonable predictions of GDP world share of major currency issuers in the next three decades.

16.4.1 *Impact of COVID-19 on GDP of the United States and China*

According to GDP data released by the IMF in April 2021, US nominal GDP decreased by 2.34% from 2019 to 2020, and Chinese nominal GDP increased by 2.67% during the same period; compound yearly growth rate of US nominal GDP is 2.86% from 2019 to 2021, and the corresponding CAGR is 7.73% of the Chinese nominal GDP during the same period. These change rates of GDP clearly show that COVID-19 has had obvious different impacts on the world's top two economies. As a result of the different impacts of COVID-19 on the two economies, the ratio of Chinese GDP over US GDP increased from 66.9% to 70.3% from 2019 to 2020.

16.4.2 *Compound annual growth rate (CAGR) of US nominal GDP in various periods*

The basis for predicting the future is historical data. Table 16.1 gives the CAGR of the nominal GDP of major currency issuers denominated in USD from 1980 to 2026 and corresponding ratios of CAGR over previous CAGR. Since COVID-19 led most economies to decrease noticeably,

Table 16.1: CAGR of Nominal GDP of the Top Eight Major International Currency Issuers and Related Ratios (1980–2020) (Unit: %)

Economy/ CAGR	1980–1990 A	1990–2000 B	2000–2010 C	2010–2020 D	2021–2026 E	B/A	C/B	D/C
US	7.63	5.57	3.87	3.39	4.75	72.94	69.55	87.63
Eurozone	7.12	1.40	6.90	0.21	5.44	19.63	493.80	3.02
Japan	10.98	4.51	1.49	(1.31)	4.39	41.07	33.00	–87.90
UK	7.05	3.36	4.10	0.88	6.82	47.67	122.12	21.39
Australia	7.12	2.13	12.11	0.83	6.80	29.87	569.75	6.83
Canada	8.00	2.25	8.07	0.16	7.00	28.11	358.47	1.98
Switzerland	8.05	0.50	7.97	2.17	5.66	6.26	1581.32	27.24
China	2.73	11.76	17.47	9.33	8.58	431.21	148.59	53.39

Source: CAGRs from 1980 to 2026 are calculated based on the data of the nominal GDP of different economies updated and forecasted by the IMF in April 2021; Euro area CAGR based on total nominal GDP of 19 Euro member countries.

CAGR from 2010 to 2020 might not represent a decade trend reliably. Therefore, it is more reasonable for us to use CAGR from 2010 to 2021 to represent the corresponding decade trend.

The ratios of decade CAGR over previous decade CAGR show that US CAGR ratio over previous decade CAGR decreased from 72.9% to 69.6% in the three decades from 1980 to 2010, yet the ratio rose back to 87.6% from 2010 to 2020 despite the obvious decline of the US GDP from 2019 to 2020 due to COVID-19. The above results show that, after the implementations of four consecutive quantitative easing (QE) policies in response to the 2008 financial crisis in the United States from 2009 to 2014 and the negative impact of COVID-19, the US GDP did not follow the three-decade long accelerating decreasing trend, but rather rebounded significantly from the decade from 2010 to 2020 compared to the previous decade from 2000 to 2010. These results show the resilience of the US GDP and USD. However, it is not possible that total debt issuance of over $6 trillion new debt in 2020 and 2021 to fight with COVID-19, more than total debt increment from 2009 to 2012 to fight the 2008 world fiscal crisis, should not have any negative impacts on future US economic development. Nevertheless, we estimate that the US nominal GDP growth rate from 2020 to 2050 will remain the product of the IMF's estimated yearly growth rate of 3.39% from 2015 to 2020 and the average CAGR ratios of 72.94% and 69.55% from 1980 to 2010 in Table 16.1, or 2.42%. Table 16.2 gives the relevant forecast results.

16.4.3 *CAGR of nominal GDP of other major economies*

The CAGRs of Eurozone, Japan, the United Kingdom, Australia, Canada, and Switzerland in Table 16.1 show that these three chief currency issuers were on clear declining trends from 1980 to 2020 as ratios of CAGR from 1990 to 1980 over that from 1980 to 1990 were all significantly below 100%. Ratios of CAGR from 2010 to 2020 over CAGR from 2000 to 2010 were largely lower than the previous corresponding ratios.

16.4.4 *CAGR of China's nominal GDP*

Table 16.1 shows that decade CAGRs of Chinese nominal GDP in USD terms from 1980 to 2020 increased from 2.73% to 11.76%, 17.46%, and 9.33%, respectively. The ratios of decade CAGR over previous decade

Table 16.2: Global Share of Nominal GDP of Top World Currency Issuers (2020–2050) (Unit: %)

Year/Economy	2020	2021	2022	2025	2030	2035	2040	2045	2050
US	24.54	24.23	24.06	23.03	22.92	23.21	23.50	23.79	23.79
Eurozone	15.30	15.58	15.59	14.84	13.66	12.60	11.35	10.48	10.48
Japan	5.89	5.75	5.67	5.47	4.83	4.23	3.71	3.25	3.25
UK	3.24	3.34	3.35	3.31	3.39	3.51	3.63	3.76	3.76
Australia	1.59	1.73	1.70	1.66	1.68	1.70	1.73	1.76	1.76
Canada	1.99	2.01	2.04	2.02	1.88	1.72	1.57	1.43	1.43
Switzerland	0.84	0.88	0.88	0.85	0.79	0.73	0.67	0.61	0.61
China	16.42	17.79	18.05	19.38	22.07	25.29	28.97	33.20	33.20

Source: Gross domestic products in current prices updated by the IMF in April 2021; average annual growth rates of US GDP is the product of US CAGR from 2010 to 2020 multiplied by the average ratios B/A and C/B in Table 16.1; average annual growth rates of other six currency issuers are obtained following the same method to obtain the US average annual growth rate; average Chinese annual growth rate is used as the product of CAGR at 9.33% from 2010 to 2020 and the lowest CAGR ratio D/C 53.39% in Table 16.1.

dropped from 431.2% to 184.6% and 53.4%, respectively, showing that China's economy evolved from low speed in the early stage of open-door policy, to medium speed in the decade before China joined the World Trade Organization (WTO) in 2001, to high speed in the first decade after China joined WTO. CAGR of China returned to high-medium speed below 10% in the second decade after China joined WTO, and it will evolve back to medium speed high-quality economic expansion in the coming decades. It is reasonable to estimate the average yearly increase rate as the product of CAGR at 9.33% from 2010 to 2020 and the lowest CAGR ratio 53.39% in Table 16.1. Table 16.2 gives the corresponding forecasting results of nominal Chinese GDP from 2025 to 2050.

16.4.5 *Global share of nominal GDP of major currency issuers from 2030 to 2050*

Using the forecast nominal GDP data of chief economies from 2020 to 2026 released by the IMF in April 2021 and the corresponding CAGRs shown in Table 16.1, we can estimate the worldwide share of nominal

GDP of eight major currency issuers from 2030 to 2050. The results are given in Table 16.2.

16.5 Anticipation of Future Sci-tech Originality Capability (OC) of Major Currency Issuers

16.5.1 *Anticipation of US sci-tech OC*

Science and technology (sci-tech) are the main driving forces for economic and trade development worldwide, and the chief factor affecting currency evaluation and globalization as shown in Chapter 14. Therefore, it is necessary to make a more accurate calculation of sci-tech OC of any currency issuer to have a more accurate forecast of the future trend of the internationalization of the currency.

Relevant data of Table 6.12 show that the US sci-tech OC increased from 81.15% to 82.03% during 1992–1994, the highest point in history, and then continued to decline to 70.25% in 2002 with an average annual decrease of 1.47%. It increased steadily to 77.44% from 2002 to 2007 with an average yearly increase of 1.44%; and then fell to 72.91% from 2007 to 2016 with an average annual decrease of 0.60%. The US sci-tech OC stayed around 73.00% from 2016 to 2020 with an average yearly decrease of 0.08%. These results show that there is no clear cycle or pattern of US sci-tech OC, yet overall, a slowly declining trend is obvious. We assume that US sci-tech OC will decline 0.04% or half of the average yearly decrease rate from 2016 to 2020. Table 16.3 shows the relevant results.

16.5.2 *Anticipation of Japan's sci-tech OC*

The relevant data in Table 7.1 show that Japanese sci-tech OC increased steadily from 17.50% in 1977 to 52.75% in 2003, the first year Japan achieved a net surplus of charges for the use of intellectual property. The average annual growth rate of sci-tech OC was 1.36% from 1977 to 2003. It continued to increase steadily to a historical high of 68.14% in 2015 with an average yearly growth of 1.28%. The steady increase of Japanese sci-tech OC shows that Japanese sci-tech OC followed almost a straight line in the 38-year period from 1977 to 2015. However, it decreased to 60.39% from 2015 to 2020 with an average yearly decrease of 1.55%. It is noticeable that Japanese sci-tech OC declined significantly with an accumulative decrease of 7.08% in 2 years from 2018 to 2020. As Japan's sci-tech OC had continued increasing for over three decades before 2015, but has only declined for 5 years since 2015, it is difficult to forecast changes of Japanese sci-tech in the next three decades. It may be appropriate for Japanese sci-tech OC to increase with the same average yearly growth rate of 0.29% from 2010 to 2020 in the next three decades. The relevant results are shown in Table 16.3.

16.6.3 *Anticipation of sci-tech OC in the Eurozone*

Table 6.12 shows that only Germany, France, and Finland have a net surplus of charge for the use of intellectual property of 19 Euro members, and the total surplus of these three countries was less than half of the surplus of Japan from 2005 to 2014, and slightly more than that of Japan from 2015 to 2020. All other Euro member countries are net importers of charges for the use of IP. Thus, the sci-tech OC of Eurozone has been largely below 40%.

Considering the two cycles of sci-tech OC changes of Eurozone from 2005 to 2013 and 2013 to 2020 largely within the range of 37% to 40%, we assume that sci-tech OC of Eurozone will increase slightly beyond the upper bound of the previous two cycles 40% in the next three decades.

16.5.4 *Prediction of Swiss and British sci-tech OC*

Switzerland and the United Kingdom have been the fourth and fifth largest net exporters of charges for the use of IP, and the total net exports of charges for the use of IP of these two countries are comparable to that of German from 2016 to 2020. Exports and imports of costs for the use of IP in these two countries are largely comparable with Swiss net exports of charges for the use of IP which has been slightly higher than UK. The average surplus of $10.8 billion shows that the overall level of sci-tech in Switzerland slightly exceeds that of the United Kingdom. Data in Table 6.12 show that average yearly change of Swiss sci-tech OC and British sci-tech OC was 0.58% and −0.11% from 2008 to 2020, respectively. Considering factors such as Brexit, it is reasonable to assume that the average annual growth rate of British sci-tech OC will be −0.10%, which is slightly higher than the average yearly growth rate of British sci-tech OC from

2008 to 2020. Table 16.3 shows the forecast results of changes in Swiss and British sci-tech OC in the future.

16.5.5 *Prediction of Canadian and Australian sci-tech OC*

Although Canada and Australia have remained in the top 15 list of the world's top economies for many years, and their currencies have long been among the world's top seven currencies, sci-tech OC of these two countries is not comparable to that of chief developed economies. Relevant data in Table 6.12 show that average annual sci-tech OC of Canada and Australia was only 29.11% and 19.89% from 2005 to 2020, respectively, which was the lowest of the top seven worldwide currency issuers. As the average yearly change of Canadian and Australian sci-tech OC was −0.26% and 0.18% from 2005 to 2020, respectively, it is reasonable for us to assume that sci-tech OC changes to −0.13% and 0.09% in the coming three decades, respectively. Table 16.3 gives the corresponding forecast results.

16.5.6 *Anticipation of China's sci-tech OC*

According to data released by the State Administration of Foreign Exchange (SAFE: www.safe.gov.cn), China's yearly average sci-tech OC was only 4.23% from 2002 to 2016 with little changes; and it increased significantly from 4.64% in 2016 to 18.75% in 2020, showing continuous improvement of China's sci-tech OC in recent years. However, the 4-year period from 2016 to 2020 is too short to predict future improvement. Figure 7.5 shows that Chinese sci-tech OC at 18.75% in 2020 was like Japanese sci-tech OC 19.31% in 1978, and Chinese sci-tech OC at 20.39% in the first 8 months of 2021 was also comparable to Japanese sci-tech OC at 20.13% in 1979. Thus, it is reasonable for us to assume that Chinese sci-tech OC will follow the Japanese pattern to increase in the next three decades. As Japanese sci-tech OC increased steadily with an average annual increase of 1.30%, it may be reasonable for Chinese sci-tech OC to increase with a yearly incremental around 1.30% from 2020 to 2050. Reasonable as it may be, Chinese efforts to improve her sci-tech OC are very likely to further strengthen, yet earlier accumulation of sci-tech before the late 1970s lay necessary foundation for steady progress of Japanese sci-tech OC in the following three decades after 1970.

16.6 Prediction of Sci-tech OC of Major Currency Issuers

Based on sci-tech OC changes of major world currency issuers described above and corresponding future trends, we can estimate the changes in their sci-tech OC. Table 16.3 gives the corresponding results. Table 16.3 shows that the US sci-tech OC will decrease from 72.58% in 2020 to 71.38% in 2050 with an accumulated decrease of only 1.20%. Sci-tech OC of Eurozone will increase from 39.78% to 41.29% in 2050 with an accumulated incremental of 1.50%; Japanese sci-tech OC will increase from 60.72% to 69.42% in 2050 with an accumulated incremental of 8.70% in three decades.

British sci-tech OC will decrease from 56.97% in 2020 to 53.78% in 2050 with a total accumulated decrease of 3.30%; Australian sci-tech OC will decrease from 19.93% in 2020 to 16.03% in 2050 with a total accumulated decrease of 3.90%. Australian sci-tech OC will remain the lowest

Table 16.3: Changes in Sci-tech OC of Top Eight International Currency Issuers (2020–2050) (Unit: %)

Year/ Economy	2020	2021	2022	2025	2030	2035	2040	2045	2050
USA	72.58	72.54	72.50	72.38	72.18	71.98	71.78	71.58	71.38
Eurozone	39.79	39.84	39.89	40.04	40.29	40.54	40.79	41.04	41.29
Japan	60.72	61.01	61.30	62.17	63.62	65.07	66.52	67.97	69.42
UK	57.08	56.97	56.86	56.53	55.98	55.43	54.88	54.33	53.78
Australia	19.93	19.80	19.67	19.28	18.63	17.98	17.33	16.68	16.03
Canada	32.14	32.23	32.32	32.59	33.04	33.49	33.94	34.39	34.84
Switzerland	71.58	71.68	71.78	72.08	72.58	73.08	73.58	74.08	74.58
China (1)	19.09	20.34	21.59	25.34	31.59	37.84	44.09	50.34	56.59
China (2)	19.09	20.59	22.09	26.59	34.09	41.59	49.09	56.59	64.09
China (3)	19.09	20.84	22.59	27.84	36.59	45.34	54.09	62.84	71.59
China (4)	19.09	21.09	23.09	29.09	39.09	49.09	59.09	69.09	79.09
China (5)	19.09	21.34	23.59	30.34	41.59	52.84	64.09	75.34	86.59
China (6)	19.09	21.59	24.09	31.59	44.09	56.59	69.09	81.59	94.09

Source: Same as Table 6.12. China (1), China (2), China (3), China (4), China (5), and China (6) are the results corresponding to estimation results assuming that China's sci-tech OC will increase by 1.25%, 1.50%, 1.75%, 2.00%, 2.25%, and 2.50% annually from 2020 to 2050, respectively.

of eight major worldwide money issuers from the year 2021, and the worldwide status of Australian dollar will face challenges because of low sci-tech OC in a few years to come.

It is noticeable that although Canadian sci-tech OC will increase steadily from 2020, its ranking will become the second lowest in about a decade in 2030, and the international status of Canadian dollar will also face challenges in about a decade.

Table 16.3 shows that even if China can achieve average annual increase of 1.25% of sci-tech OC from 2020 to 2050, slightly lower than the corresponding Japanese average yearly increase of 1.30% from 1978 to 2008, its sci-tech OC will be 56.59%, slightly higher than the corresponding British sci-tech OC in 2050. If China can achieve an average annual increase of 1.50% from 2020 to 2050, slightly higher than the corresponding three-decade Japanese average yearly increase 1.30%, then Chinese sci-tech OC will be 64.09%. Three decades is a relatively long time, almost half of a traditional lifetime, predicting future with historical trends is the only way we can depend on. However, worldwide environment change, particularly trade frictions worldwide may make any long period forecast problematic.

16.7 A New Method of Currency Internationalization Forecast

16.7.1 *Limitations of traditional forecasting of currency internationalization*

Science and technology are indeed the chief factors to affect and even determine trade, foreign exchanges, currency evaluation, and money globalization as shown in Chapters 8 and 14. Data in Table 7.1 show that although sci-tech OC of Eurozone has been about half of Japan, UK, and Switzerland, yet internationalization status of Euro has been significantly higher than that of Japanese yen, British pound, and Swiss franc. These facts clearly indicate that sci-tech OC is not the only factor affecting currency globalization. The main reason for the Euro's continued maintenance of the world's second largest worldwide money is nothing more than the economic and trade scale of the Eurozone which far exceeds that of Japan and the United Kingdom. Therefore, while considering the critical factor of sci-tech OC, the economic and trade scale of money issuers is also vital in determining currency globalization.

16.7.2 *A new method to predict currency internationalization*

Results in Chapter 15 show that global trade is the main force to drive the global foreign exchange market, and therefore the decisive force in global foreign exchange market and currency internationalization. Results of Chapters 7 and 8 show that sci-tech OC is the decisive factor for exporters to choose their settlement currencies, so sci-tech OC determines exports, and the main force of imports is the main reflection of purchasing power of a country or region, or simply gross domestic product. Imports and exports are inseparable, so we can measure the total usage of a money or total autonomy of import and export by the product of sci-tech OC of a currency issuer and the worldwide share of GDP. These two factors together can better reflect the high dependence on the import and export. The total usage of a money in the global foreign exchange market is itself the meaning of currency internationalization. This indicator should be a better way to predict money globalization. Table 16.4 gives the globalization levels of chief currencies using this method compared with the traditional results in Table 4.1.

Table 16.4 shows that the product share of the product of sci-tech and GDP share of USA, Eurozone, and Japan is very close to the world share of average daily foreign exchange turnover. The ratio of the former over the latter was only 5.9%, 2.1%, and 3.1% higher than the latter. The ratio of the product share of Euro and yen to the currency's foreign exchange turnover share was slightly higher than 100%, indicating that both Eurozone and Japan have enough sci-tech OC and purchasing power to support Euro and yen. The extra import capability of Eurozone and Japan is somewhat discounted by USD settlement of imports such as crude oil due to the monopolistic power of the of the USD. Lower than 100% ratios of product share over the average daily turnover share of British pound, Australian dollar, Canadian dollar, and Swiss franc indicate that these four money issuers do not have enough sci-tech and import capability to support.

Attention should be paid to the lowest product share over the average daily turnover share of Australian dollar, the average yearly ratio 24.1% was less than a quarter, implying that Australian dollar has the weakest support of its sci-tech OC and imports, and Australian dollar's high profile in worldwide foreign exchange market has been largely the result of US support. The international positions of Canadian dollar and British pound are also the result of US support to a lesser degree. Mutually holding of

Table 16.4: Comparisons of Currency Internationalization Using Product of Sci-tech OC and World GDP Share of Currency Issuers and Share of Average Daily Turnovers in the Global Foreign Exchange Market (2013–2020) (Unit: %)

Data Type	**The Product of GDP World Share and Sci-tech OC**				**Share of Product of Eight Currencies**				
Year/Currency	**2013**	**2016**	**2019**	**2020**	**2013**	**2016**	**2019**	**2020**	**Annual Average**
USD	0.166	0.179	0.180	0.180	53.0	55.3	53.0	52.2	53.4
EUR	0.064	0.058	0.059	0.061	20.5	18.0	17.4	17.7	18.4
JPY	0.043	0.043	0.038	0.036	13.8	13.4	11.2	10.5	12.2
GBP	0.020	0.022	0.019	0.018	6.4	6.8	5.7	5.3	6.1
AUD	0.004	0.003	0.003	0.003	1.1	1.0	1.0	0.9	1.0
CAD	0.006	0.006	0.006	0.006	1.9	1.7	1.9	1.8	1.8
CHF	0.005	0.006	0.006	0.006	1.8	1.8	1.9	1.8	1.8
RMB	0.005	0.007	0.027	0.033	1.6	2.1	7.8	9.7	5.3
Total	0.314	0.325	0.339	0.344	100.0	100.0	100.0	100.0	100.0
Currency	**World Share of Average Daily Turnover**				**World Average Daily Turnovers of Eight Currencies**				**Annual Average**
USD	43.52	43.79	44.15	43.88	49.48	50.27	51.56	50.22	50.38
EUR	16.70	15.70	16.14	14.10	18.99	18.02	18.85	16.14	18.00
JPY	11.52	10.81	8.40	10.51	13.10	12.41	9.81	12.02	11.84
GBP	5.91	6.40	6.40	5.90	6.72	7.35	7.47	6.75	7.07
AUD	4.32	3.44	3.38	3.45	4.91	3.95	3.95	4.10	4.23
CAD	2.28	2.57	2.52	2.82	2.59	2.95	2.94	3.22	2.93
CHF	2.58	2.40	2.48	3.59	2.93	2.76	2.90	3.94	3.13
RMB	1.12	1.99	2.16	3.15	1.27	2.29	2.52	3.60	2.42
Total	87.95	87.10	85.63	87.39	100.00	100.00	100.00	100.00	100.00
Currency					**Ratio of Share of Product and Share of Average Daily Turnover**				
USD					107.0	110.0	102.8	104.2	105.9
EUR					107.8	99.6	92.5	109.5	102.1
JPY					105.0	107.6	114.0	87.6	103.1

Table 16.4: (*Continued*)

Currency					**Ratio of Share of Product and Share of Average Daily Turnover**				
GBP					95.5	92.0	76.6	78.8	85.6
AUD					22.9	25.7	25.5	22.7	24.1
CAD					73.5	58.8	64.1	56.3	62.7
CHF					59.7	65.5	66.1	46.6	58.4
RMB					126.8	91.5	310.9	268.3	219.1
Total					100.0	100.0	100.0	100.0	100.0
Correlation Coefficient between the Product of eight currencies and the Average Daily Turnover	99.72	99.87	98.87	98.54					

Source: Sci-tech OC is from Table 8.3, world GDP share from Table 16.2; world share of average daily turnovers of major currencies is from Table 4.1.

net long-term securities positions of the US and Australia, UK, and Canada given in Table 13.7 provide evidence.

16.7.3 *Explanation of the inconsistency between the ratio of the RMB product and the average daily turnover*

Table 16.2 shows that the ratio of the product of China's global GDP share and sci-tech OC to the average daily foreign exchange turnover was 126.8%, 91.5%, 310.9%, and 268.3% in 2013, 2016, 2019, and 2020, respectively. The annual average is as high as 219.1%, which is significantly higher than the corresponding ratios of all other seven currencies. RMB ratio significantly higher than 100% indicates that it is inappropriate to estimate China's independent imports by its purchasing power using GDP data. This is due to the high proportion of foreign-invested enterprises in China's imports as analyzed by Zhang (2021), and foreign-invested imports in China are not Chinese imports, which naturally have little effect on the internationalization of the RMB. In addition, as shown in Table 16.4, from 2016 to 2019, the ratio of the product of China's GDP and sci-tech OC to the average daily foreign exchange turnover more than tripled from 90.1% to 307.2%, reflecting the significant increase of China's sci-tech OC in the past 4 years. These results also provide another basis for the analysis in Chapter 12 that the level of RMB globalization in 2019 increased by two to being sixth in the worldwide ranking from eighth in 2016.

Table 16.4 also shows that the ratio of the product of China's GDP share and sci-tech OC to the average daily foreign exchange turnover decreased slightly from 310.9% to 268.3% from 2019 to 2020, which is also consistent with the result that the international status of the RMB in 2020 slightly dropped from the sixth rank in 2019 to seventh.

Therefore, the product of sci-tech OC and GDP world share is a good substitute to estimate money internationalization. We will use this method to forecast changes in the worldwide status of chief world currencies in the coming three decades.

16.8 Changes in the Internationalization Positions of Major World Currencies in the Future

16.8.1 *Problems with forecasting currency internationalization in the future and methods to resolve such problems*

Most research papers or textbooks use historical data to forecast future progress of any area or subject. Historical average daily turnovers of currencies in the worldwide foreign exchange market are used to forecast future changes of currency internationalization. There are obvious problems to forecast future development of internationalization of major currencies. The first problem starts with the starting point in history, or how far back history can go; different numbers of historical periods yield different historical average growth rates. The second related problem that cannot be avoided is how far into the future. The third problem is that different currencies have different maturing stages related to the progress statuses of the money issuers. Thus, choosing the same historical data, different average historical growth rates may not maintain to the same degree in the same future target time. Therefore, different degrees of subjective factor must be considered such as the historical time selection and the extent to which the selected historical time will maintain the historical growth rate in the future. These factors will affect the prediction results, and the uncertainty and errors of the calculation results are unavoidable.

However, the worldwide share of GDP of major money issuers can be more easily forecast, and sci-tech OC of most chief currencies issuers can also be estimated more reliably because most of such economies have already reached their relatively matured status, and their sci-tech OC has also reached relatively stable stages. Therefore, we can forecast future changes of internationalization of major currencies using the method shown in Table 16.4 more reliably.

16.8.2 *Forecast results of internationalization positions top eight world currencies*

Table 16.4 shows correlation coefficients between the product of the worldwide GDP share and the product of sci-tech OC of a global currency and its average daily foreign exchange turnover share was over 99% on average from 2013 to 2020. The high correlation coefficient shows that the product of the world GDP share and sci-tech OC of the currency issuer are good substitutes for its average daily turnover in global foreign exchange market. Using this new method, we can forecast the internationalization positions of major eight world currencies from 2019 to 2050. Table 16.5 gives the results.

16.8.3 *Prediction of USD in the next three decades*

Table 16.5 shows that despite the steady decline in the share of world foreign exchange turnover, USD will continue dominating global foreign exchange market in the next three decades with around more than 10% higher share than RMB in 2050 despite the fact that Chinese economy may return to top world economy around 2030 as shown in Table 16.2 and Chinese sci-tech OC may become similar to the corresponding US sci-tech OC in 2050 as shown in Table 16.3. The difference between CNY world share 16.97% is just over half the corresponding USD share of 31.29% in 2050 even if China continues improving sci-tech OC of 1.75% in the next three decades. We will discuss related reasons later in this chapter with longer historical evidence.

Table 16.5: Internationalization Positions of World's Top Eight Currencies (2019–2050) (Unit: %)

Year/ Currency	2019	2020	2021	2022	2025	2030	2035	2040	2045	2050
USD	44.15	43.88	42.89	42.41	40.73	39.16	37.43	35.38	32.87	31.29
EUR	16.14	14.10	14.39	14.36	13.79	12.37	10.88	9.23	7.88	7.57
JPY	8.40	10.51	10.15	10.02	9.87	8.62	7.32	6.15	5.07	4.94
GBP	6.40	5.90	6.13	6.11	6.03	5.94	5.76	5.52	5.20	4.91
AUD	3.38	3.59	3.83	3.72	3.59	3.39	3.14	2.88	2.59	2.37
CAD	2.52	2.82	2.92	2.95	2.98	2.71	2.38	2.06	1.75	1.69
CHF	2.48	3.45	3.44	3.41	3.35	3.05	2.66	2.29	1.94	1.87
RMB (1)	2.61	3.15	3.42	3.67	4.65	6.40	8.31	10.39	12.51	13.42
RMB (2)	2.61	3.15	3.46	3.76	4.88	6.90	9.14	11.57	14.06	15.20
RMB (3)	2.61	3.15	3.51	3.84	5.11	7.41	9.96	12.75	15.61	16.97
RMB (4)	2.61	3.15	3.55	3.93	5.34	7.92	10.79	13.92	17.16	18.75
RMB (5)	2.61	3.15	3.59	4.02	5.57	8.42	11.61	15.10	18.72	20.53
RMB (6)	2.61	3.15	3.63	4.10	5.80	8.93	12.43	16.28	20.27	22.31

Source: Calculated using the method in Table 16.3 and data in Tables 16.2 and 16.3. Share of eight major currencies in 2020 average daily average turnovers is from Table 12.7; the six different scenarios of RMB are the same as in Table 18.3 with assumed annual growth rate of sci-tech OC of China 1.25%, 1.50%, 1.75%, 2.00%, 2.25%, and 2.50% from 2021 to 2050.

16.8.4 *Time when RMB becomes world's fifth major currency*

Table 12.5 shows that RMB may become the world's fifth currency in a year or two when the share of RMB foreign exchange turnover will exceed that of AUD in 2022 with an average yearly growth rate of sci-tech OC of China at 1.50%.

16.8.5 *Time when RMB becomes fourth and third international currency*

Table 16.5 shows that RMB share in global foreign exchange market turnover at 6.4% may exceed that of British pound at 5.94% for the first time in 2030 even with an average yearly growth rate of sci-tech OC at 1.25% from 2020 to 2030, becoming the fourth international money in or before

2030. Table 16.5 also shows that RMB share in global foreign exchange market turnover at 8.31% may exceed that of Japanese yen at 7.32% in 2035 even with an average annual growth rate of sci-tech OC at 1.25% from 2020 to 2035; thus, RMB may become the third international money before 2035.

16.8.6 *Time when RMB becomes world's second international currency*

Table 16.5 shows that RMB share of worldwide foreign exchange turnover of 10.39% may exceed that of Euro at 9.23% in 2040 even with average annual growth rate of sci-tech OC at 1.25% from 2020 to 2040; thus, RMB may replace Euro as the second international currency before 2040.

16.9 Historical Evidence of Changes of Major International Currencies

Table 16.5 shows that about two decades after China returns to the top world economy around 2030, RMB will remain the third international currency in 2030. It takes more than 5 years for RMB to replace Euro to become the second world currency before 2040. Two decades after China returns to the world's top economy in 2050, RMB will still have a gap of more than 10% with that of the USD in 2050. These forecast results seem incomprehensible, but historical evidence of changes of major world currencies in the past century relative to their economic sizes can give us some convincing answers.

"Reserve currencies have come and gone. In the past 2500 years, there have been more than a dozen reserve currencies in the world, and they have all withdrawn from the stage of history. The pound lost its reserve status in the first half of the 20th century, and the U.S. dollar will lose in the first half of the 21st century ... The loss of reserve status will lead to a series of economic and political crises in the United States" Perasud (2004). The history of many reserve currencies should give us an insight of today's worldwide finance. However, due to the lack of related data, most of the introductions and studies or statements about international currencies before the 19th century are problematic to corroborate, which is beyond the scope of this book.

16.9.1 *Changes in international status of pound sterling*

As the United Kingdom led the worldwide industrial revolution and the British maritime hegemony made the United Kingdom the world's largest trading nation, it also made the pound sterling a well-deserved chief global money in the 19th century. Statistics show that in 1860, the United Kingdom absorbed 30% of worldwide imports. By 1890, the proportion had dropped to 20% Inlah (1958). At the same time, the United Kingdom was the world's largest exporter of processed goods and services, as well as a worldwide consumer of food and raw materials. Large amounts of imports and exports and re-exports have naturally made London the origin and concentration of global commodity trading and forward/futures exchanges, and the discovery of major commodity spot and forward prices. These prices were naturally denominated in British pounds. About 60% of the world trade was settled in British pounds from 1860 to 1914 (Williams, 1968). The large amount of trade made the United Kingdom the world's largest credit country. London also became the world's long-term investment and financing center, and then became the world's largest fiscal center. In addition, the British Empire began to encourage the use of pound sterling throughout the empire as early as the early 18th century to simplify and standardize various transactions. The worldwide monopoly of the British pound declined before the beginning of World War I for the first time (Table 1, Eichengreen, 2005). The overall decline began before the war, but it took nearly half a century until the end of the 1950s when the British pound's status as the world's number one worldwide currency was replaced by the USD.

16.9.2 *Pound sterling spillover effect and its enlightenment*

With the rise of Western European countries such as France and Germany, Britain's monopoly on worldwide trade and money gradually declined. Historical data show (the output value priced in 1990 International Geary-Khamis dollars) that, the second year after the reunification of Germany in 1871, that is, in 1873, the German output of 79.981 billion German Mark surpassed France for the first time. German output surpassed France by 31.9% by 1899. Yet, 15% of Deutsche Mark reserves was still slightly lower than 16% of francs in 1899 (Table 1, Eichengreen, 2005). Germany's output surpassed Britain by 1.4% for the first time in 1908, and Germany's output surpassed Britain and France by 5.7% and 64.3% in 1913, respectively, yet mark reserve ratio remained unchanged at 15% in 1899 during the same period, 33% and 18% lower than 48% and 31% of the British pound and French franc the same year. These results show that the economic size of a money issuer is not the only determinant of the currency's worldwide status. The international status of any money lags its economic status for years or even decades.

16.9.3 *The rise of the USD*

The replacement of the British pound by the USD as the worldwide monopoly money is the most recent and only historically documented currency takeover. Nevertheless, the data on the initial stage of the replacement of the British pound by the USD are still not detailed and accurate. As a matter of fact, industrial production of the United States of 106.36 billion (International Geary–Khamis dollars in 1900) surpassed the United Kingdom's 105.80 billion for the first time as early as 1872. However, the USD had not yet entered the top three worldwide currencies in the world for over four decades until 1913. The main reason was that there was no modern central bank in the United States during the period. The establishment of the Federal Reserve in 1914 improved the liquidity of the New York market and the status of New York as an international economic center and created necessary conditions for the global promotion and popularization of the USD. Studies have shown that World War I led the United States to become a net foreign creditor country for the first time (Eichengreen, 2000). USD replaced German mark as the third international money in the 1930s, yet USD was still far behind French franc then. According to the calculation results of Triffin (1964), the USD reserves were $600 million in 1928, accounting for 19.0% of world total, and the British pound and franc accounted for 56.7% and 24.3% the same year. The output of the United States was 3.26 times and 4.37 times that of the United Kingdom and France, respectively, in 1928.

Due to the collapse of the gold standard system in 1933, total USD reserves plummeted to $60 million, and its share dropped sharply to 2.8%, which was much lower than corresponding share of the British pound and the French franc at 66.2% and 28.4%, respectively. Output of the United States was 2.46 times and 3.39 times that of the United Kingdom and France, respectively, during the same year. These results show that more than 60 years after the United States replaced UK as the world's largest economy in 1872, there was still a huge gap between USD reserves and that of the secondly ranked French franc.

Shortly after World War II, the US's leading position in worldwide military, economy and trade, finance, and technology has significantly surpassed that of any other country, yet the worldwide status of the USD did not naturally coincide with its military, economic and technology status. Data show that the British pound still accounted for more than half of the worldwide reserves in 1949, but the British proportion fell to 36% in 1957. USD completely replaced the British pound as the world's number one reserve currency until the end of the 1950s (Eichengreen, 2005). Thus, it took USD nearly 90 years after the United States replaced the United Kingdom as the world's largest economy to replace British pound as the world's top international money when the US economy was 4.67 times the size of the United Kingdom.

The USD has maintained its dominant currency status for more than half a century, and the US military, economy, trade, science and technology and other factors all contributed to USD's dominant status. However, chief developed countries such as Germany, Japan, and France have not actively promoted the globalization of their currencies in consideration of their economic advances and financial market stability before the 1990s. This is also an important reason for the USD to maintain its dominant position (Eichengreen, 2005).

As early as 2005, 3 years before the 2008 economic crisis broke out, Eichengreen (2005) raised doubts and concerns about the sustainability of the attractiveness of USD reserves. Eichengreen was worried that the United States owes worldwide debt more than 25% of US GDP and the US current account deficit and 6% of GDP. What was worrying was that the United States had to allow high inflation to increase its debt-to-GDP ratio. High inflation may lead the US dollar a repeat of British pound's loss of worldwide reserves. The ratio of US government debt to GDP has increased significantly in the years following 2008 world recession crisis and it increased faster in 2020 and 2021. Eichengreen's doubts and concerns should become stronger with the faster growing US debt ratios.

16.9.4 *Winner takes all or a few coins to share?*

The monopoly of British pound in the worldwide financial system before 1914 and the second half of the 19th century had led many scholars to conclude that the "winner takes all" the main reserve money and "the fertilizer does not flow to outsiders" once this monopoly is obtained. The conclusion is that the status is difficult to shake. "At any moment in history, there is always one money that dominates worldwide reserves, not two or more" (Persaud, 2004). However, Eichengreen (2005) believes that the dominance of a currency is not convincing enough, and it is more likely that a few currencies will share the worldwide reserve status, which is also proven by data from many historical periods. In fact, the two conclusions are not totally contradictory to each other. When the dominant money's position drops, sharing becomes the norm.

16.9.5 *Trend of international currencies in the future*

Eichengreen (2005) considered the economic and trade scale of the Eurozone and other factors, and pointed out that in the future, only the Euro can share the status of the reserve money with the USD, and the conditions for the RMB to share the global reserve function were not yet mature. Eichengreen's article was published in 2005. China's GDP was only 19.2% of the GDP of Eurozone in 2004, 1 year before Eichengreen (2005) wrote his article, yet China's GDP surpassed the Eurozone for the first time in 2018, and the former exceeded the latter by 14.0% in 2020. Thus, RMB's potentiality as the chief world money has increased significantly in the past two decades.

The above results show that the USD replaced the British pound as the world's dominant global currency almost 90 years after the US output surpassed that of the UK for the first time in 1872. Even after deducting the 42 years before the establishment of the Federal Reserve in 1914, it still took USD nearly half a century to replace British pound as the top global exchange. In addition, although Germany surpassed France and the United Kingdom in output in 1873 and 1908, respectively, the global reserve status of the German mark was still less than that of the French franc and the British pound in 1913.

These results show that the international status of a chief world money lags at least a few decades behind the ranking of its issuer's world economic ranking. As world economy and trade will be driven more by science and technology progress, global currency usage inertia may be shortened, and thus future may not follow the historical pattern. However, historical inertia cannot be removed. Relevant historical evidence certainly has great enlightenment for us to judge the global changes of chief currencies in the future.

16.10 Major Currency Circles

International currencies have been widely used and studied. Yet, chief international money circles are not discussed as much in either professional or academic fields. We introduce and discuss three major worldwide currency circles in this section. Table 16.6 gives the correlation coefficients among the top 20 global currencies from 2001 and 2019.

Table 16.6: Correlation Coefficients among Daily Average Turnovers of Top 30 International Currencies (2001–2019) (Unit: %)

Currency	USD	ERU	JPY	GBP	AUD	CAD	CHF	CNY	HKD	NZD
USD	—	98.14	94.67	98.57	96.85	98.99	95.27	90.24	82.64	99.49
EUR	98.14	—	92.19	97.63	97.34	97.89	98.84	81.48	81.79	96.95
JPY	94.67	92.19	—	90.13	97.57	92.95	87.83	82.02	60.47	94.25
GBP	98.57	97.63	90.13	—	93.79	97.49	96.52	87.82	85.39	98.60
AUD	96.85	97.34	97.57	93.79	—	94.95	94.78	78.98	70.02	95.71
CAD	98.99	97.89	92.95	97.49	94.95	—	94.57	90.39	83.15	97.87
CHF	95.27	98.84	87.83	96.52	94.78	94.57	—	74.97	81.24	94.83
CNY	90.24	81.48	82.02	87.82	78.98	90.39	74.97	—	81.94	90.32
HKD	82.64	81.79	60.47	85.39	70.02	83.15	81.24	81.94	—	81.65
NZD	99.49	96.95	94.25	98.60	95.71	97.87	94.83	90.32	81.65	—
SEK	95.69	95.41	86.02	97.88	89.33	95.88	95.85	85.49	84.83	96.85
KRW	95.28	92.28	82.69	95.29	85.71	96.74	88.49	94.73	92.17	94.08
SGD	97.93	94.06	90.63	96.23	90.85	98.73	89.81	95.89	84.97	97.46
NOK	95.76	92.89	84.66	97.45	87.99	93.71	92.77	89.38	88.35	97.45
MXN	92.96	89.13	98.30	87.71	96.36	88.98	84.69	81.02	60.09	92.89
INR	95.01	91.28	82.08	93.94	85.80	95.19	87.24	94.94	93.69	93.84
RUB	93.63	91.04	98.51	88.29	97.73	90.23	86.60	79.84	61.56	92.87
ZAR	97.88	93.59	93.66	94.90	94.88	94.69	90.05	90.96	80.45	98.04
TRY	92.70	87.11	97.43	86.75	92.15	92.34	80.20	89.33	61.20	92.01
BRL	96.81	92.04	95.72	91.59	94.68	95.50	86.04	92.41	75.19	95.71

Table 16.6: (*Continued*)

Currency	USD	ERU	JPY	GBP	AUD	CAD	CHF	CNY	HKD	NZD
TWD	91.77	86.84	77.27	91.49	80.29	92.36	82.21	96.00	93.81	90.56
DKK	93.11	87.45	95.56	90.51	91.64	89.57	84.64	86.19	63.37	95.37
PLN	95.49	97.98	93.15	94.39	96.43	95.74	97.75	76.63	73.07	95.32
THB	94.56	88.09	84.58	92.68	85.53	93.21	82.91	97.65	88.35	94.05
IDR	87.79	82.84	71.00	87.47	75.80	87.63	78.37	92.87	95.68	86.28
HUF	96.50	98.43	92.02	93.95	97.73	95.92	95.76	79.44	79.58	94.01
CZK	96.39	91.55	90.36	92.94	92.33	93.33	87.08	92.07	83.39	95.82
ILS	94.47	88.22	84.05	93.62	83.86	94.60	83.66	98.70	88.04	94.59
CLP	95.41	89.91	93.28	90.06	92.83	93.26	83.57	92.44	76.51	94.15
PHP	91.22	89.17	75.44	90.41	82.11	91.65	85.64	89.68	96.51	89.17

Source: Calculated using data of daily average foreign exchange turnovers of world's major currencies from 2001 to 2019 updated by the Bank for International Settlements in December 2019.

16.10.1 *USD currency circle*

Table 16.6 shows that USD has correlation coefficients between foreign exchange turnover of USD and British pound GBP, Canadian dollar CAD, and New Zealand dollar NZD at 98.57%, 98.99%, and 99.49% from 2001 to 2019. These correlation coefficients were higher than the correlation coefficients between USD and all other currencies. These high correlation coefficients indicate that these four currencies of English-speaking countries belong to the world's top money circle led by the world's top currency USD.

16.10.2 *Euro currency circle*

Table 16.6 also shows that the correlation coefficient between Euro and Swiss franc was 98.84%, higher than the corresponding correlation coefficient of 98.57% between USD and GBP at the same time. The correlation coefficient between Euro and Swedish krona and Norwegian krone was 95.41% and 92.89%, respectively, from 2001 to 2019. Although these two correlation coefficients were slightly lower with Euro than with USD at the same time, Swedish krona and Norwegian krone do not belong to the USD Currency circle as introduced earlier. Thus, we may consider that Euro, Swiss franc, Swedish krona, and Norwegian krone form the second major world currency circle led by the second chief world currency Euro.

16.10.3 *Japanese yen currency circle*

Table 16.6 shows that although correlation coefficients between Japanese yen and USD, Euro, and British pound (GBP) were 94.67%, 92.19%, and 90.13%, these correlation coefficients were lower than those among USD currencies circles and among chief Euro money circles introduced above. Thus, USD, Euro, and GBP do not belong to Japanese yen circle. With the only exception of Australian dollar, all other top 14 currencies do not belong to Japanese yen circle as they either belong to USD circle or Euro circle or their correlation coefficients with Japanese yen were significantly below 90% or lower than correlation coefficient between Chinese yuan with the top 14 currencies. It is noticeable that correlation coefficients between Japanese yen and chief Easter Asian currencies Chinese yuan, South Korean won (KRW), Hong Kong Dollar (HKD), Taiwan dollar (TWD), Thailand baht (THB) were either very low or lower than correlation coefficients between Chinese yuan and these currencies. These correlation coefficients show that Japanese yen is not a major global currency with high correlation coefficients with its cultural neighbor currencies as the USD money circle or with its geological neighbor currencies as the Euro money circle. Despite high correlation coefficients between Japanese yen and Mexican peso, Russian ruble, Turkish lira (TRY), Brazilian real (BRR) and other currencies, these currencies do not seem to belong to Japanese yen money circle as there are neither geological nor cultural connections between these currencies and Japanese yen is not so close. Thus, there is no clear currency circle for the third world currency yen.

16.10.4 *RMB currency circle*

Although RMB was ranked No. 8 world money by BIS in Table 4.1, RMB has already had its currency circle according to results shown in Table 16.6. Table 16.6 shows that correlation coefficients between RMB and Taiwan dollar (TWD), Singaporean dollar (SGD), and Korean won (KRW) were 96.00%, 95.89%, and 94.73% from 2001 to 2019, respectively. These three correlation coefficients were all higher than the corresponding correlation coefficients between these three Eastern Asian currencies with Japanese yen. Thus, we may consider RMB, and these three Asian "Little Dragon Currencies" form the RMB currency circle led by RMB. Besides these three East Asian currencies, correlation coefficients between RMB and Israeli shekel (ILS) at 98.70%, Thailand baht (THB) at 97.65%, and Saudi Arabian Riyal (SAR) were higher not only than correlation coefficients between these three currencies with Japanese yen but also higher than correlation coefficients between these three currencies with USD and EUR. Thus, we may consider that these three currencies also belong to RMB currency circle.

16.10.5 *Major world currency circles in a broader sense*

Table 16.6 shows that the correlation coefficient between USD and Australian dollar (AUD) at 86.85% was slightly lower than the corresponding correlation coefficients between AUD with Euro at 97.34% and with JPY at 97.57%. As three other currencies in the USD currency circle such as the GBP, CAD, and NZD are all English-speaking or Anglo-Saxon currencies, it is natural to include AUD into the USD currency circle, thus the USD currency circle has all five Anglo-Saxon currencies. The correlation coefficient between EUR and Danish krone (DKK) at 87.45% was slightly lower than the corresponding correlation coefficients between DKK with USD at 93.11% and with JPY at 95.56%. As three other currencies in the EUR currency circle such as the CHF, SEK, and NOK are all European currencies, it is natural to include DKK into the EUR currency circle, thus the EUR currency circle has five major European currencies other than GBP.

Similarly, Table 16.6 shows that as the correlation coefficient between RMB and Hong Kong dollar (HKD) at 81.94% was slightly lower than the corresponding correlation coefficient between HKD with USD at 82.64%, it is higher than the corresponding correlation coefficients between HKD and EUR at 81.79% and HKD with JPY at 60.47%. As three other currencies in RMB currency circle, KRW, SGD, and TWD, are all "Little Dragon" currency and HKD is the other "Little Dragon" money, it is natural to include HKD into the RMB currency circle, thus RMB currency circle includes five "Dragon" currencies. As correlation coefficients between RMB and ILS, THB, and SAR were higher than the corresponding coefficients between these three currencies with USD, EUR, and JPY, these three Asian currencies may also be considered in RMB currency circle.

16.11 Evidence of Contribution of Currency Internationalization to Net Exports of Charges for the Use of Intellectual Property

It is intuitive that exports and net exports of charges for the use of IP are the results of sci-tech OC or sci-tech internationalization. The higher the sci-tech OC, the higher the net exports of charges for the use of IP of a currency issuer. However, net exports of charges for the use of IP of any currency issuer are not the sole result of sci-tech OC, currency internationalization has its own contribution because imports and imports of charges for the use of IP are booked in terms of currency.

16.11.1 *Distribution of global net exports of charges for the use of intellectual property*

Chapter 6 introduced exports and imports of costs for the use of intellectual property of most countries and regions of the world. Table 6.12 shows that only the United States, Japan, Germany, Switzerland, the United Kingdom, Finland, France, Denmark, Israel, and Sweden have maintained positive net exports of costs for the use of IP over 200 countries and regions of the world from 2005 to 2020 most of the time. In other words, only these 10 countries in the world have more than 50% sci-tech OC, and all the 10 countries with positive net exports of charges for the use of IP are developed countries. All other developed countries and regions and all progressing countries are in deficit of charges for the use of IP, or sci-tech OC less than 50%.

Table 6.12 shows that the United States net exports of costs for the use of IP has remained at the highest level, and its share of total world net exports of charges for the use of IP decreased about 20% from over 70% to over 50% from 2005 to 2020, showing the relative worldwide monopoly of US intellectual property. Germany and Japan are the second and third net exporters of costs for the use of IP; the sum of net exports of charges for the use of IP of these two exporters has been just over that of US since 2016.

Switzerland and UK form the third-tier technology providers of the world as their total net exports of charges for the use of intellectual property are about half of the total net exports of charges for the use of IP of Germany and Japan. Other five countries like France, Finland, Denmark,

Sweden, and Israel form the fourth tier of technology providers as their total net exports of costs for the use of IP are about half of the total net exports of charges for the use of IP of Switzerland and UK.

16.11.2 *Impact of US quantitative easing policies on US net exports of charges for the use of intellectual property*

Using US exports and imports of charges for the use of IP, we can find the compound yearly growth rates of net US export of charges for the use of IP were 15.68%, 4.11%, and −1.77% in 3–6-year periods from 2002 to 2008, 2008 to 2014 and from 2014 to 2020, respectively. The highest CAGR in the 6-year period before 2008 indicated that US enjoyed the fastest growth of net exports of charges for the use of intellectual property before the 2008 world rescission crisis. Yet, CAGR declined dramatically after the financial crisis during the 6-year period when United States implemented its quantitative easing policies from 2009 to in 2014, and the CAGR decreased further to negative 1.77% after US withdrew of its last quantitative easing policy in 2014. These results clearly indicate that the US monetary policies in response to 2008 world rescission crisis or the globalization of the US dollar has a significant impact on the net exports of costs for the use of IP. In other words, the net US exports of costs for the use of IP not only reflect intellectual property itself, but are also closely related to US monetary policies or US globalization. The reason that net US exports of costs or the utilization of IP grew significantly before 2008 was that those exports of charges for the use of IP went together with US investment or US capital when USD was relatively weak from 2002 to 2008.

16.11.3 *Competition among major world technology providers*

Careful study of data related to Table 6.12 finds that the CAGR of total net exports of charges for the utilization of IP of other nine net exporters was 10.69% from 2005 to 2008, which was lower than the corresponding CAGR of US net exports of costs for the use of IP at 14.35% during the same period. CAGR of total net exports of charges for the use of IP of other nine net exporters increased to 11.76% from 2008 to 2014, much higher than the corresponding CAGR of US net exports of charges for the use of IP at 4.11% in the same period. CAGR of total net exports of charges for the use of IP of other nine net exporters declined to 3.68% from 2014 to 2020, yet still higher than the corresponding CAGR of US net exports of charges for the utilization of IP at −1.77% during the same period.

These results show that while the 2008 global financial crisis had a significant impact on the US net exports of charges for the use of intellectual property, it also gave other chief developed countries a rare opportunity to catch up or share global net exports of charges for the use of IP. These results also indicate that competition among world's major technology providers has become more intensified after the 2008 world rescission crisis.

16.12 Contribution of Sci-tech and Currency to Global Net Exports of Charges for the Use of Intellectual Property

Imports and exports of charges for the use of intellectual property include all usefulness of intellectual property of a currency issuer. Therefore, data of costs for the utilization of intellectual property are more comprehensive than global patent information when analyzing sci-tech OC. Chapter 12 defined sci-tech OC and sci-tech internationalization using data of charges for the use of IP. Sci-tech OC and sci-tech internationalization are good quantitative measures for us to compare sci-tech levels of different currency issuers. Sci-tech OC is highly related to the surplus and deficit of charges for the use of intellectual property, but sci-tech OC reflects the level of technological levels of different currency issuers. Despite the extreme importance of sci-tech on economic, and trade and financial markets, the net exports of charges for the use of IP contain not only the contribution of sci-tech but also the contribution of currency internationalization. We will analyze the contribution of sci-tech and currency to the net export of charges for the use of IP in this section.

16.12.1 *Brief analysis of contribution of sci-tech and currency to the net exports of charges for the use of intellectual property*

Above arguments show that net exports of charges for the utilization of intellectual property of a currency issuer are the results of not only sci-tech of the currency issuer itself but also the results of monetary policies or internationalization of the currency. Results of mutual influence between sci-tech and currency internationalization in Section 14.5 show that the former has an average impact on the latter (corresponding to the traditional currency internationalization in Table 14.1) at 50.43%, while the latter has an average impact on the former at 49.57%. Corresponding to the better currency internationalization measurement (the currency internationalization measurement result with a discount of "31.5%" in Table 13.5), the former has an average influence of 50.13% on the latter, and the latter has an average influence of 49.87% on the former.

Therefore, we intuitively find that the contribution of sci-tech for the net exports of charges for the use of IP in Table 6.12 should be directly multiplied by 50.43% or 50.87% to get the contribution of sci-tech and be multiplied by 49.57% or 49.13% to get the corresponding currency contribution. However, this intuition is incorrect. The 50.13% and 49.87% represent mutual influence between sci-tech internationalization and currency internationalization given in Chapter 14 are the overall average mutual influence between eight chief worldwide currencies and the sci-tech OC from 2001 to 2019. The contribution to the net surplus of charges for the use of IP of a particular currency issuer should be higher if the currency internationalization is higher. In other words, the higher the degree of currency internationalization, the higher the contribution of the currency issuer. Currencies with various levels of internationalization have various contributions to net exports of charges for the use of IP.

16.12.2 *Contribution analysis of sci-tech and currency to the net surplus of charges for the use of intellectual property of major currency issuers*

Using net exports of charges for the use of IP of major currencies issuers given in Table 6.12 multiplied by the corresponding currency internationalization results in Table 4.1, we can calculate values of net surpluses of charges for the use of IP of chief currency issuers from 2007 to 2019. Table 16.7 gives the results. Table 16.7 shows that currencies of USA and the Eurozone (Germany, France, and Finland together). Japan, UK, and Switzerland together contributed $27.67 billion, $30.19 billion, $38.15 billion, $37.33 billion, and $39.48 billion from 2007 to 2019 every 3 years, respectively, representing 29.66%, 27.50%, 27.27%, 27.48%, and 26.99%

of the total net exports of charges for the use of IP the same time. The 5-year average ratio of all currency contribution was 28.08%, which was much lower than 49.57%, the average contribution of currency (corresponding to traditional currency internationalization in Section 14.5). Therefore, we need to increase the global share of the average daily turnover share of major currencies given in Table 4.1 by 49.57%/28.08 = 1.7655 to match the total currency contribution 49.57%. By multiplying 1.7655% to the currency internationalization in Table 4.1, we can find corresponding currency contributions to net exports of charges for the use of IP, the results are given in Table 16.7.

Table 16.7 shows that multiplying the traditional currency internationalization share of USD, Euro, Japanese yen, British pound, and Swiss franc given in Table 4.1 by 1.6755 matches the total internationalization of the top five currencies contributing to the average of 49.57% of all currencies from 2007 to 2019. The corresponding USD average contribution increased from 43.39% to 76.60%, or 23.29% higher than the average internationalization of the USD at 43.34% from 2007 to 2019, also 27.03% higher than the corresponding average currency contribution of the eight major currencies of 49.57%.

Euro's contribution share to net costs for the use of IP of Germany, France and Finland together was 29.04%, which was 3.59% higher than Euro's average contribution 16.45% from 2007 to 2019, but 20.53% lower than the corresponding average currency contribution of the eight major currencies 49.53%. Japanese yen and the British pound contributed 17.40% and 11.51% to net exports of expenses for the use of intellectual property in the same period. Share of these two currencies was 7.54% and 5.99% higher than their average currency internationalization from 2007 to 2019, yet 32.17% and 38.06% lower than the corresponding total currency contribution of 49.57%, respectively. The average currency contribution share of Swiss franc was merely 5.00%, 2.17% higher than the corresponding average currency contribution 2.83%, 44.57% lower than the corresponding total currency contribution of 49.57%.

These results clearly show that only the USD, the global monopolistic currency, has contributed significantly more than the average contribution of $8 to the net exports of charges for the use of intellectual property, Euro, Japan, British pound, and Swiss franc have contributed slightly more to net exports of charges for the use of intellectual property. Net exports of charges for the use of IP of currency issuers other than the USD are mainly resulted with their sci-tech rather than currency.

Table 16.7: Distribution of Contribution Share to Net Surplus of Charges for the Use of Intellectual Property by Currency and Sci-tech of Major Currency Issuers (2007–2019) (Unit: USD billion, %)

Based on Corresponding Results of Currency Internationalization Given in Table 4.1									
Year/Economy	**US**	**Japan**	**Germany**	**Switzerland**	**UK**	**France**	**Finland**	**Eurozone**	**Total**
2007	25.63	0.56	−0.44	0.36	0.70	0.82	−0.03	0.35	27.67
2010	27.09	0.75	0.23	0.53	0.62	0.70	0.20	1.13	30.19
2013	34.18	1.59	0.81	0.30	0.58	0.35	0.27	1.43	38.15
2016	31.09	2.04	2.74	0.23	0.47	0.36	0.30	3.41	37.33
2019	32.97	1.74	3.30	0.30	0.53	0.07	0.50	3.87	39.48
Total Currency contribution	150.96	6.68	6.64	1.72	2.91	2.31	1.24	10.19	172.81
Total Net Surpluses	347.94	67.79	41.57	60.71	44.70	12.89	7.47	61.93	615.48
Share of Currency Contribution	43.39	9.86	15.98	2.83	6.52	17.92	16.55	16.45	28.08
Total Contribution of Sci-tech	196.98	61.11	34.93	58.99	41.79	10.58	6.23	51.74	442.67
Share of Contribution of Sci-tech	56.61	90.14	84.02	97.17	93.48	82.08	83.45	83.55	71.92
Contribution of Sci-tech World Share	44.50	13.81	7.89	13.33	9.44	2.39	1.41	11.69	97.52
Based on Result of Multiplying Currency Internationalization Given in Table 4.1 by 1.7655									
Year/Economy	**US**	**Japan**	**Germany**	**Switzerland**	**UK**	**France**	**Finland**	**Eurozone**	**Total**
2007	45.25	1.00	−0.78	0.63	1.24	0.12	−0.06	0.61	48.85
2010	47.83	1.33	0.40	0.93	1.10	0.11	0.35	1.99	53.29
2013	60.34	2.80	1.43	0.54	1.03	0.12	0.48	2.53	67.35

(*Continued*)

Table 16.7: (*Continued*)

Based on Result of Multiplying Currency Internationalization Given in Table 4.1 by 1.7655									
Year/Economy	**US**	**Japan**	**Germany**	**Switzerland**	**UK**	**France**	**Finland**	**Eurozone**	**Total**
2016	54.90	3.61	4.84	0.41	0.83	0.14	0.53	6.01	65.90
2019	58.20	3.07	5.83	0.52	0.94	0.12	0.88	6.84	69.69
Total Currency contribution	266.51	11.80	11.73	3.04	5.14	0.61	2.18	17.99	305.09
Total Net Surpluses	347.94	67.79	41.57	60.71	44.70	32.40	7.47	61.93	615.48
Share of Currency Contribution	76.60	17.40	28.21	5.00	11.51	1.89	29.23	29.04	49.57
Total Contribution of Sci-tech	81.42	56.00	29.84	57.68	39.56	31.78	5.28	43.94	321.60
Share of Contribution of Sci-tech	23.40	82.60	71.79	95.00	88.49	98.11	70.77	70.96	50.43
Contribution of Sci-tech World Share	25.32	17.41	9.28	17.93	12.30	9.88	1.19	9.93	70.86
Based on Results of Better Currency Internationalization Given in Table 13.5									
Year/Economy	**US**	**Japan**	**Germany**	**Switzerland**	**UK**	**France**	**Finland**	**Eurozone**	**Total**
2007	35.31	0.88	−0.67	0.58	1.01	0.12	−0.05	0.53	38.44
2010	34.62	1.02	0.33	0.69	0.87	0.11	0.29	1.64	38.95
2013	44.03	2.41	1.12	0.35	0.74	0.12	0.37	1.98	49.63
2016	42.86	2.99	3.81	0.28	0.65	0.14	0.42	4.73	51.66
2019	47.33	2.58	4.64	0.40	0.74	0.12	0.70	5.43	56.60
Total Currency contribution	204.14	9.89	9.22	2.30	4.01	0.61	1.73	14.32	235.28
Total Net Surpluses	347.94	67.79	41.57	60.71	44.70	32.40	7.47	61.93	615.48
Share of Currency Contribution	58.67	14.59	22.19	3.79	8.98	1.89	23.19	23.12	38.23

Total Contribution of Sci-tech	143.80	57.90	32.35	58.41	40.69	31.78	5.74	47.61	391.41
Share of Contribution of Sci-tech	41.33	85.41	77.81	96.21	91.02	98.11	76.81	76.88	61.77
Contribution of Sci-tech World Share	36.74	14.79	8.26	14.92	10.40	8.12	1.47	12.16	86.24

Based on Result of Multiplying Currency Internationalization Given in Table 4.1 by 1.3046

Year/Economy	US	Japan	Germany	Switzerland	UK	France	Finland	Eurozone	Total
2007	46.06	1.15	−0.88	0.76	1.32	0.16	−0.07	0.69	50.14
2010	45.16	1.34	0.43	0.90	1.14	0.15	0.38	2.14	50.82
2013	57.44	3.15	1.46	0.46	0.96	0.16	0.49	2.58	64.75
2016	55.92	3.90	4.97	0.37	0.85	0.18	0.54	6.18	67.39
2019	61.74	3.37	6.05	0.52	0.97	0.15	0.91	7.09	73.84
Total Currency contribution	266.31	12.91	12.03	3.00	5.24	0.80	2.26	18.68	306.94
Total Net Surpluses	347.94	67.79	41.57	60.71	44.70	32.40	7.47	61.93	615.48
Share of Currency Contribution	76.54	19.04	28.95	4.95	11.71	2.47	30.25	30.17	49.87
Total Contribution of Sci-tech	81.63	54.89	29.54	57.71	39.47	31.60	5.21	43.25	319.74
Share of Contribution of Sci-tech	23.46	80.96	71.05	95.05	88.29	97.53	69.75	69.83	50.13
Contribution of Sci-tech World Share	25.38	17.07	9.18	17.94	12.27	9.82	1.62	13.45	70.45

Source: Currency internationalization results from Tables 4.1 and 13.5, and net exports of charges for the use of intellectual property data from Table 6.12.

16.12.3 *Re-analysis of contribution of major currency issuers and sci-tech to the net exports of charges for the use of intellectual property*

The above analysis of currency and sci-tech contribution to net charges for the use of IP is based on currency internationalization using traditional currency internationalization measures. Considering that this chapter has found evidence that the better currency internationalization results are more reasonable compared with traditional currency internationalization, it is necessary for us to find currency and sci-tech contribution corresponding with the better currency internationalization measures. Table 16.7 gives the results.

Table 16.7 shows that with better currency internationalization measures, USD, Euro, Japanese yen, British pound, and Swiss franc had similar contribution to their net exports of charges for the use of IP as with traditional currency internationalization measures because total average contrition of currency with the former at 49.87% was similar to that with traditional measure at 49.57%.

16.13 Summary

To overcome subjective issues such as choosing historical data periods to forecast currency internationalization in the coming decades, this chapter finds an alternative way to measure relative long-term currency internationalization. The new method uses the product of sci-tech OC and nominal GDP world share of a currency issuer as a substitute of foreign exchange turnover of the currency. As sci-tech OC represents export capability and nominal GDP world share represents import potentiality of any money issuer, their product can well represent total trade capability of any currency issuer. Empirical results show that products of sci-tech OC and nominal GDP world share are highly correlated to foreign exchange turnovers of major currencies well enough. Since both economies and sci-tech OC are relatively stable for major currency issuers, sci-tech OC and nominal GDP world share can be better forecast. Therefore, forecasting results using this new method are more liable than results using historical foreign exchange turnovers.

Forecasting results show that despite steady economic growth and sci-tech OC in China in the coming decades, CNY international position will still lag far behind the USD long after Chinese GDP returns to the top world economy about a decade even China makes faster progress in sci-tech OC than Japan in the past three decades. Currency usage inertia plays its role as evidenced by British pound before the 1950s. Winner takes all sometimes, yet a few coins to share most of the time.

As a by-product of this chapter, we find currency contribution and sci-tech contribution share of major world currency issuers to their net exports of charges for the use of IP using the overall mutual influence of currency internationalization and sci-tech internationalization results from 2001 to 2019. Analysis shows that the USD contributed more to the US net charges for the use of IP than US sci-tech itself, yet all other currencies including Euro, Japanese yen, British pound, and Swiss franc contributed much less to corresponding net charges for the use of IP. In other words, sci-tech of other four major world currency issuers than USA makes greater contributions to their net charges for the use of IP, the corresponding contribution of these currencies to their net exports of charges for the use of IP is limited. In the sense of currency contribution to net exports of charges for the use of IP, it is still true that winner takes all.

Bibliography

Eichengreen, B., From Benign Neglect to Malignant Preoccupation: U.S. Balance of Payments Policy in the 1960s, in George L. Perry and James Tobin eds., *Economic Events, Ideas and Policies: The 1960s and After*, The Brookings Institution, 2000, pp. 185–242.

Eichengreen, B., *Sterling's Past, Dollar's Future: Historical Perspectives On Reserve Currency Competition*, National Bureau of Economic Research, 2005.

Chan, Norman T. L., Opening Remarks at the Second Hong Kong–Australia RMB Trade and Investment Dialogue, May 22, 2014, Hong Kong Monetary Authority.

Federal Reserve Bank of New York, The Foreign Exchange and Interest Rate Derivatives Markets: Turnover in the United States, April 2001 to April 2013.

Inlah, A., *Economic Elements in the Pax Britannica*, Harvard University Press, 1958.

Mussa, M., Exchange Rate Adjustments Needed to Reduce Global Payments Imbalances," in C. Fred Bergsten and J. Williamson (eds.), *Dollar Adjustment: How Far? Against What?*, Institute for International Economics, 2004, pp. 113–138.

Perasud, A., When Currency Empires Fall, October 11, 2004, www.321gold.com/editorials.

Triffin, R., The Evolution of the International Monetary System: Historical Reappraisal and Future Perspectives, Princeton Studies in International Finance no. 12, International Finance Section, Department of Economics, Princeton University, 1964.

Williams, D., The Evolution of the Sterling System, in C.R. Whitlesey and J.S.G Wilson eds., *Essays in Money and Banking*, Oxford University Press, 1968, pp. 266–297.

Xu Jiangshan, Looking at China's Interest Rate Marketization from Foreign Experience, *Futures Daily*, March 10, 2011.

Zhang, Guangping (Peter G.), *Exotic Options — A Guide to Second Generation Options*, World Scientific Publishing Co Pte Ltd, 1997.

Zhang Guangping (Peter G.), *RMB Internationalization and Product Innovation* (Ninth Edition), China Finance Press, 2019.

Zhang, Guangping (Peter G.) and Ziyang Tan, *CNY Internationalization and Product Development*, 10th Edition, China Financial Press, 2021.

Concluding Remarks

Most results of this book are based on statistical or regression methods. After the manuscript of this book was handed over to the publisher, I thought of applying exotic options from my earlier book *Exotic Options — A Guide to Second Generation Options*, first published in 1997, to the study of impacts of science and technology on exports, stock market capitalizations, gross domestic products, and foreign exchange turnovers of major economies. This idea has brought a series of new research papers with many new results related to the major results of this book. As most of these research papers are highly mathematical, it is not appreciated to include them in detail in this book. Yet, it is useful to introduce them briefly before the end of this book. Although the new results are much more mathematical, we can obtain all corresponding results in this book and much more with mathematical formulas rather than simple regressions.

Exotic options are over-the-counter (OTC) options in major world financial centers for over three decades. Zhang (1997) introduced and priced over 30 types of OTC options. Many of these options have good potentiality to be used to analyze comparative advantages of sci-tech of various economies. Using exotic option pricing mechanisms, I have published a dozen academic papers that analyze comparative advantages of sci-tech of one economy over another and other related applications. Results show that many option parameters can be better indicators of science and technology progresses than sci-tech OC, therefore applications of exotic options deepen our understanding of sci-tech of various economies.

Zhang (2021a) used the export and import of charges for the use of IP of one economy as assets and found impacts of imports of charges for the use of IP on exports of charges for the use of IP, or stimulus of imports on exports of charges for the use of IP of major economies; Zhang (2021b) found comparative advantages of sci-tech or exports of charges for the use of IP of one economy over another. Zhang (2021c) extended Zhang (2021a) to analyze comparative values of gross national products (GDPs) of one economy compared to another. More importantly, the GDP sensitivity of one economy with respect to the GDP of another economy can be obtained accordingly. This analytical method has been used to find impacts of sci-tech on human capital, capital accumulation and total factor productivity as shown in Zhang and Lin (2021).

Besides comparative advantages of sci-tech or GDP of one economy over another, Zhang (2021d) analyzed mutual influence of risk of sci-tech of one economy over another. This method can be applied to find risk influence of one stock market over another, etc.

The applications of the pricing mechanism of exotic options into the analysis of science and technology deepen most regression or statistical results of this book into the domain of mathematical formulas with more accuracy. Various parameters of related exotic options provide us with many sophisticated parameters to measure science and technology. As most of these results are highly mathematical, I decided not to include them in this book for the time being. Interested readers may wait for these papers to be published before they can be added to a potential second edition of this book or a new book before long.

Bibliography

Zhang, Guangping (Peter G.), *Exotic Options — Guide to Second-Generation Options*, World Scientific Publishing Co Pte Ltd., 2nd ed. 1998, 1997.

Zhang, Guangping (Peter G.), Science & Technology Originality Capability Implied in Prices of Exchange Options to Exchange Export and Import of Charges for the Use of Intellectual Properties for One Another, Unpublished Working Paper, 2021a.

Zhang, Guangping (Peter G.), Comparative Advantages of Science & Technology of Major Exporters and Importers of Charges for the Use of IP, Unpublished Working Paper, 2021b.

Zhang, Guangping (Peter G.), Alternative Method to Price Exchange Options and Export Sensitivity to Import of Charges for the Use of IP, Unpublished Working Paper, 2021c.

Zhang, Guangping (Peter G.), Alternative Method to Price Exchange Options and Export Uncertainty to Import Uncertainty of Charges for the Use of IP, Unpublished Working Paper, 2021d.

Zhang, Guangping (Peter G.) and Ken Lin, Empirical Evidence of Impacts of Science & Technology on Gross Domestic Products and Their Major Components Including Total Factor Productivity, unpublished working paper, 2021.

Index

B

based on science and technology OC, 331

bank internationalization, 470, 473–476, 478, 488

better currency internationalization, 599, 642–643

C

charges for the use of intellectual properties (IPs), 239, 271, 273–274, 277–279, 289, 346, 355, 600, 630, 661, 680–682, 688–689

China's science and technology OC, 321

CNY internationalization, 116, 122, 165, 414, 474, 476, 491, 532–533

currency circle, 676, 679

currency globalization, 196, 577, 664

currency internationalization, 3–4, 6, 16, 19–20, 143, 166, 170, 173, 292, 294, 333, 341, 459, 487, 532, 551, 555, 557–564, 566, 568–570, 576–586, 588, 591–592, 600, 608–609, 623, 631–633, 641–647, 665, 683–684, 688–689

currency OC, 623, 626–627, 631–635, 637, 640–643, 645–647

currency valuation and internationalization, 23

D

degrees of IP sufficiency, 282

E

exports and imports data of IP charges, 330

exports and imports of charges for the use of IP, 344–345, 360

G

government effectiveness, 358

I

imports of charges for the use of IP, 275, 343

insufficiency of IPs, 315

intellectual property sufficiency, 323

internationalization of BRICS currencies, 163
internationalization of currencies, 166
IP insufficiency, 282, 284, 324
IP sufficiency, 282

J
Japanese sci-tech OC, 303–304, 306

K
Korean sci-tech OC, 312

M
measurement of currency internationalization, 173

N
net export of charges for the use of IPs, 290

O
originality capability (OC), 19, 232, 295

P
patent internalization, 197
patent internationalization, 228, 233, 295, 327
patent OC, 296, 324
per patent family, 290

R
relative, 166
RMB internationalization, 105–106, 293, 363, 411

S
science and technology (sci-tech) independence or origination capability, 295, 298
science and technology (sci-tech) internationalization, 19, 292, 295, 327, 329–330, 333–334, 336–338, 341, 551–552, 555, 557–559, 561, 564, 568–570, 576–586, 588, 591–592, 599–601, 607–609, 641, 643–647, 680, 682, 689
science and technology originality capability (sci-tech OC), 295–296, 298–300, 302,–304, 307–316, 318–324, 329–331, 334–338, 343, 356–358, 360, 551, 623, 627, 633–635, 637, 640–641, 643–647, 660–665, 667–671, 680, 682–683, 688–689
sci-tech globalization, 608, 680, 682

T
technology independence or OC, 330
the five offices, 179, 182
traders of charges for use of IP, 281

U
US science and technology OC, 302

Y
yen internationalization, 569

www.ingramcontent.com/pod-product-compliance
Lightning Source LLC
LaVergne TN
LVHW010321220926
848484LV00004BB/825

* 9 7 8 9 8 1 1 2 5 4 0 8 6 *